Communications
in Computer and Information Science   585

Commenced Publication in 2007
Founding and Former Series Editors:
Alfredo Cuzzocrea, Dominik Ślęzak, and Xiaokang Yang

More information about this series at http://www.springer.com/series/7899

Mohammad S. Obaidat · Pascal Lorenz (Eds.)

E-Business
and Telecommunications

12th International Joint Conference, ICETE 2015
Colmar, France, July 20–22, 2015
Revised Selected Papers

 Springer

Editors
Mohammad S. Obaidat
Department of Computer and Information
  Science
Fordham University
Bronx, NY
USA

Pascal Lorenz
IUT
University of Haute Alsace
Colmar
France

ISSN 1865-0929   ISSN 1865-0937 (electronic)
Communications in Computer and Information Science
ISBN 978-3-319-30221-8   ISBN 978-3-319-30222-5 (eBook)
DOI 10.1007/978-3-319-30222-5

Library of Congress Control Number: 2015952067

Printed on acid-free paper

This Springer imprint is published by SpringerNature
The registered company is Springer International Publishing AG Switzerland

Preface

The present book includes extended and revised versions of a set of selected best papers from the 12th International Joint Conference on e-Business and Telecommunications (ICETE), which was held in July 2015, in Colmar, Alsace, France. This conference reflects a continuing effort to increase the dissemination of recent research results among professionals who work in the areas of e-business and telecommunications. ICETE is a joint international conference integrating four major areas of knowledge that are divided into six corresponding conferences: DCNET (International Conference on Data Communication Networking), ICE-B (International Conference on e-Business), OPTICS (International Conference on Optical Communication Systems), SECRYPT (International Conference on Security and Cryptography), SIGMAP (International Conference on Signal Processing and Multimedia), and WINSYS (International Conference on Wireless Information Systems).

The program of this joint conference included several outstanding keynote lectures presented by internationally renowned distinguished researchers who are experts in the various ICETE areas. Their keynote speeches have contributed to heightening the overall quality of the program and significance of the theme of the conference.

The conference topic areas define a broad spectrum in the key areas of e-business and telecommunications. This wide-view reporting made ICETE appealing to a global audience of engineers, scientists, business practitioners, ICT managers, and policy experts. The papers accepted and presented at the conference demonstrated a number of new and innovative solutions for e-business and telecommunication networks and systems, showing that the technical problems in these closely related fields are challenging and worth approaching in an interdisciplinary perspective such as that promoted by ICETE.

ICETE 2015 received 248 papers in total, with contributions from 53 different countries, in all continents, demonstrating its success and global dimension. To evaluate each submission, a double-blind paper evaluation method was used: Each paper was blindly reviewed by at least two experts from the International Program Committee. In fact, most papers had three reviews or more. The selection process followed strict criteria in all tracks. As a result only 26 papers were accepted and orally presented at ICETE as full papers (11.9 % of submissions) and 37 as short papers (16.9 % of submissions). Additionally, 52 papers were accepted for poster presentation. With these acceptance ratios, ICETE 2015 continues the tradition of previous ICETE conferences as a distinguished and high-quality international conference.

We hope that you will find this collection of the best ICETE 2015 papers an excellent source of inspiration as well as a helpful reference for research in the aforementioned areas.

July 2015

Mohammad S. Obaidat
Pascal Lorenz
Joaquim Filipe

Organization

Conference Co-chairs

Mohammad S. Obaidat   Fordham University, USA
Pascal Lorenz   University of Haute Alsace, France

Program Co-chairs

DCNET

Jose Luis Sevillano   Universidad de Sevilla, Spain
Christian Callegari   University of Pisa, Italy

ICE-B

Peter Dolog   Aalborg University, Denmark
Marten van Sinderen   University of Twente, The Netherlands

OPTICS

Panagiotis Sarigiannidis   University of Western Macedonia, Greece

SECRYPT

Pierangela Samarati   Università degli Studi di Milano, Italy

SIGMAP

Enrique Cabello   Universidad Rey Juan Carlos, Spain

WINSYS

Petros Nicopolitidis   Aristotle University, Greece
Dimitrios D. Vergados   University of Piraeus, Greece

DCNET Program Committee

Ishfaq Ahmad   University of Texas at Arlington, USA
Mohiuddin Ahmed   International Islamic University Malaysia, Malaysia
Nancy Alonistioti   The University of Athens, Greece
Baber Aslam   National University of Sciences and Technology (NUST), Pakistan
Julio Barbancho   Universidad de Sevilla, Spain
Christian Callegari   University of Pisa, Italy
Maurizio Casoni   University of Modena and Reggio Emilia, Italy

Nasser-Eddine Rikli	King Saud University, Saudi Arabia
Joel Rodrigues	Instituto de Telecomunicações, University of Beira Interior, Portugal
Francisco J. Ros	University of Murcia, Spain
Paulo Salvador	Instituto de Telecomunicações/University of Aveiro, Portugal
Jose Luis Sevillano	Universidad de Sevilla, Spain
Hangguan Shan	Zhejiang University, China
Giovanni Stea	University of Pisa, Italy
Tatsuya Suda	University Netgroup Inc., USA
Ljiljana Trajkovic	Simon Fraser University, Canada
Vicente Traver	ITACA, Universidad Politécnica de Valencia, Spain
Sandrine Vaton	Telecom Bretagne, France
Luis Javier García Villalba	Universidad Complutense de Madrid, Spain
Ping Wang	Symantec Corporation, USA
Sabine Wittevrongel	Ghent University, Belgium
Bernd E. Wolfinger	University of Hamburg, Germany
Christos Xenakis	University of Piraeus, Greece
Gaoxi Xiao	Nanyang Technological University, Singapore
Jianbin Xiong	Guangdong University of Petrochemical Technology, China
Laurance T. Yang	Huazhong University of Science and Technology, China, and Saint Francis Xavier University, Canada
Zhongming Yang	Guangdong University of Petrochemical Technology, China
Bo Zhang	Hisense Group USA, USA
Si-Qing Zheng	University of Texas Dallas, USA
Cliff C. Zou	University of Central Florida, USA

ICE-B Program Committee

Andreas Ahrens	Hochschule Wismar, University of Technology Business and Design, Germany
Dimitris Apostolou	University of Piraeus, Greece
Anteneh Ayanso	Brock University, Canada
Ana Azevedo	ISCAP - IPP and Algoritmi R&D Center, Portugal
Elarbi Badidi	United Arab Emirates University, United Arab Emirates
Michael R. Bartolacci	Pennsylvania State University, USA
Morad Benyoucef	University of Ottawa, Canada
Ilia Bider	DSV, Stockholm University, Sweden
Freimut Bodendorf	University of Erlangen-Nuremberg, Germany
Efthimios Bothos	Institute of Communication and Computer Systems, Greece
Rebecca Bulander	Pforzheim University of Applied Science, Germany
Christoph Bussler	Oracle Corporation, USA

Gustavo Rossi	University of La Plata, Argentina
Jarogniew Rykowski	The Poznan University of Economics (PUE), Poland
Ahm Shamsuzzoha	Sultan Qaboos University, Oman
Marten van Sinderen	University of Twente, The Netherlands
Hassan A. Sleiman	Commissariat à l'énergie atomique et aux énergies alternatives (CEA), France
Riccardo Spinelli	Università degli Studi di Genova, Italy
Athena Stassopoulou	University of Nicosia, Cyprus
Zhaohao Sun	PNG University of Technology, Federation University Australia, Papua New Guinea
Ruppa K. Thulasiram	University of Manitoba, Canada
Anthony Townsend	Iowa State University, USA
Christina Tsagkani	University of Athens, Greece
Yiannis Verginadis	ICCS, National Technical University of Athens, Greece
Moe Thandar Wynn	Queensland University of Technology, Australia
Qi Yu	Rochester Institute of Technology, USA
Wlodek Zadrozny	University of North Carolina, Charlotte, USA
Edzus Zeiris	ZZ Dats Ltd., Latvia

ICE-B Additional Reviewers

Meriem Laifa	University Mohamed El-Bachir El-Ibrahimi Bordj Bou Arreridj, Algeria
Kem Zhang	University of Ottawa, Canada

OPTICS Program Committee

Tiago Alves	Instituto Superior Técnico/Instituto de Telecomunicações, Portugal
Hercules Avramopoulos	National Technical University of Athens, Greece
Luis Cancela	ISCTE-IUL, Portugal
Adolfo Cartaxo	Instituto de Telecomunicações, Instituto Superior Técnico, Portugal
Bernard Cousin	University of Rennes, France
Ivan B. Djordjevic	University of Arizona, USA
Anna Manolova Fagertun	Technical University of Denmark, Denmark
Matteo Fiorani	Royal Institute of Technology, Sweden
Habib Hamam	Université de Moncton, Canada
Sang-Kook Han	Yonsei University, Korea, Republic of
Miroslaw Klinkowski	National Institute of Telecommunications, Poland
Tsuyoshi Konishi	Osaka University, Japan
Ai-Qun Liu	Nanyang Technological University, Singapore
Malamati Louta	University of Western Macedonia, Greece
Guido Maier	Politecnico de Milano, Italy
Akihiro Maruta	Osaka University, Japan

Tetsuya Miyazaki   National Institute of Information and Communications, Japan
Maria Morant   Universitat Politècnica de València, Spain
Syed H. Murshid   Florida Institute of Technology, USA
Nabil Naas   University of Ottawa, Canada
Thas A. Nirmalathas   The University of Melbourne, Australia
Yasutake Ohishi   Research Center for Advanced Photon Technology, Japan
Satoru Okamoto   The University of Electro-Communications, Japan
Haldun M. Ozaktas   Bilkent University, Turkey
Albert Pagès   Universitat Politècnica de Catalunya, Spain
Jordi Perelló   Universitat Politècnica de Catalunya (UPC), Spain
João Rebola   Instituto de Telecomunicações, ISCTE-IUL, Portugal
Enrique   Universidad Autónoma Metropolitana, Mexico
  Rodriguez-Colina
Panagiotis Sarigiannidis   University of Western Macedonia, Greece
Surinder Singh   Sant Longowal Instituite of Engineering and Technology, Longowal, India
Salvatore Spadaro   Universitat Politecnica de Catalunya, Spain
Stefan Wabnitz   Università degli Studi di Brescia, Italy
Naoya Wada   National Institute of Information and Communications Technology, Japan
(John) Xiupu Zhang   Concordia University, Canada
Zuqing Zhu   University of Science and Technology of China, China
Kyriakos E. Zoiros   Democritus University of Thrace, Greece

OPTICS Additional Reviewer

Paolo Martelli   Politecnico di Milano, Italy

SECRYPT Program Committee

Alessandro Armando   FBK, Italy
Prithvi Bisht   Adobe, USA
Carlo Blundo   Università di Salerno, Italy
Andrey Bogdanov   Technical University of Denmark, Denmark
Francesco Buccafurri   University of Reggio Calabria, Italy
Sherman S.M. Chow   Chinese University of Hong Kong, Hong Kong, SAR China
Frederic Cuppens   TELECOM Bretagne, France
Nora Cuppens-Boulahia   Institut Mines Telecom/Telecom Bretagne, France
Jun Dai   California State University, USA
Tassos Dimitriou   Computer Technology Institute, Greece and Kuwait University, Kuwait
Josep Domingo-Ferrer   Universitat Rovira i Virgili, Spain
Bao Feng   Security and Privacy Lab, Huawei, Singapore

Nicolas Sklavos	University of Patras, Greece
Einar Snekkenes	Gjøvik University College, Norway
Alessandro Sorniotti	IBM Research - Zurich, Switzerland
Willy Susilo	University of Wollongong, Australia
Juan Tapiador	Universidad Carlos III de Madrid, Spain
Vicenc Torra	University of Skövde, Sweden
Jaideep Vaidya	Rutgers Business School, USA
Luca Viganò	University of Verona, Italy
Sabrina de Capitani di Vimercati	Università degli Studi di Milano, Italy
Cong Wang	City University of Hong Kong, Hong Kong, SAR China
Haining Wang	The College of William and Mary, USA
Lingyu Wang	Concordia University, Canada
Ping Wang	Symantec Corporation, USA
Xinyuan (Frank) Wang	George Mason University, USA
Edgar Weippl	SBA Research/TU Wien, Austria
Meng Yu	Virginia Commonwealth University, USA
Lei Zhang	Thomson Reuters, USA
Hang Zhao	Columbia University, USA
Jianying Zhou	Institute for Infocomm Research, Singapore

SECRYPT Additional Reviewers

Waqas Aman	Gjøvik University College, Norway
Gregory Blanc	Institut Mines-Télécom, Télécom SudParis, France
Stanislav Dashevskyi	Fondazione Bruno Kessler/University of Trento, Italy
Jintai Ding	University of Cincinnati, USA
Russell W.F. Lai	Chinese University of Hong Kong, Hong Kong, SAR China
Liran Lerman	Université Libre de Bruxelles, Belgium
Yang Lu	Hohai University, China
Reza Malekian	University of Pretoria, South Africa
Elisa Mannes	UFPR, Brazil
Alessio Merlo	E-Campus University, Italy
Alexios Mylwnas	Staffordshire University, Greece
Sergio Pastrana	Carlos III University of Madrid, Spain
Slobodan Petrovic	Gjøvik University College, Norway
Nikos Pitropakis	Department of Digital Systems University of Piraeus, Greece
Naim Qachri	Université Libre de Bruxelles, Belgium
Yves Roggeman	Université Libre de Bruxelles (ULB), Belgium
Vishal Saraswat	CRRao AIMSCS, India
Giada Sciarretta	FBK, Italy
Federico Sinigaglia	FBK, Italy
Hari Siswantoro	Fondazione Bruno Kessler, Italy

Guillermo Suarez-Tangil	Carlos III University of Madrid, Spain
Aggeliki Tsohou	Ionian University, Greece
Luca Verderame	University of Genoa, Italy
Tao Zhang	CUHK, Hong Kong, SAR China
Ye Zhang	Penn State University, USA
Yongjun Zhao	The Chinese University of Hong Kong, Hong Kong, SAR China

SIGMAP Program Committee

Harry Agius	Brunel University, UK
Rajeev Agrawal	North Carolina Agricultural and Technical State University, USA
Zahid Akthar	University of Cagliari, Italy
João Ascenso	Instituto Superior de Engenharia de Lisboa, Portugal
Pradeep K. Atrey	University at Albany - State University of New York, USA
Arvind Bansal	Kent State University, USA
Chidansh Amitkumar Bhatt	Indian Institute of Technology, India
Gennaro Boggia	Politecnico di Bari, Italy
Adrian Bors	University of York, UK
Enrique Cabello	Universidad Rey Juan Carlos, Spain
Wai-Kuen Cham	The Chinese University of Hong Kong, China
Amitava Chatterjee	Jadavpur University, India
LG Chen	National Taiwan University, Taiwan
Wei Cheng	Garena Online Pte. Ltd., Singapore
Jean-luc Dekeyser	UMR8022 Laboratoire d' Informatique Fondamentale de Lille, France
Wu-Chi Feng	Portland State University, USA
Borko Furht	Florida Atlantic University, USA
Jakub Galka	University of Science and Technology, Poland
Seiichi Gohshi	Kogakuin University, Japan
William Grosky	University of Michigan - Dearborn, USA
Amarnath Gupta	University of California San Diego, USA
Malka Halgamuge	The University of Melbourne, Australia
Wolfgang Hürst	Utrecht University, The Netherlands
Razib Iqbal	Missouri State University, USA
Yu-Gang Jiang	Fudan University, China
Mohan Kankanhalli	National University of Singapore, Singapore
Sokratis Katsikas	University of Piraeus, Greece
Constantine Kotropoulos	Aristotle University of Thessaloniki, Greece
Gabriele Kotsis	Johannes Kepler University Linz, Austria
Konrad Kowalczyk	AGH University of Science and Technology, Poland
Adnane Latif	Cadi Ayyad University, Morocco
Chengqing Li	Xiangtan University, China
Jing Li	Nanchang University, China

Guifeng Liu	Electrical and Computer Engineering, USA
Zhu Liu	AT&T, USA
Zitao Liu	University of Pittsburgh, USA
Martin Lopez-Nores	University of Vigo, Spain
Pavel Loskot	Swansea University, UK
Ilias Maglogiannis	University of Piraeus, Greece
Hong Man	Stevens Institute of Technology, USA
Daniela Moctezuma	Rey Juan Carlos University, Mexico
Chamin Morikawa	Yubi Interactions, Japan
Alejandro Murua	University of Montreal, Canada
Hiroshi Nagahashi	Tokyo Institute of Technology, Japan
Francesco De Natale	University of Trento, Italy
Ioannis Paliokas	Centre for Research and Technolgoy - Hellas, Greece
Peter Quax	Hasselt University, Belgium
Maria Paula Queluz	Instituto Superior Técnico - Instituto de Telecomunicações, Portugal
Rudolf Rabenstein	University of Erlangen-Nuremberg, Germany
Martin Reisslein	Arizona State University, USA
Gerardo Reyes	Instituto Tecnológico de Cuautla, Mexico
Luis Alberto Morales Rosales	Instituto Tecnológico Superior de Misantla, Mexico
Simone Santini	Universidad Autónoma de Madrid, Spain
Kaushik Das Sharma	University of Calcutta, India
Oscar S. Siordia	Universidad Rey Juan Carlos, Spain
George Tsihrintzis	University of Piraeus, Greece
Aristeidis Tsitiridis	University of Rey Juan Carlos, Spain
Andreas Uhl	University of Salzburg, Austria
Steven Verstockt	Ghent University, Belgium
Zhiyong Wang	The University of Sydney, Australia
Sanjeewa Witharana	Max Planck Institute for Solar System Research, Germany
Xin-Shun Xu	Shandong University, China
Kim-hui Yap	Nanyang Technological University, Singapore
Magda El Zarki	University of California Irvine, USA
Yongxin Zhang	Qualcomm R&D, USA
Bartosz Ziolko	AGH University of Science and Technology/Techmo, Poland

SIGMAP Additional Reviewers

Kostas Delibasis	University of Thessaly, Greece
Wencan Luo	University of Pittsburgh, USA
Ronald Poppe	Utrecht University, The Netherlands
Yan Shang	Duke Univeristy, USA

WINSYS Program Committee

Ali Abedi	University of Maine, USA
Taufik Abrão	Universidade Estadual de Londrina, Brazil
Fatemeh Afghah	Northern Arizona University, USA
Ramon Aguero	University of Cantabria, Spain
Aydin Akan	Istanbul University, Turkey
Vicente Alarcon-Aquino	Universidad de las Americas Puebla, Mexico
Nancy Alonistioti	The University of Athens, Greece
Josephina Antoniou	University of Central Lancashire Cyprus, Cyprus
Francisco Barcelo Arroyo	Universitat Politecnica de Catalunya, Spain
Jose M. Barcelo-Ordinas	Universitat Politècnica de Catalunya (UPC), Spain
Bert-Jan van Beijnum	University of Twente, The Netherlands
Kostas Berberidis	University of Patras, Greece
Luis Bernardo	Universidade Nova de Lisboa, Portugal
Gennaro Boggia	Politecnico di Bari, Italy
Matthias R. Brust	Louisiana Tech University, USA
Juan-Carlos Cano	Universidad Politécnica de Valencia, Spain
Gerard Chalhoub	Clermont University, France
Chi Chung Cheung	The Hong Kong Polytechnic University, SAR China
James M. Conrad	University of North Carolina at Charlotte, USA
Roberto Corvaja	University of Padova, Italy
Orhan Dagdeviren	Ege University, Turkey
Luis Rizo Dominguez	Universidad del Caribe, Mexico
Christos Douligeris	University of Piraeus, Greece
Martin Drozda	Slovak University of Technology, Slovak Republic
Amit Dvir	BME-HIT, Hungary
Mohammed El-Hajjar	University of Southampton, UK
Jocelyne Elias	Paris Descartes University, France
Abolfazl Falahati	Iran University of Science and Technology, Iran, Islamic Republic of
Marco Di Felice	University of Bologna, Italy
Panayotis Fouliras	University of Macedonia, Greece
Antonio Grilo	INESC/IST, Portugal
Dirk Grunwald	University of Colorado Boulder, USA
Alexander Guitton	University Blaise Pascal, France
Aaron Gulliver	University of Victoria, Canada
Zygmunt Haas	Cornell University, USA
Aissaoui-Mehrez Hassane	Mines-Telecom Institute/Telecom-ParisTech, France
Jeroen Hoebeke	UGent-IBCN, Belgium
Cynthia Hood	Illinois Institute of Technology, USA
Chih-Lin Hu	National Central University, Taiwan
Ali Abu-el Humos	Jackson State University, USA
Esa Hyytiä	Aalto University, Finland
Hong Ji	Beijing University of Post and Telecommunications (BUPT), China

Tao Jiang   Huazhong University of Science and Technology,
                             China
Josep Miquel Jornet   University at Buffalo, USA
Georgios Kambourakis   University of the Aegean, Greece
Akimitsu Kanzaki   Shimane University, Japan
Majid Khabbazian   University of Alberta, Canada
Charalampos   University of Piraeus, Greece
  Konstantopoulos
Gurhan Kucuk   Yeditepe University, Turkey
Abderrahmane Lakas   UAEU - United Arab Emirates University,
                             United Arab Emirates
Chong Hyun Lee   Jeju National University, Korea, Republic of
Wookwon Lee   Gannon University, USA
Alessandro Leonardi   AGT International, Germany
Ju Liu   Shandong University, China
Elsa Macias López   University of Las Palmas de G.C., Spain
Pavel Loskot   Swansea University, UK
Spiros Louvros   Institution of Western Greece Patras, Greece
Chung-Horng Lung   Carleton University, Canada
Hsi-pin Ma   National Tsing Hua University, Taiwan
Pietro Manzoni   Universidad Politecnica de Valencia, Spain
Enrico Masala   Politecnico di Torino, Italy
Luis Mendes   Instituto de Telecomunicações and Instituto Politécnico
                             de Leiria, Portugal
Aikaterini Mitrokotsa   Chalmers University of Technology, Sweden
Ali Movaghar   Sharif University of Technology, Iran, Islamic
                             Republic of
Marek Natkaniec   AGH University of Science and Technology, Poland
Amiya Nayak   University of Ottawa, Canada
Cristiano Panazio   Escola Politécnica of São Paulo University, Brazil
Grammati Pantziou   Technological Educational Institution of Athens,
                             Greece
Georgios Papadimitriou   Aristotle University of Thessaloniki, Greece
Evangelos Papapetrou   University of Ioannina, Greece
Al-Sakib Khan Pathan   IIUM, Malaysia and Islamic University in Madinah,
                             KSA, Bangladesh
Jordi Pérez-Romero   Universitat Politècnica de Catalunya (UPC), Spain
Symon Podvalny   Voronezh State Technical University, Russian
                             Federation
Adam Postula   The University of Queensland, Australia
Guy Pujolle   LIP6 of University Pierre and Marie Currie France,
                             France
Nancy El Rachkidy   LIMOS, France
Jörg Roth   University of Applied Sciences Nuremberg, Germany
Angelos Rouskas   University of Piraeus, Greece
Hamid R. Sadjadpour   University of California Santa Cruz, USA

Manuel García Sánchez	Universidade de Vigo, Spain
Nicola Santoro	Carleton University, Canada
Susana Sargento	Universidade de Aveiro, Portugal
Christian Schindelhauer	University of Freiburg, Germany
Alvaro Suárez-Sarmiento	University of Las Palmas de Gran Canaria, Spain
Zhili Sun	University of Surrey, UK
Claude Tadonki	Mines ParisTech - Centre de Recherche en Informatique, France
Cesar Vargas-Rosales	Tecnologico de Monterrey, Campus Monterrey, Mexico
Vasos Vassiliou	University of Cyprus, Cyprus
Dimitrios D. Vergados	University of Piraeus, Greece
Natalija Vlajic	York University, Canada
Jean Pierre De Vries	RWTH Aachen University, USA
Sheng-Shih Wang	Minghsin University of Science and Technology, Taiwan
Anne Wei	CNAM Paris, France
Jie Wu	Temple University, USA
Tadeusz A. Wysocki	University of Nebraska - Lincoln, USA
Qin Xin	University of the Faroe Islands, Faroe Islands
Hyoung-Sun Youn	HCAC, University of Hawai'i, USA
Chang Wu Yu	Chung Hua University, Taiwan
Theodore Zahariadis	TEI of Sterea Ellada, Greece
Magda El Zarki	University of California Irvine, USA
Dimirios Zorbas	Inria Lille - Nord Europe, France

WINSYS Additional Reviewers

Janusz Gozdecki	AGH University of Science and Technology, Poland
Pawel Kulakowski	AGH University of Science and Technology, Poland
Amanda de Paula	UFRPE, Brazil

Invited Speakers

Anthony C. Boucouvalas	University of the Peloponnese, Greece
Eleni Karatza	Aristotle University of Thessaloniki, Greece
Andrew Moore	University of Cambridge, UK
John Domingue	The Open University, UK

Contents

Security and Cryptography

Signal Processing and Multimedia Applications

Wireless Information Networks and Systems

Invited Paper

Integrating Retail and e-Commerce Using Web Analytics and Intelligent Sensors

Anthony C. Boucouvalas[✉], Constantine J. Aivalis,
and Kleanthis Gatziolis

University of Peloponnese, Tripolis, Peloponnese, Greece
acb@uop.gr

Abstract. Retailers offer their products via e-Commerce applications in order to promote them better, globalize their clientèle, enhance and support sales. This paper explores and proposes techniques that will collect data from the physical shopping floor mainly via low cost mobile technologies and promote them for processing to a customized sophisticated e-Commerce Analyzer. This Analyzer connects the two worlds of physical and virtual shopping. The information is collected automatically during the physical store customer interaction with the support of iBeacons and Near Field Communications, used for data acquisition in the retail shop floor. The generated retail data is pushed to the Analyzer in near real time. This data enhances the Analyzer input with physical store data and can be used in order to enrich the customer experience, provide customer clustering and precise behavioral analysis, by enhancing the available operational data sets, collected by a Web Analytics application, providing better overview and supporting decision making for the entire corporation.

The consumer has a choice to shop on-line from home via a browser or mobile app or go alternatively in person to a store and accomplish a shopping goal. The latter is usually without the need of any on-line device. The two approaches are not integrated into one system. The consumer always seeks value for money to satisfy his need, also to be inspired and to have a great uplifting shopping experience. The store requires increasing profits while trying to excel in satisfying any customer requirement. The future customer will always be connected. The customer will enjoy a shopping experience, receiving personalized services leading to building loyalty and trust with the shop. This vision of the future is based on the interplay of a set of technologies which will combine the interaction of mobile data with store items in real time. This merging not only must it work well, but also be well optimized. The talk will cover the marriage of the local store together with the store electronic presence (e-shop) into one whole, smoothly operating system, from both the administrator of the system point of view and the customer. We envisage developments in physical shopping where sensors intelligently will interact, using a number of devices and techniques to assist this process, such as mobile phones or other devices using audio directions.

A real time customer servicing system will be coupled to the e-shop system of the company business. The use of web Analytics and User Profiling is crucial to e-shopping in identifying customer profiles and to offer vital statistics to the management for the state of the business as well as traffic, speed, throughput diagrams and faults of the e-shop in need of improvement. This paper will

© Springer International Publishing Switzerland 2016
M.S. Obaidat and P. Lorenz (Eds.): ICETE 2015, CCIS 585, pp. 3–35, 2016.
DOI: 10.1007/978-3-319-30222-5_1

describe an architecture we envisage for this holistic system of managing both e-shop as well as physical shop offering good prospects for profitable management for a 24/7 service. The system requirements for real time or near real time Analytics also for the physical shopping mode, sets new requirements for the sensory interpretation and data fetching/pushing into devices. A real time customer servicing application must immediately provide offers and discounted articles in conjunction with the location of the customer in the store. Since the lifetime of the customer needs is short, the system must identify the customer profile, guess the customer need, process the need and push for an inspiring solution to this need to the customer device, before the customer has walked passed this product range, ideally. The talk will describe the status of our architecture for integrated shopping, our research on Web Analytics, Intelligent sensing and other complementary technologies and applications required for shopping experiences of the future [1].

Keywords: E-Commerce · Retailing · E-Shopping · Mobile shopping · User profiling · Analytics

1 Introduction

Web Analytics measurement and visualization techniques provide excellent tools and techniques in order to analyze, document, visualize and report almost every aspect of customer interaction and performance detail of any e-shop and any web application. Analytics applications are based upon measurements and logging of the customers actions. They are complicated software systems, with the ability to accurately record user actions, key-clicks and responses to databases and access log files. Many e-commerce sites have been implemented in order to enhance and complement physical retail shops. Their goal is to extend the operation capabilities and the customer base, providing services parallel to those of the physical shop. They provide low cost availability beyond working hours by offering 24/7 services and eliminate the time zone restrictions and customer location problems.

Physical stores use multiple techniques in order to analyze client behavior. The majority of these techniques, are based on capturing the data at the cash register, during the checkout process, when the customer is about to pay. If the customer uses a credit card the purchaser is uniquely identified. Even customers that pay with cash can be monitored to some extend precisely via discount coupons and the use of loyalty cards.

Every business transaction and step, generate a large number of data. As indicated by Provost and Foster [2], Data Mining is used for general customer relationship management to analyze customer behavior in order to manage attrition and maximize expected customer value. The finance industry uses data mining for credit scoring and trading, and in operations via fraud detection and workforce management. Major retailers from Amazon to Walmart apply data mining throughout their businesses, from marketing to supply-chain management. Many firms have differentiated themselves strategically with data science, sometimes to the point of evolving into data mining companies.

A versatile Log File Analyzer (LFA) is the tool that provides operational meta-data that allow the management to identify the way customers approach the offered products and measures their behavior and generates Customer Behavior Model Graphs [3]. The LFA used for this research was implemented with the ability to import and operate on both log file and e-shop data extracted either on demand or in near real time from the e-shop application.

The data visualization component of the LFA is customizable to a large extend, since requirements are fairly fluid, and produces mainly:

- Graphical reports about products and actions,
- PDF output,
- Statistic Reports,
- Exception Reports and
- Traffic, Speed and Throughput Diagrams [4]

All reports are built around database queries and are fully customizable and extensible in order to provide visualization mechanisms that will allow the administrator or the management to extract knowledge about specific time spans and periods of operation. A typical report example is visible in Fig. 1. Here the distribution of user actions per product is visualized. The red slice of the pie is representing an 11 % of all selected actions. This is the "add product to the cart" action, for a specific time range.

Item Code 28	MIN.S.001-Silver
Action	**Count**
AddToCartFromProdId.do	36
Login.do	38
SelectProd.do	139
SetNotification.do	24
ShowCartItems.do	15
ShowImage.do	28
ShowReviews.do	29
WriteReview.do	18

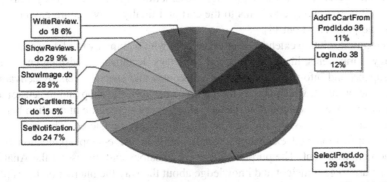

● AddToCartFromProdId.do 36 11% ● Login.do 38 12% ● SelectProd.do 139 43% ● SetNotification.do 24 7%
● ShowCartItems.do 15 5% ● ShowImage.do 28 9% ● ShowReviews.do 29 9% ● WriteReview.do 18 6%

Fig. 1. Distribution of preselected user actions per product [4].

2 The Scene

This section includes a general description of the current situation, as well as the purpose of the double application. Similarities and facilities that can be used commonly are shown. The double usage of the same Analyzer is explained.

On-line and in-store shopping are usually viewed as two distinct forms of business operation, although they can easily be integrated. Distinct software applications deal with either retailer procedures or e-shops. It is beneficial to provide solution suited for retailers which either operate e-shops, or are ready to integrate e-commerce functionality to their businesses

Extending the shop floor functionality electronically provides a better shopping experience to the physical customer, making it easy to also offer any reasonable mix of products of the physical shop available via e-commerce, through the Internet, to address large numbers of clients make this option popular. The shop extension provides the necessary tools to the physical customer for a better shopping experience.

IBIS World [5], the Australian business information provider, forecasts an 8.6 % per year increase in on-line revenues over the next five years [6]. This makes operating e-shops a very attractive goal for every retailer.

It is a fairly straight forward and relatively simple procedure for any brick and mortar retail store to implement and operate an e-commerce site, because the items to be offered are already available. A digital infrastructure is usually also already provided since retail stores run Management Information Systems and Customer Relationship Management applications. The e-shop can be viewed as an on-line product catalog with purchase policies and capabilities. It can be viewed as an extension of the retail store.

The goal of any business to customer (B2C) e-shop application is to promote retail sales and create profit. A virtual store allows buying products or services through a website, in analogy to a bricks-and-mortar retailer or a shopping mall. The Internet is no longer a niche technology – it is mass media and an utterly integral part of modern life. Over 85 per cent of the world's online population has used the Internet to make a purchase. More than half of Internet users are regular online shoppers making online purchases at least once a month [7]. The e-shop must have a fairly minimal interface, consisting of search engines and product presentation mechanisms. They must also have the ability to quickly add items to the cart and finally allow secure payments and possibly one page checkout [4].

The proposed solution extends the physical store with commonly used, low cost mobile technology components, like i-Beacons and NFC tags. It allows the visiting customer to receive support and information and loyalty discounts and special offers by activating a mobile phone or tablet, which acts as the interface between the shop and the customer.

When a prospective customer visits an e-shop, every step of the interaction between this customer and the e-shop site can be fairly precisely registered. This is done via Analytics application and extensions, usually built in the e-shop application or the application environment. The purpose of these extensions and the use of the Analytics application are to gain insight and knowledge about the way the interaction takes place. This will allow the study, deeper knowledge and evaluation of the e-commerce application. In parallel to this, the customer behavior analysis may lead to conclusions that can be used in order to improve the system in various levels.

The mobile extensions used in the physical store, are capable of capturing all details of the customers selections at a similar granularity level like the ones captured by the e-shop. This happens through the help of the mobile device, carried and used by the customer during shopping, who runs a custom made application that detects i-Beacons and NFC tags set at specific locations of the shopping floor. The user's selections and steps, time stamped together with geolocational information, are forwarded to the Analytics Application in near real time.

The collected information, along with data collected by the e-shop, allow the analytics application to profile the customer visiting the store in real time and proceed to provide customized discounts and offers.

3 Retail and E-Retail and Markets

The volumes of both retail shopping and e-commerce are constantly increasing (Figs. 2 and 3). The combined application, proposed in the current research, gains in importance, because of this growth, since it provides a solid Analytics tool, similar to the ones applied on web stores that is also applicable on the retail floor.

Retail is a 23 trillion dollar worldwide business as estimated in 2015, while the volume of e-commerce is a 1.5 trillion.

Internet sales represent a quite important part of the overall retail sales. This percentage is constantly growing (Figs. 4 and 5).

4 User Scenarios and Transforming Technologies

Describes how the customer uses the compound system. A step by step shopping procedure description example is given.

The incentive of applying such a system is based on the need of the elderly for easy and less stressful shopping, and speedier shopping for the younger. Social Networks support the shopping platforms by providing links to items and information and opinions.

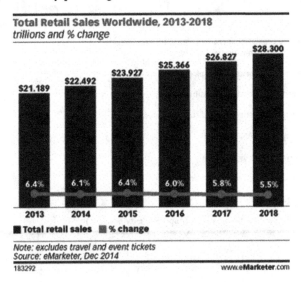

Fig. 2. Total Retail Sales Worldwide 2013-2018

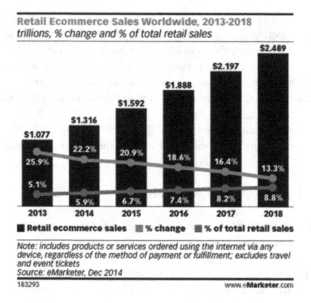

Fig. 3. Retail Ecommerce Sales Worldwide, 2013-2018

The shopping experience and the information made accessible by the mobile technologies are enhancing the customer satisfaction.

Customer loyalty discounts and offers can be very well customized. A customer can receive message alerts and product information on the shopping floor. Awards and discounts can be viewed and used during checkout. The retail market is merged with electronic market.

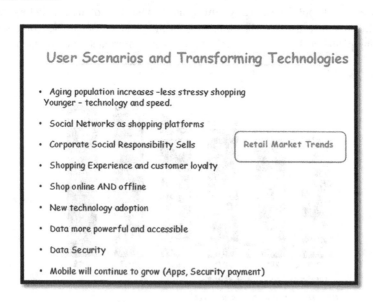

Retail Ecommerce Sales as a Percent of Total Retail Sales in Select Countries, 2013-2018

	2013	2014	2015	2016	2017	2018
UK*	11.6%	13.0%	14.4%	15.6%	16.9%	18.0%
China**	8.3%	10.1%	12.0%	13.8%	15.5%	16.6%
Finland	9.2%	9.8%	10.4%	10.8%	11.2%	11.5%
Norway	8.8%	9.7%	10.7%	11.5%	12.1%	12.7%
South Korea	8.1%	9.0%	9.8%	10.5%	11.3%	12.0%
Denmark	7.7%	8.6%	9.3%	9.9%	10.4%	10.8%
Germany	6.1%	7.3%	8.4%	9.4%	10.4%	11.2%
US*	5.8%	6.5%	7.1%	7.7%	8.3%	8.9%
Canada	4.5%	5.2%	5.9%	6.6%	7.4%	8.2%
Japan	4.4%	4.9%	5.4%	5.8%	6.2%	6.7%
France	4.2%	4.6%	5.1%	5.4%	5.8%	6.2%
Netherlands	3.8%	4.3%	4.6%	4.9%	5.1%	5.3%
Australia	3.6%	4.1%	4.5%	4.9%	5.3%	5.6%
Spain	3.6%	4.1%	4.8%	5.4%	6.0%	6.5%
Brazil	3.4%	3.8%	4.1%	4.4%	4.6%	4.8%
Sweden	3.2%	3.5%	3.8%	4.1%	4.4%	4.6%
Russia	2.0%	2.2%	2.4%	2.6%	2.8%	3.0%
Italy	1.5%	1.7%	1.9%	2.1%	2.2%	2.3%
Argentina	1.3%	1.4%	1.6%	1.9%	2.2%	2.5%
Mexico	1.0%	1.2%	1.5%	1.9%	2.2%	2.6%
India	0.6%	0.7%	0.9%	1.1%	1.3%	1.4%
Indonesia	0.5%	0.6%	0.8%	1.0%	1.2%	1.4%

Note: includes products or services ordered using the internet via any device, regardless of the method of payment or fulfillment; excludes travel and event tickets; *forecast from Sep 2014; **excludes Hong Kong
Source: eMarketer, Dec 2014

183110 www.eMarketer.com

Fig. 4. Retail Ecommerce Sales as a Percent per Country, 2013-2018

The implemented application, as described in this paper, supports the in store customer during shopping, via sensors, that will make use of mobile devices. The consumer has two shopping choices:

- In store and
- On-line shopping.

Internet sales 2013-2016 - values in billions						
	2013	2014	2015	2016	Increase 2014-15	Increase 2014-16
UK	£38.84	£44.97	£52.25	£60.25	16.2%	15.3%
Germany	£28.98	£36.23	£44.61	£54.60	23.1%	22.4%
France	£22.65	£26.38	£30.87	£36.24	17,0%	17.4%
Spain	£5.75	£6.87	£8.15	£9.66	18.6%	18.6%
Italy	£4.48	£5.33	£6.35	£7.60	19,0%	19.7%
Netherlands	£4.48	£5.09	£5.94	£6.92	16.8%	16.5%
Sweden	£3.13	£3.61	£4.17	£4.87	15.5%	16.8%
Poland	£2.92	£3.57	£4.33	£5.30	21,0%	22.5%
Europe	£111.23	£132.05	£156.67	£185.44	18.4%	18.7%
U.S.	£165.30	£189.26	£215.38	£245.96	13.8%	14.2%
Canada	£11.81	£12.84	£14.53	£16.65	13.2%	14.5%

Fig. 5. Internet Sales 2013–2016 in billions

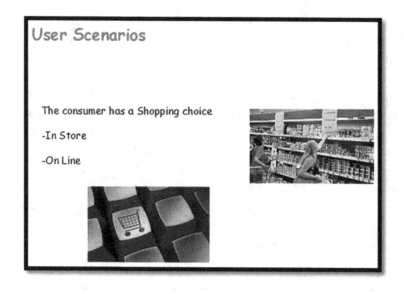

User Scenario

User Scenario.

- Shopper enters the store, launches a mobile app provided by retailer.

- The application automatically logs on, retrieves customer info (including loyalty program info), and based on their preferences and loyalty program tier or customer profile,

- May alert store employees to the customer's presence in the store.

The shopper enters the physical store carrying a mobile device and launches a mobile application on her mobile phone or tablet, which is provided by the retailer. The application allows the user to log on if the user wants. In this case it retrieves customer information, including personal loyalty program info, and based on their preferences and loyalty program tier or customer profile. It also may alert store employees to the customer's presence in the store.

During shopping the customer application receives customized message alerts in either text or voice, which are based on the user's product selections and location. The system checks for awards and discounts and presents them via the mobile app to the customer. It also alerts customer's presence to appropriate salesperson, if programmed to do so.

The user can obtain product information, information about special offers and promotions etc. The user can also connect to social networks and ask for advice from friends, request price comparisons and evaluation reviews about the product.

A novelty of the proposed solution lies in the way the integration of the technologies is achieved. Retailing practices have evolved over time, but have not changed significantly. Gradually transformational technologies are adapted to retail in store shopping. Internetworked devices, sensors and mobile technologies are capturing transactional data. Their application allows the in store customer data to apply advanced data Analytics and user profiling techniques as well as apply intelligent systems of any type, like the ones used in traditional e-commerce because of the automated data capturing provided by them.

Customer Message Alerts

The customer application can receive message alerts (text or voice)

- Check for awards
- Discounts
- Alerts customer's presence to favourite salesperson
- Product Information
- Special offers
- Promotions etc
- Could connect to social network to ask advice from friends

Transforming Technologies

Retailing practices have not changed significantly over time.

Gradually transformational technologies are adopted such as
Internetworked Devices
Sensors
Mobile Technologies
Advanced Data Analytics
User Profiling
Intelligent Systems

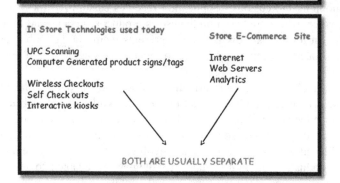

In Store Technologies used today

UPC Scanning
Computer Generated product signs/tags

Wireless Checkouts
Self Check outs
Interactive kiosks

Store E-Commerce Site

Internet
Web Servers
Analytics

BOTH ARE USUALLY SEPARATE

In Store Technologies used today
    UPC Scanning
    Computer Generated product signs/tags
    Wireless Checkouts
    Self Check outs
    Interactive kiosks
Store E-Commerce Site
    Internet
    Web Servers
    Analytics

Both technologies are usually separate. This project serves as an integration example. Integrating Retail and e-Commerce using Web Analytics and Intelligent Sensors

NEED FOR INTEGRATION
The future requires support for
BOTH Online and OFFLINE Shopping
There is a need for integration of E-Commerce system with Offline Shop MIS.

5 Management/Administrator Needs and Requirements for Analytics and User profiles

The Management should be able to
- Generate Store Performance Metrics in Near Real Time
- Derive Customer profile and segment tendencies,
- Determine Prior purchase behaviours
- Inventory stock levels
- Manufacturer promotions
- Formulate highly relevant offers in real time
- Respond in Real Time
- Customer Behavior Model Graphs

System Admin must know the
- System stability scalability and performance on low and high volume traffic

Integrating Retail and e-Commerce using Web Analytics and Intelligent Sensors
Need for Real Time Systems
Back end real time analytics can utilize factors such as customer lifetime value (Fig. 6)

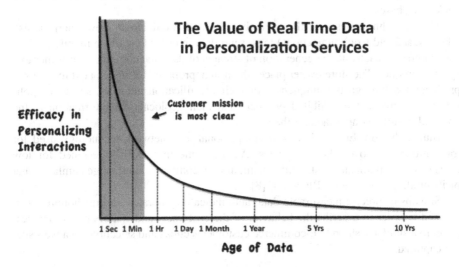

Fig. 6. Value of real time data in personalized services.

6 Intelligence and Sensors

Two technologies essential for this integration

- Intelligent Sensors
- Analytics and
- Customer Profiling.

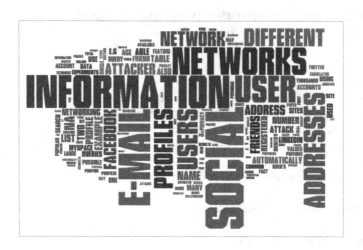

7 E-Commerce and Retail Shop Analytics Using Intelligent Sensors

We can obtain the necessary analytics information from sensors, keystrokes, mouse clicks, databases.

Mobile technologies, like iBeacons, based on BLE (Bluetooth Low Energy), also NFC (Near Field Communications) tags, send data in order to activate mobile devices and support and activate the generation of streams of data that correlate a customer to a specific product. The store owner places them in appropriate locations, next to exposed products and through the uniqueness of their identification numbers, software applications can match the exhibited products and their geolocational information to the physical customers approaching them.

Bluetooth Low Energy is a wireless personal area network technology used for transmitting data over short distances. As the name implies, it's designed for low energy consumption and cost, while maintaining a communication range similar to that of its predecessor, Classic Bluetooth [8].

Streams of precise measurable data, automatically generated during shopping, can be used in order to describe the behavior of the customers and visitors of the physical store, in a similar fashion to e-commerce customer's clicks and selections in a web-site, are captured.

The main difference between the two technologies lays in the necessary proximity between the mobile device and the source. iBeacons are used in order to automatically activate apps on the smartphone of the shop, visitor while NFC tags require higher proximity. Both technologies leverage existing networks and enhance customer support and provide accurate product information.

Back in the times where computers were introduced to the corporate world, among the first applications that became very quickly popular were Management Information Systems (MIS) for businesses. MIS's dealing with inventory, customer-maintenance, accounting, purchasing, invoicing etc., were introduced in the late fifties and have been widely used since the early sixties, running primarily on mainframe computers at that time. This fairly long evolution, lead to today's contemporary highly integrated Enterprise Resource Planning (ERP) Systems, involving almost any hardware, software and networking technological innovation that has been achieved during the past 60 years. The centralized mainframe-based application model used initially has shifted to modern distributed systems, heavily based on the Internet, mobile communications and finally the Cloud and Internet of Things.

A general data flow diagram of the basic operations performed by a typical retail system supporting the operations at the shopping floor, mainly customer purchases, is shown in the next figure. The very basic operations shown are: buying an item, payment processing and receiving an invoice. Customer transactions lead to inventory and

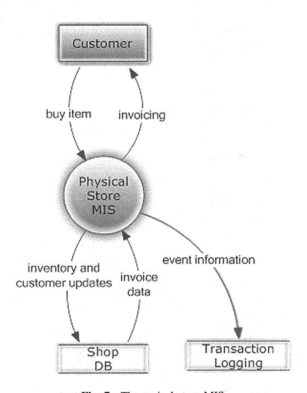

Fig. 7. The typical store MIS.

customer data updates. In order to gain full auditing ability, for future data mining and analysis of transactions, the event information is captured and stored in a log file.

This research is focused on the type of e-commerce site operators, which operate both physical stores as well, and use their e-shop in order to enhance sales, expand clientele and improve customer support. Web sites usually are multilingual, deal with multiple currencies and operate 24/7 and are cheap.

Certainly, since the introduction of the Cloud as a new form of computing, there is a change in the way traditional MIS's are viewed conceptually. The desktop applications seem to evolve into web pages. The physical location of the server seems to become irrelevant.

The Electronic Commerce Site. A typical e-commerce site can easily be viewed as a metaphor of an MIS. The physical presence of the customer is not required and the Similarities between their DFDs shown in Figs. 7 and 8, are obvious, since the e-commerce site deals and supports product purchases like a typical MIS does. The e-commerce site operates on similar data repositories, including inventory and customer data as well. For any corporation that operates both a physical and a virtual shop, the virtual shop repository could be automatically fed by inventory data from the physical store database.

The goal of a business to customer (B2C) e-shop application is to promote retail sales and create profit. A virtual store allows buying products or services through a

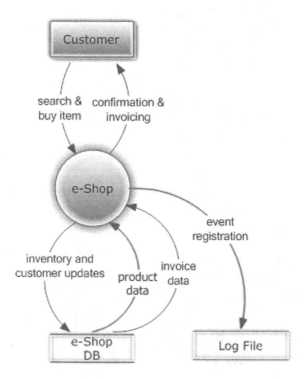

Fig. 8. The typical e-commerce application.

website, in analogy to a bricks-and-mortar retailer or a shopping mall [3]. e-Commerce is big business and getting bigger every day. Growth estimates from eMarketer report that business-to-consumer (B2C) e-commerce sales worldwide will reach $1.5 trillion in 2014, increasing nearly 20 % over 2013 [9].

The customer accesses the e-shop web page, searches the web site for a product and adds it to a shopping cart metaphor. This procedure is repeated and finally the customer checks out and the invoice is issued. The item search procedure is assisted by the e-shop categories, manufacturer selection, advanced search mechanisms and related product proposals. The customer of the physical store picks the items straight from the shelves.

Emphasis is given to the registration of events, which leads to full accountability of the operation and allows a toolbox of analytics to extract customer and system behavioral information.

The Log File Analyzer. The log file analyzer (LFA), shown in Fig. 9, is a toolbox, consisting of a menu driven application, with graphical user interface. The LFA is written in Java, in order to be portable across operating systems and architectures. It can reside on a separate server or on the server where the e-shop is running.

It is essential for the e-shop administrator to be given a user friendly application to work with. It can quickly track the transaction histories of any e-shop, measure the required parameters, the performance of actions of the entire shop and reveal the results of measurements under various load conditions.

The architecture was chosen to be expandable in order to allow easy inheritance of the classes that do the data imports and the negotiations with the various web servers, so that whenever e-shops that run on new web server architectures are needed, their respective log files and any e-shop application databases can be adapted and evaluated relatively fast. In order to be usable, the toolbox contains a tool with the ability to load log file deltas as easy as possible and get the e-hops latest status for evaluation at any time.

The requirements for results, measurements, data mining and visualization of data etc. are under constant change, therefore the LFA is easily customizable and extensible, allowing standard interactive report generators to provide customized and semi-customized reports.

The Log File Analyzer operates like a typical Extract Transform Load (ETL) application [10]. Its basic input is extracted straight from the log file of the e-shop and includes all requested events and transactions that took place during its operation. The LFA allows the administrator to configure the e-Shop in order to produce the appropriate log file details.

The analyzer application allows merging together information from the e-shop database with the log file entries. This feature allows the system to enrich the log file entries with familiar product codes, names and descriptions and produce easy comprehensible visualizations of the data.

The transformed information is stored to the LFA database transaction file, and is used in order to produce statistics, graphs and measurements.

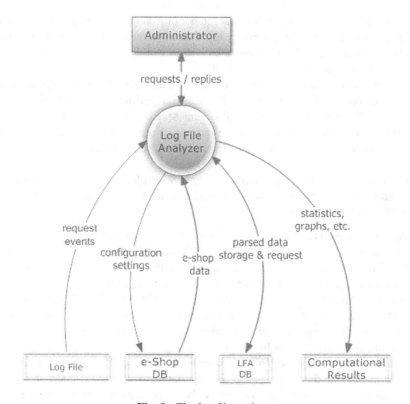

Fig. 9. The log file analyzer.

The Analyzer is designed in the "Near Real Time ETL" fashion, described by Vassiliadis and Simitsis, [11] since it is compliant to the Quality-of-Service (QoS) characteristics:

- Maximum freshness of data.
- Minimal overhead of the source systems.
- Guaranteed QoS for the warehouse operation.
- Controlled environment.
- Scalability in terms of sources involved, queries posed by end users and volumes of data to be processed.
- Stable interface at the warehouse side.
- Smooth upgrade of software at the sources.

The Combined Analyzer. Typical physical store and e-shop combo systems are comprised of two usually separate applications, which require some form of data communication bridges between them. Although the MIS and the e-shop are two distinct applications, viewed from the executive point of view, they are seen as facets of the same information system. Daily sales figures, price and inventory updates, product reorder levels and stock from one system have to update the other. In Fig. 10 the interconnection between the log files can be seen. The analyzer reads data from the e-shop and the MIS databases, but the main data bulk is read from the two log files. The entries in the two log files are parsed in accordance to their layout format, which is customizable by the application and are merged into the LFA database. From then and on the data can be used for mining, cross-correlation and any analysis and visualization necessary.

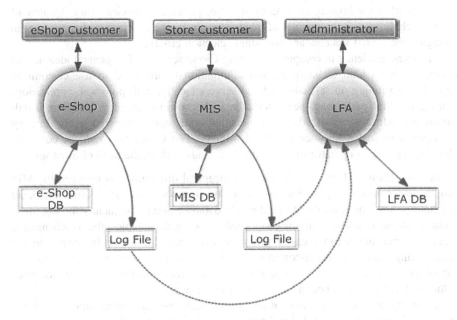

Fig. 10. The log file analyzer combining e-shop and MIS.

The quality and precision and timeliness of the reported results by the LFA depend heavily on the quality and timeliness of its input.

Data collected by the e-shop, is pushed to the LFA DB in three distinct fashions [12]:

- On demand from-to: The administrator requires from date and time and to date and time.
- On demand, based on dates or sizes, where entire rotatable log files are loaded to the DB and
- Automatically in near real time.

All three methods are available to the administrator, with the third fashion being the most convenient one, since it requires no administrator intervention. It parses and loads all required data into the LFA DB immediately after the data are collected as they are generated, allowing for real time measurements, warning and alarm generation in case of the occurrence of a problem or an exception event.

The topology of such a combined system is absolutely flexible. These three communicating applications could even reside on the same computer in small scale businesses, or even on three distinct servers with separate database servers and communication servers, all located in different locations. A large amount of companies operating e-shops prefer using virtual private networked (VPN) servers hosted by third party Internet hosting service providers, located geographically in different countries in order to lower operational costs.

The market for hosting companies is large, prices and services vary. Quality of service, reliability and the amount of freedom given by the provider to the customer to configure the rented systems are important selection criteria.

The latest tendency in computing is using Cloud services. The general idea behind moving to the Cloud is based on full elimination of the need to use customized applications running on self administered servers locally, with pure web applications running on third party machines externally, with zero investment in hardware installations and administration, other than personal computers connected to the Internet equipped with just a browser and local printers. The Cloud also reduces costs, by allowing the e-shop operator to deal with peak loads without the need of huge servers.

Enhancing Input. There is a significant conceptual differentiation between the MIS and the e-commerce application, regarding the log file level of information detail granularity they can generate. While the MIS database and consequently the log file is updated whenever a transaction is committed to the database tables, that is whenever a retail customer moves to the cash register and every item of the cart is scanned by the clerk during checkout, the e-commerce system, as a pure web application has the capability of registering every single key click and every selection of any visitor, even if the visitor does never become a customer and leaves.

For every session a vast amount of data are registered, including time stamps and the entire history of requested items and categories. This information is pushed to the analyzer and allows an analyst administrator to evaluate the visitors' behavioral patterns and correlate information according to location, time, period of the year and gain insight into the complex selection mechanisms of the public that visits the e-shop. In order to gap this detail granularity differentiation between an MIS and an e-shop, receptors from the mobile telephony world can be used in the retail store floor, in order to capture and provide interaction information, similar to the detail information of the key clicks of the e-commerce application. This way the shopping cycle of any visitor of the store can be analyzed with a detail granularity equivalent to the one found in e-commerce applications.

The smart phone can either connect via the mobile network or any in house Wi-Fi network in order to obtain information about any product, discount coupons and price offers. The customer can also proceed to the e-shop link, complete the purchase online and pick up the products on the way out. In any case, the LFA is registering all transaction details and information and enhancing the patterns required for an accurate customer behavior analysis, in real time.

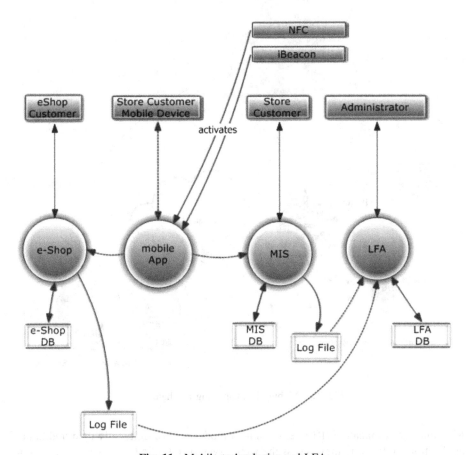

Fig. 11. Mobile technologies and LFA.

Figure 11 shows the combined extended application architecture. A custom mobile application senses the iBeacon or the NFC tag and allows the customer to connect to either the MIS or the e-Shop multiple times during the shopping session as the customer moves in the shop. The iBeacons operate automatically via Bluetooth, while the NFC only when the user selects a specific product and wishes to obtain additional information about it, or has the intention of purchasing it. This connection is either established via General Packet Radio Service (GPRS) or Wi-Fi if available.

Either way, they activate the mobile phone and allow its user to enhance the shopping experience by acquiring additional product information (Fig. 12). The actions are recorded into the log file and are being transferred, in near real time, over to the LFA for further processing. This way the physical store obtains sensors that can trace the steps of a customer during in the same fashion as the e-shop can.

An important issue that involves the evolution of web application frameworks has been resolved by the LFA we are developing. Web application systems, featuring the

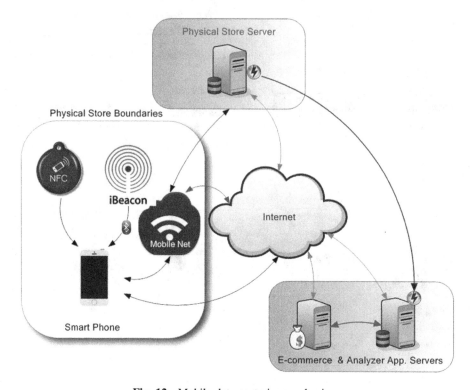

Fig. 12. Mobile data capturing mechanism.

Rich Internet Application (RIA) environment model behave differently than traditional applications in the way they access the web server. The traffic to the web server is not as detailed as necessary, in order to capture user interaction to the same level as with non RIA applications [12]. This new model of architecture shifts complicated graphical user interface (GUI) issues to the client. This way it allows using complicated widgets, similar to the ones used in desktop environments and allows the development of easier and more versatile user interfaces.

We use a specific queuing technique in order to implement the necessary near real time feed of data from the application to the Analyzer Application [12]. In addition to this data, entries obtained from the database log file are packaged and sent to the analyzed too [13]. The traditional application sends log file data via a named queue to the analytics application server. The RIA applications, on the other hand, have a less "interesting" log file to send. We try to avoid modifying the measured application and in order to generate the needed data, the applications database is being enhanced with triggers by the analyzer. An additional data table set is created. Once the triggers are activated, they write to the appropriate tables of this additional data table set the necessary information. This new set of data tables is constantly being polled by a data producer daemon and the information is fed to the analyzer in near real time.

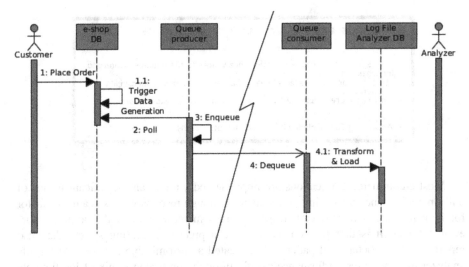

Fig. 13. NRT order processing.

A typical aspect of this implementation is presented in Fig. 13. This example describes the steps that take place whenever the Customer places an order.

This following scenario takes place when the user places an order:

1. The placement of the order by the customer starts this cycle, and is the event of interest for this metric.

   1.1 In order to automatically intercept the order data, an after-insert trigger is placed in the orders table. This trigger copies the order-id auto number unique key to the new table "transmitted", which has to be have been added to the e-shop database. This new table could also reside in a separate database, in case the database administrators want to keep the e-shop database changes and additions to a minimum. The contents of the transmitted table are kept simple. It includes just:

   - An auto number as a primary key.
   - The foreign key order number.
   - One bit, indicating that the transmission to the LFA is pending.

2. This table is polled periodically for any pending records by the queue producer.

3. If pending entries are located, based on the order number, all required additional information is gathered with the appropriate left joins with other e-shop database tables and appropriate log file data and the resulting data structure is enqueued.

4. The queue consumer at the LFA server-side dequeues the information and

   4.1 Transforms and loads the data to the LFA database. From there the order data is made available to the web application for presentation to the user.

> ## E-Shops usually do not get Analytics Reports
>
> - Only successful sales transactions are visible to the administration and management.
> - Most e-Commerce systems have no built-in performance measuring mechanisms.
> - Only registered-customer actions are taken into consideration.
>
> HOWEVER
> - Access log files include all interaction data details.

Most e-commerce applications are implemented without any significant means of built-in performance measuring mechanisms, although responsiveness is a major factor for high revenue. Often, overall response times increase without the administrators even noticing. It is therefore crucial to have a precise measuring system that also reports customer behavioral patterns. We created a customizable e-commerce log file analyzer that measures performance mainly through combining a mix of log file data with e-shop information. It is capable of supporting multiple e-shops and can perform cross comparisons between them. It is easy to use and the software is extendable in order to support different web server architectures. It displays patterns taken by the user interaction with the e-shop and allows the administrators to locate less visited pages and make improvements or promote them better. This way an e-shop may benefit since it may lead to higher user satisfaction and profitability. The administrator can regularly study the readings and take the appropriate actions, if overall performance decay is observed [4].

> # The Solution
>
> - **Parsing and "cleaning"** log files.
>   Extraction and transfer into a DBMS. Information Generation. (Extract Transform Load)
> - **Cross correlation of log file and e-Commerce site data** for seamless integration.
> - **Anonymous and registered visitor** hits can be analyzed through their IP-addresses.
> - **Crawlers and Web-Bots** can be recognized via IP-address and their behavioral patterns.
> - Implementation of a software tool that directly measures the operational performance of the e-shop in **nearly real time**.

The log analyzer toolbox is an application built with a graphical user interface. It is menu driven and fairly simple to operate since it is essential for the e-shop administrator to be given a user friendly application to work with. It can quickly track the transaction histories of any e-shop, measure the required parameters, the performance of actions of the entire shop and reveal the results of measurements under various load conditions.

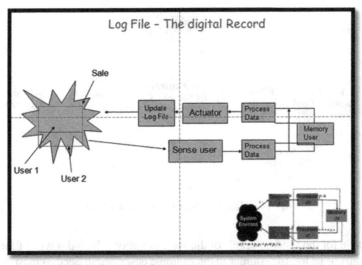

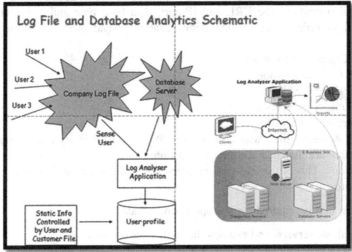

The functionality is shown in Fig. 14. The architecture was chosen to be expandable in order to allow easy inheritance of the classes that do the data imports and the negotiations with the various web servers, so that whenever e-shops that run on new web server architectures are needed, their respective log files and any e-shop application databases can be adapted and evaluated relatively fast.

In order to be usable, the toolbox contains a tool with the ability to load log file deltas as easy as possible and get the e-shops latest status for evaluation at any time.

The analyzer is based on a database, which consists of following tables:

- Servers: Stores information about the standard locations of different web servers supported (log file directory, configuration file name and location etc.).

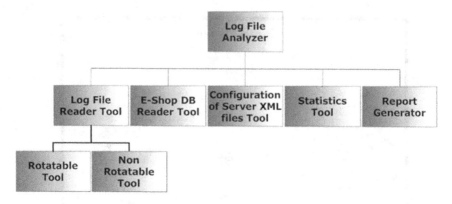

Fig. 14. Main functions of the log analyzer.

- Site: Table for the specific details of the various e-shops. Includes type of the server and details of its log file (similar to the example described in Sect. 3) must be stored here. It also contains the URL and IP-port, data base type and a username and password in order to access the items, categories and orders from the e-shop database.
- Product Categories for every e-shop
- Products for every e-shop
- Orders for every e-shop
- Order Statuses for every e-shop
- Customers of every e-shop
- Business-Actions: (like "add To Cart" or "Pay" etc.) for every e-shop implementation. They are matched with the transactions.
- Transactions: This is the table where every line of information from the log file is parsed into.

  The input that is required for the operation includes:

- Settings about servers, and e-shops that will be processed
- Rotatable or non rotatable log file deltas
- Import of Items, categories, customers, statuses and orders from the e-shop databases
- The processing that is done by the analyzer is:
- Intelligent log file import
- Preprocessing of the log file and import into the transactions table, in batches.
- Log file Analysis
- Statistical Information generation
- Chart and graph generation
- Robot analyzer
- Output produced:
- Graphical reports
- PDF output
- Various Printouts

Since Java Swing is portable on a very large variety of computing platforms, it was selected as the programming environment for the development. Java offers also a large base of application programming interfaces and offers convenient web access APIs.

The analyzer is able to accommodate data from multiple e-shops simultaneously. These e-shops should not necessarily have to be of the same architecture or framework and evaluations and cross comparisons of performance data are easily feasible.

All data can easily be replicated to the tool's database. This way, selections, comparisons and measurements become portable, easy and flexible. Extensive user access data reports can reveal customer behavior, customer-selections and navigation paths through the various pages and offerings.

The physical location of the e-shop data should be irrelevant, as long as the server host provides accessibility to download and adapt the necessary data to the toolbox's own database. This way putting extra load on the web server can be avoided. The analyzer reads the relevant data and loads it to its own database which was described earlier. In order to be able to name the log file data and provide exact information, the toolbox is offered read permission to a few database tables of the e-shop, like product categories and inventory items and orders [4].

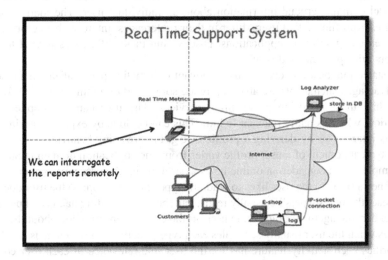

8 User Profiles

The rapidly growing amount of information on the Web makes difficult for internet users to find-access desired information. This case may be even worse if users don't have the ability to use efficiently, appropriate search engines for information discovery. But even if they do use a search engine, and submit a query, they get millions of results that most of the time are irrelevant to their needs. These results are chosen and ordered in a predefined order based on an algorithm of the search engine. If two users enter the query "apple" they get exactly the same results, from a search engine, even if the first one is a farmer and the second an IT specialist that wishes to buy some famous products from "Apple". On the other hand the number of Web services rapidly grows, so is web personalization more than before, in demand.

Google, indexes more than 1 Trillion Unique Web URLs. Looking at these numbers it is clear that an average internet-user is in need of some kind of personalized access to some topics, which are relevant to him. It is the quality of the provided information which determines whether a user is satisfied with a certain web-service, not the quantity.

The way of achieving that is by user profiling. Web personalization can help internet users with the problem of information overload. The Web nowadays is both a technical and a social phenomenon. It affects everybody's daily life, businesses and leads to considerable social implications. Businesses want to deliver valuable material to their online customers, like products services or adverts, in order to raise their profits, whereas web users do not want to receive huge amount of unrelated information resulting from a Web search. Besides the fact that a web user can get lost on the cyberspace with so much information available, he of course would not like to spend all his available time on useless browsing over the Internet to find his desire. The solution to both problems described above, is user profiling [15].

A profile is a description of someone containing the most important or interesting facts about him or her. In the context of users or software applications, a user profile or user model contains crucial information about an individual user. The motivation of building user profiles is that users differ in their preferences, interests, background and goals when using software applications. Discovering these differences is vital to provide users with personalized services.

It is stated that besides access to user-relevant information personalization has some other advantages such as we are able to provide some kind of a familiar feeling for our users, while they are using personalized services. The user can be supplied with information, which is really relevant to him. This can be done by explicitly asking him about his interests or by deriving a profile of e.g. his browsing behavior.

The typical content of a user profile varies from one application domain to another. For example, if we consider an online newspaper domain, the user profile contains the types of news (topics) the user likes to read, the types of news (topics) the user does not like to read, the newspapers he usually reads, and the user's reading habits and patterns. In a calendar management domain the user profile contains information about the dates and times when the user usually schedules each type of activity in which he is involved, the priorities each activity feature has for the user, the relevance of each user contact and the user's scheduling and rescheduling habits. In other domains personal information about the user, such as name, age, job, and hobbies might be important.

User profiling will become more and more important in the future with heterogeneous devices used to access all kinds of information and services. It is important for both the user and the service provider to have more customized ways of accessing services. All kinds of devices, especially mobile device users and service providers can have benefits from profiling.

The basic rational is that service according to individual needs benefits the customer, who then will be using services more often and will be willing to pay extra for good services. This will eventually lead to higher profitability and long-term success in the businesses providing these services as they can keep their profitable customers.

Companies are therefore interested in providing their customers with better service and user profiling is needed in order to be able to provide more personalized content.

Users face also motivation for profiling. New devices introduce new services and new technologies that provide lots of possibilities to interaction. Users will probably also need multiple profiles according to their status. Work and free-time usage and high and low-band usage must be differentiated.

Competition increases in the area of information dissemination. Supplying customers with valuable and unique services is essential. When considering different users, capabilities like bandwidth, displays or text-writing must be taken into account.

When same information and services are published in heterogeneous devices, poses lots of challenges on providing customized view on information. This demands good separation of data. Segmenting users to user groups is also important. Directed services are generally better and knowing end users is increasingly important especially those with small devices. Thus, creating different views to same information is needed to serve different users as well. What is shown and what is left out can be decided depending on user preferences and devices used for access.

Personalization is key point to providing. It is many times important for the user to affect on its own profile. This can be achieved using registrations or other methods. Users can often be very cautious at providing personal information, so privacy issues can get very important. Also users must have the possibility to alter their profiles if they want to. In latest mobile phones profiles exist to help users adjust phone settings to match situations.

Lots of work and research is needed to bring easily controllable and widely used services in place for the use in all these new pervasive devices. User profiles and their management is one of the key issues in providing intelligent services to the end users that use a variety of devices.

The following figure shows the data that could be assembled from the data sensors, which could, in turn, be processed with the assistance of an intelligent user profiling algorithm. The data analysis will give us information about the user i.e. to get a description of someone containing the most important or interesting facts about him or her. The main goal is to create "personal" software applications based on users' preferences, interests, background and goals.

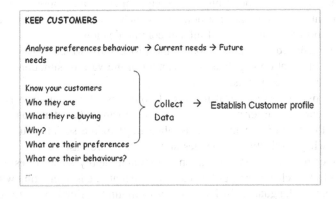

In order to focus on user profiling, we should first have a look on nowadays technology. Given the fact that heterogeneous devices that exist on the market, it is certain that technology can be sufficient enough to supply us with the tools for the management of individual's user profiling at most cases. Users with different devices that have different capabilities, make it harder for the developers to create efficient applications. These applications should operate on all devices such as PC, PDA, mobiles, and smart-TVs. Except for the case of simple files-services that can run to all the devices, it is still unfeasible to have common applications-services to operate to all of them.

Mobiles nowadays connect to the web via Wi-Fi, 3G and 4G networks. The connection speeds alter dramatically depending on how our mobile is connected to the web, so the developers should create "intelligent" applications that would alter the way they operate based on the connection speed, like increasing or decreasing the characteristics that are shown to the end-user. However, user profiling and Intelligence will be presented later in this paper.

Storing, retrieving and manipulating user profiling, under different devices and operating systems, requires a huge amount of computational power. This is both a scientific and engineering problem, thereby driving the development of new bit-device technologies and circuit architectures. Motivated by this positive feedback loop between increasing demand and improving technology, computational efficacy has improved steadily and rapidly since computing inception. Furthermore, the ultimate limits have yet to be set.

9   Emotional Analysis

Emotions play important role in human intelligence, rational decision making, social interaction, perception, memory, learning, creativity, and more. Given the importance of computer mediated communication (CMC), a lot of researches have been done on emotion recognition. At the same time, textual emotion recognition is increasingly attracting attention.

In human face-to-face communication the use of 'appropriate language', 'tone of voice', 'facial expressions', proximity and 'body language' are important audio-visual input components in space and time domains, which when complemented with other sensory input form the 'channels' of human communications.

Computer mediated communication is the process by which a group of 'social actors' in a given situation negotiate the meaning of the various situations which arise between them, using computers.

Within the psycho sociological models of communication, language is no longer seen as merely carrier of information from one mind to another, but also as 'an essential dimension of the culture to which are ascribed most of the social values and representations on which collective exchanges and practices are based'.

In computer mediated communication, individuals apply social rules and the literature points to five characteristics that cue the idea that one is interacting with a social actor. These are (a) language, (b) interactivity to multiple prior inputs, (c) computers fulfilling social roles, (d) Use of human sounding speech, and (e) The possession of a human or human-like face.

Text has traditionally been the standard medium of real time internet communications, with various chat software available. Written text sentences are rich in conveying emotional information, which is open to interpretation by the reader.

Various real time chat application programs have been developed for use and are available freely over the internet. The majority of them focus on the use of real time text communication. The growth of those basic applications is significant with the advent of low cost internet communications. Online conversations are typical in collaboration between groups, and many are entirely text-based. Text is rich inexpressiveness but it needs to be read, and people have to be focused to read and comprehend text. Text based real time communication applications can be enhanced with the use of text, images, 'emoticons' and some also use audio. Users however cannot see the participants present at a glance nor their expressions.

Sentences can be broken down into two groups of words: function words and content words. Function words include nouns, adjectives, verbs and adverbs, while content words are prepositions, conjunctions and auxiliary verbs. All these groups contain sub classes, which can be represented by tree diagrams. According to what groups the words belong to and the words preceding and subsequent the sentences can be decomposed and be analyzed.

Sentence Structure and Analysis. A sentence may only consist of a single word or a group of words. In order to analyze sentences the sentence definition groups have been developed. E.g., one of the sentence definition groups is: Article + noun + verb + preposition General sentence constructions are identified in. The constructions include: Declarative statement, Interrogative statement, finite verb phrases and negative statement.

Declarative statement: This kind of statement usually contains a subject and a verb where the subject precedes the verb. E.g., I am running.
Interrogative statement: A question, e.g., was he angry?
Finite verb phrases: Expresses statement or directives. E.g., Sit down.
Negative statements: This kind of statement expresses anything but what the sentence mean. E.g., I am not happy.

The Tagging System. Although some tagging systems already exist, these tagging systems do not fulfill the engine's requirement. The engine requires the entire word to be properly tagged in order to keep a minimum response time. For every possible emotional word and its related intensity, the engine also requires particular marks. Typical traditional tagging systems only specify the suffixes or prefixes to differentiate between different word groups

Tagged Dictionary. Daily communications involve about two thousand words. In order to identify the words, a special designed dictionary should be set up. The database includes three fields: word field, word category field and emotional tag field. Word field contains all the words and word category contains the corresponding tag. To extract emotional word as quickly as possible, the emotional tag field was added.

Word Analysis. When receiving the input sentence, the tagging system will split the sentence into words and check through the tagged dictionary to find each word and the corresponding tag category. If a word is not found in the dictionary, the engine will undergo a suffix and prefix analysis. By examining the suffix and prefix of the word, the assumed tag may be derived. The output of the tagging system includes the words and corresponding categories.

The emotion extraction engine can be used in numerous applications, for example in realtime communication systems, and real time internet games.

10   An Integrated Architecture

Certainly, since the introduction of the Cloud as a new form of computing, there is a change in the way traditional MIS's are viewed conceptually. The desktop applications seem to evolve into web pages. The physical location of the server seems to become irrelevant.

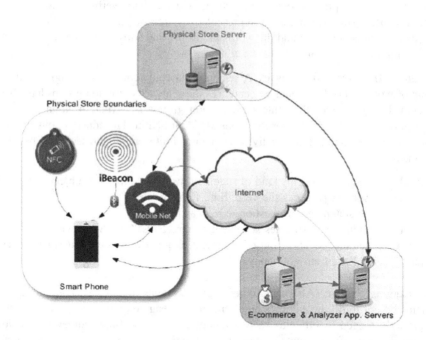

The functionality of the Integrated System

The Physical Store server:
- Intelligent System
- User Identification
- Location Determination (sensors)
- Intelligent Decisions on Offers
- Messaging to Smart Phone

E-Commerce and Analyzer Application Services
- Customer File Access
- Product Info Access

Smart Phone
- Applications
- Interfacing Sensors
- Messaging

11 Conclusions

Mobile technologies and communication techniques, commonly used in e-commerce applications can be extended in such a way that will significantly enhance the shopping experience of traditional commerce. They can be extended and can become hybrid systems, offering much better service to customers of traditional brick and mortar shops.

Typically a consumer spends some time searching the Internet before making a purchase, comparing specifications and reading reviews. When visiting a traditional shop, the customer has to rely on the words of the salesman. Three relatively low cost techniques make product information available to customers that carry portable devices like smart-phones or tablets:

- Use of NFC tags for each product
- Use of iBeacons and
- Use of Quick Response codes (QR code) tags, attached to the exhibited products.

NFC tags provide the customer with a link which redirects the mobile web client to the product's web site entry, providing all necessary information and details about the specific item, also allowing the customer to complete the purchase electronically. The web server, hosting the e-shop, can only then have clues about the whereabouts of the customer, when special NFC-tags are being used, intended for specific locations of the product.

iBeacons on the other hand, are low cost indoor operating devices, acting as micro-location awareness and positioning systems, that transmit constantly in simplex fashion packages via Bluetooth low energy (BLE). Appropriate scanner-applications on the mobile device notify the customer automatically upon approaching the product or place. Multiple beacons can be processed simultaneously and their unique codes can be used in order to identify the approximation of the customer to specific items. The constant package transmission enables the web server to easily measure the time a customer has spent studying any specific tagged item. The customer can automatically receive discount coupons or offers in order to make any seemingly product of interest more attractive. Accessing beacons provides a fairly accurate geographical location of the customer inside the premises of the business and this geolocation is guaranteed. The mobile application can automatically offer technical specifications, details and information about the product as well as similar or cross selling products. Finally the electronic payment can take place via the mobile phone and the personnel can arrange for the invoice, packaging and delivery of the product as soon as the customer reaches the exit gate. In other words the customer can start a transaction on-line and conclude it off-line.

At the same time the route of each customer and the times she spends deciding what to purchase can be analyzed, similarly to the way it is analyzed by checking out the clicks on an e-shop browser. This can enhance the accuracy of the profile of the customer, and add additional granularity if used together to other techniques, without requesting anything from the customer. If combined with data, extracted by the e-shop web analytics application will allow the company to provide better and more accurate services and make products proposals, which can lead to a more gratifying interaction and raise sales.

QR code tags can also allow the customer to receive information about products by redirecting straight to the e-shop page of the specific item. If approached this way, then the location of the customer is not guaranteed, since accessing through the special QR code could be requested by using a photograph of the code at any later time.

NFC and QR code reading are procedures that need to be demanded by the customer explicitly, while iBeacons will work automatically if the customer has the Bluetooth of her mobile device turned on.

The customer must receive adequate information about the advantages of using the system as well as the information that will be collected by the analytics application that will process the resulting interaction data.

We have seen that user profiles are vital in many areas, many of them in constant evolution and some new ones. Thus, researchers in the area of user profiling have to fulfill the expectations of these new trends and include new components as part of a profile and develop new techniques to build them.

As regards user profile contents, in recent years there has been increasing interest in modeling users' emotions and moods as part of the user profiles in areas such as social computing and intelligent agents. With respect to contextual information about a user, the developments in the areas of ubiquitous computing, mobile devices, and physical sensors enable the incorporation of new features in user profiles such as the focus of user attention (detected via eye-tracking), users' mood and emotions (detected analyzing facial expressions and body posture), temperature and humidity of the user's location, among others.

References

1. ICETE 2015. Integrating Retail and e-Commerce using Web Analytics and Intelligent Sensors. http://www.icete.org/PreviousInvitedSpeakers.aspx#2015, September 2015
2. Provost, F., Fawcett, T.: Data Science for Business, p. 2. O'Reilly, Sebastopol (2013)
3. Menascé, D.A., Almeida, V.A.F.: Challenges in scaling E-business sites. In: Proceedings of 2000 Computer Measurement Group Conference, Sect. 4, p. 5, Orlando, FL, 10–15, December 2000
4. Boucouvalas, A.C., Aivalis, C.J.: An e-shop log file analysis toolbox. In: CSNDP 2010 Newcastle. IEEE (2010)
5. http://www.ibisworld.com/, September 2015

6. http://www.wwwmetrics.com/shopping.htm, October 2015
7. Trends in Online Shopping. A Global Nielsen Consumer Report, p. 2. http://th.nielsen.com/site/documents/GlobalOnlineShoppingReportFeb08.pdf, February 2008
8. A Guide to Beacons. http://www.ibeacon.com/what-is-ibeacon-a-guide-to-beacons/, February 2015
9. e-Commerce Shifts into Higher Gear. A Global Nielsen Consumer Report, p. 2. http://ir.nielsen.com/files/doc_financials/Nielsen-Global-E-commerce-Report-August-2014.pdf, February 2015
10. Kimball, R., Ross, M.: The Data Warehouse Toolkit, 2nd edn, p. 35. Wiley Computer Publishing, Hoboken (2002)
11. Vassiliadis, P., Simitzis, A.: Near real time ETL. In: Wrembel, R., Kozielski, S. (eds.) New Trends in Data Warehousing and Data Analysis, pp. 25–28. Springer, New York (2009)
12. Aivalis, C.J., Boucouvalas, A.C.: Future proof analytics techniques for web 2.0 applications. In: TEMU 2014. IEEE (2014)
13. Aivalis, C.J., Boucouvalas, A.C.: Log file analysis of e-commerce systems in rich internet web 2.0 applications. In: PCI 2011. IEEE (2011)
14. Boucouvalas, A.C., Xu, Z., John, D.: Emotional Momentum and Text to Emotion Analysis Engines -Theory and Practice Submitted to Special issue on Journal of Visual Languages and Computing (2003)
15. Gaziolis, K., Boucouvalas, A.C.: Discovering the impact of user profiling in e-services. In: 2014 International Conference on Telecommunications and Multimedia, TEMU 2014, pp. 208–213, Heraklion Crete, Greece. IEEE (2014)

Data Communication Networking

High Level Policies in SDN

Libor Polčák[1(✉)], Leo Caldarola[2], Amine Choukir[2], Davide Cuda[2],
Marco Dondero[2], Domenico Ficara[2], Barbora Franková[1], Martin Holkovič[1],
Roberto Muccifora[2], and Antonio Trifilo[2]

[1] Faculty of Information Technology, Brno University of Technology,
Božetěchova 2, 612 66 Brno, Czech Republic
{ipolcak,ifrankova,iholkovic}@fit.vutbr.cz
[2] Cisco Systems Sarl, Rolle, Switzerland
{lcaldaro,amchouki,dcuda,mdondero,dficara,rmuccifo,antrifil}@cisco.com

Abstract. Policies for network traffic handling define packet routes
through networks, enforce required quality of service, and protect networks
from security threats. When expressing a policy, one needs to characterise
the traffic to which the policy applies by traffic identifiers. Low level traffic identifiers, such as IP addresses and port numbers, are available in each
packet. Indeed, low level traffic identifiers are perfect for data plane routing and switching. However, high level traffic identifiers, such as user name
and application name, are better for the readability and clarity of a policy.
In this paper, we extend software defined networks with high level traffic identifiers. We propose to add additional interface to SDN controllers
for collecting traffic meta data and high level traffic identifiers. The controller maintains a database that maps high level traffic identifiers to a set
of flows defined by low level traffic identifiers. SDN applications can apply
policies based on both high level and low level traffic identifiers. We leave
the southbound protocols intact. This paper provides two examples of High
Level SDN paradigms – Application-Aware Networks and Identity-Aware
Networks. The first paradigm enables policies depending on application
names and characteristics. The latter allows policies based on user names
and their roles.

1 Introduction

Recently, Software Defined Network (SDN) emerged [21] as a new paradigm
based on the separation of the network control logic (control plane) from the
forwarding fabric (data plane). The network control plane is orchestrated by a
central SDN controller or a set of cooperating SDN controllers. The data plane
is independently implemented in each network device and it allows to forward
data as fast as possible, preferably on the line speed. Current SDN controllers
are often modular, open source, extensible, and provide so called northbound
interface that allows network operators and service providers to simplify network
management operations with custom SDN applications that controls the policies
followed by the controller, and consequently, the network.

SDN handles traffic [21] with respect to low level *traffic identifiers*, such
as header field values and physical identifiers, e.g., an interface identifier.

M.S. Obaidat and P. Lorenz (Eds.): ICETE 2015, CCIS 585, pp. 39–57, 2016.
DOI: 10.1007/978-3-319-30222-5_2

SDN has no insight on the relations between flows. Due to the lack of high level traffic identifiers, it is not possible to directly and consistently specify policies for all flows belonging to a specific application or define policies for specific persons that are a part of a communication.

This paper extends SDN with high level traffic identifiers that are used to specify rules to control network traffic. The suggested high level traffic identifiers include the name of the application that generated a flow, the user name of the person that is a part of the communication, the required bandwidth for a specific flow and others. The network administrator can define specific policies for specific persons or applications, hence, the administrator does not need to specify policies for each flow separately. The extended SDN is called High Level SDN.

Currently, the predominant way of managing and configuring network is on a per-network-node and per-endpoint-type basis, irrespective of the commonalities that traffic patterns exhibit. Another painful point is the decentralised policy configuration. This configuration and management model is error prone, not flexible and cumbersome. High Level SDN unifies and centralizes the configuration. Our major contribution is in the abstraction of network traffic handling. High Level SDN recognizes relations between different flows originating from the same application, the same machine or the same user. Therefore, it is possible to handle traffic of the same application, the same machine, or the same user in a consistent manner. High Level SDN introduces high level traffic identifiers, such as application name or a user name. A network administrator specifies policies based on the high level traffic identifiers. High level policies allow for instance:

- To develop application-aware quality of service capabilities matching business-critical applications traffic and to set its priority higher. In addition, the quality of service can be further tweaked according to priorities associeted with the person that generates or produces the traffic (e.g., calls of a manager have higher priority compared to lower-level staff);
- To precisely reserve network bandwidth according to the expected traffic rate of the flows generated by specific applications;
- To deploy application-dependent or identity-related dynamic service chaining, i.e., routing of flows of a specific application or a specific person through specific network services (e.g., IPS/IDS, packet filtering, load balancing or caching).

High Level SDN does not require any specific SDN controller. However, High Level SDN requires additional sources of information — *traffic metadata*, it does require a modular and extensible SDN controller or a specialized High Level SDN controller. The differences between an SDN controller and a High Level SDN controller are following:

- High Level SDN controller provides additional interface for traffic metadata.
- High Level SDN provides traffic metadata via northbound interface to SDN applications.
- High Level SDN converts rules with high level traffic identifiers to standard SDN rules.

This paper extends the paper *Towards a real application-aware network* [3] presented at the 6th International Conference on Data Communication Networking (DCNET-2015), in which we presented the idea of an Application-Aware Network (AAN) — an SDN extension that process traffic for each application in a consistent manner. In this paper, we generalise the idea and introduce Identity-Aware Networks (IAN) as another example of high level extensions for SDN.

We evaluated the feasibility of the High Level SDN in several testbeds. We employed several SDN controllers: Opendaylight, POX, and Pyretic. One testbed was composed of real routers. High Level SDN allowed to simplify the network policies by reducing the number of rules in the policies enforced by SDN applications.

This paper is organized as follows. Section 2 introduces High Level SDN architecture and basic building block of a High Level SDN controller. Section 3 describes two examples of a High Level SDN – AAN and IAN. Section 4 lists use cases for High Level SDN along with examples of High Level SDN policies. Testbeds are described in Sect. 5. Section 6 reviews related literature. Section 7 discusses the contribution of this paper. The paper is concluded in Sect. 8.

2   High Level SDN Architecture

Controllers manage routers and switches in a plain SDN network via a southbound interface, whereas SDN applications instruct controllers via a northbound interface. Unfortunately, all current SDN southbound protocols, such as OpenFlow or OnePK, limit the amount of information exposed to a controller and consequently to SDN applications: only low level network traffic identifiers and metrics are available. The controller does not have information about the applications that produce the flows, about the relations between flows (e.g., the relation between a SIP control channel and associated RTP streams), or about the users that produce the flows.

Network endpoints do know the meta information about flows they produce or consume. An SDN application that can utilize additional high level traffic identifiers can achieve better traffic handling than a plain SDN application leveraging only low level traffic identifiers.

Figure 1 depicts building blocks of a High Level SDN network, described in detail in the following subsections.

2.1   Network and Hosts

Network is any SDN network controlled by a controller. There are no limits on the SDN network. The network connects hosts and servers. The hosts run applications that can communicate with server applications, e.g., a call manager – SIP server. In this paper we call server applications *application managers*.

2.2   SDN Control Plane

We do not assume any specific SDN controller. However, we assume that the controller provides at least basic OpenFlow functionalities, i.e., it is able to

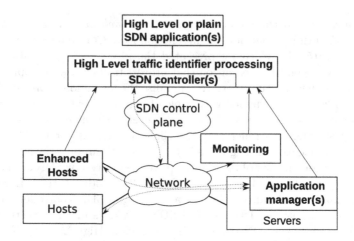

Fig. 1. Architecture of a High Level SDN network.

provide visibility and statistics about the flows crossing the SDN nodes and support basic actions to set quality of service or select the output interface.

2.3 Sources of High Level Information

Besides information provided by the control plane, we consider three additional information sources:

Enhanced Hosts: are equipped with a middle layer that passes locally known information to the controller, e.g., the name of the application that produces a specific flow or the bandwidth requirements of the flow, memory or CPU utilization.

Application Managers: (e.g., the Microsoft Exchange Server, Microsoft Lync or Cisco Unified Communications Manager for VoIP, VMWare's VSphere and OpenStack) are another source of information about application flows. A general trend is to move application managers toward cloud solutions coupled with provisioning of APIs to advertise and control flows.

Monitoring Tools: monitor network and its flows and extract high level information. Monitoring tools include DPI engines, IPFIX probes and collectors, or custom monitoring applications.

2.4 High Level SDN Controller and SDN Applications

A High Level SDN controller provides a consolidated and coherent view on the network traffic, merging flow information gathered from several sources. Any extensible modular SDN controller can be extended to handle high level traffic identifiers. See Fig. 2 for details.

Firstly, data incoming from high level information sources has to be evaluated and processed. As different sources of flow information may provide different

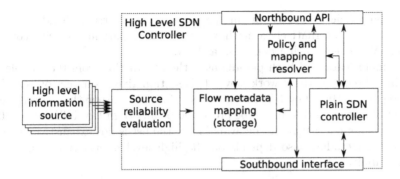

Fig. 2. High Level SDN controller internals.

information, the controller needs to merge the information consistently. One possibility is to rate the reliability of the source, e.g., information learnt from a DPI engine are less reliable than information provided by an application manager.

The controller stores gathered high level information as a mapping that maps high level traffic identifiers (such as application name, user identity) to a set of low-level traffic identifiers. The mapping is internally stored by the controller. The northbound APIs are extended to provide the high level information to SDN applications.

Finally, a High Level SDN controller incorporates a policy and mapping resolver module that converts high level policies (installed by SDN applications) to plain SDN flows by evaluating the stored mapping of the high level traffic identifiers and known traffic flows. Another task of the module is to compute statistics for high level traffic identifiers, e.g., bytes sent and received. Policy and mapping resolver can access the southbound interface either directly or delegate the network control to the plain SDN controller via its northbound API.

A High Level SDN controller provides northbound API that allows to handle traffic according to high level identifiers. A network operator can install specific SDN applications that handle traffic according to high level policies incorporating high level traffic identifiers. Hence, the High Level SDN controller abstracts the complexity of traffic handling. Moreover, the High Level SDN controller design ensures rule consistency across the SDN network.

In addition to reliability, each metadata source depends on a specific trust model that prevents the possibility of false metadata injection. Therefore, the interface from enhanced hosts, application managers, and monitoring tools to the enhanced SDN controller should employ a two-way authentication mechanisms. In our experiments, we did not focus on authentication security, or, we used Medianet authentication model [6], which provides a two-way authentication.

3   High Level SDN Examples

During our research, we examined two High Level SDN paradigms. Firstly, we focused on AAN [3]. The main aim is to provide consistent handling of application traffic. Secondly, in this paper, we analyze traffic handling based on a person (or alternatively a machine) that takes a part in a specific communication. We denote such a paradigm as IAN.

The main feature of both paradigms is the abstraction from the complexity of dealing directly with network flows. This section gives examples of metadata processed by a High Level SDN controller. However, rather than specifying a fixed set of metadata that has to be processed by any High Level SDN controller, we suggest metadata that can be available — the list is not exhaustive. The set of available metadata also depends on the high level information sources and their capabilities.

3.1 Application-Aware Networks

The number of network services and applications is constantly growing. As each application shows different requirements in terms of bandwidth and latency, it becomes critical for network operators to be able to map traffic to applications.

Getting the right insight into the different applications allows network operators to plan their network capacity and policies to deliver the right quality of service satisfying the application requirements. For example, applications such as VoIP and video conferencing need low jitter and latency whereas peer-to-peer file transfer require high throughput to minimize the download time.

An AAN needs to provide enough high level traffic identifiers to differentiate the traffic according to its application, type, and business priority. The traffic identifiers should include at least:

Application Name – a string that uniquely identify the application that produces the traffic. The application name can be accompanied by additional information describing the specific application, such as application version, its vendor etc.

Application Category – the nature of the application, e.g., Voice over IP (VoIP), video streaming service, web pages, etc.

Device Class – type of the device that generated the traffic, e.g., a general purpose computer, surveillance camera, VoIP phone, etc.

Media Type – characteristics of the transferred data, such as audio, video, text, image, etc.

For each traffic flow, it is desirable to gather additional metadata, such as required bandwidth, latency, and traffic identification.

A High Level SDN application can create policies referring to high level traffic identifiers. For example, it can restrict access to specific links for a specific application, category or a device class to specific links: `Prefer links with bandwidth of 1 Gbps and higher for traffic of (application VLC or category Business-Critical)`. A High Level SDN application can also reserve bandwidth, etc.: `Reserve bandwidth of 10 Mbps for traffic of type PhoneCall`.

3.2   Identity-Aware Networks

A typical business network is accessed by employees of the company, contractors, visitors, customers, etc. Typically, each role is associated with specific privileges. The categories can be further subdivided, e.g., the employees can be distinguished based on their department, importance for the company, etc.

The assignment of correct privileges to each network user is important to maintain the security of the network or to asses a specific quality of service to each user group.

An IAN has to provide high level traffic identifiers identifying users in the network, their importance and role. The supported traffic identifiers should include at least:

Personal ID – unique identification of a person.
Name – the name of the person.
Groups – the role of each user, e.g., employee, contractor, etc. Users and roles can be grouped together and form groups and subgroups, e.g., management, accounting department, etc.

Beside personalised services, IAN can profit from machine identification. For example, one can prepare specific policies for specific servers, e.g., `Drop traffic from device DatabaseServer leaving the network`.

The SDN application can create policies referring to the above mentioned traffic identifiers, for example, it can prioritize communication of specific persons or machines, e.g., traffic of the management or business-critical servers. An example of an identity-based policy is: `Reserve bandwidth of 1 Gbps at egress links for management`.

3.3   Other Traffic Identifiers and Combinations

Naturally, there are more than the two above-mentioned paradigms of High Level SDN. For example, the network operator might want to fine tune traffic handling in the network according to the geographical location of the communicating parties.

Moreover, AAN and IAN does not need to be deployed separately. On the contrary, their co-deployment allows to define even more precise policies, for example: `Drop traffic from device DatabaseServer leaving the network except traffic of application called System Updater`.

4   Use Cases

High Level SDN can be applied in a number of use cases. This section highlights the advantages of high level policies. Each use case is accompanied with examples of policies benefiting from high level traffic identifiers.

4.1   Remote Intrusion Detection System

An intrusion detection system (IDS) analyzes a copy of network traffic for anomalies. A remote IDS can analyse traffic gathered from many network links from different geographical locations. In addition, an IDS can be specialized for a certain type of traffic, or, the network operator is interested only in scanning the traffic of certain users (e.g., guests) or a specific type of devices (e.g., devices not managed by the company). This use case deals with the remote IDS scanning a specific type of traffic. Consider the following policy examples:

- `Duplicate data from applications called (Jabber or Thunderbird) to device IDS.`
- `Duplicate data from users in groups (Guest or Unknown) to device IDS.`
- `Duplicate data from devices (SmartPhone or SmartWatch) to device IDS.`

The SDN application processing, in cooperation with the High Level SDN controller, has to ensure the following:

- Select SDN switches that duplicates the traffic, for example, based on traffic load, path of the original traffic, or the location of the IDS.
- The network has to distinguish between the original traffic and its copy, for example by a VLAN ID or an MPLS tag.
- Populate the switching table of devices on the path with rules handling original traffic and the copy.

4.2   Packet Filter

Packet filters are a special type of a firewall, they drop malicious or unwanted traffic based on a set of rules. For example, a packet filter can be configured to drop traffic to a server from departments that should not access the server. Consider the following examples:

- `Drop data from users not in group IT department to application device SQLServer.`
- `Drop data from users in group Guest to any other user.`
- `Drop data from user Unknown to device Printer.`

The packet filtering SDN application has to instruct the controller to configure SDN switches to drop the traffic. The controller usually configure devices as close to the traffic source as possible. Another option is to optimize the number of SDN rules offloaded to SDN switches and drop the traffic close to the destination.

4.3   Path Load Balancing

Redundant links in network topologies often offer alternative paths from a source to a destination. Nevertheless, the available bandwidth or latency can differ on each path. Path load balancing aims at distributing traffic to available paths to improve quality of experience (QoE). For example, consider the following policies:

- Route data from application FTP Client along path with most available bandwidth.
- Route data of users from department Hotline along path with lowest delay.
- Route data from devices VoIP Telephone along best QoE path.

The implementation should monitor load, latency, and other characteristics of traffic links and paths. In case of a congestion, the High Level SDN application should reroute the traffic to another path meeting the policy, if available.

4.4 Traffic Monitoring

Network administrators have to monitor user behavior [12], for example, for conformance with legislation [8,26], for security incident tracking, potential future planning, and service access billing. In all cases, the controller should provide flow and derived statistics to High Level SDN applications, either gathered using southbound protocol or from external source, such as a IPFIX probe. High Level SDN controller should derive statistics for high level traffic identifiers by linking low-level-traffic-identifier statistics. Consider the following examples:

- Monitor traffic statistics of users accessing device ProtectedServer.
- Monitor traffic statistics of application Backup for data exchanged with device BackupServer.
- Monitor traffic statistics of group Servers for data exchanged with device DatabaseServer.

After a High Level SDN application subscribes for statistics, the Policy and Mapping Resolver converts high level traffic identifiers to a set of low level traffic identifiers. Then, the Policy and Mapping Resolver instructs the SDN controller to monitor the set of low level traffic identifiers. Every few seconds, the SDN controller polls statistics from SDN switches. In the case of IPFIX statistics, probes continuously send statistics to the SDN controller. After the SDN controller receives fresh statistics, it passes them to the Policy and Mapping Resolver, which combines statistics from low level traffic identifiers to statistics of high level traffic identifiers. The High Level SDN controller sends the result to subscribed High Level SDN applications.

5   Testbeds

During our research we have created application-aware testbed and identity-aware testbed to validate our high level SDN concept. We implemented the use-cases from Sect. 4 in our testbeds using several SDN controllers: Opendaylight[1], POX[2] and Pyretic[3].

---

[1] https://www.opendaylight.org/.

[2] http://www.noxrepo.org/pox/about-pox/.

[3] http://frenetic-lang.org/pyretic/.

5.1 Application-Aware Testbed

The application-aware testbed (depicted in the Fig. 3) is composed of different types of endpoint devices and applications, including both proprietary and open sources devices. Two Cisco phones and two Jabber clients are registered with a Cisco Unified Communication Manager and adopted SIP to establish audio/video sessions. Phones and Jabber clients make video calls, thus each producing two media network flows for each call: audio and video. In addition, a video and audio stream were multiplexed in a single network flow from a server to a VLC[4] client. Jabber and VLC have been enhanced with the adoption of the Media Service Interface (MSI) library [6], thus becoming application-aware endpoints.

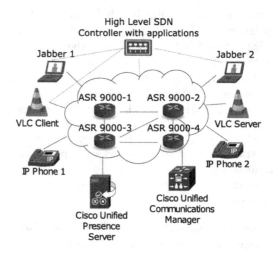

Fig. 3. Topology used in our application-aware testbed.

The ASR 9000 routers punt SIP packets produced by the Cisco IP phones and the Jabber clients to the SDN controller. Those SIP packets are then passed to a DPI module. Because Cisco phones are configured not to encrypt signaling traffic, their SIP packets are then parsed by the DPI module. The DPI module, in turn, collects SIP session details and pushes them to the common database thus mapping network flow details to application.

Jabber flows are instead announced by MSI to the appliaction-aware end-point manager that, similarly to DPI module, stores the Jabber application to network flows mapping into the common database. The same mechanism is adopted for the VLC client that announces RTP flows carrying the video and audio through MSI to the High Level SDN controller.

Normalisation is then applied on all the acquired data, according to the degree of reliability and completeness of the sources. For example, SIP packets generated by Jabber clients are not only advertised by MSI but also by the

----

[4] http://www.videolan.org/vlc/index.html.

DPI module (if they are not encrypted). This happens because the SIP packets are punted to the SDN controller and handled to the DPI module. Therefore normalisation enables for merging of the information coming from both sources, giving higher priority to the information provided by MSI as it is more reliable. The testbed treats the information sources according to the following priorities:

- Application managers are operated by network administrators and are the most reliable source. Information about both encrypted and unencrypted traffic is visible. They cover only the applications provided inside the testbed.
- Application-aware enhanced hosts have a little bit lower reliability as the endpoint can provide false information as a result of a virus infection or malicious tampering with the MSI library. Nevertheless, MSI signals information about relations between flows. Application-aware enhanced hosts also provide information about both encrypted and unencrypted traffic.
- DPI is the less reliable source as it cannot decrypt encrypted flows and there is a risk of false positive or false negative identification of a protocol.

We created two presentations [4,25] from the experiments with the testbed. The first one [4] focuses on quality of service management. The network operator is able to assign priorities to each running application and consequently provide desired quality of experience during congestion.

The latter presentation [25] focuses on path load balancing. The presented application-aware High Level SDN applications distributes traffic flows of selected applications to available paths. The goal of the High Level SDN application was to show that it is possible to operate the AAN even if not all flows are recognized by the High Level SDN controller.

Two sets of applications were operated in the testbed: (1) those running on enhanced hosts and (2) those that initiated flows that were not advertised to the High Level SDN, i.e. those that created background traffic.

The aim of the High Level SDN application [25] was to load balance the traffic of the business-critical applications across all possible paths between the source and destination. In case the High Level SDN application detected that a link carrying priority traffic was congested, it automatically rerouted the traffic to links with available capacity. Hence, even if the link was congested because of traffic from legacy endpoints (that were not application-aware), the AAN architecture allowed to ensure that the priority traffic reaches its destination without unnecessary retransmits.

5.2   Identity-Aware Testbed

The identity-aware testbed (see Fig. 4) consists of SDN switches, hosts, servers, an SMTP DPI probe and an IDS. From the hosts, several users access multiple services on the servers. Servers provide HTTP web service for user authentication, SMTP mail service for sending e-mails and FTP file service for data storage. The web service is configured to send user login name to controller after each successful authentication. DPI probe analyzes the SMTP traffic and sends user authentication login names from each SMTP session to the SDN controller.

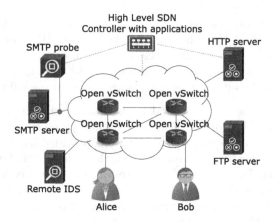

Fig. 4. Topology used in our identity-aware testbed.

The controller configures switches proactively to minimize the delay of packet processing. The controller detects mapping between IP addresses, MAC addresses and attachment points of each device from ARP packets. By default, all devices belong to user *Unknown*. When a user of a device authenticates to the web server or sends an e-mail, the controller learns the user login name and lower traffic identifiers from the high level information sources (HTTP authentication module and SMTP DPI probe).

We tested [14,16] several use cases in this testbed. The implementation of the remote IDS use case [14] dynamically selects the SDN switch that copies data to be monitored according to (1) the distance from the monitored user or device and (2) the number of rules installed to the SDN switch. The goal is to spread the rules across multiple SDN switches.

6   Related Work

It is already possible to control network traffic by high level identifiers. Network vendors offer solutions providing network application meta data (e.g., Medianet [27]) or custom identity-aware network control (e.g., Identity Driven Management [15]). This section focuses on the current state of research and on existing solutions analysing high level traffic identifiers.

Historically high level processing used heuristics [1,10], which inspect and infer flow characteristics. Heuristics may be based on port ranges [13], IP subnetting (special network subnets for specific applications, e.g., phones), or deep packet inspection (DPI) [22], e.g., application level gateway. Port based solutions suffer [22] from port overloading and inconsistent port usage. IP subnetting solutions are error prone and result in network management hassle. DPI is computationally expensive and becomes a challenge with the wider adoption of encrypted signaling and secured traffic. In addition, DPI-provided insights are hardly shared between network nodes on the path of the flow.

Network vendors proposed different solutions to make the network application-aware, such as Medianet [27], Application Visibility and Control [7] or Junos Application Aware [19]. A common characteristic of these solutions is the decoupling of flow identification from flow policies (prioritization, routing and others) through application specific tags. These tags can be either explicitly signaled as in the case of Medianet or locally produced by deep packet inspection as in the case of the Junos Application Aware solution. Based on the information about the requirements of the flows gathered from these tags, network nodes can decide the policies to be applied; in principle, this allows for a smooth collaboration between the applications and the network. However, today these solutions are mainly vendor specific. The lack of standards leads to a poor or a non-existing interoperability.

Recently Cisco introduced Medianet [27]: a solution that makes the network aware of the application traffic that it is carrying. In more details, Medianet endpoints leverage a proprietary middle layer (namely MSI) to advertise flows Metadata tags, e.g., application name, traffic type, media type and business importance. Network devices such as routers and switches take local decisions to handle the advertised flows in the desired way.

In identity controlled networks, vendors provide Identity Driven Management [15], Identity Service Engine [5], Identity and Policy Control [18]. End users submit their credentials to an autentification server (RADIUS, web), which forwards the credentials to centralized control of network configuration. Identity Service Engine [5] focuses on controlling access to network resources, while Identity and Policy Control [18] also implements accounting and tracking users activity. Identity Driven Management [15] can limit bandwidth and assign QoS based on user identities. Similarly to application-aware networks, these solutions are proprietary and lack interoperability.

6.1   Application Awareness in SDN

The usage of Software Defined Network technology to enable Application-Aware Networks is a fairly novel concept in both industry and academia. Jarschel et al. [17] showed a QoS boosting application that monitor the Youtube streaming experience. If certain quality thresholds are crossed, the application requests the BigSwitch SDN controller to enforce a routing change for the affected Youtube network flows.

Solutions such as that of Insieme (Application Visibility and Control [7]) also combine Application Awareness and SDN: DataCenter deployment and management of applications, databases and their traffic is unified through a unique controller that is drivable with a set of APIs. Similarly, PlumGrid [24] provides network abstraction for data-centers with comparable promises to those of Insieme. Curtis et al. [9] propose new ways to provide flow scheduling in Data Centers through OpenFlow. Das et al. [11] adopt OpenFlow to dynamically aggregate flows according to flow properties such as bandwidth, latency, jitter; thus providing different levels of QoS to applications. In the same spirit of using OpenFlow to aggregate traffic according to application knowledge,

Zhang et al. [28] propose an extension to the OpenFlow protocol to enable application optimization in Optical Burst Switching networks. Finally, Bredel et al. [2] show a viable way to coordinate Traffic-Engineering for traffic generated by scientific collaborations like the CERN's LHC.

Application awareness we present in this paper is similar to that of Jarschel et al. [17]. However, our approach is suited for a broader range of applications. In addition, we adopt carrier-grade IOS-XR hardware and Medianet, application-aware feature developed by Cisco.

6.2 Identity Awareness in SDN

Several recent studies investigated network control based on user identities. Resonance [23] uses OpenFlow switches to enforce high level dynamic acces control policies based on flow-level information and real-time alerts. Users authenticate through a credential based web site. The research, however, focused only on security, specifically on detecting potentially infected computers and taking appropriate action if one was found (e.g., dropping its traffic).

AuthFlow [20] also combines authetication and an access control mechanism. AuthFlow links user credentials from RADIUS server to a set of flows belonging to the authenticated host. AuthFlow denies access to network resources from unauthenticated users. Moreover, the application is able to allow or deny traffic based on different privilege level of each authenticated host.

The main goal of current identity-based software defined networks is (1) to find the most secure way to authenticate users, (2) to secure network resources and enable access to specified authenticated users or groups of users only. In this paper, we generalize the latter by using the knowledge of user identity in universal applications. Besides access control, our use cases include routing (e.g., data of a manager goes though a priority path), load balancing and duplicated packet delivery to IDS.

7 Discussion

In this section, we compare the High Level SDN to a classical distributed network and to an SDN network without high level traffic identifiers. Moreover, we describe a possible behaviour of a High Level SDN in typical network scenarios.

7.1 Evaluation

Being built on top of an SDN network, the High Level SDN maintains main advantages of the SDN architecture while reducing the complexity of applying the correct policies to related flows (typically belonging to a single application, a class of applications, or specific groups of users).

When expressing a policy, one needs to characterise the traffic to which the policy applies by certain traffic identifiers. The traffic identifiers define a class of traffic (a.k.a. class-map). Low level traffic identifiers, such as IP addresses and port numbers, are available in each packet. Hence traffic handling on nodes is traditionally defined by low level traffic identifiers. However, network administrators tend to define traffic in more abstract form, e.g., in relation to the person that generated the traffic or for specific applications.

We define the policy complexity as the number of network nodes where a class-map must be explicitly declared multiplied by the number of entries in the policy itself. Let us consider a network of N nodes with the number of applications denoted as A, each application carrying F_A different flows in average.

An alternative view on network traffic handling is based on user identities. Imagine the same network with N nodes with the number of attached users denotes as U, each user opens F_U active flows in average.

The policy complexity can be evaluated in the following way:

- In a conventional network, a rule has to be distributed for each flow of each application or each user on every network node. Therefore, the total complexity can be evaluated as $\mathcal{O}(A \times F_A \times N + U \times F_U \times N)$.
- In high-level-traffic-identifiers-aware distributed networks (HL-distributed networks), for instance Metadata-aware network, the complexity reduces to $\mathcal{O}(A \times N + U \times N)$ since the network can deal directly with applications and specific user traffic instead of flows.
- In SDN, the controller (or the set of cooperating controllers) abstracts the complexity of programming each node separately. However, a rule for each flow must be explicitly declared; thus, the total complexity in this case becomes $\mathcal{O}(A \times F_A + U \times F_U)$.
- In High Level SDN, application policies are handled in a straightforward manner since the complexity with flows is abstracted by the high level SDN controller; thus, the number of class-maps that need to be specified reduces to $\mathcal{O}(A + U)$.

Feature velocity in distributed environments depends on the number of different operating systems and different hardware platforms to be supported. In the case of SDN, the decoupling of the capabilities exposed by the network platforms and the flow characteristics allows for an increased velocity in delivering high-level-traffic-identifiers-aware features. This is achieved through writing software (an SDN application) once rather than integrating software into different network platforms. Hence, the feature velocity of SDN is fast compared to conventional or HL-distributed networks.

The control plane abstraction ensures that there is a single set of policies applied to all SDN switches in the network. In comparison, the cumbersome management of consistent rules on each node might result in inconsistent configuration, unpredictable behaviour of the network, and complicated troubleshooting. The network administrator has to maintain N configurations consistently.

In a conventional deployment, the policy complexity often results to a high number of class-map rules. The class-map rules has to be managed directly on the network nodes in a consistent manner. The maintenance of the consistency incorporates high operational costs accompanied with slow feature velocity. Despite lower complexity of HL-distributed deployment, it still requires medium operational costs as it requires big effort to maintain consistent behaviour. The decoupling of control and data plane and the abstracted complexity of the network lowers the operation costs of SDN-based paradigms. Moreover, High Level SDN treats traffic of specific high level characteristics in a consistent manner.

The comparison is summarized in Table 1.

Table 1. Comparison of available solutions to enforce policies for specific flows related to user identity and applications.

	Conventional	HL-Distributed	SDN	High Level SDN
Policy complexity $\mathcal{O}(\dots)$	$A \times F_A \times N +$ $+U \times F_U \times N$	$A \times N + U \times N$	$A \times F_A +$ $+U \times F_U$	$A + U$
Feature Velocity	Slow	Slow	Fast	
Consistent behavior	Cumbersome	Cumbersome	Automatic	
Operational cost	High	Medium	Low	Lowest

7.2   Typical Scenarios

Let us consider some specific scenarios to illustrate the benefits deriving from the deployment of a High Level SDN.

Network Congestion. Although congestion of a link is easy to detect in a distributed network, none or few network technologies exist to react and reroute flows in a timely way.

With SDN, the controller can immediately re-route traffic depending on queue occupancy or interface load increase. However, the information available to an SDN controller are limited to low level identifier (up to the transport layer).

Compared to the SDN, the High Level SDN offers two main advantages. Firstly, the routing operations can be based on high level requirements; thus all flows of a single application or a single user can be handled in a consistent way without the complexity of mapping flows by the SDN application. The second, and more significant advantage, is that the High Level SDN controller can potentially access high level metrics and eventually, it can detect the looming resource insufficiency for specific traffic in advance.

Topology Change. In the event of a topology change that impacts the path of flows with specific requirements, a regular Medianet solution requires a new distribution of Medianet tagging in the new path. If the change reoccurs with some frequency because of physical impairments, it can result in a flapping behavior and degraded quality. High Level SDN controller with complete network and application view can instead choose a stable path that avoids the prevents periodic rerouting.

Application Policy Change. In a Medianet network, whenever application requirements change, the new requirements are pushed by administrator to the network devices through configuration. Administrator has to foresee possible problems in advance so that the change targets only affected devices; and avoids changes to unrelated traffic so that a single change does not trigger an avalanche of changes. In High Level SDN, the new application requirements are enforced on all affected devices by the High Level SDN controller, which has the complete view of all flows and their paths.

8 Conclusion

Network policies are complex and, typically, they are based on abstract identifiers, such as application name, application class, user name, or user role. Users demand consistent application behavior and high quality of multimedia streams. Business environment requires traffic handling based on user role, e.g., access to some resources is limited for unpriviliged users. Conventional policy management requires to consistenly maintain configuration of many network nodes, however, on top of routing and switching according to the information carried in packet header fields, several solutions aims to simplify the configuration based on abstract traffic characteristics. SDN does not offer high level characteristcs and traffic identifiers.

This paper introduced High Level SDN architecture achieving several goals:

- The architecture is generic, extensible, and compatible with current SDN controllers. We demonstrated its suitability on an application-centric and user-centric paradigm.
- High level policies simplify traffic management.
- High level SDN is applicable to many use cases.

The testbed evaluation of the implemented High Level SDN applications confirmed that the idea of High Level SDN applications is easily applicable in real networks. During the project, we brought application-awareness Cisco IOS-XR routers, specifically, ASR 9000. Additionally, tesbeds proved fast application velocity. We were able to develop custom SDN applications in several days or weeks without the need to wait for a new version of a network operating system.

Acknowledgements. This work was supported by Cisco Systems Switzerland where the idea of AAN emerged, was implemented, tested and evaluated. The work focusing on IAN and generic High Level SDN is a part of the project VG20102015022 supported by Ministry of the Interior of the Czech Republic and it was also supported by the BUT project FIT-S-14–2299.

References

1. Bendrath, R.: Global technology trends and national regulation: explaining variation in the governance of deep packet inspection. Technical report, Delft University of Technology (2009), Paper originally prepared for the International Studies Annual Convention

2. Bredel, M., Barczyk, A., Newman, H.: Application-aware traffic engineering for wide area networks using openflow. In: SuperComputing Conference, Emerging Technologies (2013)
3. Caldarola, L., Choukir, A., Cuda, D., Dondero, M., Ficara, D., Muccifora, R., Polčák, L., Trifilo, A.: Towards a real application-aware network. In: Proceedings of the 6th International Conference on Data Communication Networking (DCNET-2015), pp. 5–12. SciTePress - Science and Technology Publications (2015)
4. Choukir, A., Caldarola, L., Cuda, D., Dondero, M., Ficara, D., Muccifora, R., Polčák, L., Trifilo, A.: Towards a real application aware network (2013). http://youtu.be/QHYPhAhIwVw
5. Cisco: Cisco identity services engine (2015). http://www.cisco.com/c/en/us/products/security/identity-services-engine/
6. Cisco Systems: Cisco MSI Deployment Guide (2013). http://www.cisco.com/web/solutions/medianet/docs/Cisco_MSI_Installation_Guide.pdf
7. Cisco Systems: Application Visibility and Control (2014). http://www.cisco.com/c/en/us/products/routers/avc_control.html
8. Council of Europe: Convention on Cybercrime (2001), ETS No. 185
9. Curtis, A.R., Kim, W., Yalagandula, P.: Mahout: low-overhead datacenter traffic management using end-host-based elephant detection. In: IEEE INFOCOM (2011)
10. Dainotti, A., Pescape, A., Claffy, K.: Issues and future directions in traffic classification. IEEE Network **26**(1), 35–40 (2012)
11. Das, S., Yiakoumis, Y., Parulkar, G., McKeown, N.: Application-aware aggregation and traffic engineering in a converged packet-circuit network. In: Optical Fiber Communication Conference and Exposition (OFC/NFOEC) and the National Fiber Optic Engineers Conference (2011)
12. ETSI: ETSI ES 201 158: Telecommunications security; Lawful Interception (LI); Requirements for network functions. European Telecommunications Standards Institute (2002), version 1.2.1
13. Fraleigh, C., Moon, S., Lyles, B., Cotton, C., Khan, M., Moll, D., Rockell, R., Seely, T., Diot, S.: Packet-level traffic measurements from the sprint IP backbone. IEEE Network **17**(6), 6–16 (2003)
14. Franková, B.: Lawful Interception in Software Defined Networks (2015). Master's thesis (in Czech), Brno University of Technology, CZ
15. Hewlett-Packard: Identity driven management: technical brief (2015). http://www.hp.com/rnd/pdf_html/IDM_technical_brief.htm
16. Holkovič, M.: SDN Controlled According to User Identity (2015). Master's thesis, Brno University of Technology, CZ
17. Jarschel, M., Wamser, F., Hohn, T., Zinner, T., Tran-Gia, P.: SDN-based application-aware networking on the example of youtube video streaming. In: European Workshop on Software Defined Networks (2013)
18. Juniper Networks: Identity and policy control (2015). http://www.juniper.net/us/en/products-services/ipc/
19. Juniper Networks Inc: Junos Application Aware: Deep packet Inspection (2015). http://www.juniper.net/us/en/products-services/network-edge-services/service-control/junos-application-aware/
20. Mattos, D.M.F., Ferraz, L.H.G., Duarte, O.C.M.B.: AuthFlow: Authentication and Access Control Mechanism for Software Defined Networking, Technical Report, Electrical Engineering Program, COPPE/UFRJ, April 2014. http://www.gta.ufrj.br/ftp/gta/TechReports/MFD14.pdf

21. McKeown, N., Anderson, T., Balakrishnan, H., Parulkar, G., Peterson, L., Rexford, J., Shenker, S., Turner, J.: Openflow: enabling innovation in campus networks. SIGCOMM Comput. Commun. Rev. **38**(2), 69–74 (2008)

22. Moore, A.W., Papagiannaki, K.: Toward the accurate identification of network applications. In: Dovrolis, C. (ed.) PAM 2005. LNCS, vol. 3431, pp. 41–54. Springer, Heidelberg (2005)

23. Nayak, A.K., Reimers, A., Feamster, N., Clark, R.: Resonance: dynamic access control for enterprise networks. In: Proceedings of the 1st ACM workshop on Research on Enterprise Networking, pp. 11–18, ACM (2009)

24. PLUMgrid: PLUMgrid: virtual network infrastructure (2014). http://plumgrid.com

25. Polčák, L.: Integration of SDN and medianet metadata (2014). http://youtu.be/CqDYn4-DKn8

26. The Council of the European Union: COUNCIL RESOLUTION of 17 January 1995 on the lawful interception of telecommunications (96/C 329/01) (1996)

27. Wilkins, S.: Designing for Cisco Internetwork Solutions (DESGN) Foundation Learning Guide (CCDA DESGN 640-864). Pearson Education, Boston (2011)

28. Zhang, D., Mai, S., Guo, H., Tsuritani, T., Wu, J., Morita, I.: Openflow-based control plane for the application-aware lobs network. In: OptoElectronics and Communications Conference (2013)

What a Difference a Year Makes: Long Term Evaluation of TLS Cipher Suite Compatibility

Stefan Prinz[1], Silvie Schmidt[1], Manuel Koschuch[1], Alexander Glaser[2],
Taro Fruhwirth[2], and Matthias Hudler[1(✉)]

[1] Competence Centre for IT-Security, FH Campus Wien,
University of Applied Sciences, Favoritenstrasse 226, 1100 Vienna, Austria
{stefan.prinz,silvia.schmidt,matthias.hudler}@fh-campuswien.ac.at,
manuel.koschuch@gmail.com
[2] FH Campus Wien, University of Applied Sciences,
Favoritenstrasse 226, 1100 Vienna, Austria
{alexander.glaser,taro.fruhwirth}@stud.fh-campuswien.ac.at

Abstract. The Transport Layer Security (TLS) protocol is still the de-facto standard for secure network connections over an insecure medium like the Internet. But its flexibility concerning the algorithms used for securing a channel between two parties can also be a weakness, due to the possible agreement on insecure ciphers. State of the art cipher suites are not supported by all websites. We relate on an existing white paper (Applied Crypto Hardening) giving recommendations on how to securely configure SSL/TLS connections with regard to the practical feasibility of these recommendations. In addition, we propose an additional configuration set with the aim of increasing compatibility as well as security. We also developed a small Cipher Negotiation Crawler (CiNeg) to test TLS-handshakes using given cipher configurations with Alexa's top websites and show its practical usability. In this work we examine the trend regarding supported cipher suites on webservers over time. To analyze this, we performed the scans twice with a one year gap. We compared the outcome of the two scans to see if we can determine a trend to better security as time goes by. And indeed, we found explicit enhancements in our reevaluations.

Keywords: OpenSSL · O-Saft · Bettercrypto · Openssl-compare · Applied crypto cardening · Cipher suite · Cipher string

1 Introduction

Since its initial public specification in 1995, the Transport Layer Security (TLS) protocol [7], originally and until v3.0 known as Secure Sockets Layer (SSL) [10], has become the de-facto standard for secure network communications over an insecure channel. One of the main reasons for its widespread usage (from web-browsers to mobile apps to embedded systems) is the flexibility this protocol offers with regard to the cryptographic algorithms used in a session.

© Springer International Publishing Switzerland 2016
M.S. Obaidat and P. Lorenz (Eds.): ICETE 2015, CCIS 585, pp. 58–78, 2016.
DOI: 10.1007/978-3-319-30222-5_3

To achieve this flexibility, the concept of *cipher suites*, described by *cipher strings*, is employed. Section 2 gives an overview of these strings and how they are used in the SSL/TLS handshake process. But this mechanism also creates practical problems: due to compatibility issues, or simple misconfiguration, a potentially very large number of SSL/TLS secured systems using insecure configurations exist. In addition, the cipher suites that — given a specific cipher string configuration — are actually negotiated with a specific server often remain unclear.

Several guides exist to support administrators on how to choose secure and compatible cipher strings, usually mostly focused on a single (or small range of) product(s). One guide that tries to take a broader approach to this topic is the *Applied Crypto Hardening (ACH)* white paper [3], which is currently (10/2015) still in draft status and in near constant flux. In Sect. 2.4 we give a more detailed description of the recommendations presented in this guide.

Our main motivation for this work was now to determine how well the cipher strings recommended in [3] are usable in practice, how they scale with different SSL/TLS versions, and what cipher suites are effectively negotiated when using the given strings in a practical setting. We also developed a small Cipher Negotiation Crawler (CiNeg) to perform TLS-handshakes with a given list of websites and show its practical usability. We repeated the scans with CiNeg again one year later, to see if time brings improvements to security and compatibility. Especially after some severe security issues, [1] and [2], were published in the beginning of 2015. Section 3 details our results.

Finally, we propose another cipher string, trying to find a balance between security and compatibility. Again, we performed tests with this string, each in 2014 and 2015, to evaluate its practical applicability and compatibiliy changes over time in Sect. 4. Section 5 sums up our results and findings.

2   Transport Layer Security Protocol

TLS is, as well as its predecessor SSL, a hybrid cryptographic protocol (SSL specifications were last updated in [10], TLS is specified in [5] and was most recently updated in [18]). It employs asymmetric cryptography during the initial handshake phase to verify the authenticity of usually at least one (the server side) of the communicating parties, as well as to exchange a symmetric key between those parties. The data communication itself is then encrypted and integrity protected using symmetric techniques.

The initial handshake can be divided into four phases, as detailed in Fig. 1, where the individual phases perform the following functions:

During *phase 1* security capabilities are established. This includes information about the protocol version, session ID, cipher suite, compression method, as well as the initial random number.

Phase 2 contains three optional messages by the server, i.e. certificate, key exchange, and the request for a client certificate. Usually, in the context of a web-server communicating with a client via HTPP over SSL (HTTPS), at least the server certificate is sent to authenticate the server.

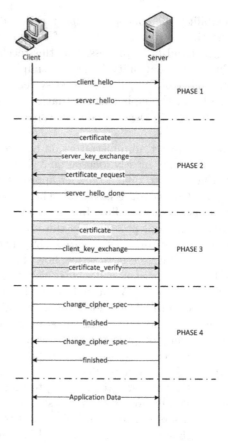

Fig. 1. TLS Basic Handshake (cf. [20]). The shaded messages are optional or situation dependent.

In *phase 3* the client may send its certificate if requested by the server. In any case the client sends key exchange information, depending on the actual cipher suite agreed upon in phase 1. At the end of phase 3 the client may send a certificate verification (forcing it to employ the private key corresponding to the one present in the client's certificate).

During *phase 4* the *change_cipher_spec* messages are sent both ways, and the handshake is finished by exchanging a message symmetrically encrypted with the agreed key and cipher.

The most interesting part of this handshake for our work is phase 1, in particular the negotiation of the cipher suites. Usually the client offers a list of supported suites in its *client_hello* message, with the server selecting a suite from its own configuration shared with the client and communicates it back to the client in the *server_hello* message. The cipher suites supported by server and client depend on their respective configuration, as well as on the SSL/TLS version used.

2.1 Cipher Suites

A cipher suite defines the cryptographic algorithms used during an SSL/TLS connection, and usually contains information about the primitives for key exchange, authentication, symmetric encryption, and integrity protection.

An example suite, given in the format used by OpenSSL, would be DHE-RSA-AES128-SHA: ephemeral Diffie-Hellman [8] is used for agreeing on a symmetric key, RSA [19] signatures for checking the authenticity of the parties involved, AES [16] with a 128-bit key for symmetric bulk data encryption, and SHA-1 [17] for calculation of the HMAC integrity protection value.

Supported cipher suites vary by SSL/TLS version and specific implementations, and are, among others, specified in [4–6,9,12,13,15].

The most commonly used algorithms for the different cryptographic primitives are:

Key Exchange: RSA, or Diffie-Hellman (DH) or its equivalent over elliptic curves (ECDH), both in ephemeral and non-ephemeral varieties ((EC)DH(E))
Authentication: RSA, or the Digital Signature Algorithm (DSA) or its equivalent over elliptic curves (ECDSA)
Encryption: AES, RC4, or CAMELLIA
Hash: MD5, or a member of the SHA family (-1,-2,-256,-384)

Most of the software products employing SSL/TLS allow for some kind of control over which cipher suites are available for negotiation, thereby enabling the users and/or administrators for enforcing certain minimum security requirements or enabling compatibility with a wider range of devices. The desired cipher suites can either be explicitly enumerated or, as in the case of OpenSSL, given as logical compositions of classes of algorithms (e.g. *"no SHA-1 AND no RC4 AND AES"*, see https://www.openssl.org/docs/apps/ciphers.html for a detailed discussion of the expressions allowed).

Regardless of the approach taken, in practice it is often unclear or at least quite cumbersome to determine which actual cipher suite is being negotiated when connecting to a particular server. In this work we try to introduce a structured tool-assisted approach to answer this question, as well as use this approach to evaluate the practical applicability and compatibility of an existing project [3] giving cipher string recommendations.

2.2 OpenSSL

The OpenSSL[1] project offers an open source toolkit written in C to implement SSL/TLS protocols, together with comprehensive utilities for creating and verifying digital certificates. OpenSSL is also the default cryptographic library used in the Apache[2] and nginx[3] HTTP servers. Both servers combined comprise about 67,26 % of current domains served (according to Analyzer.cc[4]).

---

[1] https://www.openssl.org/.

[2] http://httpd.apache.org/.

[3] http://nginx.org/.

[4] http://technology.analyzer.cc/application/openssl.

Table 1. Top 5 OpenSSL versions in use (according to http://technology.analyzer.cc/application/openssl).

OpenSSL version	Installations	%
0.9.8e	119,839	25.31 %
1.0.0	67,937	14.35 %
0.9.8g	62,510	13.20 %
1.0.1e	56,580	11.95 %
0.9.8o	36,191	7.64 %
other	130,343	27.53 %

Analyzer.cc also gives the most used version (as of 1/2015) as 0.9.8e (25.3 %), followed by version 1.0.0 and 0.9.8g, with 14.3 % and 13.2 %, respectively. Table 1 shows the top five OpenSSL versions according to Analyzer.cc.

2.3 SSL/TLS Version Distribution and Vulnerabilities

To get recent statistics on SSL/TLS usage and its versions' dissemination we used SSL Pulse[5]. As of December 2014, 1.5 million public websites are SSL/TLS enabled; due to efficiency concerns SSL Pulse recently decided to use the top 200,000 sites (according to Alexa's list[6]) for its monitoring and the resulting statistics. SSL Pulse offers various statistics concerning SSL/TLS trends. From that we find that - as of Dec.7th, 2014 - almost a quarter (22.6 %) of the websites scanned uses weak or insecure cipher suites, i.e. these sites support symmetric ciphers with a key length lower than 128 bits. This percentage of websites is 1.1 % less than a month earlier, i.e. there is a positive trend concerning cipher strength. Furthermore, SSL Pulse examines the usage of SSL/TLS versions, i.e. SSL v2.0, SSL v3.0, TLS v1.0, TLS v1.1, and TLS v1.2.

Table 2. SSL/TLS Trends: absolute and relative numbers of sites supporting the respective version. (Data from https://www.trustworthyinternet.org/ssl-pulse/, 1/2015 and 10/2015).

Protocol	Dez.2014 abs	Dez.2014 %	Sept.2015 abs	Sept.2015 %	Trend
SSL v2.0	25,096	15.5 %	15,337	10.8 %	- 4.7 %
SSL v3.0	80,085	53.5 %	48,864	33.8 %	- 20.0 %
TLS v1.0	150,293	99.6 %	143,352	99.2 %	- 0.41 %
TLS v1.1	70,933	47.4 %	92,924	64.3 %	+ 16.9 %
TLS v1.2	75,022	50.1 %	96,175	66.5 %	+ 16.4 %

---

[5] https://www.trustworthyinternet.org/ssl-pulse/.
[6] http://www.alexa.com/.

Table 2 shows the usage of SSL/TLS versions in December 2014 compared to September 2015. It is obvious that SSL support is declining and the percentage of sites deploying TLS is growing. But this significant decrease of SSLv3 and increase of TLSv1.1 and 1.2 speaks for itself. It is obvious that recently published problems in SSL/TLS are pushing people to enforce stronger security. Yet there is still a small number of servers available that are able to fallback to SSL when a client requests to do so, making it more important to choose cipher strings in a way to avoid this.

According to SSL Pulse the amount of vulnerable servers to Poodle [14] also decreased by 5.4 % since December 2014.

2.4   Available Tools

As already mentioned before, several projects exist, trying to give administrators guidelines on how to securely configure SSL/TLS installations by deploying specifically crafted cipher strings. In this work our interest is threefold: first we want to examine the recommendations given in the Applied Crypto Hardening (ACH) project [3] on their practical usability and compatibility. In addition, we try to define our own new cipher string, trying to strike a balance between the two configurations given in [3]. Finally, we want to investigate differences in negotiated cipher suites in 2014 and 2015. We chose the ACH project mainly for two reasons: the decision finding process is open and well documented on a public mailing list (http://lists.cert.at/cgi-bin/mailman/listinfo/ach) as well as in the corresponding Git repository (https://git.bettercrypto.org/ach-master.git).

And the contributors to the document come from academic research as well as from the industry, giving a broad perspective on the topic. These two properties lend credibility to the notion that a configuration created and recommended this way is actually sensible in practice. Two cipher strings are provided by ACH (as of draft revision 1333f7a):

Cipher String A is a configuration for strong security, i.e. using strong ciphers, but offering less compatibility, i.e. fewer clients [3]: EDH+ aRSA +AES256: EECDH +aRSA +AES256: !SSLv3.

Cipher String B is configured with weaker ciphers, but it offers better compatibility [3]: EDH+ CAMELLIA: EDH +aRSA: EECDH +aRSA +AESGCM: EECDH +aRSA +SHA256: EECDH: +CAMELLIA128: +AES128: +SSLv3: !aNULL: !eNULL: !LOW: !3DES: !MD5: !EXP: !PSK: !DSS: !RC4: !SEED: !IDEA: !ECDSA: kEDH: CAMELLIA128 -SHA: AES128 -SHA.

More detailed explanation for selecting these ciphers and their compatibilities can be found in [3].

To evaluate these two strings in practice we used two additional tools: Openssl-compare[7], allowing us to test a given cipher string against a certain OpenSSL version and determining the resulting supporting cipher suites. And O-Saft[8] to test a given cipher string against a server.

---

[7] https://github.com/azet/openssl-compare.

[8] https://www.owasp.org/index.php/O-Saft.

3   Practical Evaluation

In this section we describe the practical tests performed and all the results and conclusions we derive from these. We start with estimating the practical compatibility of cipher string A and B from [3], and conclude by examining the available cipher suites in different OpenSSL versions. We scanned the websites twice. First in December 2014 and then again in October 2015. We wanted to see if recently published security issues, like Logjam [1] or Freak [2], had an impact on SSL/TLS compatibilities or not. The effect is visible in different ways. An increased number of TLS 1.2 supported websites, an increased amount of SSL/TLS supported sites at all and of course a better compatibility for string A and our own cipher string.

3.1   Methodology

We first try to estimate the percentage of websites a client with a given cipher string configuration can successfully connect to, taking into account the distribution of SSL/TLS versions as well as the cipher suites described by the cipher string. To do this we use openly available tools as detailed in Sect. 2.4 as well as our own command line application CiNeg, detailed in the next Subsection.

We then try to verify our estimations by using CiNeg to connect to Alexa's top 1,000/top 25,000 sites and record the negotiated cipher suites. We compare the results from the test in 2014 and 2015 to derive conclusions regarding the trend of SSL/TLS support and therefore security, awareness for security and the impact of such massive security issues.

Finally, we specify a new cipher string and verify its usability and compatibility by also performing the scans.

3.2   Compatibility Estimation for ACH's Cipher Strings

In addition to the tools listed in Sect. 2.4, we developed the tool CiNeg, which creates an SSL/TLS session for a given list of websites with a chosen cipher string. CiNeg only tries to connect once. We established sessions with timout periods in order to evaluate the influence casued by a connection timout of 2.5 s. We concluded, that there is no significant difference in SSL/TLS handshake errors or timeouts. CiNeg only uses the given URL and does not try connecting to any sub-domains. The tool uses the installed OpenSSL client, version 1.0.1f in our case. The output shows the negotiated cipher suite and the protocol version used.

We estimate the compatibility of the cipher strings A and B with web servers which support SSL or TLS, using the results from scans with our CiNeg tool given in Table 3.

Compatibility Estimation for Cipher String A. Cipher string A only supports TLS 1.2 cipher suites. This massively reduces the number of compatible sites. According to SSL-Pulse data, with a source of about 200,000 SSL/TLS webistes, from December 2014 stated, that only 50.1 % of SSL/TLS-enabled sites support TLS 1.2. A second scan by Securitypitfalls[9] from November 2014, which uses 441,636 SSL/TLS websites from Alexa's top list[10], indicates that 66.2 % support TLS 1.2.

In July 2015 Securitypitfalls[11] scanned Alexa's top 1 million again. The result was, that 78 % of SSL/TLS enabled websites support TLS 1.2 now. In September 2015 SSL-Pulse measured a compatibility of 65.5 % to TLS 1.2 scanning about 150,000 sites. Our own measurements in October 2015 using CiNeg showed, that 82.93 % of Alexa's Top 25,000 support TLS 1.2 if a certificate is available. The obvious conclusion is, that there is a visible increase of TLS 1.2 supported sites over time.

Based on the numbers of the previous results and the compatibility values from Table 3 we estimate that the compatibility for this cipher string is between 50 % and 60 % in 2014. For 2015 we can forecast an increase of compatibility. We estimate the current compatibility between 65 % and 75 % percent.

We used CiNeg to verify these values and ran a scan with the top 1,000 and top 25,000 websites according to Alexa's top list. There are 603 (60 %) websites in the top 1,000 that support SSL/TLS and about 14,500 (58 %) in the top 25,000 in 2014. In October 2015 about 65 % of Alexa's top 1,000 support SSL/TLS. The compatibility for Alexa's Top 25,000 stayed about the same.

We first performed a scan with the cipher string 'ALL' to see how many websites return an error within the handshake, even when the cipher suites are not limited. This value may vary slightly according to the number of no responses on port 443, but this should not severely skew our estimations.

We subtract the number of the errors within the handshakes with all possible cipher suites from the number of errors in the handshake with the limited cipher suites, i.e. we removed cipher suites with limitations, such that the errors caused by these cipher suites do not occur any more. The results for the scan in December 2014 is as follows. The shared cipher suite percentage of cipher string A, when using the top 1,000 websites according to Alexa, is 54.3 %. The result for the top 25,000 websites is 56.1 %. An increased support for TLS 1.2 also means an increased compatibility for cipher string A. Currently 69.68 % from Alexa's 1,000 and 70.5 % of Alexa's 25,000 sites can establish a successful TLS/SSL-connection with string A. This is a raise of about 15 % in comparision to the elder scan. So 70 % of all webservers are capable of establishing state of the art SSL/TLS communication which is considered secure.

These results confirm our initial estimations. This quite limited compatibility is in line with the goal of cipher string A, to focus on security and not on compatibility with older systems. However this changed over time. A 70 % compatibility cannot be seen as limited compatibility anymore. As a forecast one can say that more and more servers will be capable of TLS 1.2 and therefore compatible with string A.

---

[9] https://securitypitfalls.wordpress.com/2014/12/.
[10] http://www.alexa.com/topsites.
[11] https://securitypitfalls.wordpress.com/2015/07/.

The results of the CiNeg scan also include the negotiated cipher suites. Figure 2 shows the distribution of negotiated cipher suites for the top 25,000 websites in 2014. This chart shows that `ECDHE-RSA-AES256-GCM-SHA384` is used in about 65 % of the successful negotiations, although the DHE cipher suites are preferred by the client. Possible reasons for this might be caused by the stronger support of the ECDHE cipher suite or the fact, that - according to the scan by Securitypitfalls - 67 % of the websites use their own priority order regarding their ciphers. It is also notable that about 95 % of the negotiated cipher suites use AES-GCM.

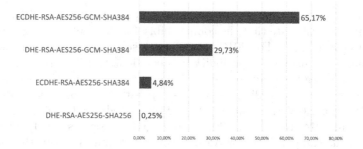

Fig. 2. Percentage of cipher suites negotiated using cipher string A with Alexa's top 25,000 websites in 2014. Compatibility at 56.1 %.

Thou the compatibility increased strongly, the distribution of negotiated Cipher Suites in 2015 is very similar to the previous scan and can be seen in Fig. 3.

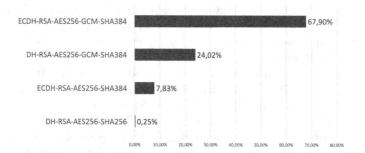

Fig. 3. Percentage of cipher suites negotiated using cipher string A with Alexa's top 25,000 websites in 2015. Compatibility at 70 %.

Compatibility Estimation for Cipher String B. Cipher string B offers better compatibility than cipher string A. The main reason for this fact is the support of cipher suites which use RSA for key exchange. This cipher string shares cipher suites with SSLv3, TLSv1, TLSv1.1 and TLS1.2. The results of SSL-Pulse show that nearly all of the websites support at least one of these protocol versions and only 1.3 % of the websites support RC4 in 2014.

According to a scan by Securitypitfalls from November 2014, which used 441,636 SSL/TLS websites, only 0.02 % of the SSL/TLS websites from Alexa's top 1 million sites only support SSLv2. The results of this scan also show that RSA for key exchange is supported by 94.2 % of the websites, followed by ECDHE with 56.7 % and DHE with 49.5 %. AES for encryption is supported by 93.6 %. In this scan there are no different results for AES128 and AES256. A different work [11] using older data also found similar results concerning the distribution of AES128/256, so this seems also valid for the newer values.

In July 2015 the scan from Securitypitfalls stated, that only 0.0048 % of websites support SSLv2 only. Still 91.5 % of servers support RSA for key exchange followed by ECDH with now 74.4 %. The trend is going towards ECDH and away from RSA for not supporting perfect forward secrecy. AES is supported by 98.1 % in total.

According to the previous numbers and the compatibility values from Table 3 we estimate that this cipher string is compatible with about 95 % of the SSL/TLS websites. We don't expect a significant change in compatibility for 2015.

We used CiNeg to verify this estimation in the same way as described in the previous section. The result for 2014 for the shared cipher suite percentage of cipher string B, when using the top 1,000 websites according to Alexa's list, is 98.3 %. The result for the top 25,000 websites is 97.2 %, i.e. the compatibility is slightly better regarding the tested websites than estimated. Our scans in October 2015 showed, that string B is now compatible to 97.62 % of Alexa's top 1,000 and 98.78 % of Alexa's top 25,000. As estimated there are no significant differences compared to 2014. But it can be seen, that websites which only support SSLv2 decreased.

Figure 4 shows the distribution of negotiated cipher suites for the top 25,000 websites when using cipher string B in 2014. This chart shows that about 26.5 % of the websites negotiated the cipher suite AES128-SHA, which does not offer perfect forward secrecy (since using RSA as the key exchange method); this cipher suite is the main reason for the better compatibility compared to cipher string A.

The negotiated Cipher Suites changed in some ways comparing to the previous scans as you can see in Fig. 5. Where in our last scans, AES128-SHA was the most frequent chosen cipher suite, it is now ECDHE-RSA-AES128-GCM-SHA256, which provides state of the art security and perfect forward secrecy. So even with the same cipher string the results have changed. This might be caused by the fact, that 67 % of the servers use their own cipher suite priority, regarding to a scan from Securitypitfalls in 2014. This indicates that server administrators changed the priority in their servers to more secure cipher suites. A reasonable explanation for this is an increased security awareness due to recent events.

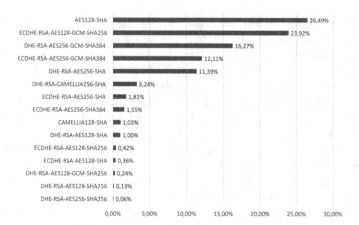

Fig. 4. Percentage of cipher suites negotiated using cipher string B with Alexa's top 25,000 websites in 2014. Compatibility at 97.2 %.

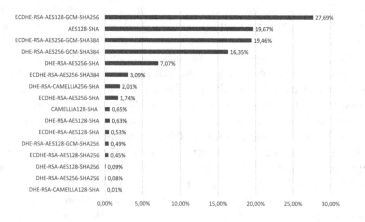

Fig. 5. Percentage of cipher suites negotiated using cipher string B with Alexa's top 25,000 websites in 2015. Compatibility at 98.78 %.

3.3 OpenSSL Support for Various Cipher Suites

Openssl-compare, available at https://github.com/azet/openssl-compare, provides the opportunity to install, execute and compare different OpenSSL versions. It offers the functionality to test a cipher string against all OpenSSL versions present on the current host. The command `ciphersuite` returns all the shared cipher suites. To determine which cipher suite of the shared cipher suites is actually negotiated during a handshake, the command `negotiate` is used.

This tool was used to elaborate which cipher suite is supported by which OpenSSL version. We also used openssl-compare to test which cipher suite is used for the different OpenSSL versions when a handshake is executed with the cipher strings A and B of the ACH project. The shared cipher suites where also identified within these tests.

The following OpenSSL versions and sub-versions where used:

- 0.9.6 (e,i-m)
- 0.9.7 (a-m)
- 0.9.8 (a-y,za,zb,zc)
- 1.0.0 (a,b,beta1-beta5,c-o)
- 1.0.1 (a,b,beta1-beta3,c-j)
- 1.0.2 (beta1-beta3)

Supported Cipher Suites. To determine the oldest OpenSSL version supporting a specific cipher suite we used the command `openssl-compare ciphersuite -s 'ALL'`. The cipher string 'ALL' matches all the cipher suites that are supported by default.

Table 3 shows an excerpt of supported cipher suites. The compatibility values are the results of scans using our CiNeg tool with the top 1,000 websites according to Alexa's list. The compatibility percentage is computed as described above.

Table 3 shows that AES is supported since version 0.9.7. It is also notable that ECDH and ECDHE are supported since version 1.0.0. In version 1.0.1 major modifications were made by introducing AES-GCM (128 and 256), SHA256, and SHA384. AES256-GCM is always used in a cipher suite with SHA384. In TLS v1.2 AES256 is usually used in a cipher suite with SHA256, except for cipher suites that include ECDH(E), where SHA384 is used.

OpenSSL Support for Cipher String A. The command `openssl-compare ciphersuite -s` was used to find the OpenSSL versions which share cipher suites with the cipher string A. The result shows that this cipher string shares cipher suites only with OpenSSL versions 1.0.1 and 1.0.2. These shared cipher suites are:

- DHE-RSA-AES256-GCM-SHA384
- DHE-RSA-AES256-SHA256
- ECDHE-RSA-AES256-GCM-SHA384
- ECDHE-RSA-AES256-SHA384

The three beta versions of version 1.0.1 do not support the cipher suite DHE-RSA-AES256-SHA256. This cipher string only supports TLSv1.2. To examine which cipher suites are negotiated in a handshake the command `openssl-compare negotiate -s` was used. The negotiated cipher suite for all supported OpenSSL versions is DHE-RSA-AES256-GCM-SHA384.

OpenSSL Support for Cipher String B. There is no shared cipher suite for any of the 0.9.6 OpenSSL versions. This cipher string causes problems with some of the older versions. In OpenSSL versions 0.9.7 to 0.9.7l the cipher suite

Table 3. OpenSSL versions' cipher suite support and estimated compatibility for a given suite according to the top 1.000 Alexa websites. "×" denotes support for a cipher suite, "-" lack thereof.

OpenSSL identifier	0.9.6	0.9.7	0.9.8	1.0.0	1.0.1	1.0.2	Compatibility [%]
RC4-SHA	×	×	×	×	×	×	65.6
DES-CBC3-SHA	×	×	×	×	×	×	87.4
AES128-SHA	-	×	×	×	×	×	96.1
AES256-SHA	-	×	×	×	×	×	94.0
EDH-RSA-DES-CBC-SHA	×	×	×	×	×	×	27.3
DHE-RSA-AES128-SHA	-	×	×	×	×	×	34.2
DHE-RSA-AES256-SHA	-	×	×	×	×	×	27.5
DHE-RSA-CAMELLIA128-SHA	-	-	-	×	×	×	17.1
DHE-RSA-CAMELLIA256-SHA	-	-	-	×	×	×	17.0
DHE-RSA-AES128-SHA256	-	-	-	-	×	×	16.9
DHE-RSA-AES256-SHA256	-	-	-	-	×	×	16.9
DHE-RSA-AES128-GCM-SHA256	-	-	-	-	×	×	19.0
DHE-RSA-AES256-GCM-SHA384	-	-	-	-	×	×	17.4
ECDHE-RSA-AES128-SHA	-	-	-	×	×	×	60.7
ECDHE-RSA-AES256-SHA	-	-	-	×	×	×	56.2
ECDHE-RSA-AES128-SHA256	-	-	-	-	×	×	51.2
ECDHE-RSA-AES256-SHA384	-	-	-	-	×	×	50.5
ECDHE-RSA-AES128-GCM-SHA256	-	-	-	-	×	×	52.1
ECDHE-RSA-AES256-GCM-SHA384	-	-	-	-	×	×	51.1

AES256-SHA is incorrectly included. This is caused by parsing problems[12] and is fixed in 0.9.7m. 0.9.7m includes the following cipher suites when tested with cipher string B:

- AES128-SHA
- DHE-RSA-AES128-SHA
- DHE-RSA-AES256-SHA

The parsing problems also exist in versions 0.9.8 to 0.9.8d and the shared cipher suites are:

- AES128-SHA
- **AES256-SHA**
- DHE-RSA-AES128-SHA
- DHE-RSA-AES256-SHA
- **ECDHE-RSA-AES128-SHA**
- **ECDHE-RSA-AES256-SHA** (not in 0.9.8(a))
- **ECDH-RSA-AES128-SHA**
- **ECDH-RSA-AES256-SHA**

---

[12] https://www.openssl.org/news/changelog.html.

The five shared cipher suites, indicated in bold in the listing above, should not be included in the shared cipher suites in versions 0.9.8 to 0.9.8d. The ECDHE cipher suites are according to the cipher string, but they are not included by the default lists and should not be used in version 0.9.8.

The parsing problems are fixed in version 0.9.8e. The versions 0.9.8e to 0.9.8zc share the following cipher suites:

- AES128-SHA
- DHE-RSA-AES128-SHA
- DHE-RSA-AES256-SHA

In versions 1.0.0, 1.0.1 and 1.0.2 there are no problems regarding parsing or negotiation of the cipher suite. The 1.0.0 versions share the following cipher suites:

- AES128-SHA
- CAMELLIA128-SHA
- DHE-RSA-AES128-SHA
- DHE-RSA-AES256-SHA
- DHE-RSA-CAMELLIA128-SHA
- DHE-RSA-CAMELLIA256-SHA
- ECDHE-RSA-AES128-SHA
- ECDHE-RSA-AES256-SHA

This list shows that in version 1.0.0 CAMELLIA is also used in DHE cipher suites. The versions 1.0.1 and 1.0.2 also share the cipher suites of the 1.0.0 versions. Additional shared cipher suites in 1.0.1 and 1.0.2 are:

- DHE-RSA-AES128-GCM-SHA256
- DHE-RSA-AES128-SHA256
- DHE-RSA-AES256-GCM-SHA384
- DHE-RSA-AES256-SHA384
- ECDHE-RSA-AES128-GCM-SHA256
- ECDHE-RSA-AES128-SHA256
- ECDHE-RSA-AES256-GCM-SHA384
- ECDHE-RSA-AES256-SHA384

This list shows that AES-GCM, SHA256, and SHA384 are supported since OpenSSL 1.0.1 (used by only about 12 % of installations, according to Table 1).

We then again utilized the openssl-compare tool to find the actual cipher suite negotiated when using cipher string B; Table 4 lists our results.

This test shows that the priority settings of the cipher suites does not work properly for the versions 0.9.8 to 0.9.8d, because ECDHE is preferred, but cipher suites including DHE should be preferred instead and ECDHE should not be used with versions 0.9.8.

The following cipher string fixes most of cipher string B's problems:
EDH +CAMELLIA: kEDH +aRSA +AES: EECDH +aRSA +AESGCM: EECDH +aRSA +SHA256:
EECDH: +CAMELLIA128: +AES128: +SSLv3: !aNULL: !eNULL: !LOW: !3DES: !MD5: !EXP:
!PSK: !DSS: !RC4: !SEED: !IDEA: !ECDSA: CAMELLIA128 -SHA: AES128 -SHA.

Table 4. Negotiated cipher suite when using cipher string B.

Cipher suite	OpenSSL
ECDHE-RSA-AES128-SHA	0.9.8(a)
ECDHE-RSA-AES256-SHA	0.9.8b-d
DHE-RSA-AES256-SHA	0.9.8e-zc
DHE-RSA-CAMELLIA256-SHA	1.0.0
DHE-RSA-AES256-GCM-SHA384	1.0.1, 1.0.2

The remaining problem with this cipher string is that the cipher suite AES256-SHA is included in the shared cipher suites for versions 0.9.7h-k and 0.9.8a. This is caused by parsing problems of these versions. The negotiated cipher suites using the modified cipher string B are listed in Table 5. These results are according to the priorities of the cipher suites in the cipher string, i.e. it is working as intended.

Table 5. Negotiated cipher suite when using modified cipher string B.

Cipher suite	OpenSSL
DHE-RSA-AES256-SHA	0.9.7 - 0.9.8
DHE-RSA-CAMELLIA256-SHA	1.0.0
DHE-RSA-AES256-GCM-SHA384	1.0.1, 1.0.2

If this cipher string should include all the cipher suites mentioned for string B in [3], CAMELLIA256-SHA:AES256-SHA has to be added at the end of the cipher string.

3.4   Analyzing Available Cipher Suites Using O-Saft

In order to get all supported cipher suites of web servers we used the tool O-Saft from https://www.owasp.org/index.php/O-Saft. To automate the O-Saft scans we wrote a tool which executes the O-Saft command `cipherraw` for a given list of URLs and a tool which parses the results.

Figure 6 shows the results for the top 100 sites according to Alexa. 58 websites of the 100 support SSL/TLS. The cipher suite with the highest compatibility (96.6 %) is AES128-SHA. It is also notable that 67.2 % of the sites support RC4-SHA and 44.8 % support RC4-MD5. Some of these values differ slightly to results of other scans; this is caused by the small sample size.

4   Cipher Suite Proposal

After having evaluated the practical compatibility of cipher string A and B from [3], our goal was to create a cipher string that offers high security and is

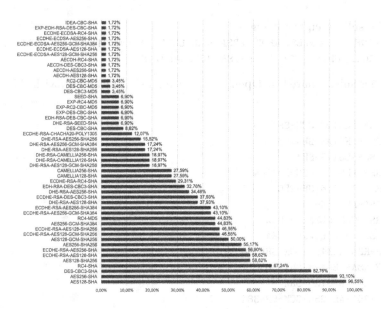

Fig. 6. Results of the O-Saft scans, indicating how many percent of Alexa's top 100 websites use a specific cipher suite in 2014.

compatible with a wide range of websites. Since the two cipher strings by [3] are designed for different requirements — one of them for high security and one for best compatibility — the created cipher string should be placed in the middle between these two.

The first condition for the cipher string is that it only uses cipher suites that support forward secrecy. These are cipher suites using DHE or ECDHE for key exchange. This reduces the compatibility, but is a very important point. (Perfect) Forward Secrecy [11] uses the private key of the web server to sign a Diffie-Hellman (DH) key exchange message. When using DH, the server always uses the same key pair: i.e. when the private key gets stolen, all sessions recorded in the past could be decrypted. When using Diffie-Hellman ephemeral (DHE) a new key pair is created for each session and the private key of the session is never stored on the server after the session has terminated. Gaining access to the private keys of a server now only enables decryption of the sessions currently in progress, but not of the ones recorded in the past.

In our cipher string proposal, TLS 1.2 cipher suites are preferred. If the cipher suites have the same protocol version, then ECDHE is preferred, because according to [11] only 0.3 % of the websites support DH parameters with a size of 2048 bits. 99.3 % of the websites support a parameter size of 1024 bits and even 34 % support a parameter size of 512 bits, trend decreasing.

The chosen encryption methods are AES and CAMELLIA with key lengths of 128 and 256 bits, respectively. These ciphers offer high security and are widely supported; as MAC we only allow hash functions from the SHA family.

The resulting cipher string is:

EECDH: kEDH +aRSA +AES: kEDH +aRSA +CAMELLIA: +SSLv3: !aNULL: !eNULL: !3DES:
!IDEA: !RC4: !MD5: !EXP: !PSK: !DSS: !ECDSA: !DES

The cipher suites shared by OpenSSL from version 1.0.1 and up with this string
are:

- DHE-RSA-AES128-GCM-SHA256
- DHE-RSA-AES128-SHA256
- DHE-RSA-AES128-SHA
- DHE-RSA-AES256-GCM-SHA384
- DHE-RSA-AES256-SHA256
- DHE-RSA-AES256-SHA
- DHE-RSA-CAMELLIA128-SHA
- DHE-RSA-CAMELLIA256-SHA
- ECDHE-RSA-AES128-GCM-SHA256
- ECDHE-RSA-AES128-SHA256
- ECDHE-RSA-AES128-SHA
- ECDHE-RSA-AES256-GCM-SHA384
- ECDHE-RSA-AES256-SHA384
- ECDHE-RSA-AES256-SHA

Table 6 gives an overview of the cipher suites negotiated by the different
OpenSSL versions when using this newly proposed string. When compared to
cipher strings A and B from above, our string prefers AES over CAMELLIA and
elliptic curve versions of Diffie-Hellman over the integer ones.

Table 6. Negotiated cipher suite when using our proposed cipher string.

Cipher suite	OpenSSL
DHE-RSA-AES256-SHA	0.9.7 - 0.9.8
ECDHE-RSA-AES256-SHA	1.0.0
ECDHE-RSA-AES256-GCM-SHA384	1.0.1, 1.0.2

CiNeg was used to get an approximate value for the compatibility. The 2014
result for the shared cipher suite percentage of our cipher string proposal, when
using the top 1,000 websites according to Alexa, is 74.8 %. The result for the
top 25,000 websites is 77.9 %. Our reevaluation in 2015 results in an even better
compatibility. 87.9 % of Alexa's top 1,000 and 87.5 % of Alexa's top 25,000 are
compatible with our proposed string. These results are showing that — in line
with the goal of the cipher string proposal — the compatibility is ranked between
ACH's cipher string A and B (see also Table 7).

Figure 7 shows the distribution of negotiated cipher suites for the top 25,000
websites when using the cipher string proposal in 2014. 71 % of the negotiated
cipher suites are TLS 1.2 cipher suites and this is according to the priorities in

Table 7. 2014: Cipher Strings A - B - Proposal, comparing the percentage of Alexa's top 25,000 websites in 2014 and 2015 sharing at least one cipher suite with the given cipher string (i.e. a TLS handshake with a site would succeed for the respective cipher string).

	December 2014	October 2015
Cipher String A	56.10 %	70.04 %
Cipher String B	97.17 %	98.89 %
Proposed Cipher String	77.9 %	87.94 %

the cipher string. It is also notable that 66 % of the negotiated cipher suites use AES-GCM.

As Fig. 8 states, the most secure cipher Suite, `ECDHE-RSA-AES256-GCM-SHA384`, is the most frequently negotiated one in 2015. In our first tests the version with AES128 was used most. Anyways, both suites offer good security but also here it can be seen, that the outcome of the negotiation changed over time and became even more secure. In 81.1 % of negotiations, a TLS 1.2 cipher is used.

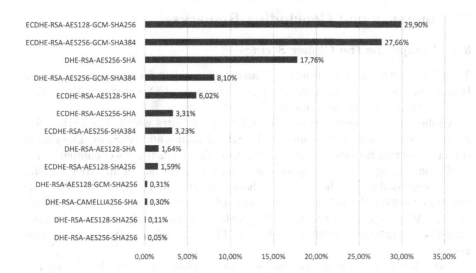

Fig. 7. Percentage of cipher suites negotiated using our cipher string proposal with Alexa's top 25,000 websites in 2014.

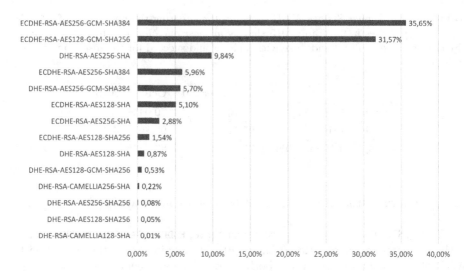

Fig. 8. Percentage of cipher suites negotiated using our proposed cipher string with Alexa's top 25,000 websites in 2015.

5   Summary and Concluding Remarks

5.1   Comparing the Cipher Strings

Table 7 indicates the percentage of shared cipher suites for the cipher string A, B and our proposal. These are the results from the CiNeg scans with Alexa's top 25,000 websites in 2014 and 2015.

Cipher string A only supports TLS 1.2 cipher suites which offer perfect forward secrecy, uses hash-functions of the SHA-2 family and AES256. The goal of this cipher string is to use strong cipher suites. This leads to a lower compatibility.

Cipher string B does support some weaker cipher suites in order to offer better compatibility. The two fall back cipher suites are `AES128-SHA` and `CAMELLIA128-SHA`; the other cipher suites offer perfect forward secrecy. While in 2014 `AES128-SHA` was the most frequently negotiated cipher suite, in 2015 `ECDH-RSA-AES128-GCM-SHA256` is preferred. TLS 1.2 cipher suites are preferred generally.

Our cipher string proposal supports only cipher suites which offer perfect forward secrecy, but it is not limited to TLS 1.2 cipher suites, i.e. ciphers suites using AES128 and CAMELLIA128 are also supported. This offers a wider range of support than cipher string A, with only a minor reduction in security.

5.2   Conclusion

Bruce Schneier's words "Security is a process, not a product[13]" clearly sums up that there will never be a final solution regarding security issues.

---

[13] https://www.schneier.com/crypto-gram/archives/2000/0515.html.

Anyways, one can say that there were explicit security improvements in SSL/TLS since 2014. Generally, going towards newer TLS versions is most likely not the only reason for this significant increase in security over one year. Another reason for this is the raising security awareness from people due to recent events.

Everything concerning security underlies fast development and rapidly changing requirements; therefore any security issues depend on individual conditions. In this work we evaluated the practical usability and compatibility of two OpenSSL cipher strings publicly proposed by members of academia and industry, using existing tools like O-Saft and Openssl-compare, as well as our newly developed CiNeg tool.

In addition, we propose a new cipher string which provides better compatibility than ACH's cipher string A and stronger security than cipher string B, with the caveat of being less secure than A and lacking compatibility compared to B.

The tests have been performed again after a year to see what a difference a year makes. Nevertheless, there is no perfect compatibility for secure cipherstrings yet and perhaps there never will be.

This again underlines the problem that there is no single perfect cipher string which meets all possible requirements; administrators have to find the right cipher string by balancing security strength and compatibility regarding their individual needs, using the tools available at their disposal.

Considering this complexity as well as recently discovered attack vectors against TLS like FREAK [2] and Logjam [1], a point of further research should be to determine if the algorithm variability present in the TLS protocol might in fact be a severe weakness and different approaches on selecting cryptographic primitives could be considered.

References

1. Adrian, D., Bhargavan, K., Durumeric, Z., Gaudry, P., Green, M., Halderman, J.A., Heninger, N., Springall, D., Thom, E., Valenta, L., VanderSloot, B., Wustrow, E., Zanella-Bguelink, S., Zimmermann, P.: Imperfect Forward Secrecy: How Diffie-Hellman Fails in Practice. Technical report, INRIA Paris-Rocquencourt and INRIA Nancy-Grand Est, CNRS and Universit de Lorraine and Microsoft Research and University of Pennsylvania and Johns Hopkins and University of Michigan (2015)
2. Beurdouche, B., Bhargavan, K., Delignat-Lavaud, A., Fournet, C., Kohlweiss, M., Pironti, A., Strub, P.Y., Zinzindohoue, J.K.: A Messy State of the Union: Taming the Composite State Machines of TLS. In: IEEE Security & Privacy 2015, preprint (2015)
3. Breyha, W., Durvaux, D., Dussa, T., Kaplan, L.A., Mendel, F., Mock, C., Koschuch, M., Kriegisch, A., Pschl, U., Sabet, R., San, B., Schlatterbeck, R., Schreck, T., Wrstlein, A., Zauner, A., Zawodsky, P.: Applied Crypto Hardening. Technical report (2015). https://bettercrypto.org/static/applied-crypto-hardening.pdf
4. Chown, P.: RFC3268 - Advanced Encryption Standard (AES) Ciphersuites for Transport Layer Security (TLS). Technical report, Network Working Group (2002)

5. Dierks, T., Allen, C.: RFC2246 - The TLS Protocol Version 1.0. Technical report, Network Working Group (1999). https://www.ietf.org/rfc/rfc2246.txt
6. Dierks, T., Rescorla, E.: RFC4346 - The Transport Layer Security (TLS) Protocol Version 1.1. Technical report, Network Working Group (2006)
7. Dierks, T., Rescorla, E.: RFC5246 - The Transport Layer Security (TLS) Protocol Version 1.2. Technical report, Network Working Group (2008)
8. Diffie, W., Hellman, M.: New directions in cryptography. IEEE Trans. Inf. Theor. **22**(6), 644–654 (2006). http://dx.doi.org/10.1109/TIT.1976.1055638
9. Eronen, P., Tschofenig, H.: RFC4279 - Pre-Shared Key Ciphersuites for Transport Layer Security (TLS). Technical report, Network Working Group (2005)
10. Freier, A., Karlton, P., Kocher, P.: RFC6101 - The Secure Sockets Layer (SSL) Protocol Version 3.0. Technical report, Internet Engineering Task Force (IETF) (2011)
11. Huang, L., Adhikarla, S., Boneh, D., Jackson, C.: An experimental study of TLS forward secrecy deployments. In: IEEE CS Security and Privacy Workshops (2014)
12. Lee, H., Yoon, J., Lee, J.: RFC4162 - Addition of SEED Cipher Suites to Transport Layer Security (TLS). Technical report, Network Working Group (2005)
13. Medvinsky, A., Hur, M.: RFC2712 - Addition of Kerberos Cipher Suites to Transport Layer Security (TLS). Technical report, Network Working Group (1999)
14. Moeller, B., Thai Duong, K.K.: This POODLE Bites: Exploiting The SSL 3.0 Fallback(2014)
15. Moriai, S., Kato, A., Kanda, M.: RFC4132 - Addition of Camellia Cipher Suites to Transport Layer Security (TLS). Technical report, Network Working Group (2005)
16. NIST: Advanced Encryption Standard (AES) (FIPS PUB 197) (2001)
17. NIST: Secure Hash Standard (SHS) (FIPS PUB 180–4) (2012)
18. Popov, A.: RFC7465 - Prohibiting RC4 Cipher Suites. Technical report, Internet Engineering Task Force (IETF) (2015)
19. Rivest, R.L., Shamir, A., Adleman, L.: A method for obtaining digital signatures and public-key cryptosystems. Commun. ACM **21**(2), 120–126 (1978). http://doi.acm.org/10.1145/359340.359342
20. Stallings, W.: Cryptography and Network Security, 4th edn., p. 539. Pearson (2008)

e-Business

ARM: Architecture for Recruitment Matchmaking

Bruno Coelho[1]([✉]), Fernando Costa[2], and Gil M. Gonçalves[1,3]

[1] INOVA+, Centro de Inovação de Matosinhos,
Rua Dr. Afonso Cordeiro, 567, 4450-309 Matosinhos, Portugal
{bruno.coelho,gil.goncalves}@inovamais.pt
[2] Department of Informatics Engineering,
Superior Institute of Engineering of Porto,
Rua Dr. António Bernardino de Almeida, 431, 4249-015 Porto, Portugal
fernando.costa@inovamais.pt
[3] Department of Informatics Engineering, Faculty of Engineering,
University of Porto, Rua Dr. Roberto Frias, 4200-465 Porto, Portugal

Abstract. In modern days people search job opportunities or candidates mainly online, where several websites for this purpose already do exist (LinkedIn, Guru and Freelancer, to name a few). This task is especially difficult because of the large number of items to look for and the need for manual compatibility by human resources. What we propose in this paper is an architecture for recruitment matchmaking that considers the user and opportunity models (content-based filtering) and social interactions (collaborative filtering) to improve the quality of its recommendations. This solution is also able to generate adequate teams for a given job opportunity, based not only on the needed competences but also on the social compatibility between their members, both using user-generated content and automatic platform data. This article is the extended version of ICE-B's Hyred - HYbrid Job REcommenDation System, which means that it includes updated information and new advances, especially in Chap. 5.

Keywords: Recommender systems · Decision support systems · Match-making algorithms · Jobs · Employment · Work · Teams · User modelling · Content-based filtering · Collaborative filtering

1 Introduction

Social professional networks have had an exponential growth in the last few years, mainly due to the banalization of internet access. LinkedIn, created in 2003, is now the most relevant professional network platform; it has reached 380 million users in 2015 [1], being that 210 million were registered between 2009 and 2014 [2]. As LinkedIn allows the input of job opportunities, if someone is looking for the most suitable job, the universe of search is pretty vast: 3 million jobs vast, to be more precise [3]. Of course that one can focus this job search to only one specific activity area, or search on an existing recommended jobs list.

However, there is still a need for an extensive and manual analysis of each one of the job specifications (e.g. analyse required experience, technical skills, education, etc.)

© Springer International Publishing Switzerland 2016
M.S. Obaidat and P. Lorenz (Eds.): ICETE 2015, CCIS 585, pp. 81–99, 2016.
DOI: 10.1007/978-3-319-30222-5_4

to know which jobs really are the most adequate to the candidate, or if we are what the opportunity really needs (opposite perspective of the recommendation).

These job search platforms lack in features that could attenuate or even eliminate all this trouble: a precise Recommendation System (RS) that takes in consideration all the parameters that a human resources (HR) specialist would normally take when searching for the best opportunity or candidate. Also, they lack on a very relevant matter – team recommendation. This would represent a very efficient and useful way of searching all the best candidates and verifying which of them would probably make a good work-related team together. Also, this could help an HR specialist finding a perfect fit for an existent team.

In this job search context, the main objective is the recommendation between entities of the domain: users and opportunities. On almost any type of situation where recommendations need to be calculated, one issue automatically arises – possible large volume of items to compare (similarity calculation) and consequently low speed in the recommendations calculation. In this scenario, speed is especially relevant, because of the complexity that entities can reveal. E.g. a user can have multiple professional experiences, soft skills and technical skills associated, so the similarity calculation can be as complex as the complexity of its profile plus its interactions with the system. The same logic applies to the opportunities that can be characterized by the same dimensions. The size of the solution space is a problem especially in the team recommendation context, because of the large number of possible combinations that can be done with a small number of users (e.g. for 15 users, combined in 10 element groups, 15c10 = 3003), only to generate user/team associations alone. Another problem has to do with the known cold-start issue [4], that consists on having little to none information about the entities at play, especially when they start off.

2 Related Work

In this chapter we present you some examples of previous research made within the scope of the same job recommendation area, i.e. job recommendation systems (JRSs). These endeavors have helped ARM immensely by providing excellent problem-resolution thinking and analysis, as well as an overall experience when trying to tackle the same difficulties. It is believed that ARM has made good use of those examples and has improved upon some of the features made available by them.

Reference [5]: This research has some similarities to our solution, being that this is a hybrid RS that uses both content-based and interaction-based data to make recommendations. Based on that information, it creates a graph that relates all the entities involved and then, using that graph, calculates similarities. The main differences between this system and our solution are: (1) this system does not have the ability to make team recommendations; (2) profile similarity calculations are made using Latent Semantic Analysis (LSA) tools and (3) the system cannot inference new information. This tool analyses text files that contain the content of profiles (instead of directly comparing each entity's profile characteristics), leading to less precise results.

Reference [6]: This project consists on a framework characterized by three sets: individuals I, expertise areas EA and social dimensions SD. The elements of such sets are captured using three graphs: competence graph, social graph and history graph. This is an interesting approach, because it divides the content into three different data structures, so the content in each one of the graphs is more specialized. However, because the information is partitioned into various graphs, one cannot infer new knowledge that uses information from more than one graph (or at least the database cannot). Although, because the platform information has a simplified structure, the recommendation of teams can be executed relatively fast. This solution continues to have the same combination explosion problem already explained, because all the team combinations must be individually calculated, as well as their members' compatibility. Also, there are several sources of information used for the team recommendation calculations; the quantity of information available is vast, leading to more complexity and thus poor performance.

Reference [7]: In this project it is suggested a team RS oriented to the academic context. Team suggestions are based on the competence revealed by the possible team members and by their cohesiveness. It is then calculated a global score related to those variables. This solution has several limitations, such as: (1) incapacity to generate new knowledge and include it in the similarities' calculation; (2) it does not consider important information that would be somewhat obvious for this domain, such as co-authorship, members of the same department, participant in the same event or conference, amongst others. It also does not consider interpersonal information usually encountered on a social network, such as *likes*, *posts* or *follows*. This kind of information is extremely relevant because it is a clear demonstration of the user's tastes that could improve greatly the precision and accuracy of the user model and, consecutively, improve the recommendation's quality.

Reference [8]: This project makes two-way recommendations (between jobs and users), which is also exactly what ARM performs. To make suggestions, they perform the following steps: (1) use explicit information extracted from user résumés and jobs' attribute information and convert them to vector space models (VSM), in order to calculate the similarity of explicit preference (it is not very clear if the job entity is also described through a résumé); (2) they use all the other résumés that exist in the platform to locate implicit preference, according to the proportion of each of the attributes being compared. These steps are followed by similarity calculations, using explicit and implicit information. This solution has as main advantages the simplicity and efficiency of the similarity calculation, while giving users total freedom to input whatever they like without using rigid forms for profile definition. However, the use of VSMs for the similarity calculations has some issues: (1) user résumés with similar context but different term vocabulary won't be associated; (2) the order in which the terms appear in the document is lost in the VSM representation; (3) keywords must precisely match résumés' items and (4) words' substrings might result in a "false positive match" (e.g. 'program' and 'programs').

3   Concept and Architecture

ARM is part of a broader web platform that has the purpose of bringing together entities which can execute tasks and entities which have the need to have those tasks executed. The overall architecture is represented in Fig. 1.

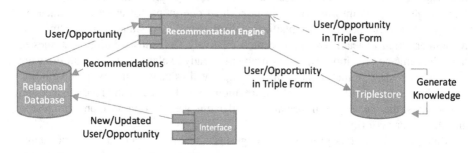

Fig. 1. Components diagram.

In the next subsections these components are explained in some detail, before diving into the most important aspect of ARM: recommendations made in the scope of the Recommendation Engine.

3.1   RDB (Relational Database)

The RDB component consists on a SQL Server relational database that contains all the data from the platform. Only some of this information is needed for recommendations. Some attention was paid as to not overload this component for the sake of recommendations, since the most important criteria for the availability of the database is the end-user interface (see next section).

3.2   Interface

The interface refers to the web portal/application that is publicly available for users to interact with and that ultimately uses the features made available by the RS. As users interact with it, the information in the RDB is updated, triggering recommendation calculations on the Recommendation Engine component. This app has many of the typical features found today on similar-themed platforms, such as social network, badges, messaging, LinkedIn integration and more. One of the most interesting scenarios is the capability of any LinkedIn user to import some parts of its profile into the devised platform, eliminating the so-called cold start problem explained earlier.

3.3   Triple Store

A study was conducted about the best option for the persistence of information of the platform's entities, which would at the same time enable for a fast recommendation generation without having an impact in the web app. Two possibilities were found: a RDB (another one or the same one presented earlier) or a Triple Store (TS). After analyzing the pros and cons, the TS was chosen. This approach to data storage has many advantages over RDB databases, and most of those are very relevant in this context. The most relevant advantages are schema flexibility, reasoning power, standardization and cost. There are some disadvantages on the use of a TS though, such as data duplication and maintenance of inference rules. A TS stores data in a graph-like structure, where entities are directly connected to each other and to their characteristics. A simple example of a data structure stored in a TS is showed in Fig. 2.

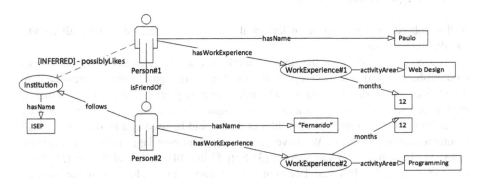

Fig. 2. Graph inference example.

The TS contains all the data related with the entities that are relevant for the recommendations calculation. This data contains not only the data related with the characteristics of the entities but also the relations between them (e.g. user's friends, user's likes, followed entities, etc.). This information can then be used by the TS itself to infer new information.

As an example, a TS can infer that a person possibly likes a certain institution if (1) a person X is friend of a person Y and (2) a person Y follows some institution Z. This can be visualized in the Fig. 2. Inference rules are created using the Semantic Web Rule Language (SWRL).

3.4 Recommendation Engine

This component is the most important of all and is responsible for the recommendations' calculations and the conversions between the RDB and the triple format (for the TS). These actions are triggered for some entity that is either added or updated in the database, therefore only operating when necessary. The recommendations are calculated for every possible combination of entities in the platform, so that end users have all of this important and useful data when navigating through the web app in a general purpose or with any of the most typical goals of the job market. These calculations are made originally made for all the elements present, with no restrictions made to the universe of search.

Conversions between the database and TS are made for every dimension related with the entities that are later used for recommendation. So users/opportunities are completely "converted" to the TS, including not only their characteristics but also their interactions with the system; this means that after the conversion is made, the RDB is no longer necessary and thus the system is completely free to attend web requests from users. After that, similarities between entities are calculated offline, so that there is no noticeable delay in the user interface. As soon as an entity is modified, all their similarities related to every other entity in the system are recalculated.

4 RS Algorithms

In this subsection we describe in technical and mathematical detail how all recommendations are made.

The core component of the devised work is a set of heterogeneous data blocks (content-based data) that make up for the most important part of the recommendation calculation. We started by defining which information pieces to attach to each one of the entities involved in the recommendation context (users and opportunities) and by streamlining that data into common blocks that would be used in a modular way in all recommendation scenarios. We have defined the following large information dimensions: (1) Education; (2) Languages; (3) Soft Skills; (4) Technical Skills; (5) Work Experience and (6) Physical Location. These dimensions (along with the simpler activity area and optional likeability ratio) are the basis of the similarity calculation between entities, and thus the basis for the more advanced forms of recommendation referred later. The fact that these dimensions are shared between entities eases and fastens the similarity calculation, while increasing precision. The dimensions of an entity "Opportunity" refer to the needed specifications for the related job opportunity; as for the entity "User", they refer to personal characteristics of human candidates (users). With the aforementioned structure in place, we will now present how we calculate the most basic kind of recommendation.

4.1   Entity Recommendations

We make singular entity recommendations (SER) by calculating the similarity between one instance of any of the basic entities involved in the job search scenario: user and opportunity; therefore we have the following combinations/types of recommendations: **user-opportunity**, **user-user** and **opportunity-opportunity**. **User-group** recommendations can also be obtained by going through the **user-user** recommendations of the respective group members (using the average). These calculations take into consideration all the dimensions associated with each one of the entities being compared. Using those similarities, we then calculate a final one that sets a weight to each one of them and then aggregates them all. In Fig. 3 we summarily demonstrate how this similarity calculation works. We now explain in detail each one of the dimensions' similarity calculations (each one of the squares contained in the central part of Fig. 3.).

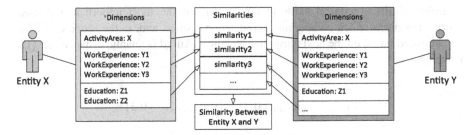

Fig. 3. Entities' similarity calculation.

Educations. Educations refer to the academic background related with the entities; at the current time only more formal types of formations are supported. When calculating their similarity, the compared attributes are: institution, activity area (compared based on the semantic distance between them, using (1) [9]), grade (numeric distance) and degree (numeric distance).

$$sim_{semanic} = \frac{1}{hierarchy_{distance} * b} \qquad (1)$$

The semantic distance between two entities of the same type is performed in the following dimensions: activity areas (used in their own similarity and within experience and education) and technical skills. The variable $hierarchy_{distance}$ is the number of levels in the hierarchy that separate both concepts, while b can act as 1 or 2 depending on whether the comparing entity is a superclass or a subclass of the comparison target respectively (i.e. we gave more importance to specialization rather to generalization).

$$sim_{edu} = (sim_{institution} * 0.2) + (sim_{actarea} * 0.5) + (sim_{grade} * 0.15) + \\ (sim_{degree} * 0.15) \qquad (2)$$

Languages. Languages refer to language skills that entities possess. Compared attributes are the language id and proficiency (numeric distance).

$$sim_{lang} = 1/proficiency_{difference} \qquad (3)$$

Soft Skills. Soft skills (SSs) are personal traits and human characteristics that play an important part in the job search problem. Because SSs can be completely defined only by its Id (i.e. the existence of that skill), the comparison is directly made.

$$sim\_ss = (shared\_ss)/(total\_ss) \qquad (4)$$

Technical Skills. Technical skills (TSs) are one of the most important and used information pieces when comparing candidate/job profiles and, in the scope of ARM, are compared based on the next attributes: technical skill id (semantic distance, i.e. (1)) and proficiency.

$$sim_{tech} = \left(sim_{wp} * 0.7\right) + \left(sim_{proficiency} * 0.3\right) \tag{5}$$

Work Experience. Work experiences possessed by people or required by opportunities are compared based on the next attributes: activity area (1) and duration.

$$sim_{we} = \left(sim_{we} * 0.7\right) + \left(sim_{months} * 0.3\right) \tag{6}$$

Physical Location. The physical location is compared based on the real distance between the locations of the compared entities. This distance is more relevant when calculating **user-user** similarities because of the *propinquity* factor [10] (please check 4.1.4 - **Physical Location of Team Members**).

$$sim_{location} = \left(sim_{city} * 0.9\right) + \left(sim_{country} * 0.1\right) \tag{7}$$

Activity Area. The activity area to where the entity belongs to can have a relevant importance in the similarity between entities. Therefore it is compared based on its semantic distance to other areas, using (1).

Likeability Ratio. Unlike other dimensions, which are explicit profile parts of each one of the entities, the likeability is an indirect value that measures the relationship between a user and an institution related with an opportunity (thus it's not used for user-user or opportunity-opportunity calculations). (8) shows a part of that likeability; however, that equation may still add some additional conditions, such as (1) if the user follows that institution or (2) if he is a member of it.

$$likeability_{ratio} = \frac{log\left(liked_{posts} + 1\right)}{\left(log\left(100 + liked_{posts}\right)\right)} * 0.3 \tag{8}$$

Final Similarity Calculation. The final similarity calculation weights each one of the explained dimensions with an almost-equal distribution; these weights are configurable through a configuration file, so that they can be further refined (attributes of each one of the dimensions are not currently configurable). We have defined the weights with the values shown in Fig. 4.

By using all of the previously explained formulae, the final similarity value is then given by (9).

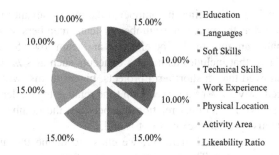

Fig. 4. SER weights.

$$entity_{similarity} = (sim_{edu} * 0.15) + (sim_{lang} * 0.1) + (sim_{ss} * 0.1) +$$
$$(sim_{tech} * 0.15) + (sim_{we} * 0.15) + (sim_{location} * 0.15) + \qquad (9)$$
$$(sim_{actarea} * 0.1) + (sim_{like} * 0.10)$$

4.2 Team Recommendations

Teams are groups of people; however, not all groups are teams, because a team is so much more than just a set of people together and that fact alone triggers all sorts of changes and interactions between people that otherwise wouldn't happen. With that in mind, we have studied which are the concepts and human traits that may have an influence in achieving the perfect group of users that can make up a good team for a certain opportunity (i.e. only those related with the job domain). Based on a number of different studies, our research has come up with the following four upper-level components that, when combined, are able to distinguish one good team from a simple/plain group of people: (1) number of team members, (2) team cohesion, (3) required competences and (4) physical location of team members. In the next sections we thoroughly detail the research and nature of these components in the scope of team recommendations, as well as how we use them in ARM.

Number of Team Members. How many people does the team have is one of the major variables to consider, not only because of resources to be allocated for the project but also because it has an impact on the rest of the variables. We have analyzed some previous studies on the subject that have helped us reach a more grounded concrete idea for the team member number.

References [11, 12] have researched, through a simple rope-pulling test, the relationship between the number of team members and the individual member's average performance. The results were surprising, demonstrating that, as new members were added to the team, the average effort by each member actually decreased. This is related with a known phenomenon called "social loafing" (SL) that happens when people exert less effort to achieve a goal when they work in a group rather than alone [13]. [14], that had also studied the SL phenomenon, said that the ideal number of team members is somewhere between 5 and 12, being the number 6 the most relevant in his studies. In [15] it is considered that the maximum number of team members should be 4 or 5. Teams with less than 4 are too small to be effective and teams over 5 are non-efficient. A study made by [16] (that includes as metrics concepts such as size, time, effort and detected defects) showed that in short term projects, bigger teams (with an average of 8.5 workers) reduced only 24 % of the execution time relative to smaller teams (with an average of 2.1 workers), i.e. a direct relationship between the number of people in a team and the productivity (increase) was not found.

Based on the aforementioned literature, we chose to define the number of team members to a maximum of ten. This is the top number of people suggested that a team working together must have, having in consideration productivity maximization and team inefficiency minimization. We also suggest 6 as the number of optimum team size for projects which necessarily will be multi-people, but we enable people to refine that number as they please.

Team Cohesion. Groups, as all living creatures, evolve over time. Initially a group is just an agglomerate of people who happened to work together, but the uncertainty eventually gives place to cohesion as the members bond with each other through strong social connections. Cohesion depends essentially on how well people relate with one another, as pairs and as groups; it is what keeps a team together after the presence of relationships between all the members. It prevents team fragmentation, keeping its members in a constant state of bonding, as well as avoids problems and animosities.

Reference [11] defends that there is a clear distinction between the individual and the group when one talks about team cohesion. For one, there is the attraction of the individual to the group – how much he/she wants to be a part of it. Then there is the group aspect, represented by a set of perceptions/features that consist, e.g. in the degree of proximity, similarity and union inside the group. Widmeyer also defends that there is a clear distinction between social cohesion and task cohesion. While social cohesion refers to the motivation to develop and maintain social relations with a group, task cohesion refers to the motivation of reaching company or project goals. We can conclude that the ideal scenario would be when both cohesions exist; indeed, the existence of only one is a bad omen for low cohesion in the long run. In the proposed solution, we chose not to calculate task cohesion, since the detection of this kind of psychological trait is difficult based on existing data. The best way to identify it is analyzing/monitoring the physical behavior of a person when working on a certain task; also, in the context of team recommendation, this variable does not have that much relevance, since people can have a very high cohesion on a certain task and very low on others.

Social Cohesion. A way of detecting team cohesion is analyzing the social cohesion, since a team is a form of social interaction. We reach this by using a formula that appears in [4]. This *social$_{score}$* combines all the following variables:

- Shared Projects: the number of projects that each person has in common with other team members (this has a very direct relationship with his/her interpersonal or emotional connection)

- Friendship relations: friendship/contact relationships between team members (just like in Facebook or LinkedIn) are one of the most obvious pieces of information for probable likeability between people
- Shared interests: if team members share the same interests or tastes (if they *follow* the same entities in the network, such as people and institutions), attended the same institutions, etc.

Next we describe the approach that was used in each one of the defined variables, in order to make them ready to be included in the *social*$_{score}$ equation.

Shared Projects. Consider $C = \{c_1, \ldots, c_m\}$ as being the group of connections between elements of a certain group of people. Each element of C connects two persons and has an associated weight p relative to the number of shared projects between them. Consider also *max* as being the heaviest weight of the C set and n representing the number of elements contained in that same set. Let U be the set of users that are related in the C set's connections. Based on this statements, we obtained (10), that we called *familiarity*$_{score}$.

$$familiarity_{score(U)} = 1 - \frac{\sum_{i=1}^{|n-1|} |p_i - \max|}{|n-1| * \max}, \forall max \geq 1; \forall n > 2 \qquad (10)$$

Friendship Relations. Consider the set of friendship connections between users from the team being analyzed $R = \{r_1, \ldots, r_m\}$. We represent the number of elements of the R set using the *nf* (number of friendships) variable. Consider also the number of all the possible combinations of relations between those users represented by n. With this, we have defined a *friendship*$_{score}$ that represents the friendship between all the elements from a team in (11).

$$friendship_{score(G)} = \frac{na}{n}, \forall n \in [0, +\infty], \forall na \in [0, +\infty], na \leq n \qquad (11)$$

Shared Interests. One important step in the team cohesion calculation is the analysis of their members' shared interests/tastes (when in the scope of job-related matters). We have made this calculation using the following connections:

- *Likes* to the same *posts* (e.g. two persons show that they *like* the same *post* submitted in the system)
- *Follows to* the same entity (e.g. two persons *follow* the same company in which they are interested in)
- Frequency of the same scholar institution or even the same course (in their respective profiles)

For the sake of brevity, the underlying assumptions regarding likeability and compatibility about these variables were left out. (12) is the one that handles all these variables and puts them together.

$$shared_{interests} = likes_{score} * 0.4 + follows_{score} * 0.3 + academic_{similarity} * 0.3 \qquad (12)$$

We have then defined in (13) how to calculate the final score related with the social cohesion. Consider a certain set $P = \{p_1, \ldots, p_n\}$ that contains a group of people. We have also set weights for the three components mentioned before such as that shared projects and friendship relations are both 25 % important, while shared interests are 50 %.

$$social_{cohesion(P)} = familiarity_{score} * 0.25 + friendship_{score} * 0.25 + tastes_{score} * 0.5$$
$$(13)$$

Required Competences. Reference [7] – "If a set of people do not provide complete coverage, then they cannot form a legitimate team by themselves". This means that at least one of their members must fulfil each one of the required competences. In order to calculate a numeric value representative of a team's competence ($competence_{score}$), we use (14) presented by [7].

$$competence_{score(T)} = \sum_{j=1}^{|C_m|} \Omega_{i=1}^{|P_m|} e(p_i, c_j) \qquad (14)$$

We now explain how the formula above works. Consider a group of people $P = \{p_1, \ldots, p_m\}$, a group of key competences $C = \{c_1, \ldots, c_n\}$, and a function $e : P \times C \rightarrow Value$ that allows to calculate the value of a person P related with a C competence. Now consider also the Ω possible values, so that $\Omega \in \{max, min, avg\}$, that helps quantifying the value of the competences of a person according to indicated preferences. The *max* value gives more importance to the existence of experts in a certain competence, while the *avg* gives more relevance to the existence of a balanced team on each of the required competences. The *min* usage gives more importance to the minimization of "weakest links".

With the objective of reducing the number of combinations to be calculated (i.e. avoiding using the whole universe of search), we've considered only the top 15 candidates for a given opportunity. These candidates are obtained through the already calculated similarities (SERs). This way, we limit the number of combinations to be analyzed to a maximum of $15C7 = 6435$. There is the clear understanding that this kind of limitation may leave out some excellent teams; a great team may not necessarily be composed of the very best of the best, nor can ARM (or any platform for that matter) predict particular types of problems that may happen between teams (such as psychological disorders). It is being tried to come up with some techniques to be able to relax this constraint in the medium/long run. Some examples may be the use of artificial intelligence techniques related with the analysis of long-term data (such as neutral networks and case-based reasoning) which end up providing us with inferred patterns, the clustering of data regarding any of the information pieces that describe entities (as mentioned before), the explicit filtering of data through the web interface, amongst others.

Physical Location of Team Members. In the context of virtual teams (teams that do not work in the same physical space), the physical proximity of their members can still have a big influence on its success; one of the main reasons is the fact that, as explained before, people's *propinquity* ends up influencing their similarity. This means not only people's personality plays a role on this likeability, but also their culture/background, easing the interpersonal relations between them. With the goal of calculating the similarity between team members related with their geographical location, we have created (16). In this formula, we sum up the averages of the distances between each pair of team members (15) and we divide that number by the squared number of people.

$$avg_{distance} = \frac{\frac{\sum_{i=1}^{n} d_1}{n^{\circ}people-1} + \cdots + \frac{\sum_{i=1}^{nm} d_m}{n^{\circ}people-1}}{(n^{\circ}people - 1)^2} \tag{15}$$

$$location_{similarity} = -\frac{\log(avg_{distance} + 1)}{\log(100 + avg_{distance})} + 1 \tag{16}$$

Team Score Formula. After the description of all variables that come into play when we evaluate the recommendation of a team of people, we then present the final formula that aggregates them all (17). We have distributed the weights this way: team cohesion (35 %), needed competences (50 %) and physical location (15 %). This equation is the basis for the **opportunity-team** recommendations that will join the other ones already presented earlier.

$$team_{score} = social_{cohesion} * 0.3 + competence_{score} * 0.5 + location_{similarity} * 0.15 \tag{17}$$

5   Testing and Validation

In order to evaluate ARM, we have made tests regarding recommendations' calculations. Because the system is still not live and publicly available, we had to build a dummy data set for this purpose; this set (300 dummy users and 300 opportunities) is characterized by regarding different profiles (all of them with at least one item per information block). We have also created 10 users that are a perfect fit for 10 opportunities, to better evaluate the recommendation adequacy.

5.1   Access Speed

The first test performed was related to access speed; specifically, we wanted to evaluate the benefits of using the TS for storing user and opportunity data in the triple structure. Therefore we have created fully-detailed users in ARM, synched those users into the TS and later made access speed tests targeting both systems: the RDB and the TS. Results are displayed in Fig. 5.

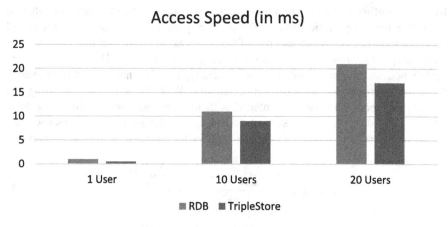

Fig. 5. Access speed tests' results.

As one can verify, there is a marginal advantage in the TS access. However, the TS's inference engine is turned on, which negatively affects its response speed, so this difference could be even greater.

5.2   Recommendation Speed

The first test is about the speed of recommendation's generation, i.e. the time it takes for the ARM algorithm to be run against a particular user or opportunity. Figures 6 and 7 show the calculation speeds for SERs (explained in Sect. 4.1) and team recommendations (explained in Sect. 4.2) respectively. This test was conducted on a machine with

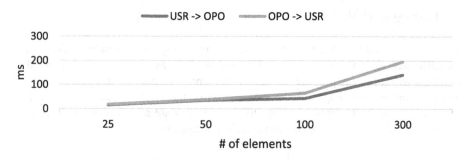

Fig. 6. Entity recommendation speed.

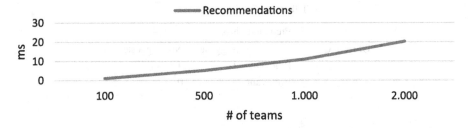

Fig. 7. Team recommendation speed.

the following specifications: CPU Intel Core i7-3630QM, RAM 6 GB 1600 MHz and HDD 500 GB 5400 RPM.

These obtained recommendation times are acceptable, as they are calculated offline (please check Sect. 3) and are not needed in real-time by the application user. However, as the number of entities in the database increases, this time delay can be a problem. As one can infer by analyzing Fig. 6 and considering that it takes 100 ms to process 43 users, if there were 100.000 elements in the database, then the average time that would be required to do this calculation would be approximately 232 s ($\sim$4 min) (applying a simple rule of three), which clearly is high. We have to take into consideration that we are making an extensive complex analysis to all possible combinations in the RDB. This is mainly due to the need for accuracy and precision of the recommendations' generation. Knowing these bottlenecks, we can make some improvements, such as: (1) more processing power, (2) multi-threading and (3) clustering. Regarding cluster- ing, one can restrict entities based on the following criteria:

- **Location** in terms of the physical distance between them (i.e. only calculate rec- ommendations for the closest items)
- **Activity area** in terms of the logical distance between them (i.e. only calculate recommendations for items with the same activity area or "compatible" activity areas, i.e. activity areas in the same hierarchical path)

NOTE: both examples above (location and activity area) are important and upper-level content-based pieces of information shared by entities, so they can propose themselves as good starting points for filtering items. They do not, in any means, necessarily translate into a trustful or adequate filtering technique (many other criteria could be used), that being the reason as to why currently no filtering is made. An option/possibility would be to allow the user to choose this parameter in the web interface.

5.3   Precision

As the main goal in a RS is the interest of the recommendations themselves for the user who receives them, we have made a classic precision test to evaluate this matter. In this test, we started by defining 25 very different user and opportunity profiles (different backgrounds). We then calculated SERs between all of those entities and manually evaluated the obtained results, which are demonstrated in Table 1.

Table 1. Confusion matrix.

Objective class	Predicted class		
		Suggested	Not suggested
	Relevant	21	4
	Irrelevant	0	0

Using this data we have calculated some metrics that help us evaluating in a more precise manner the quality of the obtained recommendations. This measures can be analyzed in the Table 2.

Table 2. Evaluation metrics.

Metric	Result [0–1]
Recall	$21/(21+4) = 0,84$
Precision	$21/(21+0) = 1$
F-measure (relates precision and recall) $2 \times \frac{Precision \times Recall}{Precision + Recall} = 2 \times \frac{1 \times 0.84}{1 + 0.84} = 0,45$	

Analyzing the calculated metrics, we can conclude that the SERs obtained through the RS have a very high quality and so a very high relevance for the application users. Although manual evaluation and the overall precision testing scenario lacks a more formal and objective approach (please check the next section), the results obtained were very promising, surpassing at least one of the related work's research numbers ([5]) had an average of 0.5 for precision.

5.4   Validation Scenarios

The aforementioned tests were made primarily to assess the robustness of algorithms and the overall concept of the platform, which at the moment has been deployed with a Minimum Viable Product (MVP) designation and approach. However, ARM also needed to be validated using other means, such as with real scenarios and more intensive needs. To this end, the following pilots were planned to be executed: (1) a real use-case of a company in need of freelance consultants in the IT sector and (2) the dissemination of the platform into several consultancy companies/technology and business hubs in order to promote the use of the system in such extremely dynamic and demanding job market scenarios:

- The first pilot has already been executed with the following parameters: one real recruitment opportunity (from the company INOVA+) which had already previously gathered the profiles of 35 candidates. Results from the execution of the RS against the aforementioned resources have found that: (1) results generation is fast, (2) there is a correlation between the number of candidates which are found acceptable to get the job and the 1–5 star system used (4 stars and above) and

(3) some design choices made in the platform should be enhanced for future use, such as unused fields and optimization of the content taxonomies. The more qualitative evaluation also made to the HR responsible for the pilot (using a questionnaire) also showed that the overall platform and opportunity management were deemed very effective and innovative in the recruitment scenario;

- The second pilot is still underway and features the definite adoption by the ARM platform (commercially designated as WORKINTEAM) by a consultancy company called INOVA+ in everything related to its recruitment efforts. Therefore, opportunities will be posted on job-related websites, whereas candidates will be invited to make their applications using the new solution. This pilot is significantly different from the first one and will generate new knowledge for the project, because: (1) multiple opportunities are at stake, (2) opportunities are public, (3) all the platform's user base is invited to participate, as well as new users and (4) since the more traditional way of applying is still doable (by email/CV), user engagement and usability will also be clear.

5.5 ICE-B Feedback

The submission of HYRED/ARM in the 12th International Joint Conference on e-Business and Telecommunications was a success on many levels, including the public presentation of the article and its underlying project, the consideration for the best paper award of the event and this very extended version of the article. Regarding the showcasing of the article, which was the timeframe where the most feedback was ever made regarding the platform, there were the following insights provided:

1. The RS could eventually be deceived/made biased, especially in the team-generation mode, if some users knew about the inner workings of the process and could make the effort to produce the necessary influential data, such as creating a group of fictional users;
2. In the RS team-generation algorithm, most of the underlying blocks of content-based filtering are possible to be generated on the fly ("ad-hocly") just excepting the presence of historical WORKINTEAM past developed projects (please check 4.2 for all of the team generation content-based mechanisms).

The above-mentioned insights are highly related to each other and as far as counter-measures to those subjects, or at least arguments to from ARM's points of view, the following needs to be explained:

1. The inner-workings of the RS were revealed in the article and in the conference as part of the research-based nature that those two contexts are related to. As with any typical final product/service, they will not be shared with the future users of the platform in a public, open or unrequested way, nor any further updates that the RS may be subject to;
2. The team behind ARM considers that the RS-nature envisaged in the bullet 2 above some have advantages though, namely the easing or elimination of the typical cold-start problem found in RSs and thus the balance of old and new users. Still,

and acknowledging the unbalance found through the analysis of the RS in that point of view, new building blocks will be considered to strengthen the historical/not real-time generated information sources of the RS. Some of the considered data blocks may be "age of user" inside WORKINTEAM, rate/speed of generated information about the user in recent times, the relationship of these items between different users, amongst others.

6 Conclusions

ARM is a system that is able to make suggestions, in an accurate and precise manner, between users and opportunities. It can also generate team suggestions for a particular opportunity, based on its complex description requirements. These recommendations are made based on: (1) explicit information from user and opportunity profiles (not only directly compared but based on their semantic distances); (2) social network interactions – e.g. shared *likes*, shared *follows* and item visualizations and (3) implicit information, through inference of new knowledge (using the TS discovery capabilities). Our tests so far have found out that, being a RS more closely related to the content-based nature, it correctly recommends items with a fairly high precision and, since we have moved our most resource-intensive processes into an offline component, recommendations can be used in a real-time application with great success as far as RS-related features and usability are concerned.

However, there is still a lot to be made in order to improve, above all, the recommendation mechanism. For instance, it will be tried to improve the recommendation's calculation **speed** both by increasing the server's hardware capabilities as well as using the server's multi-threading feature. Also, we want to use clustering techniques to reduce the universe of search – e.g. when trying to find the top candidates (or teams) to an opportunity, only calculate similarities to the 1000 closest users. It is also expected to improve the **accuracy** and **recall** of the recommendations by inferring more knowledge about users and opportunities. This new knowledge can be easily inferred through the addition of more knowledge rules into the TS, after careful study of existing recruitment/web likelihood patterns and/or through the analysis of ARM analytics itself. This evidently increases the calculation load of the TS; however, it does not make much difference in response times and user perception.

In addition, work team search configurations will also be implemented (cohesiveness, competence, creativity, etc.) and make them available to the final user without losing much speed in the similarity calculations. These features will allow the platform users to search, in a more precise way, for the exactly kind of team profile they want given their requirements. Despite SERs' weights being already currently configurable, it would be very interesting to also analyze the effectiveness of the present chosen parameters, as well as to come up with a methodology to improve these values with time and maybe to automatically suggest optimizations to them based on the actual use of the platform.

Since the platform is still in its early stages, some issues are yet to be dealt with, such as scalability, user acceptance, improvements following the first validation scenario, analysis on the currently running validation scenario (the second one presented earlier), analysis as to how the solution is actually used as it consolidates into the market, etc. On the other hand, research into the whole area of JRSs will not halt with study that grounded the final platform, so we expect to continue making significant progress into ARM by embedding more found evidence and work done (including feedback received from public presentations, such as ICE-B and workshops), either by the authors or market-related.

Acknowledgements. This work has been supported by the project WorkInTeam, funded under the Portuguese National Strategic Reference Programme (QREN 2007-2013) under the contract number 2013/38566.

References

1. Smith, C.: By the Numbers: 125+ Amazing LinkedIn Statistics (2015) [Online]
2. Wagner, K.: LinkedIn Hits 300 Million Users Amid Mobile Push (2014) [Online]
3. Smith, C.: By the Numbers: 12 Interesting LinkedIn Job Statistics (2015) [Online]
4. Sahebi, S., Cohen, W.: Community-Based Recommendations: a Solution to the Cold Start Problem. s.l., s.n. (2011)
5. Lu, Y., Helou, S. E., Gillet, D.: A recommender system for job seeking and recruiting website. s.l., s.n. (2013)
6. Datta, A., Braghin, S., Yong, J.T.T.: The Zen of Multidisciplinary Team Recommendation. J. Assoc. Inf. Sci. Technol. s.l.:s.n. (2013)
7. Datta, A., Yong, J.T.T., Ventresque, A.: T-RecS: Team Recommendation System through Expertise. s.l., s.n. (2011)
8. Yu, H., Liu, C., Zhang, F.: Reciprocal Recommendation Algorithm for the Field of Recruitment. J. Inf. Computat. Sci. s.l.:s.n. (2011)
9. Blanchard, E., Harzallah, M., Briand, H., Kuntz, P.: A typology of ontology-based semantic measures. s.l., s.n. (2005)
10. Rauch, K. L., Scholar, M., University, P.S.: Human Mate Selection: An Exploration of Assortative. s.l., s.n. (2003)
11. Widmeyer, W.N., Brawley, L., Carron, A.: The measurement of cohesion in sport teams: the Group Environment Questionnaire. s.l.:s.n. (1985)
12. Ringelmann, M.: Recherches sur les moteurs animés: Travail de l'homme. In: Annales de l'Institut National Agronomique. s.l.:s.n. (1913)
13. Simms, A., Nichols, T.: Social Loafing: A Review of the Literature. J. Manage. Policy Pract. s.l.: s.n. (2014)
14. University, W.: Is Your Team Too Big? Too Small? What's the Right Number? (2006)
15. de Rond, M.: Why Less Is More in Teams. Harvard Business Review (2012)
16. Putnam, D.: Haste Makes Waste When You Over-Staff to Achieve Schedule Compression (2015)

Understanding Local mGovernment Applications: A Business Model Approach to the Case of Brussels

Nils Walravens[(⊠)]

iMinds-SMIT, Vrije Universiteit Brussel,
Pleinlaan 9, 1050 Brussels, Belgium
nils.walravens@vub.ac.be

Abstract. This paper uses business model theory as a framework to approach modern mobile government (mGov) applications and explore the role of public bodies within the volatile and complex mobile services sector. We propose and apply a new mapping methodology with a basis in business modelling that allows the comparison of mobile app initiatives by governments and can support the development or adjustment of a mobile strategy. We zoom in on the official applications released by different public administrations in the Capital Region of Brussels, Belgium. We find that the laggard position Brussels is currently in could be an opportunity to leapfrog in the field of mobile services, but that a focused vision, quadruple helix approach and clearly formulated mobile strategy is quintessential to achieving this.

Keywords: Mobile applications · mGovernment · Brussels · Business models · Public value

1 Introduction

The public sector has always been under some form of pressure to innovate along the speed of the market, both internally as an organisation and externally, towards the services it provides to citizens. In recent times, that high expected pace of innovation has only grown, together with demands and expectations from the public [35]. As a strategy geared towards meeting some of these demands, organisations at different levels of government have begun to initiate or commission the development of mobile applications ("apps") as a new or complementary channel of (two-way) communication with citizens [20], or as a means of increasing citizen participation in government processes [12]. Shifting public service provision to mobile devices has also been referred to as mGovernment (as an evolution of the field of eGovernment) [28].

However, the mobile services and application sector is a highly volatile one, perhaps even more so than the ICT industry. Public administrations and cities are faced with a significant challenge in this regard, which mainly pertains to the high speed of innovation, a shift in culture and mindset of the organisation and the actual organisational aspects related to creating, providing and supporting mobile applications in a

© Springer International Publishing Switzerland 2016
M.S. Obaidat and P. Lorenz (Eds.): ICETE 2015, CCIS 585, pp. 100–123, 2016.
DOI: 10.1007/978-3-319-30222-5_5

complex ecosystem that is – at least in the Western hemisphere – dominated by two US companies (Apple and Google) [27].

It is in this complex context we propose business model thinking as a framework to tackle some of these challenges. Business models need to be defined in their wider context here and not for example be confused with business cases or the revenue models of single enterprises [23]. Rather, we consider the entire value network surrounding a particular mobile service and offer a framework that allows public organisations to find their "strategic fit" [34] within this complex ecosystem [1]. To better frame the discussion and help governments prioritise their mobile strategy, we propose a new mapping methodology that allows the direct comparison of mobile apps, based on the level of government involvement required in their development, as well as the potential public value they may generate. We apply this method to the Brussels Capital Region. As the capital of Belgium and Europe, the region is faced with many challenges that are representative of major metropolitan areas around the world. Additionally, the Region has a unique organisational and political structure that makes taking joint initiative challenging.

The main contribution of this paper then is to introduce this mapping methodology based in business model theory and immediately apply it to Brussels. This approach will give more insight into how business model thinking can help frame local m-government strategies and support government in setting up mobile service initiatives.

2 Business Models and M-Government

This section will briefly explore the role that business models may play in researching mGov strategies. It also develops the set of parameters that will be used as the foundation of the mapping methodology.

2.1 Business Model Thinking in mGov

We approach the concept of a business model similarly to e.g. [8, 16, 26] as a value network consisting of actors, roles and relationships that need to find a strategic fit [34] to deliver value to end users. Using this operationalisation of the concept, the underlying logic when applying it to technological innovation is that it is not the technology as such that is a determinant of success, but rather the way in which the network of actors is configured in generating added value around the technology [32].

In this sense, business modelling can serve as a means of bridging the gap between theoretical work and the daily practice of policy makers and government representatives. Applying a business model logic or thinking to the public sector does not have to be contradictory and business modelling as a concept has already proved useful in the context of eGovernment [22–24]. [40] also shows how the concept of value proposition (an integral part of business modelling theory) can be a guideline in developing an integrated framework for analysing and designing mGov strategies. Although the term business model is naturally associated with a purely commercial ecosystem, applying it in the context of government does not necessarily imply imposing a "business logic" to the public sector [32]. As mentioned, it rather serves as a framework that allows policy makers and government organisations to think about their position within a complex value network and prepare strategies as a response to potential issues of control and value. This idea is built upon in the following section, where the business model framework we will use to design the mapping methodology is explained.

2.2 mGov Business Model Parameters and Mapping Methodology

In recent years, the focus of business modelling [18] has gradually shifted from the single firm to networks of firms, and from simple to much more all-encompassing concepts (see e.g. [15, 29]). Due to this shift, the guiding question of a business model has become "Who controls the value network and the overall system design" just as much as "Is substantial value being produced by this model (or not)" [3].

Based on the tension between these two questions, [3] proposes a holistic business modelling framework that is centred around control on the one hand and creating value on the other. It examines four different aspects of business models: the value network, the functional (technical) architecture, the financial model and the value proposition. We build on these foundations, but expand the matrix to include qualitative parameters that are of additional importance when a public entity contributes to the value proposition. Given these organisations' non-commercial logic, it is imperative we take these additional parameters into account when discussing (mobile) service business models that involve public actors [39]. We propose an update to Ballon's business model matrix, represented in Fig. 1. The left-hand side of the matrix offers parameters

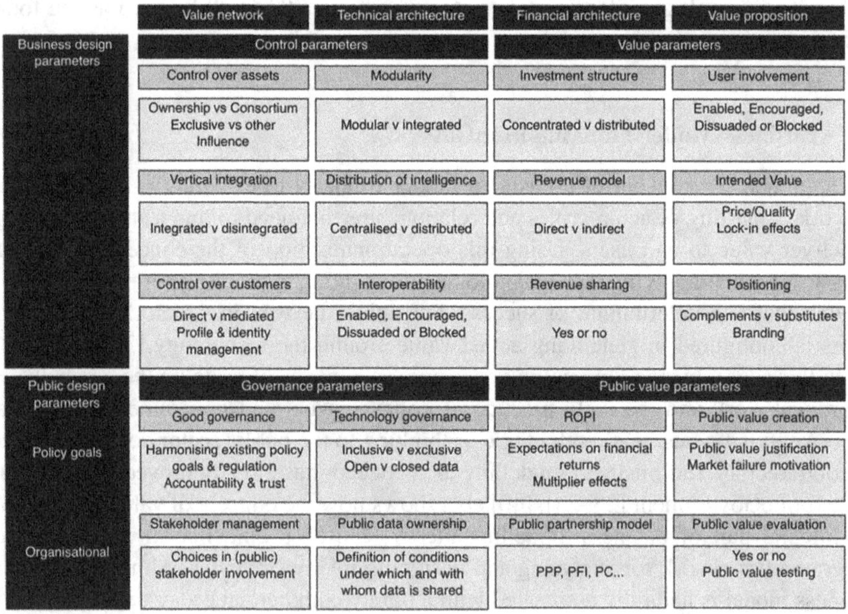

	Value network	Technical architecture	Financial architecture	Value proposition
Business design parameters	Control parameters		Value parameters	
	Control over assets	Modularity	Investment structure	User involvement
	Ownership vs Consortium Exclusive vs other Influence	Modular v integrated	Concentrated v distributed	Enabled, Encouraged, Dissuaded or Blocked
	Vertical integration	Distribution of intelligence	Revenue model	Intended Value
	Integrated v disintegrated	Centralised v distributed	Direct v indirect	Price/Quality Lock-in effects
	Control over customers	Interoperability	Revenue sharing	Positioning
	Direct v mediated Profile & identity management	Enabled, Encouraged, Dissuaded or Blocked	Yes or no	Complements v substitutes Branding
Public design parameters	Governance parameters		Public value parameters	
Policy goals	Good governance	Technology governance	ROPI	Public value creation
	Harmonising existing policy goals & regulation Accountability & trust	Inclusive v exclusive Open v closed data	Expectations on financial returns Multiplier effects	Public value justification Market failure motivation
Organisational	Stakeholder management	Public data ownership	Public partnership model	Public value evaluation
	Choices in (public) stakeholder involvement	Definition of conditions under which and with whom data is shared	PPP, PFI, PC...	Yes or no Public value testing

Fig. 1. Expanded business model matrix.

pertaining to control and governance, whereas the right-hand side parameters offer more insight into value and public value issues.

The detailed, qualitative description of all the parameters of this expanded matrix allows for the thorough analysis and direct comparison of complex business models that involve public actors in the value network. The parameters are quickly outlined below.

Value Network.

- Control over assets: anything tangible or intangible that could be used to help an organisation achieve its goals.
- Vertical integration: the level of ownership and control over successive stages of the value chain.
- Control over customers: looks into the party maintaining the customer relationship and keeping the customer data.
- Good governance: refers to a striving towards consensus and harmonization of interests (and related rhetoric).
- Stakeholder management: refers to the choices that are made related to which stakeholders (be they public, semi-public, non-governmental, private etc.) are involved or invited to participate in the process of bringing a service to end-users.

Technical Architecture.

- Modularity/integration: refers to the design of systems and artefacts as sets of discrete modules that connect to each other via predetermined interfaces.
- Distribution of intelligence: refers to the particular distribution of computing power, control and functionality across the system.
- Interoperability: refers to the ability of systems to directly exchange information and services with other systems.
- Technology governance: highlights the importance of transparency, participation and emancipation in making technological choices and relates to the digital divide.
- Public data ownership: concerns the terms under which data is opened up and to which actors.

Financial Architecture.

- Investment structure: deals with the necessary investments (both capex and opex) and the parties making them.
- Revenue model: deals with the trade-off between direct/indirect revenue models.
- Revenue sharing model: refers to agreements on whether and how to share revenues among the actors involved in the value network.
- ROPI: refers to the question whether the expected value generated by a public investment is purely financial, public, direct, indirect or combinations of these, and how a choice is justified.
- Public partnership model: explores how the financial relationships between the private and public participants in the value network are constructed.

Value Proposition.

- Positioning: refers to marketing issues including branding, market segments and identifying competing services.
- User involvement: refers to the degree in which users can contribute to the value proposition.
- Intended value: lists the basic attributes that the product or service possesses, or is intended to possess, and that together constitute the intended customer value.
- Public value creation: refers to the justification a government provides initiating a specific service, rather than leaving its deployment to the market.
- Public value evaluation: questions whether an evaluation of the generated public value takes places and if this occurs ex-ante or ex-post.

A purely textual description of all these parameters is not easily accessible and inspired us to translate this into a mapping grid, which finds its basis in the theoretical work of the matrix, but reduces the complexity of representation. In this grid, it becomes possible to compare divergent cases based on the two central parameter sets of the matrix: control and governance on the one hand and (public) value on the other. The grid represented in Fig. 2 allows us to map different cases of (in our case mobile) city services and identify how they compare to one another.

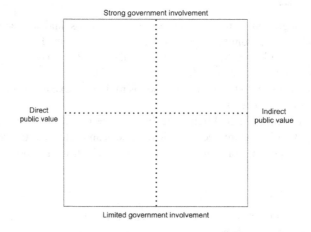

Fig. 2. Governance and public value grid.

The vertical axis refers to the governance parameters described in the two left columns of the business model matrix and provide an indication of the level of control the city government has in providing the service to citizens. The horizontal axis provides insight into the type of value that is generated by the services (the two right columns of the matrix) and whether this public value is direct or indirect: direct public value refers to a more individual, short-term value and relates to "what the public values"; while indirect public value is more collective and long term, and relates to "what adds value to the public sphere" [4]. This grid has been validated in [39] and will be used to map the official Brussels mobile city apps further on in this article.

To determine the precise relative position of the cases on the grid, a value or weight is attributed to each of the parameters in the updated business model matrix (see Sects. 4 and 5). In this sense, qualitative indicators are translated to quantitative ones in order to allow their direct comparison in a structured way (see for example [31]). This approach is detailed and applied in Sects. 4 and 5.

While this comparison is represented in a simple fashion, it is based on an extensive qualitative analysis that is based in literature, desk research, policy document analysis and expert interviews with stakeholders involved in the cases. A total of twenty-two expert interviews was carried out in 2013 and 2014, tapping both national and international expertise on mobile apps in general, as well as specific insight into the Brussels cases.

3   The Brussels Context

Although its de facto role as capital of Europe, the capital of Belgium and an interesting political construction in a rather small geographical area, Brussels is often neglected as a research topic in some fields, precisely due to this complexity. The Brussels Capital Region consists of the City of Brussels, combined with the 19 municipalities that encircle it and, with over one million inhabitants, makes up the third Region of Belgium next to the Flemish and Walloon Region. Each Region has its own government, as do the individual municipalities, next to the federal Belgian government and of course the European layer of governance. This interesting but difficult governance structure sometimes poses significant challenges in the context of Brussels in setting out a common approach for the Region, be it in the domain of ICT or otherwise. This became painfully clear for example when the Brussels Region implemented much stricter radio tower emission standards for mobile cellular networks on its quite limited geographical area, preventing the quick and smooth roll-out of 4G there, while Flanders and the Walloon Region moved much quicker in this regard [33]. Additionally, the City and Region face a wide range of urban challenges, of which a high unemployment rate and problematic mobility are only two examples. In 2013, an average of 19,3 % of the registered Brussels inhabitants was unemployed, growing from around 17 % in the two preceding years. This compares to the 5,1 % of unemployment found in the Flemish Region and 11,4 % in Wallonia in the same year. However, the numbers are particularly dramatic among youngsters under the age of 25; with 42,9 % of males and 36 % of women unemployed [38]. Another particular challenge for Brussels is its mobility, with at least 350.000 commuters travelling in and out of the city on a daily basis (over half of all employed people in Brussels do not live there) ([10]: p. 131) and the highest amount of traffic jams on a global scale (beating Los Angeles, London and Paris) [6]. These are only some of the urban challenges faced by the Region in the coming years.

As mentioned above, the Region, the City and the municipalities all hold competences related to ICT: for example, the City and the municipalities are responsible for their own websites and any online services they wish to offer to citizens (e.g. social media communications), but the Region operates an e-administration service called Irisbox, where citizens can download documents related to the Region's competences (e.g. regional tax forms and soil certificates), as well as documents related to municipal competences (e.g. birth certificates, parking permits and so on), although the availability of these documents depends on the municipality. These distributed competences can make the development of common policies a challenge and some translations of this will be illustrated below.

Although the city is known for many of its positive and negative facets and scores quite well on its competitiveness [37], it is generally not perceived as a Smart City and usually scores very low – or is not present at all – in the various Smart City rankings and indices created by many different stakeholders like technology vendors, network vendors and consultancy groups (e.g. [9, 14, 17, 21]). Brussels does take some initiatives related to ICT and innovative services, but for now they remain rather limited and often without much consequence. Although an ICT policy plan is in place for the period 2010–2014 it lacks an integrated vision related to mobile and in some cases in the execution of its promises.

One example of this is the city's approach to open data. While the cooperation models and exact terms are still crystallizing across Europe and the world, it is accepted that open data is and will be an important component of innovative Smart City services (whether they be mobile or not) [30]. As a reminder, the open data philosophy has also been translated into European law. The Re-use of Public Sector Information Directive (PSI), created by the European Commission was a first step to open up data from the public sector to citizens. The 2003 Directive was implemented into national law of the 27 Member States by May 2008 and *"encourages the EU Member States to make public sector information available for private and public organizations as well as for citizens"* [13]. In December 2011, the European Commission again stressed the importance of open data, even describing it as "the new gold" with the launch of an "Open Data Strategy", building on the work in the 2003 PSI Directive [13]. PSI was converted into the different governance levels of Belgium between 2006 and 2008: into national law in March 2007, in Wallonia and the German Communities in December 2006, in the Flemish Community in April 2007 and the last Region to adopt the PSI Directive in March 2008, was Brussels [25]. A second Directive called INSPIRE is related to opening geographical and GIS information, and was adopted into law in the Brussels Region in April 2011.

In Brussels, the resulting and other open data initiatives are distributed, depending on the competences of the different levels of government, making an integrated approach very difficult. GIS data is managed by the Brussels Region Informatics Centre (CIRB-CIBG) and made available to the public via an interactive map, as direct downloads or as several web services for developers. However, these are the only datasets managed and opened up by this non-profit organization. Other datasets are the responsibility of the Regional administrations or the municipalities; in this case the city of Brussels and the 19 municipalities that make up the Brussels Capital Region. The data for the City of Brussels - like its website - is not managed by the CIRB-CIBG, but by GIAL (Centre de Gestion Informatique des Administrations Locales), a non-profit that provides ICT-services to local administrations, including the City of Brussels. Since February 2012, the city website offers some open data sets ranging from Wi-Fi locations, over public toilets, ATM locations, parking spaces for the disabled, to locations of remarkable trees. These datasets are mostly provided in CSV, HTML or XLS formats under an open license, but provide little else and usually range between two or three stars on the well-known open data star scale by Tim Berners-Lee [36]. Although the data itself is not of a bad quality or irrelevant, little is done to promote it to the public or developers. Additionally, separate regional administrations also open up their own data sets, e.g. Brussels Mobility, which hosts open data such as regionally operated bike lanes, taxi stops, traffic intensity, trees next to lanes, fountains and monuments [5]. This information is not centralised in any way.

The Brussels ICT policy plan by the competent minister Grouwels (in place at the time) mentioned the organization of a hackathon for Brussels to promote the data ([7]: p. 29), but the Apps for Geo event that was organized in April 2013 focused only on apps with a geographical component and did not specifically touch on or promote the Brussels Region [11]. Only in the 2014 the City organised the first Apps for Brussels hackathon, although other cities in Belgium and Flanders are already organizing their third or fourth event (e.g. the city of Ghent). Of course, organizing these events is not sanctifying, but they can be important moments of promotion for the city and serve as inspiration for developers to create something innovative for the city. As it is currently handled, it is difficult to create an atmosphere of enthusiasm for digital and mobile initiatives in Brussels. This is reflected in the only statistic we have on the basis of operations of mobile app developers in Belgium: with a very heavy focus on Flanders (Antwerp and Ghent mostly), only around 16 % of Belgian professional mobile app developers are based in the capital [11]. Additionally, the ICT policy plan uses a very broad definition of what could be considered open and might offend open data proponents. It claims that the real-time travel information of the public transport company STIB is open to citizens, since it is provided via Google and the Google Maps service: *"Open data strategy related to real-time mobility data: Thanks to a cooperation between Google and STIB, statistical data on the bus, tram and metro network is freely exchanged with Google, so users can plan their trajectories using Brussels public transport."* ([7]: p. 28) (translated from Dutch). Many would argue that providing this data to Google, but not to citizens and independent developers in open formats hardly constitutes an open data policy or strategy.

While there are certain issues and questions to be raised, the Region also takes positive initiatives in the area of mobile services. In 2013, an adapted version of FixMyStreet was launched in Brussels. The service originates in the UK and was developed by the charity organization MySociety. It allows citizens to report issues with city infrastructure, such as broken traffic lights, potholes, graffiti and so on. The service started out as a website that allowed anyone in the UK to register complaints that were then sent to the correct local authority by FixMyStreet. Today, the service offers mobile reporting tools and offers cities the opportunity to integrate FixMyStreet into their local websites as well as the back end systems the city might use in order to efficiently treat issues, by sending them to the correct city service and making sure their resolution is followed up on. FixMyStreet is now the largest service of its kind in the UK, sending over 5.000 reports to local governments each month. The source code for FixMyStreet is open source and free to implement for interested cities. The Brussels Region took the Canadian version of the software code and developed an own version of the app built on the city's GIS mapping system [2]. The Brussels version is more limited than the original as it only allows four types of complaints from citizens: potholes, bad road surface or missing road markings and in its first year of operation was only available in less than half of the municipalities of the Brussels Region due to the different levels of interest from this level of governance. Today however, all municipalities of the Brussels Region are present in FixMyStreet although this was not an easy undertaking: *"The difficulties are rarely technical. The biggest difficulty is the change management that is behind it. [...] There was a lot of fear related to transparency and responsibility"* [2]. At a price of 200.000 euros to implement and connect to the various existing back-end systems, it was a rather expensive undertaking [19], but the service appears to be slowly picking up in the Region. Other positive initiatives by the City's and Region's administrations include the Visit Brussels app by the Communications and Tourism Department and the Brussels Gardens app, highlighting green spaces throughout the city from the Environmental Department. These official applications are studied in more detail in what follows.

4   Official Brussels Apps

The number of official apps by the City of Brussels, the Region or any of its institutions is limited. Table 1 provides an overview of the official apps for Brussels. For each case, all the parameters of the expanded business model matrix described above are discussed in a table, available in annex to this paper. The material for the cases was gathered from policy documents, publicly available information and expert interviews with people involved with them. From this analysis, a score on a 5-point Likert scale is given to each of the parameters that help determine the position of the case on the governance and public value grid. This scale ranges from −2 (strongly disagree) to 2 (strongly agree), indicating the level of agreement with the statements in the tables in annex. This scoring allows us to compare the cases with each other and draw some conclusions on the Brussels approach to mGov services.

Table 1. Overview of official Brussels mobile applications.

Name	Dev.	Platform	Last update	Category	Rating iOS (by x users)	Rating android (by x users)	Downloads (April 2014 android)
Be. Brussels	BRIC	iOS/ Android	2012-12	Utilities	2 (1)	3,8 (29)	100–500
Brussels gardens	Tapptic	iOS/ Android	2014-02	Lifestyle	4 (3)	3,9 (18)	1.000–5.000
City of Brussels	GIAL	Android	2015-02	Travel and local	NA	3,3 (7)	1.000–5.000
Fix My Street Bxl	BRIC	iOS/ Android	2015-01	Social	1,5 (9)	3,5 (44)	1.000–5.000
STIB mobile	STIB	iOS/ Android	2013-02	Travel	2,5 (229)	4 (3391)	100.000– 500.000
Visit Brussels	Visit Brussels	iOS/ Android	2012-12	Travel	3,5 (14)	2,2 (132)	10.000–50.000

4.1   Be.Brussels

The Be.Brussels app developed by BRIC applies to the Brussels Capital Region and offers a map with points of interest and useful phone numbers, as well as direct access to the Region's social media streams.

Given that the main goal of the app is providing information to individual citizens, we see a score that leans towards a direct public value. Although their relation is very strong, the fact that this app was developed by an individual organisation and not within a Brussels administration is reflected in the government involvement score. Since our data gathering phase, this app has been removed from Google Play and the iTunes App Store for unclear reasons. The breakdown of all parameters and scores can be found in annex to this paper.

4.2   Brussels Gardens

Brussels Gardens was created by Brussels Environment (IBGE), one of the Region's administrations responsible for the study, monitoring and management of air, water, soil, waste and nature. The app provides an overview of the green spaces and their uses in the Region as well as information on the history of the green spaces, their special characteristics and the conservation of plants and wildlife.

The almost neutral score in the public value column can in this case be explained by the fact that the app provides information to individuals, but its broader goal is to increase appreciation and use of green spaces in Brussels.

4.3   City of Brussels

The City of Brussels app only pertains to this level of government (the City and not the Region) and is developed by a different non-profit organization (GIAL) than the one working for the Region (BRIC). It provides news, public transport information, contact information, the city's social media and a map with points of interest.

Similarly to the Be.Brussels app, the fact that the app is not developed by a Regional administration is reflected in the lower government involvement score and the public value it generates is more direct.

4.4   FixMyStreet Brussels

FixMyStreet Brussels is the local implementation of the well-known issue reporting service, first developed in the UK. It allows citizens to report issues with city furniture or in the public space, but was until very recently limited to potholes, bad road surface or missing road markings in the case of the Brussels Region.

In this case a very high level of government involvement was required to make the app possible and the public value is aimed at the collective.

4.5 STIB Mobile

STIB mobile is the official app of the Brussels public transport company and allows users to consult real time departures and timetables at STIB stops.

Since the STIB acts as an independent company from the city government (even though it is publicly funded), the level of government control is lower in this case and the created public value is direct.

4.6 Visit Brussels

The final official app is Visit Brussels by the tourism department of the Region, bringing together all kinds of touristic information and offering a comprehensive city guide. The app was developed by Visit Brussels and is based on an internal database of points of interest.

Similarly to the Brussels Gardens app, we notice a balance between a direct and indirect value in the case of Visit Brussels. This can be explained as a result of the combination of the individual information the app provides to visitors and the more long-term and collective goal of boosting tourism and the attractiveness of the city.

5 Mapping

Bringing together the scores of the six publicly developed Brussels applications (see annex) allows us to map them on the governance and public value grid introduced in Sect. 2. The scores are directly translated to coordinates on the grid, which consists of two 20-point axes. The coordinates and the mapping are represented in the Table 2 and Fig. 3.

Table 2. Coordinates.

	Public value (x-axis)	Government involvement (y-axis)
Be.Brussels	−5	7
Brussels gardens	−1	13
City of Brussels	−9	5
FixMyStreet Brussels	14	17
STIB mobile	−7	−10
Visit Brussels	−1	10

Although we of course expected most apps to score quite highly when it comes to government involvement (as all are developed by official government organisations), this is slightly more nuanced. In the cases of FixMyStreet, Brussels Gardens and Visit Brussels the official Brussels administrations were directly involved in the ideation, development or commissioning of the apps. Be.Brussels, City of Brussels and STIB

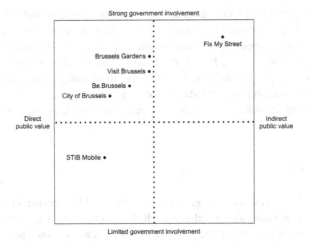

Fig. 3. Governance and public value grid mapping Brussels' cases.

Mobile were created by semi-public organisations that work directly for the Brussels Capital Region. As such and depending on their role, they score lower on the government involvement axis.

We clearly see that most apps were created with a direct public value in mind, meaning they are aimed at individuals and on providing information, without much possibility for interaction or a long-term approach. The only exception is FixMyStreet, which allows citizens to report issues that are acted upon by the local administration. The system has been integrated as a single point of contact into the daily operations of the Brussels Mobility administration and it is part of a long-term vision to add more types of reports (and related stakeholders) to the list of options for citizens. The end goal is increasing communication with citizens and at the same time improving the general quality of life around the City and Region, pointing again to the app's indirect public value. By most definitions and operationalisations of the mGovernment concept (laid out in the first two sections of this paper), FixMyStreet is probably one of the better examples of what mobile government services (should) look like.

When interpreting the scores for these six official Brussels applications, we come to the conclusion that basic information provision to individual citizens appears to be the most popular strategy amongst administrations. This is also the most careful one. It is not surprising in the context of budgetary constraints that (local) governments face today, that more long-term, structural and participatory initiatives such as FixMyStreet are more exception than rule. Nevertheless, the interview round showed that the administration involved is serious about the service and that the investment made is too important to view it as an experiment. The other apps under discussion are more easily referred to as first try-outs in mGovernment and in most cases leave features or uptake to be desired. While experimentation certainly needs to be encouraged, we argue that in order to make a long-term impact in this area and begin tackling governance challenges through mobile services, the mobile application market and related economy has now sufficiently matured for governments to move beyond experimentation and take the lessons learned locally and internationally to develop a true mobile strategy. Since Brussels is playing something of a laggard role when it comes to both Smart City initiatives and mobile application creation, the opportunity to leapfrog in this space should be valorised today. The FixMyStreet case illustrates that involving all relevant stakeholders (municipal administrations, mayors, local energy and telecom players, citizens and civil society) in a quadruple helix approach is key to a successful and broadly supported mobile government service, but one that may require higher investments.

6 Discussion

A government body can use the grid to map any mobile service initiatives it has running or plans to undertake, to identify whether their level of involvement has the desired results related to the public value it wants to generate, and thus if the actions they take are aligned with the policy goals they want to achieve. The different quadrants of the grid give insight into the approach taken by government: the strategy in the bottom-right quadrant focuses on creating a positive climate for long-term innovation and improvements to the general quality of life for as many citizens as possible; the bottom-left quadrant aims to stimulate projects and initiatives that have a more immediate and clear benefit to citizens that potentially show signs of engagement themselves; while the top-right quadrant sees a more integrated approach to solving long-term issues typical to major metropolitan areas, wherein the city takes a leading role; compared to the final top-left quadrant that sees an applied approach by the city to create some immediate value for individual citizens, by increasing the ease-of-life and attractiveness of their city. These represent four quite different strategies to providing mGov services to citizens to be considered by government authorities and public bodies looking towards or providing those services.

While this mapping offers a visual representation of the Brussels Region's mGov initiatives, the main value of the analysis lies in the business model approach taken to this challenge. By considering all the business model aspects pertaining to a modern mobile service initiative, and including parameters that are specific to public sector involvement, it has been our aim to provide policy makers at the local, regional or national level with a way to better consider the implications of a mobile strategy. As was mentioned earlier, business modelling as a framework should not only be associated with commercial initiatives, but rather be seen in a broader context. When operationalised in a methodology comparable to the one presented in this paper, business modelling can provide more insight into the challenges pertaining to mobile in the public sector as well.

A limitation of this work pertains to the focus of the original matrix on the relations between firms and organizations and not so much on the internal organizational structures of companies or agencies. Since the newly introduced parameters build on the original matrix, there is no specific attention to internal organizational processes. As government is also a system of systems with different actors and roles, this aspect should be further explored.

7 Conclusions

This article set out to frame how business modelling may also provide a framework to mGovernment, rather than being confined to purely commercial initiatives. We did this by expanding on an existing business model framework to include parameters specific to the public sector. We then apply this to all official Brussels apps, map them on the newly-developed grid and come to the conclusion that these apps are mostly aimed at short-term public value generation and providing localised information to individual citizens. FixMyStreet is the only Brussels case that shows a mid to long-term strategy that has a mobile application at its core. It is then also a showcase of how an urban challenge can (begin to) be tackled through a qualitative mGov application that is well thought out and enables citizen participation.

Our conclusion then is that Brussels is taking careful steps when it comes to smart mGov apps, but that this hesitance can for the most part be explained by the institutional complexity of the Region and the (for now) lack of a single mobile strategy as a consequence. The FixMyStreet case shows that it is possible for the Region to set up a long-term and integrated approach, but this is likely to take more time and resources. Nevertheless, we believe Brussels can learn from the increasing maturity in the mGovernment and apps sector and leverage its potential to leapfrog in this space. To do so and label itself as "smarter" than before, an integrated and open-minded approach to mobile services, which involves all relevant stakeholders in the city through a quadruple helix approach, will be a conditio sine qua non to achieving this.

Acknowledgements. This research was performed at the Vrije Universiteit Brussel and iMinds, and supported by an Innoviris PRFB grant (Brussels Capital Region).

Annex

The business model parameter descriptions and the scores of each case are appended to this paper (Tables 3, 4, 5, 6, 7, 8, 9, 10, 11, 12, 13 and 14).

Table 3. Business model parameters for Be.Brussels.

Control and governance parameters		Value and public value parameters	
Value network	**Technical architecture**	**Financial architecture**	**Value proposition**
Control over assets: with BRIC, gathering official information	Modularity: not particularly modular approach, uses BRIC's URBIS maps	Investment structure: budgeted in short term by BRIC	User involvement: limited to social networking links

(Continued)

Table 3. (*Continued*)

Control and governance parameters		Value and public value parameters	
Vertical integration: quite integrated into the city organisation, although BRIC is an independent entity	Distribution of intelligence: an internet connection is required to access main functions	Revenue model: indirect, public funds	Intended value: access to POIs and city contact information
Control over customers: with the Region, marketed as the Region's app	Interoperability: available for the two most important platforms	Revenue sharing: no revenue sharing	Positioning: towards individual citizens looking for information
Good governance: not particularly used in surrounding rhetoric	Technology governance: inclusion not emphasised, distribution of info	ROPI: one-way information channel	Public value creation: mainly one-way information channel
Stakeholder management: BRIC is the only involved stakeholder	Public data ownership: all used data is publicly available elsewhere	Public private partnership model: no structural PPP present	Public value evaluation: internally evaluated

Table 4. Scorecard for Be.Brussels.

Limited to strong government involvement		Direct to indirect public value	
Value network		**Financial architecture**	
Control over assets with city	1	Investment structure goal is long term/collective	−2
Vertically integrated within city organisation	−1	Revenue model is direct or indirect	0
Control over customers with city	2	Revenue sharing set up over long term	0
Good governance aspects emphasised	−1	ROPI is long term	1
Stakeholder management organised by city	1	PPP model is structural	0
Technical architecture		**Value proposition**	
Modularity: control over modules with city	2	User involvement: individual or collective	1
Distribution of intelligence: centralised with the city	1	Intended value: short or long term	1

(*Continued*)

Table 4. (*Continued*)

Limited to strong government involvement		Direct to indirect public value	
Interoperability emphasised	1	Positioning aimed at collective	−2
Technology governance: inclusion and openness emphasised	0	Public value creation aimed at long term/collective	−2
Public data ownership defined by city	1	Public value evaluation organised	−2
Score	7		−5
higher = more involvement		higher = indirect	

Table 5. Business model parameters for Brussels Gardens.

Control and governance parameters		Value and public value parameters	
Value network	**Technical architecture**	**Financial architecture**	**Value proposition**
Control over assets: almost completely with Brussels Environment	Modularity: not particularly modular, but uses Google Maps	Investment structure: in short-term budget of IBGE	User involvement: limited to none
Vertical integration: app was created by external developer but is managed by IBGE	Distribution of intelligence: internet connection required to load data	Revenue model: no revenue model	Intended value: access to green spaces and environment
Control over customers: free app clearly from IBGE	Interoperability: both iOS and Android versions available	Revenue sharing: indirect, public funds	Positioning: towards individual citizens looking for green space
Good governance: quite present given the topic of the app and focus on sustainability	Technology governance: inclusion not specifically emphasised	ROPI: information distribution	Public value creation: promote green spaces in Brussels
Stakeholder management: IBGE is the only main stakeholder	Public data ownership: most presented data is publicly available but not centralised	Public private partnership model: no structural PPP in place	Public value evaluation: evaluated internally

Table 6. Scorecard for Brussels Gardens.

Limited to strong government involvement		Direct to indirect public value	
Value network		**Financial architecture**	
Control over assets with city	2	Investment structure goal is long term/collective	−2
Vertically integrated within city organisation	1	Revenue model is direct or indirect	0
Control over customers with city	1	Revenue sharing set up over long term	0
Good governance aspects emphasised	2	ROPI is long term	1
Stakeholder management organised by city	0	PPP model is structural	0
Technical architecture		**Value proposition**	
Modularity: control over modules with city	1	User involvement: individual or collective	1
Distribution of intelligence: centralised with the city	2	Intended value: short or long term	2
Interoperability emphasised	1	Positioning aimed at collective	−2
Technology governance: inclusion and openness emphasised	1	Public value creation aimed at long term/collective	1
Public data ownership defined by city	2	Public value evaluation organised	−2
Score	13		−1
higher = more involvement		higher = indirect	

Table 7. Business model parameters for City of Brussels.

Control and governance parameters		Value and public value parameters	
Value network	**Technical architecture**	**Financial architecture**	**Value proposition**
Control over assets: based on public information, developed by GIAL	Modularity: not particularly modular	Investment structure: short-term budget of GIAL	User involvement: very limited to none
Vertical integration: internally developed	Distribution of intelligence: need for internet connection	Revenue model: indirect revenue, public funding	Intended value: information channel, static
Control over customers: with the City of Brussels	Interoperability: only Android, based on open data sets	Revenue sharing: no revenue sharing	Positioning: marketed as the city's app
Good governance: not particularly	Technology governance: only	ROPI: information distribution	Public value creation: wider

(*Continued*)

Table 7. (*Continued*)

Control and governance parameters		Value and public value parameters	
emphasised, info distribution	available on Android		access to information
Stakeholder management: GIAL is the only main stakeholder	Public data ownership: publicly available data (as open data)	Public private partnership model: no structural PPP	Public value evaluation: limited internal evaluation

Table 8. Scorecard for City of Brussels.

Limited to strong government involvement		Direct to indirect public value	
Value network		**Financial architecture**	
Control over assets with city	1	Investment structure goal is long term/collective	−2
Vertically integrated within city organisation	−1	Revenue model is direct or indirect	0
Control over customers with city	2	Revenue sharing set up over long term	0
Good governance aspects emphasised	−1	ROPI is long term	1
Stakeholder management organised by city	1	PPP model is structural	0
Technical architecture		**Value proposition**	
Modularity: control over modules with city	1	User involvement: individual or collective	−2
Distribution of intelligence: centralised with the city	1	Intended value: short or long term	−2
Interoperability emphasised	1	Positioning aimed at collective	−1
Technology governance: inclusion and openness emphasised	−1	Public value creation aimed at long term/collective	−2
Public data ownership defined by city	1	Public value evaluation organised	−1
Score	5		−9
higher = more involvement		higher = indirect	

Table 9. Business model parameters for FixMyStreet Brussels.

Control and governance parameters		Value and public value parameters	
Value network	**Technical architecture**	**Financial architecture**	**Value proposition**
Control over assets: shared between BRIC, cabinet and Mobile Brussels	Modularity: quite modular architecture, links to other services possible	Investment structure: public funds from regional ICT cabinet	User involvement: primordial to use of the service

(*Continued*)

Table 9. (*Continued*)

Control and governance parameters		Value and public value parameters	
Vertical integration: growing internally	Distribution of intelligence: centrally hosted, data connection required	Revenue model: indirect, public funds	Intended value: increased internal efficiency and fixing issues
Control over customers: with the city/region	Interoperability: open source, middleware required to link to existing systems	Revenue sharing: no revenue sharing	Positioning: branded as government service
Good governance: emphasised, transparency highlighted	Technology governance: Android and iOS, phone number available but differently branded	ROPI: both internal and external efficiency gains, transparency	Public value creation: increased citizen interaction, fixing issues
Stakeholder management: challenging and organised by external consultant	Public data ownership: collected reports not open data	Public private partnership model: not present	Public value evaluation: internally evaluated, stimulation towards municipalities

Table 10. Scorecard for FixMyStreet Brussels.

Limited to strong government involvement		Direct to indirect public value	
Value network		**Financial architecture**	
Control over assets with city	2	Investment structure goal is long term/collective	2
Vertically integrated within city organisation	2	Revenue model is direct or indirect	0
Control over customers with city	2	Revenue sharing set up over long term	0
Good governance aspects emphasised	2	ROPI is long term	2
Stakeholder management organised by city	1	PPP model is structural	0
Technical architecture		**Value proposition**	
Modularity: control over modules with city	2	User involvement: individual or collective	2
Distribution of intelligence: centralised with the city	2	Intended value: short or long term	2
Interoperability emphasised	2	Positioning aimed at collective	2

(*Continued*)

Table 10. (*Continued*)

Limited to strong government involvement		Direct to indirect public value	
Technology governance: inclusion and openness emphasised	1	Public value creation aimed at long term/collective	2
Public data ownership defined by city	1	Public value evaluation organised	2
Score	17		14
higher = more involvement		higher = indirect	

Table 11. Business model parameters for STIB Mobile.

Control and governance parameters		Value and public value parameters	
Value network	**Technical architecture**	**Financial architecture**	**Value proposition**
Control over assets: with STIB	Modularity: app links to real-time position system of STIB	Investment structure: public funds	User involvement: not enabled
Vertical integration: integrated with STIB location system	Distribution of intelligence: internet connection required	Revenue model: no revenue model present	Intended value: access to real-time information
Control over customers: with STIB, no explicit reference to city or region	Interoperability: no open data, closed approach	Revenue sharing: no revenue sharing	Positioning: branded as STIB service
Good governance: not particularly emphasised	Technology governance: Android, web and iOS apps	ROPI: access to real-time location of public transport	Public value creation: increased and real-time information provision
Stakeholder management: STIB is only main stakeholder	Public data ownership: closed data owned by STIB	Public private partnership model: not present	Public value evaluation: no public evaluation of app

Table 12. Scorecard for STIB Mobile.

Limited to strong government involvement		Direct to indirect public value	
Value network		**Financial architecture**	
Control over assets with city	−1	Investment structure goal is long term/collective	−2
Vertically integrated within city organisation	−1	Revenue model is direct or indirect	0
Control over customers with city	0	Revenue sharing set up over long term	0

(*Continued*)

Table 12. (*Continued*)

Limited to strong government involvement		Direct to indirect public value	
Good governance aspects emphasised	0	ROPI is long term	−2
Stakeholder management organised by city	−1	PPP model is structural	−1
Technical architecture		**Value proposition**	
Modularity: control over modules by city	−2	User involvement: individual or collective	−1
Distribution of intelligence: centralised with the city	−1	Intended value: short or long term	−2
Interoperability emphasised	−2	Positioning aimed at collective	1
Technology governance: inclusion and openness emphasised	0	Public value creation aimed at long term/collective	1
Public data ownership defined by city	−2	Public value evaluation organised	−1
Score	−10		−7
higher = more involvement		higher = indirect	

Table 13. Business model parameters for Visit Brussels.

Control and governance parameters		Value and public value parameters	
Value network	**Technical architecture**	**Financial architecture**	**Value proposition**
Control over assets: mostly with Visit Brussels	Modularity: uses Open Street Map	Investment structure: public funds	User involvement: none, apart from social media sharing
Vertical integration: integrated in Visit Brussels organisation	Distribution of intelligence: a large initial download is required, offline	Revenue model: no revenue model present	Intended value: providing touristic information on map
Control over customers: with Visit Brussels/the region	Interoperability: closed system	Revenue sharing: potential revenue sharing with event organisers	Positioning: branded as City/Regional service
Good governance: present in general communication	Technology governance: Android, iOS, no web app	ROPI: increasing information on and attractiveness of Region	Public value creation: individual information provision
Stakeholder management: Visit Brussels is main stakeholder	Public data ownership: no open data for POIs, Open Street Map	Public private partnership model: not present	Public value evaluation: internal evaluation

Table 14. Scorecard for Visit Brussels.

Limited to strong government involvement		Direct to indirect public value	
Value network		**Financial architecture**	
Control over assets with city	1	Investment structure goal is long term/collective	−1
Vertically integrated within city organisation	2	Revenue model is direct or indirect	0
Control over customers with city	2	Revenue sharing set up over long term	1
Good governance aspects emphasised	1	ROPI is long term	2
Stakeholder management organised by city	1	PPP model is structural	0
Technical architecture		**Value proposition**	
Modularity: control over modules with city	1	User involvement: individual or collective	−1
Distribution of intelligence: centralised with the city	1	Intended value: short or long term	−2
Interoperability emphasised	−1	Positioning aimed at collective	−2
Technology governance: inclusion and openness emphasised	1	Public value creation aimed at long term/collective	1
Public data ownership defined by city	1	Public value evaluation organised	1
Score	10		−1
higher = more involvement		higher = indirect	

References

1. Al-Debei, M.M., Avison, D.: Developing a unified framework of the business model concept. Eur. J. Inf. Syst. **19**(3), 359–376 (2010)
2. Auquière, E.: Expert Interview, CIRB-CIBG, Brussels, 6 May 2013
3. Ballon, P.: Control and value in mobile communications. Ph.D. thesis, Vrije Universiteit Brussel, Belgium (2009)
4. Benington, J.: From private choice to public value? In: Benington, J., Moore, M. (eds.) Public Value: Theory and Practice, pp. 31–49. Palgrave MacMillan, Basingstoke (2011)
5. Brussels Mobility. Open Data, Brussels Mobility (2013). http://www.mobielbrussel.irisnet. be/content/opendata/
6. Brussel Nieuws. Brussel Nog Maar Eens Wereldkampioen File, Brussel Nieuws, 29 August 2013. http://www.brusselnieuws.be/nl/nieuws/brussel-nog-maar-eens-wereldkampioen-file
7. Grouwels, C.M.B.: Beleidsplan Informatica 2010–2014: Brussel: Een Pragmatische Ambitie (2012). http://www.brigittegrouwels.com/?niv=4&menuid=16&paginaid=114&subniv=0
8. Chesbrough, H.: Open Business Models: How to Thrive in the New Innovation Landscape. Harvard Business School Press, Boston (2006)
9. Cohen, B.: The Top 10 Smart Cities on the Planet, Co.EXIST, 11 January 2012. http://www. fastcoexist.com/1679127/the-top-10-smart-cities-on-the-planet
10. Corijn, E., Vloeberghs, E.: Brussel!, p. 311. VUB Press, Brussels (2009)
11. De Lestré, T.: Expert Interview, Agoria, Brussels, 4 September 2013

12. De Reuver, M., Stein, S., Hampe, J.F.: From eparticipation to mobile participation: designing a service platform and business model for mobile participation. Inf. Polity **18**(1), 57–73 (2013)
13. EC-Press Release: Digital Agenda: Turning government data into gold, European Commission, 12 December 2011. http://europa.eu/rapid/pressReleasesAction.do?aged=0&format=HTML&guiLanguage=en&language=EN&reference=IP%2F11%2F1524
14. Ericsson: Networked Society City Index 2013. Research Report (2013). http://www.ericsson.com/news/131119-networked-society-city-index_244129226_c
15. Faber, E., Ballon, P., Bouwman, H., Haaker, T., Rietkerk, O., Steen, M.: Designing business models for mobile ICT services. In: Proceedings of 16th Bled E-Commerce, Bled, Slovenia (2003)
16. Gawer, A.: Towards a general theory of technological platforms. In: Proceedings of DRUID 2010, Imperial College London Business School, 16–18 June 2010
17. GSMA: Smart Cities, Mobile Industry Report, GSMA (2013). http://smartcitiesindex.gsma.com/smart-cities/
18. Hawkins, R.: The business model as a research problem in electronic commerce. In: STAR Project Issue Report No. 4, SPRU – Science and Technology Policy Research, Brighton (2001)
19. Hillenius, G.: Jurisdiction stops brussels region from sharing FixMyStreet. Joinup, European Commission, 14 June 2013
20. Hung, S.Y., Chang, C.M., Kuo, S.R.: User acceptance of mobile e-government services: an empirical study. Gov. Inf. Quart. **30**(1), 33–44 (2013)
21. IBM: How Smart Is Your City? IBM Institute for Business Value, Executive Report (2009). http://public.dhe.ibm.com/common/ssi/ecm/en/gbe03248usen/GBE03248USEN.PDF
22. Janssen, M., Kuk, G.: E-government business models for public service networks. Int. J. E-Gov. Res. **3**(3), 54–71 (2007)
23. Janssen, M., Kuk, G.: E-government business models: theory, challenges and research issues. In: Khosrow-Pour, M. (ed.) E-government Diffusion, Policy, and Impact: Advanced Issues and Practices, pp. 1–12. IGI Global, Hershey (2008)
24. Janssen, M., Kuk, G., Wagenaar, R.: A survey of web-based business models for E-government in the Netherlands. Gov. Inf. Quart. **25**(2), 202–220 (2008)
25. Janssen, K.: PSI in Belgium: a slow journey towards open data? Topic Report No. 2011/1, European Public Sector Information Platform (2011)
26. Jullien, B.: Two-sided markets and electronic intermediation. In: IDEI Working Papers 295. Institut d'Économie Industrielle (IDEI), Toulouse, France (2004)
27. Kahn, J.: iOS and Android increase duopoly on smartphone market to 96 %. 9 to 5 mac, 24 February 2015
28. Kushchu, I., Kuscu, M.: From E-Government to m-government: facing the inevitable. In: Proceedings of the 3rd European Conference on E-Government. Dublin, Ireland, pp. 253–260 (2003)
29. Linder, J., Cantrell, S.: Changing business models: surveying the landscape. Accenture Institute for Strategic Change Report, New York, NY (2000)
30. Matthews, B.: How to use open data to connect local government with the public. The Guardian, 17 September 2013
31. Michailidis, G., de Leeuw, J.: Multilevel homogeneity analysis with differential weighting. Comput. Stat. Data Anal. **32**(3/4), 411–442 (2000)
32. Panagiotopoulos, P., et al.: A business model perspective for ICTs in public engagement. Gov. Inf. Quart. **29**(2), 192–202 (2012)
33. Schievink, B.: Belgacom komt nog dit jaar met 4G dienst, Tweakers.net, 3 July 2012. http://tweakers.net/nieuws/82919/belgacom-komt-nog-dit-jaar-met-4g-dienst.html

34. Stabell, C., Fjeldstad, O.: Configuring value for competitive advantage. Strateg. Manage. J. **19** (5), 413–437 (1998)
35. Stylianou, A.: Mobile by default? leveraging mobile technology to extend Egovernments reach and scope, Workshop Policy Brief, ePractice, European Commission, 30 June 2014
36. Summers, E.: The 5 Stars of Linked Open Data, Inkdroid, 4 June 2010. http://inkdroid.org/journal/2010/06/04/the-5-stars-of-open-linked-data/
37. The Economist: Hotspots 2025: benchmarking the future competitiveness of cities. Research Report (2013). http://www.citigroup.com/citi/citiforcities/pdfs/hotspots2025.pdf
38. Thys, S.: Evolutie van de Brusselse Arbeidsmarkt. Actiris Maandverslag Mei (2014). http://www.actiris.be/Portals/36/Documents/NL/MV05-2014.pdf
39. Walravens, N., Ballon, P.: Platform business models for smart cities. IEEE Commun. Mag. **51**(6), 2–9 (2013)
40. Yu, C.-C.: Value proposition in mobile government. In: Wimmer, M.A., Janssen, M., Scholl, H.J. (eds.) EGOV 2013. LNCS, vol. 8074, pp. 175–187. Springer, Heidelberg (2013)

Understanding the Use of Location Sharing Services on Social Networking Platforms in China

Shang Gao[1,2(✉)] and Xuemei Zhang[2]

[1] Department of Computer and Information Science,
Norwegian University of Science and Technology, Trondheim, Norway
shanggao@idi.ntnu.no
[2] School of Business Administration,
Zhongnan University of Economics and Law, Wuhan, China
xuemo123@foxmail.com

Abstract. Along with the development of information communication technology, there are more and more location sharing services on social networking platforms. Although China has the largest number of Internet users in the world, users just started to use location sharing services in the last couple of years. This study aims to have a better understanding of the use of location sharing services on social networking platforms in China. To address this, four research questions are presented and 43 in-depth face-to-face interviews are carried out in China. According to the results, the drivers and barriers for using location sharing services on social networking platforms were identified. Some of the key findings were presented as follows. Firstly, most users were concerned about privacy issues when they were using location sharing services on social networking platforms. Secondly, somewhat surprisingly, some of non-users indicated that they were not aware of the availability of the location sharing services on social networking platforms and they did not know how to use location sharing services. Last but not least, some interviewees wanted to use authority management to deal with private issues raised by the shared location information on social networking platforms.

Keywords: Location sharing services · Social networking platforms · Check-in · Privacy · Contextual integrity

1 Introduction

Along with the development of information communication technology, location based services on mobile devices are getting more and more popular [8, 9]. There are an increasing number of mobile applications on social networking platforms that can sense and share users' location information with others. Location sharing services have the potential to support people in many different occasions. For example, people sometime post a new message on social networking platforms to share their experience about a specific location. People also want to recall memories by sharing their location-based experience on social networking platforms.

© Springer International Publishing Switzerland 2016
M.S. Obaidat and P. Lorenz (Eds.): ICETE 2015, CCIS 585, pp. 124–136, 2016.
DOI: 10.1007/978-3-319-30222-5_6

We have seen a significant amount of research conducted to understand users' location sharing privacy preferences when they are using location sharing services on social networking platforms [18]. For example, Lindqvist et al. [19] has studied why people use the location sharing application Foursquare. Zhu [29] has investigated the privacy have social effects of location sharing. However, we found that the usage of location sharing services has been mainly studied in developed countries in the last couple of years. The usage of location sharing services in developing countries is still an open research question. Thus, we aim to have a better understanding of the use of location sharing services on social networking platforms in China.

Social networking services are getting more and more popular in China. Weibo (a Twitter-alike service in China) and WeChat [7] (one of the most popular instant messaging services in China) are the two of most popular social networking services in China. Unlike the service of automated tracking [17], users can choose whether to attach their location information with the messages or photos on social networking platforms. According to the 2013 annual report from China Internet Network Information Center, the users of Weibo and Wechat reached a penetration rate of 43.6 % and 65 % at the end of 2013 in China respectively.

The objective of this study is to study the use of location sharing services on social networking platforms (e.g., Weibo and WeChat) in China. To address this, four research questions are presented and 43 in-depth face-to-face interviews are carried out in China. The remainder of this paper is organized as follows: the literature review is provided in Sect. 2. Section 3 proposes the research questions. This is followed by the illustration of the research method in Sect. 4. The research findings are presented in Sect. 5. In Sect. 6, we conclude this study with a discussion on the research findings and an outline for future research directions.

2 Literature Review

The related literature is discussed in this section.

2.1 The Adoption of Location-Based Services

An important and long-standing research question in information systems research is how we can accurately explain user adoption of information systems [5]. Several models have been developed to test the users' attitude and intention to adopt new technologies or information systems. These models include the Technology Acceptance Model (TAM) [4], Theory of Planned Behavior (TPB) [1], Innovation Diffusion Theory (IDT) [23], Unified Theory of Acceptance and Use of Technology (UTAUT) [26]. Among the different models that have been proposed, TAM, which is the extension of the Theory of Reasoned Action (TRA) [6], appears to be the most widely accepted model. TAM focus on the perceived usefulness (PU) and perceived ease of use (PEOU) of a system and has been tested in some domains of E-business and proved to be quite reliable to predict user acceptance of some new information technologies, such as intranet [14], electronic commerce [22], online shopping [12], mobile information services [8], and mobile tourism services [11].

Compared to the rapid development of mobile technology, the research on location-based services adoption is still in the infancy stage. It appears that only a few studies about the adoption of location-based services have employed theoretical and methodological approaches when compared with the technology diffusion research on other mobile services (e.g., mobile information services). Based on our literature review, some existing research on location-based services adoption is summarized in Table 1.

Table 1. Literature review on location-based services adoption.

Literature	Research purpose	Country and sample size	Method	Key variables	Key findings
Zhou 2012 [28]	Examine users' adoption of location based services from perspectives of UTAUT and privacy risk in China	China (191 respondents)	SEM	Performance expectancy, effort expectancy, social influence, facilitating conditions, privacy concern, trust, perceived risk, usage intention	The results indicated that usage intention is affected by both enablers such as performance expectancy, and inhibitors such as perceived risk. This implies that service providers need to concern both perspectives of technological perceptions and privacy risk in order to facilitate user adoption of location based services
Xu and Gupta 2009 [27]	Explored the effects of privacy concerns and personal innovativeness to the adoption of location based services	Singapore (176 participants)	SEM	Personal innovativeness, privacy concern, effort expectancy, performance expectancy, intention to use	The results indicate that privacy concerns significantly influence continued adoption as compared to initial adoption. But, personal innovativeness did not moderate the relationship between privacy concerns and behavioral intention
Junglas et al. 2008 [15]	Explored the potential factors likely to influence concern for privacy (CFP) in the context of location based services	USA (378 participants)	SEM	Agreeableness, conscientiousness, emotional stability, extraversion, openness to experience, and CFP	The results indicated that personality traits are influential in the formation of CFP. These traits (agreeableness, conscientiousness, and openness to experience) were found to influence CPF; the other two traits (extraversion and emotional stability) were not found to be influence

According to the summarized literature review in Table 1, we found that most previous research on the adoption of location-based services tended to focus on users' behavior on general location-based services. Most research was based on technology diffusion theories presented above to explore potential factors affecting users' adoption of location-based services. For example, Xu and Gupta [27] developed a research model to examine the effects privacy concerns and personal innovativeness on consumers' adoption of a location-based taxi calling services in Singapore. The results indicated that privacy concerns significantly influence continued adoption as compared to initial adoption. Junglas et al. [15] found that personality traits including agreeableness, extraversion, emotional stability, openness to experience and consciousness have significant effects on user behavior of general location-based services. Last but not least, Zhou [28] investigated users' adoption of Location based services from perspectives of UTAUT and privacy risk in China. The findings indicated that the usage intention is affected by both enablers, such as performance expectancy, and inhibitors, such as perceived risk.

This research aims to complement and extend existing research by focusing on the use of location sharing services on social networking platforms. More specifically, In this exploratory study on the use of location-sharing services on social networking platform, we do not aim to generalize results by carrying out an empirical study with a large sample in China, but to further explore possible drivers and barriers for the use of location sharing services on social networking platforms. Therefore, it is very important to distinguish between users and non-users when investigating the use of location sharing services. To our best knowledge, we have not found any studies completely focused on the use of location sharing services on social networking platforms in China. Therefore, it is worth to examine it in this study.

2.2 Contextual Integrity

In order to investigate how people use location sharing services in social networking platforms and how people concern about private issues in the process, the theory contextual integrity is used. The contextual integrity proposed by Nissenbaum [21] is based on two principles. Firstly, people are living in various social contexts; and secondly, every context has a set of social norms matching with it. Moreover, Nissenbaum [21] identified two types of information norms. The first norm is appropriateness, which measures whether the disclosure of information is proper in a certain context. The information type [2] is a factor to judge appropriateness. The second norm is distribution, which decides whether the distribution of information is allowed under the conditions and restrictions in the flow of information. The contextual integrity asserted that the reason for privacy issues is the violation of appropriateness or distribution principles.

In this study, the contextual integrity is used to clarify the privacy concern on the location sharing service on the social networks by exploring whether the violation of the appropriateness or distribution principles has accrued and how do people deal with privacy concerns.

As shown in Table 2, contextual integrity has been widely used to study about the Internet privacy issues in the previous studies. Lipford et al. [20] investigated privacy mechanisms on social network sites and examined privacy issues with the following four elements: profile, photos, newsfeed and the application platform. Grodzinsky et al. [13] researched personal bloggers' privacy issues. Shi et al. [24] studied users' privacy concerns of Friendship pages. Last but not least, Zimmer [30] examined users' privacy issues regarding Google's search engine in terms of contextual integrity theory.

Table 2. Literatures used contextual integrity to study about the Internet privacy issues.

Literature	Research purpose	Theory used	Findings
Lipford et al. 2009 [20]	Investigate privacy mechanisms on social network sites	Contextual integrity	The way to design a better privacy mechanism is to make the flows of information visible
Grodzinsky et al. 2010 [13]	Research personal bloggers' privacy issues	Contextual integrity	The privacy of these whose names are on the personal bloggers of others has been violated
Shi et al. 2013 [24]	Check the privacy concerns of friendship pages	Contextual integrity	Users' interpersonal privacy concerns can arise if contexts, actors, attributes and transmission principles are violated or changed in context-relative information norms
Zimmer 2008 [30]	Clarify the private threats of Google search	Contextual integrity	Google's quest for the perfect search engine has changed personal information flows. Thus, users' privacy was threatened

2.3   Privacy Concerns in Location Sharing Services

Several researchers have examined the privacy issues in location sharing services on social networking platforms. We found that the most studied platform was Foursquare. In-depth interviews and surveys were most used in previous studies (e.g., [19]). While people are sharing their locations on social networking platforms, the personal information of where you are and what you are doing at a certain time are disclosed. Cramer et al. [3] examined the conflicting norms in check-in services. The results indicated that these norms about when and where to check-in sometimes conflicted with each other since people might have different motivations in using check-in services. Furthermore, privacy attacks in location sharing services on social networking platforms were studied by Kostakos et al. [16]. The result indicated that users who were most likely to know your real location were the users who communicated most frequently with you. Last but not least, Tsai et al. [25] investigated the privacy in the perception of risks and benefits on social networking platforms. The results revealed that people cared about privacy control mechanism on social networking platforms.

This research can be seen as a continuing effort by applying context integrity to study users' privacy concerns in using location sharing services on social networking platforms in China.

3 Research Questions

The objective of this research is to understand the use of location sharing services on social networking platforms in China. As indicated in the last section, previous research found that privacy is a barrier to influence the use of location sharing services on social networking platforms. We would like to have an in-depth study on the drivers and barriers of using location sharing services on social networking platforms. Further, we would like to use the theory of contextual integrate to further investigate the norms of location information sharing on social networking platforms in China.

Our research questions are presented as follows.

1. What is the motivation for people to use location sharing services on social networking platforms?
2. What are the potential barriers for users to use location sharing services on social networking platforms?
3. When and where do users tend to share their location?
4. How do people deal with the private concerns? What is users' preference on using location sharing services on different social networking platforms (e.g., WeChat, Weibo)?

4 Method

To address the four research questions proposed in Sect. 3, we conducted a qualitative research in terms of face-to-face interviews in China. We recruited the interview participants by posting announcements on social networking platforms in the biggest city in the central part of China in October 2014. Fifty users agreed to participate in the interview. However, some users did not appear in the scheduled interview time slots. As a result, we had conducted 43 in-depth face-to-face interviews with users of social networking platforms in China. The interviews were semi-structured and also included a set of open questions for all interviewees. Each interview lasted around 25 min. The interviews were digitally recorded. And the notes were also taken during the interviews. The transcriptions and notes were analyzed by using open coding.

Based on the collected results, we have divided the sample into users and non-users of location sharing services on social networking platforms. Among the participants, 27 (numbered as A1 to A27) had some experience with using location sharing services on social networking platforms. This group was regarded as the actual users of location sharing services. 16 (numbered as A28 to A43) of the participants were users of social networking platforms. However, they never used location sharing services on social network platforms before. This group of users was seen as non-users of location sharing services. For this group of non-users, we explored the reasons behind that by asking them some open questions. 20 of the participants were male, and 23 were female. Three of the participants are under 20 years old, and 40 of them are between 20 and 25.

5 Research Findings

The research findings are presented in this section.

5.1 Motivations to Use Location Sharing Services

The frequent indicated motivations during the interviews were summarized as follows: (1) telling friends where the interviewee has been (the most indicated), (2) arriving at a new place or doing something interesting, (3) being at a place where is fun to tell his/her friends. The purpose is to inform their friends about the change of his/her geographic location. However, sometimes, people check-in at a place where they are not actually in (A6), "Sometimes, I checked-in to cheat on my boyfriend, Actually, I was not there". This means that the location information can be edited by the user.

Sometimes doing something romantic can enable users to share location information on social networking platforms. A11 shared his location in a cinema because he was with his girlfriend at that time. He said that he tended to share the location when he was dating with his girlfriend. Visiting places of interest can also motivate users to use location sharing services on social networking platforms. Some people shared location information to record their daily routines in their personal life. A14 said that, "I checked-in when I wanted to share my daily routines with my friends".

Most interviewees in the users group pointed out that they found potential added value by using location sharing services (e.g., making their location information available to their friends on social networking platforms). For instance, one of the interviewee (A4) indicated that he purchased a new mobile device with the GPS feature specifically for the needs of location sharing services to his friends on social networking platforms.

Further, some interviewees (A7, A15, A18) indicated that they were addicted to location sharing services because this was a new fashion to communicate with their friends on social networking platforms. Another two interviewees (A3, A9) mentioned that sharing location information on social networking platforms could also give them a feeling of safety, since their friends are aware of their location information.

5.2 Barriers to Use Location Sharing Services

There are 16 interviewees never used location sharing services on social networking platforms before. Six of them indicated that they never heard of this service or did not know how to use this location sharing service (A34, A36, A37, A40, A42, and A43). Three interviewees indicated that they thought sharing location is useless and meaningless (A28, A29. A33). There were also 5 interviewees who worried about the privacy and safety issues raised by using location sharing services (A30, A35, A39, A40, A41). A30 mentioned that "I don't like the feeling of being watched by sharing my location information on social networking platforms". A35 said that, "In some cybercrime cases, location information on WeChat or Weibo were used to find the object". Further, four interviewees indicated that they did not want to use location sharing services on social networking mainly due to unwillingness to share private information. For example, they did not want their location information to be seen by their parents.

Another interviewee (A38) pointed out that "although he owned an old mobile device, he did not use location sharing services because it made his device slow". This means that he did not see the added value of using location sharing services on his present mobile device.

5.3   The Information Norms of Sharing Location

Information norm is an important concept in the contextual integrity theory. It represents the norm of where and when to share location in the general accepted way.

5.3.1   Where Do People Check-in?

Interviewees were asked to rank the types of locations that they were likely to share according to their past experience. The ranking scores of each type of location were presented in Fig. 1.

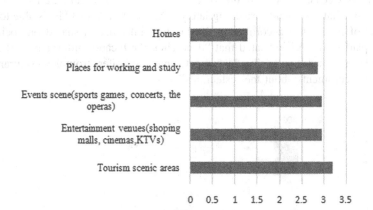

Fig. 1. The ranking scores of each type of location.

It can be seen from the bar chart that the users were most likely to share their locations at tourism scenic areas. The event scenes and entertainment venues have the same score, both of which are the second frequent places to check-in. The third most likely check in location is the places for working and studying. Home was ranked as the most unlikely place to be shared by end users.

The findings from Sect. 5.1 are of help to further explain the results in Fig. 1. The most indicated motivation is to tell friends where the interviewee has been. The tourism scenic areas are often the places of interests. Users are interested to share this information to their friends. Entertainment venues and event scenes are places that are fun and appropriate for sharing information on their daily lives. The places for working and studying, and homes are regarded as users' routine places. According to the results, it seemed that end users did not like to share location information of their routine places. Given the fact that some interviewees (A33, A39) were worried about privacy issues, they did not want to disclose their specific location information (e.g., being at a hotel/restaurant) on social networking platforms, but to only share which city they have been on the platforms.

5.3.2   When Do People Check-in?

Participants A2, A12 and A13 indicated that they intended to share their location information on social networking platforms when having group events. A7 and A24 tended to check-in when they felt funny about new places. A1, A3, A4, A10, A11, A25 and A26 shared their location information when they arrived at a place of interest.

5.3.3   What Information Can Be Gained in Friends' Shared Location Information?

Figure 2 presents the information that their friends wanted to know by viewing the shared location. All the participants chose the option "where my friend has been". 46 % of the interviewees believed they could know their friends' opinions of the places. 15 % of the interviewees chose the option "others". Moreover, A21 and A22 indicated that, "I can guess what my friends are doing lately". A5 mentioned that "he is able to know the status of his friends according to the location information shared on social networking platforms". A8 indicated that "if he click the location information of restaurants his friends shared on Weibo, he can get some good offers from the restaurants and other users' comments about the restaurants".

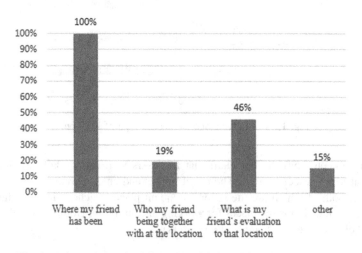

Fig. 2. Information gained from friends' shared location information.

5.4 Applying Contextual Integrity to Analyze the Privacy Concern

5.4.1 Potential Audiences

In the theory of contextual integrity, inappropriate audience of a certain context could invade privacy [2]. When the participants were asked about potential audiences, they tended to use authority management (A11, A13) to deal with private issues with potential audiences. Six interviewees said that, "If I do not want some friends to see my location, I will block them to see my location information".

Figure 3 presents the privacy concerns of the interviewees who have used the location sharing service. Three of them said that they did not have privacy concerns on using location sharing services on social networking platforms. 63 % of the interviewees indicated that they were worried about the issue that the shared location information could be accessed by some unknown merchants. 58 % of the interviewees were afraid that the location information could be seen by some unwanted friends. 42 % of the interviewees were concerned about tracing by others, while 21 % of the interviewees were concerned about possible security issues raised by strangers on social networking platforms.

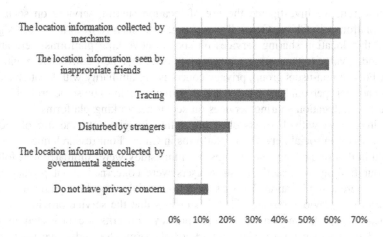

Fig. 3. Privacy concerns of the interviewees who have used the location sharing service.

5.4.2 Violation of Appropriateness

According to the previous research [8], the type of information can influence peoples' judgment on whether the appropriateness principle has been violated. When the users' current location is regarded as private, they are less likely to discourse the location information to others.

When it comes to the appropriateness, interviewees were asked to compare the difference between WeChat and Weibo. Most interviewees believed that WeChat did a better job than Weibo with respect to the privacy issue (A2, A5). The message posted on WeChat can only be seen by verified friends, while the message posted on Weibo can be seen by anyone. Users are able to look for any users with the same interest on a specific location and follow them on Weibo. This can be seen as a way of meeting new people through Weibo. The number of interviewees who tended to check-in on WeChat (44.4 %) is more than the number of interviewees who tended to check-in on Weibo (18.5 %).

5.4.3   Violation of Distribution

The principle of distribution is another important concept in the contextual integrity theory. According to the interviews, 13 users indicated that they did not have private concerns when they were using location sharing services on social networking platforms. A1 said, "I don't have privacy concerns because I never shared private location information on social networking platforms". Some interviewees who have privacy concern said that they would ask his friends to not re-post his massages any more or delete the massage (A3, A12, A13, A15, A19, A21). Other interviewees (A10, A18, and A23) chose to limit their check-in behavior because of possible distribution of the shared private location information.

6   Conclusion and Future Work

In this research, we investigated the use of location sharing services on social networking platforms in China. Generally speaking, most interviewees in the users group indicated that location sharing services on social networking platforms were able to provide added value to them (e.g., a new way of opening a new conversation with their friends). For the non-users group, privacy concerns, unfamiliarity with location sharing services and their personal knowledge and experience seem to be some critical barriers for them to use location sharing services on social networking platforms.

Our interviews with 43 users shed interesting insights into the use of location sharing services on social networking platforms in China. Four research questions were addressed in this study. The key findings from this study were summarized as follows. Firstly, our findings indicated that most users were concerned about privacy issues when they were using location sharing services on social networking platforms. This is in line with the previous research [19]. It suggests that the service providers need to setup clear interpretations on how users' privacy concerns are protected in using location sharing services on social networking platforms. Secondly, we found many motivations as to why users use location sharing services, including fun, connecting with best friends, remembering daily routines in peoples' life. Thirdly, somewhat surprisingly, some of the interviewees did not know the location sharing services on social networking platforms and did not know how to use them. The social networking services providers need to have some marketing campaigns to further promote location sharing services to the end users. Fourthly, with respect to privacy protection, most interviewees indicated that WeChat did a better job than Weibo in China. Last but not least, we found that users wanted to use authority management (A11, A13) to deal with private issues raised by the shared location information on social networking platforms.

However, we were also aware of some limitations of this research. First, the sample size in this study was quite narrow in terms of age range since all participants in our interviews were under 25 years old. This sample might not be fully representative of the entire population in China. For example, the generalizability of the findings to other groups of users (e.g., older adults) remains to be determined. This may give us very different results (e.g., middle aged adults and older adults have different intentions to use smartphones [10]). Second, the self-reporting nature of this study is another limitation. Last but not least, we only studied location sharing services on two popular social networking platforms in China. This may limit the generalizability of our findings.

Continuing with this stream of research, we plan to test other age groups to see the generalizability of our findings in this study. Future research is also needed to empirically examine potential factors influence users' adoption of location sharing services in terms of a research model with larger samples in China. We also would like to record users' historical behavior on using location sharing services to further analysis users' usage patterns.

References

1. Ajzen, I.: The theory of planned behavior. Organ. Behav. Hum. Decis. Process. **50**(2), 179–211 (1991)
2. Barth, A., Datta, A., Mitchell, J.C., et al.: Privacy and contextual integrity: framework and applications. In: 2006 IEEE Symposium on Security and Privacy, 15 pp. 184–198. IEEE (2006)
3. Cramer, H., Rost, M., Holmquist, L.E.: Performing a check-in: emerging practices, norms and 'conflicts' in location-sharing using foursquare. In: Proceedings of the 13th International Conference on Human Computer Interaction with Mobile Devices and Services, pp. 57–66. ACM (2011)
4. Davis, F.D.: Perceived usefulness, perceived ease of use and user acceptance of information technology. MIS Q. **13**(3), 319–340 (1989)
5. DeLone, W., McLean, E.: Information systems success: the quest for the dependent variable. Inf. Syst. Res. **3**(1), 60–95 (1992)
6. Fishbein, M., Ajzen, I.: Belief, Attitude, Intention and Behavior: An Introduction to Theory and Research. Addison-Wesley, Reading (1975)
7. Gao, S., Krogstie, J.: Understanding business models of mobile ecosystems in China: a case study. In: The Proceedings of the 7th International Conference on Management of Computational and Collective IntElligence in Digital EcoSystems (MEDES 2015). ACM (2015)
8. Gao, S., Krogstie, J., Siau, K.: Adoption of mobile information services: an empirical study. Mob. Inf. Syst. **10**(2), 147–171 (2014)
9. Gao, S., Krogstie, J., Thingstad, T., et al.: A mobile service using anonymous location-based data: finding reading rooms. Int. J. Inf. Learn. Technol. **32**(1), 32–44 (2015)
10. Gao, S., Krogstie, J., Yang, Y.: Differences in the adoption of smartphones between middle aged adults and older adults in China. In: Zhou, J., Salvendy, G. (eds.) ITAP 2015. LNCS, vol. 9193, pp. 451–462. Springer, Heidelberg (2015)
11. Gao, S., Roinend, P.C., Krogstie, J.: The adoption of mobile tourism services: an empirical study. In: The Proceedings of the 10th International Conference on Advances in Mobile Computing and Multimedia (MoMM 2012), pp. 47–56. ACM (2012)
12. Gefen, D.: TAM or just plain habit: a look at experienced online shoppers. J. End User Comput. **15**(3), 1–13 (2003)

13. Grodzinsky, F., Tavani, H.T.: Applying the "contextual integrity" model of privacy to personal blogs in the blogoshere (2010)
14. Horton, R.P., Buck, T., Waterson, P.E., et al.: Explaining intranet use with the technology acceptance model. J. Inf. Technol. **16**, 237–249 (2001)
15. Junglas, I.A., Johnson, N.A., Spitzmüller, C.: Personality traits and concern for privacy: an empirical study in the context of location-based services. Eur. J. Inf. Syst. **17**(4), 387–402 (2008)
16. Kostakos, V., Venkatanathan, J., Reynolds, B., et al.: Who's your best friend?: targeted privacy attacks In location-sharing social networks. In: Proceedings of the 13th International Conference on Ubiquitous Computing, pp. 177–186. ACM (2011)
17. Li, M., Zhu, H., Gao, Z., et al.: All your location are belong to us: breaking mobile social networks for automated user location tracking. In: Proceedings of the 15th ACM International Symposium on Mobile Ad Hoc Networking and Computing, pp. 43–52. ACM (2014)
18. Lin, J., Benisch, M., Sadeh, N., et al.: A comparative study of location-sharing privacy preferences in the United States and China. Pers. Ubiquit. Comput. **17**(4), 697–711 (2013)
19. Lindqvist, J., Cranshaw, J., Wiese, J., et al.: I'm the mayor of my house: examining why people use foursquare-a social-driven location sharing application. In: Proceedings of the SIGCHI Conference on Human Factors in Computing Systems, pp. 2409–2418. ACM (2011)
20. Lipford, H.R., Hull, G., Latulipe, C., et al.: Visible flows: contextual integrity and the design of privacy mechanisms on social network sites. In: International Conference on Computational Science and Engineering 2009, (CSE 2009), pp. 985–989. IEEE (2009)
21. Nissenbaum, H.: Privacy as contextual integrity. Wash. Law Rev. **79**(1), 101–139 (2004)
22. Pavlou, P.A.: Consumer acceptance of electronic commerce: integrating trust and risk with the technology acceptance model. Int. J. Electron. Commerce. **7**(3), 101–134 (2003)
23. Rogers, E.M.: The Diffusion of Innovations. Free Press, New York (1995)
24. Shi, P., Xu, H., Chen, Y.: Using contextual integrity to examine interpersonal information boundary on social network sites. In: Proceedings of the SIGCHI Conference on Human Factors in Computing Systems, pp. 35–38. ACM (2013)
25. Tsai, J.Y., Kelley, P.G., Cranor, L.F., et al.: Location-sharing technologies: privacy risks and controls. ISJLP **6**, 119 (2010)
26. Venkatesh, V., Morris, M.G., Davis, G.B., et al.: User acceptance of information technology: toward a unified view. MIS Q. **27**(3), 425–478 (2003)
27. Xu, H., Gupta, S.: The effects of privacy concerns and personal innovativeness on potential and experienced customers' adoption of location-based services. Electron. Markets **19**(2–3), 137–149 (2009)
28. Zhou, T.: Examining location-based services usage from the perspectives of unified theory of acceptance and use of technology and privacy risk. J. Electron. Commer. Res. **13**(2), 135–144 (2012)
29. Zhu, C., Wat, K.K., Fang, B., et al.: Privacy and social effects in location sharing services. In: 2012 IEEE First International Conference on Services Economics (SE), pp. 62–65. IEEE (2012)
30. Zimmer, M.: Privacy on planet Google: using the theory of contextual integrity to clarify the privacy threats of Google's quest for the perfect search engine. J. Bus. Tech. L. **3**, 109 (2008)

Large Scale Evaluation of an Adaptive E-Advertising User Model

Alaa A. Qaffas[(✉)] and Alexandra I. Cristea

Department of Computer Science, The University of Warwick, Coventry, CV4 9LX, UK
{aqaffas,acristea}@dcs.warwick.ac.uk

Abstract. The user model is considered the core content of any adaptive system. The process that is most challenging in an adaptation system is the modelling of user data. This paper is focused on creating a user model that can be suitably adapted to advertisement applications. To integrate data from different publicly available sources, a social component has been added to the user model, to support advertisements adaptation. In addition, a straightforward and lightweight user model has been targeted, which should be easy to integrate into any existing system. A tool based on this model is introduced and a study that assesses the effectiveness of it via a trial run of a prototype of the tool with different users is described.

Keywords: E-Advertising · E-Commerce · Personalisation · Adaptive advertising · User model · User profile

1 Introduction

Technological advancements have led to a significant increase in web-based promotions and online marketing, as target audiences can now be accessed regardless of time or location. The adaptation of advertising adds significant benefits to customer satisfaction and business profits [1]. Availability and the easiest way to manage the adaptation of advertising with minimal effort on any commercial site has become a key demand for businesses. Many models exist, e.g., the Dexter model [2], AHAM [3], and LAOS [4], but they are proposed mainly for personalising the educational experience. Lessons learned from them may be applied here, to some extent. Moreover, these models do not feature the lightweight integration of adaptive features on any website as their main purpose. Therefore, a new model - the *Layered Adaptive Advertising Integration* – has been proposed, based on prior ones, in order to introduce an easier approach to integrating adaptation features into any commercial website. Some of its components differ from those in traditional models. In particular, the user modelling in the proposed model is separated into storage and delivery parts, the latter is not covered in this paper, the latter having been implemented, but data is still being analysed. This separation can potentially enhance the generalisation, portability and efficiency of the user model and delivery model. The storage part is encapsulated and manipulated via XML representation, to allow the system to be integrated into any website easily and with only minor

© Springer International Publishing Switzerland 2016
M.S. Obaidat and P. Lorenz (Eds.): ICETE 2015, CCIS 585, pp. 137–157, 2016.
DOI: 10.1007/978-3-319-30222-5_7

changes to the original database of the website. In addition to the separation, the storage of the user model and its operation is added to the delivery model, in order to facilitate the integration process on any website. This separation also allows the new model to be easily expanded.

Our research aims to address the following main research question:

How can we support website owners in the creation of adaptive advertising?

This main research question can be addressed by answering the following sub-research questions:

A. *What type of tools do website owners need, to be able to efficiently add adaptive advertising in a lightweight manner (as an add-on) to their website?*
B. *What kind of support do website owners need, to be able to use these tools?*

To answer these questions, we recommend a collection of tools, Adaptive E-Advertising Delivery System (AEADS), which facilitate the creation of adaptive e-advertising. This paper in particular focuses on one of the vital components in any adaptive systems, the *User Model (UM)*. In this paper, we propose a lightweight UM, with a set of features and attributes that we consider essential to adaptive advertising, and which can be easily added to any static commercial website. Furthermore, this model is implemented and evaluated with real Internet users and customers.

The following sections discuss the related research, the user model tool and its evaluation, and finally provide a conclusion.

2   Related Research

Adaptive hypermedia systems allow for personalisation, thus improving the efficiency and accuracy of information distribution [5]. This process consists of three major types of tasks: acquisition, representation and secondary inference, and production [6]. The *acquisition tasks* identify information regarding users' characteristics, computer usage and environment, in order to construct an initial model of the user. The *representation and secondary inference tasks* inference and express the content of the user model and makes assumptions about them, such as their behaviours and the environment. The *production tasks* generate the adaptation of the contents and structure of the system to meet the users' needs. We use the classification of the data in a user model by user, usage, environment, hardware, software, and location. According to [7], an adaptive model considers user's characteristics in developing a user model and the data captured can be categorised as knowledge, interests, goals and tasks, background, individual traits, and context of work.

A user model is a basic component in any personalised system and is a representation of user data stored for any adaptive changes to the system's behaviour. All adaptive hypermedia frameworks and models have a user model as one of their components. For instance, in AHAM [3], the user model contains concepts with attributes storing user preferences, while in LAOS [4] the user model is even more complex.

There have been many systems proposed to facilitate adaptation, including AHA! [8, 9], GALE [10], ADE [11], AdROSA [12], ADWIZ [13], MyAds [14], and WHURLE [15]. A generic user model based on variable-value pairs that facilitate required adaptations form the basis of ADE, AHA! and GALE and this is suitable for online advertising purposes as well. In particular, according to [16] a model is suggested for the delivery of hypermedia content that considers the types of users, the devices used by customers to gain access, the types of access, the state of the network and the current load on the server. Nonetheless, these are all standalone systems, which cannot be integrated into existing ones in a lightweight manner. XML-based pipelining, as used by WHURLE for applying lightweight solutions and standards, is efficient for adding minor modifications to existing systems, and is, therefore, utilised in our approach. However, user modelling in WHURLE is not as extended.

AdSense [17, 18], unlike our approach, cannot provide advertisements to clients directly, it just lets advertisers in the Google Network deliver advertisements to the content site to be presented to users automatically. It specialises in banner advertisements and uses location to personalise content [19]. However, this process does not utilise any form of user-based modelling, or the assimilation of user information for personalisation purposes. Among the potential approaches to selecting the best form of advertisement, adaptive hypermedia may be used to link the advertisement to the consumer's taste, via user modelling, and is a significant element within systems that adapt to the user [20].

Another example, AdROSA [12], that makes automatic personalised web banners, depends mostly on specific browsing behaviours of a user. It is similar to AdSense, the portal model of advertising uses AdROSA to deliver the advertisements. More recent systems emerged, such as ADWIZ, and MyAds, which are adaptive advertisement systems. ADWIZ concentrates on the adaptation of web banners and is mainly dependent upon keywords, supplied via a search-service query, in order to select advertisements. Furthermore, this system does not require the use of cookies or, indeed, any user-related information within its database, with which to identify a particular user. The MyAds system concentrates on those advertisements within a public-display scenario by dynamically adapting them for an audience within a certain proximity of the display. A more recent system also called MyAds [21] is a social adaptive hypermedia system used for online advertising. It is a standalone system based on its own theoretical framework, build as five main layers. The theoretical framework is rooted in the adaptive hypermedia theory.

Social networks are good sources of user information [22], from which user behaviour and characteristics for personalising advertisements can be retrieved. Although the type of content posted on these websites varies, it is generally indicative of a user's preferences, attitudes and behaviours.

Facebook is one of the most popular social networking sites, with 1.35 billion monthly active users from around the world [23]. Users can create a personal profile, add friends, send messages, post status updates and comments to friends' "walls". They can chat together and upload photos and videos that their friends can comment on and "like" [24]. For these reasons, Facebook has been used as the first social medial data-gathering source for the first version of the system described in this paper, follow-up versions look into other sources though.

Many existing semantic web-authoring systems can be used in conjunction with other delivery or authoring systems [25, 26]. In our case, XML was selected to generate the user model tool's internal representation.

The modelling of user profiles involves acquisition, representation and secondary inference. Data acquisition can be performed using a variety of different methods depending on class, including user data acquisition methods, usage data acquisition methods and environment data acquisition methods. This includes user-supplied information acquired through questions asked by the system, acquisition rules, stereotype reasoning, and plan recognition, a process which predicts future actions based on previous patterns [27]. A simple method for making a first assessment of others is to classify them into groups sharing the same interests, according to a set of criteria – a stereotype [28]. We use the stereotype technique, as it makes inferences based on limited observations.

3   Authoring Adaptive E-Advertising

The overall Authoring model of Adaptive E-Advertising, as informed by prior research and implementations, especially in the area of personalised e-learning, includes:

1. The *Domain Model* - used by businesses to organise, label and categorise advertisements. As it has been described elsewhere [29], it is not further detailed here.
2. The *Adaptation Model* [30] - enabling businesses to adapt the advertisements they have organised, using the domain model tool for their customers' needs.
3. The *User Model* - representing the personal data of an individual user, stored for any adaptive changes to system's behaviours. For example, it can be used to predict the most relevant items for the user, when they search for information, as described below. This is the focus of our paper.

Here, the social input data component has been added to the user model, and then some functions of this model were separated, (e.g., the inference function) to be used in the delivery engine to support the integration process.

The user (customer) modelling tool has been designed to be simple (to have few user model features), in order to be lightweight, and to integrate with any potential website user model. With this tool, we implement the first steps of the user modelling, including its acquisition data, and retrieve explicit and implicit data. We use the explicit data supplied by users, and retrieve data from social networks, by using the social networks authorisation, and authentication APIs. We also conduct implicit data acquisition, by using several techniques, including *stereotype reasoning* [31], and *plan recognition* [27] to be used in the delivery Engine.

All of the data about users in the user model is stored in XML files. Storing all of the data in a lightweight fashion (XML) facilitates the integration into any commercial webpage, as XML allows for pipeline processing and independence to any other processing on the website. Users can login into the system via two methods: register (Fig. 1), and Facebook login (Fig. 2). By logging in via the latter, the user model can be automatically populated with the necessary information for the adaptation of advertisements. The user information is arranged in an XML file with attributes such as id, name, password, email, age, gender, location, number of logins to site, total number of clicks on each advertisement, device used, and software used. All users can update their information on their profile page. This data will be stored in the users.xml file (Fig. 3). The social data from the social login allows us to retrieve sufficient information about users and to infer from specific to general cases.

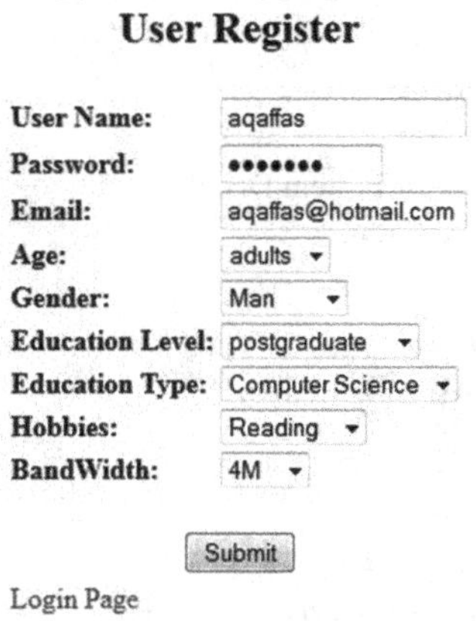

User Register

User Name:	aqaffas
Password:	•••••••
Email:	aqaffas@hotmail.com
Age:	adults ▾
Gender:	Man ▾
Education Level:	postgraduate ▾
Education Type:	Computer Science ▾
Hobbies:	Reading ▾
BandWidth:	4M ▾

Submit

Login Page

User Login

User Name:	aqaffas
Password:	•••••••
Use Cookie:	☐

Login

Register   Login with Facebook

Fig. 1. User registration.

Fig. 2. User login.

```
- <User>
    <userId>1095288034</userId>
    <userName>aqaffas</userName>
    <password>n/a</password>
    <email>aqaffas@hotmail.com</email>
    <age>kids</age>
    <gender>man</gender>
    <loginNumber>6</loginNumber>
    <totalClick>1</totalClick>
    <hobbies>Reading</hobbies>
    <educationLevel>postgraduate</educationLevel>
    <educationType>None</educationType>
    <bandWidth>2M</bandWidth>
    <softwareUsed>Mozilla/5.0 (Windows NT 6.1; rv:28.0) Gecko/20100101 Firefox/28.0</softwareUsed>
    <location>NamedFacebookType[id=106076586099038 metadata=null name=Coventry, United Kingdom type=null]</location>
    <deviceUsed>Computer</deviceUsed>
  </User>
</Users>
```

Fig. 3. User model XML file sample.

The implementation of the user modelling is made by creating servlets to be used in JSP pages, adding data to the user_item.xml file, such as the number of clicks on advertisement for each user, and the number of times each advertisement is shown, for each user attribute (Fig. 4 a, b and c). The number of clicks and shows will be utilised to apply plan recognition. Plan recognition refers to the task of inferring the plan of an intelligent agent (here, the human customer) from observing the agent's actions or their effects [27]. In addition, this process will depend on the plan library that businesses create in the authoring part. The delivery engine checks the clicked items and the plan library to acquire a sequence of advertisements to be presented to the user. The latter process belongs to the delivery engine part and no further details are given here. Moreover, a new XML file named users_items_sequence.xml tracks each user's selection sequence of advertisements, albeit only the final ten selections will be stored in this file. The threshold of 10 selections was decided based on trial and error on the testing phase of the system. This file will be used to predict user actions for current and similar users.

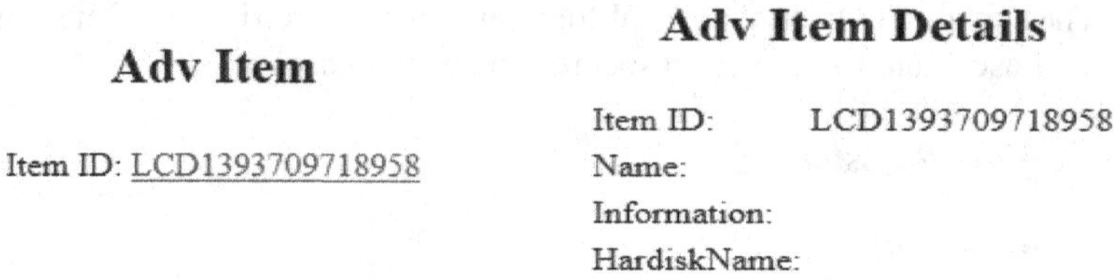

Adv Item

Item ID: LCD1393709718958

a. Show Item

Adv Item Details

Item ID: LCD1393709718958
Name:
Information:
HardiskName:

b. Item Details

```
- <UserItems>
  - <Item>
      <User_Id>1397838625271</User_Id>
      <Item_ID>LCD1393709718958</Item_ID>
      <NumberOfClicked>2</NumberOfClicked>
      <NumberOfShow>2</NumberOfShow>
   </Item>
  - <Item>
      <User_Id>1397838625271</User_Id>
      <Item_ID>AdvertRoot1393709791989</Item_ID>
      <NumberOfClicked>4</NumberOfClicked>
      <NumberOfShow>4</NumberOfShow>
   </Item>
  - <Item>
      <User_Id>1397838625271</User_Id>
      <Item_ID>LCD1393709721749</Item_ID>
      <NumberOfClicked>2</NumberOfClicked>
      <NumberOfShow>2</NumberOfShow>
   </Item>
  - <Item>
      <User_Id>1095288034</User_Id>
      <Item_ID>LCD1393709718958</Item_ID>
      <NumberOfClicked>1</NumberOfClicked>
      <NumberOfShow>1</NumberOfShow>
   </Item>
</UserItems>
```

c. User Item.XML file

Fig. 4. User model instantiation example.

Many formats can be used in a user model, for example attribute-value pairs, Booleans, lists, references to external objects, and so on. The knowledge in a user model can be represented in different ways, such as overlay models, semantic nets, user profiles and stereotype-based models. For example, in an overlay model the user's knowledge is represented as a subset of the domain model of the application.

Furthermore, for advertising adaptations, we used, as said, the stereotype technique, as it makes inferences based on limited observations. Each user is assigned to a group (stereotype), according to the types of advertisements on websites (a website owner arranges his advertisements into groups and subgroups). The system then determines the activation conditions for applying the stereotype to a user. For example, if the user model shows that the user is interested in computers and televisions, then the system activates the stereotype "technology". From the usage data, if, for instance, the user has bought at least two electronic items or computers, then the stereotype "technology" can be activated. The administrator can create and control (add- update - delete) stereotypes.xml from the stereotype page (Fig. 5). Based on hypotheses H1 (described below), an initial minimal set of necessary dimensions for an advertising user model are defined, and include *age, gender, bandwidth, device type, number of clicks on advertisements, education level, education type,* and *hobbies*. Each dimension has its own attributes. In addition, action sequencing is used in this research to predict the future actions of the user, to recommend actions based on the action sequences of other users, or to perform some of these actions on behalf of the user.

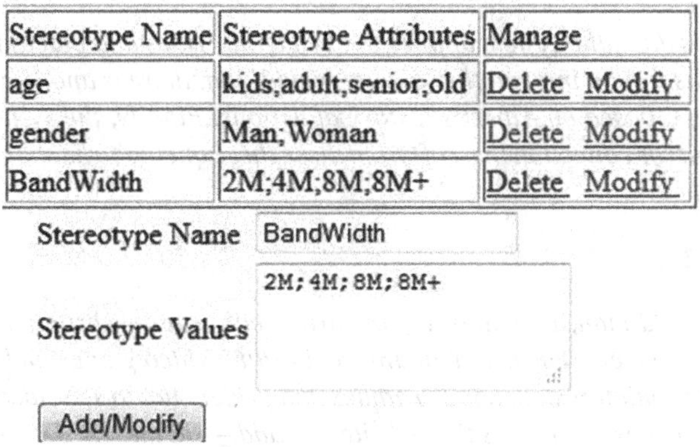

Stereotype Name	Stereotype Attributes	Manage
age	kids;adult;senior;old	Delete Modify
gender	Man;Woman	Delete Modify
BandWidth	2M;4M;8M;8M+	Delete Modify

Stereotype Name   BandWidth

Stereotype Values   2M; 4M; 8M; 8M+

Add/Modify

Fig. 5. Stereotype.

4 Scenario

To better understand the usage of the user modelling tool and the application of the data it stores, we describe two usage scenarios as follows.

4.1 Scenario 1

When the login page is loaded, Albert, a 20-year-old man, and a customer of a given company, enters his username and password. He could click the login button or he can login using his Facebook account. In both cases, bandwidth, location, device type, and software used for Albert are automatically obtained by the system. Login with a Facebook account will simplify access to the website and allows systems to automatically obtain important data.

Albert is using a smart phone with bandwidth lower than 1 M (as extracted by the system). If Albert logs into the website for the first time, then only the general rules will be applied. All of the advertisements that are not appropriate for Albert (based on general rules: e.g., advertisements targeted to women, to higher or lower ages, higher bandwidth, or another device type) will be excluded. All of the advertisements that are appropriate for Albert, and all of the advertisements that are not assigned any rules, will be placed in the queue, to be shown to Albert.

However, if Albert logs into the website more than once, the behaviour rules and some inference processes will be applied. In order to apply behaviour rules and inference processes, the system needs to store all of Albert's behaviour, the advertisements that are shown to him and not clicked, the numbers of his actions, as well as advertisements that were shown and clicked, and the number of times they were clicked. When Albert clicks on any advertisement link, or the advertisement is shown to him, the system stores all of this data in two fields (number of shows, and number of clicks for each advertisement). In addition, the system stores the last ten clicks for Albert to be used to infer his actions.

Based on this data, the system applies the behaviour rules and places the advertisements that results from it into another queue; in addition, there is another queue for the inference process, based on Albert's history of actions. Finally, the system decides on an advertisement (or collection thereof) from these three queues to be shown on the page that Albert loaded.

4.2   Scenario 2

John, a 30-year-old man, logs into his favourite real estate website that displays an array of different advertisements including real estate, video games and movie advertisements. John is uninterested in video games and prefers not to see video game advertisements. The business that owns the website can add—via the AEADS user model and its tools—a 'like' or 'stop' button for every advertisement featured on the website. Consequently, if John presses a 'stop' button for a video game advertisement, then, on the basis of the rules of the business, the inference engine is able to stop the same advertisement, or indeed, all advertisements that belong to the same category.

Conversely, if John presses the 'like' button for any given movie advertisement, the inference engine will display this advertisement a few more times, according to, and determined by, his business preferences, and will also display a number of advertisements located within the same group as the advertisement. The system will then automatically infer that John likes items in the same group and mark them with 'like'. John's activity can then be stored within the social component of the user model and, based on business rules, his preferences will prevail through follow-up log-ins.

5   Case Study

5.1   Hypotheses

The following hypotheses have been defined to evaluate the user model tool:

H0a: The user model (UM) concept for advertising (as illustrated by the UM tool) is _useful_ for constructing a user model for recommendation of advertisements.
H0b: The UM concept for advertising (as illustrated by the UM tool) is _easy to use_ for constructing a user model for recommendation of advertisements.

H0x are the basic hypotheses, and the rest are derived from them:

H1: The attributes of the proposed UM are _useful_ for recommending advertisements (username, password, email, age, gender, education level, education type, hobbies, bandwidth, location, device type and software used).
H2: The data in the user model is adequate for the advertisements delivery engine decision.
H3: Automatically generating user model data (location, device type, and software used) is useful.
H4: Social networks used as a source for user data are an appropriate data source for recommending advertisements.
H5: A user's advertisement preferences can be predicted, by tracking the user's behaviour sequence when they use the system.
H6a: The input and output mechanisms of the user model tool are useful.
H6b: The input and output mechanisms of the user model tool are easy to use.
H7: The stereotypes for users with respect to advertisements recommendation are useful and appropriate.
H8: The stereotypes for users with respect to advertisements recommendation are easy to use.
H9: It is useful to integrate the user model creation tool in any JSP website.
H10: It is easy to integrate the user model creation tool in any JSP website.
H11: Any website administrator can understand, use, and update the stereotypes.

These hypotheses were evaluated by surveying a sample group of Internet users and analysing their answers, as further described below.

5.2   Case Study Setup

The user model tool was evaluated from a functionality and ease of use perspective by students studying different subjects and modules (Introduction to Business, Principles of Marketing, Management Information System and E-Marketing) at King Abdul-Aziz University in Jeddah, Saudi Arabia. Students were deemed appropriate as a testing population because, first, all of them are Internet users, and regular online shoppers, who are familiar with the current online providers. The other reason was to get a large number of users. Note that, whilst our users were familiar with the Internet, their study of a variety of subjects ensured that they were not only Computer Science specialists, and that the tool was tested with a wide variety of backgrounds, knowledge and interests.

Consequently, a sample of 285 Internet users were asked to evaluate the user model tool. In assessing the tool, they were asked to do the following.

First, the respondents were introduced to the user model tool and given a general overview of adaptive advertising. Next, the participants were instructed to use the tool and assess its effectiveness. The three-part questionnaire was provided at this point, to guide the evaluation process. The first section collects data on the personal details of each user. The second part presents a series of Likert scale [32] questions, to encourage the users to rate the effectiveness of the system in terms of functionality and application. The Likert scale offered each respondent a series of five options when evaluating the user model tool, with the first scale option being 'not at all useful' or 'very difficult' and the last scale option being 'very useful' or 'very easy to use', respectively. A series of qualitative questions were posed in the final section, for respondents to speak freely about their experiences using the user model tool.

Table 1. Authoring tool features.

A	Whole User model Tool	G	Saving Information in XML as Export Format
B	User Registration Process	H	Facebook User Profile Import
C	Login Process	I	Match User Characteristic with Stereotype
D	Facebook Login Process	J	Adding own Stereotype
E	Submitting Information	K	Modifying existing Stereotype
F	Updating User Profile	L	Deleting Stereotype

Table 2. User model attributes.

1	Location	10	Education Type
2	Device Type	11	Hobbies
3	Software Used on Device	12	Bandwidth
4	Username	13	Get Location Automatically
5	Passwords	14	Get Device Type Automatically
6	Email	15	Get Software Used Automatically
7	Age	16	Getting Number of Shows for Each User
8	Gender	17	Getting Number of Clicks for Each User
9	Education Level	18	Getting Last 10 Sequence of Clicks for Each User

5.3   Results

A number of 134 survey questionnaires of the total 305 questionnaires that had been distributed were returned completed. The reason why less than half of the distributed questionnaires were completed may have been the fact that, prior to the survey, the participants were informed that it was not compulsory for them to answer the questionnaire and that if they did not, their academic activities or outcomes would not be affected in the least. The majority of the participants who completed the questionnaire were in the age group 18–24 years (61.2 %), whereas most of the rest were in the age group 25–34 years (38.1 %). Furthermore, the proportion of male participants was 70.9 % while the proportion of female participants was 29.1 %. Moreover, results reveals that the bachelor's degree was the level of education of the majority of the participants, although a small percentage of participants (11.2 %) were educated to postgraduate level. Due to these participant statistics, the research data may have been somewhat biased in favour of young adults with a good level of education. Nonetheless, the data are not erroneous, as this section of the demographic is the one that is dominating current and future demand, and therefore should be prioritised by web developers.

In order to make it as easy as possible for the participants to evaluate the features and functions of the tool, the Likert scale (Fig. 6) has been employed. Results showed that there were positive reactions to every main feature (A–L, as indicated in Table 1). Most participants gave the features a rating of no less than four, with a standard deviation of 0.46–0.51 and mean value of 4.47–4.69; this suggests that the features of the tool were considered by the participants to be practical. Overall, then, the user model tool can be classified as 'useful', because all scores were greater than three. In addition, the Cronbach's Alpha score is $0.91 \in [\geq 0.9]$, meaning that the reliability of the psychometric test is excellent [33]. However, despite the general positive welcome, some features proved to be more popular than others with the participants. Thus, 'Saving Information in XML as Export Format' and the 'Facebook Login Process' were the features with the highest level of overall popularity, whilst on the other hand, 'Match User Characteristic with Stereotype' and 'Modifying existing Stereotype' were the features that enjoyed less popularity. This may have been due to the fact that the intended function of these features was not understood clearly by the participants (especially terms such as 'stereotype'). Nevertheless, the less popular features are still considered very useful, because all of them received a score higher than four. Consequently, hypotheses H6a and H7 are validated by these results, highlighting not only the usefulness of the input and output mechanisms of the user model tool, but also the usefulness and relevance of user stereotypes associated with advertisements suggestion.

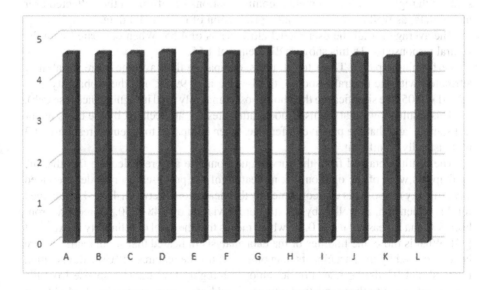

Fig. 6. Usefulness for features (Ox axis detailed in Table 1).

There was wide agreement among the participants with regard to the idea that, in order to select suitable advertisements that are compatible with their profile and preferences, every user model attribute should be collected. As can be seen in Fig. 7, the participants classified the attributes of the user model as either useful or very useful, which has been confirmed by their mean score of 4.46–4.68 and the standard deviation of 0.47–0.51. In addition, the Cronbach's Alpha score is $0.92 \in [\geq 0.9]$, meaning that the reliability of the psychometric test is excellent [33]. However, two attributes of the user model were considered to be more useful than the others, and those were "Education Level" and "Bandwidth", both of which received extremely high ratings. To a certain degree, therefore, hypotheses H1 and H2 are confirmed by these results, as they argued in favour of the utility of the attributes of the proposed user model for advertisement suggestion. On the other hand, there were two attributes that were associated with notably low scores, and these attributes were 'Get Software Used Automatically' and 'Getting Last 10 Sequences of Clicks for Each User'. In spite of scoring low, these two attributes still had scores higher than four. Furthermore, one potential explanation as to why these attributes were unpopular among the participants may be the fact that the participants were made anxious by the idea of their behaviour and activities being monitored. As a result, the attributes were not deemed to be of paramount importance, although their utility was nevertheless acknowledged. Thus, hypotheses H2 (computed from all user model attributes), H3 (computed from generated user model attributes: 13–16 in Table 2) are validated by these results. H5 needs to be analysed from tracking data, from the sequence of clicking on advertisements. Monitoring of the order in which users carry out their activities when making use of the system is an effective way of anticipating what kind of advertisements the users prefer [34]. Moreover, engine decisions with regard to advertisement recommendations benefit from the collected user model data, as well as from automatic production of user model data.

The average for all the user model attributes is of 4.55. When compared with the neutral response (of 3), this shows a difference of 1.55.

Performing a paired T-test for all users, comparing their average score for all user attributes, with the neutral response, the T-value is of 99.29, and the probability is of $0.0001 < 0.05$ (the significance threshold most commonly used in significance research).

This result shows that the user model attributes are appreciated by the users in our test sample, and that the positive difference, when compared to a neutral response of 3 is statistically significant.

The results obtained from the survey questionnaire also revealed the fact that the participants were of the opinion that no feature of the proposed user model presented any difficulty of use. This was confirmed by the mean scores between 4.46–4.63 attained for this dimension, as well as by the standard deviation of 0.48–0.50. Moreover, Cronbach's Alpha for ease of use is 0.90, which means that the level of reliability is excellent [33]. What is more, the findings of the data analysis indicated that some features were better received by the participants than others. Thus, the features of 'User Registration Process' and 'Updating User Profile' enjoyed a highly favourable response from the participants; on the other hand, the features of 'Adding own Stereotype' and 'Modifying existing Stereotype' were less favourably looked upon by the participants. Hence, these findings serve to confirm hypotheses H7 and H8, which put forth the argument that the advertisement recommendations were suitable and did not pose any obstacle to use.

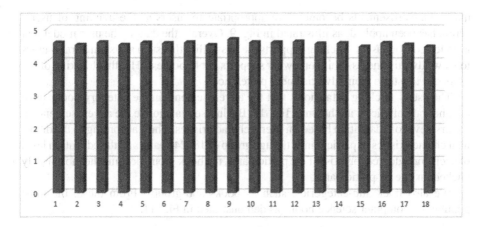

Fig. 7. Usefulness for UM attributes (Ox axis detailed in Table 2).

It must be noted that, despite being less well-received by the participants, the latter two features still scored above four, meaning that they are not difficult to use. On the whole, the ease of use of the user model tool is supported by the results of the analysis of the survey data (Fig. 8).

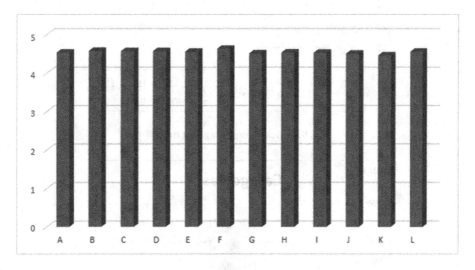

Fig. 8. Ease of use for features (Ox axis detailed in Table 1).

5.4   User Tracking

The survey questionnaire explains that during tracking user's actions, the number of clicks is increased with increasing the time of system usage. This information can reflects the predilections of the use for our system with time progress. Thus, we can conclude that the advertisements become more appropriate for users as the tracking of user's action has been applied, as illustrated in Fig. 9. Overall, the data in the user model that is collected from users' tracking supports the possibility that such a system attracts users to view advertisements. This somewhat supports out hypothesis H5, that tracking of the users can illustrate their advertisement preferences.

The users' tracking data shows that the advertisements in the category books have a higher rate of clicks, as shown in Fig. 10. Businesses categorise the advertisements in the first level of adaptation based on user's characteristics. Thus, according to the dominant characteristics of participants, the age group of 18–24 years, and the education level of bachelor's degree for most of the participants, the book group become the most highly clicked on one by participants.

We also track sub-categories, such as books sub-groups. From these, the most popular are computer science books as demonstrated in Fig. 11.

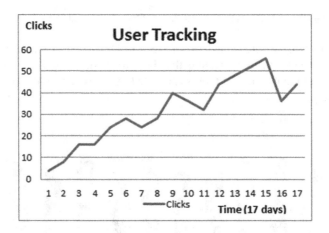

Fig. 9. Clicks progress against time.

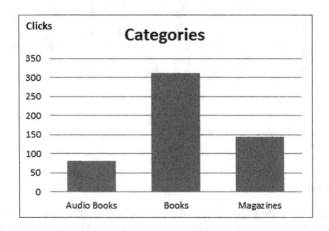

Fig. 10. Number of clicks for different groups.

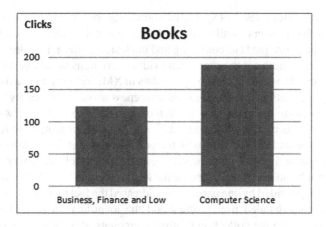

Fig. 11. Number of clicks for books sub-groups.

5.5 Participant Feedback

In addition to the questions that were designed to shed light on the participants' views with regard to the various features and functions of the user model tool, the survey questionnaire also included a section in which the participants were requested to provide feedback about the tool, so as to help identify the dimensions that required improvement. Such feedback was considered to be an essential part of the study, due to the fact that it assisted in the resolution of any emerging problems with the system, and therefore it aided in increasing the performance of the user model tool. Thus, important insight and recommendations were derived from the feedback provided by the participants. As remarked by a number of participants, the expansion of the scope of targeted campaigns could be achieved through the diversification of the spectrum of hobbies and leisure activities supplied by the tool in the form of features. Meanwhile, other participants expressed their satisfaction with the feature for Facebook login, which most web-authoring applications have incorporated. The great usefulness of such a feature resides in the fact that it not only supports the user model becoming better integrated with other web-based systems, but it also makes the model more functional and easy to use, since users can gain access to a range of different applications by entering their identification details only a single time. To some degree, these findings are in line with hypothesis H4, which maintained that advertisement recommendations could draw on the source of user data that is supplied by platforms of social networking. An additional suggestion of relevance that was made by one participant was that the model tool should not specify age in letters but in numbers. On the other hand, no remarks with regard to potential improvements that could be brought to the tool were made by some participants, although they did express their agreement that such research is necessary and significant, particularly as online marketing systems and tactics are constantly being innovated and transformed. On the basis of such feedback, it can be inferred that the user model tool should be amended so as to become not so much a highly technical process that cannot be used without a certain level of specialist knowledge, but more of a mechanism that is easily accessible to users in all aspects. Meanwhile, calculation of bandwidth was reported by some participants as confusing and unclear; therefore, in order to be able to better monitor bandwidth for the users, bandwidth restrictions should be automatically taken into account. In addition, the storage of data in XML rather than in a database was questioned by one participant, which raised awareness about the necessity to provide a clear explanation as to the manner in which the transfer of XML data between various programmes can be achieved without any difficulty. To some extent, these results serve to validate hypotheses H6a and H6b, which argued in favour of the usefulness and ease of use of the input and output processes of the user model tool. Moreover, the system can be easily run by all users, regardless of the level of system knowledge they possess.

The feedback provided by one participant addressed the fact that the creation of more comprehensive and detailed user profiles and the identification of particular target groups of users require the collection of greater amounts of demographic data. Along similar lines, a different participant recommended that the tool should be diversified through the introduction of a larger range of dimensions and the formulation of more clear-cut rules with the purpose of devising marketing strategies of higher efficiency. However, despite the fact that all the feedback provided by the participants was relevant and helpful, care should be exercised when taking these recommendations on board, since the aim was the creation of a user model characterised by flexibility, ease of use, applicability, and transferability. Careful implementation of suggestions is essential, as previous experience with adaptive hypermedia has proven that confusion and lack of clarity may be exacerbated rather than diminished by the addition of more features. One solution to this that was put forth within the setting of adaptive education [35] is to enable users to customise and adapt the different features in accordance with their needs as well as their experience and understanding of adaptive processes and systems. In addition, it is important to remember that the purpose of this study is not to formulate related strategies but to create a user model. Last but not least, with respect to interface and usability, one participant observed that the user interface of the system needs to be made more appealing and attractive; it cannot be doubted that improving the aesthetic appearance of the user interface would have a positive impact on users' attitudes and responses, but it does not represent a priority in the current phase of the research process.

On the basis of the findings obtained in this study, it is argued that, by relying on a range of pre-established demographic characteristics and rules, the proposed user model tool could enhance the precision of advertisement targeting and therefore boost business sales and profitability. Adaptive advertising systems could be made more portable by the proposed user model, which is compatible with any website. Thus, hypotheses H9 and H10 regarding the ease of incorporation of the user model tool in any JSP website hold true. Furthermore, the tool could not only help existing systems to expand, but also supply the flexibility needed by businesses to achieve advertisement customisation whilst eliminating the necessity of current model revamping. Additionally, the model could allow websites to request a method that can be found in a particular location on those websites, whilst at the same time organising and amending all the advertisements on a specific page with the help of a single code and in conformance with established adaptation rules [36] as well as maintaining a record of the advertisements that have been shown and accessed by users. To some degree, these aspects are in agreement with, and therefore validate, hypothesis H11, which maintained that stereotypes could be easily comprehended, applied and updated by all administrators of websites.

6 Discussion

As stated in the above hypotheses, the of the user model structure introduced is considered suitable for advertisements by the participants to the study, who agree that it can be constructed and used in an easy way. The most popular features were the portability, and thus the lightweight structure of the data representation, in terms of export facility in XML, and the multi-system login facility, as well as connection with social networks, via the introduction of the social networks login. Importantly, users considered that the user characteristics that are collected by the proposed user model positively affect the selection of the appropriate advertisements for them. Moreover, the additional user model information that is obtained by tracking the users positively affects and enhances the delivery of appropriate advertisements.

Courses, multimedia, and advertising, among others, can all be adapted for users by many adaptation systems designed for this purpose. Indeed, ADE, ADROSA, ADWIZ, MyAds, and more recent MyAds are all examples of adaptive systems. ADWIZ [13] possesses a trivial user model structure. It relies only on search keywords supplied by a user to a search engine. Similarly, MyAds [14] possesses a trivial user model structure since a receptor component receive the user profiles (no storage for data) through several means, including wireless, and evaluates which content should actually be allocated to which displays. The AdROSA system depends on the categorisation of web banners for groups, based on similarities between individuals, it only processes a minimum of data about users, from the local session, to categorise them, so as such, it is also a relatively trivial user model. Such trivial implementations for the user model don't allow for enough information to make useful decisions about recommending the appropriate advertisements to users. The user model in these three systems represents short-term interests, since it uses fixed static characteristics of the users, like search words. The design of the user model in AEADS is attained by separating it into four components, in order to make the adaptation process easier and reusable. The user's data is arranged as three components: user's data, behaviour data, and social data. This type of construction and the permanency of data support allows the system to predict not only short-term, but also long-term, for future sessions, the desired advertisements that will be relevant to users, based on businesses rules. The future advertisement is the fourth component that contains advertisements that will be shown in the future, at the next login, to each user.

Another example of an adaptive system, ADE, as a generic adaptive delivery system, supports a rich user model, which runs however in-session only. It often is used to deal with user model parameters such as: how many times a user has visited a concept; the active time spent by the user on each page; and clicks on links, among others. However, the ADE user model is non-persistent between sessions, which is something that was considered essential for the business case. Moreover, ADE runs as a standalone system, which was not considered appropriate for the paradigm used in this research, which needed to allow businesses to use their original websites, enhanced with AEADS features. On the other hand, the user model in the more recently developed, standalone system MyAds [37] contains information concerning the buyers and their viewing history - the ads they have seen. It is initialised by registration process or Facebook login, before being updated by the user's clicking action, to assign a related advertisement to the current user. The users are then able to declare their specific interests, by labelling categories with numbers from 1 to 10. Later on, they can annotate the recommendations, to specify if they would be willing to purchase such items or not.

Overall, in the user model in AEADS all functions of the user model are separated from storage and located within the delivery section of the AEADS system. This separation aims to increase portability and should allow an easy extension of the system, without affecting the system as a whole. AEADS can additionally deal with users that have no identification, as well as with users with identification. AEADS uses two algorithms for each of the two types and, in the case of those users that have no identification, the system starts by showing all advertisements randomly, and then monitoring the user's clicks on each advertisement, in order to allow some adaptation. The comparison of the different adaptive systems discussed in this section is summarise.

Table 3. User model in different systems.

System	Purpose	UM Size	UM Initialisation	UM Structure	UM Maintenance	UM Implementation
AEADS	Advertisement	Short - Term Long - Term	Social Login – Registration - Automatically	4 components represent levels of information	Modifier Engines Separated in Delivery model	Inference Engines Separated in Delivery model
ADE	Courses	Short - Term	Registration	Any user data (variable-value)	Presentation handler	Adaptation engine
AdROSA	Advertisement	Short - Term	Automatically	vectors database	Web (ad) usage mining	Web (ad) content mining
ADWIZ	Advertisement	Short - Term	Get only recent activity – search word	Trivial-search word	---	Ad server
MyAds	Advertisement	Short - Term	Automatically	Trivial - receptors	----	Information Processing Component
recent MyAds	Advertisement	Short - Term Long - Term	Social Login – Registration -	2 components represent users and companies	----	Ads Contents Manager on server side

7   Conclusions and Future Work

In this paper, a lightweight user modelling approach has been proposed. It could help Internet users to register to any web-based e-commerce system, and thus help companies' access their target audience more directly, by tailoring their marketing campaigns towards specific consumer demographics and focusing their advertisements on users who satisfy a predetermined range of criteria. Based on the outcome of theoretical considerations and practical testing, a minimum set of user model dimensions have been validated. The evaluation results indicate that the initial functionality and usability of the small prototype system is promising. Further modifications are planned, based on the suggestions offered by survey respondents. The user modelling tool can be refined further, by taking into account user feedback and creating a lightweight adaptive system that is more customisable, and based on the needs and preferences of Internet users. As an immediate next step, in our follow-up studies, the delivery engine has been implemented, which is resident on the same website server, to deliver the advertisements to Internet users. This part parses the contents in the XML file and uses adaptation strategies to send the appropriate advertisements to the appropriate user, based on their user model.

References

1. Internet Advertising Bureau: Internet Advertising Revenues Report 2012 full year results (2012)
2. Halasz, F., Schwartz, M., Grønbæk, K., Trigg, R.H.: The Dexter hypertext reference model. Commun. ACM **37**, 30–39 (1994)
3. De Bra, P., Houben, G.-J., Wu, H.: AHAM: a Dexter-based reference model for adaptive hypermedia. In: Proceedings of the Tenth ACM Conference on Hypertext and Hypermedia: Returning to our Diverse Roots: Returning to our Diverse Roots, pp. 147–156. ACM (1999)
4. Cristea, A.I., de Mooij, A.: LAOS: layered WWW AHS authoring model and their corresponding algebraic operators. In: WWW 2003 (The Twelfth International World Wide Web Conference), Alternate Track on Education, Budapest, Hungary (2003)
5. Brusilovsky, P.: Adaptive hypermedia: an attempt to analyze and generalize. In: Brusilovsky, P., Kommers, P., Streitz, N. (eds.) MHVR 1994. LNCS, vol. 1077, pp. 288–304. Springer, Heidelberg (1996)
6. Kobsa, A., Koenemann, J., Pohl, W.: Personalised hypermedia presentation techniques for improving online customer relationships. Knowl. Eng. Rev. **16**, 111–155 (2001)
7. Brusilovsky, P., Millán, E.: User models for adaptive hypermedia and adaptive educational systems. In: Brusilovsky, P., Kobsa, A., Nejdl, W. (eds.) Adaptive Web 2007. LNCS, vol. 4321, pp. 3–53. Springer, Heidelberg (2007)
8. Bra, P.D., Calvi, L.: AHA! An open adaptive hypermedia architecture. New Rev. Hypermedia Multimedia **4**, 115–139 (1998)
9. Stash, N., De Bra, P., Cristea, A.: Adaptation to learning styles in a general-purpose system AHA! (Adaptive Hypermedia Architecture). In: Educational Technology & Society, vol. 11 (2008)
10. Smits, D., De Bra, P.: GALE: a highly extensible adaptive hypermedia engine. In: Proceedings of ACM-CHH, pp. 63–72 (2011)

11. Scotton, J., Stewart, C., Cristea, A.I.: ADE: the adaptive display environment for adaptive hypermedia. In: Proceedings of the ACM Hypertext 2011 International Conference, Eindhoven, The Netherlands (2011)
12. Kazienko, P., Adamski, M.: AdROSA—Adaptive personalization of web advertising. Inf. Sci. **177**, 2269–2295 (2007)
13. Langheinrich, M., Nakamura, A., Abe, N., Kamba, T., Koseki, Y.: Unintrusive customization techniques for Web advertising. Comput. Netw. **31**, 1259–1272 (1999)
14. Di Ferdinando, A., Rosi, A., Lent, R., Manzalini, A., Zambonelli, F.: MyAds: A system for adaptive pervasive advertisements. Pervasive Mob. Comput. **5**, 385–401 (2009)
15. Brailsford, T.J., Choo, B.S., Davies, P.M.C., Moore, A., Stewart, C.D., Zakaria, M.R.: Web-based hierarchical universal reactive learning environment (WHURLE): an overview (White Paper for the WHURLE Project) (2001)
16. Mérida, D., Fabregat, R., Marzo, J.-L.: SHAAD: adaptable, adaptive and dynamic hypermedia system for content delivery. In: Workshop on Adaptive Systems for Web Based Education, WASWE 2002. Citeseer, Málaga España (2002)
17. www.google.com/adsense/
18. Davis, H.: Google Advertising Tools: Cashing in with AdSense, AdWords, and the Google APIs. O'Reilly Media Inc., Sebastopol (2006)
19. http://w3techs.com/technologies/overview/advertising/all
20. Kobsa, A.: Generic user modeling systems. In: Brusilovsky, P., Kobsa, A., Nejdl, W. (eds.) Adaptive Web 2007. LNCS, vol. 4321, pp. 136–154. Springer, Heidelberg (2007)
21. Al Qudah, D.A., Cristea, A.I., Shi, L., Al-Sayyed, R.M.H., Obeidah, A.: MyAds: a social adaptive system for online advertisement from hypotheses to implementation. In: Proceeding of the International Conference on e-Business and e-Government (ICBG 2014), Zurich, Switzerland, pp. 154–160 (2014)
22. Faust, K.: Very local structure in social networks. Sociol. Methodol. **37**, 209–256 (2007)
23. TheStatisticsPortal.: Number of monthly active Facebook users worldwide 2008–2014, http://www.statista.com/statistics/264810/number-of-monthly-active-facebook-users-worldwide/. Accessed 10 September 2015
24. Hof, R.D.: Facebook's new Ad model: You. FORBES **188**, 106-+ (2011)
25. Cristea, A.I.: What can the semantic web do for adaptive educational hypermedia? Educ. Technol. Soc. **7**, 40–58 (2004)
26. Wu, H.: A reference architecture for adaptive hypermedia applications. Technische Universiteit Eindhoven (2002)
27. http://www.rci.rutgers.edu/~cfs/472_html/Planning/PlanRecog.html
28. Benaki, E., Karkaletsis, V.A., Spyropoulos, C.D.: Integrating user modeling into information extraction: the UMIE prototype. In: Jameson, A., Paris, C., Tasso, C. (eds.) User Modeling, vol. 97, pp. 55–57. International Centre for Mechanical Sciences. Springer, Heidelberg(1997)
29. Qaffas, A., Cristea, A.: How to create an E-Advertising domain model: the AEADS approach. In: The 2014 International Conference on e-Learning, e-Business, Enterprise Information Systems, and e-Government (EEE 2014), Las Vegas, USA (2014)
30. Qaffas, A.A., Cristea, A.I.: How to create an E-Advertising adaptation strategy: the AEADS approach. In: Hepp, M., Hoffner, Y. (eds.) EC-Web 2014. LNBIP, vol. 188, pp. 171–178. Springer, Heidelberg (2014)
31. Benaki, E., Karkaletsis, A., Spyropoulos, D.: User modeling in WWW: the UMIE prototype. In: Proceedings of the Workshop Adaptive Systems and User Modeling on the World Wide Web, 6th International Conference on User Modelling UM, vol. 97 (1997)
32. McIver, J., Carmines, E.G.: Unidimensional Scaling. Sage, Beverly Hills (1981)

33. Gliem, J.A., Gliem, R.R.: Calculating, interpreting, and reporting Cronbach's alpha reliability coefficient for Likert-type scales. In: Midwest Research-to-Practice Conference in Adult, Continuing, and Community Education (2003)
34. Kazienko, P., Adamski, M.: Personalized web advertising method. In: De Bra, P.M.E., Nejdl, W. (eds.) AH 2004. LNCS, vol. 3137, pp. 146–155. Springer, Heidelberg (2004)
35. De Bra, P., Smits, D., Van Der Sluijs, K., Cristea, A., Hendrix, M.: GRAPPLE: personalization and adaptation in learning management systems. In: World Conference on Educational Multimedia, Hypermedia and Telecommunications, vol. 2010, pp. 3029–3038 (2010)
36. Stash, N., Cristea, A.I., De Bra, P.: Adaptation languages as vehicles of explicit intelligence in adaptive hypermedia. Int. J. Continuing Eng. Educ. Life Long Learn. **17**, 319–336 (2007)
37. Al Qudah, D.A., Cristea, A.I., Hadzidedic, S., AL-Saqqa, S., Rodan, A., Yang, W.: Personalized E-advertisement experience: recommending user targeted Ads. In: 12th International Conference on e-Business Engineering, Bejing, China (2015)

Optical Communication Systems

How Do the Multiple Tunable Receivers Per Node Affect the Efficiency of a WDM LAN? A Performance Analytical Study

Peristera A. Baziana[✉]

School of Electrical and Computer Engineering,
National Technical University of Athens, Athens, Greece
baziana@central.ntua.gr

Abstract. In this study, the performance of a WDM LAN of passive star topology is explored. An effective synchronous transmission WDMA protocol is proposed that employs a pre-transmission reservation scheme in order to improve the system output. Each station is equipped with a network interface with more than one tunable receivers in order to be able to receive more than one data packets during a time frame. As a results, the average probability of packet rejection at destination is significantly reduced as compared with the single tunable receiver per station case. The system performance is mathematically modelled based on Poisson statistics and finite station population. Also, an analytical framework is adopted to evaluate the effect of the number of tunable receivers per station on the total performance. Numerical results are comparatively studied for various numbers of data channels and stations. Finally, the propagation delay latency parameter is properly modelled while its impact on the system performance is analytically evaluated.

Keywords: Wavelength division multiple access · Multiple tunable receivers · Rejection probability

1 Introduction

In modern optical high-speed networks, the Wavelength Division Multiplexing (WDM) [1] technique has been mainly preferred and used by network engineers in order to divide the inefficient high fiber data rate into multiple parallel channels of lower data rates. Different WDM access (WDMA) schemes suitable for optical networks have been studied in literature and implemented in real world aiming to improve the total system performance, by increasing the total throughput and reducing the total delay and rejection probability.

It is obvious that in WDM networks, apart from the possibility of packets collisions over the WDM channels, another possibility of packets loss arises: this of the receiver collisions [2]. Especially, a receiver collision occurs if a data packet that has been successfully transmitted over a WDM data channel cannot be picked up by the intended destination station since its tunable receiver is currently tuned to another WDM channel to receive a packet from another source station.

© Springer International Publishing Switzerland 2016
M.S. Obaidat and P. Lorenz (Eds.): ICETE 2015, CCIS 585, pp. 161–176, 2016.
DOI: 10.1007/978-3-319-30222-5_8

Although the WDM channel collisions have been extensively studied by means of analysis or simulations in local and metropolitan area networks [1], the receiver collisions evaluation provides complexity overload and for this reason they are usually ignored. Nevertheless, some studies take under consideration the receiver conflicts and provide the performance measures estimation via either analytical or simulation models. For example, the impact of the receiver collisions on synchronous and asynchronous transmission WDMA protocols is analytically examined in [2] assuming Poisson arrivals. In this protocol cases, a dedicated control channel is used to exchange control information prior to the data packets transmissions ibn order to totally avoid the destination conflicts. In [3], the receiver collisions effect on a synchronous transmission WDMA protocol is analytically studied considering Poisson arrivals. In this study, the Multichannel Control Architecture (MCA) is introduced to exchange the appropriate control information aiming to reduce the control loss probability. The use of the MCA is also introduced in [4, 5], where two synchronous transmission WDMA protocols are proposed assuming the receiver collisions effect for different access strategies on the MCA. In these studies, two different analytical Markovian models are extensively adopted for the rigorous analytical performance measures estimation.

In many cases of WDM Metropolitan Area Networks (MANs), the proposed WDMA protocols aim to avoid the receiver collisions in a slight different way. Especially, many WDMA protocols for ring MANs consider that each station around the ring is equipped with a fixed receiver that is always tuned to the dedicated channel for reception [6–10]. Although this assumption aims to face the packet loss due to the receiver collisions, it provides bandwidth consumption since it restricts the transmission of packets destined to a specific destination station over its dedicated reception channel, although there may exist other available channels for transmission in case that it is not currently free. In order to overcome the above drawback and to efficiently exploit the available fiber bandwidth, the use of a set of tunable transmitter and receiver per station is proposed in [11–15], while all WDM channels can be used for both transmission and reception. The transceivers tunability benefits to significantly reduce the dropping probability are given in [16].

It is worth mentioning that most of the proposed studies about the receiver collisions effect in WDM networks performance assume that each station is equipped with a single receiver. Since the recent technology evolutions provide us with reliable tunable receivers whose cost gradually decreases, the utilization of more than one tunable receivers per station appears as a promising implementation to reduce the packet rejection probability. This means that the utilization of a multiple tunable receivers station interface aims to provide essential reduction of packet rejection probability at destination, improving the total throughput and eliminating the total delay.

In this study, we propose a synchronous transmission WDMA protocol that takes under consideration the receiver collisions effect in a single-hop, passive star LAN that interconnects a finite number of stations. The proposed network architecture employs a dedicated control WDM channel for the control information exchange prior to the data packets transmission in order to avoid any data channel collision. Each station is equipped with a network interface that consists of a tunable transmitter and a number x of tunable receivers (TT-TR^x). Thus, each station is capable of receiving at the end of each time frame more than one (and up to x) data packets that have been successfully transmitted over the data channels and are destined to it. In this way, the receiver collisions are effectively faced while essential rejection probability reduction and performance improvement are provided, as compared to the singe tunable receiver per station case.

In this study we provide an analytical framework based on a Poisson arrival process in order to derive the performance measures of the average throughput and the average rejection probability at destination. Numerical results for various numbers of stations and WDM channels are comparatively studied, giving the total performance improvement.

This study extends the similar study of [17]. Especially, in the present study we investigate the effect of the propagation delay latency parameter on the total system performance, by properly modelling and mathematically counting its impact on the throughput achieved evaluation.

The WDMA protocol performance depends on the number of station population, WDM data channels, and tunable receivers. Their variation is extensively studied for the performance measures evaluation.

This study is organized as follows. The network model and the assumptions are described in Sect. 2. In Sect. 3 the system is mathematically modelled and the performance measures are analytically derived. The performance evaluation is given in Sect. 4. Section 5 studies the propagation delay latency effect on the system performance and the average throughput under this consideration is derived. Finally, the conclusion is outlined in Sect. 6. The mathematical study which is referred in Sect. 3, is investigated in the Appendix.

2 Network Model and Assumptions

We assume a passive star network, as in Fig. 1. The total fiber bandwidth is divided into $N + 1$ parallel WDM channels, each operating in a different wavelength $\{\lambda_0, \lambda_1, \ldots \lambda_N\}$. The channel λ_0 is called control channel and it transmits the control packets, while the remaining channels $\{\lambda_1, \lambda_2, \ldots \lambda_N\}$ are called data channels and they transmit the data packets. The passive star coupler interconnects a finite number M of stations $(M > N)$. Each station network interface is equipped with a tunable transmitter and a set of x $(1 \leq x \leq N)$ tunable receivers that can be tuned to all channels $\{\lambda_0, \lambda_1, \ldots \lambda_N\}$, as Fig. 1 shows.

The control packet transmission time is defined as time unit reference and is called control slot or mini-slot. Thus, the data packet transmission time normalized in time units is L and is called data slot $(L > 1)$. The control packet consists of the source address, the destination address and the data channel λ_k that belongs to the set of $\{\lambda_1, \lambda_2, \ldots \lambda_N\}$ and has been chosen for the corresponding data packet transmission. Both control and data channels use the same time reference which we call frame. We define as frame the time interval that includes N time units for the control packets transmissions plus the normalized data packet transmission time L, as Fig. 2 depicts. Thus, the frame time duration F_d is:

$$F_d = (N + L) \text{ time units} \tag{1}$$

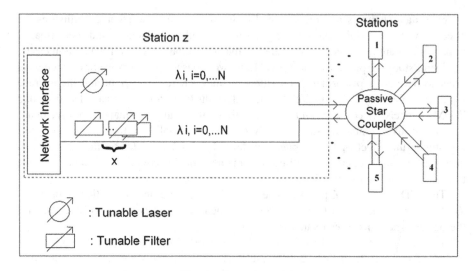

Fig. 1. Network model.

We assume a common clock to all stations. Time axis is divided into contiguous frames of equal length and stations are synchronized for transmission over the control and data channels during a frame. Each frame consists of the control and the data phase, as Fig. 2 shows. The control phase consists of N time units, while the control packets transmissions occur. The data phase that follows lasts for L time units, while the data packets transmissions take place. At the beginning of a frame data phase, each station is able to transmit at a given wavelength λ_T and simultaneously receive from a set of wavelengths $\{\lambda_{R1}, \lambda_{R2,...} \lambda_{Rx}\}$. Finally, in our analysis we assume that the tunable transceivers have negligible tuning time and very large tuning range.

We assume that each station is equipped with a buffer with capacity of one data packet. If the buffer is empty the station is said to be free, otherwise it is backlogged. Packets are collectively generated in a Poisson stream. If a station is backlogged and generates a new packet, the packet is lost. Finally, the aggregated traffic from new generated and retransmitted packets obeys Poisson statistics.

The successfully transmitted data packets are uniformly distributed among the M stations, each randomly selected with equal probability (for the sake of generality we suppose that a station may send to and receive from itself). Thus, if more than x successfully transmitted over different data channels packets are destined to the same destination, the destination is able to receive only x packets of them with its tunable receivers and rejects all the others. This phenomenon is called receiver collision.

Access Scheme. At the beginning of each frame, each station tunes one of its tunable receivers to the control channel λ_0 in order to monitor the control packets transmissions from all stations during the control phase. Also at the beginning of each frame, if it has to send a data packet to another, first it tunes its tunable transmitter to the control channel λ_0. Then, it chooses randomly one of the data channels over which the data

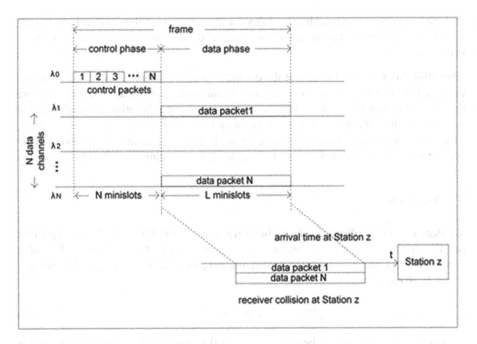

Fig. 2. Frame structure.

packet will be transmitted, let's say data channel i. Then, it informs the other stations about the i-th data channel selection, by transmitting a control packet during the i-th control mini-slot of the control phase with its tunable transmitter. The control packets from all stations compete according to the Slotted Aloha scheme to gain access over the N control mini-slots. Since the station continuously monitors the control channel with its tunable receiver during the control phase, by the end of this time period it is informed about the outcome of its control packet transmission. This means that, grace to the broadcast nature of the control channel, the station is aware of the data channel claims for transmission of all stations. Especially if one or more other stations have selected the same i-th data channel for transmission, the corresponding control packets have collided during the i-th control mini-slot and are all aborted, while all involved stations become backlogged. In the contrary if the station control packet has been successfully transmitted over the i-th control mini-slot, the station gains access to the i-th data channel for successful transmission during the frame data phase. This fact does not mean that the corresponding data packet will be correctly received by the destination. This fact depends on the number of the other data packets that are successfully transmitted over other data channels during the data phase and have the same destination. In this case, the destination station may receive up to x data packets with its tunable receivers, while the corresponding source stations become free. It is evident that the destination station aborts all the others packets destined to it due to the receiver collisions phenomenon, while the relative stations become backlogged.

We may consider several arbitration rules for the selection of the data packets that are finally correctly received by the destination while the others are aborted, such as priority etc.

Reception Scheme. At the end of the control phase, the station is informed about the data packets that will be successfully transmitted over the N data channels and are destined to it. Based on this information and the above arbitration rules, the station decides which of these data packets it is going to receive, let's say z ($z \leq x$) of them. Thus at the beginning of the frame data phase, it tunes z of its tunable receivers to the corresponding data channels while the data packets reception immediately starts.

3   Analysis

We denote as G the offered load, i.e. the average number of transmitted control packets per time unit on the control channel. According to [18], the probability P_{suc} of a successful data packet transmission over the data channel j ($j = 1,2,..., N$) during a frame is given by:

$$P_{suc} = Ge^{-G} \tag{2}$$

Let S_N be a random variable representing the number of successful data packet transmissions over the N data channels during a frame, $0 \leq S_N \leq N$.

The probability $\Pr[S_N = s]$ of finding s successfully transmitted data packets over the N data channels during a frame conforms to the binomial probability law and is given in [2]:

$$\Pr[S_N = s] = \binom{N}{s} P_{suc}^s (1 - P_{suc})^{N-s} \tag{3}$$

Also, let $A_N(s)$ be the number of the correctly received data packets at destination given that s successful transmissions over the N data channels occurred during a frame, $1 \leq A_N(s) \leq S_N$ for $S_N > 0$.

The probability $\Pr[A_N(s) = r]$ of finding r correctly received data packets at destination from s successful transmissions over the N data channels during a frame is given by (see the Appendix):

$$\Pr[A_N(s) = r] = \sum_{allsets} \frac{M!s!}{M^s \prod_{i=0}^{s} k_i! \prod_{z=1}^{s} (z!)^{k_z}} \tag{4}$$

where: the sets of integers $\{k_0, k_1, k_2, \ldots, k_M\}$ $i, k_i \in \{0, 1, 2, \ldots, M\}$ are defined in the Appendix.

Thus, the probability $S_{rc}(r)$ of finding r correctly received data packets at destination during a frame in steady state is given by:

$$S_{rc}(r) = \sum_{s=r}^{min(M,N)} \Pr[S_N = s] \Pr[A_N(s) = r] \tag{5}$$

It is obvious that:

$$min(s,x) \le r \le min(s, Mx) \tag{6}$$

We define the throughput S_{rc} as the average number of correctly received data packets at destination during a frame in steady state. Thus:

$$S_{rc} = \sum_{r=1}^{min(M,N)} r S_{rc}(r) \tag{7}$$

Also, we define the average rejection probability at destination P_{rej} in steady state, as the ratio of the average number of data packets rejected at destination due to the receiver collisions phenomenon to the average number of successfully transmitted data packets over the N data channels, during a frame. Thus, P_{rej} is given by:

$$P_{rej} = \frac{S - S_{rc}}{S} \tag{8}$$

where: S is the average number of successfully transmitted data packets over the N data channels, during a frame. In other words, S represents the average throughput per frame without the receiver collisions effect and it is given in [18]:

$$S = NP_{suc} \tag{9}$$

while its maximum value S_{max} is provided for offered load $G_{max} = 1$ and is given in [2]:

$$S_{max} = \frac{N}{e}. \tag{10}$$

Finally, we define the normalized system throughput during a frame S_{nor} as:

$$S_{nor} = \frac{L}{F_d} S_{rc}. \tag{11}$$

4 Performance Evaluation

In this section, we study the performance evaluation of the proposed WDMA protocol. For the numerical results, we consider that the data packet length is $L = 100$ time units.

Figure 3 illustrates the normalized throughput S_{nor} versus the offered load G for $M = 50$ stations, $N = 3,8,10,13$ data channels for $x = 2$ tunable receivers per station.

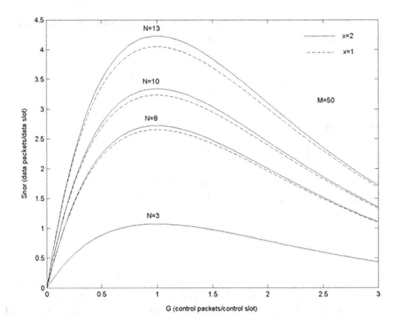

Fig. 3. S_{nor} versus G, for $M = 50$ stations, $N = 3,8,10,13$ data channels and $x = 1, 2$ tunable receivers.

The curves provided are compared with the case of a single tunable receiver per station. Let's study in Fig. 3 the S_{nor} value for $N = 13$ data channels. As it is observed the network configuration with $x = 2$ tunable receivers per station, as it is compared to the single tunable receiver case, provides higher S_{nor} value for a wide range of offered load conditions. Especially for low offered load (lower than $G = 0.2$ control packets/control slot), the S_{nor} values provided in cases of $x = 1, 2$ are almost equal. This is because, in low offered load conditions the number of transmitted control packets over the control slots is low, while the consequent control channel collisions are not few. In this case, the number of successfully transmitted data packets over the N data channels is also low, introducing low number of rejection events at destination. In other words, for low offered load conditions the impact of the receiver collisions phenomenon is not significant, providing almost equal values of throughput. On the contrary, as the offered load increases up to almost $G = 2$ control packets/control slot for values around $G_{max} = 1$ control packets/control slot, the S_{nor} in case of the $x = 2$ is essentially higher than in the $x = 1$ case, while the maximum improvement is reached for $G = G_{max}$. This behavior is explained by the fact that for offered load around the G_{max} value, the system reaches maximum number of successfully transmitted data packets over the N data channels. Thus, under these offered load conditions the number of data packets that are distributed to the M destination stations is maximum, providing higher number of rejection events at destination. Thus, the utilization of $x = 2$ instead of $x = 1$ tunable receivers per station provides maximum throughput improvement, as it is observed in Fig. 3. For high offered load conditions (higher than $G = 2$ control packets/control slot), the throughput values for $x = 1, 2$ are almost equal. This is because, for this offered load the number of control channel collisions are getting higher, while the probability of a successful data packet transmission over the N data channels is getting lower. This is the reason why the impact of the receiver collisions phenomenon on the system throughput decreases too, while the use of higher number of tunable receivers per station (from $x = 1$ to $x = 2$) does not seem to improve the throughput achieved.

Also, the above behavior is noticed for $N = 10$ and $N = 8$. Thus, in Fig. 3 it is shown that the S_{nor} maximum improvement provided by the utilization of $x = 2$ instead of $x = 1$ tunable receivers per station occurs for $G = G_{max}$, while it is analogous to the value of N. This means that as the number N of data channels decreases, the S_{nor} for $G = G_{max}$ decreases too. This can be understood since, as the N value decreases the number of successfully transmitted data packets over the N data channels decreases too, providing lower rejections at destination due to the receiver collisions. Consequently, the exploitation of more tunable receivers per station is not able to provide higher throughput values, as the number N decreases. This behavior can be representatively noticed when $N = 3$, where the probability of a control channel collision is extremely high providing almost zero probability of a receiver collision. This is the reason why, the S_{nor} values for $x = 1, 2$ tunable receivers per station are equal. The above remarks are validated by studying the S_{nor} improvement when increasing the number of tunable receivers per station from $x = 1$ to $x = 2$. For example for $G = 1.6$ control packets/control slot, the S_{nor} increases about: 0.65 % for $N = 3$, 2.25 % for $N = 8$, 2.89 % for $N = 10$, and 3.84 % for $N = 13$.

In Fig. 4 the average rejection probability P_{rej} versus the offered load G is shown, for $M = 50$ stations, $N = 8,10,13$ data channels for $x = 2$ tunable receivers per station, while

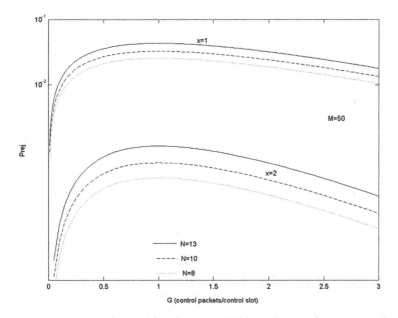

Fig. 4. P_{rej} versus G, for $N = 3,8,10,13$ data channels, $M = 50$ stations and $x = 1, 2$ tunable receivers.

the curves are compared with the case of a single tunable receiver per station. The previous results are validated in Fig. 4. Particularly, it is illustrated that the increase of the number of tunable receivers per station from $x = 1$ to $x = 2$ provides significant P_{rej} reduction that reaches almost 100 % in a wide range of offered load values, while it obtains its maximum value when $G = G_{max}$. Also, it is remarkable that the P_{rej} reduction is a decreasing function of N. This is understood since as N increases for a given number of stations, the probability of a destination conflict increases too, as previously described. As a direct result, the utilization of more tunable receivers per station provides lower rejection probability. For example, for $G = 1$ control packets/control slot, the P_{rej} reduction when increasing the number of tunable receivers per station from $x = 1$ to $x = 2$, is: 98.5 % for $N = 8$, 98 % for $N = 10$, and 97.3 % for $N = 13$.

The proposed protocol performance is studying in Fig. 5, when the station population varies. Especially, Fig. 5 depicts the average rejection probability P_{rej} versus the offered load G for $N = 13$ data channels, $M = 50,100,150$ stations for $x = 2$ tunable receivers per station, while the curves are compared with the case of a single tunable receiver per station. As in Fig. 4, the utilization of $x = 2$ instead of $x = 1$ tunable receivers per station provides essential P_{rej} reduction that becomes maximum when $G = G_{max}$, while it is almost 100 % in the whole offered load range. As Fig. 5 illustrates, P_{rej} reduction is an increasing function of M for finite number of N. This is because, as M increases the offered load to the control channel is getting higher. This means that the probability of control channel collisions increases, while consequently the number of successfully transmitted packets that are distributed to the destination stations is getting lower. This is the reason why, the P_{rej} reduction provided by the high number

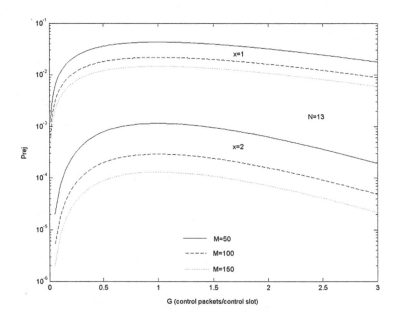

Fig. 5. P_{rej} versus G, for $M = 50,100,150$ stations, $N = 13$ data channels and $x = 1, 2$ tunable receivers.

of tunable receivers utilization increases as the station population increases. For example, for $G = 1$ control packets/control slot, the P_{rej} reduction when increasing the number of tunable receivers per station from $x = 1$ to $x = 2$, is: 97.3 % for $M = 50$, 98.4 % for $M = 100$, and 99.1 % for $M = 150$.

It is obvious that in each network implementation, the determination of the number of tunable receivers per station has to take under consideration the desired performance level achieved (in terms of P_{rej}) in conjunction with the implementation cost. Figure 6 illustrates the rejection probability maximum value $P_{rej-max}$ for various numbers of stations M and data channels N, in the cases of number of tunable receivers per station $x = 2, 3$. As expected, the increase of x from 2 to 3 provides significant performance improvement. For example for $N = 13$, the $P_{rej-max}$ reduction when increasing from $x = 2$ to $x = 3$ is: 98.2 % for $M = 50$, 98.9 % for $M = 100$, and 99.4 % for $M = 150$. In other words, the $P_{rej-max}$ reduction is an increasing function of M. This is because as M increases for fixed N, the probability of a receiver collision decreases, fact that becomes noticeable with the concurrent increase of x. Similar, for $M = 50$, the $P_{rej-max}$ reduction when increasing from $x = 2$ to $x = 3$ is: 99.1 % for $N = 8$, 98.5 % for $N = 10$, and 98.2 % for $N = 13$. This behavior is an immediate result of the above discussion. It is obvious that $P_{rej} = 0$ when $N = 3$ and $x = 3$, since there is no receiver collisions probability.

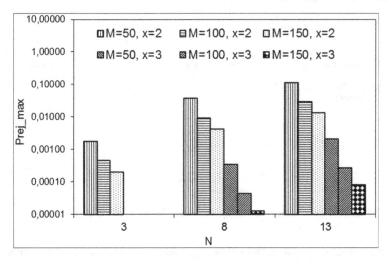

Fig. 6. $P_{rej-max}$, for $N = 3,8,13$ data channels, $M = 50,100,150$ stations, and $x = 1, 2$ tunable receivers.

5 Propagation Delay Latency Modelling

In this section, we study the effect of the propagation delay latency parameter on the system performance. In the previous sections, we modelled the system operation and we analytically derived the performance measures considering that the propagation delay latency for a packet transmission between two stations is negligible. It is obvious that this assumption is not correct in real world, since it ignores the key role that the propagation delay parameter plays to the high-speed WDM networks performance.

Thus in the followings, we take under consideration the propagation delay latency. Especially, we assume the normalized round trip propagation delay time between two stations and we denote it by R data slots ($R \times L$ time units). Also, in order for our analysis to take under consideration the propagation delay parameter, we properly extend the frame duration modeling it influence as follows: We change the frame definition and we define as frame the time interval that includes N time units for the control packets transmissions followed by the normalized round trip propagation time R and the data packet transmission time. Thus, the frame duration is shown in Fig. 7 and equals to:

$$F_{d\_R} = N + (R+1)L \text{ time units} \tag{12}$$

In order to derive the protocol performance measures taking into consideration the propagation delay latency, we follow the same assumptions like in Sect. 3. It is obvious that the propagation delay parameter affects the frame duration of Eq. (1). As a result, it influences the normalized throughput definition. This is because the normalized throughput is defined as the time percentage that the system is occupied with successful data packets transmissions.

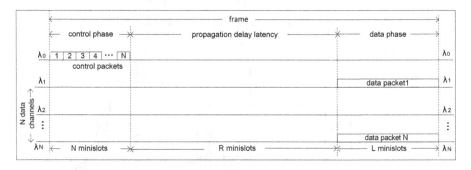

Fig. 7. Frame structure, having modelled the propagation delay latency.

So, the normalized system throughput S_{nor-R} during a frame taking into account the propagation delay latency parameter is defined as:

$$S_{nor-R} = \frac{L}{F_{d\_R}} S_{rc} \tag{13}$$

Figure 8 depicts the normalized throughput S_{nor-R} versus the offered load G for $M = 50$ stations, $N = 3,8,13$ data channels for $x = 2$ tunable receivers per station, while the curves are compared with the case of a single tunable receiver per station. For the numerical solutions, we assumed that $R = 100$ time units. The results about the use of

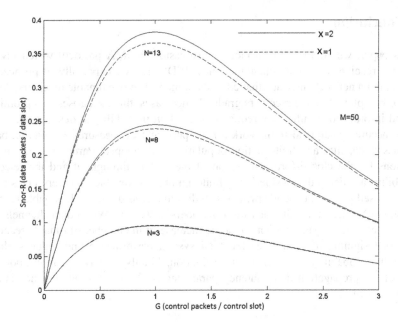

Fig. 8. S_{nor} versus G, for $M = 50$ stations, $N = 3, 8, 13$ data channels and $x = 1, 2$ tunable receivers, taking into account the propagation delay latency.

$x = 2$ instead of $x = 1$ tunable receivers per station are similar to those of Fig. 3 in Sect. 4.

The effect of the propagation delay latency parameter on the normalized throughput is representatively shown by comparing Figs. 3 and 8. Thus, for a dedicated number of data channels N and for the same offered load G, the normalized throughput S_{nor-R} when counting the propagation delay is significantly lower than the normalized throughput S_{nor} when we ignore it. This is a direct result that comes from the study of Eqs. (11) and (13). Especially when the propagation delay latency parameter is taken into account, the frame duration is longer according to Eq. (12), as compared to the frame duration when we ignore it according to Eq. (1). Thus, the normalized throughput S_{nor-R} taking into account the propagation delay latency parameter has lower value, as Eq. (13) shows.

It is remarkable that the normalized throughput S_{nor-R} taking into account the propagation delay is a decreasing function of R, as Eqs. (12) and (13) present. This is because as the R value increases, the frame duration increases too. For this reason, the frame time percentage that the system is occupied with successful data packets transmissions is lower. This fact results to lower normalized throughput S_{nor-R} values.

Finally, it is worth mentioning that the propagation delay latency parameter does not influence the probability of rejection at destination P_{rej}. This comes as a direct result of Eq. (8).

6   Conclusion

In this paper, we study a synchronous transmission WDMA protocol which investigates the receiver collisions phenomenon in WDM LANs. Especially, it proposes at each station a network interface that consists of more than one tunable receivers. As the cost of the optical tunable receivers gradually decreases, this idea arises as a promising method in order to significantly reduce the rejection probability at destination.

An accurate analytical framework for the performance measures evaluation, based on Poisson statistics and finite station population is developed. Particularly, analytical equations for the closed-form estimation of the system throughput and the rejection probability are derived, considering a finite number of tunable receivers per station. The proposed protocol expands previous studies that consider a single tunable receiver per station. Numerical results for various numbers of stations, WDM data channels, and tunable receivers per station depict that the increase of the number of tunable receivers about one significantly improves the total system performance and reduces almost 100 % the probability of conflicts at destination. Finally, an investigation about the effect of the propagation delay latency parameter on the system performance is analytically given.

Appendix

We assume the model that consists of N data channels and M stations. We aim to analytically describe the distribution of the successfully transmitted data packets over the N data channels to the M stations. This model corresponds to the occupancy problem of the distribution of indistinguishable balls (data packets) to cells (destination stations), supposing that the arrangements should have equal probabilities. We consider indistinguishable packets transmitted to indistinguishable destination stations using Maxwell-Boltzman statistics [19].

We are interested in the probability $\Pr[A_N(s) = r]$ of r correctly received data packets at destination when s data packets have been successfully transmitted over the N-channel system, during a time frame, $1 \leq s$.

Let's suppose that each station may transmit to any of the M stations (for the sake of generality we suppose that a station may send to and receive from itself). According to the Maxwell-Boltzman statistics, there are M^s possible arrangements of the s successfully transmitted data packets to the M destination stations, each with equal and constant probability: $1/M^s$.

We consider that the distribution of s data packets to M stations provides the following result by the end of a frame:

- there are k_0 of M destination stations, $k_0 \in \{0, 1, 2, \ldots, M\}$: for each of them there is no successfully transmitted data packet destined to it,
- there are k_1 of M destination stations, $k_1 \in \{0, 1, 2, \ldots, s\}$: for each of them there is 1 successfully transmitted data packet destined to it, and so on. In general,

- there are k_i of M destination stations, $i, k_i \in \{1, 2, \ldots, s\}$: for each of them there are i successfully transmitted data packets destined to it.

It is obvious that:

$$\sum_{i=0}^{s} k_i = M \tag{14}$$

and:

$$\sum_{i=0}^{s} i k_i = s \tag{15}$$

Since each destination station is capable of receiving up to x data packets per frame, it is:

$$\sum_{i=0}^{x-1} i k_i + \sum_{i=x, k_i \neq 0}^{s} i x = r. \tag{16}$$

For each set of integers $\{k_0, k_1, k_2, \ldots, k_M\}$ that satisfy Eqs. (14), (15), and (16) and it is $k_0, k_1, \ldots k_M \in \{0, 1, 2, \ldots, M\}$, the probability P_{ki} that: no data packet is destined to k_0 stations, one data packet is destined to k_1 stations, and so on; and generally, i data packets are destined to k_i stations is given in [20]:

$$P_{ki} = \frac{M! s!}{M^s \prod_{i=0}^{s} k_i! \prod_{z=1}^{s} (z!)^{k_z}}. \tag{17}$$

Thus, the probability $\Pr[A_N(s) = r]$ is defined as the sum of the probabilities P_{ki}, for all possible sets of integers $\{k_0, k_1, k_2, \ldots, k_M\}$ that satisfy Eqs. (14), (15), and (16) and it is $k_0, k_1, \ldots k_M \in \{0, 1, 2, \ldots, M\}$, i.e.:

$$\Pr[A_N(s) = r] = \sum_{\text{allsets}} \frac{M! s!}{M^s \prod_{i=0}^{s} k_i! \prod_{z=1}^{s} (z!)^{k_z}}. \tag{18}$$

References

1. Zheng, J., Mouftah, H.T.: Optical WDM Networks: Concepts and Design Principles. Wiley, IEEE Press, New York (2004)
2. Pountourakis, I.E.: Performance evaluation with receiver collisions analysis in very high-speed optical fiber local area networks using passive star topology. IEEE J. Lightwave Technol. **16**(12), 2303–2310 (1998)

3. Baziana, P.A.: An approximate protocol analysis with performance optimization for WDM. Optical Fiber Technol. **20**(4), 414–421 (2014)
4. Baziana, P.A., Pountourakis, I.E.: Performance optimization with propagation delay analysis in WDM networks. Comput. Commun. **30**(18), 3572–3585 (2007)
5. Baziana, P.A., Pountourakis, I.E.: A transmission strategy with protocol analysis for performance improvement in WDM networks. IEEE Trans. Commun. **60**(7), 1975–1985 (2012)
6. Bengi, K., van As, H.: Efficient QoS support in a slotted multihop WDM metro ring. IEEE J. Select. Areas Commun. **20**, 216–227 (2002)
7. Bengi, K.: Access protocols for an efficient and fair packet-switched IP-over-WDM metro network. Comput. Netw. **44**, 247–265 (2004)
8. Bregni, S., et al.: Slot synchronization of WDM packet-switched slotted rings: the WONDER project. In: Proceedings of the ICC 2006 International Conference Communications, Istanbul, Turkey, pp. 2556–2561, 11–15 June 2006
9. Herzog, M., et al.: Metropolitan area packet-switched WDM networks: a survey on ring systems. IEEE Commun. Surveys and Tutorials **6**, 2–20 (2004)
10. Yang, H., et al.: Metro WDM networks: performance comparison of slotted ring and AWG star networks. IEEE J. Select. Areas Commun. **22**, 1460–1473 (2004)
11. Baziana, P.A., Pountourakis, I.E.: An efficient metropolitan WDM ring architecture for a slotted transmission-technique. IEEE J. Lightwave Technol. **26**(19), 3307–3317 (2008)
12. Baziana, P.A., Pountourakis, I.E.: An input traffic allocation strategy and an efficient transmission technique for collisions-free WDM ring MANs. Opt. Fiber Technol. **16**(5), 279–291 (2010)
13. Turuk, A., Kumar, R.: A scalable and collision-free MAC protocol for all-optical ring networks. Comput. Commun. **27**, 1453–1463 (2004)
14. Turuk, A., Kumar, R.: QoS provisioning in WDM ring networks with tunable transceivers. J. High Speed Netw. **14**, 317–339 (2005)
15. Turuk, A., et al.: A token-based distributed algorithm for medium access in an optical ring network. Optics Commun. **231**, 199–212 (2004)
16. MacGregor, M., et al.: The relative utility of three optical network properties in future dynamic optical networks. In: Proceedings of the IASTED WOC 2002 Wireless and Optical Communications, Banff, Alberta, Canada, pp. 191–195, 17–19 July 2002
17. Baziana, P.A.: Performance analysis of a WDMA protocol with a multiple tunable receivers node architecture for high-speed optical fiber LANs. In: Proceedings of the 6th International Conference on Optical Communication Systems 2015 (OPTICS 2015), pp. 5–13, Colmar, France, 20–22 July 2015
18. Sudhakar, G.N.M., et al.: Slotted aloha and reservation aloha protocols for very high-speed optical fiber local area networks using passive star topology. IEEE J. Lightwave Technol. **9**(10), 1411–1422 (1991)
19. Feller, W.: An Introduction to Probability Theory and Its Applications. Wiley, New York (1968)
20. Wentzel, E., Ovcharov, L.: Applied Problems In Probability Theory. Mir Publishers, Moscow (1986)

Security and Cryptography

A Scalable Honeynet Architecture
for Industrial Control Systems

Alexandru Vlad Serbanescu[1,2,3P], Sebastian Obermeier[1(✉)],
and Der-Yeuan Yu[2]

[1] ABB Corporate Research, Baden, Switzerland
sebastian.obermeier@ch.abb.com
[2] Department of Computer Science, ETH Zurich, Zurich, Switzerland
dyu@inf.ethz.ch
[3] KPMG AG, Zurich, Switzerland
avs@ines.ro

Abstract. Industrial control systems connected to the Internet represent attractive targets for remote attacks. While targeted attacks are often publicly reported, there is no clear information regarding non-targeted attacks. In order to analyse potentially malicious behaviour, we develop a large-scale honeynet system to capture and investigate network activities that use industrial protocols. The honeynet is composed of multiple honeypots that can be automatically deployed to cloud infrastructures as well as on-premises networks, and employs a modular design to support a multitude of industrial protocols. The collected data is aggregated at a series of centralised yet redundant nodes to resist single points of failure or adversarial compromise. We deploy the honeynet to demonstrate the feasibility of our approach and present our observations.

Keywords: Industrial control system security · Honeypots · SCADA security

1 Introduction

This contribution presents a novel honeynet architecture for exploring the threat landscape in critical infrastructures, ranging from power grids to water supply, transportation, and manufacturing plants. These systems were initially designed to be isolated from other networks and systems using air gaps and proprietary protocols. In order to enable various features such as remote maintenance, supervision and control, critical systems are increasingly often using the Internet as a communication channel with their operators, owners and even vendors. Typically referred to as Supervisory Control and Data Acquisition (SCADA), these systems have been also integrated into corporate networks as part of overarching resource planning solution. For example, complex systems such as advanced metering infrastructures for smart grids are a result of the industry's adoption of classical IT protocols for control and signalling purposes. However, the resulting increased connectivity has lead to a widened attack surface that breaches

M.S. Obaidat and P. Lorenz (Eds.): ICETE 2015, CCIS 585, pp. 179–200, 2016.
DOI: 10.1007/978-3-319-30222-5_9

physical isolation and protocol obscurity. As a result, the traditional security measures from the operation technology (OT) space are considered obsolete, with such systems attracting remote attacks from the Internet [12].

The interaction with networked industrial devices has become easier due to the availability of software that supports industrial protocols and even of tools specifically developed to compromise them [9]. As a result, malicious activities targeting existing infrastructures have been reported [11,14]. While targeted attacks contribute to increased security awareness in the industry, it remains unclear in the public domain how (or in some cases even if [10]) critical systems are effectively secured against opportunistic non-targeted attacks. Moreover, efforts have focused mostly on the exploitation of classical IT protocols, such as HTTP or FTP, with a lack of information on the use of industrial protocols in such attacks.

In order to understand malicious activities targeting industrial devices and systems, we design a low-interaction honeynet system to capture specific protocol-level interaction between these devices and systems, and the Internet. The honeynet consists of multiple honeypots that mimic various industrial devices in an integrated industrial setting. While some honeypot/honeynet solutions for industrial protocols have been proposed, they do not support the convenient deployment and mimicking of multiple industrial devices and protocols across large networks. Our honeynet supports an automatic deployment to heterogeneous platforms including cloud environments, enabling honeynet operation and data analysis on a global scale. Furthermore, we propose a modular design, where independent modules supporting different industrial/IT protocols can be incorporated into each honeypot to mimic real-world devices. We also seamlessly integrate port scanning detection capabilities in our honeypots to further extend our analysis of the adversarial behaviour. Our honeynet design is translated into a proof-of-concept implementation, where multiple honeypots are globally deployed on the Amazon EC2 cloud platform to demonstrate the feasibility and effectiveness of the proposed honeynet architecture.

The designed honeynet is able to capture industry-specific interactions originating from the Internet, and we aim to analyse the impact of having industrial devices openly exposed on the Internet. In particular, we investigate the influence of having these devices listed on public search engines, such as Shodan, on the adversarial behaviour observed.[1]
Our contributions can be summarized as follows:

- We present a novel SCADA honeynet architecture consisting of individual honeypots that can be automatically deployed to heterogeneous platforms on a large scale. Our honeypots simulate multiple industrial protocols, and are modularly structured to enable straightforward functionality extensions.
- A proof-of-concept implementation was developed and globally deployed to cloud environments to demonstrate the feasibility of our approach.
- We provide extended experimental results that reveal potentially adversarial behaviour from Internet-originating parties that employ industrial protocols.

---

[1] Shodan Computer Search Engine. http://www.shodanhq.com/.

Beyond our previous publications [16,17], this contribution presents extended experimental results on temporal and geographic correlations among the recorded honeynet interactions. These correlations are revealed by observations at different moments during deployment and in various locations around the world.

2   Assumptions and Research Questions

We develop our analysis based on the following assumptions and observations regarding the adversarial behaviour using ICS/SCADA protocols and targeting critical infrastructures:

1. Attempts to identify ICS/SCADA systems belonging to critical infrastructures are happening more and more frequently. One of the main techniques to achieve this goal is port scanning. This is a consequence of systems that are part of critical infrastructures attracting the attention of malicious entities, ranging from script kiddies and individual hackers to hacktivist groups and nation states, as listed in [1].
2. Publicly-available tools (e.g. nmap) and information repositories (e.g. the Shodan search engine) facilitate the aforementioned reconnaissance activities. The latter is used for what is referred to as "indirect intelligence gathering" in [6]. The work in [20] shows that many of the attacks "started out with Shodan queries, but it cannot be accurately said if these were accidental or targeted in nature."
3. If an ICS/SCADA system is identified on the public Internet (e.g. by identifying its gateway device), the classic IT components are most likely the first target and not the ICS/SCADA components. Classic and well-documented attack techniques are usually employed, such as brute forcing credentials or exploiting SQL injection vulnerabilities in a web-based GUI. In contrast, attacks on low-level ICS/SCADA equipment are currently unlikely to be observed on the public Internet. This hypothesis is in line with the experimental results in [5], in which the honeypot collected many general PC-targeting attacks, none of which being specific to programmable logic controllers (PLCs, devices typically used to control industrial processes). However, the rare attacks that do exploit the ICS/SCADA layer are targeted and sophisticated, as shown in [21] and [20].

Based on these assumptions, our goal is to answer the following questions:

1. Can we observe attempts that use industrial protocols (e.g. Modbus, IEC-104) to identify ICS/SCADA equipment that is directly (and hence wrongly) accessible from the public Internet?
2. Do ICS/SCADA components that are accessible via the Internet draw attention? If yes, are there attempts to interact with them in a short period of time (on the order of days or even hours, as observed for example in [21])?

3. How fast do information repositories (e.g., Shodan) interact with and list newly-connected industrial devices?
4. If an ICS/SCADA-specific device is identified, how is it typically interacted with (e.g., port scan, connection attempts, exchange of protocol-level data)?

3   Related Work

The SCADA HoneyNet Project[2] is among the first to implement honeypot networks in the SCADA domain for evaluating the feasibility of software-based simulation of industrial protocols in order to mimic industrial environments. It uses Honeyd, a popular low-interaction honeypot, for protocol simulation and to expose services to the Internet, including FTP, Modbus, TCP, and Telnet. The HoneyNet Project is limited in the functions implemented and does not offer support for deployments to cloud environments and, hence, for large-scale honeypot data captures.

Based on the Honeynet Project, Digital Bond proposes a refined variant[3] of SCADA honeynet, which uses two virtual machines instead of Honeyd. One virtual machine simulates popular protocols such as FTP, Telnet, Modbus, HTTP, and SNMP; the other is dedicated to network traffic monitoring and data analysis. Their honeypot incorporates proprietary intrusion detection mechanisms to identify malicious activities targeting the simulated industrial devices [18]. Later versions of the Digital Bond honeynet support the use of real hardware in addition to protocol simulation. While the overall architecture is improved, it does not provide support for modular functionality extensions or management primitives for large-scale deployments.

Conpot is a recent work in active development, providing a low-interaction honeypot that is designed to be easy to deploy and extend.[4] By default, Conpot simulates a Siemens Programmable Logic Controller (PLC) exposing HTTP, Modbus TCP and SNMP. Similar to Digital Bond's solution, it also supports the use of real industrial devices. Scott provided a case study on honeypot design and implementation using Conpot [15]. While Conpot is easy to deploy, it requires significant customization effort, issue commonly encountered in modern SCADA honeypot solutions [5].

There are additional honeynet or honeypot solutions that have been further proposed. Beeswarm focuses on simulating communication between honeypots (referred to as drones) to mimic active systems.[5] HoneyDrive is a customized Linux distribution incorporating various honeypot software to support a wide range of protocols from a single machine.[6] While these advances make improvements on attracting attackers, our approach aims at providing a solution for

---

[2] V. Pothamsetty and M. Franz. SCADA HoneyNet Project: Building Honeypots for Industrial Networks. http://scadahoneynet.sourceforge.net/.

[3] Digital Bond Inc. SCADA Honeynet. http://www.digitalbond.com/tools/scada-honeynet/.

[4] Conpot. http://www.conpot.org.

[5] The Beeswarm project. http://www.beeswarm-ids.org/.

[6] HoneyDrive. http://sourceforge.net/projects/honeydrive/.

large-scale deployment to attract non-targeted attacks employing ICS/SCADA specific protocols.

Regarding the impact of public industrial device databases such as Shodan, recent work has identified them as potential resources used by attackers when searching for targets [3,13]. It is argued that Shodan represents a powerful tool that indexes both IT and industrial devices that are newly connected to the Internet within 19 days. In addition, 1400 SCADA devices listed from Shodan have been found to use default credentials for administrative control [13]. While recent work has indicated a possible correlation between the listing of a device on Shodan and subsequent attacks [20], it remains inconclusive whether such incidents are coincidental or intended, aspect that we aim to investigate using our honeynet.

4   Approach

In order to investigate the adversarial behaviour pertaining to critical infrastructures, we choose to develop an ICS/SCADA honeynet that exposes multiple industrial protocols to the Internet. The honeynet is deployed on a global scale using the Amazon EC2 cloud environment.

The Amazon EC2 platform is chosen such that honeypots can be deployed in multiple locations around the globe, with the investigation hence benefiting from a large capture surface for targeted, automated and opportunistic attacks. Moreover, it exposes an API that can be efficiently used for automated deployment, operation and maintenance. Even if using a hosting environment whose characteristics are known (e.g. the Amazon EC2 public IP addresses) might reduce the effectiveness of a honeynet-based approach at first, as there is the risk of not detecting attackers that use such information for adjusting their target lists (e.g. not scanning cloud computing platforms for industrial devices), certain SCADA systems are increasingly being migrated to the cloud, making these environments attractive targets. For example, one power and automation technology company announced a new SCADA cloud-based solution in 2013[7], and a web-based industrial automation software company argues that cloud computing models have well-defined SCADA-specific applications[8]. Moreover, a recent survey reveals that cloud-based systems are reported to be the third most attacked target in critical infrastructures [10].

A honeynet-based approach is chosen because it enables a software-only simulation of ICS/SCADA devices from various manufacturers in large numbers and adaptable configurations. Such a design is therefore not limited by operational constraints or physical deployment aspects.

---

[7] ABB, June 2013. ABB and GlobaLogix partner to provide SCADAvantage in the cloud for oil and gas companies. http://www.abb.ch/cawp/seitp202/5e226590a23709f8c1257b790031ccb8.aspx.

[8] Larry Combs, InduSoft, 2011. Cloud computing for SCADA. http://www.indusoft.com/Portals/0/PDF/White-Papers/Whitepaper_CloudComputing.pdf.

In order to answer the questions concerning the threat landscape, we only simulate the presence of ICS/SCADA devices that support various industrial protocols. Since our research objectives concern the overall threat landscape, the simulation is not restricted to specific products. Therefore, it is not necessary to precisely and individually mimic specific industrial products. Given the lack of information on adversarial behaviour, we perform a less-detailed-but-broad initial investigation, as it offers a better overview of the threat landscape than a deep-but-narrow one. Moreover, this also provides a basis for directing and optimising future research efforts.

As capturing port scanning activities is crucial for relating the amount of adversarial interactions to the overall number of connections, our honeynet seamlessly integrates Snort, an open-source network intrusion detection system [2]. Snort not only specialises on port scan detection; it also detects attempts to fingerprint the operating system or probes/attacks using various protocols.

With regard to device simulation, we expose the following protocols that are utilised for remote SCADA/ICS communication:

- **Modbus**, a de facto standard for industrial communication, ubiquitously used in equipment ranging from small network-enabled sensors over automation controllers to SCADA system components [19].
- **IEC 60870-5-104**, frequently used in the electrical generation and distribution industry, especially in Europe (where it is the most commonly-used protocol), but also internationally (where it competes with DNP3 in English-speaking countries).

These protocols are routable through the Internet and can thus attract malicious interest.

5   Architecture

The purpose of each honeypot node is to mimic the presence of an ICS/SCADA system component and to monitor for, carry out and record interactions using communication protocols specific to the ICS/SCADA application domain. The nodes can simultaneously simulate different services, according to their individual configuration, thus being able to interact with the environment using different combinations of ICS/SCADA protocols. If a node is interacted with (e.g. port scanned) using a protocol that is not being simulated at that moment, the attempt is also logged. In addition, the honeypot nodes apply local processing to the gathered data before sending it to the "Storage, Analysis & Management" (SAM) node(s) in order to minimise the load on the latter one(s). The information to be captured and stored consists of data at OSI Layer 3 and above, both sent and received.

The internal architecture of the honeynet system used to gather the data analysed in the next section is depicted in Fig. 1, with Amazon EC2 as the deployment platform. The modular architecture allows for scalability, easy addition of functionalities and straightforward expansion of the protocols simulated.

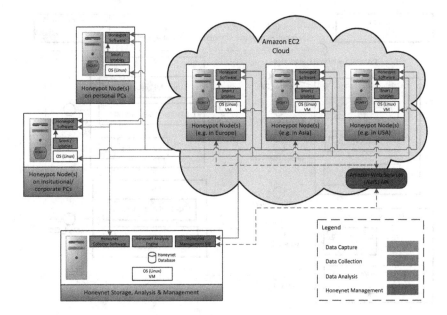

Fig. 1. Cloud-based industrial honeynet architecture.

From a high level perspective, the functionality of the honeynet is organised into *data capture*, *data collection*, *data analysis* and *honeynet management*, hence its structure follows the same logic.

Data Capture defines the recording of all interactions that occur with the surrounding environment in order to have a raw source of data that can be thereafter analysed and transformed into actionable information/knowledge. Hence, the honeynet processes all interactions, regardless of their characteristics (e.g. completeness, conformance with the corresponding standards) and captures and stores all data situated at OSI Layer 3 and above. This functionality is accomplished locally on each honeypot node at both network and application level.

Data Collection satisfies the essential need of having all information captured available at one/multiple locations in order to enable a real-time, complete and system-wide image of the honeynet and to be thus able to detect events and discover correlations. According to [7], SCADA systems require real-time threat monitoring and early warning systems to identify cyber attacks, whereas effective intrusion detection requires correlation of multiple events that are temporally and/or spatially separated. Therefore, a central data collector has been implemented to allow such correlations between multiple events.

Data Analysis embodies the key functionality of the honeynet, namely to extract information and to draw conclusions from the data collected. It is performed only on the SAM nodes in order to reduce the computational load on the honeypot nodes. Data analysis is carried out using third-party tools (i.e. Matlab) and custom Python scripts.

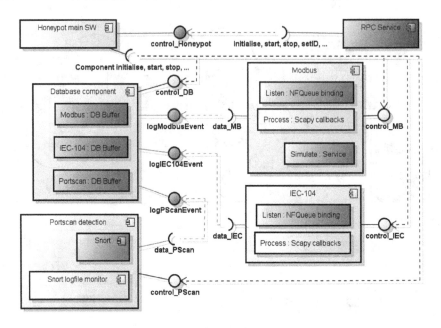

Fig. 2. Internal honeypot architecture.

Honeynet Management provides mechanisms for easy configuration, monitoring and deployment (e.g. automated deployment in the Amazon EC2 cloud) and covers all aspects of the honeypot life cycle, from honeypot node bootstrapping over secure remote management and honeynet-wide configuration/code updates to honeypot node shutdown. There are two associated data flows depicted in Fig. 1 because the honeynet SAM nodes need not only control the honeypot software itself, but also programmatically manage the hosting environment(s) employed using the API(s) exposed (e.g. provisioning a virtual machine on the Amazon EC2 cloud).

The structure of the honeypot software itself is shown in Fig. 2, using the same color coding as in Fig. 1 for the data capture, data collection and honeypot management functionalities. One of the main goals pursued with this modular structuring has been to enable simple functional extensions, therefore, it involves a minimal number of component interdependencies.

Honeypot Main SW represents the entry point, which starts in a virtual terminal environment so that its functioning is not dependent on the state of the SSH session and to also allow operator inspection/intervention at any time. The state of all other components (except for the RPC service) is controlled from here, with global commands subsequently calling the required methods in the corresponding components. For example, the command for initialising the honeypot starts with initialising the database component, followed by all protocol simulation services and finishing with the portscan detection module.

The **RPC Service** is automatically started in a separate thread for receiving commands and responding to queries from the honeynet controller, which are all tunnelled through an SSH tunnel. The most important control commands to be received using the RPC service are for initialising, starting and stopping the honeypot software, respectively for setting its unique identifier and for querying its state.

The key activity performed by the honeypot nodes – simulating services and capturing interactions – is realised with **individual components for every service/protocol simulated**. Each such component gathers data using network- and application-level mechanisms and can respond to the messages received, provided that a reply generation function is also implemented. After processing each incoming message, the extracted information is sent to the database component.

The **Portscan Detection** component employs Snort for the actual detection. Hence, the honeypot could also be extended with IPS-specific tasks done by Snort. All events detected are handed over to the database component.

The **Database Component** handles the data to be sent to the honeynet central database(s). Every simulated protocol has a specific buffer associated for storing the data gathered, which is in turn flushed when full or at regular intervals (whichever occurs first). The port scanning activity detected is also handled by such a buffer.

5.1 Data Capture

The capture of data is realised by the sensing points of the honeynet, namely the honeypot nodes, at two different levels on the OSI stack.

Network Level: For each protocol simulated, iptables entries for both incoming and outgoing traffic on the associated ports are automatically added in order to redirect the raw traffic using netfilter queues to the honeypot software residing at the application level. Here, each packet received is processed by a callback function that either stores it in a temporary buffer if the packet is still needed by other methods or sends it to the associated buffer in the database component directly. In the case of the former, after all methods have finished utilising the captured packet the last one sends the data to the buffer in the database component. This approach has been chosen as it enables using the raw capture and examination of the entire packet (using a packet manipulation tool such as Scapy). In addition, persistently storing the packet dump in the honeynet database becomes also possible – this enables a subsequent detailed inspection of the captured packets using packet analysers.

Application Level: If there are services implemented for a protocol (e.g. a Modbus server for the Modbus component), each simulated service can integrate the raw data received through the aforementioned netfilter queue redirection and use it internally. For example, the Modbus component makes use of an open-source implementation for simulating a server and by adding hooks at appropriate places.

An advantage of this data capture mechanism is that tasks such as handling TCP connections can be offloaded from the honeypot software onto the operating system through the use of standard techniques (e.g. creating a TCP socket for listening on a port), thus improving performance.

With regard to the detection of port scans, the output of the port scan detection module is redirected to a file, which is continuously monitored by the honeypot software for file system events. In this way, any port scanning occurrence detected by Snort is immediately processed by the honeynet.

5.2   Data Collection

After the data has been captured and processed by the protocol-specific or portscan detection components, it is sent to the associated buffers in the database component. These buffers inherit a base buffer that implements the logic for flushing their content to the database(s) on the SAM nodes and they specialise the structure of the data buffered, the SQL commands employed and the logging API exposed to the data-capture-responsible components. Thus, under normal operation all databases hold identical data. To assure this property under non-ideal conditions, database synchronization mechanisms can be easily added on the SAM nodes with no modification to the honeypot software itself. The logical topology of the honeynet with regard to data collection is hub(s) and spoke, with the SAM node(s) being the hub(s). Multi-threaded connection pools are created for each destination database.

5.3   Honeynet Management

Honeypot nodes are managed using a honeynet controller component, which is entirely separated form the honeypot software. This structure of the honeynet management software is depicted in Fig. 3.

Starting from the top, the *honeypot level operations* component exposes an interface for controlling the honeynet from a high-level, system-wide perspective, i.e. for executing commands such as "launch honeypot node on deployment environment X". It fulfils the role of the gateway redirecting user commands to the underlying component that can execute them according to the deployment environment they are destined for. In addition, it handles queries that request honeypot-level information, such as learning the state of the honeypot nodes or inspecting captured packets.

The next layer (blue) contains one component for each deployment environment used by the honeynet in order to handle the commands distributed by the previously mentioned gateway. High-level commands such as "add honeypot node" are broken down into the sequence of main steps to be carried out using the corresponding deployment-environment-specific mechanisms, which are implemented in the green layer below, and/or of queries to be send to the honeynet database(s). In other words, the components belonging to this level incorporate the *logic* behind all operations that the honeynet management software supports. In addition, they also expose interfaces for carrying out actions at the request

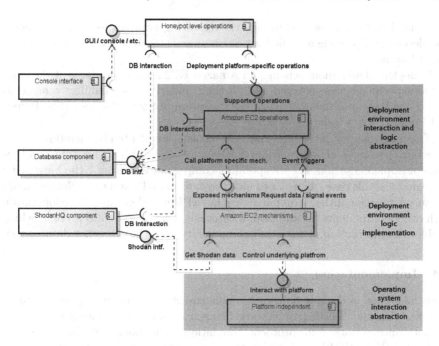

Fig. 3. Structure of the honeypot management component (Color figure online).

of the underlying mechanisms targeting the same deployment environment: for example, the illustrated *Amazon EC2 operations* component will add data to the database when the underlying component has finished updating and restarting a honeypot node running on the Amazon EC2 cloud platform.

Amazon EC2 mechanisms, together with all other components from the same layer (green), expand the steps exposed to the layer above into the actual operations that have to be executed on the target deployment environment, including possible interactions with the API provided by the latter or with other resources (e.g. the ShodanHQ component). For example, the "launchHoneypot" method will use the Amazon EC2 API to launch a new instance, request a unique identifier from the overlying component, check whether the services to be simulated by the new honeypot node are already listed on Shodan (and take appropriate actions if they are), provision the new instance, initialise and start the honeypot software. All these steps have to be translated to actual commands issued for the operating system used on the instance obtained from the deployment environment – this is done in the lowest layer of the honeypot management software, as subsequently introduced.

The (deployment) *platform-independent* component implements the entire set of operations to be carried out on the actual hosting environment, i.e. the underlying operating system. This includes, among others, installing the required software, deploying or updating the honeypot software, pushing the specified configuration files, controlling the honeypot software, and retrieving the log files.

The role of this component is to hide the operating-system specific implementation details and provide a unified set of commands to all other components that depend on it.

Using this deployment scheme, all Amazon EC2 regions available at the start of the experiment were covered and all their underlying availability zones contained one honeypot instance, with the exception of South America (Sao Paulo) and US East (N. Virginia).

The functionality of the honeynet as a whole is augmented by including access to external sources of information. Shodan has been chosen for this proof-of-concept implementation. A corresponding component is present – the *ShodanHQ component* in this case – in order to hide the external API and to implement more advanced functionalities (compared to the API-provided ones) in cooperation with other components. In addition, a *database component* is also present, which enables the interaction of the other components with the honeynet database(s).

5.4 Implementation

Both honeypot node and honeynet management software are implemented in *Python*, with the *Twisted* framework being used for asynchronous operations, network interactions and protocol simulation. The honeynet databases run on *PostgreSQL* DBMS, with which the honeypot nodes communicate through *psycopg2*. The virtual terminal environment employed for running the honeypot software is provided by *screen*.

Scapy offers the required support for packet inspection and manipulation tasks and also plays a role in the enumerated protocol simulation, with *nfqueue-bindings* alongside *iptables* being responsible for redirecting raw traffic to/from it. The Modbus server is simulated using *PyModbus*, whereas *Snort* handles the detection of port scanning attempts. In addition, information about the interaction peers is gathered using *dnspython* for reverse DNS lookups and *GeoIP* for their geographical origin.

Fabric is used for running commands remotely on the honeypot nodes, while *RPyC* and *Plumbum* enable the secure use of remote procedure calls.

6   Experimental Evaluation

We have evaluated the framework and implementation through experiments carried out using the Amazon EC2 cloud environment. The goal of this batch of experiments was to obtain a first impression about the adversarial behaviour targeting Amazon EC2, covering as many availability zones as possible and for a longer period. The protocols exposed are Modbus and IEC 60870-5-104 (IEC 104), and the duration of the experiment was 28 days.

By deploying 18 honeypot nodes, all eight Amazon EC2 regions available at the start of these experiments were covered and all of their underlying availability zones contained one honeypot instance, with the exception of South America (Sao Paulo) and US East (N. Virginia) — one availability zone in each of these two regions did not have enough resources for launching the required instances. As stated in [8], "the distribution of SCADA network nodes over the Internet helps model the large geographic scale of real-world SCADA systems".

In order to avoid loss of experimental data, two nodes were used for hosting a database each and for controlling the honeynet, as described in Sect. 5.2. This also shows the honeynet feature of simultaneously logging to multiple databases.

As a general note, the interactions are categorized using their type (new connection, request), the protocol employed and their relation to Shodan (peer belonging to the scanning infrastructure of Shodan or not). The latter characteristic is determined by performing a reverse DNS lookup of the peer's IP address and checking whether the associated PTR record is a subdomain belonging to Shodan or not. The information obtained using this method in the case of non-Shodan peers can reveal useful details, such as possible ties to different organizations, presumed owner's identity or the ISP used.

6.1   Results

A summary of the experimental data collected is shown in Table 1. The IP address, associated GeoIP source country information (if available) and corresponding DNS PTR record (if any) for each peer that has interacted with the honeynet are listed in the first three columns. The next four columns provide a breakdown of the interaction by protocol and/or type, while the last column contains the number of portscans detected by the Snort module *from the current peer*, i.e., it must not be used to assess the placement attractiveness of the honeypots/honeynet.

Observation — Influence of Shodan. Regarding the presence of portscans from the interacting peers, it can be pointed out that the peers learn about the presence of the simulated services also by other means than port scanning alone. This deduction is based on the fact that there exist peers that have not port scanned the honeypot(s) before interacting with it(them), hence they must have learned about their presence from another information source, most likely from Shodan – with only one exception, all interactions took place after being listed.

Observation — Research Activities identifed, but not on industrial protocols. Excluding the Shodan nodes, only few distinct Modbus and IEC-104 interaction peers could be observed and neither of them seems to be associated with research activities focused on adversarial behaviour using industrial protocols. This observation is supported by another experiment, during which only one peer that communicated over industrial protocols with the honeynet could be linked to research efforts (by using its DNS PTR record). Yet, the associated web site describes the overall research goal as getting an overview of servers that can be used for amplification in Distributed Denial of Service attacks[9], hence not specifically aimed at the ICS/SCADA realm.

---

[9] Amplification DDoS Tracker Project, Chair for System Security of the Ruhr University Bochum, Germany: http://scanresearch1.syssec.ruhr-uni-bochum.de/.

Table 1. Summary of data collected on Amazon EC2.

Peer IP addr.	CC	DNS PTR	Modbus		IEC-104		Pscans.
			Conns.	Reqs.	Conns.	Reqs.	
66.240.192.138	US	census8.shodan.io.	48	46	13	13	1
66.240.236.119	US	census6.shodan.io.	45	43	8	8	2
71.6.135.131	US	census7.shodan.io.	49	41	6	6	5
71.6.165.200	US	census12.shodan.io.	44	44	7	7	1
82.221.105.6	IS	census10.shodan.io.	8	8	-	-	2
82.221.105.7	IS	census11.shodan.io.	3	3	-	-	-
85.25.43.94	DE	rim.census.shodan.io.	14	12	7	7	3
85.25.103.50	DE	pacific.census.shodan.io.	10	8	-	-	1
93.120.27.62	RO	m247.ro.shodan.io.	4	4	1	1	1
95.19.182.113	ES	[...].dynamic.jazztel.es.	5	58	-	-	-
104.54.177.50	US	[...].rcsntx.sbcglobal.net.	6	-	-	-	-
108.163.245.114	US	server.albrari.com.	813	738	-	-	7
118.192.48.6	CN	-	4	3	-	-	-
198.20.69.98	DE	census2.shodan.io.	2	-	3	3	4
198.20.70.114	US	census3.shodan.io.	16	16	6	6	-
188.138.9.50	US	atlantic.census.shodan.io.	8	8	2	2	3
202.108.211.62	CN	-	13	8	-	-	4
Totals (Shodan):			251	233	53	53	23
Totals (non-Shodan):			841	807	0	0	11

6.2   Modbus — Honeynet-Level Analysis

Figure 4 uses the experiment time for the X axis and the empirical cumulative distribution of the number of occurrences for each interaction category on the Y axis. The total count for each Modbus interaction dataset is given in the legend. This way of representing the data was chosen because it makes the observation of both tendencies and isolated events, as well as the discovery of correlations, easier. The size of the bins used to count the interactions is 1 h.

Interaction Patterns. It appears that Shodan is constantly connecting and issuing Modbus requests to the honeypots, which can be deduced from the almost linear shape of the associated plots. In contrast, the other non-Shodan peers interact only from time to time with the honeypots, with one spike dominating the *new connections* and *requests* datasets. The discrete and/or batch-like interaction mode from non-Shodan peers is indicated by the isolated jumps (irregular, staircase-type pattern) of the corresponding CDF plots.

It can also be established from the figure that the honeynet (and thereby large parts of the Amazon EC2 cloud infrastructure) were port scanned at an almost constant pace during the whole duration of this round of experiments by non-Shodan peers, as the associated experimental CDF plot is almost linear as well. There were no port scans detected from Shodan peers.

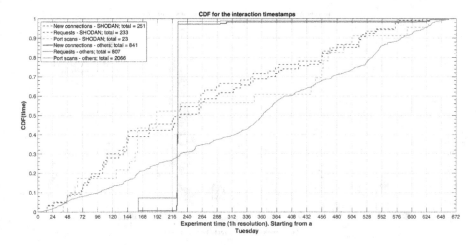

Fig. 4. Modbus: Connection, requests, port scans VS experiment time. The honeynet is port scanned by non-Shodan peers immediately after launch and at a constant rate. However, non-Shodan Modbus interaction is delayed, irregular and dominated by two spikes. Shodan peers start to regularly connect and issue Modbus requests soon after launch.

As for the port scans detected by the honeynet, those coming from non-Shodan peers started right after launching the honeypots, whereas Shodan interacts with the honeynet only after approximately 12 h. The former observation is confirmed by the work in [22], where it is concluded that "every machine on the Internet [located in the cloud or on-premises] is scanned within minutes after connecting" [22]. Moreover, the first interaction from a non-Shodan peer occurs after approximately 7 and 10 days (connection and connection+request, respectively). Therefore, it can be argued that the honeynet exhibits a *break-in period* after launch, which is to be expected.

If the two spikes were filtered out from the data to be plotted, the figure would remain similar, exhibiting the same staircase-like pattern for the non-Shodan interactions. The single representative difference would be that the first (non-filtered) interaction would occur after approximately 12 days from the launch of the honeynet (also being listed on Shodan).

Interaction Patterns — Temporal Correlations. A representation of the number of interactions and port scans captured as a function of the day of week and of time of day has been generated in Figs. 5 and 6, respectively. The goal of this representation is to reveal possible patterns caused by and specific to human-generated activities. The grouping takes the local time zones of the honeypots into consideration.

If the two spikes identified in Fig. 4, namely the connection-related (Friday) and the request-related (Tuesday) ones were filtered out, the remaining

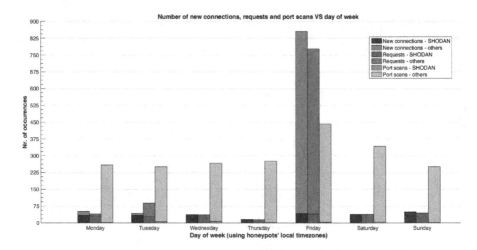

Fig. 5. Modbus: Connections, requests, port scans VS day of week. Except for the two (new connection and request) outliers caused by the aforementioned interaction spikes, no visible pattern can be observed for non-Shodan interactions. Conversely, Shodan interactions are apparently evenly distributed during the week.

interactions from non-Shodan peers would appear to take place mostly at the beginning of the week, with no visible pattern.

In contrast, Shodan-originating interactions are apparently evenly distributed during the week. There was a slight reduction of activity Thursdays, which is probably determined by the random IP address generation used by Shodan for scanning the Internet [4]. Regarding the distribution of port scans over the week, there appears to be a small activity increase Fridays and Saturdays (no convincing explanation was found), otherwise no pattern could be traced and, more significant for the purpose of this work, no correlation with the Modbus activity could be observed. Even if it appears that the connection-related activity for Fridays could reveal a correlation with port scanning, as they both present a spike then, this does not hold, as the source of the connection-related spike has only few port scans associated (less then 10 in total).

Looking at the influence of the time of day on the activity recorded by the honeynet, a relatively constant pattern can be observed in Fig. 6 for all types of interactions. The two above-mentioned spikes are, as expected, localized and the remaining activity from other non-Shodan hosts is rare and displays no visible pattern.

Interaction Levels across Amazon EC2 Availability Zones. More important from the perspective of service migration into the cloud (in this case the Amazon EC2 variant) — thus potentially becoming increasingly attractive/exposed to attackers — is the connection between the interaction intensity and the availability zone selected for deployment, which is depicted in the Fig. 7.

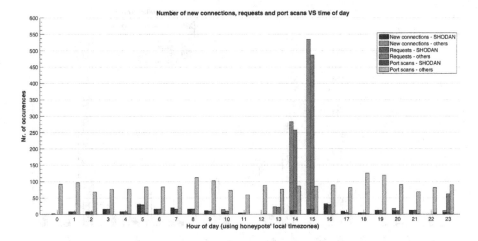

Fig. 6. Modbus: Connections, requests, port scans VS time of day. Except for the two interaction spikes, non-Shodan interactions are rare and display no visible pattern. Apart from the curious reduced interaction at noon, Shodan-originating activity is seemingly regular.

Apart from allowing the reader to identify the availability zones that have recorded the two already-mentioned spikes, this representation reveals that:

- Modbus activity from non-Shodan peers is bursty and, except for the two spikes, also low in intensity.
- Shodan-originating activities cover all availability zones except for one (eu-west-1c in this case) and appears to vary randomly but remains within the same order of measure with regard to its intensity. One possible explanation could be that it depends on the public IP address received by the underlying Amazon EC2 instance at launch; no experiments have been done in this direction because it falls outside the purpose of this study.
- Port scans from non-Shodan peers cover all availability zones except eu-west-1c and are not of negligible in terms of quantity. This represents a solid indication that the placement of the honeypots is good (port scans are considered a generally-suitable measure for evaluating it) and that there is no correlation between Modbus-/Shodan-, Modbus/non-Shodan and Modbus-/port scanning-activities, respectively. In addition, the lack of both Modbus interactions and port scans in these availability zones suggests that being listed or not on Shodan (determined from the lack of Shodan-related activity) largely determines whether Modbus interactions from non-Shodan peers will take place. In other words, it appears that the interaction targets are generally chosen using publicly-available information repositories (Shodan in this case) and not after individually carried out search actions.
- The intensity of all interaction categories varies across availability zones, with no identifiable pattern or correlation in this regard.

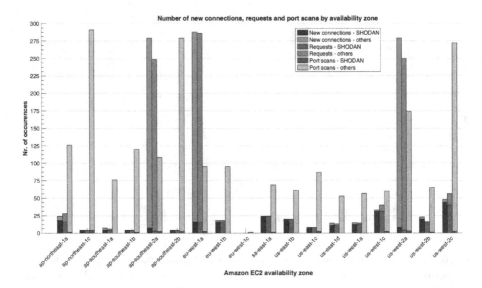

Fig. 7. Modbus: Connections, requests, port scans VS Amazon EC2 availability zone. Non-Shodan Modbus activity is bursty, low in intensity (except for the two spikes) and does not include all honeypot nodes. Port scanning and Shodan interactions, however, cover all but one of them.

Interaction Peers apparently Searching for Exposed Modbus Devices. There are instances when non-Shodan peers scan the Internet for Modbus-enabled devices by themselves, with Modbus connections and requests being captured by multiple honeypot nodes that had not been previously listed on Shodan with their Modbus service. These connections either represent TCP SYN portscans or belonged to the TCP handshakes preceding the Modbus requests. It is also worth highlighting the fact that many of the peers involved in these interactions were either related to ongoing academic research activities[10] or associated to two platforms: a developer-oriented, high-performance cloud environment[11] and a Web hosting platform known for supporting cybercrime forums and malicious websites[12]. This specificity of the interaction origins (i.e. not general-purpose platforms) and their coverage of the vast majority of honeypot nodes suggest that the interactions observed are neither accidental nor improvised, but targeted in nature and carried out meticulously.

Interaction Patterns — Arrival Rates. Another attempt to reveal any type of pattern from the data collected was to extract the inter-arrival times between two consecutive connections and requests, respectively, on a per availability zone

---

[10] University of Michigan: research aiming at a better understanding of the global use of Internet protocols. http://researchscan273.eecs.umich.edu/.

[11] Linode: https://www.linode.com/.

[12] Santrex. See http://krebsonsecurity.com/2013/10/bulletproof-hoster-santrex-calls-it-quits/ for additional details.

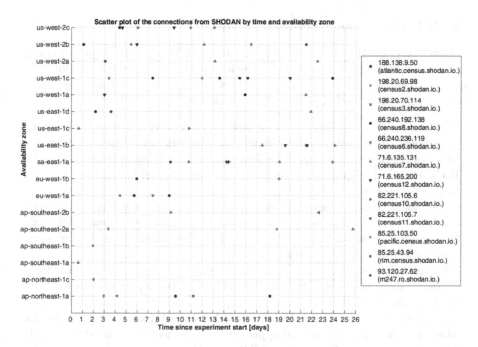

Fig. 8. Modbus: Distribution of connections from Shodan peers by experiment time and availability zone. Each peer interacts with multiple honeypot nodes in a repeated manner. This contrasts the non-Shodan interactions, which are scarcer overall and unique for each honeypot covered.

basis for both Shodan and non-Shodan peers and to compute their average and standard deviation figures. The interactions have highly variable inter-arrival times and show no clear pattern.

Interaction Patterns — Revisiting Nodes. Other explored visualization of the interactions consisted of scatter plots for each interaction type, with experiment time and the availability zone as variables, as illustrated in Fig. 8.

It can be thus observed that each Shodan peer often establishes new connections multiple times with the same honeypot and that it usually covers multiple honeypots, behaviour that is consistent with the one reported in [4]. Additionally, a higher density of the scatter plot in its upper half suggests a higher interest for the south/north American and for the European availability zones w.r.t. connect-only interactions, at least for the duration of this experimental round. The plot for Modbus request-based interactions displays the same characteristics. In comparison, the situation for non-Shodan activity is significantly scarcer and, with one exception, the non-Shodan peers interact only once with each honeypot, while still covering multiple ones.

6.3   IEC-104 — Honeynet-level Analysis

The analysis of the IEC-104 activity recorded during this batch of experiments by the honeynet follows the same structure as for the Modbus interactions. However, the corresponding figures are not included because they depict a similar situation with regard to the Shodan-sourced events, namely:

- Connections are established and messages are received constantly during the experiment. Their total number represents approximately one fifth from the Modbus figures, respectively. This indicates a lower interest from Shodan for IEC-104 than for Modbus, which may be a reflection of the public's interest in these protocols.
- The influence of both day of week and of time of day on the IEC-104 activity intensity appears to be relatively reduced, and the behaviour exhibits no clear pattern. Shodan displays also a couple more one-hour-long intervals of inactivity compared to those for Modbus.
- All availability zones but one are covered (as it was the case using Modbus).
- A subset of the peers employed by Shodan for the Modbus interaction are also used for the IEC-104 one.
- The interaction inter-arrival times for IEC-104 are significantly longer than for Modbus, with a lower bound of approximately one week compared to roughly 12 h, respectively, and similarly exhibit no pattern.
- The distribution of connections and messages displays repeated interactions with the same availability zone and a coverage of multiple availability zones for the Shodan nodes, as it was the case using Modbus. By contrast, the density of the scatter plots is visibly lower for IEC-104.

The observations above are confirmed by subsequent experiments, with the single minor difference being that Shodan covers all availability zones used (compared to all but one in the experiments analysed here). This shows once more the coverage degree achieved by Shodan and, thus, its support for identifying even singular ICS/SCADA components openly exposed to the public Internet.

With respect to the non-Shodan peers, however, the situation is completely different than for the Modbus protocol: no single IEC-104 interaction was observed during the first batch of experiments. Hence, IEC-104 is believed to be less attractive for carrying out supposedly-malicious actions on ICS/SCADA systems.

7   Conclusion

This article has presented a large-scale honeynet architecture for gaining deeper insights into the adversarial behaviour in industrial settings. We have shown that the honeynet can be automatically deployed to a cloud-based platform, and that it enables a centralised and redundant collection of data. The modular design of the honeynet enables a straightforward expansion of the industrial protocols exposed by individual nodes. We also integrated Snort seamlessly into our honeypots in order to detect port scans and (operating) system fingerprinting. The experiments carried out using a cloud platform have shown the feasibility and scalability of our approach. The honeynet was regularly probed and indexed by Shodan, and it also attracted interactions from multiple seemingly-independent peers.

Our experimental results motivate the need of having proper security mechanisms in industrial control systems that are connected to the Internet. As these systems are likely to be swiftly listed in relevant information repositories, they are further exposed to both IT-classic and ICS-specific attacks. We have also confirmed that ICS-specific protocols are used to target industrial control systems.

As future work, we plan to extend the number of protocols simulated and to evaluate the influence of search engine listings on the adversarial behaviour observed.

References

1. Asgarkhani, M., Sitnikova, E.: A strategic approach to managing security in SCADA systems. In: Proceedings of the 13th European Conference on Cyber warefare and Security, pp. 23–32. Academic Conferences and Publishing International Limited, July 2014
2. Beale, J., Baker, A., Esler, J., Kohlenberg, T., Northcutt, S.: Snort: IDS and IPS Toolkit. Jay Beale's open source security series. Syngress (2007). http://books.google.ch/books?id=M9plZZxJB_UC
3. Bodenheim, R., Butts, J., Dunlap, S., Mullins, B.: Evaluation of the ability of the shodan search engine to identify internet-facing industrial control devices. Int. J. Crit. Infrastruct. Prot. 7(2), 114–123 (2014). http://www.sciencedirect.com/science/article/pii/S1874548214000213
4. Bodenheim, R.C.: Impact of the Shodan Computer Search Engine on Internet-facing Industrial Control System Devices. Master's Thesis, AIR FORCE INSTITUTE OF TECHNOLOGY WRIGHT-PATTERSON AFB OH, March 2014. http://www.dtic.mil/cgi-bin/GetTRDoc?Location=U2&doc=GetTRDoc.pdf&AD=ADA601219
5. Buza, D.I., Juhász, F., Miru, G., Félegyházi, M., Holczer, T.: CryPLH: protecting smart energy systems from targeted attacks with a PLC honeypot. In: Cuellar, J. (ed.) SmartGridSec 2014. LNCS, vol. 8448, pp. 181–192. Springer, Switzerland (2014)
6. Byres, E.: Project SHINE: 1,000,000 internet-connected SCADA and ICS systems and counting, September 2013
7. Deng, Y., Shukla, S.: A distributed real-time event correlation architecture for SCADA security. In: Butts, J., Shenoi, S. (eds.) Critical Infrastructure Protection VII. IFIP AICT, vol. 417, pp. 81–93. Springer, Heidelberg (2013). http://dx.doi.org/10.1007/978-3-642-45330-4_6
8. Di Pietro, A., Foglietta, C., Palmieri, S., Panzieri, S.: Assessing the impact of cyber attacks on interdependent physical systems. In: Butts, J., Shenoi, S. (eds.) Critical Infrastructure Protection VII. IFIP AICT, vol. 417, pp. 215–227. Springer, Heidelberg (2013). http://dx.doi.org/10.1007/978-3-642-45330-4_15
9. ICS - CERT: Increasing threat to industrial control systems (update A), May 2013. https://ics-cert.us-cert.gov/alerts/ICS-ALERT-12-046-01A

10. Ponemon Institute: Critical infrastructure: Security preparedness and maturity. Technical report, Unysis, July 2014. http://www.unisys.com/insights/critical-infrastructure-security
11. Morris, T.H., Gao, W.: Industrial control system cyber attacks. In: Proceedings of the 1st International Symposium for ICS & SCADA Cyber Security Research (2013). http://ewic.bcs.org/content/ConWebDoc/51165
12. NIST: Guide to General Server Security - Recommendations of the National Institute of Standards and Technology, July 2008. http://csrc.nist.gov/publications/nistpubs/800-123/SP800-123.pdf
13. Patton, M., Gross, E., Chinn, R., Forbis, S., Walker, L., Chen, H.: Uninvited connections: a study of vulnerable devices on the internet of things (IoT). In: 2014 IEEE Joint Intelligence and Security Informatics Conference (JISIC), pp. 232–235, September 2014
14. Robinson, M.: The SCADA threat landscape. In: Proceedings of the 1st International Symposium for ICS & SCADA Cyber Security Research (2013). http://ewic.bcs.org/content/ConWebDoc/51166
15. Scott, C.: Designing and implementing a honeypot for a SCADA network. Technical report, The SANS Institute, June 2014
16. Serbanescu, A.V., Obermeier, S., Yu, D.: A flexible architecture for industrial control system honeypots. In: Proceedings of the 12th International Conference on Security and Cryptography, SECRYPT 2015, Colmar, Alsace, France, pp. 16–26, 20–22 July 2015. http://dx.doi.org/10.5220/0005522500160026
17. Serbanescu, A.V., Obermeier, S., Yu, D.: ICS threat analysis using a large-scale honeynet. In: 3rd International Symposium for ICS & SCADA Cyber Security Research 2015, ICS-CSR 2015. University of Applied Sciences Ingolstadt, Germany, 17–18 September 2015. http://ewic.bcs.org/content/ConWebDoc/55096
18. Wade, S.M.: SCADA Honeynets: The attractiveness of honeypots as critical infrastructure security tools for the detection and analysis of advanced threats. Master's Thesis, Iowa State University, Ames, Iowa (2011). http://lib.dr.iastate.edu/cgi/viewcontent.cgi?article=3130&context=etd
19. Wilamowski, B.M., Irwin, J.D.: The Industrial Electronics Handbook - Industrial Communications Systems, 2nd edn., vol. 2. CRC Press, Taylor & Francis Group, Boca Raton, London (2011)
20. Wilhoit, K.: The SCADA that didnt cry wolf - whos really attacking your ICS equipment? - part deux! (2013). black Hat US 2013
21. Wilhoit, K.: Whos really attacking your ICS equipment? (2013). black Hat Europe 2013
22. Zeng, Y.G., Coffey, D., Viega, J.: How vulnerable are unprotected machines on the internet? In: Faloutsos, M., Kuzmanovic, A. (eds.) PAM 2014. LNCS, vol. 8362, pp. 224–234. Springer, Heidelberg (2014). http://dx.doi.org/10.1007/978-3-319-04918-2_22

Evaluating Op-Code Frequency Histograms in Malware and Third-Party Mobile Applications

Gerardo Canfora, Francesco Mercaldo[(✉)], and Corrado Aaron Visaggio

Department of Engineering, University of Sannio, Viale Traiano 1,
82100 Benevento, Italy
{canfora,fmercaldo,visaggio}@unisannio.it

Abstract. Mobile malware has grown in scale and complexity, as a consequence of the unabated uptake of smartphones worldwide. Malware writers have been developing detection evasion techniques which are rapidly making anti-malware technologies ineffective. In particular, zero-days malware is able to easily pass signature based detection, while techniques based on dynamic analysis, which could be more accurate and robust, are too costly or inappropriate to real contexts, especially for reasons related to usability. This paper discusses a technique for discriminating Android malware from trusted applications that does not rely on signatures, but exploits a vector of features obtained from the static analysis of the Android's Dalvik code. Experiments on a sample of 11,200 applications revealed that the proposed technique produces high precision (over 93 %) in mobile malware detection. Furthermore we investigate whether the feature vector is useful to identify the malware family and if it is possible to discriminate whether an application was retrieved from the official market or third-party one.

Keywords: Malware · Android · Security · Testing · Static analysis

1 Introduction

A recent report from Gartner [13] shows that the worldwide sales of mobile phones totaled 301 million units in the third quarter of 2014; in addition, it estimates that by 2018 nine out of ten phones will be smartphones. Accordingly, the number of smartphone applications is explosively growing. Unfortunately, such popularity also attracts malware developers, determining an increased production of malware for the Android platform. Not only official marketplaces, such as Google Play [16], but a number of third-party marketplaces (AppBrain[1], Aptoide[2], Blackmart Alpha[3]) provide smartphone applications: anecdotal evidence shows that these markets are very likely to contain malware.

---

[1] http://www.appbrain.com/.
[2] http://m.aptoide.com/.
[3] http://www.blackmart.us/.

© Springer International Publishing Switzerland 2016
M.S. Obaidat and P. Lorenz (Eds.): ICETE 2015, CCIS 585, pp. 201–222, 2016.
DOI: 10.1007/978-3-319-30222-5_10

In February 2011, Google introduced Bouncer [15] to screen submitted apps for detecting malicious behaviors, but this has not eliminated the problem, as it is discussed in [18]. Existing solutions for protecting privacy and security on smartphones are still ineffective in many facets [17], and many analysts warn that the malware families and their variants for Android are rapidly increasing. This scenario calls for new security models and tools to limit the spreading of malware for smartphones.

The Fraunhofer Research Institution for Applied and Integrated Security has performed an evaluation of antivirus for Android [12], reporting that there are many techniques for evading the detection of most antivirus. An example is repackaging [27]: the attacker decompiles a trusted application to get the source code, then adds the malicious payload and recompiles the application with the payload to make it available on various market alternatives, and sometimes also on the official market. The user is often encouraged to download such malicious applications because they are free versions of trusted applications sold on the official market.

Signature-based malware detection, which is the most common technique adopted by commercial antimalware for mobile platforms, is often ineffective. Moreover, it is costly, as the process for obtaining and classifying a malware signature is laborious and time-consuming.

There is another problem affecting the ability to detect malware on Android platform. Antivirus software on desktop operating system has the possibility of monitoring the file system operations. In this way, it is possible to check whether some applications assume a suspicious behavior; for example, if an application starts to download malicious code, it will be detected immediately by the antivirus responsible for scanning the disk drive.

Android does not allow for an application to monitor the file system: every application can only access its own disk space. Resource sharing is allowed only if expressly provided by the developer of the application.

Therefore antivirus software on Android cannot monitor the file system: this allows applications to download updates and run new code without any control by the operating system. This behavior will not be detected by antivirus software in any way; as a matter of fact, a series of attacks are based on this principle (this kind of malware is also known as 'downloader').

This paper proposes a technique for malware detection, which uses a features vector, in place of the code signature. The assumption (that that will be assessed with the evaluation) is that malicious applications show values for this features vector which are different from the values shown by trusted applications. Moreover, we accomplished an analysis on third-party applications with the aim to understand if these features rise differences between apps distributed through third party markets. In fact, there is anecdotal evidence that the quality of third-party markets' apps is lower than the one of apps retrieved by the official market.

The vector includes eight features obtained by counting some Dalvik op-codes of the instructions which form the smali code[4] of the application. Specifically, we analyze some op-codes which are usually used to change the application's control flow, as these op-codes can be indicators of the application complexity. The underlying assumption is that the business logic of a trusted application tends to be more complex than the malware logic, because the trusted application code must implement a certain set of functions. On the contrary, the malware application is required to implement just the functions that activate the payload.

An approach commonly used for generating computer malware, consists of decomposing the control flow in smaller procedures to be called in a certain order, instead of following the original flow [3,4]. This technique is called 'fragmentation', and is intended to circumvent signature-based antivirus, or those kinds of antivirus which attempt to analyze the control flow for detecting malware.

The first six features aim at characterizing the fragmentation of the control flow, and compute, respectively, the number of move, jump, packed-switch, sparse- switch, invoke and if op-codes, singly taken, divided by the overall number of the occurrences of all these six Dalvik op-codes.

The last two features are based on another assumption. The classes of a trusted application tend to exhibit an intrinsic variability, because each class is designed to implement a specific part of the business logic of the overall application. Such a variability should be reflected in the distribution of the op-codes, so the same op-code should occur with different frequencies in different classes. Conversely, as the malware has not an articulated business logic, except for the malicious payload, this difference among its classes tend to be less evident than in trusted applications. For evaluating such a difference in op-codes distribution among the different classes forming the final application we use two features, which are two variants of the Minkowski distance [20], namely the Manhattan distance and the Euclidean distance. All the features are used to build a classifier which is then used to discriminate an Android malware from a trusted Android application. An advantage of using a classifier is overcoming the need to continuously collect malware signatures. However, this requires a sample of malware and a sample of trusted applications for training the classifier. Of course, the training can be run with new samples after a certain period of usage, in order to improve the accuracy and make the classifier robust with respect to the new families of malware that arise over time.

The paper poses four research questions:

- RQ1: are the features extracted able to distinguish a malware from a trusted application for Android platform?
- RQ2: is a combination of the features more effective than a single feature to distinguish an Android malware from a trusted application?
- RQ3: is the best-in-class feature set effective in identifying the malware family a malware belongs to?
- RQ4: is the best-in-class feature set effective in identifying applications taken from third-party markets?

---

[4] https://code.google.com/p/smali/.

The main contribution of this paper can be resumed in the following points:

- we provide a set of features that have been never applied to the detection of Android malware;
- the set of features consists of occurrence frequency of some specific op-codes, so the extraction of such features is easy to reproduce and does not require a great use of resources;
- we discuss extensive experimentation that shows how our detection technique is very effective in terms of precision and recall, especially if compared with the antagonist methods presented in the literature.

The rest of the paper is organized as follows: the next section provides an overview of related work; the following section illustrates the proposed features and the detection technique; the fourth section discusses the experimentation, and, finally, conclusion and future works are given in the last section.

2   Related Work

Several works address the problem of features extraction using dynamic and static analysis.

Counting op-codes is a technique used in previous works for the detection of viruses: it revealed to be successful with several variants of the W32.Evol metamorphic virus [9].

Bilar [5] proposes a detection mechanism for malicious code through statistical analysis of op-codes distributions. This work compares the statistical op-codes frequency between malware and trusted samples, concluding that malware opcode frequency distribution seems to deviate significantly from trusted applications. We accomplish a similar analysis, but for Android malware. In reference [20,21] the histograms of op-codes are used as a feature to find whether a file is a morphed version of another. Using a threshold of 0.067 authors in reference [20] correctly classify different obfuscated versions of metamorphic viruses; while in reference [21] the authors obtain a 100 % detection rate using a dataset of 40 malware instances of NGCVK family, 40 benign files and 20 samples classified by authors as other virus files.

In the literature there are a number of solutions for the detection of malicious behaviors which do not exploit op-codes occurrences.

A number of papers deals with privacy leakage, such as Pios [8], AndroidLeaks [14] and TaintDroid [11].

The purpose of TaintDroid [11] is to track the flow of privacy sensitive data, and monitor how the applications access and manipulate users personal data, in order to detect when sensitive data leave the system through untrusted applications. Authors monitor 30 third-party Android applications, founding 68 potential misuses of private information on 20 applications.

PiOS [8] and AndroidLeaks [14] perform static analysis for detecting privacy leaks in smartphones. The aim is to detect when sensitive information is collected by applications with malicious intents.

Canfora et al. [6] propose a method for detecting mobile malware based on three metrics, which evaluate: the occurrences of a specific subset of system calls, a weighted sum of a subset of permissions that the application requires, and a set of combinations of permissions. They obtain a precision of 0.74 using a balanced dataset composed by 200 trusted and 200 real malware applications.

Sahs et al. [23] use a control flow graph to detect Android Malware; their work is based on AndroGuard [1], a tool useful to extract a series of features from mobile applications in order to train a One-Class Support Vector Machine. They validate the proposed method on 2,081 benign and 91 malicious application, concluding that the trusted sample size combined with a fixed malicious sample size causes precision to decrease as the benign sample increases.

Desnos [10] presents an algorithm to detect an infected Android application using similarity distance between two applications. The similarity distance seems to be an useful index to determine whether a version of an application has potentially been pirated.

Mobile Application Security Triage (MAST) [7] ranks the maliciousness of apks by using a set of attributes, like intent filters and native code. MAST uses Multiple Correspondence Analysis to measure the correlation between declared indicators of functionality required to be present in the packages of the analyzed applications. Conversely, in this paper we focus on a set of op-codes.

CopperDroid [22] recognizes Android malware through a system call analysis: the solution is based on the observation that such behaviors are however achieved through the system calls invocation, using a customized version of the Android emulator to enable system call tracking and support system call analyses.

Wu et al. [25] propose a static feature-based mechanism that considers the permission, the deployment of components, the intent messages passing and API calls for characterizing the Android applications behavior. Zheng et al. [26] propose a signature based analytic system to automatically collect, manage, analyze and extract Android malware.

Arp et al. [2] propose a method to perform a static analysis of Android applications based on features extracted from the manifest file and from the disassembled code (suspicious API calls, network addresses and other). Their approach uses Support Vector Machines to produce a detection model, and extracts a set of features which is different from the one presented in this paper. Their dataset is composed by 5,560 malware applications and 123,453 trusted one obtaining a detection rate equal to 93.9 %.

As emerges from this discussion, and at the best knowledge of the authors, the set of features considered in this paper was never used in any of the works on Android malware in literature.

3   The Proposed Features

We classify malware using a set of features which count the occurrences of a specific group of op-codes extracted from the smali Dalvik code of the application under analysis (AUA in the remaining of the paper). Smali is a language that represents disassembled code for the Dalvik Virtual Machine[5], a virtual machine optimized for the hardware of mobile devices.

We produce the histograms of a set of op-codes occurring in the AUA: each histogram dimension represents the number of times the op-code corresponding to that dimension appears in the code. The collected op-codes have been chosen because they are representative of the alteration of the control flow. The underlying assumption is that a trusted application tends to have a greater complexity than a malicious one. We consider 6 op-codes:

- Move: which moves the content of one register into another one.
- Jump: which deviates the control flow to a new instruction based on the value in a specific register.
- Packed-Switch: which represents a switch statement. The instruction uses an index table.
- Sparse-Switch: which implements a switch statement with sparse case table, the difference with the previous switch is that it uses a lookup table.
- Invoke: which is used to invoke a method, it may accept one or more parameters.
- If: which is a Jump conditioned by the verification of a truth predicate.

In order to compute the set of features, we follow two steps. The first step consists of preprocessing the AUA: we prepare the input data in form of histograms. It is worth observing that the histogram dissimilarity has been already applied with success in malware detection in [20, 21].

At the end of this step, we have a series of histograms, a histogram for each class of the AUA; each histogram has six dimensions, each dimension corresponds to one among the six op-codes included in the model. In the second step, we compute two forms of the Minkowski distances.

In the preprocessing step, we disassemble the executable files using APK-Tool[6], a tool for reverse engineering Android apps, and generating Dalvik source code files. After this, we create a set of histograms that represent the frequencies of the six op-codes within each class.

Figure 1 shows the process of program disassembly and the corresponding breakdown into histograms.

Figure 2 represents an example of a class histogram.

The second step comprises the computation of the distances between the various histograms obtained with the step 1.

The first six features are computed as follows; let X be one of the following values:

- M_i: the number of occurrences of the 'move' op-code in the i-th class of the application;
- J_i: the number of occurrences of the 'jump' op-code in the i-th class of the application;

---

[5] http://pallergabor.uw.hu/androidblog/dalvik_opcodes.html.
[6] https://code.google.com/p/android-apktool/.

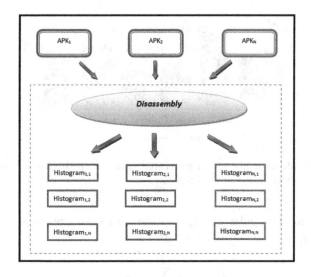

Fig. 1. A graphical representation of AUA analysis' step 1, which consists of the AUA disassembly and histograms generation.

- P_i: the number of occurrences of the 'packed-switch' op-code in the i-th class of the application;
- S_i: the number of occurrences of the 'sparse-switch' op-code in the i-th class of the application;
- K_i: the number of occurrences of the 'invoke' op-code in the i-th class of the application;
- I_i: the number of occurrences of the 'if' op-code in the i-th class of the application.

Then:

$$\#X = \frac{\sum_{k=1}^{N} X_i}{\sum_{k=1}^{N}(M_i + J_i + P_i + S_i + K_i + I_i)}$$

where X is the occurrence of one of the six op-codes extracted and N is the total number of the classes forming the AUA.

Before explaining the last two features, it is useful to recall the Minkowski distance.

Let's consider two vectors of size n, $X = (x_i, x_2, ..., x_n)$ and $Y = (y_i, y_2, ..., y_n)$, then the Minkowski distance between two vectors X and Y is:

$$d_{X,Y}^r = \sum_{k=1}^{N} |x_i - y_i|^r$$

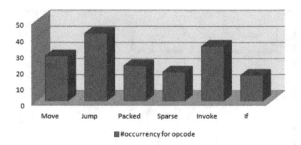

Fig. 2. An example of a histogram generated from the n-th class of the j-th AUA obtained with the processing of the step 1.

One of the most popular histogram distance measurements is the Euclidean distance. It is a Minkowski distance with r = 2:

$$d_{X,Y}^E = \sqrt{\sum_{k=1}^{N}(x_i - y_i)^2}$$

Another popular histogram distance measurement is Manhattan distance. Also the Manhattan distance is a form of the Minkowski distance, in this case r = 1:

$$d_{X,Y}^M = \sum_{k=1}^{N}|x_i - y_i|$$

The last two features are Manhattan and Euclidean distance, computed with a process of three steps. Given an AUA containing N classes, the AUA will have N histograms, one for each class, where each histograms H_i will be a vector of six values, each one corresponding to an op-code of the model ('move', 'jump', 'packed-switch', 'sparse-switch', 'invoke', 'if').

As an example, we will show an application of the model to a simplified case in which the model has only three classes and two op-codes. Let's assume that the AUA's histograms are H_1= {4,2}, H_2={2,1}, H_3={5,9}.

- *Step1*: the Minkowski distance is computed among each pair H_i, H_j with i≠j and 1≤i,j≤N. In the example we will have $d_{1,2}$=3; $d_{1,3}$=2; $d_{2,3}$=11.We do not compute $d_{2,1}$, $d_{3,1}$ and $d_{3,2}$ because Minkowski distance is symmetric, i.e. $d_{i,j}$ = $d_{j,i}$ for 1≤i,j≤N. For simplicity we consider only the Manhattan distance in the example;
- *Step 2*: the vector with all the distances is computed for each AUA, D= {$d_{i,j}$ — i≠j and 1≤i≤ N, 2≤j≤ N}. Each dimension of the vector corresponds to a class of the AUA. In the example D ={3, 2, 11}.
- *Step 3*: the max element in the vector is extracted, which is M_{AUA} = MAX (D[i]). In the example M_{AUA} is 11.

Finally the last two features are the values M_{AUA} computed, respectively, with Manhattan and Euclidean distance. Thus, M_{AUA} is a measure of dissimilarity among the classes of the AUA.

4   Evaluation: Study Design

We designed an experiment in order to evaluate the effectiveness of the proposed technique, expressed through the research questions RQ1, RQ2, RQ3, and RQ4 stated in the introduction.

More specifically, the experiment is aimed at verifying whether the eight features are able to classify a mobile application as trusted or malicious. The classification is carried out by using a classifier built with the eight features discussed in the previous section. The evaluation consists of three stages: (i) a comparison of descriptive statistics of the populations of programs; (ii) hypotheses testing, to verify if the eight features have different distributions for the populations of malware and trusted applications; and (iii) a classification analysis aimed at assessing whether the features are able to correctly classify malware and trusted applications. The classification analysis was accomplished with Weka, a suite of machine learning software[7], largely employed in data mining for scientific research.

The dataset was made by 5,560 Android trusted applications and 5,560 Android malware applications: trusted applications of different categories (call & contacts, education, entertainment, GPS & travel, internet, lifestyle, news & weather, productivity, utilities, business, communication, email & SMS, fun & games, health & fitness, live wallpapers, personalization) were downloaded from Google Play[8], while the malware applications belong to the collection of the Drebin project [2,24]. The Drebin project is a dataset that gathers the majority of existing Android malware families. The dataset includes different types of malware categorized by installation methods and activation mechanisms, as well as the nature of carried malicious payloads, in particular the dataset includes 179 Android malware families. In order to answer RQ4, 5,560 apps were retrieved from AppChina[9] and 3,000 from Gfan[10], two widespread chinese (third party) markets.

With regards to the hypotheses testing, the null hypothesis to be tested is: H_0: 'malware and trusted applications have similar values of the features'.

The null hypothesis was tested with Mann-Whitney (with the p-level fixed to 0.05) and with Kolmogorov-Smirnov Test (with the p-level fixed to 0.05). We chose to run two different tests in order to enforce the conclusion validity.

The purpose of these tests is to determine the level of significance, i.e. the risk (the probability) that erroneous conclusions be drawn: in our case, we set the significance level equal to .05, which means that we accept to make mistakes 5 times out of 100.

The classification analysis was aimed at assessing whether the features where able to correctly classify malware and trusted applications.

---

[7] http://www.cs.waikato.ac.nz/ml/weka/.
[8] https://play.google.com/.
[9] http://www.appchina.com/.
[10] http://www.gfan.com/.

Six algorithms of classification were used: J48, LadTree, NBTree, Random-Forest, RandomTree and RepTree. These algorithms were applied separately to the eight features and to three groups of features.

The first group includes the move and the jump features, the second group includes the two distances, and the third group includes all the four features (move, jump, Manhattan and Euclidean features). The features grouping was driven by the goal to obtain the best results in classification, as discussed later in the paper.

5   Evaluation: Analysis of Data

For the sake of clarity, the results of our evaluation will be discussed reflecting the data analysis' division in three phases: descriptive statistics, hypotheses testing and classification.

5.1   Descriptive Statistics

The analysis of box plots (shown in Fig. 3) related to the eight features helps to identify the features more effective to discriminate malware from trusted applications.

The differences between the box plots of malware and trusted applications for the 'move' and 'jump' features suggest that the two populations could belong to different distributions. A huge part of the trusted sample (between the second and the third quartile) has values greater than the 75 % of the malware sample for this couple of features. The reason may reside, as conjectured in the introduction, in the fact that in trusted applications these op-codes are used for implementing a certain business logic (whose complexity may vary a lot), while in the malware they can be only employed basically for code fragmentation.

This hypothesis will be confirmed by the hypothesis testing, as discussed later.

The distributions of 'sparse-switch' and 'packed-switch' op-codes seem to show a difference in the two samples, too, which is more relevant for the 'sparse-switch' box plots. This evidence strengthens the starting assumption of the paper, that will be confirmed by the results of the hypotheses testing. Switch constructs are frequently used for implementing the business logic of remote control (command and control malware are very widespread) of a victim device, or the selection criteria for activating the payload.

Instead, the box plots related to the features 'invoke' and 'if' do not produce significant differences between malware and trusted samples.

Finally, the differences between the box plots of trusted applications and malware for the Manhattan and the Euclidean distance are much more pronounced than the previous cases, suggesting that the two populations could belong to different distributions. It is interesting to observe how in both the cases the third percentile of the malware sample is lower than the first percentile of the trusted sample.

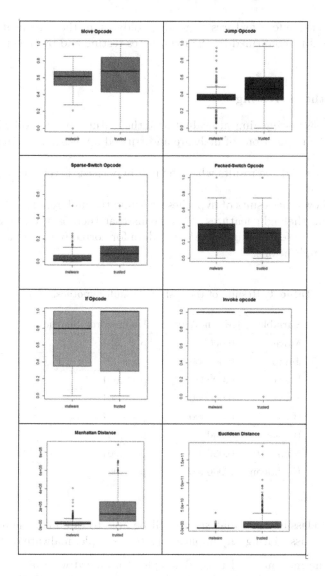

Fig. 3. Box plots for the features extracted.

The very tight box plots of the distances for malware, especially the one associated to the Manhattan distance, confirm the assumption that malware code has a lower variability (in terms of business logic) than trusted applications.

Remark 1: From descriptive statistics we find out that trusted applications box-plots (for 'move' and 'jump' opcodes, and for the two distances) range in a wider interval than the malware ones. This may reveal the fact that malware applications implement little business logic with respect to the trusted ones, and identifies these four features as good candidates for the classification phase. This result will be confirmed by the hypotheses testing and by the classification analysis.

5.2 Hypothesis Testing

The hypothesis testing aims at evaluating if the features present different distributions for the populations of malware and trusted applications with statistical evidence.

We assume valid the results when the null hypothesis is rejected by both the tests performed.

Table 1 shows the results of hypothesis testing: the null hypothesis H_0 can be rejected for all the eight features. This means that there is statistical evidence that the vector of features is a good candidate for correctly classifying malware and trusted applications.

Table 1. Results of the test of the null hypothesis H_0.

Variable	Mann-Whitney	Kolmogorov-Smirnov
Move	0,000000	$p < .001$
Jump	0,000000	$p < .001$
Packed	0,000240	$p < .001$
Sparse	0,000000	$p < .001$
If	0,000000	$p < .001$
Invoke	0,000000	$p < .001$
Manhattan	0,000000	$p < .001$
Euclidean	0,000000	$p < .001$

With the classification analysis we will be able to establish the accuracy of the features in associating any applications to a sample, malware or trusted.

Remark 2: the malware and trusted samples (produced with all the eight features) show a statistically significant difference by running both the tests.

5.3 Classification Analysis

The classification analysis consisted of building a classifier, and evaluating its accuracy. For training the classifier, we defined T as a set of labelled mobile applications *(AUA, l)*, where each AUA is associated to a label $l \in \{trusted, malicious\}$. For each AUA we built a feature vector $F \in R_y$, where y is the number of the features used in training phase *(1≤y≤8)*. To answer RQ1, we performed eight different classifications, each one with a single feature *(y=1)*, while for answering RQ2 we performed three classifications with $y>1$ (classifications with a set of features).

Using the features set that achieve best result in discriminating malware from trusted applications, for RQ3 we performed ten classifications, each of them with a different m label, where m represents the malware family $(0 < m < 10)$, in this case the label $l \in \{FakeInstaller, Plankton, DroidKungFu, GinMaster, BaseBridge, Adrd, KMin, Geinimi, DroidDream, Opfake\}$.

To answer RQ4, we used the same feature set as for RQ3: the only difference is that we classified using n label, where n represents the marketplace, i.e. trusted (GooglePlay) and 3P (AppChina and Gfan).

For the learning phase, we use a k-fold cross-validation: the dataset is randomly partitioned into k subsets. A single subset is retained as the validation dataset for testing the model, while the remaining k-1 subsets of the original dataset are used as training data. We repeated the process for k times; each one of the k subsets has been used once as the validation dataset. To obtain a single estimate, we computed the average of the k results from the folds.

We evaluated the effectiveness of the classification method with the following procedure:

1. build a training set $T \subset D$;
2. build a testing set T' = $D \div T$;
3. run the training phase on T;
4. apply the learned classifier to each element of T'.

We performed a 10-fold cross validation: we repeated the four steps 10 times varying the composition of T (and hence of T').

The results that we obtained with this procedure are shown in Table 2. Three metrics were used to evaluate the classification results: recall, precision and roc area.

The precision has been computed as the proportion of the examples that truly belong to class X among all those which were assigned to the class. It is the ratio of the number of relevant records retrieved to the total number of irrelevant and relevant records retrieved:

$$Precision = \frac{tp}{tp + fp}$$

where tp indicates the number of true positives and fp indicates the number of false positives.

The recall has been computed as the proportion of examples that were assigned to class X, among all the examples that truly belong to the class, i.e. how much part of the class was captured. It is the ratio of the number of relevant records retrieved to the total number of relevant records:

$$Recall = \frac{tp}{tp + fn}$$

where *fn* is the number of false negatives. Precision and recall are inversely related. The Roc Area is defined as the probability that a positive instance randomly chosen is classified above a negative randomly chosen.

The classification analysis suggests several considerations. With regards to the precision:

- All the algorithms are able to effectively classify both trusted applications and malicious applications (with the exception of the 'packed-switch' feature that exhibits a value of precision in the trusted classification lower than 0.5 with the NBTree classification algorithm).
- The features 'move' and 'jump' return the best results for the classification of malware applications (in particular, the precision of the 'move' is equal to 0.926 with RandomForest classification algorithm), the features Manhattan distance and Euclidean distance appear to be the best to classify trusted applications (in particular precision of the Euclidean distance for the trusted applications amounted to 0.934 with J48 and NBTree classification algorithms).
- The 'Invoke', 'Packed', 'Switch' and 'If' features are characterized by precision values smaller than the other features analyzed, but exhibit much better results with regard to the classification of malware, if compared to trusted applications. However, in any case, these values are lower than the features 'move' and 'jump' for detecting malware and Manhattan and Euclidean distance, for classifying the trusted applications.

With regards to the recall:

- All the algorithms are able to classify effectively malware (with the exception of the 'packed-switch', 'invoke' and 'if' features that exhibit a value of recall lower than 0.5 in the trusted classification).
- The recall presents high values for malware detection (the Euclidean distance allows for a recall equal to 0.98 with J48 and NBTree classification algorithms), while the trusted applications detection appears to be weaker if compared to the malware detection, in fact the maximum recall value for trusted applications distribution is equal to 0.821 (corresponding to the 'move' feature with RandomForest algorithm).
- The other features have lower values of recall for both the distributions.

With regards to the roc area:

- The performances of all the algorithms are pretty the same for malware and trusted applications.
- The 'move' feature presents the maximum rocarea value equal to 0.892 with RandomForest algorithm.
- The 'invoke' feature presents the lowest values of roc-area.

Relying on this first classification, we selected those features which had the best performance, in order to investigate if grouping them could increase the accuracy of the classification obtained with single features.

The following three groups of features were identified: (i) 'move-jump', in order to obtain the maximum precision value for detecting malware; (ii) 'Manhattan-Euclidean', in order to obtain the maximum precision value in the detection of trusted applications, and (iii) 'move-jump-Manhattan-Euclidean', in order to combine the characteristics of the two sets of features previously considered.

The classification accomplished by using these groups of features confirms our expectations: we obtained results significantly better than in the case of the classification with single features, as Table 3 shows.

The group of features 'move-jump' allows for a precision equal to 0.939 by performing the classification of malware with the J48 algorithm, while the precision of the classification of trusted applications is equal to 0.782 using the J48, the RandomForest and the RandomTree algorithm.

Combining the two features produces an improvement on the detection of malware (0.939), in fact by using only the 'move' the precision is equal to 0.926, by using the algorithm RandomForest; while the single 'jump' feature reaches a precision equal to 0.886, by using the algorithm RandomTree.

The recall is 0.911 in the classification of malware, when using the algorithm RandomForest and RandomTree, while for the classification of trusted applications is 0.853 by using the J48 algorithm.

The maximum value of rocarea is equal to 0.928 by using the algorithm RandomForest.

The group of the features 'Manhattan-Euclidean' presents a precision in the detection of malware equal to 0.912, by using the algorithm RandomForest, while with regard to the trusted applications a value equal to 0.935 is obtained by using the algorithms J48 and NBTree. Combining these two features produces an improvement for the detection of the trusted applications: in fact, the precision of the feature 'Manhattan' for trusted applications is equal to 0.888 with the algorithm NBTree, for the feature 'Euclidean' is equal to 0.934 with the algorithm J48 and NBTree.

The recall is 0.961 in the classification of malware using the algorithm J48, while in the trusted applications detection is equal to 0.77 using the algorithm RandomTree. The maximum value of rocarea is equal to 0.897 using the algorithm RandomForest.

The classification of the combination of the four features leads to optimal results for the detection of both malware and trusted applications: in fact, the value of precision for the detection of malware is equal to 0.931 by using the algorithm RandomForest and 0.902 for the trusted applications, by using the algorithm RandomForest. The recall is 0.961 using the algorithm RandomForest in the case of malware, and 0.821 using the algorithms RandomForest and RandomTree. The rocArea is maintained equal for the detection of both trusted applications and malware, using the algorithm RandomForest. This result is particularly valuable: tests producing values of ROCArea greater than 0.9 are usually considered optimal in terms of accuracy.

Table 2. Classification Results: Precision, Recall and RocArea for classifying Malware and Trusted applications, computed with the single features, with the algorithms J48, LadTree, NBTree, RandomForest, RandomTree and RepTree.

Features	Algorithm	Precision		Recall		RocArea	
		Malware	Trusted	Malware	Trusted	Malware	Trusted
move	J48	0.905	0.714	0.885	0.757	0.856	0.856
	LADTree	0.81	0.714	0.887	0.742	0.858	0.858
	NBTree	0.81	0.713	0.887	0.742	0.859	0.859
	RandomForest	0.926	0.69	0.867	0.821	0.802	0.802
	RandomTree	0.924	0.695	0.866	0.817	0.88	0.88
	RepTree	0.904	0.715	0.886	0.755	0.886	0.886
jump	J48	0.872	0.706	0.896	0.651	0.858	0.858
	LADTree	0.866	0.732	0.91	0.626	0.875	0.875
	NBTree	0.853	0.753	0.925	0.575	0.861	0.861
	RandomForest	0.887	0.735	0.903	0.697	0.876	0.876
	RandomTree	0.886	0.736	0.904	0.695	0.868	0.868
	RepTree	0.885	0.713	0.893	0.695	0.871	0.871
invoke	J48	0.765	0.598	0.935	0.227	0.569	0.569
	LADTree	0.765	0.598	0.935	0.227	0.569	0.569
	NBTree	0.765	0.598	0.935	0.227	0.569	0.569
	RandomForest	0.765	0.598	0.935	0.227	0.578	0.578
	RandomTree	0.765	0.598	0.935	0.227	0.569	0.569
	RepTree	0.765	0.598	0.935	0.227	0.569	0.569
LADTree **packed**	J48	0.67	0.576	0.937	0.201	0.619	0.619
		0.751	0.512	0.938	0.161	0.715	0.715
	NBTree	0.732	0.373	0.95	0.059	0.635	0.635
	RandomForest	0.768	0.557	0.918	0.254	0.64	0.64
	RandomTree	0.759	0.569	0.935	0.201	0.725	0.725
	RepTree	0.752	0.531	0.936	0.107	0.697	0.697
Sparse	J48	0.846	0.731	0.919	0.555	0.747	0.747
	LADTree	0.834	0.718	0.92	0.501	0.826	0.826
	NBTree	0.828	0.702	0.921	0.489	0.801	0.801
	RandomForest	0.831	0.747	0.932	0.493	0.855	0.855
	RandomTree	0.824	0.767	0.941	0.462	0.849	0.849
	RepTree	0.837	0.723	0.921	0.52	0.836	0.836
if	J48	0.766	0.6	0.935	0.229	0.621	0.621
	LADTree	0.766	0.596	0.934	0.232	0.71	0.71
	NBTree	0.765	0.595	0.926	0.227	0.71	0.71
	RandomForest	0.771	0.596	0.928	0.216	0.726	0.726
	RandomTree	0.771	0.596	0.928	0.216	0.72	0.72
	RepTree	0.768	0.598	0.932	0.241	0.708	0.708
Manhattan	J48	0.856	0.844	0.934	0.575	0.843	0.843
	LADTree	0.854	0.848	0.956	0.556	0.868	0.868
	NBTree	0.838	0.888	0.969	0.5	0.854	0.854
	RandomForest	0.885	0.783	0.921	0.686	0.852	0.852
	RandomTree	0.889	0.789	0.918	0.7	0.809	0.809
	RepTree	0.861	0.842	0.953	0.591	0.849	0.849
LADTree **Euclidean**	J48	0.833	0.934	0.98	0.478	0.71	0.71
		0.836	0.908	0.974	0.489	0.869	0.869
	NBTree	0.833	0.934	0.98	0.478	0.854	0.854
	RandomForest	0.88	0.771	0.918	0.702	0.854	0.854
	RandomTree	0.891	0.765	0.915	0.706	0.811	0.811
	RepTree	0.851	0.829	0.951	0.558	0.852	0.852

Table 3. Classification Results: Precision, Recall and RocArea for classifying Malware and Trusted applications, computed with the three groups of features, with the algorithms J48, LadTree, NBTree, RandomForest, RandomTree and RepTree.

Features	Algorithm	Precision		Recall		RocArea	
		Malware	Trusted	Malware	Trusted	Malware	Trusted
move-jump	J48	0.939	0.782	0.909	0.853	0.917	0.917
	LADTree	0.8	0.723	0.896	0.708	0.877	0.877
	NBTree	0.912	0.748	0.9	0.775	0.909	0.909
	RandomForest	0.931	0.782	0.911	0.828	0.928	0.928
	RandomTree	0.929	0.782	0.911	0.824	0.892	0.892
	RepTree	0.93	0.748	0.894	0.83	0.916	0.916
Manhattan-Euclidean	J48	0.855	0.935	0.961	0.569	0.841	0.841
	LADTree	0.85	0.853	0.958	0.551	0.868	0.868
	NBTree	0.84	0.935	0.956	0.515	0.855	0.855
	RandomForest	0.906	0.83	0.938	0.746	0.897	0.897
	RandomTree	0.912	0.807	0.927	0.77	0.849	0.849
	RepTree	0.871	0.854	0.954	0.626	0.854	0.854
Move-Jump Manhattan-Euclidean	J48	0.916	0.852	0.945	0.777	0.897	0.897
	LADTree	0.885	0.803	0.933	0.682	0.911	0.911
	NBTree	0.922	0.738	0.891	0.806	0.925	0.925
	RandomForest	0.931	0.902	0.971	0.821	0.946	0.946
	RandomTree	0.931	0.894	0.958	0.812	0.8	0.8
	RepTree	0.927	0.876	0.955	0.746	0.904	0.904

Table 5 shows the results obtained by classifying, using the 'move-jump-Manhattan-Euclidean' feature group, malware applications labelled with families.

The classification using the label of the 10 most populous families shows the following results:

- **Adrd:** best value of precision (0.824) is obtained using the J48 algorithm, this family is represented by 91 samples in our dataset;
- **BaseBridge:** best precision value(0.971) is obtained with the RandomForest algorithm, this family is represented by 330 samples in our dataset;
- **DroidDream:** best precision value (0.852) is obtained using the J48 algorithm, this family is represented by 81 samples in our dataset;
- **DroidKungFu:** best value of precision (0.571) is retrieved using the LADTree algorithm, this family is represented by 667 samples in our dataset;
- **FakeInstaller:** best precision value (0.969) is obtained using the NBTree algorithm, this family is represented by 925 samples in our dataset;
- **Geinimi:** best value of precision (0.76) is obtained using the NBTree algorithm. The family is represented by 92 samples in malware dataset;
- **Ginmaster:** best precision value (0.721) is retrieved using the RandomTree algorithm. this family is represented by 339 samples in the dataset;
- **Kmin:** best precision value (0.98) is obtained using J48 and LADTree algorithms. The family is represented by 147 samples in our dataset;

Table 4. Classification Results: Precision, Recall and RocArea for classifying Trusted and Third-Party (3P) applications, computed with the **Move-Jump-Manhattan-Euclidean** feature, with the algorithms J48, LadTree, NBTree, RandomForest, RandomTree and RepTree.

Features	Algorithm	Precision		Recall		RocArea	
		Trusted	3P	Trusted	3P	Trusted	3P
	J48	0.732	0.76	0.596	0.855	0.788	0.788
Move-	LADTree	0.73	0.729	0.515	0.873	0.739	0.739
Jump-	NBTree	0.683	0.752	0.597	0.815	0.758	0.758
Manhattan-	RandomForest	0.75	0.78	0.638	0.858	0.834	0.834
Euclidean	RandomTree	0.715	0.782	0.654	0.826	0.786	0.786
	RepTree	0.73	0.761	0.6	0.851	0.792	0.792

- **OpFake:** best precision value (0.953) is obtained using RandomForest and RandomTree algorithms. The Opfake family, the first Android polymorphic malware in the wild[11], is represented by 613 samples in our dataset;
- **Plankton**: best value of precision (0.936) obtained using the RandomForest algorithm. The Plankton family is represented in our dataset by 613 samples.

Remark 3: The results show that 5 out of 10 families obtained precision values greater than 0.9, while 4 families out of 10 obtained precision values ranging between 0.7 and 0.82, and finally just a family (DroidKungFu) obtained a precision value lower than 0.6. The features used are able to identify successfully only some families.

Table 4 shows the results obtained by classifying, using the 'move-jump-Manhattan-Euclidean' features, trusted applications and applications taken from third parties marketplaces. The best value of precision in trusted identification (0.732) is obtained using the J48 algorithm, while the best value of recall (0.654) is obtained with the RandomTree algorithm. The best precision value(0.782) in the identification of third-party applications is obtained with the RandomTree algorithm, while the best recall value (0.873) is obtained with the LADTree algorithm.

From these results it emerges that trusted applications retrieved from Google Play are rather similar to the third-party applications when we characterize them with the features belonging to our method.

Remark 4: The selected features are not able to recognize apps taken from third party markets.

Table 5. Classification Results: Precision, Recall and RocArea for classifying Malware families, computed with the **Move-Jump-Manhattan-Euclidean** feature, with the algorithms J48, LadTree, NBTree, RandomForest, RandomTree and RepTree.

Family	Algorithm	Precision	Recall	RocArea
	J48	0.636	0.157	0.795
	LADTree	0.5	0.011	0.755
Adrd	NBTree	0.824	0.157	0.832
	RandomForest	0.696	0.18	0.824
	RandomTree	0.696	0.18	0.823
	RepTree	0.737	0.157	0.815
	J48	0.963	0.706	0.925
	LADTree	0.884	0.63	0.882
BaseBridge	NBTree	0.942	0.697	0.932
	RandomForest	0.971	0.709	0.938
	RandomTree	0.95	0.703	0.922
	RepTree	0.952	0.667	0.915
	J48	0.852	0.613	0.871
	LADTree	0	0	0
DroidDream	NBTree	0.783	0.627	0.898
	RandomForest	0.831	0.653	0.939
	RandomTree	0.731	0.653	0.864
	RepTree	0.678	0.533	0.897
	J48	0.424	0.934	0.909
	LADTree	0.571	0.497	0.855
DroidKungFu	NBTree	0.421	0.942	0.916
	RandomForest	0.425	0.945	0.922
	RandomTree	0.425	0.954	0.91
	RepTree	0.414	0.925	0.908
	J48	0.961	0.847	0.959
	LADTree	0.854	0.814	0.928
FakeInstaller	NBTree	0.969	0.857	0.965
	RandomForest	0.776	0.864	0.973
	RandomTree	0.963	0.864	0.964
	RepTree	0.94	0.852	0.959
	J48	0.5	0.212	0.843
	LADTree	0	0	0.76
Geinimi	NBTree	0.76	0.224	0.843
	RandomForest	0.773	0.259	0.856
	RandomTree	0.629	0.259	0.829
	RepTree	0.708	0.2	0.836
	J48	0.629	0.456	0.811
	LADTree	0.342	0.193	0.695
Ginmaster	NBTree	0.641	0.447	0.86
	RandomForest	0.705	0.483	0.904
	RandomTree	0.721	0.399	0.783
	RepTree	0.59	0.378	0.818
	J48	0.98	0.204	0.885
	LADTree	0.98	0.014	0.857
Kmin	NBTree	0.97	0.204	0.817
	RandomForest	0.968	0.204	0.885
	RandomTree	0.777	0.825	0.723
	RepTree	0.968	0.204	0.885
	J48	0.928	0.633	0.935
	LADTree	0.367	0.89	0.877
OpFake	NBTree	0.854	0.627	0.937
	RandomForest	0.953	0.635	0.942
	RandomTree	0.953	0.637	0.937
	RepTree	0.899	0.613	0.929
	J48	0.918	0.838	0.945
	LADTree	0.833	0.686	0.909
Plankton	NBTree	0.928	0.846	0.96
	RandomForest	0.936	0.864	0.971
	RandomTree	0.912	0.845	0.935
	RepTree	0.89	0.821	0.946

6   Conclusions and Future Works

The aim of this work is to understand whether a features vector obtained by the counting of some op-codes occurrences can be used to classify a mobile application as malware or trusted and if the app is taken from a third party market.

The experiment allowed us to provide the following answers to the research questions we posed:

- RQ1: the features extracted are able to discriminate malware from trusted applications. In particular, the features 'move' and 'jump' produced values of precision equal to 0.9 in the identification of malware, while the 'Manhattan' and 'Euclidean' distance revealed to be the best ones for detecting the trusted applications.
- RQ2: grouping the features may increase precision and accuracy of classification. In fact the classification with all the features allows for benefits for both malware and trusted applications classification, achieving a precision of 0.931 in the detection of malware and 0.902 in detection of trusted applications. Additionally, the accuracy of the tests is equal to 0.95, which is considered optimal.
- RQ3: classifying the top 10 most populous families, we obtain a precision value greater than 0.7 for 9 families, and a value greater than 0.9 for 4 families, suggesting that the features extracted may be helpful to identify the malware family.
- RQ4: the features extracted are not effective in discriminating trusted and third-party applications. From this study we note that the trusted and third-party applications are more similar in terms of the frequency of op-codes than malware ones.

Unfortunately code morphing techniques could be employed in order to alterate op-codes histograms. This is usually accomplished by adding junk code which does not alter the behaviour of malware, but just the distribution of op-codes.

This evasion technique can be contrasted by two ways: first, by applying methods for finding junk code within malware, which is part of future work. Second, by identifying precise patterns and sequences of op-codes that could be recurrent in malicious malware's code. This latter technique could also help to understand which is the family each malware instance belongs to, which is a further improvement of interest in the area of malware detection.

An undeniable advantage of our technique is the easiness of implementation and the correspondent lightness in terms of requested resources: basically the proposed method needs to extract the occurrence frequency of a set of op-codes. The method can be straightforward reproduced and this fosters the replications of our study for confirming the outcomes or finding possible weakness points.

We can compare our work with [2] and [19], as these are the closest works to ours for technique among the considered related works. Arp et al. [2] obtained a precision (94 %) which is almost identical than the one obtained with our approach (93.9 %), while Peng et al. [19] reported a ROC AREA of 95 %, which coincides with our best ROC AREA (95.6 %.) The best deployment of the proposed classifier is a client-server architecture, where the classifier resides in a server and a client app is installed on the user device and requires the analysis of a certain app to the server.

The main limitation of the evaluation stands in the external validity, as we have considered a sample of applications collected in 2012. Running our method on newest samples could produce different results. However, some mitigation factors must be taken into account for this experimental threat. First, we have considered a large set of samples, amounting to 11,200 units. This could assure a wide coverage of many kinds of malware and trusted applications, so the sample could be considered well representative of the original population. Additionally, in order to enforce the validity of the used dataset, we should consider that malware traditionally evolves by improving existing malware with (a few) new functions, or merging fragments of existing malware applications.

References

1. Androguard (2014). https://code.google.com/p/androguard/
2. Arp, D., Spreitzenbarth, M., Hubner, M., Gascon, H., Rieck, K.: Drebin: effective and explainable detection of android malware in your pocket. In: NDSS 2014, Network and Distributed System Security Symposium. IEEE (2014)
3. Attaluri, S., McGhee, S., Stamp, M.: Profile hidden markov models and metamorphic virus detection. J. Comput. Virol. Hacking Tech. 5(2), 179–192 (2008)
4. Baysa, D., Low, R.M., Stamp, M.: Structural entropy and metamorphic malware. J. Comput. Virol. Hacking Tech. 9(4), 179–192 (2013)
5. Bilar, D.: Opcodes as predictor for malware. Int. J. Electron. Secur. Digital Forensics 1(2), 156–168 (2007)
6. Canfora, G., Mercaldo, F., Visaggio, C.: A classifier of malicious android applications. In: IWSMA 2013, 2nd International Workshop on Security of Mobile Applications, in conjunction with the International Conference on Availability, Reliability and Security, pp. 607–614. IEEE (2013)
7. Chakradeo, S., Reaves, B., Traynor, P., Enck, W.: Mast: triage for market-scale mobile malware analysis. In: WISEC 2013, 6th ACM Conference on Security in Wireless and Mobile Networks, pp. 13–24. ACM (2013)
8. Chandra, D., Franz, M.: Fine-grained information flow analysis and enforcement in a java virtual machine. In: ACSAC 2007, 23rd Annual Computer Security Applications Conference, pp. 463–475. IEEE (2007)
9. Choucane, M., Lakhotia, A.: Using engine signature to detect metamorphic malware. In: WORM 2006, 4th ACM workshop on Recurring malcode, pp. 73–78. ACM (2006)
10. Desnos, A.: Android: static analysis using similarity distance. In: HICSS 2012, 45th Hawaii International Conference on System Sciences, pp. 5394–5403. IEEE (2012)
11. Enck, W., Gilbert, P., Chun, B., Con, L., Jung, J., McDaniel, P., Sheth, A.: Taintdroid: an information-flow tracking system for realtime privacy monitoring on smartphones. In: OSDI 2010, 9th USENIX Symposium on Operating Systems Design and Implementation (2010)

12. Fedler, R., Schütte, J., Kulicke, M.: On the effectiveness of malware protection on android: An evaluation of android antivirus apps, (2014). http://www.aisec. fraunhofer.de/, http://www.aisec.fraunhofer.de/content/dam/aisec/Dokumente/ Publikationen/Studien_TechReports/deutsch/042013-Technical-Report-Android-Virus-Test.pdf
13. Gartner (2014). http://www.gartner.com/newsroom/id/2944819
14. Gibler, C., Crussell, J., Erickson, J., Chen, H.: Androidleaks: automatically detecting potential privacy leaks in android applications on a large scale. In: Katzenbeisser, S., Weippl, E., Camp, L.J., Volkamer, M., Reiter, M., Zhang, X. (eds.) Trust 2012. LNCS, vol. 7344, pp. 291–307. Springer, Heidelberg (2012)
15. GoogleMobile   (2014).   http://googlemobile.blogspot.it/2012/02/android-and-security.html
16. GooglePlay (2014). https://play.google.com/
17. Marforio, C., Aurelien, F., Srdjan, C.: Application collusion attack on the permission-based security model and its implications for modern smartphone systems (2011). ftp://ftp.inf.ethz.ch/doc/tech-reports/7xx/724.pdf
18. Oberheide, J., Miller, C.: Dissecting the android bouncer. In: SummerCon (2012). https://jon.oberheide.org/files/summercon12-bouncer.pdf
19. Peng, H., Gates, C., Sarma, B., Li, N., Qi, Y., Potharaju, R., Nita-Rotaru, C., Molloy, I.: Using probabilistic generative models for ranking risks of android apps. In: CCS 2012, 19th ACM Conference on Computer and Communications Security, pp. 241–252 (2012)
20. Rad, B.B., Masrom, M.: Metamorphic virus variants classification using opcode frequency histogram. Latest Trends on Computers (Volume I) (2010)
21. Rad, B., Masrom, M., Ibrahim, S.: Opcodes histogram for classifying metamorphic portable executables malware. In: ICEEE 2012, International Conference on E-Learning and E-Technologies in Education, pp. 209–213 (2012)
22. Reina, A., Fattori, A., Cavallaro, L.: A system call-centric analysis and stimulation technique to automatically reconstruct android malware behaviors. In: EUROSEC 2013, 6th European Workshop on Systems Security (2013)
23. Sahs, J., Khan, L.: A machine learning approach to android malware detection. In: EISIC 2012, European Intelligence and Security Informatics Conference, pp. 141–147 (2012)
24. Spreitzenbarth, M., Ectler, F., Schreck, T., Freling, F., Hoffmann, J.: Mobilesandbox: looking deeper into android applications. In: SAC 2013, 28th International ACM Symposium on Applied Computing (2013)
25. Wu, D., Mao, C., Wei, T., Lee, H., Wu, K.: Droidmat: android malware detection through manifest and api calls tracing. In: Asia JCIS 2012, 7th Asia Joint Conference on Information Security, pp. 62–69 (2012)
26. Zheng, M., Sun, M., Lui, J.: Droid analytics: a signature based analytic system to collect, extract, analyze and associate android malware. In: TrustCom 2013, International Conference on Trust, Security and Privacy in Computing and Communications, pp. 163–171 (2013)
27. Zhou, Y., Jiang, X.: Dissecting android malware: characterization and evolution. In: SP 2012, IEEE Symposium on Security and Privacy, pp. 95–109 (2012)

Automated Verification of e-Cash Protocols

Jannik Dreier[1,2,3], Ali Kassem[4,5(✉)], and Pascal Lafourcade[6]

[1] Inria, 54600 Villers-lés-Nancy, France
[2] CNRS, Loria, UMR 7503, 54506 Vandoeuvre-lés-Nancy, France
[3] Université de Lorraine, Loria, UMR 7503, 54506 Vandoeuvre-lés-Nancy, France
jannik.dreier@loria.fr
[4] University Grenoble Alpes, VERIMAG, 38000 Grenoble, France
[5] Ascola Team (Mines Nantes, Inria, Lina) DAPI,
École des Mines de Nantes, Nantes, France
ali.kassem@mines-nantes.fr
[6] University Clermont Auvergne, LIMOS, Clermont-Ferrand, France
pascal.lafourcade@udamail.fr

Abstract. Electronic cash (e-cash) permits secure e-payments by providing security and anonymity similar to real cash. Several protocols have been proposed to meet security and anonymity properties of e-cash. However, there are no general formal definitions that allow the automatic verification of e-cash protocols. In this paper, we propose a formal framework to define and verify security properties of e-cash protocols. To this end, we model e-cash protocols in the applied π-calculus, and we formally define five relevant security properties. Finally, we validate our framework by analyzing, using the automatic tool ProVerif, four e-cash protocols: the online and the offline Chaum protocols, the Digicash protocol, and the protocol by Petersen and Poupard.

Keywords: e-Cash · Formal verification · Double spending · Exculpability · Privacy · Applied π-calculus · ProVerif

1 Introduction

Although current banking and electronic payment systems such as credit cards or, *e.g.*, PayPal allow clients to transfer money around the world in a fraction of a second, they do not fully ensure the clients' privacy. In such systems, no transaction can be made in a completely anonymous way, since the bank or the payment provider knows all details of the clients' transactions. By analyzing a clients payments for, *e.g.*, transportation, hotels, restaurants, movies, clothes, and so on, the payment provider can typically deduce the client's whereabouts, and much information about his lifestyle.

Physical cash provides better privacy: the payments are difficult to trace as there is no central authority that monitors all transactions, in contrast to most

This research was conducted with the support of the "Digital trust" Chair from the University of Auvergne Foundation.

© Springer International Publishing Switzerland 2016
M.S. Obaidat and P. Lorenz (Eds.): ICETE 2015, CCIS 585, pp. 223–244, 2016.
DOI: 10.1007/978-3-319-30222-5_11

electronic payment systems. This property is the inspiration for "untraceable" e-cash systems. The concept of "untraceable" e-cash was introduced by David Chaum [8]. The general e-cash system involves three main parties: client, bank and seller. A client withdraws an electronic coin from the bank, which blindly signs it. The bank is the only party capable to create coins. The client then can use the coins to pay a seller. Finally, the seller deposits the coin he received from client in his bank account. At deposit the bank verifies that the coin was not deposited before. If the coin was deposited before, the banks verifies whether the seller deposited the same coin twice, or the client double-spent the coin. In the former case the bank reject the deposit, while in the latter case the bank takes actions depending on the type of the system (online or offline). In online e-cash systems, *i.e.*, those where a seller has to contact the bank at payment before accepting the coin, the bank acknowledge the seller to reject the coin at payment. Thus, in such systems normally double spending is not possible. In contrast, in offline systems the bank runs a procedure to disclose the client's identity. This can be achieved due to the fact that offline systems usually support the encoding of client's identity into the coin at its withdrawal. To protect the client, an e-cash system must also ensures that the bank cannot frame a honest client for double spending. We identify the following main security properties of e-cash protocols:

- *Unforgeability*, which says that clients cannot spend more coins than they withdrew.
- *Double Spending Identification* ensures that the bank can identify the double spender.
- *Exculpability* ensures that an attacker cannot forge a double spend, and hence incorrectly blame an honest client for double spending.
- *Weak Anonymity* ensures that the attacker cannot link a client to a payment.
- *Strong Anonymity* ensures, additionally to weak anonymity, that the attacker cannot decide whether two payments were made by the same client.

Contributions. In this paper, we propose a general formalization for e-cash protocols in the applied π-calculus [1]. Our definitions are amenable to automatic verification using ProVerif [5], and cover all the identified unforgery and privacy properties: *Unforgeability, Double Spending Identification, Exculpability, Weak Anonymity, Strong Anonymity*. Finally, we validate our approach by analyzing the online protocol proposed by Chaum *et al.* [8], as well as, a real implementation based on it [26]. We also analyze the offline variant of this e-cash system [9], and the protocol by Peterson and Poupard [23]. Some of the results have been published in a previous paper [16]. This paper extends our results, and provides an additional case study.

Related Work. Several e-cash protocols have been proposed [2,6,9,11–13,17, 19,23] since the seminal work by David Chaum [8], which introduces the blinding signature primitive to allow the anonymous withdrawal of coins. Chaum *et al.* [9] presented an offline variant of Chaum [8] protocol. Berry Schoenmakers has described a real e-cash protocol that is implemented by DigiCash based on online

Chaum protocol [8]. Abe *et al.* [2] have introduced a scheme based on partial blind signature, which allows the bank to include certain information in the blind signature of the coin, for example the expiration date or the value of the coin. Kim *et al.* [19] have proposed an e-cash system that supports coin refund and assigns them a value, based again on partial blind signature. Peterson and Poupard [23] have proposed a protocol to prevent extortion attacks by relying on additional party, the trustee, which publishes, in case of coin or key extortion, some information that can be used by the sellers to reject illegal coins.

However, several attacks have been found against various existing e-cash protocols: for example Pfitzmann *et al.* [24,25] break the anonymity of [11–13]. Cheng *et al.* [10] show that Brand's protocol [6] allows a client to spend a coin more than once without being identified. Aboud and Agoun [3] show that [17] cannot ensure the anonymity and unlinkability properties that were claimed. These numerous attacks triggered some work on formal analysis of e-cash protocols in the computational [7] and symbolic world [21,27]. Canard and Gouget [7] provide formal definitions for various privacy and unforgeability properties in the computational world, but only with manual proofs as their framework is difficult to automate. In contrast, Luo *et al.* [21] and Thandar *et al.* [27] both rely on automatic tools (ProVerif [5], and AVISPA [4] respectively). Yet, they only consider a fraction of the essential security properties, and for some properties Luo *et al.*only perform a manual analysis. Moreover, much of their reasoning is targeted on their respective case studies, and cannot easily be transferred to other protocols.

Outline. In Sect. 2, we model e-cash protocols in the applied π-calculus. Then, in Sect. 3, we formalize the security properties. In Sect. 4, we validate our framework by analyzing, using ProVerif [5], the online and the offline e-cash systems by Chaum *et al.* [8,9], the implementation based on the online protocol [26], and the protocol by Peterson and Poupard [23]. Finally, in Sect. 5, we discuss our results and outline future work.

2   Modeling e-Cash Protocols in the Applied π-Calculus

An e-cash system involves at least the following parties: the *client* C who has an account at the *bank* B, the *seller* S who accepts electronic coins, and the bank, which certifies the electronic coins. A protocol can has several authorities that run in parallel with the bank. A typically e-cash protocol runs in three phases:

1. *Withdrawal*: the client withdraws an electronic coin from the bank, which debits the client's account.
2. *Payment*: the client spends the coin by executing a transaction with a seller.
3. *Deposit*: the seller deposits the transaction at the bank, which credits the seller's account.

In addition to these three main phases, some systems allow the clients to return coins directly to the bank without using them in a payment, or to restore coins that have been lost. As these functionalities are not implemented by all protocols, our model does not require them. Moreover, we assume that the coins are neither transferable nor divisible.

We model e-cash protocols in the applied π-calculus. We refer to the original paper [1] for a detailed description of its syntax and semantics. We assume a Dolev-Yao style attacker [15], which has a complete control to the network, except the private channels. He can eavesdrop, remove, substitute, duplicate and delay messages that the parties are sending to one another, and even insert messages of his choice on the public channels. Parties other than the attacker can be either honest or corrupted. Honest parties follow the protocol's specification, do not reveal their secret data (e.g., account numbers, keys etc.) to the attacker, and do not take malicious actions such as double spending a coin or generating fake transactions. Honest parties are modeled as processes in the applied π-calculus. These processes can exchange messages on public or private channels, create fresh random values and perform tests and cryptographic operations, which are modeled as functions on terms with respect to an equational theory describing their properties. Corrupted parties are those that collude with the attacker by revealing their secret data to him, taking orders from him, and also making malicious actions. We model corrupted parties as in Definition 15 from [14]: if the process P is an honest party, then the process P^c is its corrupted version. This is a variant of P which shares with the attacker channels ch_1 and ch_2. Through ch_1, P^c sends all its inputs and freshly generated names (but not other channel names). From ch_2, P^c receives messages that can influence its behavior. We define an e-cash protocol as a tuple of processes each representing the role of a certain party.

Definition 1 (e-Cash Protocol). *An e-cash protocol is a tuple $(B, S, C, \tilde{n}_p)$, where B is the process executed by the bank, S is the process executed by the sellers, C is the process executed by the clients, and $\tilde{n}_p$ is the set of the private channel names used by the protocol.*

To reason about privacy properties we use runs of the protocol, called e-cash instances.

Definition 2 (e-Cash Instance). *Given an e-cash protocol, an e-cash instance is a closed plain process:*

$$CP = \nu\tilde{n}.(B|S\sigma_{ids_1}|\ldots|S\sigma_{ids_l}|(C\sigma_{idc_1}\sigma_{c_{11}}\sigma_{ids_{11}}|\ldots|C\sigma_{idc_1}\sigma_{c_{1p_1}}\sigma_{ids_{1p_1}})|$$

$$\vdots$$

$$|(C\sigma_{idc_k}\sigma_{c_{k1}}\sigma_{ids_{k1}}|\ldots|C\sigma_{idc_k}\sigma_{c_{kp_k}}\sigma_{ids_{kp_k}}))$$

where $\tilde{n}$ is the set of all restricted names which includes the set of the protocol's private channels $\tilde{n}_p$; B is the process executed by the bank; $S\sigma_{ids_i}$ is the process executed by the seller whose identity is specified by the substitution σ_{ids_i}; $C\sigma_{idc_i}\sigma_{c_{ij}}\sigma_{ids_{ij}}$ is the process executed by the client whose identity is specified by the substitution σ_{idc_i}, and which spends the coin identified by the substitution $\sigma_{c_{ij}}$ to pay the seller with the identity specified by the substitution $\sigma_{ids_{ij}}$.

Note that, idc_i can spend p_i coins. Note also that, the bank process B can be structurally equivalent to $B_1, \ldots, B_k$, thus several authorities can be captured by our definition.

To improve the readability of our definitions, we introduce the notation of context $CP_I[\_]$ to denote the process CP with "holes" for all processes executed by the parties whose identities are included in the set I. For example, to enumerate all the sessions executed by the client idc_1 without repeating the entire e-cash instance, we can rewrite CP as $CP_{\{idc_1\}}[C\sigma_{idc_1}\sigma_{c_{11}}\sigma_{ids_{11}} | \cdots | C\sigma_{idc_1}\sigma_{c_{1p_1}}\sigma_{ids_{1p_1}}]$.

Finally, we use the notation C_w to denote a client that withdraws a coin, but does not spend it in a payment: C_w is a variant of the process C that halts at the end of withdrawal phase, *i.e.*, where the code corresponding to the payment phase is removed.

3 Formalizing Security Properties

In this section, we propose formal definitions for the three forgery-related properties: *Unforgeability*, *Double Spending Identification*, and *Exculpability*, as well as, for the two privacy properties: *Weak Anonymity* and *Strong Anonymity*.

3.1 Forgery-Related Properties

In an e-cash protocol only the bank should be able to create coins. A client must not be able to forge a coin, or to double spend a valid coin. This is ensured by *Unforgeability*, which we define using the following two events:

- *withdraw(c)*: is an event emitted when the coin c is withdrawn. This event is placed inside the bank process just before the bank outputs the coin's certificate (*e.g.*, a signature on the coin).
- *spend(c)*: is an event emitted when the coin c is spent. This event is placed inside the seller process just after he receives and accepts the coin.

Note that, events are annotations that mark important steps in the protocol execution, but do otherwise not change the behavior of processes.

Definition 3 (Unforgeability). *An e-cash protocol ensures* Unforgeability *if, for every e-cash instance CP, each occurrence of the event* spend(c) *is preceded by a distinct occurrence of the event* withdraw(c) *on every execution trace.*

If a fake coin is successfully spent, the event *spend* will be emitted without any matching event *withdraw*, violating the property. Similarly, in the case of a successful double spending the event *spend* will be emitted twice, but these events are preceded by only one occurrence of the event *withdraw*. Since a malicious client might be interested to create fake coins or double spend a coin, it is particularly interesting to study *Unforgeability* with an honest bank and corrupted clients. A partially corrupted seller, which *e.g.*, gives some information to the attacker but still emits the event *spend* correctly, could also be considered to check if a seller colluding with the client and the attacker can results in a coin forging. Note that, if the seller is totally corrupted then *Unforgeability* will be trivially violated, since a corrupted seller can simply emit the event *spend* for a forged coin, although there was no transaction.

In the rest of the paper, we illustrate all our notions with the *"real cash"* system (mainly coins and banknotes) as a running example. We hope that it helps the reader to understand the properties but also to feel the difference between real cash and e-cash systems.

Example 1 (Real Cash). In real cash, unforgeability is ensured by physical measures that make forging or copying coins and banknotes difficult, for example by adding serial numbers, using special paper, ultraviolet ink, holograms and so on.

In case of double spending, the bank should be able to identify the responsible client. This is ensured by *Double Spending Identification* (in short, DSI), which says that a client cannot double spend a coin without revealing his identity. To deposit a coin at the bank the seller has to present a *transaction* which contains, in addition to the coin, some information certifying that he received the coin in a payment. A *valid transaction* is a transaction which could be accepted by the bank, *i.e.*, it contains a correct proof that the coin is received in a correct payment. The bank accepts a valid transaction if it does not contain a coin that is already deposited using the same or a different transaction. In the following, we denote by TR the set of all transactions, and we define the function transId which takes a transaction $tr \in$ TR and returns a pair (s, c), where s identifies tr and c is the coin involved in tr. Such a pair can usually be computed from a transaction. We also denote by ID the set of all client identities, and by D a special data set that includes the data known to the bank after the protocol execution, *e.g.*, the data presents in the bank's database.

Definition 4 (Double Spending Identification). *An e-cash protocol ensures DSI if there exists a test* $\mathsf{T_{DSI}}$: TR $\times$ TR $\times$ D $\mapsto$ ID $\cup \{\bot\}$ *satisfying: for any two valid transactions tr_1 and tr_2 that are different but involve the same coin (i.e.,* transId$(tr_1) = (s_1, c)$, *and* transId$(tr_2) = (s_2, c)$ *for some coin c with $s_1 \neq s_2$), there exists $p \in$ D such that* $\mathsf{T_{DSI}}(tr_1, tr_2, p)$ *outputs $(idc, e) \in$ ID $\times$ D, where e is an evidence that idc withdrew the coin c.*

DSI allows the bank to identify the double spender by running a test $\mathsf{T_{DSI}}$ on two different transactions that involves the same coin. For example, consider a protocol where after a successful transaction the seller gets $x = m.id + r$ where id is the identity of the client (*e.g.*, his secret key), r is a random value (identifies the coin) chosen by the client at withdrawal, and m is the challenge of the seller. So, if the client double spends the same coin then the bank can compute id and r using the two equations: $x_1 = m_1.id + r$ and $x_2 = m_2.id + r$. The data p could be some information necessary to identify the double spender or to construct the evidence e. This data is usually presented to the bank at withdrawal or at deposit. The required evidence depends on the protocol. Note that, e is an evidence from the point of view of the bank, and not necessarily a proof for an outer judge. Thus, the goal of DSI is to preserve the security of the bank by enabling him to identify the responsible of a double spending. Note also that, if a client withdraws a coin and gives it to an attacker which double spends it, then the test returns the identity of the client and not the attacker's identity.

Example 2 (Real Cash). In real cash, double spending is prevented by ensuring that notes cannot be copied. However, DSI is not ensured: even if a central bank is able to identify copied banknotes using, *e.g.*, their serial numbers, this does not allow it to identify the person responsible for creating the counterfeit notes.

DSI gives rise to a potential problem: what if the client is honest and spends the coin only once, but the attacker (*e.g.*, a corrupted seller) is able to forge a second spend, or what if a corrupted bank is able to simulate a coin withdrawal and payment, *i.e.*, to forge a coin withdrawal and payment that seems to be made by a certain client. For instance, in the example mentioned above, the two equations are enough evidence for the bank. However, if the bank knows *id* he can generate the two equations himself and blame the client for double spending. So, to convince a judge, an additional evidence is needed, *e.g.*, the client's signature.

If any of the two situations mentioned above is possible, then a honest client could be falsely blamed for double spending, and also it gives raise to a corrupted client which is responsible of double spending to deny it. To solve this problem we define *Exculpability* which says that the attacker, even when colluding with the bank and the seller, cannot forge a double spend by a certain client in order to blame him. More precisely, provided a transaction executed by a client *idc*, the attacker cannot provide two different valid transactions which involves the same coin, and the data p necessary for the test $\mathsf{T}_{\mathrm{DSI}}$ to output the identity *idc* with an evidence. Note that *Exculpability* is only relevant if DSI holds: otherwise a client cannot be blamed regardless of the ability to forge a second spend or to simulate a coin withdrawal and payment, as his identity cannot be revealed.

Definition 5 (Exculpability). *Assume that we have a test* $\mathsf{T}_{\mathrm{DSI}}$ *as specified in Definition 4, i.e. DSI holds, and that the bank is corrupted. Let idc be a honest client (in particular he does not double spend a coin), and ids be a corrupted seller. Then,* Exculpability *is ensured if, after observing a transaction made by idc with ids, the attacker cannot provide two valid transactions* tr_1, tr_2 *that are different but involve the same coin c, and some data p such that* $\mathsf{T}_{\mathrm{DSI}}(tr_1, tr_2, p)$ *outputs* (*idc, e*) *where e is an evidence that idc withdrew the coin c.*

The intuition is: if after observing a transaction executed by a client *idc*, the attacker can provide a different valid transaction which involves the same coin, and the required data p, then the test will return the identity *idc* with the necessary evidence, thus the property will be violated. Similarly, in the case where the attacker can forge a coin withdrawal and payment seems to be made by a client *idc*, together with the necessary data p. Then the attacker can obtain two transactions satisfying the required conditions, and the test will return the identity *idc* with an evidence.

Note that, *Double Spending Identification* and *Exculpability* are only relevant in case of off-line e-cash systems where double spending might be possible.

3.2 Privacy Properties

We define the privacy properties using observational equivalence, a standard choice for such kind of properties. We use the *labeled bisimilarity* ($\approx_l$) to express the equivalence between two processes [1]. Informally, two processes are equivalent if an attacker interacting with them has no way to tell them apart.

To ensure the privacy of the client, the following two notions have been introduced by cryptographers, *e.g.*, [7,18,26].

1. *Weak Anonymity*: the attacker cannot link a client to a spend, *i.e.*, he cannot distinguish which client makes a payment.
2. *Strong Anonymity*: a stronger notion than weak anonymity, which additionally requires that the attacker cannot decide whether two spends were done by the same client.

Canard *et al.* [7], have defined *Weak Anonymity* using the following game: two honest clients each withdraw a coin from the bank. Then one of them (randomly chosen) spends his coin to the adversary. The adversary already knows the identities of these two clients, and also the secret key of the bank. It wins the game if it guesses correctly which client spends the coin. Inspired by this definition, we define *Weak Anonymity* in the applied π-calculus as follows.

Definition 6 (Weak Anonymity). *An e-cash protocol ensures* Weak Anonymity *if for any e-cash instance CP, any two honest clients idc_1, idc_2, any corrupted seller ids, we have that:*

$$CP_I[C\sigma_{idc_1}\sigma_{c_1}\sigma_{ids}|C_w\sigma_{idc_2}\sigma_{c_2}|S^c\sigma_{ids}|B^c]$$

$$\approx_l$$

$$CP_I[C_w\sigma_{idc_1}\sigma_{c_1}|C\sigma_{idc_2}\sigma_{c_2}\sigma_{ids}|S^c\sigma_{ids}|B^c]$$

where c_1, c_2 are any two coins (not previously known to the attacker) withdrawn by idc_1 and idc_2 respectively, $I = \{idc_1, idc_2, ids, id_B\}$, id_B is the bank's identity, and C_w is a variant of C that halts at the end of the withdrawal phase.

Weak anonymity ensures that a process in which the client idc_1 spends the coin c_1 to a corrupted seller ids_1, is equivalent to a process in which the client idc_2 spends the coin c_2 to a corrupted seller ids_1. We assume a corrupted bank represented by B^c. Note that, the client that does not spend his coin still withdraws it. This is necessary since otherwise the attacker could likely distinguish both sides during the withdrawal phase, as the bank is corrupted and typically the client reveals his identity to the bank at withdrawal. We also note that, we do not necessarily consider other corrupted clients, however this can easily be done by replacing some honest clients from the context CP_I (*i.e.*, other than idc_1 and idc_2) with corrupted ones.

Example 3 (Real Cash). Real coins ensure weak anonymity as two coins (assuming the same value and production year) are indistinguishable. However, banknotes do not ensure weak anonymity according to our definition, as they include serial numbers. Since the two clients withdraw a note each, the notes hence have different serial numbers which the bank can identify. In reality this is used by the bank to trace notes and detect suspicious activities, *e.g.*, money laundering. Note however that banknotes ensure a weaker form of anonymity: if two different clients use the same note, one cannot distinguish them.

Strong Anonymity is defined in [7] using the same game as for *Weak Anonymity*, with the difference that the adversary may have previously seen some coins being spent by the two honest clients explicitly mentioned in the definition. We define *Strong Anonymity* as follows.

Definition 7 (Strong Anonymity). *An e-cash protocol ensures* Strong Anonymity *if for any e-cash instance CP, any two honest clients idc_1, idc_2, any corrupted seller ids, we have that:*

$$CP_I[\|_{0 \leq i \leq m_1} C\sigma_{idc_1}\sigma_{c_1^i}\sigma_{ids}|_{0 \leq i \leq m_2} C\sigma_{idc_2}\sigma_{c_2^i}\sigma_{ids}|$$
$$C\sigma_{idc_1}\sigma_{c_1}\sigma_{ids}|C_w\sigma_{idc_2}\sigma_{c_2}|S^c\sigma_{ids}|B^c]$$
$$\approx_l$$
$$CP_I[\|_{0 \leq i \leq m_1} C\sigma_{idc_1}\sigma_{c_1^i}\sigma_{ids}|_{0 \leq i \leq m_2} C\sigma_{idc_2}\sigma_{c_2^i}\sigma_{ids}|$$
$$C_w\sigma_{idc_1}\sigma_{c_1}|C\sigma_{idc_2}\sigma_{c_2}\sigma_{ids}|S^c\sigma_{ids}|B^c]$$

where c_1 and $c_1^1 \ldots c_1^{m_1}$ are any coins withdrawn by idc_1, c_2 and $c_2^1 \ldots c_2^{m_2}$ are any coins withdrawn by idc_2, $I = \{idc_1, idc_2, ids, id_B\}$, id_B is the bank's identity, and C_w is a variant of C that halts at the end of the withdrawal phase.

Strong Anonymity ensures that the process in which client idc_1 spends $m_1 + 1$ coins, while idc_2 spends m_2 coins and additionally withdraws another coin without spending it, is equivalent to the process in which client idc_1 spends m_1 coins and withdraws an additional coin, while idc_2 spends $m_2 + 1$ coins. The definition assumes that the bank is corrupted, and that the seller receiving the coins from the two clients idc_1 and idc_2 is also corrupted. Note that, we consider C_w to avoid distinguishing from the number of withdrawals by each client. Again, we can replace some honest clients from CP_I by corrupted ones.

Example 4 (Real Cash). Again, real coins ensure strong anonymity as, assuming the same value and production year, two coins are indistinguishable. Yet, for the same reason as in weak anonymity, banknotes do not ensure strong anonymity according to our definition: the serial numbers allow an attacker to identify the different clients.

We note that any protocol satisfying *Strong Anonymity* also satisfies *Weak Anonymity*, as *Weak* Anonymity is a special case of *Strong Anonymity* for $m_1 = m_2 = 0$, *i.e.* when the two honest clients do not make any previous spends.

4 Case Studies

In this section, we describe and analyze the online [8] and the offline [9] variants of the protocol, the online protocol implemented by DigiCash [26], and the protocol by Peterson and Poupard [23]. To perform the automatic protocol verification we use ProVerif [5]. ProVerif uses a process description based on the applied π-calculus, but has syntactical extensions, for example its language is enriched by *events* to check reachability and correspondence properties; besides it can check *observational equivalence* properties. All the verification presented in the paper are carried out on a standard PC (Intel(R) Pentium(R) D CPU 3.00 GHz, 2 GB RAM).

4.1 Chaum Online Protocol

The Chaum Online Protocol was proposed in [8] and detailed in [9]. It allows a client to withdraw a coin blindly from the bank, and then spend it later in a payment without being traced even by the bank. The protocol is "online" in the sense that the seller does not accept the payment before contacting the bank to verify that the coin has not been deposited before, to prevent double spending. We start by giving a description of the protocol.

Table 1. Equational theory for Chaum Online Protocol.

$$getmess(sign(m, k)) = m$$
$$checksign(sign(m, k), pk(k)) = m$$
$$unblind(blind(m, r), r) = m$$
$$unblind(sign(blind(m, r), k), r) = sign(m, k)$$

Withdrawal Phase. To obtain an electronic coin, the client communicates with the bank using the following protocol:

1. The client randomly chooses a value x, and a coefficient r. The client then sends to the bank his identity u and the value $b = \mathtt{blind}(x, r)$, where $\mathtt{blind}$ is a blinding function.
2. The bank signs the blinded value b using a signing function $\mathtt{sign}$ and his secret key skB, then sends the signature $bs = \mathtt{sign}(b, skB)$ to the client. The bank also debits the amount of the coin from the client's account.
3. The client verifies the signature and removes the blinding to obtain the bank's signature $s = \mathtt{sign}(x, skB)$ on x. The coin consists of the pair $(x, \mathtt{sign}(x, skB))$.

Payment (and Deposit) Phases. To spend a coin:

1. The client sends the pair $(x, \text{sign}(x, sk_B))$ to the seller.
2. After checking the bank's signature, the seller sends the coin $(x, \text{sign}(x, sk_B))$ to the bank to verify that it is not deposited before.
3. The bank verifies the signature s, and that the coin is not in the list of deposited coins. If these checks succeed the bank credits the seller's account with the amount of the coin and informs him of acceptance. Otherwise, the payment is rejected.

Modeling in ProVerif. The equational theory depicted in Table 1 models the cryptographic primitives used within Chaum on-line protocol. It includes well-known model for digital signature (functions *sign*, *getmess*, and *checksign*). The functions *blind/unblind* are used to blind/unblind a message using a random value. We also include the possibility of unblinding a signed blinded message, so that we obtain the signature of the message – the key feature of blind signatures.

Analysis. The result of the analysis is summarized in Table 2. We model *Unforgeability* as an injective correspondence between the events *withdraw* and *spend*, they are placed in their appropriate positions, according to the Definition 3, inside the bank and seller processes respectively. We consider a honest bank and honest seller but corrupted clients. We assume that the bank sends an authenticated message through private channel to inform the seller about a coin acceptance. Otherwise, the attacker can forge a message which leads the seller to accepting an already deposited coin. However, ProVerif still finds an attack against *Unforgeability* when two copies of the same coin spent at the same time. In this case the bank makes two parallel database lookups to check if the coin was deposited before. If the parallel deposit was not finished yet and thus the coin is not yet inserted in the database, then each lookup confirms that the coin was not deposited before which results in acceptance of two spends of the same coin. This attack may be avoided with some synchronization like locking the table when a coin deposit is initiated and then unlocking it when the operation is finished. ProVerif does not support such an feature. Protocols that rely on state could be analyzed using the Tamarin Prover[1] thanks to the SAPIC[2] tool. However, it is difficult to model, using Tamarin, rewriting rules that are not subterm-convergent, which is the case of the equation that supports blind signature primitive. Note that corrupted clients cannot create a fake coin as the correspondence holds without injectivity. *Double Spending Identification* and *Exculpability* are not relevant in the case of on-line protocols as their countermeasure against double spending is the online calling of the bank at payment, and thus they do not have any kind of test to identify double spenders.

For privacy properties, we assume a corrupted bank and a corrupted seller, but honest clients. ProVerif confirms that the privacy of the client is preserved, as both *Weak Anonymity*, and *Strong Anonymity* are satisfied. This due to the

---

Table 2. Analysis of the Chaum online protocol. A ($\checkmark$) indicates that the property holds. A ($\times$) indicates that it fails (ProVerif shows an attack).

Property	Result	Time
Unforgeability	$\times$	$< 1s$
Weak Anonymity	$\checkmark$	$< 1s$
Strong Anonymity	$\checkmark$	$< 1s$

fact that the coin is signed blindly during the withdrawal phase, and thus cannot be traced later by the attacker even when colludes with the bank and the seller. Note that, for *Strong Anonymity*, we consider an unbounded number of spends by each client and one spend that is made by either the first client or by the second one.

4.2   DigiCash Protocol

The online Chaum protocol has been implemented by DigiCash[3]. Latter, the specifications of the DigiCash protocol outlined in [26]. It has the same withdrawal phase as Chaum online protocol, except that the client sends an authenticated coin to be signed by the bank, however the paper does not specify the way of authentication. We ignore this authentication as its purpose is to ensure that the bank debits the correct client account. Hence, we believe that it does not effect the privacy and unforgeability properties (analysis confirms that as we can see in Table 2). The payment and deposit phases are different from those of Chaum online protocol. They are summarized as follows.

Payment (and Deposit) Phases in DigiCash

1. The client sends the seller $pay = enc((id_s, \mathrm{h}(pay\text{-}spec), x, \mathtt{sign}(x, sk_B)), pk_B)$ which is the encryption, using the public key of the bank pk_B, of the seller's identity id_s, hash of the payment specification $pay\text{-}spec$ (specification of the sold object, price etc.), and the coin $(x, \mathtt{sign}(x, sk_B))$.
2. The seller signs $(\mathrm{h}(pay\text{-}spec), pay)$ and sends it along with his identity id_s to the bank.
3. The bank verifies the signature, decrypts pay then verifies the value of $\mathrm{h}(pay\text{-}spec)$ and that the coin is valid and not deposited before. If so it informs the seller to accept the coin, and to reject it otherwise.

Modeling in ProVerif. Additionally to the equational theory of the Chaum online protocol (Table 1), the equational theory of DigiCash protocol includes well-known model of the public key encryption represented by the following equation: $dec(enc(m, pk(k)), k) = m$.

---

[3] DigiCash declared bankruptcy in 1998, and was sold to Blucora.

Table 3. Analysis of DigiCash protocol. A ($\checkmark$) indicates that the property holds. A ($\times$) indicates that it fails (ProVerif shows an attack).

Property	Result	Time
Unforgeability	$\times$	$< 1s$
Weak Anonymity	$\checkmark$	$< 1s$
Strong Anonymity	$\checkmark$	$< 1s$

Analysis. The result of analysis of DigiCash protocol using ProVerif is summarized in Table 3. ProVerif shows the same results as obtained for Chaum online protocol. Namely, it shows that *Weak Anonymity*, and *Strong Anonymity* are satisfied, and it outputs the same attack presented in Sect. 4.1 against *Unforgeability*. Again *Double Spending Identification* and *Exculpability* are not relevant. Note that, obtaining the same result for the two protocols, even that they have different payment and deposit phases, confirms that the blinding signature used during the withdrawal phase plays the key role in preserving the privacy of the client, as claimed by David Chaum.

4.3   Chaum Offline Protocol

The offline variant of the Chaum protocol is proposed in [9]. It removes the requirement that the seller must contact the bank during every payment. This introduces the risk of double spending a coin by a client.

Withdrawal Phase. To obtain an electronic coin, the client randomly chooses a, c and d, and calculates the pair $H = (\mathtt{h}(a, c), \mathtt{h}(a \oplus u, d))$, where u is the client identity and $\mathtt{h}$ is a hash function. The client then proceed as in the Chaum online protocol, but with x (the potential coin) replaced by the pair H. Namely, the client blinds the pair H and sends it to the bank. Then the bank signs and returns it to the client. The main difference from the Chaum online protocol is that the coin has to be of the following form

$$(\mathtt{h}(a, c), \mathtt{h}(a \oplus u, d))$$

where the client identity is masked inside it. This aims to reveal the identity if the client double spends the coin. In order for the bank to be sure that the client provides a message of the appropriate form, Chaum *et al.*used in [9] the well known "*cut-and-choose*"technique. Precisely, the client computes n such a pair H where n is the system security parameter. The bank then selects half of them and asks the client to reveal their corresponding parameters (a, b, c and r). If n is large enough the client can cheats with a low probability.

At the end of this phase the client holds the electronic coin composed of the pair H, and the bank's signature $S = \mathtt{sign}(H, sk_B)$. The client also has to keep the random values a, c, d which are used later to spend the coin.

Payment Phase. For a client to spend a coin to a seller:

1. The client presents the pair H and the bank's signature S to the seller. The seller checks the signature, if it is correct then he chooses and sends a random binary bit y, a challenge, to the client. The client returns to the seller:
   - The values a and c if y is 0.
   - The values $a \oplus u$ and d if y is 1.
2. The seller checks the compliance of the values sent with the pair H. If everything (the signature and the values) is correct, the payment is accepted.

At the end of the payment phase, the seller holds the pair H, the signature S, the values of either (a, c) or $(a \oplus u, d)$, and the challenge y. All these data together compose the transaction that the seller has to present to the bank at deposit.

   Note that, in case where n pairs are used for the coin, the challenge y will be n bit string and for each bit either the corresponding values of (a, c) or $(a \oplus u, d)$ are revealed to the seller.

Deposit Phase. To deposit a coin at the bank:

1. The seller contacts the bank and provides it with the transaction $(H, S, y, (a, c))$ or $(H, S, y, (a \oplus u, d))$.
2. The bank checks the signature and also whether the values (a, c) or $(a \oplus u, d)$ correspond to their hash value in H. If any of these values is incorrect, the fault is on the seller's part, as he was able to independently check the regularity of the coin at payment. If the coin is correct, the bank checks its database to see whether the same coin had been used before. If it has not, the bank credits the seller's account with the appropriate amount. Otherwise, the bank rejects the transaction.

Chaum offline protocol does not prevent double spending, however it preserve client's anonymity only if he spend a coin once. Note that, a double spender can be identified when the coin has the form $(\mathbf{h}(a, c), \mathbf{h}(a \oplus u, d))$. However, the bank can simulate the coin withdrawal and payment (as the bank knows the identities of all the clients), thus the bank can blame a honest client for double spending. As a countermeasure, the authors propose to concatenate two values z and z' with u inside the pair H to have $(\mathbf{h}(a, c), \mathbf{h}(a \oplus (u, z, z'), d))$ and provide to the bank, at withdrawal, additionally the client's signature on $\mathbf{h}(z, z')$.

Modeling in ProVerif. To model the Chaum off-line protocol in ProVerif, in addition to the equational theory used for the Chaum online protocol (Table 1), we use the function *xor* to represent the exclusive-or ($\oplus$) of two values. Given the first value, the second value can be obtained using the function *unxor*. Such an – admittedly limited – modeling for $\oplus$ operator is sufficient to catch the functional properties of the scheme required by Chaum offline protocol, but does not catch all algebraic properties of this operator. However, there are currently no tools that support observational equivalence – which we need for the anonymity properties – and all algebraic properties of $\oplus$. Kuesters *et al.* [20] proposed a way to extend ProVerif with $\oplus$. Their tool translates a model of the protocol to a ProVerif input where all $\oplus$ are ground terms to enable automated reasoning. However, this tool can only deal with secrecy and authentication properties, and does not support equivalence properties. The *xor* function is only used to hide the client's identity u using a random value a ($a \oplus u$), which we model as $xor(a, u)$. The bank then uses a to reveal the client's identity u if he double spends a coin. This is modeled by the following two equations

$$unxor(xor(a, u), a) = u$$
$$unxor(a, xor(a, u)) = u$$

which represents the various ways: $((a \oplus u) \oplus a) = u$, or $(a \oplus (a \oplus u)) = u$. We always assume that identity is the second value, and this is how we model it inside honest processes.

Analysis. As expected ProVerif confirms that *Unforgeability* is not satisfied, a corrupted client can double spend a coin. In fact the seller cannot know whether a certain coin is already spent or not, he accepts any coin that is certified by the bank. However, a collusion between the client and the attacker cannot lead to forging a coin.

In case of double spending, the bank may receive two transactions of the form $tr_1 = (h, hx, sign((h, hx), skB), 0, a, c)$ and $tr_2 = (h, hx, sign((h, hx), skB), 1, xor(a, u), d)$. Then, the bank can apply a test to obtain the identity u. This is done using the *unxor* function as $unxor(xor(a, u), a) = u$. The evidence here is showing that the identity of the client is masked inside the coin. This can be done thanks to the values of $(a, c, xor(a, u), d)$ which are initially known only to the client. Spending the coin only once reveals either (a, c) or $(xor(a, u), d)$ which does not allow to obtain the identity u. Note that, if the two sellers provide the same challenge, the two transactions will be exactly equal. In this case no double spending is detected, and the second transaction will be rejected by the bank which considers it as a second copy of the first transaction. In practice this can be avoided with high probability if n pairs coin is used and thus n bits challenge. Note that ProVerif consider all the possibilities.

We model the output of an identity and an evidence of the test T_{DSI} by an emission of the *event OK*. The test emits *event KO* otherwise. To say that *Double Spending Identification* is satisfied, (i) the test T_{DSI} should not emit the *event KO* for every two valid transactions tr_1, tr_2 that are different but involves the same coin, *i.e.*, it always emits *event OK* for such transactions; (ii) the test should not emit the *event OK* for any two transactions that do not satisfy these conditions. ProVerif shows that the test can emit the *event KO* for certain two transactions satisfy the required conditions. Actually, a corrupted client can withdraw a coin that does not have the appropriate form (*e.g.*, client's identity is not masked inside it), thus the bank cannot obtain the identity in case of double spending. Note that, if the bank only certifies coins with the appropriate form at withdrawal (*i.e.*, of the form $(h(a, c), h(a \oplus u, d))$), then the property holds, ProVerif

Table 4. Analysis of Chaum offline protocol. A ($\checkmark$) indicates that the property holds. A ($\times$) indicates that it fails. ($*$) Only coins with the appropriate form are considered. ($\dagger$) After applying the countermeasure.

Property	Result	Time
Unforgeability	$\times$	<1s
Double Spending Identification	$\times$	<2s
Double Spending Identification*	$\checkmark$	<2s
Exculpability*	$\times$	< 6s
Exculpability†	$\checkmark$	< 6s
Weak Anonymity	$\checkmark$	<1s
Strong Anonymity	$\checkmark$	<1s

confirms that. Again, in practice applying the "cut-and-choose" technique can guarantee with high probability that the coin is in the appropriate form. However, applying this technique using ProVerif does not make any difference since ProVerif works under symbolic world, which deals with possibilities and not with probabilities. For instance, the attacker still can guess the pairs that the bank will request to reveal and construct them in the appropriate form, but cheat with the others which will compose the coin (Table 4).

We analyze *Exculpability* in case where only coins of appropriate forms are considered *i.e.*, the case where *Double Spending Identification* holds. ProVerif confirms that a corrupted bank can blame a honest client. The bank can simulate the withdrawal and the payment since the bank knows the identity of the client. Thus it can obtain two transactions satisfying the required conditions. This is due to the fact that the evidence obtained by the test, which is showing that the client's identity is masked inside the coin, is not strong enough to act as a proof. However, the attacker cannot re-spend a coin withdrawn and spent by a honest client. After applying the countermeasure that is including some terms z and z' so that the client signs $h(z, z')$, ProVerif confirms that *Exculpability* holds. Applying the countermeasure results in a new test which takes, in addition to the two transactions, the client's signature on $h(z, z')$. The test shows, in case of double spending, that the identity u and the preimage (z, z') of the hash signed by the client are masked inside the coin. This represents a stronger evidence which acts as a proof that the client withdrew the coin since the bank cannot forge the client's signature.

We note that, Ogiela *et al.* [22] show an attack on Chaum offline protocol: when a client double spends a coin, the sellers can forge additional transactions involving the same coin, so that the bank cannot know how many transactions are actually result from spends made by the client and how many are forged by the sellers. In such a case, according to our definition, *Unforgeability* does not hold since the client has to spend the coin at least twice. Moreover, the bank can still identify the client and punish him as the bank can be sure that he at least spend the coin twice. Yet, corrupted sellers can blame a corrupted client who double spends a coin for further spends.

Concerning privacy properties, ProVerif shows that Chaum off-line protocol still satisfies both *Weak Anonymity* and *Strong Anonymity*.

To sum up, ProVerif confirms the claim about preserving client's anonymity. ProVerif also was able to show that a client can double spend a withdrawn coin but cannot forge a coin, and that the bank can identify the double spender if the coin is in the appropriate form. ProVerif also shows, in case of coin with appropriate form, that the bank can simulate a withdrawal and payment, and thus can blame him for double spending. After applying the countermeasure no attack against *Exculpability* is found.

4.4   Protocol by Peterson and Poupard

In this section, we give the description of the protocol due to Peterson and Poupard [23], which we call concisely P&P protocol. Then, we present the results of our analysis. The protocol has two variants for electronic purse payments and internet payments, which are slightly differ in few steps. We analyze the internet payments schemes.

The protocol aims, to met the usual security properties, and to prevent extortion attacks, in which a criminal forces the bank to issue coins or reveal secret keys through kidnapping. To this end, the protocol consider an additional authority, the trustee, at which a client has to register using a pseudonymous keypair (PS_x, PS_y). Then, public part of the client's pseudonym PS_y is embedded into the coin. The main rule of the trustee is to take some actions (*e.g.*, publishes list of illegal coins) when an extortion attack is reported. Accordingly, the protocol has an additional phase, *Registration Phase*, in which the client open an account at the bank and registers at the trustee. Note that similar to Chaum protocols, P&P protocol uses a blind signature scheme in order to withdraw anonymous coins, and uses a "challenge-and-response" procedure at payment. In the following, we provide the description of the P&P protocol.

Registration Phase. To open an account:

1. The client id_C registers at the bank and obtains an account number acc_C.
2. The bank stores (id_C, acc_C) in his database.

For the client to identify himself to the trustee:

1. The client and the trustee obtain an authentic session key k_{CT} using an authentic key exchange protocol.
2. The client generates a pseudonymous keypair (PS_x, PS_y), computes the signature $\sigma_C = sign((id_C, PS_y), sk_C)$, and sends $enc((id_C, PS_y, \sigma_C), k_{CT})$ to the trustee, where enc is a symmetric encryption function.
3. The trustee verifies the signature σ_c, calculates $\sigma_T = sign(PS_y, sk_C)$, and sends $enc(\sigma_T, k_{CT})$ to the client. The trustee also stores (id_C, PS_y, σ_C) in his database.
4. The client verifies the signature σ_T, and stores all the values.

These steps might be processed several times to obtain several pseudonymous keypairs (PS_x, PS_y).

Withdrawal Phase. The client can withdraw a coin from the bank according to the following steps:

1. The client and the bank first obtain an authentic session key k_{CB} using an authentic key exchange protocol.
2. The client generates random coin c, computes $bc = blind(h(c, PS_y))$ and $e_T = aenc(h(c, PS_y), pk_T)$ where h is a hash function and $aenc$ is a probabilistic asymmetric encryption function, and sends bc and e_T to the bank. Note that, e_T is mainly used in case of an extortion attack against the bank which then sends all the stored values e_T to the trustee.
3. The bank signs the blinded coin by computing $\tilde{\sigma}_B = sign(bc, sk_B)$ and sends it to the client. The bank also subtracts the value of the coin from the client's account acc_C and stores (id_C, bc, e_T).
4. The client unblind the signature $\tilde{\sigma}_B$ to obtain σ_B and verifies it. The client keeps (c, σ_B) as his coin and notices the relation to the tuple (PS_x, σ_T).

Payment Phase. To spend a coin, the client communicates with the seller according to the following steps:

1. The seller sends the client a uniquely generated message *mess*.
2. The client generates the signature $\sigma_{coin} = sign((c, id_S, mess, PS_y), PS_x)$, and sends the payment transcript $(c, PS_y, \sigma_T, \sigma_B, aenc(\sigma_{coin}, pk_S))$.
3. The seller verifies σ_T, σ_B, and σ_{coin}, and stores the payment transcript together with *mess* in his database.

Note that in addition the protocol consider three extortion cases: extortion of client's secret key PS_x, extortion of bank's secret key sk_B, and extortion of trustee's secret key sk_T. In case of extortion of PS_x, the trustee distributes the corresponding key PS_y among the sellers so that the seller rejects all the coins withdrawn under PS_y. The trustee also issues the signature $sign((id_C, PS_y), sk_T)$ which allows the client exchange unspent coins withdrawn under PS_y at the bank. In case of extortion of bank's secret key, he sends e_T to the trustee which in turn decrypts it and publishes the legal coins among the sellers so that they can verify the coin at payment. In case of extortion trustee's secret key , he signs PS_y and publishes it, then the seller verifies the signature and check if PS_y is among the published list before accepting. We consider these additional checks in our model.

Deposit Phase. To deposite a coin at the bank:

1. The seller sends the tuple $(c, PS_y, id_S, acc_S, mess, \sigma_B, \sigma_T, \sigma_{coin})$ to the bank.
2. The bank verifies the signatures σ_B, σ_T and checks whether the coin was already deposited under the same PS_y. If it is the case, then:
    - If $\sigma'_{coin} = \sigma_{coin}$, the seller is accused for double deposite. The bank sends the tuple (c, σ'_{coin}) to the seller as a proof.

– If $\sigma'_{coin} \neq \sigma_{coin}$, the bank verifies σ_{coin}. If it is valid, then the coin has been overspent. In this case, the bank sends the trustee the transcripts $(c, PS_y, mess_1, \sigma_B, \sigma_T, \sigma_{coin,1}) \ldots (c, PS_y, mess_k, \sigma_B, \sigma_T, \sigma_{coin,k})$. To prove that the coin c was overspent, the trustee verifies all transcripts. If they are correct, he looks for the tuple (id_C, PS_y, σ_C) in his database and sends (id_C, σ_C) to the bank. The bank checks the signature σ_C.

Otherwise, If every thing is okay the bank stores the payment transcript in his database and credits the seller's account acc_S by the value of c.

Modeling in ProVerif. To model the P&P protocol in ProVerif, we use the equational theory depicted in Table 5. It includes the well-known equational theory for digital signature (functions *sign*, *getmess*, and *checksign*), symmetric encryption (functions *enc* and *dec*), and asymmetric encryption (functions *aenc* and *adec*). We also use two equations for the blinding function (*blind* and *unblind*) similar to the one we use for previous protocols.

Table 5. Equational theory for P&P Protocol.

$$getmess(sign(m,k)) = m$$
$$checksign(sign(m,k), pk(k)) = m$$
$$dec(enc(m,k),k) = m$$
$$adec(aenc(m, pk(k), r), k) = m$$
$$unblind(blind(m,r),r) = m$$
$$unblind(sign(blind(m,r),k),r) = sign(m,k)$$

Analysis. The result of the analysis is summarized in Table 6. Similarly to the previous protocols, we model *Unforgeability* as an injective correspondence between the two events *withdraw* and *spend*. We consider a honest bank and honest seller but corrupted clients. As expected for offline protocols, ProVerif finds an attack against *Unforgeability*. A corrupted client can double spend a coin, However, a collusion between the client and the attacker cannot lead to forging a coin as the correspondence holds without injectivity.

In case of double spending, the bank may receive two transactions of the form $(c, PS_y, mess_1, \sigma_B, \sigma_T, \sigma_{coin,1})$ and $(c, PS_y, mess_2, \sigma_B, \sigma_T, \sigma_{coin,2})$, and additionally he receives from trustee (id_C, σ_C). Then bank checks that the two transactions are valid and that the signature σ_C is computed by the client on (id_C, PS_y). Thus linking PS_y (under which the coin is withdrawn) to the client identity id_C. To verify *Double Spending Identification*, similar to the Chaum offline protocol, we model the test outputs *event OK* when it finds an identity and an evidence, and *event KO* when it fails. ProVerif shows that P&P satisfies *Double Spending Identification*. ProVerif also shows that *Exculpability* is satisfied as the bank cannot forge the client signature σ_C.

For privacy properties, we assume a corrupted bank and a corrupted seller, but honest clients. ProVerif confirms that *Weak Anonymity* is satisfied by P&P

Table 6. Analysis of P&P protocol. A ($\checkmark$) indicates that the property holds. A ($\times$) indicates that it fails. ($*$) Only one coin was withdrawn per a pseudonymous keypair.

Property	Result	Time
Unforgeability	$\times$	$< 1s$
Double Spending Identification	$\checkmark$	$< 1s$
Exculpability	$\checkmark$	$< 1s$
Weak Anonymity	$\checkmark$	$< 1s$
Strong Anonymity	$\times$	$< 1s$
Strong Anonymity*	$\checkmark$	$< 2s$

protocol. However, *Strong Anonymity* is satisfied only if the client use a distinct pseudonymous keypair for each coin. Otherwise, the seller can easily links two payments to the same client since PS_y is revealed to him at payment.

5   Conclusion

E-cash protocols aim at emulating real cash by offering anonymous payments. Several protocols have been proposed to ensure client's anonymity, as well as, the standard forgery-related properties. However, multiple flaws were discovered on claimed secure protocols. To avoid further bad surprises, formal verification can be used to improve confidence in e-cash protocols.

In this paper, we proposed a formal framework to automatically verify e-cash protocols with respect to multiple essential privacy and forgery-related properties. Our framework relies on the applied π-calculus and uses ProVerif as the verification tool. As a case study, we analyzed the online protocol proposed by Chaum, as well as a real implementation based on it (the DigiCash protocol). We also analyze the offline variant of this system, and the protocol due to Peterson and Poupard. For Chaum online protocol and DigiCash protocol, we found a weakness concerning *Unforgeability*: the attacker can double spend a valid coin when there is a lack of synchronization. Concerning Chaum offline protocol, we re-discover some known attacks which confirms the correctness of our model. Namely we re-discover, the attack against *Unforgeability* (double spending), the attack against *Double Spending Identification* when the coin does not have the proper form, and the attack against *Exculpability* when the counter-measure is not considered. With respect to P&P protocol, we found an expected attack on *Unforgeability* as double spending is usually possible in case of offline protocols. We also found an attack on *Strong Anonymity* when more than one coin is withdrawn under the same pseudonymous keypair.

As future work, we would like to investigate further case studies and to extend our model to cover transferable protocols with divisible coins. Also we would like to use the tool SAPIC, which is based on Tamarin, in order to see how it can help to analyze e-cash protocols.

References

1. Abadi, M., Fournet, C.: Mobile values, new names, and secure communication. In: The 28th Symposium on Principles of Programming Languages, UK, pp. 104–115. ACM (2001)
2. Abe, M., Fujisaki, E.: How to date blind signatures. In: Kim, K.-C., Matsumoto, T. (eds.) ASIACRYPT 1996. LNCS, vol. 1163, pp. 244–251. Springer, Heidelberg (1996)
3. Aboud, S.J., Agoun, A.: Analysis of a known offline e-coin system. Int. J. Comput. Appl. 98(15), 27–30 (2014)
4. Armando, A., et al.: The AVISPA tool for the automated validation of internet security protocols and applications. In: Etessami, K., Rajamani, S.K. (eds.) CAV 2005. LNCS, vol. 3576, pp. 281–285. Springer, Heidelberg (2005)
5. Blanchet, B.: An efficient cryptographic protocol verifier based on prolog rules. In: 14th IEEE Computer Security Foundations Workshop (CSFW 2014), Canada, pp. 82–96 (2001)
6. Brands, S.: Untraceable off-line cash in wallets with observers. In: Stinson, D.R. (ed.) CRYPTO 1993. LNCS, vol. 773, pp. 302–318. Springer, Heidelberg (1994). http://dl.acm.org/citation.cfm?id=646758.705703
7. Canard, S., Gouget, A.: Anonymity in transferable e-cash. In: Bellovin, S.M., Gennaro, R., Keromytis, A.D., Yung, M. (eds.) ACNS 2008. LNCS, vol. 5037, pp. 207–223. Springer, Heidelberg (2008)
8. Chaum, D.: Blind signatures for untraceable payments. In: Chaum, D., Rivest, R.L., Sherman, A.T. (eds.) Advances in Cryptology: Proceedings of CRYPTO 1982, pp. 199–203. Springer, US (1983)
9. Chaum, D., Fiat, A., Naor, M.: Untraceable electronic cash. In: Goldwasser, S. (ed.) CRYPTO 1988. LNCS, vol. 403, pp. 319–327. Springer, Heidelberg (1990)
10. Cheng, C.Y., Yunus, J., Seman, K.: Estimations on the security aspect of brand's electronic cash scheme. In: 19th International Conference on Advanced Information Networking and Applications (AINA 2005), Taipei, Taiwan, 28–30 March 2005, pp. 131–134 (2005)
11. Crescenzo, G.D.: A non-interactive electronic cash system. In: Bonuccelli, M.A., Crescenzi, P., Petreschi, R. (eds.) CIAC 1994. LNCS, vol. 778, pp. 109–124. Springer, Heidelberg (1994)
12. Damgård, I.B.: Payment systems and credential mechanisms with provable security against abuse by individuals. In: Goldwasser, S. (ed.) CRYPTO 1988. LNCS, vol. 403, pp. 328–335. Springer, Heidelberg (1990)
13. D'Amiano, S., Di Crescenzo, G.: Methodology for digital money based on general cryptographic tools. In: De Santis, A. (ed.) EUROCRYPT 1994. LNCS, vol. 950, pp. 156–170. Springer, Heidelberg (1995)
14. Delaune, S., Kremer, S., Ryan, M.: Verifying privacy-type properties of electronic voting protocols. J. Comput. Secur. 17, 435–487 (2009). http://www.lsv.ens-cachan.fr/Publis/PAPERS/PDF/DKR-jcs08.pdf
15. Dolev, D., Yao, A.C.: On the security of public key protocols. IEEE Trans. Inf. Theory 29(2), 198–208 (1983)
16. Dreier, J., Kassem, A., Lafourcade, P.: Formal analysis of e-cash protocols. In: Proceedings of the 12th International Conference on Security and Cryptography, SECRYPT 2015, Colmar, Alsace, France, 20–22 July 2015, pp. 65–75 (2015). http://dx.doi.org/10.5220/0005544500650075

17. Fan, C.I., Huang, V.S.M., Yu, Y.C.: User efficient recoverable off-line e-cash scheme with fast anonymity revoking. Math. Comput. Modell. **58**(1–2), 227–237 (2013)
18. Ferguson, N.: Single term off-line coins. In: Helleseth, T. (ed.) EUROCRYPT 1993. LNCS, vol. 765, pp. 318–328. Springer, Heidelberg (1994)
19. Kim, S., Oh, H.: A new electronic check system with reusable refunds. Int. J. Inf. Sec. **1**(3), 175–188 (2002). http://dx.doi.org/10.1007/s10207-002-0015-z
20. Küsters, R., Truderung, T.: Reducing protocol analysis with xor to the xor-free case in the horn theory based approach. J. Autom. Reason. **46**(3), 325–352 (2011)
21. Luo, Z., Cai, X., Pang, J., Deng, Y.: Analyzing an electronic cash protocol using applied pi calculus. In: Katz, J., Yung, M. (eds.) ACNS 2007. LNCS, vol. 4521, pp. 87–103. Springer, Heidelberg (2007)
22. Ogiela, M.R., Sulkowski, P.: Improved cryptographic protocol for digital coin exchange. In: Soft Computing and Intelligent Systems (SCIS), pp. 1148–1151 (2014)
23. Peterson, H., Poupard, G.: Efficient scalable fair cash with off-line extortion prevention. In: Han, Y., Quing, S. (eds.) ICICS 1997. LNCS, vol. 1334. Springer, Heidelberg (1997)
24. Pfitzmann, B., Schunter, M., Waidner, M.: How to break another "Provably Secure" payment system. In: Guillou, L.C., Quisquater, J.-J. (eds.) EUROCRYPT 1995. LNCS, vol. 921, pp. 121–132. Springer, Heidelberg (1995)
25. Pfitzmann, B., Waidner, M.: How to break and repair a "Provably Secure" untraceable payment system. In: Feigenbaum, J. (ed.) CRYPTO 1991. LNCS, vol. 576, pp. 338–350. Springer, Heidelberg (1992)
26. Schoenmakers, B.: Security aspects of the Ecash^{TM} payment system. In: Preneel, B., Rijmen, V. (eds.) COSIC 1997 Course. LNCS, vol. 1528, pp. 338–352. Springer, Heidelberg (1998)
27. Swe, A.T., Kyaw, K.K.K.: Formal analysis of secure e-cash transaction protocol. In: International Conference on Advances in Engineering and Technology, ICAET 2014, Singapore (2014)

Theoretical Foundation for Code Obfuscation Security: A Kolmogorov Complexity Approach

Rabih Mohsen[1(✉)] and Alexandre Miranda Pinto[2,3]

[1] Department of Computing, Imperial College London, London, UK
r.mohsen11@imperial.ac.uk
[2] Information Security Group, Royal Holloway University of London, London, UK
[3] Instituto Universitário da Maia, Maia, Portugal

Abstract. The main problem in designing effective code obfuscation is to guarantee security. State of the art obfuscation techniques rely on an unproven concept of security, and therefore are not regarded as provably secure. In this paper, we undertake a theoretical investigation of code obfuscation security and its adversary model based on Kolmogorov complexity and algorithmic mutual information. We introduce a new definition of code obfuscation that requires the algorithmic mutual information between a code and its obfuscated version to be minimal, allowing for controlled amount of information to be leaked to an adversary. We argue that our definition avoids the impossibility results of Barak et al. and is more advantageous than the obfuscation indistinguishability definition in the sense it is more intuitive, and is algorithmic rather than probabilistic.

1 Introduction

Malicious reverse engineering represents a great risk to software confidentiality, especially for software that runs on a malicious host controlled by a software pirate intent on stealing intellectual artifacts. Thwarting vicious reverse engineering, using software protection techniques such as code obfuscation, is vital to defend programs against malicious host attacks. An obfuscating transformation attempts to transform code so that it becomes unintelligible to human and automated program analysis tools, while preserving their functionality.

One of the major challenges of code obfuscation is the lack of a rigorous theoretical background. The absence of a theoretical basis makes it difficult to formally analyse and certify the effectiveness of these techniques against malicious host attacks. In particular, it is hard to compare different obfuscating transformations with respect to their resilience to attacks. Often, obfuscation transformation techniques are proposed with no provable properties presented.

Software developers strive to produce structured and easy to comprehend code, their motivation is to simplify maintenance. Code obfuscation, on the other hand, transforms code to a less structured and intelligible version. It produces more complex code that looks patternless, with little regularity and is difficult to understand. We argue that irregularities and noise makes the obfuscated code difficult to comprehend. Kolmogorov complexity [11] is a well known theory that can measure

© Springer International Publishing Switzerland 2016
M.S. Obaidat and P. Lorenz (Eds.): ICETE 2015, CCIS 585, pp. 245–269, 2016.
DOI: 10.1007/978-3-319-30222-5_12

regularities and randomness. The size of the shortest program that describes a program tends to be bigger as more noise and irregularities are present in a program. Kolmogorov complexity is the basic concept of algorithmic information theory, that in many respects adapts the viewpoint of well-established Information Theory to focus on individual instances rather than random distributions. In general, algorithmic information theory replaces the notion of probability by that of intrinsic randomness of a string. Kolmogorov complexity is uncomputable; however it can be approximated in practice by lossless compression [9,11], which helps to intuitively understand this notion and makes this theory relevant for real world applications. Our aim in this paper is to provide a theoretical framework for code obfuscation in the context of algorithmic information theory: to quantitatively capture the security of code obfuscation, to discuss its achievability and to investigate its limitations and resilience against an adversary.

We introduce the notion of unintelligibility to define confusion in code obfuscation and argue this is not good enough. We then propose our notion of security and compare both definitions. We also present a model for a code obfuscating adversary, specifying the adversary's capabilities, goals and winning conditions.

We argue that our model of security is fundamentally different from the virtual black-box model of Barak et al., and that because of this their impossibility result does not apply. Then, we show that under reasonable conditions we can have secure obfuscation. Finally, we study the security of two main approaches to obfuscated code in software, *encoding* and *hiding*, at the subprogram level.

To the best of our knowledge, this paper is the first to propose algorithmic information theory as a theoretical basis for code obfuscation and its threat model; we believe our work is the first step to derive consistent metrics that measure the protection quality of code obfuscation. The framework can be applied to most code obfuscation techniques and is not limited to any obfuscation method or language paradigm.

Paper Structure. In Sect. 2, we provide an overview of related work. Section 3 provides the preliminaries and the required notations. In Sect. 4, we discuss the intuition behind our approach, propose the formal definition of code obfuscation, the adversary model and present some results for security code obfuscations against passive attackers. In Sect. 5, we study the security of two main approaches to code obfuscation at the subprogram level. Section 6 concludes with the proposed future work.

2   Related Work

Collberg et al. [3] were the first to define obfuscation in terms of a semantic-preserving transformation. Barak et al. [2] introduced a formal definition of *perfect* obfuscation in an attempt to achieve well-defined security, which is based on the black-box paradigm. Intuitively, a program obfuscator $\mathcal{O}$ is called *perfect* if it transforms any program P into a virtual black box $\mathcal{O}(P)$ so that anything that can be also efficiently computed from $\mathcal{O}(P)$, can be efficiently computed given just oracle access to P. However, they also proved that the black-box definition cannot be met by showing the existence of set of functions that are impossible to obfuscate. On the other hand, a recent study conducted by Garg et al. [5] provided positive results, using indistinguishability obfuscation, for which there are no known impossibility results. However, as argued by [7] there is a disadvantage of indistinguishability obfuscation: it does not give an intuitive guarantee about the security of code obfuscation.

3 Preliminaries

We use the U as the shorthand for a universal Turing machine, x for a finite-length binary string and $|x|$ for its length. We use ϵ for a negligible value, and Λ for an empty string. We use the notation $O(1)$ for a constant, $p(n)$ for a polynomial function with input $n \in \mathbb{N}$. $\|$ is used to denote the concatenation between two programs or strings. $\mathcal{P}$ is a set of binary programs and $\mathcal{P}'$ is a set of binary obfuscated programs, $\mathcal{L} = \{\lambda_n : \lambda_n \in \{0,1\}^+, n \in \mathbb{N}\}$ is a set of (secret) security parameters used in the obfuscation process[1]. $\mathbb{A} = \{\mathcal{A}_n\}_{n \in \mathbb{N}}$ represents a set of adversaries (deobfuscators) where an adversary $\mathcal{A} \subseteq \mathbb{A}$ uses a set of deobfuscation techniques (e.g. reverse engineering); the term adversary is used interchangeably with deobfuscator. Given two sets, I an input set and O an output set, a program functionality (meaning) is a function $[\![.]\!] : \mathcal{P} \times I \to O$ that computes the program's output given an input and terminates.

We consider only the prefix version of Kolmogorov complexity (prefix algorithmic complexity) which is denoted by $K(.)$. *Complexity* and *Kolmogorov complexity* terms are sometimes used interchangeably; for more details on prefix algorithmic complexity and algorithmic information theory, we refer the reader to [11]. The necessary parts of this theory are briefly presented in the following.

Definition 1. Let $U(P)$ denote the output of U when presented with a program $P \in \{0,1\}^+$.

1. The *Kolmogorov complexity* $K(x)$ of a binary string x with respect to U is defined as: $K(x) = \min\{|P| : U(P) = x\}$.
2. The Conditional Kolmogorov Complexity relative to y is defined as: $K(x \mid y) = \min\{|P| : U(P, y) = x\}$.

Definition 2. Mutual algorithmic information of two binary programs x and y is given by : $I_K(x; y) = K(y) - K(y \mid x)$.

Theorem 1 (chain rule [4]). *For all x, $y \in \mathbb{N}$*

1. $K(x; y) = K(x) + K(y \mid x)$ *up to an additive term* $O(\log K(x, y))$.
2. $K(x) - K(x \mid y) = K(y) - K(y \mid x)$ *i.e.* $I_K(x; y) = I_K(y; x)$, *up to an additive term* $O(\log K(x, y))$.

---

[1] The security parameter may include the obfuscation key, the obfuscation transformation algorithm or any necessary information that the obfuscation function can use.

Logarithmic factors like the ones needed in the previous theorem are pervasive in the theory of Kolmogorov complexity. As commonly is done in the literature, we mostly omit them in our results, making a note in the theorem statements that they are there. This also "hides" smaller constant terms, and for this reason we regularly omit them in the derivations.

Definition 3. The Mutual algorithmic information of two binary strings x and y conditioned to a binary string z is defined as: $I(x; y|z) = K(y|z) - K(y|x, z)$

Theorem 2 ([11]). *There is a constant c such that for all x and y*

$$K(x) \leq |x| + 2\log|x| + c \quad and \quad K(x\,|\,y) \leq K(x) + c.$$

Theorem 3 ([13]). *Given a recursive computable function $f : \{0,1\}^* \to \{0,1\}^*$, for all x the algorithmic information content of $f(x)$ is bounded by:* $K(f(x)) \leq K(x) + O(1)$.

If we are aware that x belongs to a subset S of binary strings, then we can consider its complexity $K(x|S)$. Also, we can measure the level of randomness (irregularities) using randomness deficiency.

Definition 4. [11] The randomness deficiency of x with respect to a finite set S containing x is defined as $\delta(x|S) = \log \#S - K(x|S)$.

Lemma 1. [11] *Let S be an enumerable binary set of programs such that $x \in S$, Then, $K(x) \leq K(S) + \log \#S + O(1)$.*

4   Code Obfuscation Using Kolmogorov Complexity

The main purpose of code obfuscation is to confuse an adversary, making the task of reverse engineering extremely difficult. Code obfuscation introduces noise and dummy instructions that produce irregularities in the targeted obfuscated code. We believe that these make the obfuscated code difficult to comprehend. Classical complexity metrics have a limited power for measuring and quantifying irregularities in obfuscated code, because most of these metrics are designed to measure certain aspects of code attributes such as finding bugs and code maintenance. Human comprehension is a key in this case; an adversary has to understand the obfuscated code in order to recover the original. Measuring code obfuscation has to take into consideration this human factor. Although measuring code comprehension is very subjective, there were some successful attempts to measure human cognitive reasoning and cognitive science based on Kolmogorov complexity [6].

Code regularity (and irregularity) can be quantified, as was suggested in [8,10], using Kolmogorov complexity and compression. Code regularity means a certain structure is repeated many times, and thus can be recognized. Conversely, irregularities in code can be explained as the code exhibiting different types of structure over the code's body. Regularities in programs were introduced

``
while(i<n){
  i=i+1;
  x=x+i;}
``
 	
(a) Sum code
	``
	while(i<n){
	  i=i+1;
	  if (7*y*y-1==x*x){ //
	    false
	    y=x*i;
	  else
	    x=x+4*i;}
	  if (7*y*y-1==x*x){
	    y=x*i;
	  else
	    x=x-2*i;}
	  if (7*y*y-1==x*x){
	    y=x*i;
	  else
	    x=x-i;}}
	``

(b) One opaque predicate

```
while(i<n){
  i=i+1;
  if (7*y*y-1==x*x){ //
    false
    y=x*(i+1);
  else
    x=x+4*i;}
  if (x*x-34*y*y==-1){ //
    false
    y=x*i;
  else
    x=x-2*i;}
  if ((x*x+x)mod 2==0){
    //true
    x=x-i;
  else
    y=x*(i-1);}}
```

(c) Three opaque predicate

Fig. 1. Obfuscation example: (a) is the original code for the sum of n integers; (b) is an obfuscated version of (a) with one opaque predicate and data encoding which has some patterns and regularities; (c) is another obfuscated version of (a) with three opaque predicate and data encoding, which has less patterns and regularities comparing to (b).

by Jbara et al. in [8] as a potential measure for code comprehension; they experimentally showed using compression that long regular functions are less complex than the conventional classical metrics such as LOC (Line of Code) and McCabe (Cyclomatic complexity) could estimate.

The main intuition behind our approach is based on the following argument: if an adversary fails to capture some patterns (regularities) in an obfuscated code, then the adversary will have difficulty comprehending that code: it cannot provide a valid and brief, i.e., simple description. On the other hand, if these regularities are simple to explain, then describing them becomes easier, and consequently the code will not be difficult to understand.

We demonstrate our motivation using the example in Fig. 1. We obfuscate the program in Fig. 1-(a) that calculates the sum of the first n positive integers, by adding opaque predicates[2] with bogus code and data encoding. If we apply Cyclomatic complexity (McCabe [12]), a classical complexity measure, to Fig. 1-(b) the result will be 6. Cyclomatic complexity is based on control flow graph (CFG), and is computed by: $E - N + 2$, where E is the number of edges and N is the number of nodes in CFG. Figure 1-(b) contains $N = 8$ nodes, $E = 13$ edges then the Cyclomatic complexity is $(13 - 8 + 2) = 7$. We can see some regularity here: there is one opaque predicate repeated three times. Furthermore, the variable y is repeated three times in the same place of the

---

[2] An opaque predicate is an algebraic expression which always evaluates to same value (true or false) regardless of the input.

If-branch. We conjecture that we can find the short description of the program in Fig. 1-(b), due to presence of regularity by using lossless compression.

We take another obfuscated version in Fig. 1-(c) (of the same program); this code is obfuscated by adding three different opaque predicates. The patterns are less in this version comparing to Fig. 1-(b); the shortest program that describes Fig. 1-(c) is likely to be very similar to the code itself, where the Cyclomatic complexity is the same 7, and it does not account for the changes that occurred in the code. Assuming the opaque predicates of Fig. 1-(c) are equally difficult to break, attacking this code requires at least twice more effort than the code in Fig. 1-(b), as we need to figure out the value of two more opaque predicates. Furthermore, Fig. 1-(b) can be compressed at higher rate than Fig. 1-(c); again, this is due to the inherent regularity in Fig. 1-(b). We argue that an obfuscated program which is secure and confuses an adversary will exhibit a high level of irregularity in its source code and thus require a longer description to characterize all its features. This can be captured by the notion of Kolmogorov Complexity, which quantifies the amount of information in an object. An obfuscated program will have more non-essential information, and thus higher complexity, than a non-obfuscated one. Thus, we can use Kolmogorov Complexity to quantify the level of confusion in obfuscated programs due to the obfuscation process.

4.1   Applying Kolmogorov Complexity to Code Obfuscation

In this section, we present a novel approach for code obfuscation based on notions from algorithmic information theory. We start with an intuitive definition that is inspired by practical uses of obfuscation. The rationale behind this definition is that an obfuscated program must be more difficult to understand than the original program. This uses the separate notion of c-unintelligibility:

Definition 5. A program P' is said to be c-unintelligible with respect to another program P if it is c times more complex than P, i.e. the added complexity is c times the original one, and thus more difficult to understand. Formally:

$$K(P') \geq (c+1)K(P),$$

for some constant $c > 0$.

Definition 6. A c-Obfuscator $\mathcal{O} : \mathcal{P} \times \mathcal{L} \to \mathcal{P}'$ is a mapping from programs with security parameters $\mathcal{L}$ to their obfuscated versions such that $\forall P \in \mathcal{P}, \lambda \in \mathcal{L}$. $\mathcal{O}(P, \lambda) \neq P$ and satisfies the following properties:

- **Functionality:** $O(P, \lambda)$ and P compute the same function, such that $\forall i \in I$. $[\![P]\!](i) = [\![\mathcal{O}(P, \lambda)]\!](i)$.
- **Polynomial Slowdown:** the size and running time of $\mathcal{O}(P, \lambda)$ are at most polynomially larger than the size and running time of P, i.e. for polynomial function p. $|\mathcal{O}(P, \lambda)| \leq p(|P|)$, and if P halts in k steps on an input i, then $O(P, \lambda)$ halts within $p(k)$ steps on i.
- **Unintelligibility:** $\mathcal{O}(P, \lambda)$ is c-unintelligible with respect to P.

It is interesting to ask to what extent unintelligibility is related to the quality of the obfuscation parameter λ. Is a large λ *necessary* for high unintelligibility? Is it *sufficient*? We answer the first question in the positive by showing that c-unintelligibility sets a lower bound on the size of λ.

Lemma 2. *Consider a program P and an obfuscated version $P' = \mathcal{O}(P, \lambda)$ such that P' is c-unintelligible with respect to P. Then, $|\lambda| \geq cK(P) - O(1)$.*

Proof. By assumption, $K(\mathcal{O}(P, \lambda)) \geq (c+1)K(P)$. To compute P', we only need P, λ and the obfuscator program $\mathcal{O}$ and so we can upper bound $K(P')$:

$$K(P) + K(\lambda|P) + K(\mathcal{O}) \geq K(\mathcal{O}(P, \lambda))$$
$$\geq (c+1)K(P)$$
$$\Rightarrow K(\lambda|P) \geq cK(P) - K(\mathcal{O}).$$

Assuming the obfuscator program is simple, that is, $K(\mathcal{O}) = O(1)$, we have by basic properties of Kolmogorov complexity: $|\lambda| \geq K(\lambda) \geq K(\lambda|P) \geq cK(P) - O(1)$.

To answer the second question, we show a counter-example. So far, we have not addressed the nature of $\mathcal{O}$ and how well it uses its obfuscation parameter. It could well be the case that $\mathcal{O}$ only uses some bits of λ to modify P. In an extreme case, it can ignore λ altogether and simply return $\mathcal{O}(P, \lambda) = P$. The result satisfies the first two properties of an obfuscator, but can be considered unintelligible only in the degenerate case for $c = 0$ and surely we would not call the resulting code obfuscated. Another extreme case is when $\lambda = P$. Now, we would have at most $K(\mathcal{O}(P, \lambda)) \leq K(P) + K(\mathcal{O}) + O(1)$ which again would lead to a very small c. These two cases, although extreme, serve only to show that the quality of an obfuscator depends not only on λ but also on the obfuscation algorithm itself, $\mathcal{O}$. This is addressed later in Theorem 7.

Definition 6 is perhaps the first natural definition one can find, but it has one shortcoming. Merely requiring the obfuscated program to be complex overall does not mean that it is complex in all its parts, and in particular, that it hides the original program. To illustrate this point, consider the following example.

Example 1. Consider an obfuscated program $P' = \mathcal{O}(P, \lambda) = P \parallel \lambda$, which is a simple concatenation of P and λ. Define $n = |P'|$. We know $K(P \parallel \lambda) \simeq K(P, \lambda)$ within logarithmic precision (see [11] page 663). Then, by applying the chain rule of Theorem 1, $K(P') = K(P \parallel \lambda) \simeq K(P) + K(\lambda|P) + O(\log n)$. For large λ independent of P, this might signify a large unintelligibility, but the original program can be extracted directly from the obfuscated version requiring only $O(\log n)$ to indicate where P ends and λ starts.

This leads us to our second definition, where we require not that the obfuscated program be more complex than the original but rather, that it reveal almost no information about the original. This is captured by the notion of algorithmic mutual information and can be stated formally as:

Definition 7. Consider a program P and its obfuscated program $P' = \mathcal{O}(P, \lambda)$. We say P' is a γ-secure obfuscation of P if the mutual information between P and P' is at most γ, that is:

$$I_K(P; \mathcal{O}(P, \lambda)) \leq \gamma.$$

We say P' is a secure obfuscation of P if is γ-secure and γ is negligible.

It is common to consider, in the literature about Kolmogorov Complexity, that logarithmic terms are negligible. Thus, if both P and P' have lengths of order n, we might consider that P' would be a secure obfuscation for $\gamma = \log n$. This intuition, however, is bound to fail in practice.

Programs are typically redundant, written in very well-defined and formal languages, with common structures, design patterns, and even many helpful comments. It is expected that the complexity of a non-obfuscated program be low, compared to its length. Consider then the case that for a given P and $n = |P|$ we have $K(P) = O(\log n)$. Consider a scenario like that of Example 1, where the obfuscated reveals the original program and so the mutual information between both programs is maximum, i.e., $I_K(P; \mathcal{O}(P, \lambda)) = K(P) - O(\log n) = O(\log n)$. Even though this obfuscation can not be considered secure, the resulting mutual information is so small that Definition 7 would declare it secure. We have two ways out of this:

- we do not consider programs with $K(P) = O(\log n)$, since this is the error margin of the important properties of Kolmogorov complexity, and at this level we can not achieve significant results;
- or we consider a relative definition of security, requiring that the mutual information be only at most a negligible fraction of the information in P.

The second option leads us to the following definition:

Definition 8. Consider a program P and its obfuscated program $P' = \mathcal{O}(P, \lambda)$. We say P' is a ϵ-secure obfuscation of P if the mutual information between P and P' is at most $\epsilon K(P)$, that is: $I_K(P; \mathcal{O}(P, \lambda)) \leq \epsilon K(P)$, for $0 \leq \epsilon \leq 1$.

We say P' is a secure obfuscation of P if is ϵ-secure and ϵ is negligible in some appropriate sense.

4.2 Adversary Model

To properly define security we need to specify the capabilities of our attacker. The most basic case we want to capture is that of a human who seeks to obtain some original code from an obfuscated version thereof, without the assistance of any automated tools. The difficulty of the analyst's task is measured by the amount of information that s/he lacks to obtain the target code. If the obfuscation is weak, this will be small. A good obfuscation will force the analyst to obtain more information to reach its target, possibly some of the randomness used to execute the obfuscation.

At the other extreme, we have an analyst with access to the complete range of analysis tools. It can execute the obfuscated code (the 'challenge'), it can run any program on the challenge to obtain static analysis information on that code or it can produce variations of the challenge and subsequently run them. The adversary is not restricted in how many times s/he runs these programs nor in what order. Ultimately, with all the information gathered from this process, the adversary will attempt to produce the original code that was obfuscated into the challenge. This model equally captures automated reverse-engineering analysis techniques, such as static program analysis (e.g., data flow, control flow, alias analysis, program slicing, disassemblers, and decompilers), and dynamic program analysis (e.g., dynamic testing, profiling, and program tracing).

While the first adversary is too limited to be realistic, the powers of the second are too broad to be useful. Every obfuscated program that is obtained by a deterministic transformation (taking clear code and auxiliary randomness as input) can be reversed by undoing the exact same steps in the opposite order. Therefore, for each instance there will be at least one computable function that is able to return the original code. To achieve a meaningful model we have to establish limits to the adversary power and exclude such situations that would make any obfuscation trivially impossible.

A distinction commonly made in the literature is whether the attacker is passive or active. The first kind of adversary is limited to analysing the source code of the challenge, but can't run it nor modify it. The second adversary can execute the challenge code and modified versions thereof. We model these two kinds of adversary in the choice of computable functions available to the adversary.

To define our adversary model, we take inspiration from the game-based definitions of adversary capabilities commonly used in cryptography, although there are important differences. As standard, we have a game played between two parties, a challenger and an adversary, to assert the security of a particular instance of the obfuscation process $\mathcal{O}$. While $\mathcal{O}$ is known to both parties, only the challenger knows P, who chooses a random λ and produces $P' = \mathcal{O}(P, \lambda)$. (P, P') are the instance of the game.

It is customary to first fix an adversary and then select the challenge at random, so that the adversary can not be tailored to a specific instance, i.e., the adversary has no information at all about the messages that are used to construct the challenge. This then leads to a probabilistic analysis of the success of the adversary.

Kolmogorov Complexity theory is often used to analyse individual instances and avoid the analysis of probabilistic ensembles, and this is the route we follow in our approach. We of course also intend to guarantee that the adversary holds no information about the plain code, but instead of requiring this to be picked at random, we simply state that the *mutual information* between the plain code and the code of a *legitimate adversary* must be very low.

Thus our model of security is focused on individual instances of an obfuscation process, instead of considering at the same time all possibilities. This makes analysis much easier in a practical setting, since we can choose a particular case of obfuscated code and analyse its security without having to consider all other cases. This also shifts the focus of the security definition in the direction of actual examples of obfuscated code, and away from the obfuscator algorithm *per se*.

According to this reasoning, we say an adversary is *legitimate* if and only if its code, $\mathcal{A}$, satisfies[3]. $I_K(P; \mathcal{A}) = O(1)$.

This excludes the trivial case where a particular adversary already knows the source code or a good deal of it, and could therefore win the game without having any "intelligence" to undo the obfuscation. We mentioned before that for a particular instance, it is always possible to find a deterministic algorithm that trivially undoes the obfuscation: for example, an algorithm that simply "knows" the solution and prints it. This case is excluded by this mutual information requirement. Since $\mathcal{A}$ can print P even without knowledge of P', $K(P|\mathcal{A}) = O(1)$ and so $I(P; \mathcal{A}) = K(P) - O(1)$.

Another trivial algorithm is one that does not have any particular intelligence for a general obfuscated program: it just has a hard-coded list of changes that revert P' to P, for example, a list of the steps in obfuscation process detailing the state before and after that step. But then, this means $\mathcal{A}$ already contains in its code parts that are specific to P: some algorithm can look into $\mathcal{A}$ and thus reconstruct these parts of P even without knowing P'. The complexity of these parts is the information contained in $\mathcal{A}$ about P and if P and P' are reasonably different, the complexity of this list will be larger than $O(1)$.

This case is subtly different from one where the obfuscation process is so weak that it is possible to write a simple reversal algorithm, say, R, that simply undoes each step of O. In this case, $\mathcal{A}$ would use R as a list of steps to turn P' into P, much like in the previous case, but with the difference that these can be applied to any instance (P, P') of this obfuscator. For example, containing instructions that convert a particular structure into another, or that add or remove specific letters to a variable name. In this case, $\mathcal{A}$ knows R, but this does not have any information about a specific P, which makes $\mathcal{A}$ a legal adversary, giving evidence that $\mathcal{O}$ is a bad obfuscator and instances computed from it are weak.

On the other hand, there is also some lee-way in the adversary's goal. The most strict goal is to produce the original code. More relaxed conditions would allow the adversary to succeed if it could produce code that was close enough to the original source and had the same functionality. In our scenario, the adversary already knows the functionality to a large degree. If s/he did not, an adequate winning condition would be simply to produce as simple an equivalent version of the obfuscated code as possible, which would mean the adversary had understood the functionality and found a more compact implementation for it. But this does not mean the adversary's implementation is better than the original in some practical terms, for example, that it is more efficient. Our aim is to represent a situation where the obfuscated implementation of a specific functionality holds some value for the attacker: although the latter might know the full functionality,

---

[3] It is possible to parameterize the amount of information, but we think it would add much complication for little gain.

the way in which this is implemented is not known, and might be better in some practical terms than all the implementations the adversary currently knows.

So, the attacker will succeed if it can produce code that, although not the original, satisfies some properties chosen by the attacker in the same way the original code does. Finally, the result code should not be significantly more complex than the true original. That means they must have similar Kolmogorov complexities. Even if they might not be easily derived from the other, these two conditions guarantee that the adversary's solution and the true solution are equivalent in practice.

Definition 9 (Victory Conditions). For some program P and security parameter λ, given parameter ϵ, a program $P' = O(P, \lambda)$ and set of properties $\Pi = \pi_1, \ldots, \pi_n$, the adversary wins if it is able to produce a program P^* such that:

- $\pi_i(P^*) = \pi_i(P)$ for all properties π_i in Π;
- P^* is δ−close to P, that is, $|K(P) - K(P^*)| \leq \delta K(P)$ for $0 \leq \delta$.

The properties in Π represent the characteristics that the adversary values in the target program and that his/her solution should, therefore, preserve. These could be, for example, "P belongs in complexity class X", or "P uses at most n bits of randomness". In general terms they might even not be efficiently computable, so for a particular definition to be viable these properties should be chosen with care: that is, they should be represented by programs that compute those properties.

We thus summarize our adversary model:

- the adversary has no information about the source code used to produce the challenge;
- the adversary can run for an unlimited amount of time;
- the adversary can execute auxiliary algorithms that it can use to analyse the challenge;
- the adversary breaks the obfuscation if it can produce code close enough to the original, and the information it used is less, by some amount, than that of the clear code.

We give a more formal description below:

Definition 10 (Adversary's Game Parameters)

- $(P, P' = \mathcal{O}(P, \lambda))$
- Capabilities of the adversary:
  - The type of adversary, i.e., *passive* or *active*.
- Adversaries goals:
  - A set of properties that the target source code satisfies: $\Pi = \pi_1, \ldots, \pi_n$;
  - A proximity parameter δ.
- Security parameter:
  - A measure of the adversary's advantage against the defender.

Definition 11 (Adversary Model)

- Phase 0:
  - The adversary A must satisfy $I(P; A) = O(1)$, otherwise it is not legitimate and the game is meaningless.
- Phase 1:
  - The adversary selects a set of computable functions representing the analysis techniques s/he intends to use: $F = F_1, \ldots, F_k$. These functions can be constants (i.e., they are simply advice strings).
    * If the adversary is passive, no function is chosen in F, and move to phase 3.
    * If the adversary is active, the adversary can choose any function that takes code and produces other code (static or dynamic analysis).
    * If the adversary is *active*, P' is added to the set F.
- Phase 2:
  - The adversary executes any function in F as many times and in any order it wishes, under the sole constraint that the total execution time does not take more than $t(|P'|)$.
- Phase 3:
  - The adversary outputs its guess at the original code: P^*.

The adversary succeeds for security parameter ϵ if:

- The functionality of P^* and P' is equal[4], and P^* is close to P, that is, $|K(P) - K(P^*)| \leq \delta K(P)$.
- $\pi_i(P^*) = \pi_i(P)$, for all $1 \leq i \leq q$.
- Kolmogorov complexity of the adversary's information, $K(A, F_1, \ldots, F_k)$, is less than $(1 - \epsilon)K(P)$.

This adversary model using the security game is compatible with our mutual based security definition in Definition 8: if the last condition is true, the adversary successfully produces P from P'. Therefore, $K(P|P') \leq K(A, F_1, \ldots, F_k) < (1 - \epsilon)K(P)$ and so $I_K(P; P') > \epsilon K(P)$.

Notes:

- The amount of information used by the adversary is the upper limit to the length of the adversary's own code, plus that of any algorithm the adversary chooses in phase 1. In strict terms, this quantity should be measured by the Kolmogorov complexity of the above. In practice, this can be approximated by the length of a compression thereof or, in the worst case, the original strings.

The next proposition provides an example of how to test the security of an obfuscated code against an adversary.

---

[4] If this can not be checked, e.g. due to a large function domain, the adversary must provide a formal proof that the functionality is the same.

Proposition 1. *Consider a clear program P of length n with $K(P) \geq n - O(\log n)$ and $\mathcal{A}$ an adversary that extracts at least $m \leq n$ consecutive bits of P from $P' = \mathcal{O}(P, \lambda)$ then:*

1. $K(P|P') \leq n - m + O(\log n)$.
2. $I_K(P; P') \geq m - O(\log n)$

Proof. We prove this proposition by building the following algorithm:
Algorithm:

- Build $\mathcal{A}$ of length $O(1)$.
- Compute $\mathcal{A}(P')$, we obtain $m \leq n$ bits of P. Denote these by string ω.
- Now, build a program β such that $P = \beta(\omega)$ which computes two blocks of bits: those that come before and those that come after ω.
  To produce P, β needs at most to produce a pair of two strings (s_1, s_2) with combined length $n - m$. To describe the pair, we need at most $O(\log n)$ bits saying where to divide s_1 from s_2. Thus, $K(\beta) \leq n - m + O(\log n)$.

By construction, $K(P|\mathcal{O}(P, \lambda)) + O(1) \leq K(\beta) + O(1) \leq n - m + O(\log n)$. Using the assumption about $K(P)$, it is straight forward to compute

$$I_K(P; P') \geq m - O(\log n)$$

On the other hand, the adversary can fully obtain P, with only a logarithmic error, if it knows λ the security parameter, as the next theorem shows.

Theorem 4. *Let $P' = \mathcal{O}(P, \lambda)$, for an adversary $\mathcal{A}$ who knows λ:*

1. $K(P|P', \lambda) = O(\log n)$.
2. $I_K(P, P'|\lambda) = K(P|\lambda) - O(\log n)$.

where n is the maximum length of P, P' and λ.

Proof. If λ contains all the knowledge that $\mathcal{A}$ requires to obtain P given P', then the shortest program for a universal Turing machine U that describes P given $\mathcal{A}, P'$ and λ, is negligible i.e. empty string. It is sufficient for U to describe P from $\mathcal{A}, P'$ and λ with no need of any extra programs i.e. $U(\Lambda, \mathcal{A}(P'), \lambda) = P$ where Λ is an empty string. $O(\log n)$ is needed as an overhead cost required by U to combine $\mathcal{A}, P'$ and λ and to locate them on U tape. The advantage of $\mathcal{A}$ given λ is obtained as follows:

$$I_K(P; P'|\lambda) = K(P|\lambda) - K(P|P', \lambda)$$
$$= K(P|\lambda) - O(\log n)$$

These results are not surprising. Intuitively, an adversary can easily recover the original code from the obfuscated version once the security parameter that is used for obfuscation is known.

4.3   On the Impossibility of Obfuscation

There exist other definitions of obfuscation in the literature. Of particular importance to us is the work of [1], due to its famous impossibility result. As the authors argue in that paper, the black-box model they propose for obfuscation is too strong to be satisfiable in practice. The black-box model considers a program[5] P' obfuscated if any property that can be learned from P' can also be obtained by a simulator with only oracle access to P'. This essentially states that P' does not give any particular information about that property, since it is possible to learn it without having access to P'. Notice that this model does not compare an obfuscated program with an original one, but rather with its functionality. This is different from the definitions that we have proposed so far. Our definitions can be used to capture this purpose, namely, measuring how much information a program P' gives about the function it computes, which we denote by $[\![P']\!]$.

It suffices to note that every function F has a minimal program for it, say, Q. Then, its Kolmogorov complexity is the size of Q and for every other program P' computing F we have $K(F) = |Q| \leq |P'|$.

For every such program it must be that $K(F) \leq K(P') + O(1)$, otherwise we could build a program R of size $K(P')$ that produced P' and then ran in succession R and $U(R)$.[6] This composition of programs is itself a program with complexity $K(P') + O(1)$ which would be smaller than the assumed minimal program F, i.e., a contradiction. Therefore, our definition can be changed to compare the obfuscated program not with any simpler program but with *the simplest* program computing the same function.

Definition 12. Consider a program P'. We say P' is ϵ-securely obfuscated if

$$I_K([\![P']\!]; P') \leq \epsilon K([\![P']\!]),$$

for $0 \leq \epsilon \leq 1$.

We say P' is a secure obfuscated program if is ϵ-secure and ϵ is negligible.

We believe our definitions of obfuscation differ from the simulation black-box model in important ways, allowing us to avoid the impossibility result of [1].

Our definition is a less stringent form of obfuscation rather than a weak form of black box obfuscation. We assume the functionality of an obfuscated program is almost completely known and available to an adversary, and only require hiding the implementation rather than the functionality itself. This approach to obfuscation is very practical and pragmatic, especially for software protection obfuscation, as usually the customer likes to know exactly what a product does, although s/he might not care about how it was implemented.

---

[5] Or rather, a circuit or a Turing machine representation thereof.

[6] That is, we run R to produce P' then we execute the result of this first execution, that is P itself.

Our definition for security takes a program P (clear code), which supposedly is an easy and smart implementation of functionality F, and compares it with P', which is a different and supposedly unintelligible implementation of F, such that the original P can not be perceived or obtained from P'. The defenders' aim is not to prevent an adversary from understanding or finding F, but to prevent her/him from finding their own implementations P.

This intuition best matches the idea of *best possible obfuscation* which was advanced by Goldwasser and Rothblum [7]. According to [7] an obfuscator $\mathcal{O}$ is considered as best possible if it transforms a program P so that any property that can be computed from the obfuscated program P', can also be computed from any equivalent program of the same functionality. However, despite the close intuitive correspondence, our definition also differs from best possible obfuscation, in the sense that it relies on some form of black-box simulation. It was proved in [7] that best possible obfuscation has a strong relation with *indistinguishability obfuscation* [2,5], if $\mathcal{O}$ is an efficient obfuscation i.e. run in polynomial time.

In contrast, the black box model definition requires that all properties of a given obfuscated program P must be hidden from any adversary that ignores its source code but has access to at most a polynomial number of points of $[\![P]\!]$.

1. We can see that in our case, the adversary knows more about the functionality. Since the functionality is mostly public, this would be equivalent to giving the simulator in the black-box model access to this extra knowledge, reducing the advantage of the adversary and possibly making some functions obfuscatable.
2. On the other hand, our definition allows the leakage of a small, but non-zero, amount of information. Compare with the black-box model where a single-bit property that is non-trivially computed by an adversary, renders a function un-obfuscatable. Our definition requires the adversary to be able to compute more than a few bits in order for obfuscation to be broken.
3. Our definition considers only deterministic adversaries, again making adversaries less powerful and reducing their advantage.

We can try to model the implications for our definition of a successful black-box adversary against obfuscation. Consider an adversary $\mathcal{A}$ attacking a predicate π by accessing an algorithm A , such that $A(P') = 1$ if and only P' satisfies π. In this case, $\mathcal{A}$ is able to compute 1 bit of information about P', and we want to measure how much this helps $\mathcal{A}$ in describing some simpler program P that implements the same function $[\![P']\!]$. Since the adversary $\mathcal{A}$ knows A, s/he can enumerate the set S of all programs that satisfy A. Then, for some program $P \in S$, we would have $K(P|A) \leq K(S|A) + \log |S|$.

Note that the set S may be infinite, and so enumeration is the best that can be done: we enumerate all relevant programs and run A with each of them, noting the result. We could try to avoid this infinity problem by noticing we are only interested in programs simpler than the original, and thus satisfying $K(P) \leq K(P') \leq |P'|$. This does not give absolute guarantees, since in general there are programs with $|P| > |P'|$ and $K(P) \leq K(P')$, but our hope is that these are few and far between as they increase in length. Thus, even if we make this assumption and disregard a whole class of possibly relevant programs, we still have in the order of 2^n specimens. If A were a deterministic algorithm, we would have $K(S|A) = O(1)$, and if S has less than a half of all possible programs, then indeed we would find that $K(P|A) \leq K(S|A) + \log|S|/2 \leq n - 1$.

However, A is randomized, and in order to accurately produce S, for each program q, A must be run with a set of random coins r such that $A(q, r) \Leftrightarrow q \in S$. One way to describe S from A would need a polynomial number of bits for each program in S. Now, we no longer have the comfort of a negligible $K(S|A)$ term, and we can no longer be sure that knowing this property would in any way reduce the complexity of our target program.

We can still try to go around this problem, by allowing our enumerator to list not only all programs but also all possible random strings, and choosing the majority vote for each program. The length, and therefore the number, of possible random strings is bound by the running time of the program, which in turn is bound by a function of its length. Therefore, if we limit the length of our programs we limit the number of random strings to search.

This would eliminate the necessity of considering the extra information due to the random coins, but on the other hand the running time would increase exponentially. Any successful adversary would be very different to the PPT adversaries of [2], and although our definition has been made, for ease of exposition, with unbounded Kolmogorov complexity (for unbounded adversaries), it is easy to change it to consider polynomially-bounded adversaries by using an alternative definition of mutual information:

$$I_K^*(P; P') = K(P) - K^{t()}(P|P'),$$

where $t()$ is a polynomial on the length of P' that acts as a hard limit to the number of steps the universal machine can be run for. This notion of information can be negative in some cases, but clearly limits the ability of any adversary trying to find P from P' in a consistent way with the black-box model. With this definition of obfuscation, the above reasoning would lead to examples where non-obfuscatability by the black-box model does not prevent obfuscatability in the algorithmic information-theoretic model.

4.4   Security and Unintelligibility

Our first attempt to characterize obfuscation was based on *unintelligibility*, and then we evolved to a notion of security based on *mutual information*. The first notion seemed more immediately intuitive, traditional obfuscation techniques seem to rely only on making the code as complex as possible in an attempt to hide its meaning. But precisely this notion of "hiding meaning" is nothing more than reducing the information that the obfuscated program leaks about the original one, and so we believe the second approach to be the correct one. However, we can ask the natural question: is there any relation between these two concepts? Does high unintelligibility imply high security, or vice-versa?

`\\ variable that holds authentication`
`    password`
`string user-Input = input();`
`string secure-password = ...;`
`if secure-password ==  user-Input {`
`  grant-access();`
`else`
`  deny-access();}`
	`string O@ = x0();`
	`string $F=...;`
	`if O@== $F{`
	` x1();`
	`else`
	` x2(); }`

P: simple password checker	P': obfuscating P

Fig. 2. An example for obfuscating a program using renaming technique.

We give a partial answer to this question. In certain situations, high unintelligibility will imply high security, as stated in the following theorem.

Theorem 5. *Consider a program P of length m and its obfuscated version $P' = \mathcal{O}(P, \lambda)$ of length $n > m$ (where n is at most polynomially larger than m), satisfying c-unintelligibility for $c \geq \frac{n}{K(P)}$. Assuming that the obfuscation security parameter λ satisfies $K(P'|P) \geq K(\lambda|P) - \alpha$, then up to $O(\log n)$:*

$$I(P; \mathcal{O}(P, \lambda)) \leq \alpha - O(1)$$

Proof. By Theorem 3, $K(P') = K(\mathcal{O}(P, \lambda)) \leq K(P, \lambda) + K(\mathcal{O}) = K(P, \lambda)$[7] and by assumption $K(P') \geq (c+1)K(P)$. Then,

$$K(P, \lambda) \geq (c+1)K(P)$$
$$K(P, \lambda) - K(P) \geq cK(P)$$
$$K(\lambda|P) \geq cK(P)$$

Now, for mutual information, we have

$$I(P; P') = K(P') - K(P'|P)$$
$$\leq K(P') - K(\lambda|P) + \alpha \text{ (by assumption)}$$
$$\leq n - cK(P) + \alpha$$
$$\leq n - n + \alpha \text{ (by assumption)}$$
$$= \alpha$$

Intuitively, if we consider an optimal obfuscation key (it has all the information needed to produce P' from P, but not much more than that), we can say that if P' is c-unintelligible for large enough c, then P' is a secure obfuscation of P.

The above theorem shows when high c-unintelligibility implies security of code obfuscation. It turns out that the reverse implication does not exist, as the following theorem illustrates.

---

[7] The $O(1)$ term is absorbed by the logarithmic additive term that we are not notating.

Claim. There are obfuscated functions $\mathcal{O}(P, \lambda)$ that are arbtrarily secure and yet do not satisfy c-unintelligibility for $c \geq 0$.

Proof. Consider first the case of program P of Fig. 2, that simply checks a password for access, and its obfuscated version P', which was computed using layout obfuscation [3]: variable and function renaming and comment deleting. The obfuscated variable and function names are independent of the original ones and so the information that P' contains about P is limited to the unchanging structure of the code: assignment, test and if branch.

The complexity of the original code can be broken in several independent parts: the comment, the structure, the variable and function names, and therefore we can write $K(P) = n_c + n_s + n_v$. The only thing that P' can give information about is the structure part, since all the other information was irrevocably destroyed in the process: there is no data remaining that bears any relation to the lost comment or the lost function names. Therefore, $I_K(P; P') \leq n_s = \frac{n_s}{n_c+n_s+n_v} K(P)$. We can make the fraction $\frac{n_s}{n_c+n_s+n_v}$ as small as necessary by inserting large comments, long names and representing structure as compactly as possible, for example, keeping names in a dictionary block and indicating their use by pointers to this.

However the complexity of P' is less than that of P, since there is less essential information to describe: the same structure, no comments and the function names could be described by a simple algorithm. Therefore, we have that c-unintelligibility can not be satisfied for any non-negative value of c. This shows that high ϵ-security does not imply high unintelligibility.

The next theorem shows how we can obtain security if the obfuscated code is complex enough and the obfuscation key is independent of the original program.

Theorem 6. *Let P be a program of length n and λ an independent and random obfuscation key, satisfying $K(\lambda) \geq n - \alpha$ and $K(P, \lambda) \geq K(P) + K(\lambda) - \beta$, where $\alpha, \beta \in \mathbb{N}$. Suppose the obfuscation $\mathcal{O}(P, \lambda)$ satisfies $K(\mathcal{O}(P, \lambda)|P) \geq K(\lambda|P) - O(1)$. Then up to a logarithmic factor: $I_K(P; \mathcal{O}(P, \lambda)) \leq \alpha + \beta$.*

Proof.

$$\begin{aligned}
I_K(P; \mathcal{O}(P, \lambda)) &= K(\mathcal{O}(P, \lambda)) - K(\mathcal{O}(P, \lambda)|P) \\
&\leq K(\mathcal{O}(P, \lambda)) - K(\lambda|P) \\
&\leq K(\mathcal{O}(P, \lambda)) - K(\lambda, P) + K(P) \quad \text{(By Theorem 1)} \\
&\leq n - K(P) - n + \alpha + \beta + K(P) \leq \alpha + \beta
\end{aligned}$$

The first two assumptions are natural: picking λ at random and independently of P will satisfy high complexity and low mutual information with high probability, so we can simply assume those properties at the start. The third assumption, however, is not immediately obvious: it describes a situation where the obfuscation key is *optimal*, in the sense that it contains just the amount of information to go from P to P', within a small logarithmic term. The following lemma shows how λ must have a minimum complexity to allow the derivation of P to P'.

Lemma 3. *Consider* $P' = \mathcal{O}(P, \lambda)$ *is the result of obfuscating a program* P. *Then,* $K(\lambda|P) \geq K(P'|P) - O(1)$

Proof. Given the obfuscator $\mathcal{O}$ and any λ, construct the function $q_\lambda(\cdot) = \mathcal{O}(\cdot, \lambda)$. Let Q_λ be a program that implements it. Then, clearly, $U(Q_\lambda, P) = P'$ and so $|Q_\lambda| \geq K(P'|P)$. To describe Q_λ, we only need to specify λ and instructions to invoke $\mathcal{O}$ with the proper arguments, but since P is already known, we can use it to find a shorter description for λ. This gives $K(P'|P) \leq K(\lambda|P) + O(1)$.

An optimal obfuscation key λ is then the one that uses as little information as possible. Obfuscation techniques can use randomness or not. In Sect. 4.4, we showed one case where names could be obfuscated in a deterministic way, without any randomness. However, we could equally have used instead highly random names, with the same effect in security but increasing unintelligibility as well. We can as well consider that the set of obfuscation techniques is finite and describe each of them by a unique number. This way, we can characterize a single application of obfuscation by a key composed of the technique's index and the randomness needed.

We now proceed to show that it is possible to achieve obfuscation security according to our definitions, but restricted to a passive adversary, that is, one that does not realize transformations over the intercepted code. The intuition is to use obfuscation techniques that behave as much as possible as secure encryption functions, namely, using random keys that are independent from the code and large enough that they obscure almost all original information. The crucial difference that enables security is that because an obfuscation technique preserves functionality, we do not need to decrypt the obfuscated code and so don't need to hide the key.

First, we prove the effect of obfuscating an elementary piece of code, by application of a single obfuscation technique. Then, we reason about the case of a full program, composed of several of these independent blocks.

Theorem 7. *Let* p *represent a program block,* $\mathcal{O}$ *an obfuscation technique and* $\lambda \in \mathcal{L}$ *an obfuscation key with fixed length* n. *Let* $p' = \mathcal{O}(p, \lambda)$ *be the obfuscated block. Assume* $\mathcal{O}$ *produces an output with length* $\ell \leq n + \gamma$ *and is "nearly-injective" in the following sense: for every* p, *any subset of* $\mathcal{L}$ *of keys with the same behaviour for* p *has cardinality at most polynomial in* n. *That is, for all* p *and* $\lambda_0 \in \mathcal{L}$, $|\{\lambda : \mathcal{O}(p, \lambda) = \mathcal{O}(p, \lambda_0)\}| \leq n^k$, *for some positive integer* k.

Then, if the key is random, $K(\lambda) \geq n - \alpha$ *and independent from* p, $K(\lambda|p) \geq K(\lambda) - \beta$, *the obfuscated code* p' *is* $(\alpha + \beta + \gamma)$-*secure up to a logarithmic term.*

Proof. By symmetry of information, we can write $K(p|p') = K(p'|p) + K(p) - K(p')$. Since $p' = \mathcal{O}(p, \lambda)$, it's easy to see that $K(p'|p) \leq K(\mathcal{O}) + K(\lambda|p) = K(\lambda|p)$, since $K(\mathcal{O})$ is a constant independent of p, λ or p'. As well, we can show the reverse inequality. To produce λ from p, we can first produce p' from p

(with a program that takes at least $K(p'|p)$ bits) and then build the set $S_{p,p'} = \{\lambda : |\lambda| \leq n, \mathcal{O}(p,\lambda) = p'\}$ of all compatible λ, by a program whose length is $O(1)$. Finally, we just have to give the index of λ in this set, and so $K(\lambda|p) \leq K(p'|p) + \log \#S_{p,p'}$. Then, by assumptions on λ, $K(p'|p) \geq K(\lambda|p) - \log \#S_{p,p'} \geq n - \alpha - \beta - \log \#S_{p,p'}$. By assumption on the output of $\mathcal{O}$, $K(p') \leq |\mathcal{O}(p,\lambda)| \leq n + \gamma$. This gives $K(p|p') \geq K(p) + n - \alpha - \beta - O(\log n) - K(p') \geq K(p) - \alpha - \beta - \gamma - O(\log n)$.

The randomness and independence conditions for the keys are natural. The other two conditions may seem harder to justify, but they ensure that $\mathcal{O}$ effectively mixes p with the randomness provided by λ: the limit on the size of subsets of $\mathcal{L}$ implies a lower bound on the number of possible obfuscations for p (the more the better); on the other hand, the limit on the length of the output of $\mathcal{O}$ forces the information contained in p to be scrambled with λ, since it can take only a few more bits than those required to describe λ itself. The extreme case is similar to One-Time Pad encryption[8], when both the output and λ have the same size n, and $\mathcal{O}$ is injective for each p: there are 2^n keys, as well as possible obfuscations for each p. Furthermore, because the obfuscated code has the same length of λ, the exact same obfuscated strings are possible for each p, maximizing security.

In general, a program is composed of several of these minimal blocks in sequence. The above proof shows when the obfuscated block p' gives no information about its original block, say p_0. As well, p' can not give any more information about any other block p_1, as there is no causal relation between p_1 and p'. At best, there is some information in p_1 about p_0, but then the information given by p' about p_1 should be at most that given by about p_0. Therefore, we conclude that if all the sub-blocks in a program are securely obfuscated, then the whole program is. The above theorem, then, shows that secure obfuscation is possible under very reasonable assumptions.

4.5   Normalized Kolmogorov Complexity

Kolmogorov Complexity is an absolute measure, which is problematic when we want to compare two programs with different sizes. For example consider a program P of 1000 bits size that can be compressed to 500 bits, take another program Q of 10^6 bits size, which is compressed to 1000 bits. By using the absolute measure of Kolmogorov complexity, Q is more complex than P. However, P can be compressed to almost half of its size, where Q can be compressed to $\frac{1}{1000}$ of its size, which clearly indicates that Q has more regularities than P, and hence that makes P more complex than Q. In order to overcome this issue, we suggest a normalized version of Kolmogorov Complexity that is relativized by the upper bound of Kolmogorov complexity i.e. the maximum complexity a certain obfuscated code can achieve. Kolmogorov complexity is upper bounded by the length of its program, the subject of measure, according to Theorem 2; this bound

---

[8] Which is proved to be an unconditionally secure symmetric cypher.

can be used as the maximum Kolmogorov complexity. Normalized Kolmogorov complexity can be useful demonstrating the divergence of obfuscated code complexity before and after a given attack, in terms of information content (high variability of text content), from the maximum value of that complexity.

Definition 13. The normalised Kolmogorov complexity NK of a program P is given by:

$$NK(P) = \frac{K(P)}{|P| + 2\log(|P|)}$$

Where $|P|$ is the length of P.

A high value of NK means that there is a high variability of program content structure, i.e. high complexity. A low value of NK means high redundancy, i.e. the ratio of repeating fragments, operators and operands in code. Since Kolmogorov complexity can be effectively approximated by compression ([9]), it is possible to estimate NK by using a standard compressor instead of a minimal program:

$$NC(P) = \frac{C(P)}{|P| + 2\log(|P|)},$$

implying $0 \le NC \le 1$.

5 Individual Security of Code Obfuscation

Studying the security of individual instances of obfuscated code provides more granularity. Even if the obfuscated program is considered secure according to our definition, it may have parts which can provide some information about other obfuscated parts, which reduce the security of the obfuscated code. It could be that a program is obfuscated but that some module is not: some part of the obfuscated code stays still in its original form. We can demonstrate this relation by providing some boundaries on the complexity of subprograms in the same program.

We can view (obfuscated) programs as finite, and therefore recursively enumerable, sets of subprograms (blocks or modules) such that $P' = \{p'_n\}_{n \in \mathbb{N}}$. Given an obfuscated program P', it may consist of obfuscated and unobfuscated modules, that is: $\exists p'_j, p'_i \in P'$, where p'_i is an obfuscated module and p'_j is an unobfuscated module. Theorem 6 demonstrates the effect of security parameters λ on the whole obfuscation process. The following results show the effect of each individual security parameter on each obfuscated subprogram. Choosing a good λ (with a good source of randomness) requires a minimum amount of information to be shared with obfuscated code and the clear code. It is important to study the relation between the security parameter and the original (clear) code. In the following theorem, we use a simple way to check the independence between λ and P on the subprogram level.

Theorem 8. *Let P' be a set of obfuscated subprograms and P a set of clear subprograms, such that each subprogram p' of P' has length at most n, and is the obfuscation of a corresponding block in P: $\exists p_i \in P, \kappa_i \in \lambda$. $p' = \mathcal{O}(p_i, \kappa_i)$. If $K(\kappa_i, p_i) \geq K(p_i) + K(\kappa_i) - \alpha$, then (up to a logarithmic term): $I_K(\kappa_i; p_i) \leq \alpha$.*

Proof. Since $K(p_i, \kappa_i) \leq K(\kappa_i|p_i) + K(p_i) + O(\log n)$, we have by assumption

$$K(p_i) + K(\kappa_i) - \alpha \leq K(\kappa_i|p_i) + K(p_i) + O(\log n)$$
$$K(\kappa_i) - \alpha \leq K(\kappa_i|p_i) + O(\log n)$$
$$K(\kappa_i) - K(\kappa_i|p_i) \leq \alpha + O(\log n)$$
$$I_K(\kappa_i, p_i) \leq \alpha + O(\log n)$$

The following two theorems address the security of two different forms of code obfuscation: obfuscation-as-encoding and obfuscation-as-hiding. In the obfuscation-as-encoding technique, the original program is transformed in such a way it changes the structure of original code, but preserving the functionality, for example Data transformation techniques such as array splitting, splitting variable, Restructure Arrays and Merge Scalar Variables [3]. The encoding process is considered as the security parameter that dictates how the obfuscation should be performed and where it should take place. Encoding differs from encryption, if somebody knows the encoding process, then the original code can be recovered. In encoding obfuscation, the clear program is not presented in the obfuscated code; what still exists, but hidden, is the encoding process. Reversing the encoded program (obfuscated) requires finding and understanding the encoding process. For instance we used a simple encoding in Fig. 1, x=x+i is encoded as x=x+4*i;x=x-2*i;x=x-i; the encoding process converts i to 4*i;-2*i;-i, to figure out x=x+i , we have to find and combine 4*i;-2*i;-i, which is the security parameter in this case. The next theorem addresses the security of obfuscation code when we apply encoding to P (as a set of subprograms), here, the encoding process is presented as a part of security parameter.

Theorem 9 (Encoding). *Let P' be a collection of obfuscated subprograms p'_i using $\kappa_i \in \lambda$, each of length at most n. Then, for $\delta_{\kappa_i} = \delta(\kappa_i|P')$: $I_K(\kappa_i; p'_i) \leq \delta_{\kappa_i} - O(1)$.*

Proof. Since P' is a collection of sub-programs, we can assume that it contains all the information in p'_i as well as that of all other sub-programs. Then,
$K(\kappa_i|P') = K(\kappa_i|p'_1, \ldots, p'_i, \ldots, p'_n) \leq K(\kappa_i|p'_i)$ and so

$$\begin{aligned} I_K(\kappa_i; p'_i) &= K(\kappa_i) - K(\kappa_i|p'_i) \\ &\leq K(\kappa_i) - K(\kappa_i|P') \\ &\leq K(\kappa_i) - (\log \#P' - \delta_{\kappa_i}) \text{ by Definition 4} \end{aligned}$$

Because each subprogram has length at most n, P' can contain at most 2^n distinct programs. Assuming that each appears at most a constant number of times, we have that $\#P' = O(2^n)$ and $\log \#P' = n + O(1)$. Then,

$$I_K(\kappa_i; p_i') \leq n - n + \delta_{\kappa_i} - O(1)$$
$$\leq \delta_{\kappa_i} - O(1)$$

In hiding obfuscation techniques the original subprogram still exists in the obfuscated program (set of obfuscated subprograms), the security of such techniques depends on the degree of hiding in the set obfuscated subprograms. An example of such technique is the control flow obfuscations such as Insert Dead basic-blocks, Loop Unrolling, Opaque Predicate and Flatten Control Flow [3]. Normally these techniques are combined and used with encoding obfuscation techniques, in order to make the code more resilient to reverse engineering techniques.

For code obfuscation, an opaque predicate is used as a guard predicate that cannot statistically be computed without running the code; however the original code still exists too in the obfuscated code, but protected by the predicate. In Fig. 1 we used opaque predicates with simple data encoding technique. Consider the following obfuscated code of Fig. 1-(a), where the encoding has been removed. Obviously, x=x+i is still in the code, but is hidden under the protection of opaque predicate.

```
while(i<n){
   i=i+1
 if (7*y*y-1==x*x){ //false
    y=x*i;
  else
   x=x+i;}}
```

Opaque predicate with no encoding.

Theorem 10 (Hiding). *Let P' be a collection of obfuscated subprograms p_i', each of length at most n. Then, for $\delta_{p_i} = \delta(p_i|P')$: $I_K(p_i; p_i') \leq \delta_{p_i} - O(1)$.*

Proof. The proof is very similar to Theorem 9. The block p_i is hidden in P' but in its original form, due to the obfuscation process. Since P' is a collection of subprograms, we can assume that it contains all the information in p_i' as well as that of all other sub-programs. Then, $K(p_i|P') = K(p_i|p_1', \ldots, p_i', \ldots, p_n') \leq K(p_i|p_i')$

$$I_K(p_i; p_i') = K(p_i) - K(p_i|p_i')$$
$$\leq K(p_i) - K(p_i|P')$$
$$\leq K(p_i) - (\log \#P' - \delta_{p_i}) \text{ by Definition 4}$$

Similarly to the proof of Theorem 9, $\#P' = O(2^n)$ and $\log \#P' = n + O(1)$. Then,

$$I_K(p_i; p_i') \leq n - n + \delta_{p_i} - O(1)$$
$$\leq \delta_{p_i} - O(1)$$

6   Conclusion and Future Work

In this paper, we provide a theoretical investigation of code obfuscation. We defined code obfuscation using Kolmogorov complexity and algorithmic mutual information. Our definition allows for a small amount of secret information to be revealed to an adversary, and it gives an intuitive guarantee about the security conditions that have to be met for secure obfuscation. We argued our definition is more lenient than the virtual black-box model of Barak et al. and for that reason the impossibility result does not apply. In contrast, we showed that under reasonable circumstances we can have secure obfuscation according to our definition.

To the best of our knowledge, this paper is the first to propose algorithmic information theory as a theoretical basis for code obfuscation and its threat model. We believe that our new definition for code obfuscation provides the first step toward establishing quantitative metrics for certifying code obfuscation techniques. Currently, we are working toward deriving new metrics based on our model, aiming to validate and apply these metrics, empirically, to real obfuscated programs using state of the art obfuscation techniques. There are still some questions we want to address in future work. For example, it is still not clear whether the complexity of security parameter (key) has always a positive effect on the the security of obfuscated programs based on algorithmic mutual information definition. Furthermore, algorithmic mutual information has a parallel counterpart based on classical information theory such as Shannon mutual information, it would be interesting to explore the relation between our definition and Shannon mutual information in the context of code obfuscation security. We are also planning to study and characterize the security of particular techniques and to analyze more carefully the scenario of active adversaries.

References

1. Barak, B., Goldreich, O., Impagliazzo, R., Rudich, S., Sahai, A., Vadhan, S., Yang, K.: On the (im)possibility of obfuscating programs. J. ACM **59**(2), 1–48 (2012). http://doi.acm.org/10.1145/2160158.2160159
2. Barak, B., Goldreich, O., Impagliazzo, R., Rudich, S., Sahai, A., Vadhan, S.P., Yang, K.: On the (im)possibility of obfuscating programs. IACR Cryptology ePrint Arch. **2001**, 69 (2001)
3. Collberg, C., Thomborson, C., Low, D.: A Taxonomy of Obfuscating Transformations (1997). https://researchspace.auckland.ac.nz/handle/2292/3491
4. Gács, P.: On the symmetry of algorithmic information. Soviet Math. Dokl **15**, 1477–1480 (1974)

5. Garg, S., Raykova, M., Gentry, C., Sahai, A., Halevi, S., Waters, B.: Candidate indistinguishability obfuscation and functional encryption for all circuits. In: FOCS (2013)
6. Gauvrit, N., Zenil, H., Delahaye, J.P.: Assessing cognitive randomness: A kolmogorov complexity approach. CoRR abs/1106.3059 (2011)
7. Goldwasser, S., Rothblum, G.N.: On best-possible obfuscation. In: Vadhan, S.P. (ed.) TCC 2007. LNCS, vol. 4392, pp. 194–213. Springer, Heidelberg (2007)
8. Jbara, A., Feitelson, D.G.: On the effect of code regularity on comprehension. In: Proceedings of the 22nd International Conference on Program Comprehension, ICpPC 2014, pp. 189–200. ACM, New York (2014). http://doi.acm.org/10.1145/2597008.2597140
9. Kieffer, J.C., Yang, E.H.: Sequential codes, lossless compression of individual sequences, and kolmogorov complexity. IEEE Trans. Inf. Theor. $42(1)$, 29–39 (1996)
10. Lathrop, J.I.: Compression depth and the behavior of cellular automata. Complex Systems (1997)
11. Li, M., Vitnyi, P.M.: An Introduction to Kolmogorov Complexity and Its Applications, 3rd edn. Springer Publishing Company, Incorporated (2008)
12. McCabe, T.J.: A complexity measure. IEEE Trans. Softw. Eng. $2(4)$, 308–320 (1976)
13. Shen, A.: Axiomatic description of the entropy notion for finite objects. VIII All-USSR Conference (Logika i metodologija nauki), Vilnjus, pp. 104–105 (1982). http://www.lirmm.fr/ashen/mathtext/1982/vilnus.pdf. The paper in Russian

The Entity Labeling Pattern for Modeling Operating Systems Access Control

Peter Amthor[✉]

Ilmenau University of Technology, P.O. Box 100565, 98684 Ilmenau, Germany
peter.amthor@tu-ilmenau.de

Abstract. To meet tightening security requirements, modern operating systems enforce mandatory access control based on formal security policies. To ensure the critical property of policy correctness, formal methods and models for both their specification and verification are used. The variety of these approaches reflects the diversity and heterogeneity of policy semantics, which makes policy engineering an intricate and error-prone process. Therefore, a common formal framework is needed that unifies both diverse access control systems on the one hand and diverse formal criteria of correctness on the other hand.

This paper presents a step towards this goal. We propose to leverage core-based model engineering, a uniform approach to policy formalization, and refine it by adding typical semantic abstractions of contemporary policy-controlled operating systems. This results in a simple, yet highly flexible framework for formalization, specification and analysis of operating system security policies. We substantiate this claim by applying our method to the SELinux system and demonstrating the practical usage of the resulting model.

Keywords: Security engineering · Security policies · Access control models · Operating system security · SELinux

1 Introduction

In the application domains of modern operating systems, such as server virtualization, mobile and ubiquitous computing or automotive computing, security requirements are more than ever of paramount importance. In order to meet these requirements, systems security engineering increasingly relies on formally specified security policies [35]. These policies define rules that, given their reliable enforcement, can be proven to achieve application-specific security goals such as confidentiality and integrity of a system and the information it processes. Consequently, their key role in a security engineering process yielded an increasing number policy-controlled operating systems over the past years [7,9,13,18,23,29,31,34].

Given their critical nature, specification and verification of OS security policies has proven to require as much attention as their design, implementation and enforcement. To this end, formal models have been developed for such policies based on two major objectives:

© Springer International Publishing Switzerland 2016
M.S. Obaidat and P. Lorenz (Eds.): ICETE 2015, CCIS 585, pp. 270–292, 2016.
DOI: 10.1007/978-3-319-30222-5_13

(1.) Modeling a particular system and
(2.) modeling a particular security property.

While the first approach seeks to precisely specify the security-related semantics of an operating system, which are determined by its respective application domain (such as roles [24] or user relationships [12]), the second takes the opposite way: formalizing and analyzing a security property, which results from the security requirements of a particular application domain (such as right proliferation [11,14] or information flows [15]). Both approaches yield models that are available to formal methods; however, models resulting from both approaches are often incompatible: when focusing on a formally analyzable property such as dynamic right proliferation, system-independent access control models based on state machines have proven to be valuable; when focusing on a formal framework for policy specification and communication on the other hand, system-specific models such as for the SELinux operating system have evolved, which may in turn sacrifice analyzability with respect to a whole family of security properties.

This problem has been addressed by the design paradigm of model-based security policy engineering [4,5,15,17,22]. Its goal is to derive a uniform pattern for designing security models, which flexibly fits (1.) diverse security policy semantics as well as (2.) diverse formal analysis goals. Such a uniform pattern would then serve as a fundamental prerequisite for both specifying and verifying security policies.

According to [4,22], this goal can be achieved through a flexible and extensible common model core based on a deterministic state machine (*core-based model engineering*). In practice, it requires to adapt domain-specific abstractions to a deliberately general formal framework. This yields a twofold result: On the one hand, core-based model engineering eliminates the need for a formal framework from scratch, whenever a given security policy is to be analyzed with one of the two objectives stated above. On the other hand, given the versatile and thus domain-independent semantics of the pattern, the actual engineering effort to create usable model instances is still significant in practice (as pointed out by [22, pp. 46 et seq.]).

This paper aims at further reducing this engineering effort—and thus the probability of errors—in the domain of policy-controlled operating systems by presenting a refinement of the core-based modeling pattern. Its idea is based on the general principle of entity labeling, which can be found in a large family of access control (AC) policies for contemporary operating systems. The resulting modeling pattern will then be applied to the SELinux operating system, which exhibits semantic features typical for OS security policies. Based on the resulting SELinux access control model, we will discuss the costs of model design and model instantiation.

Contributions and Paper Organization. To introduce the context of this paper, we briefly discuss relevant related work (Sect. 2), followed by a summary of the fundamental concepts of one typical OS representative, SELinux (Sect. 3). Section 4 focuses on a formalization of the discussed concepts: First, the fundamentals of core-based modeling are introduced (Sect. 4.1). We then present a novel, abstract policy modeling pattern based on *entity labeling* (Sect. 4.2), which enriches the core pattern by adequate access control semantics for the operating systems domain. It hence eases analysis and verification of contemporary operating system security policies with respect to an actual system's protection state (*dynamic analysis*) using existing formal methods and tools.

To substantiate this claim, we applied our pattern to SELinux. We create an entity labeling model of the SELinux access control system (Sect. 5) and discuss, how a real-world system's protection state and security policy can be transformed into an instance of this model (Sect. 6). This paves the way for subsequently applying tried and tested analysis methods for core-based models to SELinux, some of which we will discuss based on static and dynamic reachability properties. We conclude with Sect. 7.

2   Related Work

In the AC model community, considerable research has already been done to unify model semantics and formalisms. Notably, the access control meta-model by Barker [5], the Policy Machine [10], and core-based security models [17,22] provide general formal frameworks for a precise specification of access control semantics and policies. While Barker's unifying meta-model and the Policy Machine are primarily designed for policy specification, core-based modeling aims at both specifying and analyzing/verifying a policy.

Another family of formal AC models is specifically tailored to OSs. Among numerous work in this area, most is tailored to specific operating systems such as SELinux [26,36,38] or special types of OS policies such as MLS [19]. While all of these approaches emphasize policy analysis with respect to a particular formal security property, they cannot be easily adapted to other OS AC semantics or other formal analysis goals. In our approach, we aim for both: streamlined adaption to versatile OS AC semantics that share only the abstract concept of labeling, and accessibility to a bandwidth of security properties and their appropriate formal analysis methods.

The basic idea of label-based AC modeling is far from being new. Dating back to the historical BLP model [6], which effectively introduced access permissions based on labels, a whole new class of attribute-based AC models (ABAC) evolved based on this principle [16,39]. However, they usually focus policy specification in the domain of service-oriented architectures [20,28,37] rather than system architectures. To this end, both the goal of formal policy analysis and the focus on the OS domain cannot be easily incorporated into existing ABAC models.

3   SELinux Access Control

Today's operating systems increasingly rely on mandatory access control (MAC) mechanisms governed by a security policy. In large parts, their authorization semantics are based on assigning policy-specific labels to entities, which are divided into subjects (an activity abstraction such as process or thread) and objects (OS resources, described by abstractions such as files, handlers, sockets, etc.). The idea of label-based OS policies dates back to SELinux [18], one of the first policy-controlled OSs, and has been adopted by a wide range of later operating systems such as SEBSD [34], Oracle Solaris [9], Microsoft Windows [13], and Google's Android [29].

The goal of this section is to take a closer look at the security architecture and policy semantics of SELinux as a typical representative of modern policy-controlled operating systems.

3.1   Security Architecture

The original goal of SELinux was to enforce MAC in the Linux operating system. To achieve this, the *Flask* security architecture [31] was implemented, which clearly distinguishes between policy enforcement points (PEP) and a singular policy decision point (PDP). The PDP logically encapsulates the whole security policy.

Today, SELinux is implemented as a dynamically loadable kernel module. Its architecture merges into the Linux kernel through the LSM interface (*Linux Security Modules*). It provides ready-made PEP hooks for all system call implementations, which are connected to the PDP (the *Security Server*) via the SELinux kernel module. In addition to the processing logic, that translates information about an OS resource access into the policy-related data structures that are used by the security server, this module also includes a caching mechanism for previously made decisions (the *Access Vector Cache*, AVC).

To illustrate how an access request by an application process (1) is handled in SELinux, we consider the following example based on Linux kernel 3.19 (cf. Fig. 1): Once an according syscall is processed by the kernel, e.g. *read()* for accessing a file (2), the LSM hook (`security_file_permission()`) invokes the

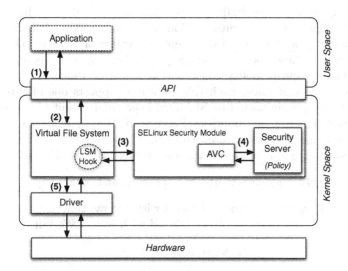

Fig. 1. Processing an access request in the SELinux security architecture.

according interface of the SELinux Security Module (3). Here, the permissions needed for authorizing the specific request (here: FILE_READ) are checked against the AVC (calling avc_has_perm()) or, in case of a miss, the Security Server's security_compute _av()-interface (4). The decision is then returned through the LSM hook and enforced by the *read()*-implementation in vfs_read() (either invoking the respective file system interface to ultimately access the storage hardware (5), or returning to the caller with an "access denied" error).

Inside the Security Server logic, access decisions are based on the policy rules and SELinux *security contexts* associated to entities. The latter is a label consisting of four attributes, which is usually represented by a string

$$user : role : type [: range]$$

where **user** is the name of an SELinux user the process belongs to, **role** is the name of an SELinux role the process assumes, and **type** is the name of the domain (or type) in SELinux type enforcement (TE) in which the process currently runs. Finally, **range** is a collection of confidentiality classes and categories used by multi-level security (MLS) policy rules based on the BLP model. Since support for the MLS mechanism is neither required by the SELinux policy semantics nor by the security server, this fourth attribute is optional. We will discuss the semantics of these attributes in a security policy in the next section.

On implementation level, security contexts of processes are stored in their management data structures, represented as a part of the non-persistent /proc file system, while those of objects such as files or sockets are stored in extended attributes of the respective file system.

3.2   Policy Semantics

As already mentioned, the PDP logic in SELinux is configured by a security policy. At runtime, a binary representation of this policy resides in kernel address space; however, as for the rest of this paper, we will refer to its human-readable specification in SELinux policy language [30] as "the (security) policy".

An SELinux security policy consists of statements, which can be classified into different types of rules. Each rule basically supports one of three fundamental AC concepts supported by SELinux: type enforcement (TE), role-based access control (RBAC), and multi-level security (MLS). The most basic authorization mechanism is implemented through TE, using TE-allow-rules which basically associate a pair of types with a set of permissions. The rule

$$allow\ system\_t\ etc\_t : file\ \{read\ execute\}$$

for example will grant any process labeled with the system_t type the right to read and execute any file-class object labeled with etc_t. We call

$$\langle system\_t, etc\_t, file \rangle$$

the *key* of above TE-allow-rule. A second authorization mechanism, whose support by an SELinux kernel is still optional, is MLS. Its rules are based on defining a dominance relation over the attributes *confidentiality class* and *category*, which is then used to limit all read- or write access to particular objects.

Lastly, the RBAC mechanism is used for restricting permitted labels of a process. It was introduced to provide a policy administrator with an additional, user-centric layer of AC configuration. RBAC rules define compatible combinations of all three major attributes: The role declaration rule

`role user_r types {user_t passwd_t}`

is necessary for a process label to include both the user_r role and any of the types user_t and passwd_t. Similarly, any role can be tied to one or more users by a user declaration rule. For instance,

`user peter roles {admin_r}`

is necessary for a process label to include both user attribute peter and the admin_r role.

Both the type- and role-attribute of a security context may change during runtime (known as *transitions*). Accordingly, there are policy rules to control these changes: For role transitions, a role-allow-rule

`allow user_r admin_r`

is necessary to change the role-attribute user_r of a process to admin_r. Note that, despite of the same keyword, this rule is not related to access authorization through TE.

For type transitions on the other hand, a special set of SELinux permissions exists that must be assigned to types through the already discussed TE-allow-rules. Rules with these permissions can be used for fine-grained control over allowed, forbidden, or even mandatory type transitions; however, it should be noted that their semantics are entirely different to rules intended for object access:

- `allow init_t apache_t : process transition` is necessary for a process to change its type from init_t to apache_t.
- `allow apache_t apache_exec_t : file entrypoint` is necessary for a process to change its type to apache_t during execution of a program file of type apache_exec_t (which is therefore called an *entrypoint* type of apache_t).
- `allow init_t apache_exec_t : file execute_no_trans` is necessary for a process with type init_t to execute a program file of type apache_exec_t *without* a type transition.

Since type transitions are intended to exclusively happen on program execution, the regular access permission execute on apache_exec_t : file will also be necessary in each case. Note that both permissions execute and execute_no_trans used as indicated above are sufficient for a program execution without type transition, yet not forbidding it.

As a last rule type, SELinux policies support constraints, that may further restrict (i.e. override) any access decision based on the mechanisms discussed so far. Supported by a limited syntax for nested boolean expressions, policy constraints can be used to explicitly forbid an access based on the security contexts of both involved entities and the given logical expression.

4   Modeling Patterns

This section introduces the two basic formal approaches we will use to model the SELinux AC system: the core-based modeling pattern by Pölck, and the novel EL pattern which aims at simplifying a domain-specific model engineering for OS AC policies. Throughout the rest of this paper, we will use the following conventions for formal notation:

- $\models$ is a binary relation between variable assignments and formulas in second-order logic, where $I \models \phi$ iff I is an assignment of unbound variables to values that satisfies ϕ. In an unambiguous context, we will write $\langle x_0, \ldots, x_n \rangle \models \phi$ for any assignment of variables x_i in ϕ that satisfies ϕ.
- For any mapping f, $f[x \mapsto y]$ denotes the mapping which maps x to y and any other argument x' to $f(x')$.
- For any mapping $f : A \to B$, $f \upharpoonright_{A'}$ denotes a restriction of f to $A' \subset A$ that maps any argument $x' \in A'$ to $f(x')$, whereas $f \upharpoonright_{A'} (x)$ is undefined for any $x \in A \setminus A'$.
- For any set A, 2^A denotes the power set of A.
- $\mathbb{B} = \{\top, \bot\}$ is the set of Boolean values, where $\top$ (*true*) is interpreted as "allow", $\bot$ (*false*) as "deny".

4.1   Core-Based Modeling

The goal of the core-based model engineering paradigm is to establish a uniform formal basis for specification, analysis and implementation of diverse security models. In this work, we build our modeling pattern on top of this paradigm to leverage its generality regarding formal analysis methods and its uniform yet flexible design.

A core-based access control model is described by an extended state machine

$$\langle Q, \Sigma, \delta, \lambda, q_0, \text{EXT} \rangle \tag{1}$$

where Q is a (finite or infinite) set of protection states, Σ is a (finite or infinite) set of inputs, $\delta : Q \times \Sigma \to Q$ is the state transition function, $\lambda : Q \times \Sigma \to \mathbb{B}$ is the output function, $q_0 \in Q$ is the initial protection state, and EXT is an arbitrary tuple of static model extensions. The state machine serves as a common basis for formalizing policy semantics, called *model core*, which can be tailored to any domain-specific security policy in terms of state members and model extensions.

Based on the abstract definition above, three steps are required to describe a particular AC system through a core-based model (cf. [22, pp. 25 et seq.]):

(1.) Specializing Q, i.e. explicitly defining the automaton's state space members (dynamic model components).

(2.) Specializing EXT, i.e. defining static model components which are not part of the automaton's state.

(3.) Specializing δ and λ, i.e. describing the dynamic behavior of the AC system.

Depending on step (1), the initial protection state q_0 has to be specified according to the particular analysis goal. Depending on both steps (1) and (2), the input alphabet Σ has to be specified according to the interface of the modeled access control system.

In step (3), protection state dynamics are described by the state transition function δ through pre- and post-conditions of every possible state transition. This is done by comparing each input with two formulas in second-order logic, PRE and POST. We then define δ by formally specifying the conditions that each pair of states q and q' has to satisfy w.r.t. an input $\sigma \in \Sigma$ for a state transition from q to q' to occur:

$$\delta(q, \sigma) = \begin{cases} q', \langle q, \sigma \rangle \models \mathsf{PRE} \wedge \langle q', \sigma \rangle \models \mathsf{POST} \\ q, \text{ otherwise.} \end{cases} \tag{2}$$

Since an access control system is usually deterministic, POST fundamentally requires that q' equals q where not redefined.

Finally, to describe authorization decisions at an AC system's interface, the automaton features an output function λ. It enables the analysis of correct policy behavior and thus supports a formally verified specification. λ defines a binary access decision based on PRE:

$$\lambda(q, \sigma) \Leftrightarrow \langle q, \sigma \rangle \models \mathsf{PRE}. \tag{3}$$

4.2   Entity Labeling

This section describes entity labeling (EL), an abstract semantic modeling pattern for the formalization of contemporary operating system security policies. Based on the observations on OS policy semantics discussed in Sect. 3, the design goal of an entity labeling model is to describe access control policies which

(1.) use attributes (labels) of system entities for access decisions,

(2.) have a dynamic protection state,

(3.) are governed by additional constraints, possibly subject to a dynamically changing context.

The domain-specific semantics of such models is directly derived from these goals: (1.) To support labeling, a basic set of possible label values is needed. Since our goal is a complete description of an access control system, a set of entity identifiers is needed as well as an association of these entities with one or more label values. Then, label-based access rules can be formalized as well. (2.) To model a dynamic protection state, these formal concepts can be mapped on the model core as discussed in Sect. 4.1. On top of it, the rules for changing labels of existing entities (which are also part of a system's policy) have to be modeled. (3.) Lastly, model constraints express time-invariant side conditions for correct behavior of the AC system. Due to their static nature, such conditions are not part of the automaton's state; however, they can of course include variables referencing any system interface outside the AC system—which is of increasing importance in mobile systems (e.g. time of day, NFC device proximity, geographic location, etc.) [8, 27].

In summary, we define six abstract components of an EL model, each of which may be specialized to concrete formal components for describing a particular policy:

Label Set (LS): A set containing legal label values.

Relabeling Rule (RR): A requirement for legal label changes.

Entity Set (ES): A set containing identifiers of entities relevant to access control decisions.

Label Assignment (LA): An association between each entity and its label (or labels).

Access Rule (AR): Rule that describes, based on two or more labels, which operations entities with these labels are allowed to perform.

Model Constraints (MC): Constraints over the other components that must be satisfied in every model state.[1]

This design follows the basic idea of model component specialization, which has been adopted by the core-based modeling paradigm from object-oriented programming.

Note that the semantics of these components do neither dictate nor imply any specific formalism (other than the extended state machine required by the model core). In practice, any suitable formalism may be chosen based on the particular security property in question as well as the established methods and tools for its formal analysis. As an example, an SELinux policy analysis could target the security property of type- or role-reachability, possibly related to some security-critical labels such as system_t or admin_r (cf. Sect. 6.4). Both graph-based and inference-based formal approaches could be used for analysis, which would effectively lead to either a directed graph or a body of logical formulas that define a deductive database for expressing relabeling rules.

For specializing these abstract model components, their semantics have to be matched to policy abstractions of a real system. In order to support model dynamics, this also includes decisions about which specialized components are modifiable during policy runtime—these should be defined within the core-based model's state—and which are not. Again, EL does not impose any restrictions on this.

---

[1] To distinguish from SELinux "constraints" mentioned in Sect. 3.2, we will keep calling them *policy constraints*, while the term *model constraints* exclusively refers to the abstract EL component discussed here.

Note that EL spans a subfamily of core-based models by adding domain-specific semantic abstractions to the calculus, which are however orthogonal to those of the core paradigm. Models in this family can be further tailored to match contemporary OS security policies. In the next section, we will show an example of this based on the SELinux security policy.

5   SELinux Security Model

In this section, we will demonstrate the application of EL on the SELinux operating system. In Sect. 5.1, the concepts of the SELinux security policy as described in Sect. 3 will be formalized using the EL modeling scheme. In Sect. 5.2, a full core-based access control model will be defined from these components. At last, Sect. 5.3 proposes a specification for the SELinux-specific commands and their impact on protection state transitions and model output.

5.1   EL Components

The abstractions of system resources that are managed by the Linux operating system are completely covered by the SELinux security policy. Therefore, we could define a separate entity set for each of these abstractions (processes, files, message queues, sockets, ...). However, the policy semantics are written on a higher level of granulariy: instead of singular entities, object classes are used to distinguish between OS abstractions. Since these classes are assigned to each system entity on runtime much similar to its respective security context, we will uniformly model these information as labels. Consequently, we define the following **label sets**:

- C is the set of SELinux object classes
- U is the set of SELinux users as defined in the policy
- R is the set of all roles as defined in the policy
- T is the set of all types and domains as defined by the policy

Moreover, a single **entity set** E represents all processes and other system resources (such as files, sockets, etc.).

To allow label changes, an SELinux policy uses special permissions such as `transition` or `entrypoint`, whose semantics drastically differ from those of other permissions used in TE-allow-rules (cf. Sect. 3). To this end, we refrain from modeling these elements of the policy language as actual access rules. Instead, type- and role-transitions are modeled by two **relabeling rules** as follows:

- $\hookrightarrow_r \subseteq R^2$ is a binary relation defined as $r \hookrightarrow_r r'$ iff a role transition from r to r' is allowed according to the policy's role-`allow`-rules
- $\hookrightarrow_t \subseteq T^3$ is a ternary relation defined as $t \overset{et}{\hookrightarrow}_t t'$ iff a type transition from t to t' via an entrypoint type et is allowed according to the policy's TE-`allow`-rules

User transitions can never be allowed by an SELinux policy and are therefore not modeled. The above notation serves as a shorthand here; for model checking purposes, both relations can be interpreted as edges (weighted in case of $\hookrightarrow_t$) of directed graphs.

Consequently, the remaining portion of TE-`allow`-rules in a policy is modeled by the following **access rule**. The mapping $allow : T \times T \times C \to 2^P$ represents the combined semantics of all TE-`allow`-rules:

$$allow(t_1, t_2, c) = \{p \mid a\, \text{TE} - \texttt{allow} - \text{rule for } p \text{ with key}$$
$$\langle t_1, t_2, c \rangle \text{ exists in the policy}\}$$

where P is the set of SELinux permissions.

As already mentioned, SELinux stores label assignments as part of its protection state rather than in the policy. Nevertheless, we need to model the following **label assignments** for a meaningful analysis of the model's dynamic protection state:

- $cl : E \to C$ is the class assignment, which labels each entity with its SELinux object class.
- $con : E \to SC$ is the context assignment, which labels each entity with its SELinux security context. Here, the set of security contexts $SC = U \times R \times T$ represents all possible security contexts (labels) for entities under the given policy.

Concluding, two further restrictions on type- and role transitions have to be taken into account: those imposed by user and role declarations. For both, we use the following **model constraints**:

- $UR \subseteq U \times R$ associates users with roles they are allowed to assume according to the security policy's user declaration statements
- $RT \subseteq R \times T$ associates roles with types they are allowed to assume according to the security policy's role declaration statements
- $\tau_{UR} :: = \forall e \in E : con(e) = \langle u, r, t \rangle \Rightarrow \langle u, r \rangle \in UR$ ensures that no role is assumed a user is not authorized for
- $\tau_{RT} :: = \forall e \in E : con(e) = \langle u, r, t \rangle \Rightarrow \langle r, t \rangle \in RT$ ensures that no type is assumed a role is not authorized for

5.2   Core-Based Model

The formal EL components defined above will be put into context of a core-based model now. Therefore, it has to be decided which component is part of the automaton's state (thus dynamic) and which is part of the extension vector (thus static). In case of SELinux, these components directly reflect the semantics of a policy that configures the security server, which again is static during runtime—except for E, cl and con. This results in the classification shown in Table 1.[2]

---

[2] For a minimal example, we did not include MLS and policy constraints in this model. To do this, additional label sets and label assignments for "classification" and "category", an authorization rule for the MLS dominance relation and another set of model constraints for expressing policy constraints is needed.

Table 1. Classification of SELX model components in EL and core-based modeling patterns.

EL component	Q members	EXT members
LS	—	C, U, R, T
RR	—	$\hookrightarrow_r, \hookrightarrow_t$
ES	E	—
LA	cl, con	—
AR	—	$allow, P$
MC	—	$\tau_{UR}, \tau_{RT}, UR, RT$

According to the basic definition of the model core (1), we define an EL model for SELinux as a tuple

$$\mathsf{SELX} = \langle Q, \Sigma, \delta, \lambda, q_0, \mathrm{EXT} \rangle$$

where

$$Q = 2^E \times CL \times CON$$
$$\Sigma = \Sigma_C \times \Sigma_X$$
$$\mathrm{EXT} = \langle C, U, R, T, \hookrightarrow_r, \hookrightarrow_t, allow, P, \tau_{UR}, \tau_{RT}, UR, RT \rangle$$

Each state $q \in Q$ of the model is a triple $\langle E_q, cl_q, con_q \rangle$ with the semantics defined above, where we use the sets $E_q \subseteq E$ of all entities in state q, $CL = \{cl_q | cl_q : E_q \to C\}$ of all state-specific class assignments, and $CON = \{con_q | con_q : E_q \to SC\}$ of all state-specific context assignments. The input set Σ is defined by a set of commands Σ_C (that may be SELinux system calls, but also operations on application level for different implementations) and a set of arbitrary parameter sequences $\Sigma_X = (E \cup C \cup P \cup U \cup R \cup T)^*$. δ and λ are defined as in definitions (2) and (3). The extensions in EXT are defined as given in Sect. 5.1.

Both δ and λ are controlled by the conditions PRE and POST, which are partially defined using the following scheme. For each element of a model-specific set of commands $cmd \in \Sigma_C$ along with its parameters vector $x_{cmd} \in \Sigma_X$, we write:

▶ $cmd(x_{cmd}) :: =$
  PRE: $\phi_0 \wedge \cdots \wedge \phi_n$;
POST: $\psi_E \wedge \psi_{CL} \wedge \psi_{CON} \wedge \psi_{MC}$

where ϕ_i and ψ_j are expressions that q, q' and x_{cmd} should satisfy. While the above notation is used to define PRE(cmd) and POST(cmd) of each command, these conditions constitute the global terms:

$$\mathsf{PRE} = \bigvee_{cmd \in \Sigma_C} \left(\sigma = \langle cmd, x_{cmd} \rangle \wedge \mathsf{PRE}(cmd) \right)$$

$$\mathsf{POST} = \bigvee_{cmd \in \Sigma_C} \left(\sigma = \langle cmd, x_{cmd} \rangle \wedge \mathsf{POST}(cmd) \right)$$

While any number of arbitrary pre-condition clauses can be used in this scheme, post-conditions require a stricter pattern due to the fact that each command definition should yield exactly one possible follow-up state: Since post-conditions describe the modifications that q' should undergo with respect to q, the first three boolean clauses ensure an unambiguous definition of the entity set (ψ_E), class assignment (ψ_{CL}), and context assignment (ψ_{CON}) of q'. This requirement has to be considered for each specific EL model based on its particular state members. The last clause ψ_{MC} is mandatory, since it ensures that model constraints are satisfied in each follow-up state. In case of SELX, it is defined as

$$\psi_{MC} :: = q' \models \tau_{UR} \wedge q' \models \tau_{RT}$$

while $q_0 \models \tau_{UR} \wedge q_0 \models \tau_{RT}$ must also hold for every correct SELX model instance.

For brevity, we will omit any of these clauses when writing command definitions iff the respective state component in q and q' is equal. ψ_{MC} will be generally considered implicit due to its mandatory nature.

5.3   Specifying SELX Commands

As an input to the state machine that triggers state transitions and output (access decisions), commands are the interface between a formalized security policy and a formalized analysis goal. As in most complex security architectures, security-relevant commands in an SELinux system may be modeled on at least two different levels of abstraction (see Fig. 2): (I) at PEP level, i.e. based on the access handling logic in the SELinux security module; (II) at API level, thus covering the rich and complex semantics of all API calls.[3]

Both semantical levels may be used depending on a particular analysis scenario: If a security engineer has the goal to verify a given policy based on the behavior of the security server, she will opt for Level I (in practice, this may be relevant e.g. if an attacker model includes control flow or code manipulation in a user process' address space). On the other hand, if the focus is on OS behavior from a user space perspective—considering kernel implementation as a black box—Level II commands have to be specified, accepting the more comprehensive and detailed degree of security-relevant interaction that is capsuled in an SELinux API call. In practice, given the huge flexibility of the Linux kernel with respect to differing library wrappers, kernel features and architectures, API implementations may vary in any case—thus yielding different command specifications in the model.

Moreover, complexity of the state transition function that results from command specification is another important point in question. As previous work on

---

[3] In practice, there is another choice to make here: either modeling library wrapper functions only, or including the syscall interface of the Linux kernel. Again, the decision depends on whether our respective analysis scenario includes applications that directly use syscalls. We will not further go into detail on when to prefer which degree of detail, and assume in the following that both are modeled.

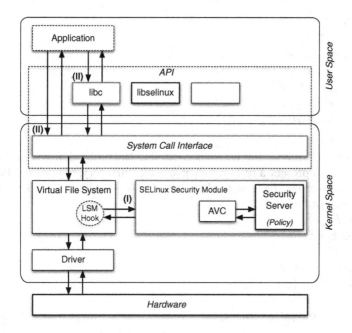

Fig. 2. Semantical levels for modeling commands.

model analysis has shown [3,14,25,32], most approaches stand or fall with a certain degree of complexity. Thus, a clean separation of Level I and Level II commands serves two goals:

I. Keep command specifications as *small* and *uniform* as possible, even across different SELinux implementations, to support dynamic model analysis.
II. Enable flexible specification of tailored, implementation-specific model dynamics that expose a high-level interface for security analyses on application level.

Since Level II commands have to partially include the semantics of Level I commands, we follow a two-step approach for modeling dynamics in **SELX**: We first specify a small number of commands on Level I (Sect. 5.3), that are general enough to be used for every SELinux implementation. We then define a pattern for specifying commands on Level II (Sect. 5.3), that leverages the previous specifications and may thus be disassembled into Level I commands.

Basic Commands. Level I commands, which we call basic commands, are *access*, *create*, *remove*, and *relabel*. They are defined as follows.

access specifies the semantics of any access decision. It does not model any state transitions and thus impacts only the automaton's output (λ). Any access by a process e to an entity e' that requires permission p is defined as

▶ **access**$(e, e', p) :: =$
  PRE: $\{e, e'\} \subseteq E_q$
    $\wedge \; cl_q(e) = \text{process}$
    $\wedge \; cl_q(e') = c'$
    $\wedge \; con_q(e) = \langle u, r, t \rangle$
    $\wedge \; con_q(e') = \langle u', r', t' \rangle$
    $\wedge \; p \in allow(t, t', c')\,;$
POST: $\top$

create specifies how a new entity is created in the protection system. In SELX, this entity may represent a resource such as a file, directory, or a socket, but also a process. Any creation of an entity e' of class c' with parent entity[4] e is defined as

▶ **create**$(e, e', c') :: =$
  PRE: $e \in E_q$
    $\wedge \; e' \in E \setminus E_q$
    $\wedge \; c' \in C$
    $\wedge \; con_q(e) = \langle u, r, t \rangle\,;$
POST: $E_{q'} = E_q \cup \{e'\}$
    $\wedge \; cl_{q'} = cl_q[e' \mapsto c']$
    $\wedge \; con_{q'} = con_q[e' \mapsto \langle u, r, t \rangle]$

Corresponding to *create*, *remove* specifies removing an entity e from the system:

▶ **remove**$(e) :: =$
  PRE: $e \in E_q\,;$
POST: $E_{q'} = E_q \setminus \{e\}$
    $\wedge \; cl_{q'} = cl_q \upharpoonright_{E_{q'}}$
    $\wedge \; con_{q'} = con_q \upharpoonright_{E_{q'}}$

In an EL model, assigning new permissions to entities is done through labels. For SELX, a last basic command is needed that describes relabeling processes with a new security context. In SELinux, such process transitions occur on the execution of an "entrypoint" program. Changing the security context of a process e to a role r' and a type t' via an entrypoint program file f is defined as

▶ **relabel**$(e, f, r', t') :: =$
  PRE: $e \in E_q$
    $\wedge \; cl_q(e) = \text{process}$
    $\wedge \; con_q(e) = \langle u, r, t \rangle$
    $\wedge \; con_q(f) = \langle uf, rf, tf \rangle$
    $\wedge \; r \hookrightarrow_r r'$
    $\wedge \; t \hookrightarrow_t tft'\,;$
POST: $con_{q'} = con_q[e \mapsto \langle u, r', t' \rangle]$

Note that, from an abstract view, this collection of basic commands expresses operations fundamental to every EL model—even though their particular PRE and

---

[4] SELinux uses the term "parent entity" to generalize the concept of label inheritance: whenever a process is created, e is its parent process; whenever a file or directory is created, it is the respective parent directory.

POST terms have been tailored to SELinux policies. This is another example for our basic assumption towards the generality of the EL model family, and how it can be leveraged to enhance the model-based engineering idea in the OS domain.

Composed Commands. Based on the specifications of basic commands, we can now give a design pattern for such commands that model a specific system's API. For this purpose, we compose such Level II commands by using the *composition operator* $\circ : \Sigma \times \Sigma \cup \{\epsilon\} \to \Sigma$, which is defined as follows:

$$\langle c_1, x_{c_1} \rangle \circ \epsilon :: = \langle c_1, x_{c_1} \rangle$$
$$\langle c_1, x_{c_1} \rangle \circ \langle c_2, x_{c_2} \rangle :: = \langle c_{12}, x_{c_1} x_{c_2} \rangle$$

where $x_{c_1} x_{c_2} \in \Sigma_X$ is a concatenated parameter sequence and $c_{12} \in \Sigma_C$ is a composed command defined as

▶ $c_{12}(x_{c_1} x_{c_2}):: =$
PRE: $\mathsf{PRE}(c_1) \wedge \mathsf{PRE}(c_2)$;
POST: $\mathsf{POST}(c_1) \wedge \mathsf{POST}(c_2)$

We can then model any interface to the SELinux security policy by the resulting *composed commands*. As an example, *fork()* and *execve()* may be composed as follows:

▷ fork(*caller*, *child*) :: =
  access(*caller*, *caller*, fork)
○ create(*caller*, *child*, process)
▷ execve(*caller*, *exec_file*, *post_r*, *post_t*) :: =
  access(*caller*, *exec_file*, execute)
○ access(*caller*, *exec_file*, getattr)
○ relabel(*caller*, *exec_file*, *post_r*, *post_t*)
where *caller* $\in E_q$, *child* $\in E_q$ are processes, *exec_file* $\in E_q$ is the program file to execute, *post_r* is the role that should be assumed by *caller* after execution, and *post_t* is the type that should be assumed by *caller* after execution.

Note that using composed commands, access control semantics of different granularity can be modeled: since basic commands cover all relevant behavior of the security policy, they can be composed on API level (outlined above), but as well on bare syscall level or even on level of a particular middleware interface.

6   Model Instantiation

The goal of this section is to demonstrate how a core-based EL model can be used in practice. Based on our SELinux model discussed in Sect. 5, we will focus on the problem of extracting model components from a real-world SELinux system. Note that this is only one of two possible model analysis use cases: the other one focuses on designing an SELinux-based AC system from scratch, including API design and the policy itself. The practical process however can be considered symmetrical to the one outlined in the following. We will conclude this section with a summary of model extraction results and ongoing work regarding model analysis.

As discussed in Sect. 4.1, there are generally three specialized definitions required to tailor a core-based model to a particular AC system: the automaton's state space (Q), model extensions (EXT), and model dynamics (δ and λ). In the following, we present our methods to perform each of these three steps in practice. We used a Linux 3.19 kernel in a Debian distribution with SELinux enabled; for most of the following steps, tools of our model engineering workbench *WorSE* [4] have been used.

6.1 State Space

A protection state in SELX consists of an entity set and label assignments. Entities in SELinux are processes, whose labels are stored in the `attr` namespace of the `/proc` file system, and files representing OS objects, whose labels are stored in extended file system attributes.

Consequently, a protection state can be extracted from an SELinux system by parsing the whole file system. In practice, we build on our previous work described in [2] and [4, p. 49]: a file system crawler, originally intended for extracting ACLs from inodes, was slightly modified to recursively scan through a file system and extract each inode number i along with its associated file type ft and the associated SELinux security context sec using `stat`. These information are then compiled to form the initial state of the model, where $i \in E_{q_0}$, $cl_{q_0}(i) = ft$, $con_{q_0}(i) = sec$.[5] For processes, the directories `/proc/`*pid*`/attr` are scanned with a similar result.

Snapshot consistency, being a major problem in this step, could be ensured by different approaches: Disabling preemption for all other user processes while running the crawler would prevent runtime changes to the protection state, but requires critical tampering with the kernel. To this end, in our approach a frozen snapshot of a virtual machine is used instead. More information about this are provided in the aforementioned papers.

6.2 Model Extensions

The static model extensions in SELX consist of authorization and relabeling rules, which are equivalent to particular rule types in the SELinux security policy, and label sets these rules are based on. Model constraints regarding user-/role-/type-compatibility correspond to another type of policy rules.

To extract model extensions, we have modified the policy compiler *sepol2hru* from [2]. It parses policy source files in plain syntax, i.e. after expanding auxiliary `m4`-macros, and produces an XML-based specification for the components of EXT. For evaluation purposes, we have applied it on a basic, non-MLS configuration of the reference policy by Tresys Technology [21].

The modified compiler is designed to isomorphically map statements in the SELinux policy language to definitions of the EXT components as follows:

---

[5] Technically, there is another, isomorphic mapping of file types to object classes that yields $cl_{q_0}(i)$ based on ft.

Elements of C, P, U, R and T are explicitly declared through the statements class, common, user, role, and type.

allow is defined by assembling all TE-allow-statements as described in Sect. 5.1. We do not take into account the neverallow rule of the policy language, since it acts similar to an assertion tested by the policy compiler, but not reflected in any way in the resulting binary policy that steers the security server.

UR and RT are defined by assembling all user- and role-statements as described in Sect. 5.1.

$\hookrightarrow_r$ is defined by assembling all role-allow-statements. For each number of parsed rules $i \geq 0$ of the form allow $\{ r_0 \ldots r_n \} \{ r'_0 \ldots r'_m \}$, $\hookrightarrow_r$ is extended iteratively as follows:

- $\hookrightarrow_r^0 = \emptyset$
- $\hookrightarrow_r^{i+1} = \hookrightarrow_r^i \cup \{r_0 \ldots r_n\} \times \{r'_0 \ldots r'_m\}$

The result is $\hookrightarrow_r = \hookrightarrow_r^n$, where n denotes the total number of parsed role transition rules.

$\hookrightarrow_t$ is defined by assembling all TE-allow-statements for one of the three permissions transition, entrypoint, and execute_no_trans (we investigated their respective semantics in Sect. 3.2). Depending on which permission p is assigned to a key $\langle t_1, t_2, c \rangle$ by the i-th parsed rule ($i \geq 0$), $\hookrightarrow_t$ is extended iteratively using the *transition graph union* operator $\sqcup$ as follows:

- $\hookrightarrow_t^0 = \emptyset$
- $p = \text{transition} \wedge c = \text{process} \Rightarrow \hookrightarrow_t^{i+1} = \hookrightarrow_t^i \sqcup \langle t_1, \epsilon, t_2 \rangle$
- $p = \text{entrypoint} \wedge c = \text{file} \Rightarrow \hookrightarrow_t^{i+1} = \hookrightarrow_t^i \sqcup \langle \epsilon, t_2, t_1 \rangle$
- $p = \text{execute\_no\_trans} \wedge c = \text{file} \Rightarrow \hookrightarrow_t^{i+1} = \hookrightarrow_t^i \sqcup \langle t_1, t_2, t_1 \rangle$

where $\sqcup : 2^{T^3} \times T^3 \rightarrow 2^{T^3}$ is defined as

$$A \sqcup \langle a_1, a_2, a_3 \rangle = \begin{cases} A \cup \{\langle a_1, a'_2, a_3 \rangle \mid \langle \epsilon, a'_2, a_3 \rangle \in A\} \cup \{\langle a_1, \epsilon, a_3 \rangle\}, & a_2 = \epsilon \\ A \cup \{\langle a'_1, a_2, a_3 \rangle \mid \langle a'_1, \epsilon, a_3 \rangle \in A\} \cup \{\langle \epsilon, a_2, a_3 \rangle\}, & a_1 = \epsilon \\ A \cup \{\langle a_1, a_2, a_3 \rangle\} & \epsilon \notin \{a_1, a_2, a_3\} \end{cases}$$

The result is $\hookrightarrow_t = \hookrightarrow_t^m$, where m denotes the total number of parsed type transition rules. Table 2 depicts a graphical representation of $\hookrightarrow_t$ as resulting from a sample set of policy rules.

6.3 Model Dynamics

The dynamic behavior of the SELinux AC system is based on the implementation of both the SELinux security module and library wrappers of API calls. While the combination of both leads to the definition of composed commands, basic commands solely depend on the PDP logic and thus stick to their fundamental semantics, independent from an actual AC interface. As already discussed in Sect. 5.3, we consider this one of their essential merits.

In contrast to the other model components, extracting the definitions of composed commands is a task that cannot be automated. It requires insight

Table 2. Examples for extracting $\hookrightarrow_t$ as a type transition graph.

Policy Rules Parsed	$\hookrightarrow_t$
`allow init_t apache_t : process transition;`	init_t $\big\downarrow \epsilon$ apache_t
`allow init_t apache_exec_t : file execute_no_trans;`	apache_exec_t $\cap$ init_t
`allow init_t apache_exec_t : file execute_no_trans;` `allow init_t apache_t : process transition;` `allow apache_t apache_exec_t : file entrypoint;`	apache_exec_t $\cap$ init_t $\big\downarrow$ apache_exec_t $\big\downarrow$ apache_t

into the implementation behind the desired interface, in our case both of the kernel and any wrapper functions. We have restricted to a subset of common syscalls in this study, such as *fork()*, *execve()*, *read()* etc. Once LSM hooks involved in a syscall have been identified, such as `security_file_permission()` in the example of *read()* in Sect. 3.1, specifying a composed command usually boils down to tracking subsequent calls of the `avc_has_perm()`-function in the SELinux security module. These give information about which parameters for the *access* basic command are needed. Moreover, protection-state-changing system calls such as *fork()* or *execve()* include more logic such as for relabeling or entity creation, and thus require the corresponding basic commands. An example of this was shown in Sect. 5.3.

Note that, when specifying composed commands, we are not interested in mere information retrieval concerning entity names and contexts, default type transitions and the like (which is why we did not consider the latter in the *execve* composed command). Instead, our goal is to model AC-related logic as precisely as possible, while any additional management logic for protection state data is deliberately excluded. This supports a clean separation of security model and analysis scenario, that may provide any of this information through the model's formal interface (i.e. via command parameters).

6.4   Results

Using the techniques described in this section, our method yields a machine-readable specification of a formal SELX model in ELM, an XML-based EL model format, which can be parsed by model analysis and verification tools such as *WorSE* (cf. [4, Sect. 4]).

To understand model complexity and scalability in real-world scenarios, we have conducted studies on different SELinux-based setups whose evaluation with respect to different analysis goals is subject to ongoing work. As a quantitative example, a real policy of one of our group's web servers included 2,847 types, 22 roles, 18 users, 4,330 relabeling rules, and 130,912 authorization rules. The corresponding protection state consists of approx. 390,000 entities, each with their associated security context labels.

Model Analysis. Based on the SELX model extracted from the mentioned web server, we are currently applying and evaluating formal analysis approaches for core-based access control models. We here focus on two fundamental classes of analysis goals: static and dynamic reachability properties. While the first class requires analysis of a finite set of possible model states (thus generally related to static model components), the second one deals with properties that can affect an unknown, potentially infinite number of states (generally related to dynamic model components).

In the first class, we are adapting a graph-based method originally intended for information flow analyses [1] to analyze type- and role-reachability with respect to certain base types and roles (based on a type- and role transition graphs such as depicted in Table 2). A possible live monitoring framework for an SELinux system using this method is subject to future work.

In the second class, we are currently working on a heuristic method for model simulation, which may lead to permission proliferation with respect to particular entities in a system (e.g. a web server process). We have developed the *DepSearch* algorithm [3] for (r)-simple-safety analysis of HRU models (cf. Tripunitara and Li [33]), which we currently modify for SELX safety analysis.

7 Conclusions

In this paper, we addressed the problem of creating a uniform yet flexible access control model for operating system security policies. We aimed at complementing the core-based model engineering approach with an abstract, label-based modeling pattern that helps in tailoring the automaton's components to an OS AC system.

After discussing essential properties of a typical policy for the SELinux OS, we have presented the design of a formal policy model for this OS based on the core-based entity labeling pattern. We have substantiated its feasibility by demonstrating a model instantiation method for a real-world system and discussing tool-based model analysis methods.

Regarding the costs of model engineering in this case study, we made two major observations: First, tailoring the core-based pattern to the SELinux AC system was streamlined considerably by using the ready-made abstract categories of the EL pattern. We thus argue that, based on these categories, other OS security policies can be formalized in a very similar manner. Second, instantiating the model for a real-world system essentially required manual effort for formalizing commands. Here, a two-stage pattern consisting of basic commands and composed commands helps to reduce modeling complexity; again, we argue for this approach to be adaptable to other policy-controlled OSs.

Ongoing work focuses on the problem of generalizing and evaluating both the modeling pattern and analysis approaches based on it with respect to a larger family of OS policies. Besides, we believe that further specialization of the analysis methods discussed in Sect. 6.4 on SELX will support SELinux administration tasks. We therefore push complementary work on policy checking and runtime monitoring tools, that can help improve correctness and quality of an SELinux security policy in practice. Future work focuses on the more formal problem of proving transformation correctness for core-based EL models. In this area, we pursue the idea of a pattern-based formal proof of model-to-policy isomorphism, that is based on fundamental automaton properties and specialized by the semantics of the EL components used for the respective OS.

References

1. Amthor, P., Kühnhauser, W.: An information flow view on privacy in social networks. ACM Trans. Internet Technol., 0: 1–0: 17 (2015). (under review)
2. Amthor, P., Kühnhauser, W.E., Pölck, A.: Model-based safety analysis of SELinux security policies. In: Samarati, P., Foresti, S., Hu, J., Livraga, G. (eds.) Proceedings of 5th International Conference on Network and System Security, pp. 208–215. IEEE (2011)
3. Amthor, P., Kühnhauser, W.E., Pölck, A.: Heuristic safety analysis of access control models. In: Proceedings of the 18th ACM Symposium on Access Control Models and Technologies, SACMAT 2013, pp. 137–148. ACM, New York (2013). http://doi.acm.org/10.1145/2462410.2462413
4. Amthor, P., Kühnhauser, W.E., Pölck, A.: WorSE: a workbench for model-based security engineering. Comput. Secur. **42**, 40–55 (2014). http://www.sciencedirect.com/science/article/pii/S0167404814000066
5. Barker, S.: The next 700 access control models or a unifying meta-model? In: Proceedings of the 14th ACM Symposium on Access Control Models and Technologies, SACMAT 2009, pp. 187–196. ACM, New York (2009)
6. Bell, D., LaPadula, L.: Secure Computer System: Unified Exposition and Multics Interpretation. Technical report AD-A023 588, MITRE, March 1976
7. Bugiel, S., Heuser, S., Sadeghi, A.R.: Flexible and fine-grained mandatory access control on android for diverse security and privacy policies. In: 22nd USENIX Security Symposium (USENIX Security 2013), USENIX, August 2013
8. Conti, M., Crispo, B., Fernandes, E., Zhauniarovich, Y.: Crêpe: a system for enforcing fine-grained context-related policies on android. IEEE Trans. Inf. Forensics Secur. **7**(5), 1426–1438 (2012)
9. Faden, G.: Multilevel filesystems in solaris trusted extensions. In: Proceedings of the 12th ACM Symposium on Access Control Models and Technologies, SACMAT 2007, pp. 121–126. ACM, New York (2007). http://doi.acm.org/10.1145/1266840.1266859
10. Ferraiolo, D., Atluri, V., Gavrila, S.: The policy machine: a novel architecture and framework for access control policy specification and enforcement. J. Syst. Archit. EUROMICRO J. **57**(4), 412–424 (2011)

11. Ferrara, A.L., Madhusudan, P., Parlato, G.: Policy analysis for self-administrated role-based access control. In: Piterman, N., Smolka, S.A. (eds.) TACAS 2013 (ETAPS 2013). LNCS, vol. 7795, pp. 432–447. Springer, Heidelberg (2013)
12. Fong, P.W., Siahaan, I.: Relationship-based access control policies and their policy languages. In: Proceedings of the 16th ACM Symposium on Access Control Models and Technologies, SACMAT 2011, pp. 51–60. ACM, New York (2011). http://doi.acm.org/10.1145/1998441.1998450
13. Grimes, R.A., Johansson, J.M.: Windows Vista Security: Securing Vista Against Malicious Attacks. John Wiley & Sons Inc, New York (2007)
14. Harrison, M.A., Ruzzo, W.L., Ullman, J.D.: Protection in operating systems. Commun. ACM **19**(8), 461–471 (1976). http://doi.acm.org/10.1145/360303.360333
15. Kafura, D., Gracanin, D.: An information flow control meta-model. In: Proceedings of the 18th ACM Symposium on Access Control Models and Technologies, SACMAT 2013, pp. 101–112. ACM, New York (2013). http://doi.acm.org/10.1145/2462410.2462414
16. Kuhn, D., Coyne, E., Weil, T.: Adding attributes to role-based access control. IEEE Comput. **43**(6), 79–81 (2010)
17. Kühnhauser, W.E., Pölck, A.: Towards access control model engineering. In: Jajodia, S., Mazumdar, C. (eds.) ICISS 2011. LNCS, vol. 7093, pp. 379–382. Springer, Heidelberg (2011). http://dx.doi.org/10.1007/978-3-642-25560-1_27
18. Loscocco, P.A., Smalley, S.D.: Integrating flexible support for security policies into the linux operating system. In: Cole, C. (ed.) 2001 USENIX Annual Technical Conference, pp. 29–42 (2001)
19. Naldurg, P., Raghavendra, K.: SEAL: a logic programming framework for specifying and verifying access control models. In: Proceedings of the 16th ACM Symposium on Access Control Models and Technologies, SACMAT 2011, pp. 83–92. ACM, New York (2011). http://doi.acm.org/10.1145/1998441.1998454
20. Park, S.M., Chung, S.M.: Privacy-preserving attribute-based access control for grid computing. Int. J. Grid Util. Comput. **5**(4), 286–296 (2014). http://dx.org/10.1504/ijguc.2014.065372
21. PeBenito, C.J., Mayer, F., MacMillan, K.: Reference policy for security enhanced linux. In: Proceedings of the 3rd Annual SELinux Symposium (2006)
22. Pölck, A.: Small TCBs of Policy-controlled Operating Systems. Universitätsverlag Ilmenau, May 2014
23. Russello, G., Conti, M., Crispo, B., Fernandes, E.: MOSES: Supporting operation modes on smartphones. In: Proceedings of the 17th ACM Symposium on Access Control Models and Technologies, SACMAT 2012, pp. 3–12. ACM, New York (2012). http://doi.acm.org/10.1145/2295136.2295140
24. Sandhu, R., Ferraiolo, D., Kuhn, R.: The NIST model for role-based access control: towards a unified standard. In: Proceedings 5th ACM Workshop on Role-Based Access Control, pp. 47–63. ACM, New York (2000). ISBN 1-58113-259-X
25. Sandhu, R.S.: The typed access matrix model. In: Proceedings of the 1992 IEEE Symposium on Security and Privacy, SP 1992, pp. 122–136. IEEE Computer Society, Washington, DC (1992). http://dl.acm.org/citation.cfm?id=882488.884182
26. Sarna-Starosta, B., Stoller, S.D.: Policy analysis for security-enhanced linux. In: Proceedings of the 2004 Workshop on Issues in the Theory of Security (WITS) (2004)
27. Shebaro, B., Oluwatimi, O., Bertino, E.: Context-based access control systems for mobile devices. IEEE Trans. Dependable Secure Comput. **PP**(99), 1 (2014)

28. Shen, H.: A semantic-aware attribute-based access control model for web services. In: Hua, A., Chang, S.-L. (eds.) ICA3PP 2009. LNCS, vol. 5574, pp. 693–703. Springer, Heidelberg (2009). http://dx.doi.org/10.1007/978-3-642-03095-6_65

29. Smalley, S., Craig, R.: Security Enhanced (SE) android: bringing flexible MAC to android. In: 20th Annual Network & Distributed System Security Symposium (NDSS), February 2013

30. Smalley, S.D.: Configuring the SELinux Policy. Technical report 02–007, NAI Labs, February 2005

31. Spencer, R., Smalley, S., Loscocco, P., Hibler, M., Andersen, D., Lepreau, J.: The flask security architecture: system support for diverse security policies. In: Proceedings 8th USENIX Security Symposium (1999)

32. Stoller, S.D., Yang, P., Gofman, M., Ramakrishnan, C.R.: Symbolic reachability analysis for parameterized administrative role based access control. Comput. Secur. **30**(2–3), 148–164 (2011)

33. Tripunitara, M.V., Li, N.: The foundational work of harrison-ruzzo-ullman revisited. IEEE Trans. Dependable Secur. Comput. **10**(1), 28–39 (2013). http://dx.org/10.1109/TDSC.2012.77

34. Watson, R., Vance, C.: Security-Enhanced BSD. Technical report, Network Associates Laboratories, Rockville, MD, USA, July 2003

35. Watson, R.N.M.: A decade of OS access-control extensibility. ACM Queue **11**(1), 20:20–20:41 (2013). http://doi.acm.org/10.1145/2428616.2430732

36. Xu, W., Shehab, M., Ahn, G.J.: Visualization-based policy analysis for SELinux: framework and user study. Int. J. Inf. Secur. **12**(3), 155–171 (2013). http://dx.org/10.1007/s10207-012-0180-7

37. Yuan, E., Tong, J.: Attributed Based Access Control (ABAC) for web services. In: Proceedings of the IEEE International Conference on Web Services, ICWS 2005, pp. 561–569. IEEE Press, Washington, DC (2005)

38. Zanin, G., Mancini, L.V.: Towards a formal model for security policies specification and validation in the SELinux system. In: Proceedings of the 9th ACM Symposium on Access Control Models and Technologies, pp. 136–145, ACM (2004)

39. Zhang, X., Li, Y., Nalla, D.: An attribute-based access matrix model. In: Proceedings 2005 ACM Symposium on Applied Computing, SAC 2005, pp. 359–363. ACM, New York (2005)

Execution Path Classification for Vulnerability Analysis and Detection

George Stergiopoulos[1], Panagiotis Katsaros[2],
and Dimitris Gritzalis[1(✉)]

[1] Information Security and Critical Infrastructure Protection (INFOSEC)
Laboratory, Department of Informatics, Athens University of Economics
and Business (AUEB), Athens, Greece
{geostergiop, dgrit}@aueb.gr
[2] Department of Informatics,
Aristotle University of Thessaloniki, Thessaloniki, Greece
panagiotis.petsanas@aueb.gr, katsaros@csd.auth.gr

Abstract. Various commercial and open-source tools exist, developed both by the industry and academic groups, which are able to detect various types of security bugs in applications' source code. However, most of these tools are prone to non-negligible rates of false positives and false negatives, since they are designed to detect a priori specified types of bugs. Also, their analysis scalability to large programs is often an issue. To address these problems, we present a new source code analysis technique based on execution path classification. We develop a prototype tool to test our method's ability to detect different types of information-flow dependent bugs. Our approach is based on classifying the Risk of likely exploits inside source code execution paths using two measuring functions: Severity and Vulnerability. For an Application Under Test (AUT), we analyze every single pair of input vector and program sink in an execution path, which we call an Information Block (IB). Severity quantifies the danger level of an IB using static analysis and a variation of the Information Gain algorithm. On the other hand, an IB's Vulnerability rank quantifies how certain the tool is that an exploit exists on a given execution path. The Vulnerability function is based on tainted object propagation. The Risk of each IB is the combination of its computed Severity and Vulnerability measurements through an aggregation operation over two fuzzy sets using a Fuzzy Logic system. An IB is charac-terized of a high risk, when both its Severity and Vulnerability rankings have been found to be above the low zone. In this case, our prototype tool called Entroine reports a detected code exploit. The tool was tested on 45 Java vul-nerable programs from NIST's Juliet Test Suite, which implement three different types of exploits. All existing code exploits were detected without any false positive.

Keywords: Code exploits · Software vulnerabilities · Source code classifica-tion · Fuzzy logic · Tainted object propagation

© Springer International Publishing Switzerland 2016
M.S. Obaidat and P. Lorenz (Eds.): ICETE 2015, CCIS 585, pp. 293–317, 2016.
DOI: 10.1007/978-3-319-30222-5_14

1   Introduction

Automated detection of potential vulnerabilities in source code is a well-known research area. Multiple techniques have been proposed, some of which have been proven effective in detecting a priori known flaws (e.g. Time Of Check and Time Of Use errors, known as TOCTOU). Yet, the National Institute of Software and Technology (NIST) published a report [1], which indicates that most tools still generate non-negligible numbers of false negatives and false positives, whereas their analysis scalability to very big programs is questionable. Nevertheless, many tools shine on specific types of vulnerabilities, but it is clear that there is no overall "best" tool with a high detection rate in multiple exploit categories [2, 28].

To cope with these issues, we propose here a different approach for detecting vulnerabilities in source code, which is based on the classification and the criticality assessment of an application's execution paths, with each path representing a sequence of program points from one location to another location of the program's control flow graph. We implemented our method in a prototype tool for the analysis of Java code to test our analysis technique. The tool, called Entroine analyses the code of an Application Under Test (AUT) for possible flaws by classifying the execution paths based on their Entropy Loss, thus producing data, which are processed by a mathematical fuzzy logic system. More precisely, Entroine processes structures called information blocks (IB), with each of them containing information for execution paths, variables and program instructions on the paths. Only a subset of all possible execution paths is examined: the paths from locations associated with input vectors to locations corresponding to information flow sinks. IB are classified in two different groups of sets as follows:

- the *Severity* sets that quantify the danger level for the execution paths (the impact that an exploit would have, if it would be manifested in the path),
- the *Vulnerability* sets that quantify detected vulnerabilities based on a variable usage analysis (tainted object propagation and validation of sanitization checks, in which the data context of variables is checked).

The method consists of the following three components: (a) A static analysis, based on the BCEL library [31, 32], which creates the control flow graph that is parsed to get information about variable usages. It is thus possible to detect input data vectors, control-flow locations and instructions that enforce context checks on variable data. Entroine then maps the execution paths for the AUT variables and, more specifically, only those locations, where the program execution can follow different paths (execution flow branching points). (b) A classification approach that combines output from (a) to create IB. Each IB is classified using statistical Entropy Loss and the two fuzzy membership sets (Severity and Vulnerability). (c) A Fuzzy Logic system for quantifying the overall Risk for each IB, based on linguistic variables, and Severity and Vulnerability classification ratings.

The main contributions of this paper are summarized as follows:

1. We introduce a program analysis technique for our classification system. Based on the control flow graph and our Fuzzy Logic ranking system only a limited number of execution paths and statements have to be analyzed.

2. We propose a Risk classification of program locations using two membership functions, one for the identified Severity (Entropy Loss) and another one for the Vulnerability level.

3. We present our prototype tool. By using the Vulnerability and Severity classifications, we realized that the number of false positives is reduced. In addition, Entroine warned for elevated danger levels in program locations where a false negative could have been occurred.

4. We provide test results from applying Entroine to the Juliet Test Suite [33] that has been proposed by NIST to study the effectiveness of code analysis tools [28]. Entroine detected all common weaknesses used upon, without having reported any false positive.

In Sect. 2, we report recent results in related research. In Sect. 3, we expose the theoretical underpinnings of our method. Section 4 provides technical details for the implementation of our method in Entroine and Sect. 5 presents our experiments and reports metrics and detection coverage in all tests.

2 Related Work

Previously proposed analysis techniques based on tainted object propagation such as the one in [3] mostly focus on how to formulate various classes of security vulnerabilities as instances of the general taint analysis problem. These approaches do not explicitly model the program's control flow and it is therefore possible to miss-flag sanitized input, thus resulting in false positives. Furthermore, there is no easy general approach to avoid the possibility of false negatives. This type of analysis does not suffer a potential state space explosion, but its scalability is directly connected to the analysis sensitivity characteristics (path and context sensitivity) and there is an inherent trade-off between the analysis scalability and the resulting precision/recall.

Regarding well-known static analysis tools, it is mentioning FindBugs [9], which is used to detect more than 300 code defects that are usually classified in diverse categories, including those analyzed by tainted object propagation. The principle of most of the FindBug's bug detectors is to identifying low-hanging fruits, i.e. to cheaply detect likely defects or program points where the programmer's attention should be focused [4].

Other tools, such as [5–7, 36] are well-known for their capability to detect numerous bugs, but related research in [8] has shown that their main focus is centered around specific bug types like null pointer exceptions, explicit import-export and not those, for which a taint analysis is required (XSS, OS executions etc.). In [8], a relatively low detection rate is reported for many of the above mentioned tools for some variants of important bug types (null pointer exception, user injections and non-black final instance). To the best of our knowledge, none of the above mentioned tools implements a mechanism to cope with the possibility of false negatives.

Pixy [10], a prototype implementing a flow-sensitive, inter-procedural and context-sensitive dataflow, alias and literal analysis, is a new tool that further develops pre-existing analyses. It mainly aims to detect cross-site scripting vulnerabilities in PHP scripts, but a false positive rate is at a-round 50 % (i.e., one false positive for each detected vulnerability) has been reported and no mechanism has been implemented to mitigate the problem.

Other researchers try to detect code flaws using program slicing. Introduced in [11] is a program slicing technique and applied it to debugging. The main drawback is that the slice set often contains too many program entities, which in some cases can correspond to the whole program.

Presented in [13], this technique that uses a threshold to prune the computed backward slice. A limitation is that this technique does not account for the strength of the dependences between program entities, nor the likelihood for each program entity to be a failure cause. Another limitation is that the slice sets can be sometimes very large. Finally, no information is provided by any of these techniques for how to start searching for a code flaw.

Researchers in [15], focus exclusively on specific flaws found in web applications as in [16], where various analysis techniques are combined to identify multi-module vulnerabilities.

None of these techniques attempts to profile the danger level in the program's behavior. In [12, 34, 35], we have presented the APP_LogGIC tool for source case analysis, but we focused on logical errors instead of program exploits and our ranking method was not based on a statistical classification of the source code.

```
public void bad() throws Throwable {
        String data = "", test = "";
        /* FLAW: data from .properties */
        data = properties.getProperty("data");
        if(System.getProperty("os.name").indexOf("win") >= 0) {
                String osCommand = "c:\\WINDOWS\\SYSTEM32\\cmd.exe
        /c dir ";
        }
        /*POTENTIAL FLAW: command injection */
        Process proc = Runtime.getRuntime().exec(osCommand +
data);
}
```

Fig. 1. NIST's command injection example.

3   Methodology

Let us consider the example shown in Fig. 1 from the Juliet Test Suite, a collection of programs for testing source code analyzers [33].

Example 1. Variable data in Fig. 1 is assigned data originated from the source properties. GetProperty. Then, it is used in the sink instruction getRuntime().exec without being checked previously or having sanitized the variable's contents, as it should have happened. Our method will detect and analyze the execution path starting from the invocation of getProperty("data") and ending with the exec() call, thus revealing the exploit present in the source code.

Definition 1. Given the set T of all transitions in the control flow graph of an AUT, an information block IB is a structure, containing a set of instructions I and a set of transitions Ti ⊆ T enabled at the corresponding program points, along with information about data assignments on variables used in sets I and Ti.

Our method outputs a Risk value (ranging from one to five) that denotes the overall danger level of an IB. The Risk is quantified by means of a source code classification system using Fuzzy Logic to flag exploits [14]. This classification technique aims to confront two important problems: the large data sets of the AUT analysis and the possible false positives and false negatives when trying to detect specific vulnerabilities. Regarding the first mentioned problem, the Entroine tool can help auditors to focus only to those instructions and paths that appear having a relatively high rating in its classification system. The second mentioned problem can be alleviated through Entroine's ratings that implement general criteria, which take into account the possibility of an exploit in execution paths (Vulnerability) and a path's danger level (Severity). Two measuring functions, namely Severity and Vulnerability create fuzzy sets reflecting gradually varying danger levels. Each IB gets a membership degree in these sets, which represents its danger level and it is thus classified within a broad taxonomy of exploits which is based on a wide variety of publications [26, 27, 37]. Membership sets act as code filters for the IB.

Example 2. Figure 2 below depicts the Entroine's output for the program of Fig. 1. Our tool detected data entry points (input vectors) and the relevant execution path, stored in the "Lines Executed" field (line numbers correspond to lines inside the source code Class file, depicting the execution path's instructions). Then, the IB has been classified in relevant Severity and Vulnerability ranks by analyzing checks and relations between variables. Figure 2's *Input Ranking* depicts the rank assigned based on the input vector classification, in this case, the readLine() instruction. Similar, Sink ranking depicts the rank assigned in the sink instruction where the exploit manifests: a rank 5 OS Injection exec() instruction.

```
Input Ranking:            4
Sink Ranking:             5
Starting at line:         54
Source:                   getProperty
Input into variable:      data bad, test bad
Sink method:              exec
Execution arguments:      osCommand, data,
Severity Rank#:           5
Lines executed:           106 83 82 81 80 79 78 77 76 75 73
                          62 60 57 56 54
Dangerous variables:      proc , test , data,
Connections between the dangerous variables:proc <-- data
Vulnerability Rank#:      4
```

Fig. 2. Information block example (from Entroine).

In the following section, we describe the way that the Severity and Vulnerability classification ranks are computed.

3.1 Source Code Profiling for Exploit Detection

Entroine classifies source code using two different classification mechanisms: Severity and Vulnerability. Entroine aggregates results from both to produce a distinct, overall Risk value for dangerous code points.

Severity. For an information block IB, `Severity(IB)` measures the membership degree of its path π in a Severity fuzzy set. `Severity(IB)` reflects the relative *impact* on an IB's execution path π, if an exploit were to manifest on π. According to [22] by the National Institute of Software and Technology (NIST), the impact of an exploit on a program's execution can be captured by syntactical characteristics that determine the program's execution flow, i.e. the input vectors and *branch conditions* (e.g. conditional statements). Variables used in each transition of the execution path are weighted based on how they affect the control flow. Thus, variables that directly affect the control flow or are known to manifest exploits (e.g. they input data, used in branch conditions or affect the system) are considered dangerous.

Definition 2. Given the information block IB, with a set of variables and their execution paths, we define Severity as

$$\texttt{Severity(IB)} = v \in [0,5]$$

measuring the severity of IB on a Likert-type scale from 1 to 5.

Likert scales are a convenient way to quantify facts [17] that in our case refer to a program's control flow. If an exploit were to manifest on an execution path within an IB, the scale-range captures the intensity of its impact in the AUT's execution flow. Statistical Entropy Loss classifies execution paths and their information blocks in one of five Severity categories, one 1–5. Categories are then grouped into Fuzzy Logic sets using labels: *high* Severity (4–5), *medium* (3) or *low* (1 or 2).

Entropy Loss as a Statistical Function for Severity Measurement. Evaluation of the membership degree of each execution path in the Severity set can be based on a well-defined statistical measure. To assign Severity ranks, continuous weights are estimated using Prior Entropy and Entropy Loss. Finally, a fuzzy relational classifier uses these estimations to establish correlations between Severity ranks and execution paths.

Expected Entropy Loss, which is also called *Information Gain*, is a statistical measure [19] that has been utilized as a feature selection technique for information retrieval [20]. Feature selection increases both effectiveness and efficiency, by removing non-relevant information based on corpus statistics [30].

Our method is based on selected *features*, i.e. source code instructions, which are tied to specific types of vulnerabilities (Sect. 4.2). For example, the `exec()` instruction is known to be tied to OS injection vulnerabilities. Thus, Entroine uses `exec()` as a feature to classify vulnerable IB as a detected type of OS Injection.

Expected entropy loss is computed for each information block and ranks each IB based on methods/features detected in its execution path. Each Severity rank corresponds to a specific taxonomy subset comprised of source code methods. A total of five (5) ranks/method sets depicting five different levels of danger exist (0 being the lowest to 4 being the highest). For example, subset 0 is comprised of instructions that are only detected in very low risk vulnerabilities, e.g. it contains the java.awt.Robot.key Release() method. This classification method considers features to be more important if they are effective discriminators of a specific danger level/rank (a.k.a. method subset) [18].

This technique was also used for source code classification in [18, 21]. Here, we use the same technique, in order to classify execution paths and corresponding IB into danger levels.

In the following paragraphs, we provide a brief description of the theory [19]. Let C be the event that indicates whether an execution path must be considered dangerous, depending on the path's transitions, and let f be the event that the path does indeed contain a specific feature f (e.g. the exec() instruction). Let $\bar{C}$ and $\bar{f}$ be their negations and $Pr()$ their probability (computed as in Sect. 4.3). The prior entropy is the probability distribution that expresses how certain we are that an execution path belongs to a specific category, before feature f is taken into account:

$$e = -Pr(C)lgPr(C) - Pr(\bar{C})lgPr(\bar{C})$$

where lg is the binary logarithm (logarithm to the base 2). The posterior entropy, when feature f has been detected in the path is

$$e_f = -Pr(C \mid f)lg\ Pr(C \mid f) - Pr(\bar{C}|f)lg\ Pr(\bar{C}|f)$$

whereas the posterior entropy, when the feature is absent is

$$e_{\bar{f}} = -Pr(C \mid \bar{f})lg\ Pr(C \mid \bar{f}) - Pr(\bar{C}|\bar{f})lg\ Pr(\bar{C}|\bar{f})$$

Thus the expected overall posterior entropy is given by

$$e_f\ Pr(f) + e_{\bar{f}}Pr(\bar{f})$$

and the expected entropy loss for a given feature f is

$$e - e_f\ Pr(f) - e_{\bar{f}}Pr(\bar{f})$$

The expected entropy loss is non-negative and higher scores indicate more discriminatory features.

Example 3. Let us compute the expected Entropy Loss used for the Severity classification of the program in Example 1. Our Severity function will classify the path's features (input vectors, sinks, branch statements like exec() and getProperty()) according to a taxonomy of features made up of dangerous coding methods (Sect. 4.2). Five probabilities Pr(C) were computed, one for each of the five Severity ranks and the IB was classified at the Severity rank 4 (maximum danger level-set of the five).

The IB's prior entropy e was then calculated for the same ranks. Prior entropy represents the current classification certainty of Entroine, i.e. the level of confidence that it has assigned the correct Severity rank. Finally, the entropy loss (information gain) was calculated for each one of the detected input vectors and sinks in the execution path, for the variable data. We are interested in the highest and the lowest observed Entropy Loss (Information Gain) values:

1. The higher value of information gain is observed, the more the uncertainty for a dangerous security characteristic is lowered and the classification to a specific Rank category is therefore more robust. Also, a relatively high information gain coupled with a high probability $Pr(C|f)$ for sanitization provides information about features within paths that lower the Vulnerability level.
2. The lowest value of information gain (highest entropy) provides information on the most widespread and distributed security methods by showing the level of danger diffused in the AUT's execution paths.

Figure 3 below depicts the Entropy Loss output for the example path. The conclusion drawn from this output is the following:

- The highest entropy loss (information gain) is detected in method `getProperty`. This shows that `getProperty` is a defining characteristic for this Rank 5 exploit.
- The lowest entropy loss in method `exec()` has highest probability of appearance, $Pr(C) = 1$, which basically means that `exec()` is being used in all execution paths analyzed as potentially dangerous. This elevates the Severity level of the detected exploit significantly, because `exec()` is prone to OS injection.

```
Prior path Entropy =                             0.8112781
Source code Severity rank:          5
Calculation exec. time:             2 seconds
Entropy Loss for getInputStream - Rank 5: 0.31127812
Entropy Loss for getProperty - Rank 5:     0.81127812
Entropy Loss for exec in Rank 5:    0.0
```

Fig. 3. OS injection rank 5 classification – Entropy calculation example.

Vulnerability. Vulnerability sets define categories based on the type of detection and the method's propagation rules and each category reveals the extent to which variable values are sanitized by conditional checks [22]. As a measuring function, Vulnerability assigns IB into vulnerability sets thus quantifying how certain the tool is about an exploit manifesting in a specific variable usage.

Definition 3. Given the information block IB, with a set of variables and their execution paths, we define Severity as

$$Vulnerability(IB) = v \in [0,5]$$

Ratings here also use a Likert scale [17] from 1 to 5. Similarly to the `Severity` (`IB`) function, our fuzzy logic system classifies IB in similar categories: "high" vulnerability, "medium" or "low".

Vulnerability Function - Object Propagation and Control Flow Heuristics. Our control flow based heuristics for assigning Vulnerability ratings to information blocks are complemented by a *tainted object propagation* analysis. Tainted object propagation can reveal various types of attacks that are possible due to user input that has not been (properly) validated [3]. Variables holding input data (*sources*) are considered tainted. If a tainted object (or any other object derived from it) is passed as a parameter to an exploitable instruction (a *sink*) like the instructions executing OS commands we have a vulnerability case [3].

Variables and checks enforced upon them are analyzed for the following correctness criterion: All input data should be sanitized before their use [22]. Appropriate checks show: (i) whether a tainted variable is used in sinks without having previously checked its values, (ii) if data from a tainted variable is passed along and (iii) if there are instances of the input that have never been sanitized in any way.

Entroine checks tainted variable usage by analyzing its corresponding execution paths and conditions enforced on them (if any) for data propagation. The tool uses explicit taint object propagation rules for the most common Java methods, such as `System.exec()`. These rules are outlined in Sect. 4.3, where the technical implementation details are discussed.

Example 4. Again, as an example, we will show how our method analyzes the program of Fig. 1 to decide in which Vulnerability rank to classify the IB of Example 2. Our tainted object analysis detects that (i) an input vector assigns data to variable data and, then, (ii) data is never checked by a conditional statement like an `if-statement` or any other instruction known to sanitize variable data. Then (iii) variable data is used in a sink (`exec()`) without further sanitization of its contents. Thus, our method will not detect any transition that lowers the Vulnerability level of the execution path in Fig. 1 and will therefore assign a high rating (4) on the Vulnerability scale for the IB containing this variable-execution path pair.

Using Severity and Vulnerability thresholds, Entroine can focus only on a subset of paths for exploit detection, thus limiting the number of paths needed to traverse during its tainted propagation analysis. The execution path set is pruned twice: (i) once based on Severity measurements and the type of instruction used ("safe" paths are discarded), and (ii) again when possible exploits have been detected by using a Vulnerability rank as threshold.

3.2 Risk

According to OWASP, the standard risk formulation is an operation over the likelihood and the impact of a finding [23]:

$$\text{Risk} = \text{Likelihood} \times \text{Impact}$$

We adopt this notion of risk into our framework for exploit detection. In our approach, for each IB an estimate of the associated risk can be computed by combining Severity(IB) and Vulnerability (IB) into a single value called Risk. We opt for an aggregation function that allows taking into account membership degrees in a Fuzzy Logic system [14]:

Definition 4. Given an AUT and an information block IB with specific input vectors, corresponding variables and their execution paths $\pi \in P$, function Risk (IB) is the aggregation

$$\text{Risk}(\text{IB}) = \text{aggreg}(\text{Severity}(\text{IB}), \text{Vulnerability}(\text{IB}))$$

with a fuzzy set valuation

$$\text{Risk}(\text{IB}) = \{\text{Severity}(\text{IB})\} \cap \{\text{Vulnerability}(\text{IB})\}$$

Aggregation operations on fuzzy sets are operations by which several fuzzy sets are combined to produce a single fuzzy set. Entroine applies defuzzification [24] on the resulting set, using the Center of Gravity technique. *Defuzzification* is the computation of a single value from two given fuzzy sets and their corresponding membership degrees, i.e. the involvedness of each fuzzy set presented in Likert values.

Risk ratings have the following interpretation: for two information blocks IB1 and IB2, if Risk(IB1) > Risk(IB2), then IB1 *is more dangerous than* IB2, in terms of how respective paths $\pi1$ and $\pi2$ affect the execution of the AUT and if the variable analysis detects possible exploits. In the next section, we provide technical details for the techniques used to implement the discussed analysis.

The risk of each information block is plotted separately, producing a numerical and a fuzzy result. It is calculated by the Center of Gravity technique [24] via its Severity and Criticality assigned values. Aggregating both membership sets, produces a new membership set and, by taking the "center" (sort of an "average"), Entroine produces a discrete, numerical output.

4   Design and Implementation

In this section, the technical details on how Entroine was developed will be presented. The tools architecture, workflow along with technical details on how Severity and Vulnerability are calculated.

4.1   Entroine's Architecture and Workflow

Entroine consists of three main components: a static source code analyzer (depicted with the colors orange and green in Fig. 4 below), an Information Block constructor and, finally, the fuzzy logic system to compute the Risk (grey and yellow colors).

- *Static Analysis:* Static code analysis uses the Java compiler to create Abstract Syntax Trees for the AUT. It provides information concerning every single method invocation, branch statements and variable assignments or declarations found in the AUT. Compiler methods (`visitIf()`, `visitMethodInvocation()`, etc.) were overridden, in order to analyze branch conditions and sanitization checks of variables. The following sample output shows the AST meta-data gathered for variable "sig_3" in a class named "Sub-system114":

```
DECLARE::12::double::sig_3::0::Main22::
Subsystem114.java
```

The ByteCode Engineering Library (Apache BCEL) [32] is used to build the AUT's control flow graph and to extract the program's execution paths. BCEL is a library that analyzes, creates, and manipulates class files.

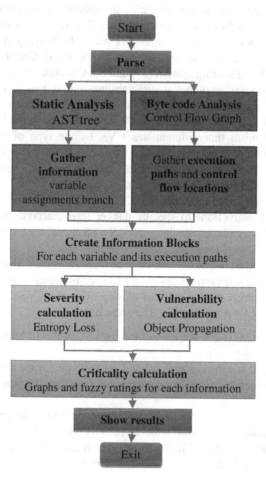

Fig. 4. Entroine's processing flowchart (Color figure online).

- *Information Block Creator:* This component combines information obtained from the static analysis to create IB that contain pairs of execution path - input vector. Information blocks are then assigned Severity and Vulnerability ranks.
- *Fuzzy Logic System:* The Fuzzy Logic system is implemented using the jFuzzy-Logic library [14]. We use it to aggregate Severity and Vulnerability sets to quantify the danger level for each IB. This aggregation classifies each IB to an overall Risk rank.

4.2   Taxonomy of Dangerous Instructions

Following Oracle's JAVA API and documentation [25–27], three categories of Java instructions were used to classify execution paths in IB. (i) *Control Flow instructions*, (ii) *Input Vector instructions* and (iii) potentially exploitable methods (sinks). 159 Java methods were reviewed and gathered from formal publications and organizations that specifically classify exploits and, consequently, any instructions used in them [26, 27, 37].

The taxonomy's methods were grouped into five *categories* of Severity corresponding to the taxonomy's Severity ranks. We based the Severity classification ranks for ranking instructions on the well-known international Common Vulnerability Scoring System (CVSS) scoring system [37] and the Common Weakness Enumeration system [38]. CVSS classifies potential vulnerabilities into danger levels and is used by NIST's National Vulnerability Database (NVD) to manage an entire database of vulnerabilities found in deployed software. The NVD is also using the CWE system as a classification mechanism that differentiates CVE by the type of vulnerability they represent. The Common Weakness Scoring System (CWSS) [40] provides a mechanism for prioritizing software weaknesses. It applies scores into vulnerabilities based on a mathematical formula of characteristics.

Entroine uses all three of these systems, NVD-CVSS, CWE and CWSS ranking to assign source code instructions to specific danger levels, according the type of vulnerability, in which they participate, its general SWSS score and corresponding ranking value in similar CVSS vulnerabilities that we found.

The method followed to classify source code methods is the following: Each source code instruction in the taxonomy is assigned to a specific feature set which represents a danger level. The correct feature set was chosen using the CVSS scores of vulnerabilities from the NVD repository [42]. The steps are:

1. For each instruction, check the lowest and highest ratings of known vulnerabilities that use it.
2. Use the CVSS 3.0 scoring calculator 2 and calculate the lowest and highest possible vulnerability scores for each instruction, based on the characteristics of known vulnerabilities.
3. Rank each instruction in a feature set corresponding to a danger level using the output calculation. Instructions with score 7 or above were grouped in Set 5. Instructions with score 6 to 7 in Set 4, those with score 5 to 6 in Set 3, those with score 4 to 5 in Set 2, those with score 1 to 4 in Set 1.

Example: The `Runtime.exec()` instruction is widely-known to be used in many OS command injection exploits. CWE and NIST provide a multitude of critical vulnerabilities based in this instruction (e.g. the CWE-78 category). Also the CVSS 3.0 scoring system [41] ranked the use of `exec()` to execute code with application level privileges very high in its scale (9.3 out of 10). Thus, Entroine's taxonomy classifies the `exec()` instruction into its very high (5) danger level category. Similar notion has been followed in organizing the rest of Entroine's taxonomy instructions into Severity levels. This way, we limit our personal intuition, in an effort to support that Entroine's ranking system is justified.

Due to space limitations, only two small Java Class group examples are given. The complete classification system can be found in the provided link at the end of the article. The symbol § corresponds to chapters in Java documentation [26].

Control Flow Statements. According to an NSA's report [28], Boolean expressions determine the control flow. Such expressions are found in the following statements:

1. if-statements
   (§14.9)
2. switch-statements
   (§14.11)
3. while-statements
   (§14.12)
4. do-statements
   (§14.13)
5. for-statements
   (§14.14)

Input Vector Methods. Java has numerous methods and classes that accept data from users, streams or file [27]. Most of them concern byte, character and stream input/output. Entroine takes into account 69 different ways of entering data into an AUT. A simple example is given in Table 1.

Table 1. Example group: Input vector methods taxonomy.

java.io.BufferedReader	java.io.BufferedInputStream
java.io.ByteArrayInputStream	java.io.DataInputStream
java.lang.System	javax.servlet.http.
java.io.ObjectInputStream	java.io.StringReader

Based on [27] and common programming experience, monitoring specific Java objects seems to be an adequate, albeit not entirely thorough, way of tracing user data inside Java applications.

Exploitable Methods (Sinks). Based on CWE, NVD [37] and common knowledge, we know that specific methods are used in exploits. We consider them as potential sinks and thus, Entroine examines them carefully. As mentioned earlier, Entroine's taxonomy of exploitable methods was based on the exploit classification and relevant source code by NIST's NVD in their CWE taxonomy [37]. Entroine takes into account 90 methods known to be exploitable as sinks, according to NIST CWEs. It then classifies them according to CWE's rank and its corresponding CVSS-CWE and CWSS rank. An example is given in Table 2.

Table 2. Example group - Sink methods taxonomy.

java.lang.Runtime	java.net.URLClassLoader
java.lang.System	java.sql.Statement
java.io. File	java.net.Socket

4.3 Classification and Ranking System

As explained in Sect. 3, the Fuzzy Logic system from [14] is used in Entroine, which provides a means to rank possible logical errors. In order to aid the end-user, Severity and Vulnerability values are grouped into three sets (Low, Medium, High), with an approximate width of each group of $5/3 = 1,66 \sim 1,5$ (final ranges: Low in $[0...2]$, Medium in $(2...3,5]$ and High in $(3,5...5]$).

Calculating Severity (Entropy Loss and Feature Selection). Entroine's classification system for execution paths uses Entropy Loss (aka Information Gain) to capture the danger level in AUT's execution paths. It takes into consideration specific method execution appearances against the total number of instructions in a given set of transitions and applies Severity ranks to execution paths and the corresponding information blocks.

Entroine detects, evaluates and classifies instructions found in execution paths. Severity ratings are applied by classifying each information block into and corresponding path into one of five Severity levels, according to the Prior Entropy and Entropy Loss of features in every execution path.

Since each information block refers to a specific execution path and its variables, the necessary metrics are calculated based on a ratio between execution paths considered dangerous (e.g. command execution instructions like exec()) and the total number of paths detected for each application. Similarly to [18], probabilities for the expected entropy loss of each feature are calculated as follows:

$$Pr(C) = \frac{numberOfPathsInCategory}{totalNumberOf\text{ExecutionPaths}}$$

$$Pr(\bar{C}) = 1 - Pr(C)$$

$$\Pr(f) = \frac{numberOfPathsWithFeatureF}{totalNumberOfPaths}$$

$$\Pr(\bar{f}) = 1 - \Pr(f)$$

$$\Pr(C|f) == \frac{numberOfPathsForSpecificRankWithFeatureF}{totalNumberOfPathsWithFeatureF}$$

$$\Pr(\bar{C}|f) = 1 - \Pr(C|f)$$

$$\Pr(C|\bar{f}) == \frac{numberOfPathsForSpecificRankWithoutFeatureF}{totalNumberOfPathsWithoutFeatureF}$$

$$\Pr(\bar{C}|\bar{f}) = 1 - \Pr(C|\bar{f})$$

numberOfPathsWithFeatureF denotes to the sum of execution paths inside the application under test that contain a specific method in them regardless of category that the path belongs to (low, medium or high), while *numberOfPathsForSpecificRankWithFeatureF* represents the sum of execution paths which belong to a specific danger level category (e.g. Severity rank 3 set), based on a specific feature F.

Entropy Loss is computed separately for each source code feature characterized by a specific token. Only tokens that are part of a variable's execution paths are analyzed. For example, in the expression "data = properties.getProperty ("data");" the tokens will be: "data", "getProperty" and "properties".

The taxonomy of Java instructions defines various features used in place of *f* in the above equations. An example of Entroine's features classification is given in Table 3. For a complete list, the reader is referred to the link at the end of the article.

Table 3. Severity classification examples.

Rank	Example of classified methods	Category
Low	javax.servlet.http.Cookie (new Cookie)	0
Low	java.lang.reflection.Field (new Field)	1
Medium	java.io.PipedInputStream (new PipedInputStream)	2
High	java.io.FileInputStream (new FileInputStream)	3
High	java.sql.ResultSet:: getString()	4

Severity is evaluated relative to the Technical Impact 5-point scale, as defined by NIST's Common Weakness Scoring System (CWSS). For better granularity, Entroine's scale is a 10-point scale, from 0 to 4 corresponding to the four Severity method subsets that depict different danger levels. The Fuzzy membership sets created by combining the CWSS scale points with the 5-point Severity rank scale are presented in Fig. 5.

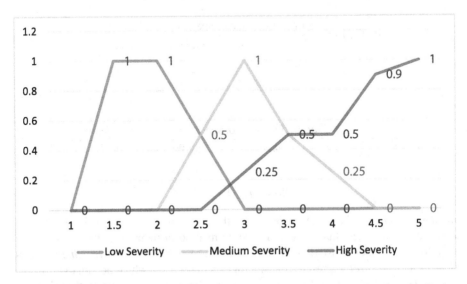

Fig. 5. Severity membership sets (Low, Medium, High rank values) (Color figure online).

The participation of values into membership sets for each part of the [1–5] scale are depicted in Table 4.

Calculating Vulnerability (Control Flow Analysis and Tainted Object Propagation).
To calculate Vulnerability, Entroine runs a Tainted Propagation algorithm that classifies the likelihood of an exploit happening in an execution path. Entroine uses BCEL [31, 32] to traverse the program's Control Flow Graph bottom-to-top, in order to gather variable execution paths.

Entroine's propagation rules are the following:

- The highest entropy loss (information gain) is detected Variables assigned data from expressions (e.g. +, −, method return) whose output depends on tainted data, are tainted.
- Literals (e.g. hardcoded strings, true declarations) are never tainted.
- If an object's variable gets tainted, only data referred by that variable are considered tainted, not all object properties.
- Methods that accept tainted variables as parameters are considered tainted.
- The return value of a tainted function is always tainted, even for functions with implicit return statements (e.g. constructors).

Table 5 depicts the check rules for exploit detection.

Table 4. Participation percentages of severity values in Fuzzy sets.

0-4 ranks (values)	% participation - Low set	% participation - Medium set	% participation - High set
1	0	0	0
1.5	1	0	0
2	1	0	0
2.5	0.5	0.5	0
3	0	1	0.25
3.5	0	0.5	0.5
4	0	0.25	0.5
4.5	0	0	0.9
5	0	0	1

Table 5. Vulnerability check rules and their categories.

Rank	Example of classified methods	Category
Low	No improper checks of variables	1
Low	Sinks NOT linked to input vectors	2
Medium	Propagation to methods	3
High	Improper checks on variables with input data – Variables used in sinks	4
High	No checks - variables used in sinks	5

Pre-calculated membership sets exist in the Fuzzy logic system that classify each IB Vulnerability value into a "Safe" or "Vulnerable" state. These two subsets are defined with fuzzy boundaries; i.e. the distinction between a "safe" flaw and a flaw that can lead to exploits is not clear. For this reason, empirical observations and examples from the National Vulnerability Database (NVD) [42] led us to believe that vulnerability scores vary due to context differentiations. To this end, we applied an empirical distribution of Vulnerability ranks into "Safe" and "Vulnerable" that leaves plenty of room for modeling uncertainty in lower ranks (1.5 to 2.5 out of 5 is a grey area). Same as with Severity, the fuzzy membership sets that classify Vulnerability ranks are depicted in Fig. 6.

The participation of values into membership sets for each part of the 1-5 scale are depicted in Table 6.

Risk. Risk represents a calculated value assigned to each information block IB and its corresponding variables, by aggregating the above mentioned Severity and Vulnerability ratings. Membership of an IB in Risk sets is calculated using Fuzzy Logic's

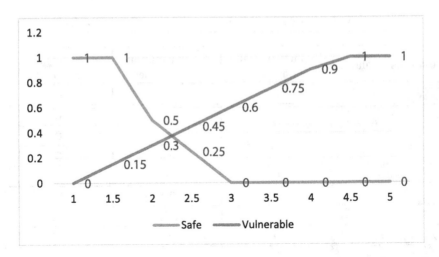

Fig. 6. Vulnerability membership sets for safe and vulnerable rank values (Color figure online).

Table 6. Participation percentages of Vulnerability values in Fuzzy sets.

0-4 ranks (values)	% participation – Safe set	% participation – Vulnerable set
1	1	0
1.5	1	0.15
2	0.5	0.3
2.5	0.25	0.45
3	0	0.6
3.5	0	0.75
4	0	0.9
4.5	0	1
5	0	1

IF-THEN rules. For clarity, all scales (Severity, Vulnerability and Risk) are divided in the same sets: "Low", "Medium" and "High". An example of how Risk is calculated using Fuzzy Logic linguistic rules is given:

$$IF Severity = \textbf{low} AND Vulnerability = \textbf{low} THEN Risk = \textbf{low}$$

Table 7 shows the fuzzy logic output for Risk, based on the aggregation of Severity and Vulnerability.

Table 7. Severity × Vulnerability = R - Risk sets.

Severity / Vulnerability	Low	Medium	High
Safe	Trifle	Trifle	Average
Vulnerable	Average	High	High

Risk output is basically the output of the fuzzy logic process, depicted in a way that provides a crisp, single-valued number to ease the end-users understanding. Fuzzy Logic is basically a logical system that expresses situations with multivalued results that do not have distinct boundaries. In our case, Fuzzy Logic is used to understand the danger-level set (rank) that an IB belongs to. Since an execution path is comprised by multiple method execution that may belong to different danger-level rank sets, pin-pointing the exact set to classify a path can be tricky. Even more, combining that classification output (Severity) with Vulnerability outputs leads to even bigger "fuzziness" concerning the overall Risk of each IB. The fuzzy membership sets that define the Overall Risk sets are depicted in Fig. 7.

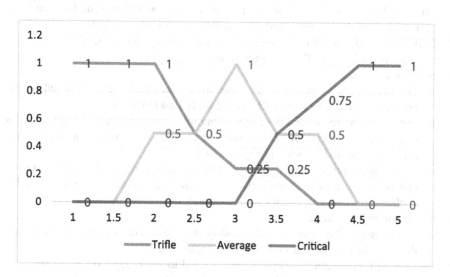

Fig. 7. Risk membership sets for Trifle (Low), Average and Critical (High) risk values (Color figure online).

The participation of values into membership sets are also depicted in Table 8 for clarification purposes.

Table 8. Participation percentages of Risk values in Fuzzy sets.

% participation	Trifle	Average	Critical
1	1	0	0
1.5	1	0	0
2	1	0.5	0
2.5	0.5	0.5	0
3	0.25	1	0
3.5	0.25	0.5	0.5
4	0	0.5	0.75
4.5	0	0	1
5	0	0	1

5   Experiments and Results

5.1   Entroine's Example Run

Let us say that Entroine runs on a small sample application based on the code in Fig. 1. The method steps would be the following:

1. Control Flow Graph analysis shows that there are 5 execution paths from an input vector (method that accepts method to a sink (method that executes data).
2. 5 IB are created, one for each execution path containing all necessary info about the code traversed in each IB's execution path.
3. Severity calculations
   a. The overall prior entropy of the program is computed ($Pr(C)$) based on the prior categorization of each IB into Severity ranks/subsets.
   b. For each feature (method) in the taxonomy, the program's Entropy Loss is calculated for the gathered paths, based on the number of paths that contain each taxonomy method, as seen in Fig. 8 below.
   c. The highest entropy loss detected points to the Severity rank (method subset) that best describes the corresponding IB and the overall danger level of the application; if a vulnerability were to manifest on these paths.
4. Vulnerability calculations
   a. IB are assigned to specific Vulnerability ranks based on the analysis of control flow statements and the sanitization of input data.
5. Severity and Vulnerability output values are fed to the Fuzzy Logic system.
6. The fuzzy membership of Risk is calculated, based on fuzzy set system.
7. Defuzzification is applied on the resulting Risk membership set to get a specific value for each detection. This is done to aid end-users in understanding Risk output (users understand a 3.7/5 scaled output quite better than a membership percentage in danger levels).
8. User can select IB flagged and check their Risk analysis.

```
////// Entropy Loss calculation //////

Entropy Loss calculation duration: 0 milliseconds
Entropy Loss for getInputStream in Rank 0: 0.0
Entropy Loss for getInputStream in Rank 1: 0.0
Entropy Loss for getInputStream in Rank 2: 0.0
Entropy Loss for getInputStream in Rank 3: 0.31127812445913283
Entropy Loss for getInputStream in Rank 4: 0.31127812445913283
Entropy Loss for readLine in Rank 0: 0.0
Entropy Loss for readLine in Rank 1: 0.0
Entropy Loss for readLine in Rank 2: 0.0
Entropy Loss for readLine in Rank 3: 0.12255624891826566
Entropy Loss for readLine in Rank 4: 0.12255624891826566
Entropy Loss for getProperty in Rank 0: 0.0
Entropy Loss for getProperty in Rank 1: 0.0
Entropy Loss for getProperty in Rank 2: 0.0
Entropy Loss for getProperty in Rank 3: 0.0
Entropy Loss for getProperty in Rank 4: 0.8112781244591328
Entropy Loss for exec in Rank 0: 0.0
Entropy Loss for exec in Rank 1: 0.0
Entropy Loss for exec in Rank 2: 0.0
Entropy Loss for exec in Rank 3: 0.0
Entropy Loss for exec in Rank 4: 0.0
```

Fig. 8. Screenshot of Entroine severity calculation outputs in eclipse console.

5.2   Experimental Results on the Juliet Test Case

In order to test our approach, we needed appropriate AUTs to analyze. We considered whether we should use open-source software or "artificially made" programs, such as those usually used for benchmarking program analysis tools. Both options are characterized by various positive characteristics and limitations.

In choosing between real AUTs and artificial code for our purpose, we endorsed NSA's principles from [28, 29] were it states that "the benefits of using artificial code outweigh the associated disadvantages". Therefore, for preliminary experimentation with Entroine we have opted using the Juliet Test Case suite, a formal collection of artificially-made programs packed with exploits [33].

The Juliet Test Suite is a collection of over 81.000 synthetic C/C ++ and Java programs with a priori known flaws. The suite's Java tests contain cases for 112 different CWEs (exploits). Each test case focuses on one type of flaw, but other flaws may randomly manifest. A bad() method in each test-program manifests an exploit. A good() method implements a safe way of coding and has to be classified as a true negative. Since Juliet is a synthetic test suite, we mark results as true positive, if there is an appropriate warning in flawed (bad) code or false positive, if there is an appropriate warning in non-flawed (good) code, similarly to [1].

This testing methodology is developed by NIST. We focus on exploits from user input, whereas other categories are not examined (e.g. race conditions). Table 9 provides a list of all Weakness Class Types used in the study. The middle column depicts the categories of exploits on which Entroine is tested (e.g. HTTP Response/Req

Table 9. Weakness classes (CWE).

Weakness (CWE)	Types of weaknesses analyzed	No. of tests
CWE-113	HTTP Response/Req HeaderServlet (add) HTTP Response/Req Cookie Servlet HTTP Response/Req HeaderServlet (set)	15
CWE-78	Operating System Command_ Injection	15
CWE-89	SQL Injection_connect_tcp SQL Injection_Environment_ execute SQL Injection_Servlet_execute	15

Header-Servlet (add): exploits that manifest on servlets when adding HTTP headers in responses and requests).

We ran Entroine on a set of vulnerable sample programs from the CWE categories depicted in Table 9. Our test data set consists of 45 total Juliet programs, 15 cases from each CWE category depicted in Table 9. Each bad method with an exploit will have to produce a True Positive (TP), whereas all good methods will have to represent True Negatives (TN).

Overall 178 tests (TP + TN) were included in all programs: 45 exploits and 133 cases of safe implementations (TNs). Entroine flags detections when both Severity and Vulnerability ranks for an IB are ranked above the Low zone (Risk >=3). Table 10 shows the overall results of our tests and, therefore, the accuracy of the tool.

Table 10. TP, TN, FP detection rate (80 samples).

Weakness Class (CWE)	TP Rate	TN Rate	TP +TN	All tests	No. of programs
CWE samples	45/ 45	133/ 133	178	178	45
Accuracy	TP = 100% , FP = 0%				

Table 11 provides a more detailed view of the results shown in Table 10. Table 11 depicts all tests per category of Juliet programs, whereas Table 7 is an overall look on

Table 11. Detection rates for each weakness type.

Weakness Class - CWE	TP	TN	TP + TN	All tests	No. of programs
CWE-89: SQL Injection	15/15	51/51	66	66	15
CWE-78: OS Command Injection	15/15	28/28	43	43	15
CWE-113: HTTP Response Split	15/15	54/54	69	69	15

the results. A total of 15 differentiated tests from each category where chosen for the Entroine's preliminary proof-of-concept.

6 Conclusions

Entroine is in pre-alpha stage. Tests act as proof-of-concept statistics, since testing real-world, big applications is not yet feasible due to package complexity, external libraries, etc. State explosion remains an issue, a problem inherited by the used analysis techniques. Yet, state explosion seems manageable using source code classification, in order to focus on specific variable paths. This is aided by Severity ranking.

Another limitation of Entroine is that it cannot detect errors based on variables' context. This can be realized by introducing semantic constructs to analyze information behind input data. A formal comparison with known tools is, therefore, needed.

We plan to use our technique to test real-world code used in cyber-physical systems (e.g. high level code that manipulates devices through SCADA systems). This will work as an adequate extension to previous work of ours [39].

Entroine runs relatively fast in comparison to what it has to do. Table 12 depicts execution times.

Table 12. Entroine's execution times.

Execution time (per 15 tests)	~ 129 s
Entropy loss calculation (per test)	~ 1 ms
Static analysis (per test)	~ 5 s

All tests were ran on an Intel Core i5 4570 PC (3.2 GHz, 8 GB RAM). A link to Entroine's taxonomy and example files can be found at: http://www.infosec.aueb.gr/Publications/Entroine_files.zip

References

1. Okun, V., Delaitre, O., Black, P.: Report on the Static Analysis Tool Exposition (SATE) IV, pp. 500–297. NIST Special Publication (2013)
2. Rutar, N., Almazan, C., Foster, S.: A comparison of bug finding tools for Java. In: Proceedings of the 15th International Symposium on Software Reliability Engineering. IEEE Computer Society, USA (2004)
3. Livshits, V., Lam, M.: Finding security vulnerabilities in Java applications with static analysis. In: Proceedings of the 14th USENIX Security Symposium (2005)
4. Ayewah, N., Hovemeyer, D., Morgenthaler, J., Penix, J., Pugh, W.: Using static analysis to find bugs. IEEE Softw. **25**(5), 22–29 (2008)
5. CodePro. https://developers.google.com/java-dev-tools/codepro/doc/
6. UCDetector. http://www.ucdetector.org/
7. Pmd. http://pmd.sourceforge.net/

8. Tripathi, A., Gupta, A.: A controlled experiment to evaluate the effectiveness and the efficiency of four static program analysis tools for Java programs. In: Proceedings of the 18th International Conference on Evaluation and Assessment in Software Engineering. ACM (2014)

9. Hovemeyer, D., Pugh, W.: Finding bugs is easy. SIGPLAN Not. **39**(12), 92–106 (2004)

10. Jovanovic, N., Kruegel, C., Kirda, E.: Static analysis for detecting taint-style vulnerabilities in web applications. J. Comput. Sec. **18**(5), 861–907 (2010). IOS Press

11. Weiser, M.: Program slicing. In: Proceedings of the International Conference on Software Engineering, pp. 439–449 (1981)

12. Stegiopoulos, G., Tsoumas, V., Gritzalis, D.: On business logic vulnerabilities hunting: the APP_LogGIC frame-work. In: Lopez, J., Huang, X., Sandhu, R. (eds.) NSS 2013. LNCS, vol. 7873, pp. 236–249. Springer, Heidelberg (2013)

13. Zhang, X., Gupta, N., Gupta, R.: Pruning dynamic slices with confidence. In: Proceedings of the Conference on Programming Language Design and Implementation, pp. 169–180 (2006)

14. Cingolani, P., Alcala-Fdez, J.: jFuzzyLogic: a robust and flexible Fuzzy-Logic inference system language implementation. In: Proceedings of the IEEE International Conference on Fuzzy Systems, pp. 1–8 (2012)

15. Doupe, A., Boe, B., Vigna, G.: Fear the EAR: discovering and mitigating execution after redirect vulnerabilities. In: Proceedings of the 18th ACM Conference on Computer and Communications Security, pp. 251–262. ACM, USA (2011)

16. Balzarotti, D., Cova, M., Felmetsger, V., Vigna, G.: Multi-module vulnerability analysis of web-based applications. In: Proceedings of the 14th ACM Conference on Computer and Communications Security, pp. 25–35. ACM, USA (2007)

17. Albaum, G.: The Likert scale revisited. Market Res. Soc. J. **39**, 331–348 (1997)

18. Ugurel, S., Krovetz, R., Giles, C., Pennock, D., Glover, E., Zha, H.: What's the code? automatic classification of source code archives. In: Proceedings of the 8th ACM SIGKDD International Conference on Knowledge Discovery and Data Mining, pp. 632–638. ACM, USA (2002)

19. Abramson, N.: Information Theory and Coding. McGraw-Hill, New York (1963)

20. Etzkorn, L., Davis, C.: Automatically identifying reusable OO legacy code. IEEE Comput. **30**(10), 66–71 (1997)

21. Glover, E., Flake, G., Lawrence, S., Birmingham, W., Kruger, A., Giles, L., Pennoek, D.: Improving category specific web search by learning query modification. In: Proceedings of the IEEE Symposium on Applications and the Internet, pp. 23–31. IEEE Press, USA (2001)

22. Stoneburner, G., Goguen, A.: SP 800-30. Risk management guide for information technology systems. Technical report. NIST, USA (2002)

23. OWASP: The OWASP Risk Rating Methodology. www.owasp.org/index.php/OWASP_Risk_Rating_Methodology

24. Leekwijck, W., Kerre, E.: Defuzzification: criteria and classification. Fuzzy Sets Syst. **108**(2), 159–178 (1999)

25. Java API: Java Standard Edition 7 API Specification. http://docs.oracle.com/javase/7/docs/api/

26. Gosling, J., Joy, B., Steele, G., Bracha, G., Buckley, A.: The Java Language Specification. Java SE 8 Edition, Oracle America Inc. and/or its affiliates, March 2015

27. Harold, E.: Java I/O, Tips and Techniques for Putting I/O to Work. O'Reilly, New York (2006)

28. National Security Agency: On Analyzing Static Analysis Tools. Center for Assured Software, NSA, Washington (2011)

29. National Security Agency: CAS Static Analysis Tool Study-Methodology. Center for Assured Software, National Security Agency (December 2012). https://samate.nist.gov/docs/ CAS%202012%20Static%20Analysis%20Tool%20Study%20Methodology.pdf
30. Yang, Y., Pederson, J.: A comparative study on feature selection in text categorization. In: Proceedings of the 14th International Conference on Machine Learning (ICML 1997), pp. 412–420 (1997)
31. BCEL, Apache Commons BCEL project page. http://commons.apache.org/proper/ commons-bcel/
32. Dahm, M., van Zyl, J., Haase, E.: The Bytecode Engineering Library (BCEL) (2003)
33. Boland, T., Black, P.: Juliet 1.1 C/C ++ and Java test suite. Computer **45**(10), 88–90 (2012)
34. Stergiopoulos, G., Tsoumas, B., Gritzalis, D.: Hunting application-level logical errors. In: Barthe, G., Livshits, B., Scandariato, R. (eds.) ESSoS 2012. LNCS, vol. 7159, pp. 135–142. Springer, Heidelberg (2012)
35. Stergiopoulos, G., Katsaros, P., Gritzalis, D.: Automated detection of logical errors in programs. In: Lopez, J., Ray, I., Crispo, B. (eds.) CRiSIS 2014. LNCS, vol. 8924, pp. 35–51. Springer, Heidelberg (2014)
36. Coverity SAVE audit tool. http://www.coverity.com
37. Mell, P., Scarfone, K., Romanosky, S.: Common vulnerability scoring system. Secur. Priv., IEEE **4**(6), 85–89 (2006)
38. The Common Weakness Enumeration (CWE), Office of Cybersecurity and Communications, US Deptartment of Homeland Security. http://cwe.mitre.org
39. Stergiopoulos, G., Theoharidou, P., Gritzalis, D.: Using logical error detection in RemoteTerminal Units to predict initiating events of Critical Infrastructures failures. In: Tryfonas, Theo, Askoxylakis, Ioannis (eds.) HAS 2014. LNCS, vol. 8533. Springer, Heidelberg (2015)
40. CWE - CWSS. https://cwe.mitre.org/cwss/cwss_v1.0.1.html
41. CWSS 3.0 scoring system. https://www.first.org/cvss/specification-document
42. National Vulnerability Database (NVD). https://nvd.nist.gov/

A Privacy-Sensitive Collaborative Approach to Business Process Development

Hassaan Irshad[1], Basit Shafiq[1], Jaideep Vaidya[2(✉)],
Muhammad Ahmed Bashir[1], Hafiz Salman Asif[2], Sameera Ghayyur[1],
Shafay Shamail[1], and Adam Nabil[2]

[1] Lahore University of Management Sciences, Lahore, Pakistan
[2] CIMIC, Rutgers University, Newark, USA
jsvaidya@rutgers.edu

Abstract. The objective of this paper is to enable organizations to generate an executable business process from high level design specifications. The basic idea is to exploit the knowledge of the existing business processes of related organizations to generate an executable business process for the given organization based on its requirements. However, this requires organizations with existing business processes to share their process execution sequences. Since the execution sequences (even after data sanitization) still include sensitive business information which organizations may not want to share with their competitors, this needs to be done in a privacy-sensitive way.

Towards this, we propose a privacy preserving approach for generating a repository of business process execution sequences. The proposed approach is based on differential privacy and does not reveal any sensitive information about individual organizations. The proposed approach is designed for a collaborative environment in which organizations share their business process details with a trusted third party called Business Process Recommendation and Composition System (BPRCS). BPRCS generates a differentially private dataset of execution sequences and employs process mining and classification techniques on this dataset to regenerate the executable business process workflow. We have implemented a prototype of BPRCS in J2EE and used it to validate the approach.

1 Introduction

Business Process (BP) development is a challenging task for small and medium enterprises (SMEs) which may not have adequate resources for coding, administration, and hosting of their BPs. Service oriented approach offers a potential solution to this problem [2, 11, 21, 22]. The emerging cloud infrastructure and service-oriented middleware can be leveraged for development, administration, and hosting of the BPs of organizations in the SME sector. The individual activities of the BP can be performed by invoking the Web services offered by 3rd parties. Especially in the e-commerce and financial domains, there are numerous 3rd party Web services covering every major functional aspect such as invoicing and billing, taxation and costing, accounting, payment processing, shipment, and

© Springer International Publishing Switzerland 2016
M.S. Obaidat and P. Lorenz (Eds.): ICETE 2015, CCIS 585, pp. 318–342, 2016.
DOI: 10.1007/978-3-319-30222-5_15

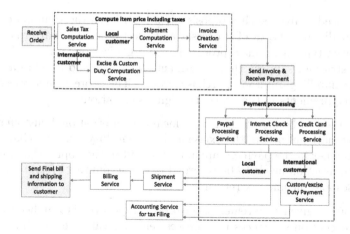

Fig. 1. Example of a business process for handling Internet purchase orders.

so on [25]. Similarly, other cloud resources (e.g., servers, compute nodes, storage, etc.) can be utilized for hosting and administration of BPs. The increased availability of such Web services has opened new opportunities for organizations for rapid and cost-effective development of their business processes even if they lack the capability to perform all of the tasks required for the business processes.

As an example, consider a business process for Internet orders processing by an online store. This is a complex process involving several tasks and each task itself can be a multi-step workflow as shown in Fig. 1. However, all these tasks can be executed by utilizing existing third party Web services. Assuming that the business process workflow is known and all the relevant Web services have been selected a priori then the process can be invoked and executed anytime. However, coming up with the implementation level business process workflow design so that each task can be mapped to an individual Web service as well as selection of third party web services for such tasks, poses significant challenges [22]. Typically, business process development involves working with a high-level process specification and manually elaborating the high-level specifications into implementation level design [10,12]. After this, partner Web services are selected and a binding is established between the workflow tasks and the selected partner Web services to generate the executable business process (e.g., BPEL process [15]).

Such business process development can be done collaboratively by exploiting the knowledge of the existing business processes of related organizations to compose an executable business process of a given organization based on its requirements and design specifications. However, this requires a repository of existing business processes that includes different types of business processes such as supply chain management, Internet purchase orders, accounting and taxation. For each type, the repository has to include the history of the business process invocations by different organizations in form of execution sequences (e.g., order in which the activities were performed and the corresponding Web services invoked). Given such a repository, we can learn the common execution patterns for different types of processes and use the learned patterns for composing a given type of business process for an organization [3,4].

For illustration, suppose that a garment store wants to develop a business process for handling Internet purchase orders. The store owner specifies the following requirements in the process design specification:

(1) Orders need to be handled for both local and international customers.
(2) For international orders the excise and custom duty must be charged from the customer in the payment amount and paid to the appropriate authority.
(3) Each transaction needs to be recorded in the accounting system for filing of the sales and income tax returns.

Based on the given requirements, the process repository is searched to retrieve the set of execution sequences that process either local orders or International orders with customs and excise duty payment. This set of execution sequences can be used to determine: (i) relevant activities in the Internet purchase order business process; (ii) controlflow and dataflow between the activities; (iii) third party web services that can perform the different activities in the business process; and (iv) trustworthiness of such third party Web services based on their invocation frequency. Given this information, an executable business process can be composed and deployed. For example, we can employ process mining on the sequence dataset to regenerate the BP workflow [27].

However, creating such a repository typically requires sharing sensitive information. Essentially, organizations with existing business processes, have to share and upload their process execution sequences to the central repository. The execution sequences (even after masking of the data values such as credit card information, social security number, etc.) include sensitive business information which organizations may not want to share [3,4,17]. For instance an organization may not want its competitors to learn: how many times the organization selects a given third party Web service as opposed to another service with the same functionality? How many times a business process failed for the organization because the requested item was not in the inventory? What is the turn-around time from order receipt to shipment?

To address this problem, we develop a privacy-preserving Business Process Recommendation and Composition System (BPRCS), that generates a differentially private dataset of execution sequences which can be published and shared with other organizations for composition and implementation of their business processes. We employ process mining and classification on the differentially private sequence dataset to regenerate the BP workflow. From this BP workflow, we can generate the executable BP code in BPEL.

As such, this paper examines the implications of privacy for business process composition while leveraging the knowledge of existing business processes from related organization. This is an important problem since there is a lot of benefit in creating business processes that utilize the available web services. We do this by employing the notion of differential privacy to protect the confidentiality of information contributed by each organization. Our key contribution is to exploit

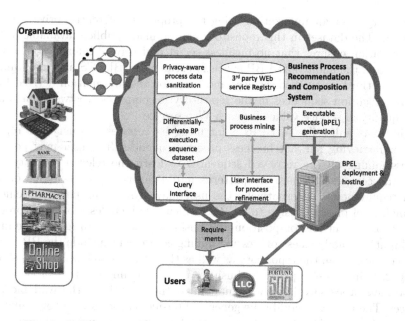

Fig. 2. Collaborative environment for business process composition.

the sequential composition property of differential private computations by modeling the execution sequences as a graph and performing random walk on this graph to regenerate comparable execution sequences that cannot be linked to a contributing organization. We have developed a prototype in J2EE and evaluated its effectiveness using two different business process execution sequence datasets. We measure the semantic correctness of the output BP workflow with respect to the termination states, dependency preservation, and branching correctness of the output workflow.

The rest of the paper is structured as follows. We first present the collaborative environment for business processes composition in Sect. 2. Section 3 outlines the privacy model, while the proposed approach is described in Sect. 4. Section 5 presents the privacy and complexity analysis of the proposed approach. In Sect. 6, we present a detailed experimental evaluation. Section 7 discusses the prototype implementation of the BPRCS system for generating an executable business process. Section 8 discusses the related work. Finally, Sect. 9 concludes the paper and discusses future work.

2   Environment

Figure 2 shows the environment for business process recommendation and composition. BPRCS is a trusted party in the cloud that provides support for collaborative composition of executable business processes in a privacy-preserving manner. Organizations from different domains register with BPRCS and publish their business process details (BP execution sequences) which are stored in a repository after anonymization using the proposed differential privacy-based approach. The dataset in this repository can be made publicly available as the anonymization ensures that no business secret and private information can be learned from the anonymized BP execution sequences. BPRCS also maintains a registry of third party Web services and based on the information derived from the BP execution sequences in the repository it computes trustworthiness and other quality of service values for each Web service.

The users subscribe to BPRCS for using its services to query the repository for retrieving relevant business process sequences. The user may perform process mining on the retrieved sequences to learn the relevant activity patterns and compose the activity patterns into a business process based on the given requirements. Alternatively, the user may provide his/her requirements and high level process design to BPRCS which also includes a business process mining component for composition of a business process in an interactive manner. Inputs to the business processing mining component include the BP execution sequences from the repository as well as the available web services as shown in Fig. 2. Using these inputs, the business process mining component generates the business process workflow with mapping of the activities to the available Web services. The user can modify the generated business process workflow using the process refinement interface. The process refinements may include changing the activity to Web service mapping or modifying the structure of the generated BP workflow. Given the business process workflow design and the activity to Web service mapping, an executable BPEL process can be easily generated and deployed on the server either at the user site or on the cloud.

One question that might occur is why would organizations participate in the BPRCS system. Basically, given an assurance of privacy, there are several incentives for these organizations to share their data in this collaborative environment, as discussed below:

1. Organizations can use the BPRCS for composing new business processes.
2. Refinement/extension of existing processes – An organization can compare its business process with comparable processes from other organizations to check for inconsistency/redundancy or identify any extension that may add more value to the process.
3. The proposed BPRCS system is also suitable for less open collaborative environments (e.g., digital government, single large organization) that require a pre-established level of trust before using third party Web services or ownership of such services [9]. In such environments, the organizations may be trustworthy; however, they may have similar privacy concerns for sharing their sensitive business process data. Also in such environments (e.g., digital government), there is typically a large number of trusted or co-owned Web services that could be used in composition of new business processes by other organizations. For example a property tax assessment Web service provided by County treasurer department can be used by the business registration department of the city. In this case, both the subscriber and user

organizations are trustworthy and use BPRCS for composition of new business processes.

3   Privacy Model

We first formally define business process execution sequences and then present the privacy model.

3.1   BP Execution Sequence

Generally, a business process is not designed for one time use only. Users execute their business processes repeatedly and each execution of the business process may be different from a prior execution of the same process. We define an execution sequence of a business process as the ordered list of activities (along with their input/output parameters) that are executed in any given execution of the business process. The activities in an execution sequence are ordered based on their invocation time. Based on BPEL formalism [15], an activity can be an invoke activity (invoking a Web service), receive activity (receiving input from a user), reply activity (sending a reply to the user), and assignment activity (for variable/value assignment). Since receive, reply, and assignment activities are primarily used to capture the data flow between Web services (invoke activities), we do not consider these activities in an execution sequence and define an execution sequence with respect to the Web services invoked. The data flow is captured by annotating each Web service with its input and output parameters in the given execution sequence. We represent the Web service invocation by the tuple

$$WS = (WS_{id}, input\_List, output\_List)$$

where WS_{id} corresponds to the unique identifier of the Web service being invoked. $input\_list = \{(input\_parameter, value)\}$ and $output\_List = \{(output\_parameter, value)\}$. Note that a given web service may provide multiple operations and in the BP execution sequence we need to capture which specific operation of the web service was invoked. However, for simplicity of discussion we assume that each Web service provides only one operation. In case a Web service provides multiple operations, we assign a unique WS_{id} to each combination of the Web service and its operation.

Definition 1 (BP Execution Sequence (ES)). *A BP execution sequence is a list of WS tuples ordered by their invocation time in the given business process execution.*

Table 1 shows a sample of BP execution sequences database including four sequences related to the Internet purchase order of Fig. 1. The Web service invocation tuples in the sequence are separated by $\rightarrow$. The sensitive information in the input list and output list is masked by the organization sharing its sequence data. Only those input and output parameter values are disclosed which are not considered sensitive. For example, in the **GetOrderFromAmazon** Web service in sequence 1 (Table 1), all the input parameter values including customer name and address are masked. Similarly, all the input and output parameter values in the Web service tuple **EasyBill** are masked to protect leakage of sensitive information.

3.2   Differential Privacy

Differential Privacy [13,14] is a well accepted privacy model that provides a formal and quantifiable privacy guarantee irrespective of an adversary's background knowledge and available computational power. A randomized algorithm is considered to be differentially private if for any pair of neighboring inputs, the probability of generating the same output, is within a small multiple of each other, for the entire output space [13]. Thus, for any two datasets which are close to one another, a differentially private algorithm will behave approximately the same on both data sets.

Definition 2 (ϵ-Differential Privacy). *A randomization algorithm $\mathcal{A}$ satisfies ϵ-differential privacy if for any two neighboring datasets D_1 and D_2 (differing in one element), and all $R \subseteq Range(\mathcal{A})$, we have $e^{-\epsilon} \leq \frac{Pr[\mathcal{A}(D_1) \in R]}{Pr[\mathcal{A}(D_2) \in R]} \leq e^{\epsilon}$.*

A standard mechanism to achieve differential privacy is based on the addition of appropriately parameterized Laplacian noise. For this, we need to define the sensitivity of the function to be computed.

Definition 3 (Sensitivity). *For any query function q over the input datasets, the sensitivity of q is $\Delta q = max||q(D_1) - q(D_2)||$ for any neighboring datasets D_1 and D_2.*

Queries with lower sensitivity can better tolerate the data modifications from added noise. The work in [14] shows that to release a (perturbed) value $q(x)$ while satisfying privacy, it suffices to add Laplace noise with standard deviation $\Delta q / \epsilon$. More specifically, for any given query function q, the mechanism $\mathcal{A}$:

$$\mathcal{A}(D) = q(D) + Laplace(\Delta q / \epsilon)$$

gives ϵ-differential privacy. Note that the above privacy guarantee requires that all the tuples in the dataset are independent [18], and may not hold if this is not true.

3.3   Privacy Requirement

Given a BP execution sequence database D and any BP execution sequence $ES \in D$, we do not want an adversary to learn if ES is the execution sequence of an organization Org_x. Thus, in terms of differential privacy, any two execution sequence databases D_1 and D_2 differing only on the inclusion of ES (i.e., D_1

Table 1. Sample BP execution sequence database.

No.	BP execution sequence
1	**(GetOrderFromAmazon**,{ }, {(Item,LevisJeans), (Qty,1) (BuyerLoc, LA)}) → **(SalesTaxSVC$_A$**,{(Item,LevisJeans), (Qty,1), (Price,50) (Buyer-Loc,LA)},{(Tax,4)}) → **(TransShip**,{(wt,0.5), (Origin,NYC), (Dest,LA) (Type,Std)},{(Charge,5)}) → **(PayPal**, {(Amount,59)},{(Result,OK) }) →**(EasyBill**, { },{ })
2	**(GetOrderFromAmazon**,{ }, {(Item,LevisJeans), (Qty,1) (BuyerLoc, London)}) → **(SalesTaxSVC$_A$**,{(Item,LevisJeans), (Qty,1), (Price,50) (BuyerLoc,London)},{(Tax,4)}) → **(UKCustoms**,{(ItemType,Clothes), (Qty,1), (Price,54),(BuyerLoc,London},{(Duty,2)})) → **(TransShip**, {(wt,0.5), (Origin,NYC), (Dest,LA) (Type,Std)},{(Charge,5)}) → **(PayPal**, {(Amount,61)},{(Result,OK) }) → **(UKDutyPymt**, {(Amount,2)}, {(Result,OK) })**(EasyBill**, { },{ })
3	**(GetOrderFromEbay**,{ }, {(Item,PoloShirt), (Qty,1) (Buyer Loc,Chicago)}) **(EasySalesTax**,{(Item,PoloShirt), (Qty,1), (Price,60) (BuyerLoc,Chicago)},{(Tax,5)}) → **(USPS**,{(wt,0.5), (Origin,NYC), (Dest,Chicago) (Type,Urgent)},{(Charge,10)}) → **(PayPal**, {(Amount, 75)},{(Result,OK) }) →**(EasyBill**, { },{ })
4	**(GetOrderFromAmazon**,{ }, {(Item,LevisJeans), (Qty,2) (Buyer-Loc,Paris)}) → **(SalesTaxSVC$_A$**,{(Item,LevisJeans), (Qty,2), (Price,100) (BuyerLoc,Paris)},{(Tax,8)}) → **(EuroCustoms**,{(ItemType,Clothes), (Qty,1), (Price,54),(BuyerLoc,Paris)},{(Duty,2)}) → **(TransShip**,{(wt, 1), (Origin,NYC), (Dest,LA) (Type,Std)},{(Charge,10)}) → **(PayPal**, {(Amount,120)},{(Result,OK) }) → **(EuroDutyPymt**, {(Amount, 2)},{(Result,OK) }) **(EasyBill**, { },{ })

includes ES and D_2 does not include ES), an ϵ-differentially private algorithm $\mathcal{A}$ satisfies:

$$Pr[\mathcal{A}(D_1) \in R] = e^\epsilon Pr[\mathcal{A}(D_2) \in R]$$

Where $R \subseteq Range(\mathcal{A})$. As stated in Sect. 3.2, this privacy guarantee is based on the assumption that all the execution sequences in the datasets D_1 and D_2 are independent. This assumption would definitely be valid if each organization contributes at most one execution sequence to the database. In case an organization (Org_x) contribute m sequences to the execution sequence database, then the adversary's probability estimate that a given execution sequence belongs to Org_x can change by at most $e^{m\epsilon}$ [18]. Note that this will only be true if the execution sequences are all based on the same underlying business process. In any case, to avoid even the potential of such disclosure, we restrict the number of execution sequences contributed by each organization to 3.

4   Proposed Approach

We first discuss how the differentially privacy repository of BP execution sequences is generated and then describe process mining for BP workflow creation.

4.1   Differentially Private BP Execution Sequences

We model the BP execution sequence database as a graph $G = (V, E)$. A node in the graph represents a Web service and an edge represents ordering relationship between invocation of two web services in some execution sequence. We formally define the execution sequence graph below:

Definition 4 (BP Execution Sequence Graph). *A BP execution sequence graph $G = (V, E)$ is a compact representation of the BP execution sequence database.*

- *Each node in V corresponds to a Web service.*
- *An edge $(WS_i, WS_j) \in E$ denotes that in some business process execution, the Web service WS_i was invoked first followed by the Web service WS_j.*
- *$c : E \to \mathbb{Z}^+$ is a count function. $c(WS_i, WS_j)$ denotes how many times WS_j was invoked after invocation of WS_i.*
- *$dist_{ip} : E \to \mathbf{X}$. For an edge $e : (WS_i, WS_j)$, $\mathbf{X}$ is a vector of distributions of all the input parameter values of WS_j given that WS_j is invoked immediately after WS_i. If WS_j has n input parameters then $\mathbf{X}$ includes n distributions.*
- *$dist_{op} : E \to \mathbf{Y}$. For an edge $e : (WS_i, WS_j)$, $\mathbf{Y}$ is a vector of distributions of all the output parameter values of WS_i given that WS_j is invoked immediately after WS_i. If WS_i has n output parameters then $\mathbf{Y}$ includes n distributions.*
- *$slen : V \to 2^{\mathbb{Z}^+ \times \mathbb{Z}^+}$. For a node v, $slen(v) = \{(length, count)\}$. $slen(v)$ returns the length of all execution sequences that originate from v. count denotes the number of occurrences of the sequence.*

In the execution sequence graph, the functions $dist_{ip}$ and $dist_{op}$ keep track of the distribution of the input and output parameter values of the Web services against each edge. This distribution of parameter values would be needed in the process mining phase to identify any conditional branches when composing the business process.

Figure 3 shows the graph of based representation of the sample BP execution sequence database of Table 1. This graph has 11 nodes corresponding to each Web service in the sample database. The edges in the graph are labeled with the count value given by the function $c()$. For example, $c(v_1, v_3) = 3$ indicating that there are three sequences in which the Web service **SalesTaxSVC$_A$** was invoked after the **GetOrderFromAmazon** Web service. The input parameters value distribution for the edge (v_1, v_2) is also shown in Fig. 3. The distribution indicates that amongst the corresponding sequences, the service **SalesTaxSVC$_A$** was invoked 3 times when the item was *LevisJeans* and quantity was in the range $[1\text{--}2]$. Also, in these three invocations the price was in the range $[50\text{--}80]$ twice and in the

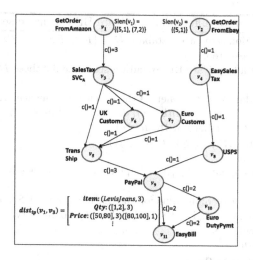

Fig. 3. Graph based representation of the sample BP execution sequence database of Table 1.

range [80–100] once. As discussed in Sect. 3.2, the values of sensitive parameters in the execution sequences would be masked by the organizations for privacy concerns. Therefore, the value distributions of those parameters are not included in $dist_{ip}$ and $dist_{op}$. The starting nodes in the sample database are v_1 corresponding to **GetOrderFromAmazon** and v_2 corresponding to **GetOrderFromEbay**. $slen(v_1) = (5,1),(7,2)$ indicating that there is one sequence of length 5 and two sequences of length 7 that originate from v_1. For all nodes other than v_1 and v_2 $slen()$ is an empty set.

We use the BP execution sequence graph to generate the differentially private database of execution sequences. The basic idea is to add Laplacian noise with appropriate ϵ value to the count value of each edge. Based on the edge count values, we compute the probability of taking an edge from a given node. For example in Fig. 3 there are three edges originating from node v_3: (v_3, v_5), (v_3, v_6), and (v_3, v_7). Each has a count value of 1, so the probability of each edge is $1/3$. Given the edge traversal probabilities, we can do a random walk from the starting nodes to regenerate the BP execution sequences. The length and the number of such execution sequences from any given starting node v is given by the $slen(v)$

Algorithm 1 shows the pseudo code for generation of differentially private BP execution sequence database. The input to this algorithm is the original sequence database and the privacy budget ϵ. The output database generated by the algorithm ensures ϵ-differential privacy. Algorithm 1 first generates the BP execution sequence graph from the given database (lines 1–4). Then noise derived from Laplace distribution with 0-mean and $\lambda = \epsilon/k$ is added to the count value for each edge (lines 6–8). k is the length of the longest sequence in the database D. The steps for regeneration of BP execution sequences by doing random walk from the start nodes are shown in lines 10–17.

Algorithm 1. Generate differentially private BP execution sequences.

Require: BP execution sequence database $D = \{ES_1, ES_2, \ldots, ES_N\}$
Require: Privacy measure ϵ
Ensure: ϵ-Differentially private BP execution sequence database $\tilde{D}$
1: $\tilde{D} \leftarrow \phi$
2: From the given database D, generate the execution sequence graph $G = (V, E)$
3: For each edge $e \in E$, label e with $c(e)$, $dist_{ip}(e)$, and $dist_{op}(e)$.
4: For each node $v \in V$, label v with $slen(v)$
5: $k \leftarrow max(\{length(ES_1), \ldots length(ES_N)\})$
6: **for** each $e \in E$ **do**
7:    $c(e) \leftarrow c(e) + Laplace(\epsilon/k)$ {Add Laplacian noise to the edge count}
8: **end for**
9: Based on the modified count value for an edge $e = (WS_i, WS_j)$, compute the probability of taking that edge, i.e., the probability of invoking service WS_j immediately after invocation of WS_i
10: **for** each $v \in V$ **do**
11:    **for** each $t \in slen(v)$ **do**
12:       **for** $i = 1$ to $t.count$ **do**
13:          Generate $\widehat{ES}$ by doing a random walk of $t.length$ steps starting from node v using the probability values of corresponding edges computed in line 9
14:          $\tilde{D} \leftarrow \tilde{D} \cup \widehat{ES}$ (this is a multiset union)
15:       **end for**
16:    **end for**
17: **end for**
18: **return** $\tilde{D}$

4.2 Process Mining and BP Workflow Generation

Once the differentially private BP sequence database is generated, it can be queried to retrieve relevant sequences based on user requirements as depicted in Fig. 2. From the retrieved BP sequences, we need to generate the BP workflow structure including the control flow and data flow. In addition the activities in the BP workflow need to be mapped to appropriate Web services.

There are several process mining tools available for discovering workflow models from event logs [24, 26–28]. We use the process mining tool ProM [27] to create this basic workflow structure from the given BP execution sequences. From this basic workflow structure, we identify all the branching points. There may exist a strong correlation between the values of some of the input/output parameters and the branch taken during business process execution. For example, with reference to the Internet purchase order example depicted in Fig. 1, if the order is made by an international customer, the business process branches to the excise and custom duty computation service. On the other hand, if the order is made by a local customer the business process execution takes the first branch. For each branching point, we build a decision tree-based classification model to discover the branching conditions. The differentially private execution dataset (used for generation of the basic workflow) serves as a training dataset for classification models generation. Essentially, each BP execution sequence in this dataset corresponds to an instance with relevant data and parameter values for building the classification model. The rules generated by the classification model corresponds to the branching conditions and are annotated on the corresponding branching path.

Note that given the workflow structure including the controlflow, dataflow, activities to Web services mapping and branching condition, we can create the executable BPEL process that can then be deployed.

5 Analysis

Privacy Analysis. As discussed in Sect. 3.3, the differential privacy guarantee requires that there must not be any correlation between multiple sequences submitted by the same organization that enables one to link such sequences to that organization. In case an organization (Org_x) contribute m sequences to the execution sequence database, then the adversary's probability estimate that a given execution sequence belongs to Org_x can change by a factor of $e^{m\epsilon}$ [18].

In our experiments, we limit the maximum number of execution sequences contributed by any organization to 3 (i.e., $m \leq 3$). Also, when considering multiple BP execution sequences from a single organization, we ensure that such sequences do not overlap or the overlap is frequent across multiple organizations such that the information about the overlapping sequences does not significantly increases the probability of linking the overlapping sequences to specific organizations.

Below, we discuss the privacy analysis with respect to generation of differentially private BP execution sequence database (Algorithm 1). The process mining step operates on this differentially-private database and therefore does not affect privacy.

To satisfy the differential privacy requirement, we add Laplace noise to the edge count values in Algorithm 1. The standard deviation λ of Laplace noise depends on two parameters *sensitivity* and the privacy budget ϵ.

Sensitivity Δq. The count value for an edge (v_1, v_2) basically gives the number of BP execution sequences in which Web service v_2 was invoked immediately after v_1. Given that the neighboring database for differential privacy differ in one record, the sensitivity value for count queries is 1 [20].

Privacy Budget. Algorithm 1 regenerates the BP execution sequences by doing random walk up to some given length. In the random walk, basically we are composing the sequence of computations that each provide differential privacy in isolation. Here, the computations are the count queries on the edges. Assuming that a computation C_i provides ϵ_i differential privacy, then by the sequential composition theorem in [20], the sequence of computations $C_i(D)$ provides $(\Sigma_i \epsilon_i)$-differential privacy. To ensure $m\epsilon$ differential privacy for the released database $\tilde{D}$, we consider a privacy budget of $m\epsilon/k$ when adding noise to count value to edges, where k is the maximum length of any execution sequence in the original database D and m is the maximum number of execution sequences contributed by any organization. Since, we can have at most k steps in the random walk for creating any execution sequence and $\Sigma_{i=1}^{k}(m\epsilon/k) = m\epsilon$, therefore our algorithm provides at least $m\epsilon$-differential privacy.

Computation Complexity. We first discuss the complexity of Algorithm 1. Lines (1–4) of Algorithm 1 generate the execution sequence graph $G = (V, E)$. The total number of nodes ($|V|$) in G is equal to the total number of web services in the BP sequence Database D and the number of edges can be at most $|V|^2$. Therefore, the size of G is $O(|D|)$. In lines (6–8) Laplace noise is added to each edge, therefore, the complexity of this step is $O(|E|)$. In the BP execution sequence regeneration step, we do a random walk as many times as the number of sequences in D. In each random walk, at most k nodes are visited, where k is the length of the longest sequence in D. Therefore, the runtime complexity of the sequence regeneration step is $O(k|D|)$. Hence, the overall complexity of Algorithm 1 is $O(k|D| + |E|) = O(k|D|)$.

The computation complexity for workflow generation from the BP execution sequences depends on the complexity of the process mining and classification model generation. We use ProM tool that incorporates α-algorithm for process mining [26]. The complexity of α-algorithm is linear in the number of sequences and exponential in the number of tasks/activities in the workflow [26]. The number of tasks/activities in a workflow does not depend on the size of the BP sequence dataset and is typically less than 100. Therefore, complexity is not a major issue for process mining. The classification model is built at each branching point to identify the branching conditions. The computation complexity of building the classifier depends on the particular classification model used. For example the cost of building an ID3 decision tree classifier is $O(|D||A||N|)$, where, $|D|$ is the number of sequences, $|A|$ is the number of attributes, and $|N|$ is the number of non-leaf nodes in the decision tree built [23].

6   Experimental Evaluation

In this section, we evaluate the utility of the proposed approach in terms of the semantic correctness of the BP workflow generated from the differentially-private dataset. We refer to the BP workflow generated from the differentially-private dataset as output BP workflow. We measure the semantic correctness of the output BP workflow with respect to the following requirements:

1. **Completion of the Output BP Workflow.** This requirement entails that the output BP workflow terminates in the correct state. We measure the utility with respect to this requirement by computing the degree of overlap between the set of terminating states of the output BP workflow and original BPs (from which the BP sequence dataset is generated).
2. **Dependency Preservation in the Output BP Workflow.** Ensuring that the output BP workflow terminates in the correct state is not sufficient to verify its correctness. We also need to make sure that in any possible execution of the output BP workflow, the ordering and dependence relationship between the different activities are maintained with respect to the original

BPs. Since there is a large number of original BPs (over 1000), we cannot perform structural comparison between the set of original BPs and the output BP workflow. Rather, we compare the overlap between the frequent sequential patterns of originals BPs and the frequent sequential patterns in the sanitized (differentially private) sequence dataset.

3. **Correctness of the branching Conditions in the Output BP Workflow.** We compare the output BP workflow and the original BPs in terms of the branching condition at each branching point.

6.1   Dataset Description

We performed experiments on two different datasets. The first dataset includes execution sequences selected from BPs related to Internet purchase orders. Since our experiments involved over a thousand BPs, we could not get these many real-world BPs. To address this issue, we first identified a large set of Web services and their categories related to Internet purchase orders in different businesses (e.g., garments/apparel, electronics). Then we identified the ordering and dependence relationships (e.g., shipment Web service is called after payment processing web service) and mutual exclusion constraints (e.g., Payment can be made using either Paypal or credit card Web service but not both) between the different Web service categories. These relationships and constraints were modeled in a dependency graph in which the nodes represent Web service categories. We consider two types of edges: i) dependence edge defining the dependence relationship between the Web service categories; and ii) constraint edges defining the mutual exclusion constraint between the Web service categories. From this dependency graph, we generated the required number of BPs by considering different combinations of alternate paths to terminal nodes as well as considering different parallel structures for independent nodes (i.e., Web services that do not have any dependence relationship). Figure 4 depicts the dependency graph of the Internet purchase order and a BP instance generated from this dependency graph. In this dependency graph, the number of web service categories is 28. From each BP, we generated all possible execution sequences.

In the second dataset, we generated multiple dependency graphs randomly with fixed number of service category nodes (total service categories = 30) and varying number of alternate paths from the start node to leaf nodes (terminating states). From each dependency graph, we generated the required number of BPs and all possible execution sequence from each BP.

6.2   Results

In the following discussion, D denotes the database of the original execution sequences generated from all the BPs of a dependency graph. The D_S denotes the database of the BP sequences used for sanitization $D_S \subseteq D$. Each BP contributes a small number (1–3) of execution sequences in D_S for privacy reasons discussed above. $\tilde{D}$ denotes the sanitized database after applying Algorithm 1 on D_S.

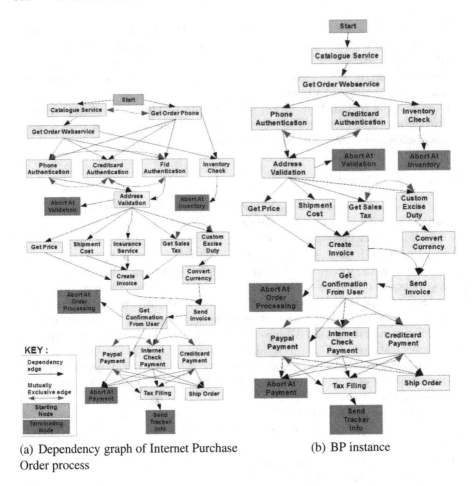

(a) Dependency graph of Internet Purchase
Order process

(b) BP instance

Fig. 4. Dependency graph and a BP instance derived from dependency graph.

Completion of the Output BP Workflow. For this requirement, we measure
the degree of overlap between the set of terminating states of the output BP workflow and original BPs (from which the BP sequence dataset is generated). Specifically, we measure the accuracy of the set of terminating states in the original BP
workflow (denoted by T) and the set of terminating states (denoted by $\tilde{T}$) in the
output BP workflow in terms of precision and recall. These values were averaged
over four runs. $\tilde{T}$ is obtained from the output BP workflow structure returned after
performing process mining on the sanitized execution sequence dataset.

Table 2 shows precision and recall values of terminating states with varying $\tilde{\epsilon}$.
For this experiment, we considered different numbers of BPs (200, 500, 1000, and
2000). These BPs were generated from the Internet Purchase Order dependency
graph. From each BP, we selected 3 execution sequences and sanitized the resulting database of selected execution sequences.

Table 2. Precision and recall of terminating states with varying $\tilde{\epsilon}$ and number of BPs related to Internet purchase order dataset.

Precision (Percent)				
$\tilde{\epsilon}$	200 BPs	500 BPs	1000 BPs	2000 BPs
0.02	100	100	100	100
0.01	100	100	100	100
0.005	100	100	100	100
0.002	100	100	100	100
Recall (Percent)				
0.02	60	60	60	60
0.01	40	60	60	60
0.005	40	40	60	60
0.002	40	60	60	60

Table 3. Recall of terminating states with varying number of distinct execution sequences in the random dataset.

Recall (Percent)				
Distinct ESs	200 BPs	500 BPs	1000 BPs	2000 BPs
2264	50	75	100	100
1467	50	25	50	75
1065	50	50	75	50
955	25	25	50	50
739	25	25	25	25

As shown in Table 2, Precision is 100 % for the Internet purchase order dataset. Recall improves as number of BPs are increased for generation of the output BP workflow. Also, recall improves as we decrease the noise (i.e., increase in $\tilde{\epsilon}$)

In Table 3, we show the recall results for the random dataset. In this table, we varied the total number of distinct sequences possible in a randomly generated dependency graph (Distinct ESs) along with total number of BPs while keeping $\tilde{\epsilon}$ fixed at 0.01 and selected 1 Execution sequence per BP. From Table 3, we can see that as the number of distinct execution sequences are reduced, it becomes harder for the process miner to correctly recall terminating states because of increase in noise to distinct execution sequences ratio. As for precision, it is consistent with Table 2 and stays at 100 % for all values of distinct execution sequences and total BPs; therefore precision results are not shown in the table.

Dependency Preservation in the Output BP Workflow. We compute the overlap between the frequent sequential patterns in D and $\tilde{D}$ in terms of

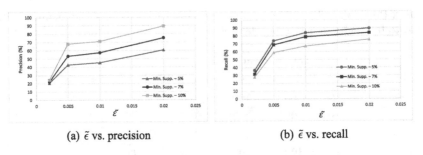

(a) $\tilde{\epsilon}$ vs. precision   (b) $\tilde{\epsilon}$ vs. recall

Fig. 5. No. of BPs = 1000 and 1 sequence per BP for Internet Purchase Order dataset.

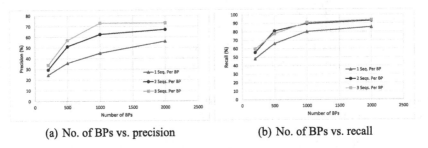

(a) No. of BPs vs. precision   (b) No. of BPs vs. recall

Fig. 6. $\tilde{\epsilon} = 0.01$ and minimum support threshold for frequent patterns in $D = 10\%$ and for $\tilde{D} = 5\%$ – Internet Purchase Order dataset.

precision and recall. For measuring recall, we considered exact matching of patterns between D and $\tilde{D}$. For measuring precision, we consider two patterns p_i and p_j to be matching if they differ by at most one element and the order of elements is preserved. This approximate matching (for precision) makes sense since business process composition is an interactive process as depicted in Fig. 2. The user will take the output of the system and refine it based on his/her requirements.

Precision and Recall of frequent Sequential Patterns w.r.t. ϵ. Figure 5a and b shows the graph of precision and recall values measured against different $\tilde{\epsilon}$ for the Internet Purchase Order BPs. $\tilde{\epsilon} = \epsilon/k$ and for the Internet Purchase Order BPs $k \leq 16$. The precision and recall values in Fig. 5 are computed by taking the average of precision and recall values of the frequent patterns with length between 5 and 10 in Fig. 5, the number of input BPs is 1000. From each of the input BP, we randomly selected 1 execution sequence for generation of the output BP workflow. We first ran the frequent sequential pattern analysis on the original; database D with a minimum support threshold of 10 % for all patterns of length between 5 and 10. For the sanitized database $\tilde{D}$, we considered 3 minimum support thresholds: 5 %, 7 %, and 10 % in Fig. 5. The reason for choosing smaller support threshold (5 % and 7 %) for differentially private dataset is that addition of noise typically decreases the support value for frequent patterns. However at 5 % minimum support and $\tilde{\epsilon} \geq 0.005$ more than 75 % of all the frequent patterns of the original dataset are retrieved as depicted in Fig. 5(b). As depicted in

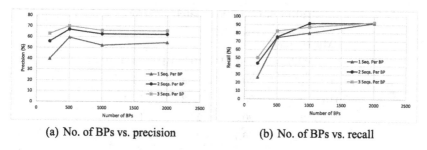

(a) No. of BPs vs. precision   (b) No. of BPs vs. recall

Fig. 7. $\tilde{\epsilon} = 0.01$ and minimum support threshold for frequent patterns in $D = 10\,\%$ and for $\tilde{D} = 5\,\%$ – Internet Purchase Order dataset.

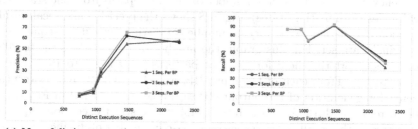

(a) No. of distinct execution sequences vs. (b) No. of distinct execution sequences vs. precision   recall

Fig. 8. $\tilde{\epsilon} = 0.01$ and minimum support threshold for frequent patterns in $D = 10\,\%$ and for $\tilde{D} = 5\,\%$ – BPs generated from random dependency graph.

Fig. 5, both precision and recall increases as the value of $\tilde{\epsilon}$ increases (i.e., lesser the noise, better the results).

Precision and Recall of Frequent Sequential Patterns w.r.t. Number of BPs. Figure 6a and b shows the graph of average precision and recall values measured against different number of input BPs for the Internet Purchase Order. Similarly, Fig. 7a and b shows the graph of average precision and recall values for BPs generated from the random dependency graph with approximately 1400 distinct execution sequences. In both graphs, $\tilde{\epsilon} = 0.01$, minimum support threshold for frequent patterns in D is set to $10\,\%$ and for $\tilde{D}$ is set to $5\,\%$. From each of the input BP, we randomly selected 1, 2, and 3 execution sequence for generation of the output BP workflow. As depicted in Figs. 6 and 7, the precision and recall improves as the number of input BPs increases. Moreover, the results improve with the increase in the number of execution sequences from each BP for generation of the output BP workflow.

Precision and Recall of Frequent Sequential Patterns w.r.t. Number of Distinct Execution Sequences in the Original Dataset D. We would like to measure the affect of variation in the original BP dataset D (i.e., number of distinct execution sequences in D) on the dependency preservation in the output BP workflow. For this purpose, we considered BPs generated from random

Table 4. Condition matching error.

CME (Percent)				
$\tilde{\epsilon}$	200 BPs	500 BPs	1000 BPs	2000 BPs
0.02	26.7	20	13.3	13.3
0.01	26.7	20	13.3	13.3
0.005	26.7	20	20	13.3
0.002	20	26.7	20	20

dependency graphs with varying number of alternate paths from the start node to leaf nodes (terminating states). Figure 8 shows the precision and recall results for random BP dataset with varying number of distinct execution sequences in the original data set. For this graph, the number of input BPs is set to 2000, minimum support threshold for frequent patterns in D is set to 10 % and for $\tilde{D}$ is set to 5 %. From each of the input BP, we selected 1, 2, and 3 execution sequence for generation of the output BP workflow. As depicted in Fig. 8, precision increases with the increase in the number of distinct execution sequences in D; whereas, the recall decreases with increase in number of distinct execution sequences.

Correctness of the Branching Conditions in the Output BP Workflow. We compare the output BP workflow and the original BPs in terms of the branching condition at each branching point. Since the branching conditions have semantic meanings, we need to have real-world business processes for evaluating the proposed approach against this metric. We used real-world Internet Purchase Order BPs and generated output BP workflow structure after sanitization and process mining. Finally at each branching point, we build the decision-tree based classification (ID3) model to infer the branching conditions. We then compare the branching conditions between the original workflow W and generated output BP workflow $\tilde{W}$ at each branching point to compute the *conditon matching error (CME)* defined as:

$$CME = \frac{\text{No. of non-matching conditions between } W \& \tilde{W}}{\text{No. of branching conditions in } W}$$

Table 4 shows the CME for the workflows generated from the Internet Purchase order dataset for different number of BPs and with varying $\tilde{\epsilon}$. As depicted in Table 4, CME decreases as the number of BPs increases. Also, when the number of BPs is fixed, CME increases with decrease in $\tilde{\epsilon}$ (i.e., increase in the noise). Note that for computing CMEs, we consider those conditions that involve comparion between a variable and a fixed value (e.g., $SalesTax > 10$). We miss those conditions that involve comparison between two variables ((e.g., $SalesTax < 0.10 * ItemPrice$)).

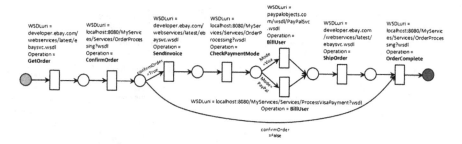

Fig. 9. Petrinet-based model of the Internet Purchase order process workflow generated after process mining and classification steps.

7 Implementation

We have developed a prototype of the Business process composition and recommendation system that implements the proposed approach in J2EE. Given a set of Business process execution sequences, the prototype first generates the Differentially private BP execution sequence dataset. It employs process minining tool ProM [27] to generate the basic BP workflow structure from the sanitized BP execution sequence dataset. PRom generates this Workflow structure in Petri Net. From this Petri Net, we identify all the branching points and discover the branching conditions using decision tree-based classification. We use Weka j48 API for building the classification model [16]. The workflow Petri Net is labeled with the branching conditions. The transitions in the Petri Net workflow correspond to Web service categories. These Web service categories are then mapped to actual Web services. Currently, we do not consider any optimalty criteria for selecting Web services; however, the Web service selection approaches given in [7,29] can be employed for optimal service selection. Figure 9 shows an example of Internet Purchase order process workflow generated after process mining and classification.

In order to generate the BPEL code from the given Workflow Petri Net with branching condition, the input and ouput variables of the selected web services need to be mapped. In the current prototype, this variable mapping is done manually by the user. A graphical interface is provided for performing variable mapping as depicted in Fig. 10(a). In this figure, the possible mappings of the *ShippingAddress* of *ShipOrder* operation of a shipping Web services are shown. The user can select the correct mapping. After performing the variable mapping, the prototype generates the BPEL code that can be executed on BPEL 2.0 Engine (e.g., Apache ODE). Figure 10(b) shows part of the BPEL process in the Eclipse IDE using the BPEL 2.0 plugin. This BPEL is generated from the Internet purchase order Petrinet workflow.

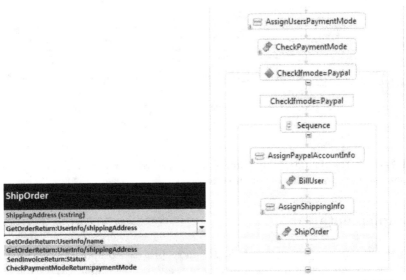

(a) Variable mapping GUI   (b) Partial view of BPEL process in Eclipse

Fig. 10. Illustration of the BPEL code generation implementation.

8   Related Work

We will discuss the related work with respect to the following aspects: (i) differential privacy for sequence dataset; (ii) collaborative business process composition; and (iii) business process management.

Differential Privacy for Sequence Dataset. [8] have proposed a differential privacy based approach for sanitization of trajectory data. In this approach they first build a prefix tree from the given trajectory dataset and then add Laplacian noise at each level of the prefix tree to satisfy differential privacy. From the noisy prefix tree, they regenerate trajectories for the sanitized dataset. Their approach can be an alternate approach for generation of the sanitized BP Execution sequence database as trajectories are essentially sequence of locations. However, in their prefix-tree based approach, there can be multiple branches in the prefix tree for sequences that overlap considerably but differ only in the beginning part of the sequences. Due to this, the memory requirement for generation of the prefix tree for BP execution sequence dataset will be high.

Collaborative Business Process Composition. Awad et al. have proposed an approach for business process composition using a repository of design patterns [1]. The basic idea is to maintain a repository that stores a variety of process components and design patterns extracted from existing processes. Given a partial process model by the process designer, this repository is queried to retrieve the process components that match with the fragments of the partial process model. These components are composed in the partial model to provide a complete process model and presented to the process designer who can accept or refine the design. This work is relevant to the querying and business process mining aspect of the collaborative business process composition environment-depicted in Fig. 2. Given the process components and patterns in the repository may come from multiple organizations, our proposed approach facilitates in developing such a repository by addressing the privacy concerns of organizations sharing their business process data.

Recently, there is some work on collaborative design and composition of business processes by utilizing social network platforms [5,6,12,19]. These social network platforms serve as a recommendation system that facilitates a process designer to complete or update a formal BP model on the basis of the prior usage of the process fragments by other peers. However, the privacy issues related to sharing of the usage patterns and process fragments are not considered.

[3,4] have proposed an anonymization-based approach for privacy preserving outsourcing of business processes in a multi-tenant cloud environment. In their approach a business process is broken down into smaller fragments for re-use in future process modeling. A fragment is disclosed for process composition only if it satisfies the K_l anonyfrag requirement. This requirement enatils that the disclosed fragment must have at least K clones distributed among l tenants. This anonyfrag approach indeed satsifies the privacy requirement. However, it requires the process designer to manually compose the business process from the available fragments. In contrast, our proposed approach generates the initial BP workflow (based on the given requirements) that can be refined by the process designer.

Business Process Management. [2,21] have described business process management approaches with self-adaptation capabilities. The idea is to monitor the execution of BPEL processes and in case of failure or service unavailability, the process is adapted automatically at execution time to deal with such failures or service unavailability. As part of the process adaptation framework, a registry of all the third party Web services is maintained with their quality of service parameters observed during the BPEL process execution. This work can be leveraged for mapping of third party Web services to the different business process activities in the BPEL generation step (Fig. 2).

9   Conclusions and Future Work

In this paper, we have described how executable business processes can be developed in a collaborative manner while preserving privacy. Essentially, business process details in the form of BP execution sequences from multiple organizations are collated together in a differentially private central repository. Process mining over this repository is used to generate business process workflows based on user requirements and high level design specifications. The results from the experimental evaluation show that the proposed approach is effective in terms of preserving utility of the original BP execution sequence database while guaranteeing privacy. This utility is measured with respect to preservation of process workflow structure and semantics as well as preservation of Web service ranking.

While this approach preserves privacy, it does require trust in the central repository which sanitizes the data before making it public. One possibility is to employ encryption based techniques to address this limitation. However, this would add significant computation and communication overhead. Since business process composition is often an iterative process, another possibility is to utilize game-theoretic techniques to create efficient solutions. In the future, we plan to explore these approaches.

Acknowledgements. The work of Shafiq and Shamail is supported by the LUMS Faculty Initiative Fund Grant and by HEC under the PAK-US Science and Technology Cooperation Program. The work of Vaidya is supported by the NSF under Grant No. CNS-1422501. The work of Adam is supported by the National Academies of Sciences, Engineering, and Medicine under the PAK-US Science and Technology Cooperation Program.

References

1. Awad, A., Sakr, S., Kunze, M., Weske, M.: Design by selection: a reuse-based approach for business process modeling. In: Jeusfeld, M., Delcambre, L., Ling, T.-W. (eds.) ER 2011. LNCS, vol. 6998, pp. 332–345. Springer, Heidelberg (2011)
2. Baresi, L., Guinea, S.: Self-supervising bpel processes. IEEE Trans. Softw. Eng. **37**(2), 247–263 (2011)
3. Bentounsi, M., Benbernou, S., Atallah, M.J.: Privacy-preserving business process outsourcing. In: 2012 IEEE 19th International Conference on Web Services (ICWS), pp. 662–663, June 2012
4. Bentounsi, M., Benbernou, S., Deme, C.S., Atallah, M.J.: Anonyfrag: an anonymization-based approach for privacy-preserving bpaas. In: Proceedings of the 1st International Workshop on Cloud Intelligence, Cloud-I 2012, pp. 9:1–9:8. ACM, NY, USA (2012)
5. Brambilla, M., Fraternali, P., Vaca, C.: BPMN and design patterns for engineering social BPM solutions. In: Daniel, F., Barkaoui, K., Dustdar, S. (eds.) BPM Workshops 2011, Part I. LNBIP, vol. 99, pp. 219–230. Springer, Heidelberg (2012)
6. Bruno, G., Dengler, F., Jennings, B., Khalaf, R., Nurcan, S., Prilla, M., Sarini, M., Schmidt, R., Silva, R.: Key challenges for enabling agile BPM with social software. J. Softw. Maintenance Evol. Res. Pract. **23**(4), 297–326 (2011)
7. Calinescu, R., Grunske, L., Kwiatkowska, M., Mirandola, R., Tamburrelli, G.: Dynamic QoS management and optimization in service-based systems. IEEE Trans. Software Eng. **37**(3), 387–409 (2011)
8. Chen, R., Fung, B.C., Desai, B.C., Sossou, N.M.: Differentially private transit data publication: a case study on the montreal transportation system. In: Proceedings of the 18th ACM SIGKDD International Conference on Knowledge Discovery and Data Mining, KDD 2012, pp. 213–221. ACM, NY, USA (2012)

9. Chun, S., Atluri, V., Adam, N.R.: Dynamic composition of workflows for customized egovernment service delivery. In: Proceedings of the Annual National Conference on Digital Government Research, pp. 1–7. Digital Government Society of North America (2002)

10. Chun, S.A., Atluri, V., Adam, N.R.: Domain knowledge-based automatic workflow generation. In: Hameurlain, A., Cicchetti, R., Traunmüller, R. (eds.) DEXA 2002. LNCS, vol. 2453, pp. 81–93. Springer, Heidelberg (2002)

11. Chun, S.A., Atluri, V., Adam, N.R.: Using semantics for policy-based web service composition. Distrib. Parallel Databases 18(1), 37–64 (2005)

12. Dengler, F., Koschmider, A., Oberweis, A., Zhang, H.: Social software for coordination of collaborative process activities. In: Muehlen, M., Su, J. (eds.) BPM 2010 Workshops. LNBIP, vol. 66, pp. 396–407. Springer, Heidelberg (2011)

13. Dwork, C.: Differential privacy. In: Bugliesi, M., Preneel, B., Sassone, V., Wegener, I. (eds.) ICALP 2006. LNCS, vol. 4052, pp. 1–12. Springer, Heidelberg (2006)

14. Dwork, C., McSherry, F., Nissim, K., Smith, A.: Calibrating noise to sensitivity in private data analysis. In: Halevi, S., Rabin, T. (eds.) TCC 2006. LNCS, vol. 3876, pp. 265–284. Springer, Heidelberg (2006)

15. Evdemon, J., Arkin, A., Barreto, A., Curbera, B., Goland, F., Kartha, G., Khalaf, L., Marin, van der Rijn, M., Yiu, Y.: Services business process execution language version 2.0. OASIS Standard, April 2007

16. Hall, M., Frank, E., Holmes, G., Pfahringer, B., Reutemann, P., Witten, I.H.: The weka data mining software: an update. ACM SIGKDD Explor. Newsl. 11(1), 10–18 (2009)

17. Kerschbaum, F., Deitos, R.J.: Security against the business partner. In: Proceedings of the ACM Workshop on Secure Web Services, SWS 2008, pp. 1–10. ACM, New York, USA (2008)

18. Kifer, D., Machanavajjhala, A.: No free lunch in data privacy. In: Proceedings of the ACM SIGMOD International Conference on Management of Data, SIGMOD 2011, pp. 193–204. ACM, New York, NY, USA (2011)

19. Koschmider, A., Song, M., Reijers, H.A.: Social software for business process modeling. J. Inf. Technol. 25(3), 308–322 (2010)

20. McSherry, F.D.: Privacy integrated queries: an extensible platform for privacy-preserving data analysis. In: Proceedings of the ACM SIGMOD International Conference on Management of data, SIGMOD 2009, pp. 19–30. ACM, New York, USA (2009)

21. Moser, O., Rosenberg, F., Dustdar, S.: Non-intrusive monitoring and service adaptation for WS-BPEL. In: Proceedings of the 17th International Conference on World Wide Web, WWW 2008, pp. 815–824. ACM, New York, USA (2008)

22. Paliwal, A.V., Shafiq, B., Vaidya, J., Xiong, H., Adam, N.: Semantics-based automated service discovery. IEEE Trans. Serv. Comput. 5(2), 260–275 (2012)

23. Quinlan, J.R.: Induction of decision trees. Mach. Learn. 1(1), 81–106 (1986)

24. Silva, R., Zhang, J., Shanahan, J.G.: Probabilistic workflow mining. In: Proceedings of the Eleventh ACM SIGKDD International Conference on Knowledge Discovery in Data Mining, KDD 2005, pp. 275–284. ACM, New York, USA (2005)

25. Turban, E., Lee, J.K., King, D., Liang, T.P., Turban, D.: Electronic Commerce 2010. Prentice Hall Press, Upper Saddle River (2009)

26. Van der Aalst, W., Weijters, T., Maruster, L.: Workflow mining: discovering process models from event logs. IEEE Trans. Knowl. Data Eng. 16(9), 1128–1142 (2004)

27. van der Aalst, W.M.P., Pesic, M., Song, M.: Beyond process mining: from the past to present and future. In: Pernici, B. (ed.) CAiSE 2010. LNCS, vol. 6051, pp. 38–52. Springer, Heidelberg (2010)

28. Wen, L., Wang, J., Aalst, W., Huang, B., Sun, J.: A novel approach for process mining based on event types. J. Intell. Inf. Syst. **32**, 163–190 (2009)
29. Yu, T., Zhang, Y., Lin, K.-J.: Efficient algorithms for web services selection with end-to-end QoS constraints. ACM Trans. Web (TWEB) **1**(1), 6 (2007)

Using OWL Reasoning for Evaluating XACML Policies

Fabio Marfia[1(✉)], Mario Arrigoni Neri[2], Filippo Pellegrini[1],
and Marco Colombetti[1]

[1] DEIB Department of Information, Electronics and Bioengineering,
Politecnico di Milano, Via Ponzio 34/5, Milano, Italy
{fabio.marfia,marco.colombetti}@polimi.it,
filippo1.pellegrini@mail.polimi.it
[2] Department of Management, Information and Production Engineering,
University of Bergamo, Viale Marconi 5, Dalmine, Italy
mario.arrigonineri@unibg.it

Abstract. We present an approach for evaluating XACML policies
using OWL technologies and DL reasoning. We explain how policies
can be mapped to an OWL axiomatization, and how it is possible to
generate answers to access requests using standard DL reasoning tools,
all of that in the context of a complete XACML-compliant framework.
Our model represents a substratum for policies presenting an expressivity that can not be captured by actual XACML engines. Furthermore,
advanced Access Control functionalities, as Policy Harmonization and
Policy Explanation, can be implemented with the use of the present
model.

Keywords: Access control · Policy languages · Description logics ·
Reasoning

1 Introduction

As data engineers decided to create application-independent logical mechanisms
of data storage in the '60s, and first database systems became available, the
chance of modeling logically-independent policy management systems has been
considered in the last decade.

As a matter of facts, an increasing number of distributed applications have
been meeting complex problems in managing distribution and access authoriza-
tions of contents in the last years (see, e.g., Ardagna et al. [1]). Description
and enforcement of policies can become a very complex task in large systems.
An independent Policy Management architecture represents a scalable and reusable environment for:

- Formally specifying policies (Policy Editing and Storing);
- Automatically asserting, according to the specified policies, whether an agent
  is authorized to commit an act, or not (Policy Evaluation, or Policy Decision);

© Springer International Publishing Switzerland 2016
M.S. Obaidat and P. Lorenz (Eds.): ICETE 2015, CCIS 585, pp. 343–363, 2016.
DOI: 10.1007/978-3-319-30222-5_16

- Automatically resolving conflicts between policies (Policy Harmonization);
- Generating human-readable explanations of the causes of a specific policy evaluation (Policy Explanation);
- Eventually enforce an agent to commit an act or perpetrate penalization acts against agents, as a response to policy violations (Policy Enforcement).

Different models are presented in literature, defining abstract frameworks and specific protocols for such tasks. While a large number of solutions have been modeled in the last years, the current *de facto* standard between Access Control models is represented by XACML [30].

XACML defines standard protocols for transmitting credentials, requesting resources, defining and storing access policies; together with the definition of a general security layer, made up of different and specialised software components [28]. Such a layer deals with the aforementioned tasks of allowing policy administrators to edit and store policies, handling conflicts between contradictory decrees, providing a ultimate response for access requests, together with an explanation of such a response eventually.

We present an implementation of an XACML-compliant framework in this paper, based on OWL and reasoning technologies. The expression and usage of deontic propositions is well known in literature (see, e.g., [7,13,21]). However, as far as we know, this is the first time they are applied with the specific aim of providing a solution for an XACML security layer, even if activities for formalizing XACML policies with Description Logics (DL) were done in the past, for Policy Harmonization purposes [12].

In parallel, there is to notice that different implementations of XACML-compliant frameworks have already been developed (e.g., Sun PDP [24], XEngine [31], SBA-XACML [15]). Again, we can notice that, as far as we know, this is the first time that OWL technology is used for implementing such a type of framework.

Description Logics allow the expression of complex and expressive policies as it is requested, we believe, from nowadays pluralistic scenarios. Moreover, OWL technology allows to store policies into complex knowledge bases that represent an interesting, alternative portrait of the normative state of a system, that can be read by agents in order to regulate their behaviour with the use of reasoning. Moreover, policy administrators can edit the normative status of the system in real-time, without revising any hard-coded software.

The main drawback of the present approach is represented by the fact that, relying many core functionalities on DL reasoning activities, requiring significant computational resources, performances are worse than every cited XACML engine's, as presented in Sect. 4. Therefore, an advancement in policy expressivity and framework functionalities is obtained with an increase of computational requirements, in respect to standard XACML engines.

Every policy example that is considered in this paper is taken from hospital unit use cases, representing a real-life scenario in which the wide policy expressivity allowed by the present work definitely represents an essential requirement for modeling data security and privacy.

The paper proceeds as follows: we present the components and the structure of the framework in Sect. 2. We explain how XACML policies are converted into a collection of DL axioms, and how policy decisions are generated in Sect. 3. Performances are evaluated in Sect. 4. Related work is presented in Sect. 5. Conclusion and future work are presented in Sect. 6.

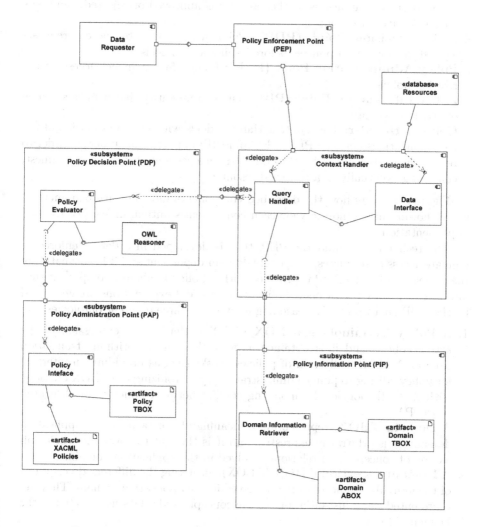

Fig. 1. OWL-based XACML Framework –Component Diagram.

2   An OWL-Based XACML Policy Framework

As described in [28], the XACML standard defines a general framework for receiving data requests and handling responses according to an arbitrarily large collection of policies, that are stored in a repository according to a standard XML-compliant model. The subsequent architectural components are defined for the framework, as described in [29]:

- **Policy Enforcement Point (PEP):** Point which intercepts user's access request to a resource, makes a decision request to the PDP to obtain the access decision (i.e. access to the resource is approved or rejected), and acts on the received decision;
- **Policy Decision Point (PDP):** Point which evaluates access requests against authorization policies before issuing access decisions;
- **Policy Administration Point (PAP):** Point which manages access authorization policies;
- **Policy Information Point (PIP):** The system entity that acts as a source of attribute values;
- **Context Handler:** The Context Handler deals with the coordination of the communications between PDP, PEP and PIP; in particular, it acts in order to return the output of the PDP to the PEP as a response for an access request, consisting eventually in a retrieved resource.

Figure 1 presents how the described components interact with one another, while showing in a synoptic view each component's outline in the OWL-based implementation.

The technology behind the PEP, that is developed in order to enforce or regulate access to resources, is strongly domain-dependent and it is not matter of the current work. The PDP is provided with a Policy Evaluator component that interfaces with a DL Reasoner. Policy decisions and explanations are generated by the PDP as a result of a reasoning activity on three different ontologies:

1. A **Policy Terminological BOX** (TBOX), that is the expression of the active policies and it is obtained as a result of an algorithmic translation from an XACML collection of policies. Tasks such as providing an interface for policy editing to policy administrators, synchronizing the TBOX ontology with XACML policies, harmonizing conflict between policies, are delegated to the PAP.
2. A **Domain TBOX**, representing a meaningful portrayal of the application domain. It is arbitrarily expressive and it is thought to cover the whole collection of concepts and relations involved in the application domain.
3. A **Domain Assertional BOX** (ABOX), gathering the different descriptions of the individuals and resources involved in the application domain. They are represented as an instantiations of the concepts and relations depicted in the Domain TBOX.

Both Domain TBOX and ABOX are stored and managed by the PIP.

3   Axiomatic Policies

As presented in Sect. 2, the PAP allows a policy administrator to edit and store policies in the form of an XACML collection. XACML represents the XML-compliant description of the policies in the environment, while the DL form of

Table 1. Policy archetypes.

ID	Reference	Description	Example
1	IBAC	A single subject is allowed to access to one or more resources	John Andrews can read Healthcare Assistant Documents
2	RBAC	A group of subjects is allowed to access to one or more resources	Medical Consultants can write a Medical Regulation Document
3	ABAC	Only subjects with specific attributes are allowed to access to one or more resources	Females can not read Andrology Documents
4	ABAC	Only subjects in a specific relation with another subject with specific attributes are allowed to access to one or more resources	A tutor of a person that is not of age can read document 305871
5	N/A	Only subjects in a specific relation with another subject are allowed to access to the resources that refer to the latter subject	A subject can read all the records of the ward he/she works in

the same collection is represented by an OWL TBOX. Policies are translated from the former representation to the latter automatically.

Kolovski et al. [12] present how to formalize XACML policies, using a more complex syntax than DL, defined DDL$^-$. That is done according to three types of XACML combining algorithms (see also [27]): *permit-overrides, deny-overrides, first-applicable*. We decided to reduce the expressivity of the XACML collection specifiable by the PAP, in respect to the aforementioned formalisation, as follows: the policy collection is reduced to a set of XACML rules, applying according to the policy combining algorithm *deny-overrides* only. The algorithm takes into consideration every rule, and, then, if both access deny and permit apply, an access deny is returned as a response. Whether nothing is found to be applied in the whole set of rules, a final general policy is defined in order to deny any access. Such approach allows to rely on standard DL technologies for reasoning without involving the DDL$^-$ formalisation, obtaining better performances and an easier policy representation. We believe that such simplification is a sufficient approach for satisfying the requirements of many real-life environments in which, for security reasons, every access is denied *ex-ante*, while policies are applied for modifying such default behaviour.

In order for the rules to be properly translated into an OWL TBOX, they can not be expressed arbitrarily: we have then identified five different policy archetypes, according to which the policies must be defined. The identified archetypes cover a wide range of expressiveness, in particular IBAC, RBAC and ABAC are fully covered by the model.

The five different policy archetypes are shown in Table 1. Each policy can be composed with others using AND or OR conjunctions in our model, as foreseen by XACML protocol, in order to generate complex rules. Furthermore, each policy can be positive or negative, allowing the policy administrator to permit or deny access to specific resources.

We describe the five policy archetypes, together with policy examples, in Sect. 3.1, while specifying how every type of policy is translated into a set of axioms. We describe how policies can be combined with AND or OR conjunctions in Sect. 3.2. We present the general algorithm for translating XACML policies in Sect. 3.3. We present how the PDP can obtain policy decisions from the generated axioms in Sect. 3.4. The syntax in which all DL axioms are presented in this Section is the Manchester OWL Syntax [11].

It is important to underline that complex DL structures (i.e. property chains, class definitions) can be present in the Domain TBOX, allowing the definition of policies based on composite relations in a concise manner. So, the reader must not be mislead in considering the whole expressive ability of the system by the simple archetypes shown. In principle, every single proposition in a policy could be obtained after a complex inference procedure, starting from the axioms expressed in the Domain TBOX and ABOX.

For example, we may want to define the tutor of an impatient I as herself, if she is of age; otherwise, her father and mother are her tutor. In order to express a policy allowing the tutor of an impatient to access to certain documents, we can simply define the subject of the policy as tutorOf I. That can be done as DL axioms are present in the Domain TBOX defining what a tutor is, according to the aforementioned definition.

3.1   Policy Archetypes

Type 1 - IBAC Simple Policy. The first policy archetype is the permission released or denied to a single subject, for the access to a resource or a group of resources. A sample XACML Type 1 rule is shown in Listing 1.1, allowing the subject John Andrews to read the group of resources HealthcareAssistantDocument. The policy is translated into a TBOX ontological policy with the subsequent procedure. First, an OWL class is generated, containing only the individual john_andrews:

```
Class:
    John_andrews_Class

equivalentTo:
    {john_andrews}
```

Then, the functional Identity Property identityOn_John_andrews_Class is defined for the generated class, representing the property of each member of the class pointing to the member itself:

```
Class:
    John_andrews_Class

equivalentTo:
    identityOn_John_andrews_Class some Self
```

The same is done for the group of resources, represented in the Domain TBOX ontology by the class HealthcareAssistantDocument:

```
Class:
    HealthcareAssistantDocument

equivalentTo:
    identityOn_HealthcareAssistantDocument some Self
```

Finally, the positive permission to be annotated, canRead, is defined as a super-property of a specific property chain, as follows:

```
objectProperty:
    identityOn_John_andrews_Class o
    topObjectProperty o
    identityOn_HealthcareAssistantDocument

SubPropertyOf:
    canRead
```

where topObjectProperty is the Universal Property, connecting each entity to each other in the ontology. The individual john_andrews is connected in this way with the property canRead to each resource belonging to the class HealthcareAssistantDocu- ment.

Type 2 - RBAC Policy. The second policy archetype is a permission released or denied to a group of subjects, for the access to a resource or a group of resources. A sample XACML Type 2 rule is shown in Listing 1.2, allow-ing every identity that is a MedicalAssistant to write a document that is a MedicalRegulationDocument. The policy is translated into a TBOX ontological policy wit subsequent procedure. First, the functional Identity Prop-erty identityOn_MedicalAssistant is defined, representing the property of each member of the class MedicalAssistant pointing to the member itself:

```
Class:
    MedicalAssistant

equivalentTo:
    identityOn_MedicalAssistant some Self
```

The same is done for the group of resources, represented in the Domain TBOX ontology by the class MedicalRegulationDocument:

```
Class:
    MedicalRegulationDocument

equivalentTo:
    identityOn_MedicalRegulationDocument
    some Self
```

Finally, the positive permission to be annotated, canWrite, is defined as a superproperty of a specific property chain, as follows:

```
objectProperty:
    identityOn_MedicalAssistant o
    topObjectProperty o
    identityOn_MedicalRegulationDocument

SubPropertyOf:
    canWrite
```

All the individuals belonging to the class MedicalAssistant are connected in this way with the property canWrite to each resource belonging to the class MedicalRegula- tionDocument.

Type 3 - ABAC Simple Policy. The third policy archetype represents the permission released or denied to a single subject characterized by one or more attributes, for the access to a resource or a group of resources. A sample XACML Type 3 rule is shown in Listing 1.3, allowing every subject with dataProperty hasGender equal to "F" to read the group of resources AndrologyDocument. The policy is translated into a TBOX ontological policy with the subsequent procedure. First, an OWL class is generated, containing only the individuals characterized by the aforementioned property:

```
Class:
    hasGender_F_Class

equivalentTo:
    hasGender value "F"
```

Then, the functional Identity Property identityOn_hasGender_F_Class is defined for the generated class, representing the property of each member of the class pointing to the member itself:

```
Class:
    hasGender_F_Class

equivalentTo:
    identityOn_hasGender_F_Class some Self
```

The same is done for the group of resources, represented in the Domain TBOX ontology by the class AndrologyDocument:

```
Class:
    AndrologyDocument

equivalentTo:
    identityOn_AndrologyDocument some Self
```

Finally, the negative permission to be annotated, `CanNotRead`, is defined as a superproperty of a specific property chain, as follows:

```
objectProperty:
    identityOn_hasGender_F_Class o
    topObjectProperty o
    identityOn_AndrologyDocument

SubPropertyOf:
    CanNotRead
```

All the individuals with the dataProperty `hasGender value "F"` are connected in this way with the property `CanNotRead` to each resource belonging to the class `Andrology- Document`.

Type 4 - ABAC Composite Policy. The fourth policy archetype differs from the simple ABAC policy as the permission is released or denied to a subject that is in relation with another subject characterized by one or more attributes, for the access to a resource or a group of resources. So, attributes are checked for the latter subject, while the permission is released or denied to the former. A sample XACML Type 4 rule is shown in Listing 1.4, allowing every subject that `isTutorOf` another subject with dataProperty `hasAge` lower than `18` to `read` the single document `document_305871`. The policy is translated into a TBOX ontological policy with the subsequent procedure. First, an OWL class is generated, containing only the individuals characterized by the aforementioned relation:

```
Class:
    isTutuorOf_subjectThat_hasAge_lowerThan18_Class

equivalentTo:
    isTutorOf some (hasAge some int[< 18])
```

Then, the functional Identity Property `identityOn_isTutuorOf_subject That_hasAge_lowerThan18_Class` is defined for the generated class, representing the property of each member of the class pointing to the member itself:

```
Class:
    isTutuorOf_subjectThat_hasAge_lowerThan18_Class

equivalentTo:
    isTutuorOf_subjectThat_hasAge_lowerThan18_Class some Self
```

Being the resource a single resource, an OWL class has to be generated for it:

```
Class:
    document_305871_Class

equivalentTo:
    {document_305871}
```

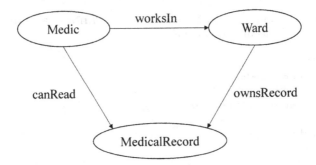

Fig. 2. Type 5 Policy example – the annotated permission is the side of a triangle in the ontological representation.

Then, the functional Identity Property `identityOn_document_305871_Class` is generated as well for the class:

```
Class:
    document_305871_Class

equivalentTo:
    identityOn_document_305871_Class
    some Self
```

Finally, the positive permission to be annotated, `CanRead`, is defined as a super-property of a specific property chain, as follows:

```
objectProperty:
    isTutuorOf_subjectThat_hasAge_lowerThan18_Class o
    topObjectProperty o
    identityOn_document_305871_Class

SubPropertyOf:
    CanRead
```

All the individuals with the objectProperty `isTutuorOf` pointing to an individual with the dataProperty `hasAge some int[< 18]` are connected in this way with the property `CanRead` to the document `document_305871`.

Type 5 - Triangular Relation Policy. The fifth policy archetype puts in relation the subject and the resource generating the permission only in the case that a common individual is in a specific connection with both of them. The added permission property represents the side of a triangle in such a case, where its vertexes are represented by the subject, the resource and the individual in common. A sample XACML Type 5 rule is shown in Listing 1.5 and in Fig. 2, allowing every subject to read every `MedicalRecord` of the ward in which he `worksIn`.

The OWL axiomatic expression of such a policy is characterized by a single property chain expressed as a subproperty of the involved permission property:

```
objectProperty:
    worksIn o
    ownsRecord

SubPropertyOf:
    canRead
```

3.2 Combining Policies

As stated, the presented policies can be also expressed together in a single XACML rule using AND or OR operators. As it can be understood, each archetype differs from the others for the way in which the subject requirements are expressed only, while the expression of permission and resources (a single one, or a group) are the same. So, a joined expression of two policies can be, for example, allowing a **Medic** that is **male** to read every AndrologyDocument. That is an expression of a Type 2 + Type 3 policy.

In case that many policies are joined with an OR conjunction, it is sufficient to translate each policy singularly into a TBOX policy.

In case that many policies are joined with an AND conjunction, the approach changes whether none, one or more Type 5 policy are present.

In case that no Type 5 policy is present, a new class is defined as an intersection of all the classes that identify the subject requirements for every policy. Then, a new Identity Property is created for the class and the positive or negative permission is assigned as a superproperty of the property chain between the created Identity Property, the topOjbectProperty and the Identity Property on the resources, as it is done for any of the Type 1 to 4 archetypes.

In case that one Type 5 policy is present, a new class is defined as an intersection of all the classes that identify the subject requirements for every policy of Type 1 to 4. Then, a new Identity Property is created for the class and the positive or negative permission is assigned as a superproperty of the property chain between the just created Identity Property and the two object properties involved in the Type 5 policy.

Expression of an axiomatic policy is not possible, using DL, in case of AND conjunction between more than one Type 5 policies. That because specification of double paths between the same identities is involved, and it is not possible, as explained in [8]. However, it is possible to address the issue defining a SWRL Rule [25].

As an example, we may want to allow a medic to read any medical record of the ward he worksIn, but only if it is about a patient he follows. That is an AND conjunction between two Type 5 policies. The subsequent SWRL rules could then be defined:

```
worsIn(x, z), ownsRecord(z, y), isMedicOf(x, a),
isAbout(y,a) -> canRead(x, a)
```

3.3 Axiomatic Policies Generation Algorithm

We present the general algorithm for translating the XACML collection of policies into an OWL TBOX, as Algorithm 3.1.

Algorithm 3.1: XACML_POLICIES_TO_DL_POLICIES.()

$\mathcal{O} = loaded\,ontology\,(Policy\,TBOX)$
$\mathcal{R} = set\,of\,rules$
for each $\langle rule : r \rangle \in \mathcal{R}$

$\mathbf{do}$ $\begin{cases} \mathcal{TS} = \emptyset \quad (set\,of\,subject\,identities\,for\,rule\,r) \\ \mathcal{S} = set\,of\,subjects\,of\,rule\,r \\ \textbf{for each } \langle subject : s \rangle \in \mathcal{S} \\ \quad \mathbf{do} \begin{cases} \mathcal{TM} = \emptyset \quad (set\,of\,subjectMatch\,identities \\ \qquad\qquad for\,subject\,s) \\ \mathcal{M} = set\,of\,subjectMatches\,of\,subject\,s \\ \textbf{for each } \langle subjectMatch : m \rangle \in \mathcal{M} \\ \quad \mathbf{do} \begin{cases} create\,objectProperty\,i\,as\,identity\,on\,m \\ \mathcal{TM} \leftarrow \mathcal{TM} \cup \{i\} \end{cases} \\ create\,objectProperty\,c\,as\,identity\,on\,the \\ \qquad conjunction\,of\,all\,elements\,in\,\mathcal{TM} \\ \mathcal{TS} \leftarrow \mathcal{TS} \cup \{c\} \end{cases} \\ \mathcal{TD} = \emptyset \quad (set\,of\,resource\,identities\,for\,rule\,r) \\ \mathcal{D} = set\,of\,resources\,of\,rule\,r \\ \textbf{for each } \langle resource : d \rangle \in \mathcal{D} \\ \quad \mathbf{do} \begin{cases} \mathcal{TM} = \emptyset \quad (set\,of\,resourceMatch\,identities \\ \qquad\qquad for\,resource\,d) \\ \mathcal{M} = set\,of\,resourceMatches\,of\,resource\,d \\ \textbf{for each } \langle resourceMatch : m \rangle \in \mathcal{M} \\ \quad \mathbf{do} \begin{cases} create\,objectProperty\,i\,as\,identity\,on\,m \\ \mathcal{TM} \leftarrow \mathcal{TM} \cup \{i\} \end{cases} \\ create\,objectProperty\,c\,as\,identity\,on\,the \\ \qquad conjunction\,of\,all\,elements\,in\,\mathcal{TM} \\ \mathcal{TD} \leftarrow \mathcal{TD} \cup \{c\} \end{cases} \\ a : objectProperty\,for\,the\,action\,specified\,in\,rule\,r \\ U : the\,Universal\,Property\,(topObjectProperty) \\ \textbf{for each } \langle objectProperty : ts \rangle \in \mathcal{TS} \\ \quad \mathbf{do} \begin{cases} \textbf{for each } \langle objectProperty : td \rangle \in \mathcal{TD} \\ \quad \mathbf{do} \begin{cases} axiom\,ax = \{ts \circ U \circ td \sqsubseteq a\} \\ \mathcal{O} \leftarrow \mathcal{O} \cup \{ax\} \end{cases} \end{cases} \end{cases}$

The procedure analyzes rule by rule and, for each rule, the approach for managing it can be divided into three main parts.

First, each subject s in the rule is analyzed: each subjectMatch m in s is taken into consideration for defining an OWL class, that corresponds to s. The definition of such class is obtained as the conjunction of all the subjectMatches in s.

Then, the same is done for each `resource` r: each `resourceMatch` in r is taken into consideration for defining a class, that corresponds to r. The definition of such class is obtained as the conjunction of all the `resourceMatches` in r.

The final part considers each (`subject, resource`) couple, and it generates a policy axiom ax defining the property chain between the identity on the `subject` class, the universal property U and the identity on the `resource` class as a subclass of the action permission a, as specified in the rule (it may be, e.g., `canRead`).

3.4   Policy Decision

Once the XACML policies are correctly translated into a Policy TBOX by the PAP, when the PDP receives an XACML access request from the Context Handler (more formally, an XACML *Context* [28]), it retrieves the Policy TBOX from the PAP and the Domain TBOX and ABOX from the PIP.

The Domain ABOX may include even thousands individuals in real environments, so, only individuals that can be useful for inferring the access permission are kept in the ABOX by the PIP before returning it. That is done by selecting a value for a $\sigma \in \mathbb{N}$ constant *ex-ante*, with $\sigma \geq 2$. Every individual in the Domain ABOX is discarded before returning it, except the requesting subject, the requested resource and every individual than can be reached from those two individuals in a maximum number of σ steps.

At the current state of the work, we are not able to calculate a suitable value for σ starting from the Domain TBOX automatically. Such value has to be set up manually by a Policy Administrator, considering the complexity of the axioms defined in the Domain TBOX. Indeed, a lower value of σ than what is needed can result in a loss of information contained in specific axioms, as, e.g., property chains defining chains of relationships with a number of steps $> \sigma$, or transitive properties. So, the value of σ must be chosen carefully by analyzing every axiom in the Domain TBOX, in order to avoid a loss of information that can take to unexpected responses. According to our experience, we expect a value $2 \leq \sigma \leq 4$ for the majority of the real environments, being that usual defined axioms allow values for σ between such constraints.

At this point, the task of Policy Decision reduces itself to the process of querying the set of the retrieved ontologies, for verifying whether they logically entail or not two specific theorems: the one stating that the subject *can do* the requested action on the requested resource (*positive permission theorem*), and the one stating that the subject *can not do* the requested action on the requested resource (*negative permission theorem*).

Whether the positive permission theorem is found only, a positive authorization is returned by the PDP to the Context Handler. A negative authorization is returned in any other case. As an example, we can assume that the permission request for `john_andrews` to `read` the document `document_305871` is received by the PDP from the Context Handler. Two DL queries [4] are sent, then, to the set of ontologies for retrieving the two subsequent theorems:

1. john_andrews canRead document_305871.
2. john_andrews canNotRead document_305871.

The response of the PDP is a positive authorization if theorem 1 is found only. Otherwise, the response is a negative authorization.

4   Performances

We developed a prototype framework using JAVA and OWL API [9], with Hermit 1.3.8 [20] as reasoning engine. The tests were done using a PC with an Intel Core 2 Duo 2.8 GHz processor, and 8 GB 800 MHz DDR2 as RAM. We set for every experiment $\sigma = 3$.

As it can be seen in Fig. 3a and b, axiomatic policies generation time is of the order of fractions of a second (e.g., 0.15 s with 1000 individuals and 75 policies), and it changes almost linearly in respect to the number of ABOX individuals, and exponentially in respect to the number of rules.

The number of ABOX individuals, as it can be seen in Fig. 3c, does not affect the Policy Decision time significantly. In fact, the time for identifying

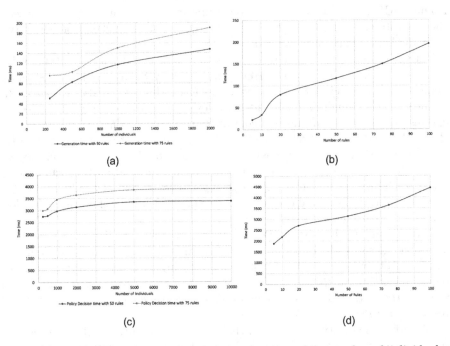

Fig. 3. (a) TBOX policies generation time as a function of the number of individuals, with 50 and 75 rules – (b) TBOX policies generation time as a function of the the number of rules, with 1000 individuals – (c) Policy Decision time as a function of the the number of individuals, with 50 and 75 rules – (d) Policy Decision time as a function of the the number of rules, with 2000 individuals.

useful individuals in the ABOX represents a small fraction of the total time, while the rest is used for the reasoning algorithms execution.

Figure 3d shows the Policy Decision time in function of the number of rules, with a 2000 individuals ABOX; e.g., the Policy Decision time with 75 rules is 3.65 s. As it can be noticed, response time starts to grow exponentially after 50 rules. It is reasonable to consider that an amount of policies of the order of dozens fits well for many real environments, so, such exponential growth does not seem to represent a major issue at the current state.

In fact, we believe that 75–100 is a realistic amount of policies for different real-life scenarios, e.g., a hospital unit. As it can be seen from Fig. 3d, a Policy Decision took about 4–5 s in such a case in our tests. That can not be considered a good performance for real-time environments. Anyway, it is reasonable to state that an optimized and compiled code, running on an advanced hardware can lower the Policy Decision time up to a performance that can be considered acceptable, as, e.g., 1 s or lower.

The Policy Decision performances of three different XACML policy engines are presented in [15]. They are SBA-XACML engine [15], XEngine [31] and Sun PDP [24]. Even with 400 rules, the Policy Decision time of every engine results under 0.1 s, while we present a Policy Decision time of 3.65 s for 75 rules with 2000 individuals. Our performances can be estimated in the order of 100x in time in respect to such standard policy engines. The estimation varies in respect to the specific engine and the number of rules.

5 Related Work

Kolovski et al. [12] use DDL$^-$ (a still-decidable extension of DL) for formalizing XACML policies. Given a set of policies, they convert their semantics into a knowledge base representation in order to apply tasks of policy harmonization. Their model foresee a wide range of XACML combining algorithms (*permit-overrides, deny-overrides, first-applicable*). However, their work does not focus on any model for storing policies, nor any way to return policy decisions to a user who requests data. They use as a reason for such a choice that nowadays computational resources are still not sufficient to provide real-time responses for policy decisions. We managed such a problem with an ABOX reduction procedure before running reasoning algorithms, as presented in Sect. 3.4.

Finin et al. [6] present a theoretical work for converting RBAC XACML policies into a DL representation. The first approach considers the roles as OWL classes, the second translates them into specific relationships that connect individuals. We adopted the first method in our model, describing roles as OWL classes in our Domain TBOX. The second representation method was adopted by Ferrini et al. [5] instead, for modeling RBAC access control within XACML. We differ from both presented works in the fact that we support a wider range of expressivity in the policies (ABAC, triangular relations). Furthermore, we have at our disposal a Domain TBOX in which more axioms can be specified for a further enlargement in the policies expressivity. Also, they use reasoning for inferring roles and separation of duties only, with no support for Policy Decision.

Ardagna et al. [2] implemented an extension of the XACML framework for adding credential-based management and privacy control. Their work is developed in the context of the PrimeLife European project [18]. They implemented a Policy Decision engine in the context of a complete solution for safe access control, with no logical approach. The framework seems not to be an appropriate substratum for managing complex tasks as Policy Harmonization and Policy Explanation. Anyway, their hard-coded approach results in better performances.

Paraboschi and Arrigoni Neri [16] present a framework for the definition of policies using OWL, in the context of the PoSecCo European project [17]. The PoSecCo project objectives are to define new tools and approaches for a service that is able to meet security requirements of a generic environment. Policies can be defined at different levels of abstraction. Paraboschi and Arrigoni Neri propose a solution for the definition of policies in the context of a specific layer that is called IT Policy Level. Policy Harmonization techniques using DL are presented and analyzed. No Policy Decision algorithm is defined.

Mourad and Jebbaoui [15] present SBA-XACML, an XACML implementation for generating efficient Policy Decisions for web services. Their aim is to obtain better performances than standard XACML engines' for real-time decision processes. Their main reference for the comparison of the results is the XACML PDP implementation by SUN [24]. They use set-based algebra for translating and processing XACML policies. Again, while their approach results in efficient performances, complex semantic tasks seem not to be manageable directly.

Between non-XACML-related security frameworks that make use of OWL or reasoning, there are KAoS [26] and OWL-POLAR [19].

KAoS is collection of user-friendly tools for editing and managing policies. Between the tools, there is a user interface for editing policies, Policy Decision services, Policy Enforcement services for different usage contexts. While their approach seems to represent an efficient background for complex semantic tasks, their framework is not directly compatible with the XACML standard. Moreover, policies are modeled in KAoS as OWL individuals and not OWL TBOX axioms. Such a choice lowers the expressivity of the policies themselves that can be captured by DL reasoners definitely.

OWL-POLAR is a framework for the general expression of permissions, prohibitions and obligations using OWL. Their Policy Decision approach consists in a set of SPARQL queries [23] for a collection of defined axioms. Policy Harmonization algorithms are provided. Again, while their semantic approach can be a valid background for complex tasks, their framework is not directly compatible with the XACML standard. Moreover, the use of reasoning is barely considered as a possibility in the OWL-POLAR context, while every functionality seems to be managed with no use of reasoning actually.

6   Conclusion and Future Work

We presented an implementation of an XACML framework in this paper, based on OWL and reasoning technologies. While policy conversion to DL is executed within a reasonable time, Policy Decision performances are worse than any known XACML engine. Anyway, we believe that our solution can be a reasonable alternative in a real-life scenario to ordinary XACML engines for the subsequent reasons:

- An optimized code and an efficient hardware can support a usable PDP engine for real-time interactions in real-life environments;
- DL expressiveness can be used to define policies which complexity can not be caught by ordinary XACML engines;
- External applications can generate interesting portrays of the regulation state by accessing to the framework semantics for an end-user;
- Automatic agents may regulate their behaviour by reading and reasoning on provided policies;
- Advanced complex tasks can be exploited that are almost impossible for ordinary XACML frameworks; as Policy Explanation, or Policy Harmonization.

Improvements can be done in the future in the Policy TBOX expressiveness, in order to support more XACML policy combining algorithms (e.g., *permit-overrides, first-applicable*), as it is done by Kolovski et al. [12]. Also, considering temporal constraints for the policies can represent a further advance (see, e.g., [3]). Also, researches can be done in order to use reasoning for calculating a suitable value for the constant σ in order to avoid the manual input of such value by a Policy Administrator.

Moreover, as stated, a Policy Explanation can be provided together with the response, using OWL Justification technology [10], as already done by Marfia [14]. OWL Justification is an OWL tool for Pellet reasoner [22] that is able to identify the minimum set of starting axioms that is needed to entail a specific theorem. Considering as final theorems the two ones that define the possibility for the requesting individual to act or not to act on the requested resource, which entailment is used to obtain a Policy Decision (see Sect. 3.4), OWL justification can be used in order to infer the minimum set of axioms that entail such theorems. It is obvious that, between all the starting axioms, policies that are involved in the decision are present, as well as other Domain TBOX axioms that have to be considered in formulating an explanation for the response. Such starting axioms can be labeled with a verbose description in the ontology using OWL annotations, and a set of ordered labels can be returned to the user as a decision explanation.

Finally, a Policy Harmonization service based on the OWL policy representation can be developed for the framework, accordingly to what presented in [16] and [12]. Special reasoning techniques are needed, in fact, for resolving conflicts between contradictory decrees, because conflicts can emerge from the exploration of possible worlds in which specific users ask for specific resources under specific states, and contradictory conclusions can emerge from starting axioms.

Appendix

We present the complete XACML code in this appendix for the example policies mentioned in Sect. 3. It is shown in Listings from 1.1 to 1.5.

Listing 1.1. Example Type 1 policy –XACML specification.

```
<!-- Rule to let john_andrews read healthCareAssistantDocument -->
<Rule RuleId="Rule1" Effect="Permit">
  <Target>
    <Subjects>
      <Subject>
        <SubjectMatch MatchId="urn:polimi:names:dbsp:1:function:ontology-id-equal">
          <AttributeValue DataType="urn:polimi:names:dbsp:1:data-type:ontology-id">
            john_andrews
          </AttributeValue>
          <SubjectAttributeDesignator AttributeId="urn:polimi:names:dbsp:1:attribute:id" MustBePresent="true"
              DataType="urn:polimi:names:dbsp:1:data-type:ontology-id"/>
        </SubjectMatch>
      </Subject>
    </Subjects>

    <Resources>
      <Resource>
        <ResourceMatch MatchId="urn:polimi:names:dbsp:1:function:ontology-id-equal">
          <AttributeValue DataType="urn:polimi:names:dbsp:1:data-type:ontology-id">
            healthcareAssistantDocument
          </AttributeValue>
          <ResourceAttributeDesignator AttributeId="urn:polimi:names:dbsp:1:attribute:class"
              DataType="urn:polimi:names:dbsp:1:data-type:ontology-id"/>
        </ResourceMatch>
      </Resource>
    </Resources>

    <Actions>
      <Action>
        <ActionMatch MatchId="urn:polimi:names:dbsp:1:function:ontology-id-equal">
          <AttributeValue DataType="urn:polimi:names:dbsp:1:data-type:ontology-id">read</AttributeValue>
          <ActionAttributeDesignator DataType="urn:polimi:names:dbsp:1:data-type:ontology-id"
              AttributeId="urn:polimi:names:dbsp:1:attribute:id" />
        </ActionMatch>
      </Action>
    </Actions>
  </Target>
</Rule>
```

Listing 1.2. Example Type 2 policy –XACML specification.

```
<!-- Rule to let medicalConsultant write medicalRegulationDocument -->
<Rule RuleId="Rule2" Effect="Permit">

  <Target>
    <Subjects>
      <Subject>
        <SubjectMatch MatchId="urn:polimi:names:dbsp:1:function:ontology-id-equal">
          <AttributeValue DataType="urn:polimi:names:dbsp:1:data-type:ontology-id">
            medicalConsultant
          </AttributeValue>
          <SubjectAttributeDesignator AttributeId="urn:polimi:names:dbsp:1:attribute:class" MustBePresent="true"
              DataType="urn:polimi:names:dbsp:1:data-type:ontology-id"/>
        </SubjectMatch>
      </Subject>
    </Subjects>

    <Resources>
      <Resource>
        <ResourceMatch MatchId="urn:polimi:names:dbsp:1:function:ontology-id-equal">
          <AttributeValue DataType="urn:polimi:names:dbsp:1:data-type:ontology-id">
            medicalRegulationDocument
          </AttributeValue>
          <ResourceAttributeDesignator AttributeId="urn:polimi:names:dbsp:1:attribute:class"
              DataType="urn:polimi:names:dbsp:1:data-type:ontology-id"/>
        </ResourceMatch>
      </Resource>
    </Resources>

    <Actions>
      <Action>
        <ActionMatch MatchId="urn:polimi:names:dbsp:1:function:ontology-id-equal">
          <AttributeValue DataType="urn:polimi:names:dbsp:1:data-type:ontology-id">write</AttributeValue>
          <ActionAttributeDesignator DataType="urn:polimi:names:dbsp:1:data-type:ontology-id"
              AttributeId="urn:polimi:names:dbsp:1:attribute:id" />
        </ActionMatch>
      </Action>
    </Actions>
  </Target>

</Rule>
```

Listing 1.3. Example Type 3 policy –XACML specification.

```
<!—— Rule to deny female access for reading andrology documents ——>
<Rule RuleId="Rule3" Effect="Deny">
  <Target>
    <Subjects>
      <Subject>
        <SubjectMatch MatchId="urn:oasis:names:tc:xacml:1.0:function:string—equal">
          <AttributeValue DataType="http://www.w3.org/2001/XMLSchema#string">F</AttributeValue>
          <SubjectAttributeDesignator AttributeId="urn:polimi:names:dbsp:1:attribute:dataProperty:hasGender"
                                MustBePresent="true" DataType="http://www.w3.org/2001/XMLSchema#string"/>
        </SubjectMatch>
      </Subject>
    </Subjects>

    <Resources>
      <Resource>
        <ResourceMatch MatchId="urn:polimi:names:dbsp:1:function:ontology—id—equal">
          <AttributeValue DataType="http://www.w3.org/2001/XMLSchema#string">
            AndrologyDocument
          </AttributeValue>
          <ResourceAttributeDesignator AttributeId="urn:polimi:names:dbsp:1:attribute:class"
                        DataType="urn:polimi:names:dbsp:1:data—type:ontology—id"/>
        </ResourceMatch>
      </Resource>
    </Resources>

    <Actions>
      <Action>
        <ActionMatch MatchId="urn:polimi:names:dbsp:1:function:ontology—id—equal">
          <AttributeValue DataType="http://www.w3.org/2001/XMLSchema#string">read</AttributeValue>
          <ActionAttributeDesignator DataType="urn:polimi:names:dbsp:1:data—type:ontology—id"
                        AttributeId="urn:polimi:names:dbsp:1:attribute:id" />
        </ActionMatch>
      </Action>
    </Actions>
  </Target>
</Rule>
```

Listing 1.4. Example Type 4 policy –XACML specification.

```
<!—— Rule to let a tutor of a person with less than 18 years read document_305871 ——>
<Rule RuleId="Rule4" Effect="Permit">
  <Target>
    <Subjects>
      <Subject>
        <SubjectMatch MatchId="urn:oasis:names:tc:xacml:1.0:function:lower—than">
          <AttributeValue DataType="http://www.w3.org/2001/XMLSchema#integer">18</AttributeValue>
          <SubjectAttributeSelector Path="urn:polimi:names:dbsp:1:attribute:objectProperty:isTutor
          Of/urn:polimi:names:dbsp:1:attribute:dataProperty:hasAge" MustBePresent="true"
                        DataType="http://www.w3.org/2001/XMLSchema#integer" />
        </SubjectMatch>
      </Subject>
    </Subjects>

    <Resources>
      <Resource>
        <ResourceMatch MatchId="urn:polimi:names:dbsp:1:function:ontology—id—equal">
          <AttributeValue DataType="http://www.w3.org/2001/XMLSchema#string">
            document_305871
          </AttributeValue>
          <ResourceAttributeDesignator AttributeId="urn:polimi:names:dbsp:1:attribute:id"
                        DataType="urn:polimi:names:dbsp:1:data—type:ontology—id"/>
        </ResourceMatch>
      </Resource>
    </Resources>

    <Actions>
      <Action>
        <ActionMatch MatchId="urn:polimi:names:dbsp:1:function:ontology—id—equal">
          <AttributeValue DataType="http://www.w3.org/2001/XMLSchema#string">read</AttributeValue>
          <ActionAttributeDesignator DataType="urn:polimi:names:dbsp:1:data—type:ontology—id"
                        AttributeId="urn:polimi:names:dbsp:1:attribute:id" />
        </ActionMatch>
      </Action>
    </Actions>
  </Target>
</Rule>
```

Listing 1.5. Example Type 5 policy –XACML specification.

```
<!— Rule to let a subject read all the records of the ward he/she works in —>
<Rule RuleId="Rule5" Effect="Permit">

  <Target>
    <Subjects>
      <Subject>
        <SubjectMatch MatchId="urn:polimi:names:dbsp:1:function:id—from—category—with—ontology—id—equal">
          <AttributeValue DataType="urn:polimi:names:dbsp:1:data—type:category">Resource</AttributeValue>
          <SubjectAttributeSelector Path="urn:polimi:names:dbsp:1:attribute:objectProperty:worksIn/urn:polimi:
          names:dbsp:1:attribute:objectProperty:ownsRecord" MustBePresent="true"
                               DataType="urn:polimi:names:dbsp:1:data—type:ontology—id" />
        </SubjectMatch>
      </Subject>
    </Subjects>

    <Actions>
      <Action>
        <ActionMatch MatchId="urn:polimi:names:dbsp:1:function:ontology—id—equal">
          <AttributeValue DataType="urn:polimi:names:dbsp:1:data—type:ontology—id">read</AttributeValue>
          <ActionAttributeDesignator DataType="urn:polimi:names:dbsp:1:data—type:ontology—id"
                               AttributeId="urn:polimi:names:dbsp:1:attribute:id" />
        </ActionMatch>
      </Action>
    </Actions>
  </Target>
</Rule>
```

References

1. Ardagna, C., Di Vimercati, S.D.C., Neven, G., Paraboschi, S., Pedrini, E., Preiss, F.-S., Samarati, P., Verdicchio, M.: Advances in access control policies. In: Camenisch, J., Fischer-Hübner, S., Rannenberg, K. (eds.) Privacy and Identity Management for Life, pp. 327–341. Springer, Heidelberg (2011)

2. Ardagna, C., di Vimercati, S.D.C., Paraboschi, S., Pedrini, E., Samarati, P.: An XACML-based privacy-centered access control system. In: Proceedings of the 1st ACM Workshop on Information Security Governance, WISG, Chicago, Illinois, USA, November 2009

3. Batsakis, S., Stravoskoufos, K., Petrakis, E.G.M.: Temporal reasoning for supporting temporal queries in OWL 2.0. In: König, A., Dengel, A., Hinkelmann, K., Kise, K., Howlett, R.J., Jain, L.C. (eds.) KES 2011, Part I. LNCS, vol. 6881, pp. 558–567. Springer, Heidelberg (2011)

4. DL Query guide - Protégé DLQueryTab (2008). http://protegewiki.stanford.edu/wiki/DLQueryTab

5. Ferrini, R., Bertino, E.: Supporting RBAC with XACML+OWL. In: Proceedings of the 14th ACM Symposium on Access Control Models and Technologies, SACMAT 2009, pp. 145–154, New York, NY, USA. ACM (2009)

6. Finin, T., Joshi, A., Kagal, L., Niu, J., Sandhu, R., Winsborough, W.H., Thuraisingham, B.: ROWLBAC - representing role based access control in OWL. In: Proceedings of the 13th Symposium on Access control Models and Technologies, Estes Park, Colorado, USA. ACM Press, June 2008

7. Fornara, N., Colombetti, M.: Ontology and time evolution of obligations and prohibitions using semantic web technology. In: Baldoni, M., Bentahar, J., van Riemsdijk, M.B., Lloyd, J. (eds.) DALT 2009. LNCS, vol. 5948, pp. 101–118. Springer, Heidelberg (2010)

8. Hitzler, P., Krötzsch, M., Rudolph, S.: Foundations of Semantic Web Technologies. Chapman & Hall/CRC, Boca raton (2009)

9. Horridge, M., Bechhofer, S.: The OWL API: a Java API for OWL ontologies. Semant. Web **2**(1), 11–21 (2011)

10. Horridge, M., Parsia, B., Sattler, U.: Laconic and precise justifications in OWL. In: Sheth, A.P., Staab, S., Dean, M., Paolucci, M., Maynard, D., Finin, T., Thirunarayan, K. (eds.) ISWC 2008. LNCS, vol. 5318, pp. 323–338. Springer, Heidelberg (2008)

11. Horridge, M., Patel-schneider, P.F.: Manchester syntax for OWL 1.1. In: OWLED 2008, 4th International Workshop OWL: Experiences and Directions Live Extraction 1223 (2008)
12. Kolovski, V., Hendler, J., Parsia, B.: Analyzing web access control policies. In: Proceedings of the 16th International Conference on World Wide Web, WWW 2007, pp. 677–686, New York, NY, USA. ACM (2007)
13. López, F.L.Y., Luck, M., D'Inverno, M.: A normative framework for agent-based systems. Comput. Math. Organ. Theory 12(2–3), 227–250 (2006)
14. Marfia, F.: Using abductive and inductive inference to generate policy explanations. In: Obaidat, M., Holzinger, A., Samarati, P. (eds.) Proceedings of International Conference on Security and Cryptography (SECRYpPT). SciTePress (2014)
15. Mourad, A., Jebbaoui, H.: SBA-XACML: set-based approach providing efficient policy decision process for accessing web services. Expert Syst. Appl. 42(1), 165–178 (2015)
16. Paraboschi, S., Neri, M.A., Mutti, S., Psaila, G., Salvaneschi, P., Verdicchio, M., Basile, A.: D2.4 - Policy Harmonization and Reasoning, PoSecCo WP2, Business and IT level policies (2013)
17. PoSecCo - Policy and Security Configuration Management (2010). http://www.posecco.eu/
18. PrimeLife - Bringing sustainable privacy and identity management to future networks and services (2008). http://primelife.ercim.eu/
19. Sensoy, M., Norman, T.J., Vasconcelos, W.W., Sycara, K.: OWL-POLAR: a framework for semantic policy representation and reasoning. Web Semant. 12–13, 148–160 (2012)
20. Shearer, R., Motik, B., Horrocks, I.: HermiT.: a highly-efficient OWL reasoner. In: Dolbear, C., Ruttenberg, A., Sattler, U. (eds.) OWLED, CEUR Workshop Proceedings, vol. 432. CEUR-WS.org (2008)
21. Singh, M.P.: An ontology for commitments in multiagent systems: toward a unification of normative concepts. Artif. Intell. Law 7, 97–113 (1998)
22. Sirin, E., Parsia, B.: SPARQL-DL: SPARQL Query for OWL-DL. In: 3rd OWL Experiences and Directions Workshop (OWLED 2007) (2007)
23. SPARQL Query Language for RDF (2008). http://www.w3.org/TR/rdf-sparql-query/
24. Sun's XACML Implementation (2004). http://sunxacml.sourceforge.net/
25. SWRL: A Semantic Web Rule Language Combining OWL and RuleML (2004). http://www.w3.org/Submission/SWRL/
26. Uszok, A., Bradshaw, J.M.: Demonstrating selected W3C policy languages interest group use cases using the KAoS policy services framework. In: POLICY, pp. 233–234. IEEE Computer Society (2008)
27. OASIS XACML Version 3.0 Specification, Combining algorithms, p. 5 (2013). http://docs.oasis-open.org/xacml/3.0/xacml-3.0-core-spec-cs-01-en.pdf
28. OASIS XACML Version 3.0 Specification, Data-flow model, pp. 19–20 (2013). http://docs.oasis-open.org/xacml/3.0/xacml-3.0-core-spec-cs-01-en.pdf
29. RFC2904 - AAA Authorization Framework Memo (2000). http://tools.ietf.org/html/rfc2904
30. OASIS eXtensible Access Control Markup Language (XACML) (2013). https://www.oasis-open.org/committees/xacml/
31. XEngine: A Fast and Scalable XACML Policy Evaluation Engine (2008). http://xacmlpdp.sourceforge.net/

Partial Key Exposure Attacks on RSA with Exponent Blinding

Stelvio Cimato[1], Silvia Mella[1(✉)], and Ruggero Susella[2]

[1] Università degli Studi di Milano, Milano, Italy
{stelvio.cimato,silvia.mella}@unimi.it
[2] STMicroelectronics, Agrate Brianza, Italy
ruggero.susella@st.com

Abstract. Partial key exposure attacks, introduced by Boneh, Durfee and Frankel in 1998, aim at retrieving an RSA private key when a fraction of its bits is known. These attacks are of particular interest in the context of side-channel attacks, where the attacker can retrieve bits of the key exploiting leakages in the implementation. In this work we analyze the effectiveness of partial key exposure when a countermeasure for side-channel attacks is adopted. In particular, we consider the exponent blinding technique, which consists in randomizing the private exponent at each execution. We address our analysis to both RSA and CRT-RSA, providing theoretical proofs and experimental results.

Keywords: RSA · Partial key exposure · Coppersmith's method · Exponent blinding · Horizontal attack

1 Introduction

Partial key exposure attacks, introduced by Boneh et al. in 1998 [7], are attacks that rely on some knowledge about the private key, for example some portion of the bits, that can be used to fully recover the key itself and break the system. The high interest for this family of attacks is motivated by the fact that, in practice, some implementations may leak some bits of the private key, as in the case of side channel attacks.

In these attacks, introduced in 1996 by Paul Kocher [14], some information can be extracted by examining the RSA computation (such as power consumption, electromagnetic emission, acoustic emission, etc.), and can be used to recover the secret key. Most side channel attacks leverage on combining the side-channel leakages, i.e. traces, of several executions of the cryptographic algorithm with same secret but different input. The first attack of this family is Differential Power Analysis (DPA) [16]. Its main feature is the ability to significantly reduce the random noise, by averaging a large amount of traces, compared to Simple Power Analysis (SPA), where only one trace is used.

In general, side channel attacks allow the adversary to gain information about some number of either consecutive most significant bits (MSBs) or least significant bits (LSBs) of the private exponent. On the basis on this knowledge,

© Springer International Publishing Switzerland 2016
M.S. Obaidat and P. Lorenz (Eds.): ICETE 2015, CCIS 585, pp. 364–385, 2016.
DOI: 10.1007/978-3-319-30222-5_17

Boneh et al. show that, for the common cases where the factorization of the public exponent is known, the given partial information on the private exponent can be used to obtain partial information on a prime factor of the modulus. In turn, those attacks rely on Coppersmith's method to find small solutions of univariate modular polynomials. This method has been presented in [4], and extended to bivariate equations, enabling the factorization of an RSA modulus given half of the bits of one of its prime factors [11].

The importance of partial key exposure attacks is given also by the consideration that in many cases some countermeasures can be adopted by implementers to thwart side channel attack and enable the attacker to obtain information on just a part of the secret exponent. Indeed, a common countermeasure used for RSA is exponent blinding, originally introduced in [14] but often attributed to [15]. This technique consists of adding a random multiple of $\phi(N)$ to the RSA private exponent at each execution. This countermeasure has the feature to change the private exponent at each computation, thus not permitting the use of multiple traces, as required for DPA. This results in the need of using a single trace to discover the secret key. A method for this was originally proposed in [17], for a particular exponentiation algorithm, and generalized for regular exponentiation algorithms in [18] and named horizontal attack.

The question as to whether partial key exposure could be applied in this setting was answered in [6]. The authors presented two techniques to recover the full exponent, knowing enough MSBs or LSBs portions of it, leaving the open question as up to which extent it is possible to apply partial key exposure when exponent blinding is applied to the Chinese Remainder Theorem variant of RSA (CRT-RSA) [21].

Our Contribution. Our contribution consists of new methods for partial key exposure when exponent blinding is used, improving the results of [6] for common RSA settings and providing novel attacks for the CRT variant. Specifically, in this work, we:

- provide a more efficient technique for the LSBs attack, requiring to reduce a lattice basis of lower dimension;
- reduce the number of required bits for the MSBs attack and make it to not rely on a common heuristic assumption;
- present novel attacks against CRT-RSA implementations that make use of exponent blinding; This particular case has never been analyzed before;
- provide experimental results using moduli of 2048 or 3072-bit length.

This work is organized as follows. At first we present some previous results on partial key exposure attacks in Sect. 2. In Sect. 3 we recall some basic information about RSA and the parameter choices commonly made for real applications. In Sect. 4 we give a brief introduction about lattices and Coppersmith's method. In Sect. 5 we present two partial key exposure attacks on RSA with exponent blinding and in Sect. 6 on CRT-RSA with exponent blinding. Experimental results are then provided in Sect. 7.

2 Related Works

In their work, Boneh, Durfee and Frankel presented several attacks on RSA based on the knowledge of the least significant bits of the private exponent or of the most significant bits of the private exponent [7]. When the LSBs are known they show that a quarter of the private exponent is sufficient to break the system if the public exponent is relatively small, i.e. smaller than $N^{\frac{1}{4}}$. When the MSBs are known, the number of bits that the adversary needs to know depends on his knowledge of e. Supposing that $N^{\frac{1}{4}} < e < N^{\frac{1}{2}}$ and its factorization is known, than at most half of the bits of d are required. The smaller e is, the smaller the number of required bits is. Indeed, when e is close to $N^{\frac{1}{4}}$ then only a quarter of bits of d are sufficient to mount the attack. When the factorization for e is not known and $e < N^{\frac{1}{2}}$, at least half of the bits of d are required. Unlike the previous case, the smaller e is, the bigger number of required bits is.

In 2003, Blömer and May presented partial key exposure attacks considering larger values of the public exponent e. They show that for $N^{\frac{1}{2}} < e < N^{\frac{3}{4}}$ the number of MSBs of d required to mount the attack increases as e grows. For instance, when e is close to $N^{\frac{1}{2}}$ then half of the bits of d suffice to mount the attack, whereas for e close to $N^{\frac{2}{3}}$ the fraction of required bits is bigger than 80 %. When LSBs of the private exponent are known, they provide results for all exponents $e < N^{\frac{7}{8}}$. When e is close to $N^{\frac{1}{2}}$, about 90 % of the bits are required, whereas when e is close to $N^{\frac{7}{8}}$, almost all the bits must be known. In this work, Blömer and May provide also results for CRT-RSA. In the case of known LSBs, for low public exponents e (i.e. $e = poly(\log N)$), half of the LSBs of d_p suffice to mount the attack. In the case of known MSBs for $e < N^{\frac{1}{4}}$ again only half of the MSBs of d_p are required.

In [8], Lu et. al. extended the attack for CRT-RSA up to $e < N^{\frac{3}{8}}$ and d_p of full-size. The bigger e is, the bigger the number of required bits of d_p is, for both the MSBs and LSBs cases.

In [3], Ernst et. al. provided new results in the case e or d is full-size and the other is relatively small. For instance, when d is close to $N^{\frac{1}{3}}$ then a quarter of its MSBs or of its LSBs are sufficient to mount the attack.

All these works consider the private exponent d smaller than N. In 2012, Joye and Lepoint [6] analyzed RSA implementations using larger exponents d, which is the scenario of exponent blinding. We will give more details about their results in the next sections when comparing our approach with their one.

3 RSA Applications

In literature, Coppersmith's method has been applied with very different, and unusual, RSA parameters. For example the case where e is of the same bitsize of N has been analyzed in [3]. In this work we preferred to focus our analysis on more common RSA settings. Before presenting them, we briefly introduce the RSA algorithm and its variant CRT-RSA.

3.1 RSA

A pair of private and public key for RSA is generated as follows.

At first, two large distinct primes p and q are chosen at random. Then the modulus $N = p \cdot q$ is defined together with $\phi(N) = (p-1)(q-1)$, where ϕ denotes the Euler's totient function. Then an integer e is chosen such that $1 < e < \phi(N)$ and $\gcd(e, \phi(N)) = 1$ (i.e., e and $\phi(N)$ are coprime). Finally the multiplicative inverse of e modulo $\phi(N)$, denoted by d, is computed. Namely, e and d satisfy

$$ed \equiv 1 \bmod N . \tag{1}$$

The pair (N, e) is released as the public key, whereas d is the private key. Notice that also p, q and $\phi(N)$ are kept private, otherwise they can be used to calculate d.

To encrypt a message, it is first turned into an integer m, such that $0 \leq m < N$ and $\gcd(m, N) = 1$ and then a modular exponentiation by e is performed. Namely, the ciphertext is computed as $c = m^e \pmod{N}$. To decrypt the ciphertext c, an exponentiation by d is performed: $m = c^e \pmod{N}$.

The correctness of the algorithm relies on the Euler's theorem, which states that for each a that is coprime with N the equation $a^{\phi(N)} \equiv 1 \bmod sN$ holds. Thus, the following equalities show that m is correctly retrieved:

$$m^{ed} \equiv m^{1+k\phi(N)} \equiv m \left(m^{\phi(N)} \right)^k \equiv m(1)^k \equiv m \bmod N . \tag{2}$$

The first equality holds since $ed \equiv 1 \bmod N$, that implies $ed = 1 + k\phi(N)$ for some integer k. By working separately modulo p and modulo q and then combing the results through the Chinese Remainder Theorem [21] it is possible to show that encryption and decryption works even when $\gcd(m, N) \neq 1$.

3.2 CRT-RSA

In order to speed up the exponentiation computation, some RSA implementations make use of a technique based on the Chinese Remainder Theorem (CRT)[21]. In particular, one can use exponents

$$d_p = d \bmod (p-1) \quad \text{and} \quad d_q = d \bmod (q-1)$$

to compute

$$m_1 = c^{d_p} \bmod p \quad \text{and} \quad m_2 = c^{d_q} \bmod q .$$

Then, the value

$$h = q^{-1}(m_1 - m_2) \bmod p$$

is computed and the message retrieved as $m = m_2 + hq$.

3.3 Exponent Blinding

The side-channel countermeasure considered in this work is the exponent blinding, introduced by Kocher [14]. It consists of adding a random multiple of $\phi(N)$ to d. In particular, RSA exponentiation is computed by using the new exponent $d^* = d + \ell\phi(N)$, for some $\ell > 0$ randomly chosen at each execution. The correctness of RSA is still valid, since

$$m^{ed^*} \equiv m^{ed+e\ell\phi(N)} \equiv m^{1+(k+e\ell)\phi(N)} \equiv m\left(m^{\phi(N)}\right)^{k+e\ell} \equiv m(1)^{k+e\ell} \equiv m \bmod N \ . \tag{3}$$

Also CRT-RSA can be protected with exponent blinding. Thus, exponentiation is computed by using $d_p^* = d_p + \ell_1(p-1)$ and $d_q^* = d_q + \ell_2(q-1)$, for some $\ell_1, \ell_2 > 0$ randomly chosen.

3.4 Common Parameters Setting

The modulus N has prime factors p and q that for security purposes are chosen of equal bit-size. We assume wlog that $p > q$, that implies

$$q < \sqrt{N} < p < 2q < 2\sqrt{N}$$

and

$$\sqrt{N} < p + q < 3\sqrt{N} \ .$$

It is common practice to choose the modulus N as 1024, 2048 or 3072-bit long.

The most common value for the public exponent e is $2^{16}+1$. This is also the default value for the public exponent in the OpenSSL library. Other common values are 3 and 17. NIST mandates that e satisfies $2^{16} < e < 2^{256}$ [12]. Therefore, to be as generic as possible but still adhering to realistic scenarios, we will consider in our analysis $3 \le e < 2^{256}$, but we will provide experiments only for the most common case $e = 2^{16}+1$.

The exponent d is commonly chosen to be full size, namely as large as $\phi(N)$. In order to speed-up the decryption process, someone suggests to use smaller d. However, this choice may lead to security problems as Wiener's attack [2]. Therefore, it is usually avoided.

The dimension of the random factor ℓ used in the exponent blinding countermeasure is a tradeoff between security and efficiency. If ℓ is 32-bit long or smaller, it allows some combination of brute-forcing and side-channel as in [19], where a brute-force on ℓ is required. Thus, it is a safer choice to use ℓ with bit-size 64. A larger dimension would make the decryption process less efficient.

In our analysis, to maintain generality, we will consider $0 \le \ell < 2^{128}$ and in our experiments we will test bit-sizes of 0, 10, 32, 64 and 100. Our methods never require the capability of brute-forcing the values of k or ℓ, sometimes needed in other works.

To recap, in this work we will consider both RSA and CRT-RSA implementations that make use of the exponent blinding countermeasure. Our RSA settings will consider moduli of 1024, 2048 and 3072 bits, public exponent such that $3 \leq e < 2^{256}$, private exponent of full size and a randomization factor up to 128 bits. To derive theoretical bounds in next sections, we prefer to express the restrictions on e and ℓ with respect to the modulus N. In general, we translate them to the less restrictive conditions: $\ell < 2N^{\frac{1}{8}}$ and $e < 2N^{\frac{1}{4}}$. When necessary, we will consider more restrictive bounds. We will run experiments by considering the widely used public exponent $e = 2^{16} + 1$ and random values ℓ of different bit-size from 0 to 100. The modulus N will be 2048 or 3072-bit long, but note that our attacks are effective also for other sizes.

4   General Strategy

Partial key exposure attacks relies on Coppersmith's method for finding roots of modular polynomials and multivariate polynomials. This method makes significant use of lattices and lattice reduction algorithms.

We give here a brief introduction to lattices and to the general strategy used in partial key exposure attacks and thus also in our attacks.

4.1   Lattices

Given a set of real linearly independent vectors $B = \{b_1, \ldots, b_n\}$ with $b_i \in \mathbb{R}^n$, a (full-rank) lattice spanned by B is the set of all integer linear combinations of vectors of B. Namely, the set $L(B) = \{\sum_i x_i b_i \; : \; x_i \in \mathbb{Z}\}$.

B is called the *basis* of the lattice and the $(n \times n)$-matrix consisting of the row vectors $b_1, \ldots, b_n$ is called basis matrix.

Every lattice has an infinite number of lattice bases. A basis is obtained from another through a unimodular transformation (i.e., by multiplying the basis matrix by a matrix with determinant ± 1). The determinant of the lattice is defined as $\det(L) = |\det(B_i)|$ and is an invariant, namely it is independent of the choice of the basis. The dimension of the lattice is $\dim(L) = n$.

The goal of lattice reduction is to find a basis with short and nearly orthogonal vectors. The LLL algorithm [20] produces in polynomial time a set of reduced basis vectors. The following theorem bounds the norm of these vectors.

Theorem 1 (Lenstra-Lenstra-Lovász). *Let L be a lattice of dimension n. The LLL-algorithm outputs in polynomial time reduced basis vectors v_i, $1 \leq i \leq n$, satisfying*

$$\|v_1\| \leq \|v_2\| \leq \cdots \leq \|v_i\| \leq 2^{\frac{n(n-1)}{4(n+1-i)}} \det L^{\frac{1}{n+1-i}} \; .$$

4.2   General Strategy

In [4], Don Coppersmith presents a rigorous method to find small roots of univariate modular polynomials. The method is based on LLL and can be extended to polynomials in more variables, but only heuristically.

In this work we use the following reformulation of Coppersmith's theorem due to Howgrave-Graham [5].

Theorem 2 (Howgrave-Graham). *Let $f(x_1, \ldots, x_k)$ be a polynomial in k variables with n monomials. Let m be a positive integer. Suppose that*

1. $f(r_1, \ldots, r_k) = 0 \mod b^m$ *where* $|r_i| < X_i \; \forall i$;
2. $\|f(x_1 X_1, \ldots, x_k X_k)\| < \dfrac{b^m}{\sqrt{n}}.$

Then $f(r_1, \ldots, r_k) = 0$ holds over the integers.

The general strategy is the following. Starting from an RSA equation we construct a multivariate polynomial $f_b(x_1, \ldots, x_k)$ modulo an integer b, such that its root $(r_1, \ldots, r_k)$ contains secret values. Our goal is to find this root, even if no classic root finding method is known for modular polynomials. So, we construct k polynomials $f_1, \ldots, f_k$ satisfying the two conditions of Theorem 2 so that such polynomials will have the same root $(r_1, \ldots, r_k)$ over $\mathbb{Z}$. Finally, we compute the common roots of these polynomials and recover the secret values.

To generate such polynomials we apply the following strategy. Starting from f_b we construct auxiliary polynomials $g_i(x_1, \ldots, x_k)$ that all satisfy condition 1 of Howgrave-Graham's Theorem. Since every integer linear combination of these polynomials also satisfies condition 1, we look for linear combinations that also satisfy condition 2. Such combinations are the polynomials $f_1, \ldots, f_k$.

In order to construct $f_1, \ldots, f_k$, we build a lattice $L(B)$ where the basis B is composed by the coefficient vectors of the polynomials $g_i(x_1 X_1, \ldots, x_k X_k)$ (with $X_1, \ldots, X_k$ bounds on the root as in Theorem 2).

By using the LLL-lattice reduction algorithm, we obtain a reduced basis for the lattice L as in Theorem 1. The first k vectors of the reduced basis have norm smaller than $\frac{b^m}{\sqrt{n}}$, if:

$$2^{\frac{n(n-1)}{4(n+1-k)}} \det L^{\frac{1}{n+1-k}} < \frac{b^m}{\sqrt{n}} .$$

We may let terms that do not depend on N contribute to an error term ϵ and consider the simplified condition

$$\det L \leq b^{m(n+1-k)} . \tag{4}$$

If this condition holds, then we can use the first k reduced-basis vectors to construct the polynomials $f_1, \ldots, f_k$ satisfying the second condition of Theorem 2. Then, in order to compute $(r_1, \ldots, r_k)$, we do the following.

If $k = 1$, then we consider the polynomial $F = f_1(x_1)$ and apply a classic roots finding algorithm for univariate polynomials over the integers.

If $k > 1$, we use the resultant computation to construct k univariate polynomials $F_i(x_i)$ from $f_1, \ldots, f_k$ and apply a classic roots finding algorithm for each of them. The effectiveness of this last method relies on the following heuristic assumption.

Assumption 1. *The resultant computation for the polynomials f_i described above yields a non-zero polynomial.*

This assumption is fundamental and widely used for many attacks in literature [3,6–9]. None of our experiments has ever failed to yield a non-zero polynomial and hence to mount the attack.

In this work we will make use of a seminal result due to Coppersmith, based on the strategy described above. We present here a more general variant of it, due to May [13], together with a sketch of its proof to illustrate how we will construct lattices for our experiments.

Theorem 3. *Let $N = pq$ with $p > q$. Let k be an unknown integer that is not a multiple of q. Suppose we know an approximation $\widetilde{kp}$ of kp with $|kp - \widetilde{kp}| \leq 2N^{\frac{1}{4}}$. Then we can factor N in time polynomial in $\log N$.*

Sketch of Proof. Define the univariate polynomial

$$f_p(x) = x + \widetilde{kp}$$

with root $x_0 = kp - \widetilde{kp}$ modulo p.

Divide the interval $[-2N^{\frac{1}{4}}, 2N^{\frac{1}{4}}]$ into 8 subintervals of size $\frac{1}{2}N^{\frac{1}{4}}$ centered at some x_i. For each subinterval consider the polynomial $f_p(x - x_i)$ and find its roots r such that $|r| \leq \frac{1}{4}N^{\frac{1}{4}}$. Among all these roots of all these polynomials there is also x_0. So, for each $f_p(x - x_i)$ set $X = \frac{1}{4}N^{\frac{1}{4}}$. Fix $m = \lceil \log N/4 \rceil$ and set $t = m$.

Define the auxiliary polynomials

$$g_{i,j}(x) = x^j N^i f^{m-i} \text{ for } i = 0, \ldots, m - 1; \ j = 0 \, ;$$
$$h_i(x) = x^i f^m(x) \text{ for } i = 0, \ldots, t - 1 \, .$$

and construct the lattice spanned by the vectors $g_{i,j}(xX)$ and $h_i(xX)$.

By applying the LLL-algorithm to L, a reduced basis is obtained. From the shortest vector construct the polynomial $f_i(x)$. Among its roots over the integers, there are also the roots of $f_p(x - x_i)$. Compute the roots of $f_i(x)$ by using a classic roots-finding algorithm. Construct the set R of all integer roots of the polynomials $f_i(x)$. The set R will contain also the root x_0.

Thus, $f(x_0) = kp$ can be computed and, since k is not a multiple of q, the computation of $\gcd(N, kp)$ gives p.

Recall that the LLL-algorithm is polynomial in the dimension of the matrix basis and in the bit-size of its entries. Since the dimension of the lattice is $m + t = \lceil \log N/2 \rceil$ and the bit-size of its entries is bounded by a polynomial in $(m \log N)$, every step of the proof can be done in polynomial time.   □

5   Attacks on RSA

In this section we present two attacks on RSA implementations, one given the most significant bits of the private exponent and the other one given its least significant bits. We assume that the private exponent d is full-size and that it is masked by a random multiple ℓ of $\phi(N)$. Thus, exponentiation is performed by using the exponent $d^* = d + \ell\phi(N)$ for some $\ell \geq 0$. When $\ell = 0$ clearly $d^* = d$, that means that no countermeasure is applied.

5.1   Partial Information on LSBs of d^*

In this section, we assume that the attacker is able to recover the least significant bits of the secret d^*. We write $d^* = d_1 \cdot M + d_0$, where d_0 represents the fraction of d^* known to the attacker while d_1 represents the unknown part. For instance, if the attacker knows the m LSB of d^*, then $M = 2^m$.

To prove our result, we generalize the method used in [9], by introducing the new factor ℓ.

Theorem 4. *Let (N, e) be an RSA public key with $e = N^\alpha \leq 2N^{\frac{1}{4}}$ and $d^* = d + \ell\phi(N)$, for some $\ell = N^\sigma \leq 2N^{\frac{1}{8}}$. Suppose we are given d_0 and M satisfying $d_0 = d^* \bmod M$ with*

$$M \geq N^{\frac{1}{3}\sqrt{1+6(\alpha+\sigma)}+\frac{1}{6}(1+6\sigma)+\varepsilon} ,$$

for some $\varepsilon > 0$. Then, under Assumption 1, we can find the factorization of N in time polynomial in $\log N$.

Proof. We start from the RSA equation

$$ed - 1 = k\phi(N) .$$

Since $d^* = d + \ell\phi(N)$, we obtain the equation

$$ed^* - 1 = (k + e\ell)\phi(N) .$$

Let $k^* = k + e\ell$, so that $ed^* - 1 = k^*\phi(N)$.

By writing $d^* = d_1 M + d_0$ and considering that $\phi(N) = N - (p + q - 1)$, we get

$$k^* N - k^*(p + q - 1) - ed_0 + 1 = eMd_1 .$$

It follows that the bivariate polynomial

$$f_{eM}(x, y) = xN - xy - ed_0 + 1$$

has root $(x_0, y_0) = (k^*, p + q - 1)$ modulo eM.

In order to bound x_0, notice that

$$k^* = \frac{ed^* - 1}{\phi(N)} < e\left(\frac{d + \ell\phi(N)}{\phi(N)}\right) < e(1 + \ell) \leq 2N^{\alpha+\sigma} .$$

In addition, recall that $p + q \leq 3N^{\frac{1}{2}}$.

We can set the bounds $X = 2N^{\alpha+\sigma}$ and $Y = 3N^{\frac{1}{2}}$ so that $x_0 \leq X$ and $y_0 \leq Y$.

To construct the lattice, we consider the following auxiliary polynomials

$$g_{i,j}(x, y) = x^i(eM)^i f_{eM}^{m-i} \text{ for } i = 0, \ldots, m; \ j = 0, \ldots, i;$$
$$h_{i,j}(x, y) = y^j(eM)^i f_{eM}^{m-i} \text{ for } i = 0, \ldots, m; \ j = 1, \ldots, t ,$$

for some integers m and t, where $t = \tau m$ has to be optimized.

All integer linear combinations of these polynomials have the root (x_0, y_0) modulo $(eM)^m$, since they all have a term $(eM)^i f_{eM}^{m-i}$. So the first condition of Theorem 2 is satisfied. In order to satisfy the second condition, we have to find a short vector in the lattice spanned by $g_{i,j}(xX, yY)$ and $h_{i,j}(xX, yY)$. In particular, this vector shall have a norm smaller than $\frac{(eM)^m}{\sqrt{\dim L}}$.

The second condition of Theorem 2 is satisfied when inequality (4) holds, i.e. if

$$\det L \leq (eM)^{m(n-1)}. \tag{5}$$

An easy computation shows that $n = \left(\tau + \frac{1}{2}\right) m^2$ and that

$$\det L(M) = \left((eMY)^{3\tau+2} Z^{3\tau^2+3\tau+1}\right)^{\frac{1}{6}m^3(1+o(1))}.$$

Considering the bounds $X = 2N^{\alpha+\sigma}$ and $Y = 3N^{\frac{1}{2}}$, we obtain the condition

$$\left((eM2N^{\alpha+\sigma})^{3\tau+2}(3N^{\frac{1}{2}})^{3\tau^2+3\tau+1}\right)^{\frac{1}{6}m^3(1+o(1))} \leq (eM)^{m(n-1)}$$

that reduces to

$$N^{\frac{m^3}{6}\left((\alpha+\sigma)(3\tau+2)+\frac{1}{2}(3\tau^2+3\tau+1)\right)(1+o(1))} \leq (eM)^{m(n-1)-\frac{m^3}{6}(3\tau+2)(1+o(1))}.$$

We know that $eM \geq N^{\alpha\frac{1}{3}\sqrt{1+6(\alpha+\sigma)}+\frac{1}{6}(1+6\sigma)+\varepsilon}$, so the above condition is satisfied if

$$9\tau^2 + 6(\alpha + \sigma + \tau) - 2\sqrt{1 + 6(\alpha + \sigma)}(1 + 3\tau) + 2 \leq 0.$$

The left-hand side is minimized, for

$$\tau = \frac{1}{3}\left(\sqrt{1 + 6(\alpha + \sigma)} - 1\right).$$

Thus, for this choice of τ condition 5 is satisfied so we can successfully apply the LLL-algorithm.

From the LLL-reduced basis, we construct two polynomials $f_1(x, y)$, $f_2(x, y)$ with the common root (x_0, y_0) over the integers. By the heuristic assumption, the resultant $res_x(f_1, f_2)$ is not zero and we can find $y_0 = p+q-1$ using standard root finding algorithms. This gives us the factorization of N.

To conclude the proof, we need to show that every step of the method can be done in time polynomial in $\log(N)$. The LLL-algorithm runs in polynomial time, since the basis matrix B has constant dimension (fixed by m) and its entries are bounded by a polynomial in N. Additionally, $res_x(f_1, f_2)$ has constant degree and coefficients bounded by a polynomial in N. Thus, every step can be done in polynomial time. $\square$

We would like to make two considerations. The first is that when $\sigma = 0$, we get the same result of [9]. Indeed, our method is a generalization of it. The second is that we obtain the same bound of [6], but our approach is more effective in practice. As we will show in Sect. 7.1, we are able to get closer to the theoretical bound by using smaller lattices.

5.2   Partial Information on MSBs of d^*

In this section, we prove that if the attacker knows a sufficiently large number of most significant bits of the protected exponent, then she can factor N. To prove this result, we show how the partial knowledge on d^* can be used to construct an approximation of p that allows to apply Theorem 3.

The advantage of this approach compared to [6] is that it does not rely on the heuristic Assumption 1 and yields to a better bound.

Theorem 5. *Let (N, e) be an RSA public key with $e = N^\alpha$ and $d^* = d + \ell\phi(N)$ for some $\ell = N^\sigma$ with $\sigma > 0$ and $N^{\alpha+\sigma} < 2N^{\frac{3}{8}}$. Suppose that $|p - q| \geq cN^{\frac{1}{2}}$, for some $c \leq \frac{1}{2}$, and suppose we are given an approximation $\widetilde{d^*}$ of d^* such that*

$$|d^* - \widetilde{d^*}| \leq cN^{\frac{1}{4}+\sigma} .$$

Then we can find the factorization of N in time polynomial in $\log N$.

Notice that, like in Theorem 4, we have $ed^* - 1 = k^*\phi(N)$ with $k^* = k + e\ell$. In order to prove Theorem 5 we need first to prove the following lemma.

Lemma 1. *With $N^{\alpha+\sigma} < 2N^{\frac{3}{8}}$, given $\widetilde{d^*}$ such that $|d^* - \widetilde{d^*}| \leq \frac{1}{4}N^{1-\alpha}$ then the approximation $\widetilde{k^*} := \left\lceil \frac{e\widetilde{d^*}-1}{N+1} \right\rceil$ of k^* is exact.*

Proof. This proof follows the same strategy used in the proof of Theorem 6 of [9]. Note that

$$|k^* - \widetilde{k^*}| < \left| \frac{ed^* - 1}{\phi(N)} - \frac{e\widetilde{d^*} - 1}{N + 1} \right|$$

$$< \left| \frac{(ed^* - 1)(N + 1) - (e\widetilde{d^*} - 1)(N + 1 - (p + q))}{\phi(N)(N + 1)} \right| .$$

Then, given that $\phi(N) > N/2$, $p+q \leq 3N^{\frac{1}{2}}$, $N^2 + N > N^2$ and $d^* < 2N^{1+\sigma}$, we obtain

$$|k^* - \widetilde{k^*}| < \left| \frac{e(d^* - \widetilde{d^*})}{\phi(N)} \right| + \left| \frac{(p + q)(e\widetilde{d^*} - 1)}{\phi(N)(N + 1)} \right|$$

$$< \left| \frac{\frac{1}{4}N^\alpha N^{1-\alpha}}{\frac{N}{2}} \right| + \left| \frac{6N^{\frac{3}{2}+\alpha+1+\sigma}}{\frac{N}{2}(N + 1)} \right|$$

$$< \frac{1}{2} + 12N^{-\frac{1}{2}+\frac{3}{8}} < \frac{1}{2} + \frac{12}{N^{\frac{1}{8}}} .$$

With RSA parameters, we have $12 \ll N^{1/8}$, so we can safely assume $|k^* - \widetilde{k^*}| < 1$. But the difference between two integers is an integer, thus we can conclude that it is zero, therefore $\widetilde{k^*} = k^*$. $\square$

It is worth to observe two facts: first, the bound $|d^* - \widetilde{d^*}| \leq \frac{1}{4}N^{1-\alpha}$ requires the attacker to get the $(\log_2(N^{\sigma+\alpha}) + 2)$ most significant bits of d^*, a result which holds even for $\sigma = 0$ (i.e. $d^* = d$); second, the assumption $N^{\alpha+\sigma} < 2N^{\frac{3}{8}}$ of Lemma 1 always holds for our choice of RSA parameters.

We can now prove Theorem 5.

Proof of Theorem 5. We begin by applying Lemma 1 to obtain the value of k^*. The condition $|d^* - \widetilde{d^*}| \leq \frac{1}{4}N^{1-\alpha}$ of the lemma is always satisfied by our choices of RSA parameters because $\frac{1}{2}N^{\frac{1}{4}+\sigma} \ll \frac{1}{4}N^{1-\alpha}$, since $N^\sigma < 2N^{\frac{1}{8}}$ and $N^\alpha < 2N^{\frac{1}{4}}$.

We can define an approximation $\tilde{s}$ of $s = p + q$ as

$$\tilde{s} := 1 + N - \frac{e\widetilde{d^*} - 1}{k^*} .$$

Reminding that k^*, with the assumption of $\sigma > 0$, is lower bounded by $N^{\alpha+\sigma}$, we obtain

$$|s - \tilde{s}| = \left| \frac{e}{k^*} \left(d^* - \widetilde{d^*} \right) \right| \leq \frac{N^\alpha}{N^{\alpha+\sigma}} cN^{\frac{1}{4}+\sigma} \leq cN^{\frac{1}{4}} .$$

We use $\tilde{s}$ to define

$$\tilde{p} := \frac{1}{2} \left(\tilde{s} + \sqrt{\tilde{s}^2 - 4N} \right)$$

as an approximation of p.

Without loss of generality, following Appendix B of [7], we now assume that $\tilde{s} \geq s$, so that $\tilde{p} \geq p$.

Observe that

$$\tilde{p} - p = \frac{1}{2}(\tilde{s} - s) + \frac{1}{2} \left(\sqrt{\tilde{s}^2 - 4N} - \sqrt{s^2 - 4N} \right)$$

$$= \frac{1}{2}(\tilde{s} - s) + \frac{(\tilde{s} + s)(\tilde{s} - s)}{2 \left(\sqrt{\tilde{s}^2 - 4N} + \sqrt{s^2 - 4N} \right)} .$$

Since $\tilde{s} \geq s$, we have $\tilde{s}^2 - 4N \geq s^2 - 4N = (p - q)^2$ and $|p - q| \geq cN^{\frac{1}{2}}$ with $c \leq \frac{1}{2}$.

Noting that $\tilde{s} \leq s + cN^{\frac{1}{4}}$, we have

$$\tilde{s} + s \leq 2s + cN^{\frac{1}{4}} \leq 2(p + q) + N^{\frac{1}{4}} \leq 6N^{\frac{1}{2}} + N^{\frac{1}{4}} \leq 7N^{\frac{1}{2}} .$$

It follows that

$$\tilde{p} - p \leq \frac{1}{2}(\tilde{s} - s) + \frac{(\tilde{s} + s)(\tilde{s} - s)}{4(p - q)}$$

$$\leq \frac{1}{2}cN^{\frac{1}{4}} + \frac{(7N^{\frac{1}{2}})(cN^{\frac{1}{4}})}{4cN^{\frac{1}{2}}} \leq \frac{1}{4}N^{\frac{1}{4}} + \frac{7}{4}N^{\frac{1}{4}} \leq 2N^{\frac{1}{4}} .$$

Since the approximation $\tilde{p}$ satisfies the hypothesis of Theorem 3 with $k = 1$, we can find the factorization of N in time polynomial in $\log N$. $\qquad\square$

From Theorem 5 we can recover the minimum number of known MSBs required. In accordance to previous sections we define this quantity as $\log_2 M$ where M is defined as

$$M = \frac{d^*}{|d^* - \tilde{d}^*|} = \frac{2N^{1+\sigma}}{cN^{\frac{1}{4}+\sigma}} = \frac{2}{c}N^{\frac{3}{4}} \geq 4N^{\frac{3}{4}} . \tag{6}$$

It is important to underline that this bound is not affected by the size of α and σ as long as the condition of Lemma 1 holds. In fact, while it might seem counter-intuitive, the presence of the countermeasure (i.e. $\sigma > 0$) improves the theoretical bound $|d - \tilde{d}| \leq cN^{\frac{1}{4}-\alpha}$ of Theorem 3.3 of [7]. However, this difference was not shown in the experimental results, probably due to low value of α when $e = 2^{16} + 1$.

Also note that Theorem (5) provides a significant improvement over the bound of [6]. In fact, for $\alpha + \sigma \leq \frac{1}{2}$ (which is always true in our setting), their bound is $|d^* - \tilde{d}^*| \leq N^{\alpha+\sigma}$, which would require knowledge of $\log_2(N^{1-\alpha})$ bits.

Considerations on C. It can be noted from equation (6) that the required number of bits to be recovered depends on c which is unknown to the attacker. It's easy to show that c is closely related to $\frac{1}{2^{i+1}}$ where i is the number of most significant bits that p and q have in common. While it is true that attacker has no a priori knowledge of c and thus can't a priori know how many bits she needs to recover before being able to apply Theorem 5, it is also true that she can get its exact value after recovering the required minimum bits $\log_2(4N^{\frac{3}{4}})$. In fact, she can compute $\tilde{p}$ and $\tilde{q} = \frac{N}{\tilde{p}}$ and retrieve c which is lower bounded by NIST in the condition $|p - q| > 2^{\log_2(N)/2-100}$ so that $\log_2(4N^{\frac{3}{4}})$ are always enough to compute it.

Attack Using Both MSBs and LSBs of d*. We want to briefly analyze also the case where the attacker might be able to detect bits in different positions of d^*. In this scenario, the attacker could obtain enough most significant bits to satisfy Lemma 1 and obtain $\frac{1}{4}\log_2 N$ least significant bits to recover half of the bits of p and factor N, as shown in [7]. Thus, the knowledge of only $(\log_2(N^{\frac{1}{4}+\sigma+\alpha}) + 2 + \epsilon)$ bits and the resolution of an univariate equation are required. We don't describe the attack in details because, once k^* is recovered applying Lemma 1, it reduces to the method of [7]. Thus, we remind the reader to it. In Sect. 7, we will provide experimental results.

6   Attacks on CRT-RSA

In this section we present two attacks on CRT-RSA implementations, where we target exponentiation by d_p^*. One is based on the knowledge of the most significant bits of the CRT private exponent and one is based on the knowledge of its least significant bits. We assume that the private exponent d_p is full-size (with respect to p) and that it is masked by a random multiple ℓ of $(p - 1)$, for some $\ell \geq 0$. When $\ell = 0$ clearly $d_p^* = d_p$, that means that no countermeasure is applied.

6.1   Partial Information on LSBs of d_p^*

Assuming that the attacker is able to recover the least significant bits of the secret d_p^*, we can write $d_p^* = d_1 \cdot M + d_0$ where d_0 is known while d_1 is unknown. The integer M is a power of two and represents the bound on the known part.

To prove our result we use a method presented by Herrmann and May to find the solutions of a bivariate linear equation modulo p [10].

Theorem 6. *Let (N, e) be an RSA public key with $e = N^\alpha$. Let $d_p = d \bmod p - 1$ and let $d_p^* = d + \ell(p - 1)$ for some $\ell = N^\sigma$ with $\sigma \geq 0$. Suppose that $N^{\alpha+\sigma} \leq N^{\frac{1}{\sqrt{2}}-\frac{1}{2}}$ and that we are given d_0 and M satisfying $d_0 = d_p^* \bmod M$ with*

$$M \geq N^{1-\frac{1}{\sqrt{2}}+\alpha+2\sigma+\varepsilon} ,$$

for some $\varepsilon > 0$. Then, under Assumption 1, we can find the factorization of N (in time polynomial in $\log N$).

Proof. We start from the equation

$$ed_p - 1 = k_p(p - 1) .$$

Since $d_p^* = d_p + \ell(p - 1)$, we obtain

$$ed_p^* - 1 = (k_p + e\ell)(p - 1) .$$

Let k_p^* denote $k_p + e\ell$. By writing $d_p^* = d_1 M + d_0$, we obtain the following equation

$$eMd_1 + k_p^* + ed_0 - 1 = k_p^* p .$$

It follows that the bivariate polynomial

$$f_p(x, y) = eMx + y + ed_0 - 1$$

has root $(x_0, y_0) = (d_1, k_p^*)$ modulo p.

In order to bound y_0, notice that

$$k_p^* = \frac{ed_p^* - 1}{(p - 1)} < e\left(\frac{d_p + \ell(p - 1)}{(p - 1)}\right) < e(1 + \ell) \leq 2N^{\alpha+\sigma} .$$

Additionally, recall that $d_1 = \frac{d_p^*}{M} - d_0$.

We can set bounds $X = N^{\frac{1}{\sqrt{2}}-\frac{1}{2}-\alpha-\sigma}$ and $Y = 2N^{\alpha+\sigma}$ so that $x_0 \leq X$ and $y_0 \leq Y$.

To construct the lattice, we consider the following auxiliary polynomials:

$$\bar{f} = x + Ry + R(ed_0 - 1) \text{ where } R = (eM)^{-1} \bmod N ;$$
$$g_{k,i} = y^i \bar{f}^k N^{\max\{t-k,0\}}, \quad k = 0, \ldots, m; i = 0, \ldots, m - k .$$

for some integers m and t, where $t = \tau m$ has to be optimized.

All integer linear combinations of these polynomials share the root (x_0, y_0) modulo p^t. Thus, the first condition of Theorem 2 is satisfied. In order to satisfy the second condition we have to find a short vector in the lattice L, spanned by $g_{k,i}(xX, yY)$. In particular, this vector shall have a norm smaller than $\frac{p^t}{\sqrt{\dim L}}$.

The second condition of Theorem 2 is satisfied when equation (4) holds, i.e. when

$$\det L \leq N^{\frac{1}{2}\tau m(n-1)} . \tag{7}$$

A straightforward computation shows that $n = \frac{1}{2}(m^2 + 3m + 2)$ and that

$$\det L(M) = (XY)^{\frac{1}{6}(m^3 + 3m^2 + 2m)} N^{\frac{1}{6}m\tau(m\tau+1)(4+3m-m\tau)} .$$

Thus, condition (7) becomes

$$(XY)^{\frac{1}{6}(m^3 + 3m^2 + 2m)} \leq N^{\frac{1}{4}\tau m(m^2 + 3m) - \frac{1}{6}m\tau(m\tau+1)(4+3m-m\tau)}$$

that reduces to

$$XY \leq N^{\frac{1}{2}(3\tau + 2\tau^3 - 6\tau^2)} .$$

Since $XY = 2N^{\frac{1}{\sqrt{2}} - \frac{1}{2}}$, the above condition is satisfied if

$$\frac{1}{\sqrt{2}} - \frac{1}{2} - \frac{1}{2}(3\tau + 2\tau^3 - 6\tau^2) \leq 0 .$$

The left-hand side is minimized for $\tau = 1 - \frac{1}{\sqrt{2}}$. For this choice of τ condition (7) is satisfied, so we can successfully apply LLL-algorithm and then find the root (d_1, k_p^*). From this values, we can obtain $p - 1$ and then the factorization of N.

To conclude the proof, we need to show that every step of the method can be done in time polynomial in $\log(N)$. The LLL-algorithm is polynomial in the dimension of the matrix, that is $\mathcal{O}(m^2)$, and in the bit-size of its entries, that are $\mathcal{O}(m \log N)$. Additionally, $res_y(f_1, f_2)$ has constant degree and coefficients bounded by a polynomial in N. Thus, every step can be done in polynomial time. □

6.2 Partial Information on MSBs of d_p^*

In this section, we prove that if the attacker knows a sufficiently large number of most significant bits of the protected exponent d_p^*, then she can factor N.

To prove this result, we show how the partial knowledge on d_p^* can be used to construct an approximation of a multiple of p that allows to apply Theorem 3.

Theorem 7. *Let (N, e) be an RSA public key with $e = N^\alpha$. Let $d_p = d \bmod p - 1$ and let $d_p^* = d_p + \ell(p-1)$, for some $\ell = N^\sigma$ with $\sigma \geq 0$. Suppose that $N^{\alpha+\sigma} \leq \frac{1}{2}N^{\frac{1}{4}}$ and that we are given an approximation $\widetilde{d_p^*}$ of d_p^* such that*

$$|d_p^* - \widetilde{d_p^*}| \leq N^{\frac{1}{4} - \alpha} .$$

Then, we can find the factorization of N in time polynomial in $\log N$.

Proof. We start from equation

$$ed_p^* - 1 = k_p^*(p - 1)$$

with $k_p^* = k_p + \ell e$.

Note that $k_p^* \leq 2N^{\alpha+\sigma} < \frac{1}{2}N^{\frac{1}{2}}$ implies that q can't divide k_p^*.
We compute an approximation

$$\widetilde{k_p^* p} := e\widetilde{d_p^*} - 1$$

of $k_p^* p$, up to an additive error of at most

$$|k_p^* p - \widetilde{k_p^* p}| = |ed_p^* - 1 + k_p^* - e\widetilde{d_p^*} + 1|$$
$$= |e(d_p^* - \widetilde{d_p^*}) + k| \leq N^{\frac{1}{4}} + 2N^{\alpha+\sigma} \leq 2N^{\frac{1}{4}} .$$

Since the approximation $\widetilde{k_p^* p}$ satisfies the hypothesis of Theorem 3, we can find the factorization of N in time polynomial in $\log N$.   □

The bound of Theorem 7 implies that an attacker has to know at least $\log_2 M$ bits, where

$$M = \frac{d_p^*}{|d_p^* - \widetilde{d_p^*}|} = \frac{2N^{\frac{1}{2}+\sigma}}{N^{\frac{1}{4}-\alpha}} = 2N^{\frac{1}{4}+\alpha+\sigma} . \tag{8}$$

This bound holds when the condition $N^{\alpha+\sigma} \leq \frac{1}{2}N^{\frac{1}{4}}$ holds, which is not always the case in our settings. For example an RSA modulus of 1024 bit with $\log_2 e = 256$ and $log_2\ell = 128$ will have $N^{\alpha+\sigma} \leq 2N^{\frac{3}{8}}$. For these cases we are unaware of successful applications of Coppersmith's method.

In [8] Sect. 4 it is presented a novel technique for the CRT case with better bound but with the requirement to have d_p not full size. This requirement also implies that no countermeasure is applied.

7   Experimental Results

In our experiments we target RSA applications with 2048 or 3072-bit modulus N and public exponent $e = 2^{16} + 1$, since this is the most common choice made for real implementations. In addition we assume that a random multiple ℓ of $\phi(N)$ (or of $(p-1)$ for CRT-RSA applications) is added to the private exponent d (respectively d_p).

For each dimension of ℓ, we first report the theoretical bound on the minimum number of bits of the secret key that the attacker needs to know to recover it entirely. This values are derived from theorems we have proved in previous sections. Then, we report the average minimum number of bits that we really needed in our tests. In fact, theoretical bounds are reached when the lattice dimension goes to infinity. In general, the smaller is the number of known bits, the bigger the lattice shall be. To concretely mount an attack, one needs to construct a lattice whose dimension is such that the LLL-algorithm runs in practical time.

Recall that the running time of LLL-algorithm depends on the lattice dimension and on the dimension of the entries of its matrix-basis. Since the dimension of the entries depends on the bounds X_i and on the modular polynomial used, the LLL-algorithm may have different running times for the same lattice dimension. We decided to fix an upper bound on the dimension of the lattices we constructed. We chose the threshold 80 as a tradeoff between efficiency and effectiveness of our attacks. Indeed, this choice allows us to get closer to the theoretical bounds as opposed to smaller dimensions. On the other hand, 80 is small enough to make the LLL-algorithm running in practical time. We fixed the same threshold for all attacks in order to compare their effectiveness when using the same lattice dimension.

We implemented our methods with the SAGE computer-algebra system [1] and run it on a 3GHz Intel Core i5. With the exception of the CRT-MSB case, where we used only 5 experiments, for all other attacks we ran 100 experiments generating different key pairs and different values of ℓ. We report the average values obtained from these experiments.

7.1   Results with Known LSBs of d*

Experimental results are presented in Table 1. For generating lattices, we used $m = 11$ and $t = \tau m$, where τ is defined in the proof of Theorem 4. Notice that τ is always very small resulting in $t = 0$ for each experiment. Thus, the dimension of the lattice is always equal to 78.

Table 1. Experimental results for partial key exposure attack given least significant bits of the secret exponent $d^* = d + \ell\phi(N)$. The public exponent is $e = 2^{16} + 1$.

$\log_2 \ell$	$\log_2 N = 2048$				$\log_2 N = 3072$			
	theo. bound	exp. bound	dim(L)	LLL	theo. bound	exp. bound	dim(L)	LLL
0	1040	1043	78	18 s	1552	1556	78	23 s
10	1060	1063	78	19 s	1572	1577	78	30 s
32	1103	1106	78	22 s	1615	1620	78	40 s
64	1164	1171	78	50 s	1678	1684	78	58 s
100	1232	1243	78	70 s	1747	1756	78	80 s

The difference between theoretical and experimental bounds is of very few bits and the LLL-algorithm's running time is really small.

It is worth to say that for $\ell = 0$ and small e, the attack in [7] is more effective than our attack. Indeed the $n/4$ least significant bits of d are sufficient to factor N. However their attack requires a brute-force search on k, that in our case is allowed only when $e + e\ell$ is small. Thus, with the introduction of exponent

Table 2. Comparison between the approach of [6] and our approach for partial key exposure attack given least significant bits of the secret exponent $d^* = d + \ell\phi(N)$. The modulus N is 1000-bit long and $e = 2^{16} + 1$.

$\log_2 \ell$	Approach of [6]				Our approach			
	theo. bound	*exp. bound*	dim(L)	LLL	*theo. bound*	*exp. bound*	dim(L)	LLL
10	535	580	16	1 s	535	540	10	1 s
100	700	760	16	1 s	700	720	10	1 s
200	871	960	16	1 s	871	920	10	1 s
300	1033	1160	16	1 s	1033	1120	10	1 s

Table 3. Experimental results for partial key exposure attack given most significant bits of the secret exponent $d^* = d + \ell\phi(N)$. The public exponent is $e = 2^{16} + 1$.

$\log_2 \ell$	$\log_2 N = 2048$				$\log_2 N = 3072$			
	theo. bound	*exp. bound*	dim(L)	LLL	*theo. bound*	*exp. bound*	dim(L)	LLL
0	1555	1555	80	112 m	2323	2331	80	203 m
10	1538	1555	80	112 m	2306	2331	80	203 m
32	1538	1555	80	112 m	2306	2331	80	203 m
64	1538	1555	80	112 m	2306	2331	80	203 m
100	1538	1555	80	112 m	2306	2331	80	203 m

blinding, or for larger dimension of e, their method can't be applied, because the brute force-search becomes impractical.

In Table 2 we report experimental results to compare our approach and the approach of [6] for the same scenario. Specifically, we consider 1000-bit modulus N, public exponent $e = 2^{16} + 1$ and $\ell \in \{10, 100, 200, 300\}$ as used in [6]. In our analysis we use a bivariate polynomial instead of a trivariate polynomial, thus we perform a single resultant computation, instead of three. The theoretical bound we obtain is the same of [6], but our approach allows us to get closer to it as shown in Table 2. Moreover, we do it by using smaller lattices.

7.2   Results with Known MSBs of d*

In Table 3 we present our results. Since this method uses an univariate polynomial, it is possible, in theory, to match the theoretical limit, although the lattice dimension would make LLL highly impractical. By imposing the threshold for the maximum dimension of the lattice equal to 80, the LLL-algorithm's running time is about 2 hours. For constructing such a lattice, we used $m = 40$ and $t = 40$.

The experiments confirmed the independence of the bound with respect to the dimension of the random integer ℓ.

Unfortunately, in this case we cannot compare our approach with the approach of [6], because they didn't provide any experimental result respecting our

Table 4. Experimental results for partial key exposure attack given most and least significant bits of the secret $d^* = d + \ell\phi(N)$. The public exponent is $e = 2^{16} + 1$.

$\log_2 \ell$	$\log_2 N = 2048$				$\log_2 N = 3072$			
	theo. bound	*exp. bound*	dim(L)	LLL	*theo. bound*	*exp. bound*	dim(L)	LLL
0	17+514	17+526	80	2 h 27 m	17+770	17+789	80	4 h 50 m
10	27+514	27+526	80	2 h 27 m	27+770	27+789	80	4 h 50 m
32	49+514	49+526	80	2 h 27 m	49+770	49+789	80	4 h 50 m
64	81+514	81+526	80	2 h 27 m	81+770	81+789	80	4 h 50 m
100	117+514	117+526	80	2 h 27 m	117+770	117+789	80	4 h 50 m

assumptions. In fact, they use very large values of ℓ, namely 500, 600 or 700-bit long for a modulus N of size 1000 bits. These settings do not satisfy our requirement of Lemma 1 for $N^{\alpha+\sigma} \leq 2N^{\frac{3}{8}}$. In any case, our approach improves their bound, as said in Sect. 5.2.

Results Using Both MSBs and LSBs. As said in Sect. 5.2, it is possible to mount an attack knowing both MSBs and LSBs of d^*. An univariate polynomial is constructed and its root is found by constructing a lattice as in the proof of Theorem 3. In Table 4 we provide some experimental results for this method.

7.3   Results with Known LSBs of d_p^*

In Table 5 we present our results, obtained by generating lattices using $m = 3$ an $t = 11$. To get closer to the theoretical bound, the lattice dimension should be significantly increased. But this makes the LLL-algorithm's running time highly impractical. By setting the threshold 80 for the lattice dimension, the LLL-algorithm's running time is about 13 minutes.

Table 5. Experimental results for partial key exposure attack against CRT-RSA, given least significant bits of the secret exponent $d_p^* = d_p + \ell(p-1)$. The public exponent is $e = 2^{16} + 1$.

$\log_2 \ell$	$\log_2 N = 2048$				$\log_2 N = 3072$			
	theo. bound	*exp. bound*	dim(L)	LLL	*theo. bound*	*exp. bound*	dim(L)	LLL
0	617	691	80	8 m	917	1019	80	14 m
10	637	712	80	10 m	937	1041	80	16 m
32	681	758	80	13 m	981	1087	80	21 m
64	745	822	80	17 m	1045	1154	80	28 m
100	817	894	80	18 m	1117	1227	80	34 m

In this case, the difference between theoretical and experimental bounds is about 80 bits for 2014-bit N and about 100 for 3072-bit N. Given a smaller number of leaked bits one can still mount the attack by constructing bigger

Table 6. Experimental results for partial key exposure attack given most significant bits of the CRT secret exponent $d_p^* = d + \ell(p-1)$. The public exponent is $e = 2^{16} + 1$.

$\log_2 \ell$	$\log_2 N = 2048$				$\log_2 N = 3072$			
	theo. bound	*exp. bound*	dim(L)	LLL	*theo. bound*	*exp. bound*	dim(L)	LLL
0	528	540	80	3 h 03 m	783	803	80	8 h 54 m
10	537	550	80	3 h 59 m	793	813	80	12 h 17 m
32	560	573	80	4 h 23 m	815	835	80	13 h 46 m
64	591	604	80	4 h 52 m	848	868	80	15 h 59 m
100	628	640	80	6 h 13 m	884	903	80	22 h 25 m

lattices, but the computation will need more time to end. For example, by setting $t = 5$ and $m = 18$ it is sufficient to obtain 50 (or 70) bits more than the theoretical bound to solve. But the corresponding lattice dimension is 190, which makes the LLL-algorithm end in about one day. By setting $t = 7$ and $m = 24$ it is sufficient to obtain 40 (or 60) bits more than the theoretical bound to solve. But the lattice dimension is around 500 and we think that the LLL-al gorithm would be highly impractical in this case.

Notice that for $\ell = 0$ and small e, Blömer and May show that a quarter of d_p is sufficient to the attacker to factor N [9]. To prove their result, they use a brute-force search on k_p, that is allowed only when $e + e\ell$ is small. Thus, for $e = 2^{16} + 1$ and $\ell = 0$ their method is better than our method, since a smaller number of leaked bits are sufficient to factor N. But, for larger dimension of e and when $\ell > 0$ their method is no more effective because the brute force-search becomes unfeasible.

7.4 Results with Known MSBs of d_p^*

Also in this case we imposed the threshold 80 for the lattice dimension, which allowed us to run the LLL-algorithm in practical time. We constructed lattices by using $m = 40$ and $t = 40$.

In Table 6 we report the theoretical and experimental number of leaked bits, the lattice dimension and the running time of LLL-algorithm.

As opposite to the case based on LSBs, this method is the most effective also for $\ell = 0$. Indeed, our method is a generalization of [9], thus for $\ell = 0$ we obtain their original result which is the most effective method in literature for this scenario.

8   Conclusions

We presented some methods to mount partial key exposure attacks on RSA with exponent blinding. We investigated both RSA and CRT-RSA, focusing on practical settings for the exponents and the blinding factor ℓ. In particular, we focused on public exponent e such that $3 \leq e < 2^{256}$, combining the upper bound provided by NIST with the frequent value of 3. Additionally, we focused on full size private exponents and $\ell < 2^{128}$, as commonly used in real implementations.

We derived sufficient conditions to successfully mount partial key exposure attacks in different scenarios and validated them providing numerical experiments, using N of size 2048 or 3072 and $e = 2^{16} + 1$, which is the most commonly used setting in real implementations.

As for RSA, we improved the results of [6] with the aim of reducing the number of bits to be recovered by the adversary through side-channel. In particular, when least significant bits are exposed, our approach allows to get closer to the theoretical bound by using smaller lattices, as shown in Table 2. Whereas, when most significant bits are exposed, we presented a method that does not rely on the heuristic assumption and that provides better bounds, as shown in Sect. 5.2.

Additionally, we provided novel results for the particular case where the adversary is able to recover non-consecutive portions of the private information.

As for CRT-RSA with exponent blinding, we provided novel results for both scenarios when either least or most significant bits are exposed.

Table 7. The number of bits that the attacker needs to know to successfully mount partial key exposure attacks. The public exponent is $e = 2^{16} + 1$. The private exponent is blinded using the random factor ℓ.

$\log_2 \ell$	$\log_2 N = 2048$					$\log_2 N = 3072$				
	LSB	MSB	MSB+LSB	CRT-LSB	CRT-MSB	LSB	MSB	MSB+LSB	CRT-LSB	CRT-MSB
0	1043	1555	17+526	691	540	1556	2331	17+789	1019	803
10	1063	1555	27+526	712	550	1577	2331	27+789	1041	813
32	1106	1555	49+526	758	573	1620	2331	49+789	1087	835
64	1171	1555	81+526	822	604	1684	2331	81+789	1154	868
100	1243	1555	117+526	894	640	1756	2331	117+789	1227	903

In Table 7, we recap the numerical results we obtained from our experiments. For each dimension of ℓ we provide the minimum number of bits of the protected exponent that is sufficient to the attacker to successfully break the system.

With the only exception of the RSA attack based on most significant bits, the number of known bits depends on the bit-size of the blinding factor ℓ.

References

1. Sage Mathematics Software (Version 6.2). http://www.sagemath.org
2. Wiener, M.J.: Cryptanalysis of short RSA secret exponents. IEEE Trans. Inf. Theory **36**, 553–558 (1990)
3. Ernst, M., Jochemsz, E., May, A., de Weger, B.: Partial key exposure attacks on RSA up to full size exponents. In: Cramer, R. (ed.) EUROCRYPT 2005. LNCS, vol. 3494, pp. 371–386. Springer, Heidelberg (2005)
4. Coppersmith, D.: Finding a small root of a univariate modular equation. In: Maurer, U.M. (ed.) EUROCRYPT 1996. LNCS, vol. 1070, pp. 155–165. Springer, Heidelberg (1996)

5. Howgrave-Graham, N.: Finding small roots of univariate modular equations revisited. In: Darnell, Michael J. (ed.) Cryptography and Coding 1997. LNCS, vol. 1355, pp. 131–142. Springer, Heidelberg (1997)

6. Joye, M., Lepoint, T.: Partial key exposure on RSA with private exponents larger than N. In: Ryan, M.D., Smyth, B., Wang, G. (eds.) ISPEC 2012. LNCS, vol. 7232, pp. 369–380. Springer, Heidelberg (2012)

7. Boneh, D., Durfee, G., Frankel, Y.: An attack on RSA given a small fraction of the private key bits. In: Ohta, K., Pei, D. (eds.) ASIACRYPT 1998. LNCS, vol. 1514, pp. 25–34. Springer, Heidelberg (1998)

8. Lu, Y., Zhang, R., Lin, D.: New partial key exposure attacks on CRT-RSA with large public exponents. In: Boureanu, I., Owesarski, P., Vaudenay, S. (eds.) ACNS 2014. LNCS, vol. 8479, pp. 151–162. Springer, Heidelberg (2014)

9. Blömer, J., May, A.: New partial key exposure attacks on RSA. In: Boneh, D. (ed.) CRYPTO 2003. LNCS, vol. 2729, pp. 27–43. Springer, Heidelberg (2003)

10. Herrmann, M., May, A.: Solving linear equations modulo divisors: on factoring given any bits. In: Pieprzyk, J. (ed.) ASIACRYPT 2008. LNCS, vol. 5350, pp. 406–424. Springer, Heidelberg (2008)

11. Coppersmith, D.: Finding a small root of a bivariate integer equation; factoring with high bits known. In: Maurer, U.M. (ed.) EUROCRYPT 1996. LNCS, vol. 1070, pp. 178–189. Springer, Heidelberg (1996)

12. NIST: FIPS PUB 186-4 Federal Information Processing Standards Publication, Digital Signature Standard (DSS) (2013)

13. May, A.: New RSA vulnerabilities using lattice reduction methods. Ph.D. thesis (2003)

14. Kocher, P.C.: Timing attacks on implementations of diffie-Hellman, RSA, DSS, and other systems. In: Koblitz, N. (ed.) CRYPTO 1996. LNCS, vol. 1109, pp. 104–113. Springer, Heidelberg (1996)

15. Coron, J.-S.: Resistance against differential power analysis for elliptic curve cryptosystems. In: Koç, Ç.K., Paar, C. (eds.) CHES 1999. LNCS, vol. 1717, pp. 292–302. Springer, Heidelberg (1999)

16. Kocher, P.C., Jaffe, J., Jun, B.: Differential power analysis. In: Wiener, M. (ed.) CRYPTO 1999. LNCS, vol. 1666, p. 388. Springer, Heidelberg (1999)

17. Walter, C.D.: Sliding windows succumbs to big mac attack. In: Koç, Ç.K., Naccache, D., Paar, C. (eds.) CHES 2001. LNCS, vol. 2162, pp. 286–299. Springer, Heidelberg (2001)

18. Clavier, C., Feix, B., Gagnerot, G., Roussellet, M., Verneuil, V.: Horizontal correlation analysis on exponentiation. In: Soriano, M., Qing, S., López, J. (eds.) ICICS 2010. LNCS, vol. 6476, pp. 46–61. Springer, Heidelberg (2010)

19. Fouque, P.-A., Kunz-Jacques, S., Martinet, G., Muller, F., Valette, F.: Power attack on small RSA public exponent. In: Goubin, L., Matsui, M. (eds.) CHES 2006. LNCS, vol. 4249, pp. 339–353. Springer, Heidelberg (2006)

20. Lenstra, A.K., Lenstra, H.W.J., Lovász, L.: Factoring polynomials with rational coefficients. Math. Ann. 261, 515–534 (1982)

21. Quisquater, J.-J., Couvreur, C.: Fast decipherment algorithm for RSA public-key cryptosystem. Electron. Lett. 18, 905–907 (1982)

A Generalized Authentication Scheme for Mobile Phones Using Gait Signals

Huan Nguyen[1], Huy H. Nguyen[1], Thang Hoang[3],
Deokjai Choi[2], and Thuc D. Nguyen[1(✉)]

[1] FIT, University of Science VNU-HCMC, Ho Chi Minh City, Vietnam
{1012158,0912182}@student.hcmus.edu.vn, ndthuc@fit.hcmus.edu.vn
[2] ECE, Chonnam National University, Gwangju, South Korea
dchoi@jnu.ac.kr
[3] EECS, Oregon State University, Corvallis, USA
hoangmin@eecs.oregonstate.edu

Abstract. Despite the reliability of authentication schemes using tokens or biometric modalities, their requirement of explicit gestures makes them less usable. On the other hand, the study on gait signals which are potential reliable for effective implicit authentication have been raised recently. Having said that, all the existing solutions fail to be applicable in reality since they rely on having sensors fixed to a specific position and orientation. In order to handle the instability of sensor's orientation, a flexible approach taking advantages of available sensors on mobile devices is our main contribution in this work. Utilizing both statistical and supervised learning, we conduct experiments on the signal captured in different positions: front pocket and waist. In particular, adopting PCA+SVM brings about impressive results on signals in front pocket with an equal error rate of 2.45 % and accuracy rate of 99.14 % in regard to the verification and identification process, respectively. The proposed method outperformed other state-of-the-art studies.

Keywords: Gait recognition · Pattern recognition · Behavioural biometrics · Implicit authentication · Accelerometer · Mobile security

1 Introduction

In recent years, mobile phones have undergone a significant evolution from communication devices into personal intelligent assistants. They are also becoming much more familiar for everyone since the forecast from a market survey shows that smart phone subscriptions will reach 5.6 billion in 2019 in a total of 9.3 billion mobile subscriptions. Nowadays, mobile phones are capable of providing a variety of utilities including entertainment, data storage and Internet transactions and are therefore gradually considered to be portable personal computers accumulating sensitive data. In addition, modern mobile devices tend to be smaller and lighter which makes them more easily lost, thus putting a huge amount of personal data at risk of being exposed to criminals. However,

© Springer International Publishing Switzerland 2016
M.S. Obaidat and P. Lorenz (Eds.): ICETE 2015, CCIS 585, pp. 386–407, 2016.
DOI: 10.1007/978-3-319-30222-5_18

despite this possible increase in security needs, the common authentication technique for mobiles currently in use is still based on traditional methods of secret number, text or visual pattern passwords [2]. Considering the drawbacks of the password-based technique including memory and security problems [2], newer alternatives relying on biometric traits have recently been introduced [3], which use fingerprint, face recognition or online signature. Nevertheless, user cooperation is a major requisite for all of these verification techniques as users are required to perform certain actions each time and when repeated this routine might become rather annoying and obtrusive. Another important issue regarding mobile phones is the different levels of security required for each function. For example, the risks involved with accessing one's own daily schedule is much less significant in comparison with carrying out online transactions; therefore, there is actually no need to apply the same authentication requirements to every application. Hence, with the increasing number of new mobile applications, different authentication schemes are necessary for user experience optimization. Accordingly, further investigation is required for an implicit authentication method and human gait signal recognition by wearable sensors is considered to be an effective alternative [3,4,24]. After a long time of research, this method of identification has recently been introduced and also achieved positive results [1,8].

ID number utilizing gait signs using wearable sensors has been acquainted in recent times. Furthermore, they are observed to attain positive and desirable results, such as [1,8]. Also, gait signals are able to capture users implicitly without interrupting their walking activities. Additionally, they are verified to have superior user-friendly design and ease of use as well as security over other biometric modalities, for instance, [16,22]. It is far more difficult to counterfeit an authentic gait pattern than replicating a copy of fingerprints or face detection with a sensor of other modalities [22]. However, most of the gait recognition systems available on the market nowadays have their sensor set up with specific orientation and positions such as the waist, ankle, or hip [1,8,11,16,18]. Undoubtedly, in the mobile context, these position captures might be confusing and inappropriate to the users.

The solution proposed in this paper aims to be able to provide reliable verification or identification using the gait of the user. Our observation indicates that the phone is usually placed in the front pocket of the user [2], and as a result we focus our effort into this particular placement of the phone. The difficulty of gait recognition lies mainly in the various orientations especially when gait pattern is something highly susceptible to external circumstances. These challenges render pattern matching an unreliable solution in recent studies [8,11,16–18,23]. On the other hand, since a mobile device tend to be carried by its user throughout the day, we realized that gait signals can be collected and processed continuously. Using the machine learning techniques mentioned in Lecture Notes in Computer Science: Authors' Instructions 3, we applied it to the gait signals created by a user during a specific period of time. In addition, experiments on a dataset of waist signal [25] are also conducted in order to analyze the effectiveness of the proposed method on different position. We want to be able to identify any significant changes in the gait pattern of the user and inform the device to update its model when identification fails consistently.

Our main goals in this paper:

- Investigate the problem of the orientation of the device and provide a simple solution that uses sensors available on most modern mobile devices (Sect. 3).
- Present a new model for gait recognition that appears to have a lower error rate than the solutions currently available (Sect. 5).

2   Related Works

Human gait data is used to detect human feet movement; thus, it contains information for human recognition. More specifically, the mechanism of human gait requires the coordination between the skeletal, neurological, and muscular systems of the human body [4]. The idea of using wearable sensors for gait verification was first introduced by H. Ailisto in 2005 [1], further researched by Gafurov [8]. Generally speaking, to record movement signals, sensors are attached to a specific position on a human body, such as ankle [6–8,18], hip [8,11,12], waist [1,25], arm [8], or multiple positions [5,9]. Accelerometers are most commonly used to capture gait signals, while other options such as gyroscopes or rotation sensors are also frequently adopted. The most popular approach is rooted in pattern matching, in which the gait signals are captured, preprocessed and separated into several different patterns. The second approach is based on machine learning, in which Feature vectors are extracted and supervised learning is adopted to construct general gait verification or identification models.

Wearable sensors, though have been experimented with a variety of success rates, have restraints, such as high price and lack of portability due to their size and weight. Lately, the development of micro electromechanical (MEM) technology has enabled scientists to miniaturize sensors and integrate them in mobile devices, which also allowed gait identification to be integrated in handheld devices [16,20]. Mobile sensors are cheaper, simpler than wearable sensors; but they are considered of unstable quality. For example, the sampling rate is unstable and low, the noise level is rather high.

Derawi et al. [11] demonstrated these deficiencies by re-implementing Holien et al.'s work [13]. The authors achieved an EER of 20.1 %, in comparison to the original EER of 12.9 %.

3   The Instability of Sensor Orientation

3.1   Problem Statement

Figure 1b–d illustrate the instability of the mobile in terms of its orientation and position when it is put freely in the pocket. Because walking is a slow activity with a moderate fluctuation, any strong acceleration is likely to last no longer than a few tenths of a second. Consequently, the impact of different positions in

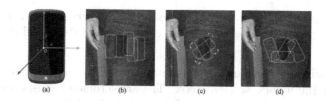

Fig. 1. (a) Mobile coordinate system, (b) misplacement error, (c) disorientation error and (d) disorientation errors and misplacement errors.

the pocket is not significant and is considered as noise. This can be mitigated by applying an effective noise filtering algorithm which will be described in Sect. 4.1.

Meanwhile, the instability of the mobile's orientation (namely the disorientation for short) significantly affects the quality of the acquired gait signals. Due to the design of the mobile accelerometer, wherein the gait signals are captured in 3 separate dimensions, the shape of the acquired signals fully depends on the relative orientation between the mobile and its carrier. So, the instability of the mobile orientation would make the gait signals in each separate dimension dissimilar. This obstacle could ruin the effectiveness of gait verification or identification systems. For instance, the accuracy rate of pattern matching approaches can be reduced when dealing with dissimilar gait signals. This circumstance will be illustrated in Sect. 5.5. Furthermore, based on our observations, gait cycle-based segmentation can be easily performed on the gait signal in the dimension which represents the vertical walking direction (viz. the Y–dimension as in Fig. 1a). Due to the disorientation problem, it is difficult to determine the correct dimension which reflects the vertical walking direction. Errors in the segmentation phase might propagate to subsequent processing phases, so that the effectiveness of the system can be compromised. Finally, extracting reliable features from dissimilar gait signals could be a problematic issue.

Generally, the main objective of resolving the disorientation problem is to maintain the accuracy rate of the mobile gait verification or identification systems under practical conditions. A small part of this problem was solved in [19]. However, there are unrealistic assumptions and constraints which could make the authors' proposed method difficult to apply in practice. We present a more flexible solution to this problem in the following section.

3.2 Proposed Solution

A simple but effective strategy to handle the disorientation is making gait signals always be represented in a fixed coordinate system which is insensitive to the device's orientation. In other words, acceleration vectors representing gait signals should be transformed from the instable mobile coordinate system to a stable one. Based on the availability of sensors in the mobile, the Earth coordinate is likely to be considered as the effective fixed system to represent the collected acceleration samples. To do that, it is mandatory to collect various kinds of sensor data during the gait sensing period. The following section describes all necessary sensors need to be activated to collect enough data used in this study.

Data Acquisition. Obviously, the first sensor needs to be activated to capture gait signal is the mobile accelerometer. The accelerometer senses forces acting on the mobile in the three orthogonal axes of X, Y, Z (Fig. 1a). A sequence of acceleration samples output by the accelerometer during walking is recognized as the gait signal. Each sample is a 3-dimensional vector, wherein each component is a combination of the forces of gravity and user motion acting on each dimension.

$$\mathbf{a} = (a^{(X)}, a^{(Y)}, a^{(Z)}), \tag{1}$$

where $a^{(D)}$ is the acceleration value sensed on the $D-$axis of the mobile.

Due to the characteristics of the accelerometer, the raw acceleration samples always comprise gravitational acceleration components. In order to obtain samples which only involve pure gait signals of individuals, we eliminate the impact of gravity by additionally activating a virtual sensor of gravity to determine the gravitational acceleration components on the 3 axes of the mobile during the gait capture process. The output of the gravity sensor is a 3-component vector

$$\mathbf{g} = (g^{(X)}, g^{(Y)}, g^{(Z)}), \tag{2}$$

where $g^{(D)}$ is the gravitational acceleration on the $D-$axis of the mobile.

Furthermore to resolve the disorientation problem, we activate a synthetic sensor of orientation, along with the two sensors above to monitor the orientation states of the mobile. As in the case of the accelerometer and gravity sensor, the output of the orientation sensor is a 3-component vector

$$\mathbf{o} = (\alpha, \beta, \gamma), \tag{3}$$

where α, β, γ represent the degrees of rotation around the $Z-, X-, Y-$ axes of the mobile respectively.

Note that both orientation sensor and gravity sensor are all virtual sensors whose outputs are normally synthesized from two physical sensors: the accelerometer and the geomagnetic field sensor. These sensors are getting more and more popular, appearing in most modern smartphones so that all mandatory sensor data needed in this study can be easily obtained in practice.

Gait Signal Transformation. Let us assume that after a gait sensing period, we obtain n vectors of acceleration $\mathbf{a}_i$, orientation $\mathbf{o}_i$ and gravity $\mathbf{g}_i$

$$\mathbf{A} = \begin{bmatrix} \mathbf{a}_1 \dots \mathbf{a}_i \dots \mathbf{a}_n \end{bmatrix}^\top \in \mathbb{R}^{n \times 3}, \qquad \mathbf{G} = \begin{bmatrix} \mathbf{g}_1 \dots \mathbf{g}_i \dots \mathbf{g}_n \end{bmatrix}^\top \in \mathbb{R}^{n \times 3},$$

$$\mathbf{O} = \begin{bmatrix} \mathbf{o}_1 \dots \mathbf{o}_i \dots \mathbf{o}_n \end{bmatrix}^\top = \begin{bmatrix} \alpha_1 \dots \alpha_i \dots \alpha_n \\ \beta_1 \dots \beta_i \dots \beta_n \\ \gamma_1 \dots \gamma_i \dots \gamma_n \end{bmatrix}^\top \in \mathbb{R}^{n \times 3}. \tag{4}$$

First, the influence of gravity on the acquired acceleration samples is eliminated to obtain the pure gait signal.

$$\mathbf{A} \leftarrow \mathbf{A} - \mathbf{G}. \tag{5}$$

For each rotation vector $\mathbf{o}_i$ in $\mathbf{O}$, we calculate a rotation matrix $\mathbf{R}_i$ which will be used to transform the acceleration vector in the mobile coordinate system to the Earth coordinate system.

$$\mathbf{R}_i = \begin{bmatrix} \cos\alpha_i \cos\gamma_i - \sin\alpha_i \sin\beta_i \sin\gamma_i & \sin\alpha_i \cos\beta_i & \cos\alpha_i \sin\gamma_i + \sin\alpha_i \sin\beta_i \cos\gamma_i \\ -\sin\alpha_i \cos\gamma_i - \cos\alpha_i \sin\beta_i \sin\gamma_i & \cos\alpha_i \cos\beta_i & -\sin\alpha_i \sin\gamma_i + \cos\alpha_i \sin\beta_i \cos\gamma_i \\ -\cos\beta_i \sin\gamma_i & -\sin\beta_i & \cos\beta_i \cos\gamma_i \end{bmatrix} \tag{6}$$

Finally, we transform the gravity-free acceleration vector representing in the mobile coordinate system to the new fixed system by multiplying the vector with the corresponding rotation matrix.

$$\mathbf{a}_i \leftarrow \mathbf{a}_i \mathbf{R}_i. \tag{7}$$

The gait signal after transformation is denoted as

$$\mathbf{A} = \begin{bmatrix} \mathbf{a}_1 \dots \mathbf{a}_i \dots \mathbf{a}_n \end{bmatrix}^\mathsf{T} = \begin{bmatrix} a_1^{(X)} \dots a_i^{(X)} \dots a_n^{(X)} \\ a_1^{(Y)} \dots a_i^{(Y)} \dots a_n^{(Y)} \\ a_1^{(Z)} \dots a_i^{(Z)} \dots a_n^{(Z)} \end{bmatrix}^\mathsf{T} = \begin{bmatrix} \mathbf{a}^{(X)} & \mathbf{a}^{(Y)} & \mathbf{a}^{(Z)} \end{bmatrix}. \tag{8}$$

The acceleration vectors after transformation are presented in the Earth coordinate system, wherein the new $Z-$dimension represents the vertical direction which is perpendicular to the ground, whereas the new $X-$ and $Y-$dimensions represent the horizontal plane which is parallel to the ground. These transformed $X-$ and $Y-$dimensions always point towards the East and the magnetic North Pole respectively regardless of the walking direction. However, due to the fact that the user can walk in any direction in the horizontal plane, gait signals in the transformed $X-$ and $Y-$dimensions which are captured from a session can be dissimilar to those captured from other sessions respectively. Therefore, instead of using the signals in each separate dimension of X and Y, we utilize the combined signal of $X - Y$

$$\mathbf{a}^{(XY)} = (a_1^{(XY)}, \dots, a_i^{(XY)}, \dots, a_n^{(XY)}), \tag{9}$$

where $a_i^{(XY)} = \sqrt{\left(a_i^{(X)}\right)^2 + \left(a_i^{(Y)}\right)^2}$.

In other words, the gait signals will be finally represented in the 2 dimensions of the Earth, wherein the transformed $Z-$ and $XY-$ axes represent the vertical and horizontal directions of walking, respectively. Moreover, the magnitude of the gait signal is additionally utilized as an additional dimension for gait representation.

$$\mathbf{a}^{(M)} = (a_1^{(M)}, \dots, a_i^{(M)}, \dots, a_n^{(M)}), \tag{10}$$

where $a_i^{(M)} = \sqrt{\left(a_i^{(X)}\right)^2 + \left(a_i^{(Y)}\right)^2 + \left(a_i^{(Z)}\right)^2}$.

In summary, the gait signal after transformation will be presented in 3 dimensions as described above.

$$\mathbf{A} = \begin{bmatrix} \mathbf{a}^{(Z)} \ \mathbf{a}^{(XY)} \ \mathbf{a}^{(M)} \end{bmatrix} = \begin{bmatrix} a_1^{(Z)} \ldots a_i^{(Z)} \ldots a_n^{(Z)} \\ a_1^{(XY)} \ldots a_i^{(XY)} \ldots a_n^{(XY)} \\ a_1^{(M)} \ldots a_i^{(M)} \ldots a_n^{(M)} \end{bmatrix}^{\top} . \tag{11}$$

Since each acceleration sample is always transformed into the Earth coordinate system according to the current orientation of the mobile determined as soon as the acceleration value is returned, it is more robust than the solution proposed in [19], in that all of the signals are likely to be transformed according to the initial orientation of the mobile, which is predetermined before the user starts to walk.

4   Gait Recognition Model Construction

In this section, we propose a novel gait verification system using statistical analysis and a supervised learning, working effectively on orientation-independent gait signals obtained by using the method presented in the previous section. Our system follows the traditional pattern recognition process consisting of mandatory steps such as data preprocessing, segmentation, feature extraction and classification.

4.1   Data Preprocessing

Linear Interpolation. As the mobile sensor is a power saving device which is simpler than standalone sensors, the sampling rate is not always stable. The time interval between two consecutive returned samples is not identical. First, we apply linear interpolation to the acquired acceleration samples to achieve gait signals at a fixed sampling rate.

Moreover, due to the design of the mobile operating system (e.g., Android OS), the triplet of acceleration sample, orientation sample and gravity sample is not yielded simultaneously. Meanwhile in the proposed solution to handle the disorientation issue, it is required that this triplet need to be yielded concurrently. Therefore, we additionally apply the same linear interpolation to the obtained orientation samples and gravity samples. The timestamp of the interpolated acceleration samples is used as the reference axis to determine the approximate orientation vector and gravity vector yielded at the same time as the acceleration vector.

Noise Elimination. Gait signals captured by the mobile accelerometer inevitably contain much noise. This can be due to the misplacement error (Fig. 1b), the quality of the sensors or bumps on the ground while walking,

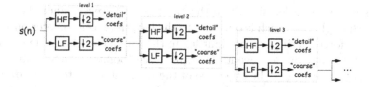

Fig. 2. Multi-level wavelet decomposition.

the difference in footwear, etc. We apply a multi-level wavelet decomposition and reconstruction method to remove the noise components in the signal. Technically, the detailed coefficients (obtained by HF filter as in Fig. 2) are set to 0 s at all decomposition levels. The signal reconstruction process involves combining the detailed coefficients of zero with the coarse coefficients from the lowest level until the level 0 is achieved. Specifically, in this study, we apply the Daubechies orthogonal wavelet (Db6) [15,21] with the decomposition at level 2 to mitigate the noise caused by the acquisition environment.

4.2   Gait Pattern Extraction

Gait Cycle Based Segmentation. Segmentation is the most important process which could directly affect the quality of the extracted gait patterns. It can be easily seen that walking is a cyclic activity so that the gait signal should be segmented into gait cycles instead of fixed-length patterns.

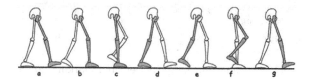

Fig. 3. Illustration of a gait cycle.

Gait cycle is commonly defined as the time interval between two successive occurrences of one of the repetitive events when walking [24]. Particularly, a gait cycle can start with initial contact of the heel and continue until the same heel contacts the ground again. We assume that the mobile device is placed at the same side with the leg which is going to contact the ground as in the phase "a" or "g" in the Fig. 3, for example the right leg. So, at the time the heel touches the ground, the association of the ground reaction force and the inertial force together will act on the right leg, which makes the acceleration value of the transformed Z-dimension signal sensed by the accelerometer strongly change and form negative peaks (illustrated as star points in the Fig. 4b). They are recognized as the starting points of the gait cycles. Note that when the event "d" happens (e.g., the left heel touches the ground), the accelerometer also generates negative peaks, similar to the "a" event. However, since the device is placed at the right leg which is opposite to the left, the accelerometer only senses insignificant forces acting on the right leg in this case. Therefore, the magnitude of peaks generated by "d" events (Fig. 4b, circle points) is not high as those generated by "a" or "g". The objective of the segmentation step is to divide the signal into separate gait cycles. So, it is required to determine peaks which are generated by the event of "a" or "g" in the Fig. 3. First of all, we determine the position of all of the negative peaks in the $Z-$dimension gait signal $a^{(Z)}$ of length n. Let

$$\Pi = \{i_j | a^{(Z)}_{i_j-1} > a^{(Z)}_{i_j}, a^{(Z)}_{i_j+1} > a^{(Z)}_{i_j}, i_j \in 1 \ldots n\} \qquad (12)$$

be the set of index of these peaks with the order preserved. Assuming that $|\Pi|$ is always larger than 1 given a gait signal of a walking session, we filter the starting points of the gait cycles in Π based on two criteria.

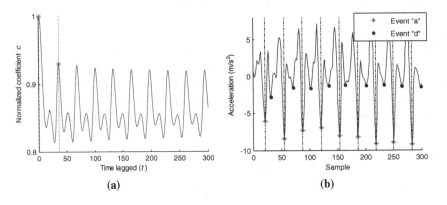

Fig. 4. (a) Auto-correlation coefficients, (b) Detected marking points in $Z-$signal.

The first criterion is based on the magnitude of the peaks. We eliminate the noisy peaks whose values are higher than a threshold δ determined by the mean and standard deviation of all of the peaks in Π.

$$\delta = \mu_\Pi - \tau \sigma_\Pi, \qquad (13)$$

where

$$\mu_\Pi = \frac{1}{|\Pi|} \sum_{i \in \Pi} a^{(Z)}_i,$$

$$\sigma_\Pi = \sqrt{\frac{1}{(|\Pi|-1)} \sum_{i \in \Pi} (a^{(Z)}_i - \mu_\Pi)^2}, \qquad (14)$$

τ is a user-defined parameter.

Table 1. List of gait features extracted in time and frequency domains.

Time domain features
Mean of the max/min value in each $s_u^{(D)}$ in $\mathbf{p}^{(D)}$ where $D = Z, XYM$; average absolute difference; root mean square; standard deviation; waveform length; 10-bin histogram distribution; average length of $s_u^{(D)}$ in $\mathbf{p}^{(D)}$
Frequency domain features
Magnitudes of first 40 FFT coefficients; first 40 DCT coefficients

The second is based on the correct positions of the gait cycle's starting points. While the distance between starting points of the gait cycle is assumed to fluctuate around a constant range in other studies [11,17], we observed that such range does not cover all possible cases since the walking speed of different individuals varies significantly. Instead, we estimate the length of the gait cycle according to the characteristics of each signal.

To determine the periodicity of the gait signal, we calculate the autocorrelation coefficients c_t $(0 \leq t < n)$ of the Z−dimension signal by

$$c_t = \frac{N}{N - t} \times \frac{\sum_{i=1}^{N-t} a_i^{(Z)} a_{i+t}^{(Z)}}{\sum_{i=1}^{N} \left(a_i^{(Z)}\right)^2}. \tag{15}$$

The moving average algorithm is then applied to smooth these coefficients. Let us assume that c_i and c_j are the 1st and 2nd peaks autocorrelation coefficients, respectively, as depicted by two stars in the Fig. 4a. Then, the length of a gait cycle can be approximated by

$$\Delta = j. \tag{16}$$

According to the two criteria of magnitude and position, we determine the peaks representing the starting points of the gait cycles. Let Ω be the set of these peaks with the order of indices preserved. Then, Ω will be given by

$$\Omega = \{i_j | a_{i_j}^{(Z)} < \delta, (\exists i_k \in \Pi, k > j, \Delta - \epsilon \leq i_k - i_j \leq \Delta + \epsilon), i_j \in \Pi\}, \tag{17}$$

where $\epsilon > 0$ is the user-defined parameter. Assuming that there are $k - 1$ where $k > 1$ gait cycles in the given gait signal, hence, $|\Omega| = k$. We separate the signal into $k - 1$ distinct segments, with each $\mathbf{S}_i$ consisting of a full gait cycle

$$\mathbf{S}_i = \begin{bmatrix} a_{\Omega_i}^{(Z)} & a_{\Omega_i}^{(XY)} & a_{\Omega_i}^{(M)} \\ \vdots & \vdots & \vdots \\ a_{\Omega_{i+1}}^{(Z)} & a_{\Omega_{i+1}}^{(XY)} & a_{\Omega_{i+1}}^{(M)} \end{bmatrix}. \tag{18}$$

Pattern Extraction. We form gait patterns by concatenating the separate one-gait-cycle segments extracted in the previous section. Each gait pattern would contain n_s consecutive segments and 50 % of them overlaps with the previous one. Let $\left[\mathbf{s}_u^{(Z)} \ \mathbf{s}_u^{(XY)} \ \mathbf{s}_u^{(M)}\right]$ be a segment consisting of a gait cycle, where $\mathbf{s}_u^{(Z)} = \left[a_{u1}^{(Z)} \ldots a_{un_u}^{(Z)}\right]^{\top}$, $\mathbf{s}_u^{(XY)} = \left[a_{u1}^{(XY)} \ldots a_{un_u}^{(XY)}\right]^{\top}$, $\mathbf{s}_u^{(M)} = \left[a_{u1}^{(M)} \ldots a_{un_u}^{(M)}\right]^{\top}$. Let

$$\mathbf{p}^{(Z)} = \left[a_{11}^{(Z)} \ldots a_{1n_1}^{(Z)} \ a_{21}^{(Z)} \ldots a_{2n_2}^{(Z)} \ldots a_{u1}^{(Z)} \ldots a_{un_u}^{(Z)} \ldots a_{s1}^{(Z)} \ldots a_{sn_s}^{(Z)}\right]^{\top},$$

$$\mathbf{p}^{(XY)} = \left[a_{11}^{(XY)} \ldots a_{1n_1}^{(XY)} \ a_{21}^{(XY)} \ldots a_{2n_2}^{(XY)} \ldots a_{u1}^{(XY)} \ldots a_{un_u}^{(XY)} \ldots a_{s1}^{(XY)} \ldots a_{sn_s}^{(XY)}\right]^{\top},$$

$$\mathbf{p}^{(M)} = \left[a_{11}^{(M)} \ldots a_{1n_1}^{(M)} \ a_{21}^{(M)} \ldots a_{2n_2}^{(M)} \ldots a_{u1}^{(M)} \ldots a_{un_u}^{(M)} \ldots a_{s1}^{(M)} \ldots a_{sn_s}^{(M)}\right]^{\top}.$$

Then, a gait pattern $\mathbf{P}$ is defined by

$$\mathbf{P} = \left[\mathbf{p}^{(Z)} \ \mathbf{p}^{(XY)} \ \mathbf{p}^{(M)}\right] = \begin{bmatrix} a_{11}^{(Z)} \ldots a_{un_u}^{(Z)} \ldots a_{sn_s}^{(Z)} \\ a_{11}^{(XY)} \ldots a_{un_u}^{(XY)} \ldots a_{un_u}^{(XY)} \\ a_{11}^{(M)} \ldots a_{un_u}^{(M)} \ldots a_{sn_s}^{(M)} \end{bmatrix}^{\top}. \tag{19}$$

4.3 Gait Model Construction

Feature Extraction. We extract the features on both time and frequency domains as used in [19] for each gait pattern $\mathbf{P}$. The list of extracted features is briefly summarized in the Table 1. Note that all of the features in the time and frequency domains are extracted for the 3 dimensions of the gait pattern (viz. $\mathbf{p}^{(Z)}, \mathbf{p}^{(XY)}, \mathbf{p}^{(M)}$ in (19)), except for the "average length of $\mathbf{s}_u^{(D)}$ in $\mathbf{p}^{(D)}$" feature since its value is identical in all 3 dimensions. All of the extracted features are concatenated to form the final feature vector for a gait pattern.

Feature Vector Dimension Reduction. Since we expect the system to run directly on the mobile phone with limited computational resources, it is necessary to reduce the dimension of the extracted feature vectors to lighten the complexity of the gait model built by using the machine learning algorithms. Thus, we adopt the Principle Component Analysis (PCA) to reduce the number of dimensions while maintaining the discriminability of the feature vectors.

Let us assume that the number of users is denoted as N. The number of feature vectors extracted from all of the gait patterns for each user is M. According to the feature extraction phase, the length of each feature vector is $n_f = 289$. The $j^{th}(j = 1 \ldots M)$ feature vector of the user $i(i = 1 \ldots N)$ is denoted as

$$\mathbf{v}_j^{(i)} = \left[f_{j,1}^{(i)}, \ldots, f_{j,k}^{(i)}, \ldots, f_{j,n_f}^{(i)}\right], \tag{20}$$

where $f_{j,k}^{(i)}$ is the kth feature component of $\mathbf{v}_j^{(i)}$. The matrix of feature vectors of all users can be formed as

$$
\mathbf{F} = \begin{bmatrix} \mathbf{v}_1^{(1)} \\ \vdots \\ \mathbf{v}_j^{(i)} \\ \vdots \\ \mathbf{v}_M^{(N)} \end{bmatrix} = \begin{bmatrix} f_{1,1}^{(1)} & f_{1,k}^{(1)} & f_{1,n_f}^{(1)} \\ \vdots & \vdots & \vdots \\ f_{j,1}^{(i)} & f_{j,k}^{(i)} & f_{j,n_f}^{(i)} \\ \vdots & \vdots & \vdots \\ f_{M,1}^{(N)} & f_{M,k}^{(N)} & f_{M,n_f}^{(N)} \end{bmatrix} = \begin{bmatrix} \mathbf{v}_1 \\ \vdots \\ \mathbf{v}_t \\ \vdots \\ \mathbf{v}_{MN} \end{bmatrix} \in \mathbb{R}^{MN \times n_f}. \tag{21}
$$

Then, a covariance matrix of $\mathbf{F}$ can be calculated by

$$
\Sigma = \frac{1}{MN} \sum_{i=1}^{MN} (\mathbf{v}_i - \bar{\mathbf{v}})(\mathbf{v}_i - \bar{\mathbf{v}})^\top \in \mathbb{R}^{n_f \times n_f}. \tag{22}
$$

Let $\vec{\lambda} = (\lambda_1, \ldots, \lambda_i, \ldots, \lambda_{n_f})$ and $\mathbf{u}_i$ be eigenvalues and eigenvectors obtained from the Σ, respectively. All eigenvalues λ_i of Σ are sorted in descending order in which the higher the eigenvalues are, the more important they are. Assuming that $\lambda_i < \lambda_{i-1}$, to reduce the number of dimensions of the original feature vector from n_f to k, k eigenvectors are taken according to the order of the eigenvalues

$$
\mathbf{U} = \begin{bmatrix} \mathbf{u}_1 \ldots \mathbf{u}_i \ldots \mathbf{u}_k \end{bmatrix} \in \mathbb{R}^{n_f \times k}. \tag{23}
$$

The dimension-reduced matrix of feature vectors can be calculated by

$$
\hat{\mathbf{F}}^\top = \mathbf{F}^\top \mathbf{U}. \tag{24}
$$

Gait Recognition Model for Verification and Identification. We adopt two schemes, namely feature vector matching and supervised learning, for both identification and verification. In the former scheme, the feature vectors extracted after using PCA are stored in the mobile storage, which will be used for user identification or verification. In the latter scheme, we apply Support Vector Machine (SVM) with a linear kernel to build a gait model for each user. An open library tool, LIBSVM [14], is used in this study for SVM-based gait model construction and evaluation.

5   Experiments

5.1   Dataset Description

We use the dataset which is an extended version of the one used in [19]. Besides our dataset, we additionally evaluate our proposed method on a well-known dataset [25] for experimental evaluation in this study. We would like to give readers a brief description of both datasets. The first dataset consists of gait signals of 38 subjects captured by using a Google Nexus One mobile phone.

Table 2. List of physical and virtual sensors activated during the gait capture process.

Sensor name	Model name	Sampling rate
Magnetic field sensor	AK 8973	25 Hz
Accelerometer	BMA 150	25 Hz
Orientation sensor	Virtual	25 Hz
Gravity sensor	Virtual	25 Hz
Linear acceleration sensor	Virtual	25 Hz
Rotation vector sensor	Virtual	25 Hz

The device is put freely inside the front trouser pocket and the sampling rate of integrated sensors is set to 25 Hz. Besides data described in the original work, the authors further provide other sensor data which are collected along with acceleration data during gait sensing period in the extended version. List of particular sensors activated in this phase is summarized in the Table 2. The second dataset is a collection of 745 subjects collected by inertial sensors (accelerometer, gyroscope). The sensors are mounted on a waist belt to measure at their maximum sampling rate 100 Hz. In this dataset, each subject has only two samples while the number of segments of several samples is not enough. The sequences for each subject are extracted automatically by using motion trajectory constraint and signal autocorrelation. Since having accelerometer and gyroscope signals with a particular sampling rate, we can easily convert the accelerometer to Earth coordinate system and proceed next steps of our algorithm. We only apply our algorithm on level-walk sequences.

5.2   Experimental Configuration

First Position: Front Pocket. Since the sampling rate of the sensor is low (25 Hz), making the number of samples in a one-gait-cycle segment small, we form each gait pattern extracted in Sect. 4.2 by concatenating $n_s = 4$ consecutive segments, in order to feasibly extract enough features in the time and frequency domains. In total, around 10226 gait patterns are extracted from the dataset. Moreover, the length of the feature vectors after applying PCA is selected to be equal to n' such that the first n' eigenvectors capture at least 99.5 % of the total variance. According to the dataset used in this study, n' is equal to 42.

Table 3. The configuration differences in between the original study and this experiment.

Method	Original setup				This experiment			
	Axes	# Subject	Position	SR (%)	Axes	# Subject	Position	SR
Rong et al.	X, Y, Z	38	Ankle	250	Z, XY, M	38	Front pocket	25
Gafurov et al.	Z	30	Ankle	100	Z	38	Front pocket	25
Derawi et al.	M	60	Hip	100	M	38	Front pocket	25

We re-implement several state-of-the-art gait recognition systems on the dataset used in this experiment ([17, 18, 23]) in order to not only evaluate the effectiveness of the solution proposed to handle the disorientation problem, but also compare with our proposed recognition schemes. The effectiveness of gait recognition systems is evaluated under two aspects: identification and verification capabilities. Note that in the comparison of the verification and identification capabilities among the studies, the disorientation problem is not taken into account so that all of the works will be evaluated on the orientation-independent gait signals (referred to as the transformed dataset). Furthermore, as Rong et al. used the gait signals of the $X-$ and $Y-$dimensions which are not available in the transformed dataset, we replace them with the gait signals of the $XY-$ and $M-$ dimensions to make sure that the number of dimensions is consistent to that in the original study. In Gafurov et al.'s method, the authors experimented on the gait signals of different dimensions and achieved various results. Based on the availability of dimensions in the transformed dataset, we select the gait signal of the $Z-$dimension (referred to as the up-down direction in the original) as the standard for evaluation and comparison. Table 3 shows the difference in the configuration settings in between the original studies and this experiment.

Second Position: Waist. Since the dataset does not provide timestamp along with signals [25], we transform the accelerometer into Earth coordinate system by gyroscope signals and sampling rate. In more detail, each gyroscope sample shows rotation angle (radian) in 0.01 s. We observe that the structure of signals will collapse if we apply the noise elimination, hence our skipping it on this dataset. Due to the limit of this dataset on the number of segment of each subject, we collect 29 from 745 subjects satisfying that both their training and testing data has at least 12 segments. Similar to the previous section, we form each gait pattern by concatenating $n_s = 4$ consecutive segments in order to feasibly extract enough features in time and frequency domains. In aggregate, there are 384 gait patterns extracted from the dataset. We also make some adjustments to make our algorithm more effective to this dataset in recognizing the first peak as well as segments more precisely. Furthermore, instead of using only three dimensions $Z-$, $XY-$, $M-$, we use gyroscope signals as three extra dimensions to enhance the result.

5.3   Verification Results

First Position: Front Pocket. We utilize Receiver Operating Characteristic (ROC) curves to illustrate the performance of the proposed system in the aspect of verification. Firstly, we experiment with different portions of the training data and testing data, ranging from $k = 5\%$ to 50%, in order to determine the influence of the number of training data on the effectiveness of the proposed schemes. Note that we apply cross-verification to overall evaluate the performance of the proposed method. Participants will be considered as the genuine user in turn. Specifically for each user i, in the PCA approach, we store randomly k gait patterns of the user i as the training data. The remaining patterns of the user i

will be utilized for testing the false rejection rate (FRR), and the patterns of all other users $j(j \neq i)$ will be used for testing false acceptance rate (FAR). Similarly in the PCA+SVM approach, k genuine gait patterns of the user i and k patterns of each other users will be used to construct the gait model for the user i, while remaining data will be used for evaluating the error rates of the constructed model.

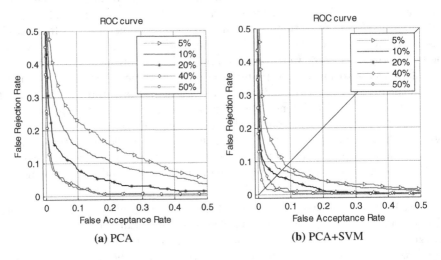

Fig. 5. ROC curves of the proposed system using two verification schemes according to different portions of training data (Color figure online).

Figure 5 depicts the error rates of the proposed method using the PCA and PCA+SVM schemes with different proportions of training data and testing data. As expected, a higher proportion of the training data yield a lower error rate. Moreover, we can see that applying a supervised learning (PCA+SVM) technique can help to enhance the accuracy of the system. The overall error rate achieved using the PCA+SVM scheme is lower than that when only using the PCA scheme. Next, we compare the proposed system with those of other studies which are re-implemented and evaluated according to the new configuration settings. The verification performance of all of these studies is investigated on two testing scenarios: Firstly, we consider each walking session as a testing trial, which is commonly used in comparing studies. Unlike in these studies, we apply majority voting to our schemes to validate each walking session. That means the user is verified if a larger portion of the gait patterns extracted in the session is recognized as being authentic. Figure 6a depicts the error rates of the proposed methods and other studies in this scenario.

From our viewpoint, session-based verification might require a lot of time and efforts from the user since he/she has to continuously walk for a long distance, in order to collect enough data to be verified. The verification process can be performed faster and more constantly if the system can immediately verify the

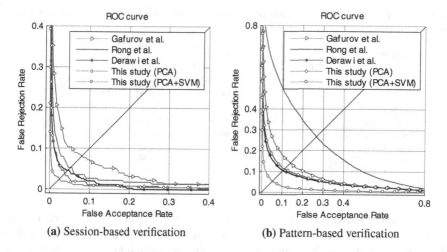

Fig. 6. The ROC curves of the proposed method and other studies which are re-implemented and evaluate on the first dataset according to the configuration in Table 3 (Color figure online).

user only using the gait pattern instead of having to wait until the walking session finishes. Therefore, we additionally investigate the performance of the methods in all of the studies when the separate gait patterns are treated as independent testing trials. As depicted in Fig. 6b, we can see that the error rates of all of the approaches are higher than those in the session-based scenario. Especially in Rong et al.'s method, the error rate is significantly increased, since the method of gait pattern extraction employed strongly relies on the whole walking session data. The error rate of our method using the PCA+SVM scheme in this scenario is approximately 5.35 %, which can help to reduce the time and effort needed to perform the verification task. Table 4 summarizes the EERs achieved in all of the studies according to two scenarios. It can be seen that in the session-based scenario, the achieved EERs with the methods proposed in the other studies after evaluating them in the transformed dataset are similar to original values. This reflects that handling the disorientation problem is mandatory in order to maintain the effectiveness of gait recognition systems because this problem might result in a significant increase of the error rates of the systems. This impact will be clearly shown in the Sect. 5.5.

Second Position: Waist. The same algorithm is applied with a few minor adjustments to be more compatible with this dataset [25]. Figure 7 depicts the error rates of the proposed method using PCA and PCA+SVM schemes. Because of the low number of sample, we skip the comparison between different proportions of training and testing data like the previous section. The result of our proposed method on this dataset is inferior to the result of the previous section. To elucidate the difference of those results, we contend that the position which a

Table 4. The error rates of session-based and pattern-based gait verification methods on the first dataset.

Method	Session-based			Pattern-based	
	EER(%) (*original*)	EER (%)	FRR (%) (*at* FAR = 1 %)	EER (%)	FRR (%) (*at* FAR = 1 %)
Rong et al.	5.6	5.28	16.47	26.67	84.27
Gafurov et al.	2.2 – 23.6	8.07	28.43	14.11	52.37
Derawi et al.	5.7	4.59	10.71	10.49	31.86
Proposed method (PCA)	–	3.83	10.75	11.23	35.03
Proposed method (PCA+SVM)	–	**2.45**	**3.75**	**5.35**	**14.38**

dataset is recorded affects strongly the result beside the quality of algorithm and dataset. In more detail, when walking, motion of our thigh is stronger than that of our waist. As we see, the supervised learning technique actually improves the accuracy of the verification system. Compared to using only PCA scheme, the overall error rate achieved using PCA+SVM scheme is lower. Similar to the previous section, we analyze the result in two testing scenarios: session-based and pattern-based. Table 5 summarizes the EERs achieved in our proposed method according to these scenarios.

Table 5. The error rates of session-based and pattern-based gait verification methods on the second dataset.

Method	Session-based			Pattern-based	
	EER(%) (*original*)	EER (%)	FRR (%) (*at* FAR = 1 %)	EER (%)	FRR (%) (*at* FAR = 1 %)
Proposed method (PCA)	–	18.87	37.08	16.07	31.51
Proposed method (PCA+SVM)	–	12.57	22.59	12.50	20.43

In contrast to the previous section, the result shows that both the EERs achieved in the session-based scenario and the FRR value when FAR is equal to 0.01 are slightly larger than those in pattern-based scenario. According to the experiments shown in [25], the EERs achieved in our proposed method is quite higher than in other studies, which varies from 5.6 % to 6.1 %. However, it is necessary to emphasize that the result of EERs cannot show the effectiveness of a particular algorithm for this dataset regularly. There are numerous subjects in this dataset and less number of samples for each subject, thus the dataset are very unbalanced. Therefore, we conduct a few experiments in identification to show readers the comprehensive result of our proposed method on this dataset. In the previous section, this issue is not mentioned because the experiment of our proposed method on our own dataset (for front pocket) shows impressive results in both verification and identification processes.

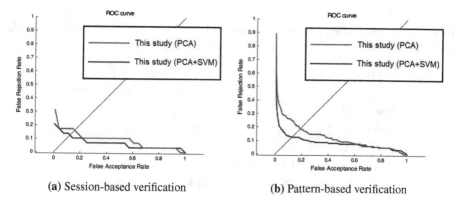

(a) Session-based verification   (b) Pattern-based verification

Fig. 7. The ROC curves of the proposed method on a subset of the second dataset (Color figure online).

5.4   Identification Results

First Position: Front Pocket. We also investigate the identification capability of the proposed method and other studies according to the two evaluation scenarios described above. The same 1-nearest neighbor algorithm is applied to all methods, except for the PCA+SVM scheme in order to measure the performance between studies. The best accuracy rate belongs to the proposed PCA+SVM scheme, with an amount of approximately 99.14 % being achieved under session-based identification aspect. Table 6 shows the identification performance of the proposed method and comparing studies. Similar to the verification results, the accuracy rate of pattern-based identification is normally lower than that of session-based identification. Especially in Rong et al.'s method, the accuracy of the system strongly decreases an amount of approximately 30 %.

Second Position: Waist. While our algorithm achieves outstanding results with our dataset recorded in front pocket, the result on this dataset does not meet the same expectations. All factors mentioned in Sect. 5.3 also affect the identification method. For instance, waist motion is more stable than thigh motion, so the step gait cycle detection for this dataset is more challenging as well. Moreover, the fact that number of subjects is high while number of samples of a subject is actually small makes a strong negative impact on the result. In fact, this issue affects identification more greatly than verification due to the difficulty of the multi-class problem. Consequently, only 29 subjects with reasonable quantity of samples are collected for this evaluation. Setting the number of folds to 5, the cross-validation accuracy is approximately 78.11 % for the set of 29 subjects consisting at least 5 patterns. The result dramatically decreases to 34.08 % for the set of 704 subjects consisting of at least 1 pattern.

Table 6. The error rates of session-based and pattern-based gait identification methods on the first dataset.

Method	Accuracy rate (%)	
	Session-based	Pattern-based
Rong et al. (+kNN)	93.12	64.82
Gafurov et al. (+kNN)	87.68	76.55
Derawi et al. (+kNN)	93.41	88.09
Proposed method (PCA+kNN)	96.56	85.48
Proposed method (PCA+SVM)	**99.14**	**94.93**

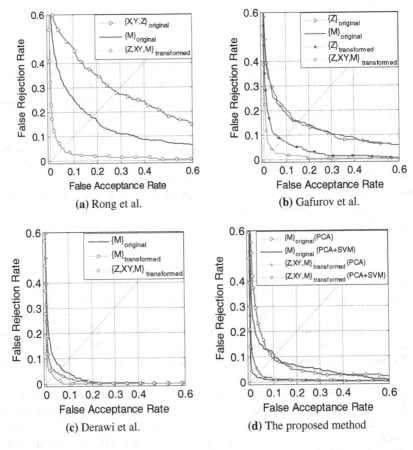

Fig. 8. The impacts of the disorientation error on the error rates of the gait verification systems on the first dataset (Color figure online).

5.5   The Impacts of Disorientation Error

Finally, we illustrate the impact of disorientation errors on the accuracy of the gait verification systems. As already mentioned, the instability of sensor orientation would cause the gait signals acquired in the 3 separate dimensions to be dissimilar. As can be seen in Fig. 8a (the triangle line), since the authors store the gait patterns of the separate dimensions, including the X-Template, Y-Template and Z-Template, as the reference set for individual matching, the error rate is significantly increased, because of the dissimilarity issues. This is similar to Gafurov et al.'s work (Fig. 8b). Looking at both Fig. 8a, b, it can be seen that protecting the similarity of the gait signals from the disorientation problem can help to maintain the accuracy rate of the system. Based on our observations, the magnitude of the gait signal is orientation-independent, so it can be used to construct the gait verification system in spite of the disorientation issues. This signal was used in the original study of Derawi et al. and achieved positive results (Fig. 8c). Therefore, we also modified the methods of Rong et al. and Gafurov et al. by only using the magnitude of the signal and found that the error rates could be enhanced. However, from our perspective, we are strongly convinced that the gait can be more distinguishable if the gait signal can be expressed in higher dimensions. Consequently, additional experiments are conducted according to the hypothesis, wherein we employ the gait signals of all dimensions, which can be obtained after overcoming the disorientation problem. As expected, the error rates achieved with the methods of all of the studies are likely to be more decreased when the gait signals in the dimensions of Z, XY, M are all used (Fig. 8). Therefore, we believe that overcoming the disorientation problem, in order to maintain the number of dimensions of the acquired gait signals, is mandatory to optimize the performance of gait verification and identification systems.

6   Conclusions

In reality, especially in the mobile context, the sensor disorientation is an obvious problem in gait verification and identification. To solve this problem, a simple but effective solution taking advantages of available sensors in mobile device was proposed. Our solution is using a gait recognition model leveraging statistical analysis and supervised machine learning to verify and identify mobile user. We also implemented our solution on signals of different positions, thigh and waist, to compare the effectiveness between them. The result we collected painted a very promising picture, especially in the case when the device is placed in the front pocket. Regard to that case, the proposed method outperformed other state-of-the-art studies in identification process. Along with the highly promising results achieved, the good potential of deploying a gait-based verification enhance the security on mobile devices. However, the result of our method on the public dataset is not good enough and the generalization problem on different positions of this subject still remains open. In fact, our proposed method is an optional to enhance the usability of mobile devices rather than a replacement for standard authentication schemes on mobile due to high expectation in privacy. In our opinion, the result can be improved if we apply a better gait segment detection strategy. In future works, we would like to develop a unique recognition model where gait models are stored directly in the device working effectively regardless of the position where a mobile device is placed in.

Acknowledgements. The research was supported by 2012-18-02TD VNU–HCMC Project.

References

1. Ailisto, H., Lindholm, M., Mantyjarvi, J., Vildjounaite E., Makela, S.M.: Identifying people from gait pattern with accelerometers. In: Proceedings of SPIE 5779, Biometric Technology for Human Identification II (2005)
2. Breitinger, F., Nickel, C.: User survey on phone security and usage. In: Proceedings of BIOSIG, vol. 164GI (2010)
3. Jain, A.K., Ross, A., Prabhakar, S.: An introduction to biometric recognition. IEEE Trans. Circuits Syst. Video Technol. **14**(1), 4–20 (2004)
4. Fish, D.J., Nielsen, J.: Clinical assessment of human gait. J. Prosthet. Orthot. **5**(2), 39 (1993)
5. Mondal, S., Nandy, A., Chakraborty, P., Nandi, G.C.: Gait based personal identification system using rotation sensor. Comput. Inf. Sci. **3**(2), 395–402 (2012)
6. Yuexiang, L., Xiabo, W., Feng, Q.: Gait authentication based on acceleration signals of ankle. Chin. J. Electron. **20**(3), 447–451 (2011)
7. Terada, S., Enomoto, Y., Hanawa D., Oguchi, K.: Performance of gait authentication using an acceleration sensor. In: Proceedings of 34th ICTSP (2011)
8. Gafurov, D., Snekkenes, E.: Gait recognition using wearable motion recording sensors. EURASIP J. Adv. Signal Process. **2009**, 7 (2009)
9. Pan, G., Zhang, Y., Wu, Z.: Accelerometer-based gait recognition via voting by signature points. IET Electron. Lett. **45**(22), 1116–1118 (2009)
10. Frank, F., Mannor, S., Precup, D.: Activity and gait recognition with time-delay embeddings. In: Proceedings of the 24th AAAI (2010)
11. Derawi, M., Nickel, C., Bours, P., Busch, C.: Unobtrusive user-authentication on mobile phones using biometric gait recoginition. In: Proceedings of the 6th IIH-MSP (2010)
12. Sprager, S., Zazula, D.: A cumulant-based method for gait identification using accelerometer data with principal component analysis and support vector machine. WSEAS Trans. Signal Process. **5**, 369–378 (2009)
13. Holien, K., Gait Recoginition under non-standard circumstances, Master thesis, Gjovik University College (2008)
14. Chang, C., Lin, C.J.: LIBSVM: a library for support vector machines. ACM Trans. Intell. Syst. Technol. **2**, 27 (2011)
15. Daubechies, I., Bates, B.: Ten lectures on wavelets. J. Acoust. Soc. Am. **93**(3), 1671–1671 (1993)
16. Derawi, M., Bours, P.: Gait and activity recognition using commercial phones. Comput. Secur. **39**, 137–144 (2013)
17. Derawi, M., Bours, P., Holien, K.: Improved cycle detection for accelerometer based gait authentication. In: 2010 Sixth International Conference on Intelligent Information Hiding and Multimedia Signal Processing (IIH-MSP), pp. 312–317. IEEE (2010)

18. Gafurov, D., Snekkenes, E., Bours, P.: Improved gait recognition performance using cycle matching. In: 2010 IEEE 24th International Conference on Advanced Information Networking and Applications Workshops (WAINA), pp. 836–841. IEEE (2010)
19. Hoang, T., Choi, D., Vo, V., Nguyen, A., Nguyen, T.: A lightweight gait authentication on mobile phone regardless of installation error. In: Janczewski, L.J., Wolfe, H.B., Shenoi, S. (eds.) SEC 2013. IFIP AICT, vol. 405, pp. 83–101. Springer, Heidelberg (2013)
20. Lu, H., Huang, J., Saha, T., Nachman, L.: Unobtrusive gait verification for mobile phones. In: Proceedings of the 2014 ACM International Symposium on Wearable Computers. ACM (2014)
21. Mallat, S.: A theory for multiresolution signal decomposition: the wavelet representation. IEEE Trans. Pattern Anal. Mach. Intell. 11(7), 674–693 (1989)
22. Mjaaland, B.B., Bours, P., Gligoroski, D.: Walk the walk: attacking gait biometrics by imitation. In: Burmester, M., Tsudik, G., Magliveras, S., Ilić, I. (eds.) ISC 2010. LNCS, vol. 6531, pp. 361–380. Springer, Heidelberg (2011)
23. Rong, L., Jianzhong, Z., Ming, L., Xiangfeng, H.: A wearable acceleration sensor system for gait recognition. In: 2nd IEEE Conference on Industrial Electronics and Applications ICIEA 2007, pp. 2654–2659. IEEE (2007)
24. Whitle, M.: Gait Analysis: An Introduction, vol. 1. Elsevier, Philadelphia (2007)
25. Ngo, T.: The largest inertial sensor-based gait database and performance evaluation of gait-based personal authentication. Pattern Recogn. 47(1), 228–237 (2014)

Signal Processing and Multimedia Applications

Signal Modelling for the Digital Reconstruction of Gramophone Noise

Christoph F. Stallmann[✉] and Andries P. Engelbrecht

Department of Computer Science, University of Pretoria, Lynnwood Road,
Hatfield, Pretoria 0002, South Africa
{cstallmann,engel}@cs.up.ac.za

Abstract. The revenue generated from gramophone records surpassed
that of ad-supported online streaming services in the United States in
2015. With the increase in popularity, a lot of old records are dug out and
digitized by private audiophiles, or remastered by music labels. These
old records are often scratched and damaged due to mishandling and
extensive playback. This article analyses various models and algorithms
than can be used to digitally refurbish the noise from gramophone records
which are often perceived as *crackles* and *pops*. Different duplication
approaches, trigonometric functions, polynomials, and time series models
are analysed according to their signal reconstruction ability. Some novel
artificial neural networks are discussed and compared to the existing
models. It was found that the neural networks outperformed the other
mathematical models, producing a more natural reconstruction of the
audio signal with little remaining noise perceivable by the human ear.

Keywords: Gramophone records · Noise reconstruction · Audio signal
modelling · Feed forward neural networks · Polynomials · Time series
models

1 Introduction

Gramophone records were the first commercial audio storage medium with the
introduction of Berliner's turntable in 1889 [40]. Records continued to be widely
used for more than seven decades, until they were replaced by the compact
disc (CD) in the late 1980s. Although downloadable digital music has become
the forerunner in the 20th century, gramophone sales have surged in the past
few years, achieving record sales since they were discontinued as main music
medium in 1993. Approximately six million records were sold in the United
States alone in 2013, an increase of 33 % from the previous year [29]. However,
the Nielsen Company indicated that only 15 % of the sales were logged, since
most gramophone records do not have a bar code which is used to track sales [7].
The Recording Industry Association of America (RIAA) reported that the revenue generated from gramophone records surpassed that of ad-supported online
streaming services such as Spotify and Pandora by 28 % in 2015 [18]. Besides

© Springer International Publishing Switzerland 2016
M.S. Obaidat and P. Lorenz (Eds.): ICETE 2015, CCIS 585, pp. 411–432, 2016.
DOI: 10.1007/978-3-319-30222-5_19

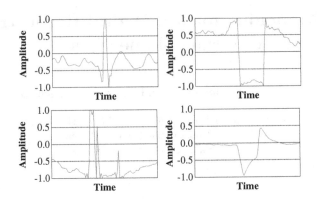

Fig. 1. Typical disruptions caused by scratches on gramophone records.

an increase in sales of new records, most recordings prior to the 1960 s are only available on gramophone. Efforts are made by both commercial music labels and private audiophiles to digitize these historic records. The digitization process is a tedious and time consuming process, since most records are damaged and need to be refurbished. Figure 1 shows typical distortions in the sound wave caused by scratches on the gramophone record.

This paper examines 29 different interpolation algorithms that are utilized for the digital restoration of audio signals that are distorted by scratches and other physical damage to the record. This research is part of a larger project aimed at automating the detection and reconstruction of noise on damaged gramophone records, removing the burden of manual labour. Although the research focuses on gramophones, the algorithms can be directly applied to other areas of audio signal processing, such as lost packets in voice over IP (VoIP) or the poor reception in digital car radios. The empirical procedure, test dataset and the measurement of the reconstruction performance and execution time used during the empirical analysis is discussed. Finally, the algorithms are benchmarked on music from eight different genres and the results are presented in the last section.

2   Algorithms

This section briefly discusses the theoretical background and mathematics of various interpolation algorithms used to reconstruct gramophone audio signals. The algorithms are categorized into duplication approaches, trigonometric methods, polynomials, time series models, and artificial neural networks.

2.1   Duplication Approaches

A simple method for reconstructing missing values is to copy a series of samples from another source or from somewhere else in the signal. Some duplication algorithms make use of equivalent sources to reconstruct the audio, where at least one of the sources is not subjected to noise [35]. However, multiple copies are mostly not available and copying samples from different parts of the same source is a more practical solution. A smart copying algorithm was proposed, able to replicate a similar fragment from the preceding or succeeding samples using an AR model with mixed excitation and a Kalman filter [27]. This section discusses four duplication algorithms, namely adjacent and mirroring window duplication, followed by a nearest neighbour approach and similarity interpolation.

Adjacent Window Interpolation. Adjacent window interpolation (AWI) reconstructs a gap of size n at time delay t by simply copying the preceding n samples from the signal y, that is,

$$y_{t+i} = y_{t-n+i} \tag{1}$$

for integer $i \in \{0, 1, \ldots, n-1\}$. This approach relies on the idea that if a certain combination of samples exists, there is a likelihood that they might be repeated at a later stage. The interpolation accuracy is improved by using bidirectional processing and taking the average between the forward and backward interpolation process.

Adjacent Window Interpolation. Volatile signals that are interpolated with adjacent windows can cause a sudden jump between sample y_t and y_{t-1} and sample y_{t+n-1} and y_{t+n}, that is, where the gap of missing samples starts and ends respectively. This sample jump is prominent for a large n, since using a forward adjacent window will only interpolate the gap with the historical data and not consider the future direction of the signal. By mirroring the samples during mirroring window interpolation (MWI), the signal is smoothed between the first and last sample of the gap as follows:

$$y_{t+i} = y_{t-1-i} \tag{2}$$

for integer $i \in \{0, 1, \ldots, n-1\}$. Similarly, the average between the forward and backward mirrored windows increases the interpolation accuracy.

Nearest Neighbour Interpolation. The nearest neighbour interpolation (NNI) reconstructs a point by choosing the value of the closest neighbouring point in the Euclidean space. NNI for a sequential dataset at time delay t is defined as

$$y_t = \sum_{i=t-k}^{t+k} h(t - i\triangle_t)y_i \tag{3}$$

where k is the number of samples to consider at both sides of y_t and $\triangle_t$ the change in time. h is the rectangular function defined as

$$h(t) = \begin{cases} 1 & \text{for } -\frac{1}{2} \leq \frac{t}{\triangle_t} < \frac{1}{2} \\ 0 & \text{otherwise} \end{cases} \tag{4}$$

Since NNI was originally intended for resampling two-dimensional grid data, the reconstructed samples in an audio signal may have a steep jump in the middle of the gap if there is a steep gradient between the last sample before and the first sample after the gap.

Similarity Interpolation. Duplication-based interpolation algorithms can produce an inaccurate reconstruction if the interpolation gap shares little characteristics with the preceding and successive samples. A more accurate approach through similarity interpolation (SI) involves the search for a sequence of samples that are similar to the samples on each side of the gap. This can be done by constructing a set of vectors $\mathbf{d}_i$ by calculating the deviation between the amplitudes of neighbouring samples in a moving window as follows:

$$\mathbf{d}_i = [(y_i - y_{i+1}), (y_{i+1} - y_{i+2}), \ldots, (y_{i+n-1} - y_{i+n})] \tag{5}$$

where y is the series of observed samples with a moving window size of $n + 1$. Given u as the number of previous and v as the number of future samples surrounding the gap, a total of $(u+v-n)$ vectors are calculated when the window moves over y. The goal of similarity interpolation is to find the vector in $\mathbf{d}_i$ that shares most of its characteristics with the samples preceding the interpolation gap. Note that, by using the amplitude deviation, the algorithm will find a sequence of samples that are similar in direction and gradient and not necessarily similar in amplitude. This ensures that sample sequences with a similar waveform are also considered and not only sequences with similar amplitudes. A series of mean squared errors between the most similar vector and last windows of samples is calculated. The errors are iteratively added to the last sample before the gap in order to reconstruct the missing values.

2.2   Trigonometric Approaches

Smoothing between two groups of samples can also be achieved through trigonometric functions such as the sine and cosine functions. This section examines Lanczos and a cosine reconstruction approach.

Lanczos Interpolation. Lanczos interpolation (LI) is a smoothing interpolation technique based on the sinc function [13]. The sinc function is the normalized sine function, that is, $\frac{\sin(x)}{x}$ [19]. The LI is defined as

$$l(x) = \sum_{i=\lfloor x \rfloor - n+1}^{\lfloor x \rfloor + n} y_i L(x - i) \tag{6}$$

where $\lfloor x \rfloor$ is the floor function of x, n the number of samples to consider on both sides of x and $L(x)$ the Lanczos kernel. The Lanczos kernel is a dilated sinc function used to window another sinc function as follows:

$$L(x) = \begin{cases} \text{sinc}(x)\text{sinc}(\frac{x}{n}) & \text{for } -n < x < n \\ 0 & \text{otherwise} \end{cases} \tag{7}$$

Lanczos interpolation is typically used for resampling where the interpolation is applied to gaps between equidistant samples. If non-equidistant gaps are reconstructed, all values of x in the Lanczos kernel are scaled to the range $[0, 1]$ and the resulting interpolate is divided by the sum of the Lanczos kernel.

Cosine Interpolation. A continuous trigonometric function like cosine can be used to smoothly interpolate between two points. Given a gap of n missing samples starting at time delay t, the cosine interpolation (CI) is defined as

$$c(x) = y_{t-1}(1 - h(x)) + y_{t+n}h(x) \tag{8}$$

where $h(x)$ is calculated with cosine as follows:

$$h(x) = \frac{1 - \cos\left(\frac{\pi(x+1)}{n+1}\right)}{2} \tag{9}$$

The cosine operation can be replaced with any other smoothing function $f(x)$, as long as $f(0) = 1$ and $f'(x) < 0$ for $x \in (0, 1)$. Alternatively, if the function has the properties $f(0) = 0$ and $f'(x) > 0$ for $x \in (0, 1)$, the points y_{t-1} and y_{t+n} in Eq. (8) have to be swapped around.

2.3 Polynomials

A polynomial is a mathematical expression with a set of variables and a set of corresponding coefficients. This section discusses the standard, Fourier, Hermite and Newton polynomials. Additionally, the standard and Fourier polynomials are applied in an osculating fashion and are utilized in spline interpolation.

Standard Polynomial. A standard polynomial (STP) is the sum of terms where the variables only have non-negative integer exponents and is expressed as

$$m_{stp}(x) = \alpha_d x^d + \cdots + \alpha_1 x + \alpha_0 = \sum_{i=0}^{d} \alpha_i x^i \tag{10}$$

where x represent the variables, α_i the coefficients, and d the order of the polynomial. x represents the time delay of the samples y in audio signals. According to the unisolvence theorem, a unique polynomial of degree n or lower is guaranteed for $n + 1$ data points [24]. STP are typically approximated using a linear least squares (LLS) fit.

Fourier Polynomial. Fourier proposed to model a complex partial differentiable equation as a superposition of simpler oscillating sine and cosine functions [17]. A discrete Fourier polynomial (FOP) is approximated with a finite sum d of sine and cosine functions with a period of one as follows:

$$m_{fop}(x) = \frac{\alpha_0}{2} + \sum_{i=1}^{d} \left[\alpha_i \cos(i\pi x) + \beta_i \sin(i\pi x)\right] \tag{11}$$

where α_i and β_i are the cosine and sine coefficients respectively. For any set of n data points, there exists a trigonometric polynomial that satisfies the Fourier series as long as there are not more points than coefficients, that is $n \le 2d + 1$. A unique solution exists if and only if the number of coefficients is equal to the number of data points, therefore $n = 2d + 1$. Depending on the data points, if $n > 2d + 1$, there might be a solution. FOP coefficients are estimated using a LLS fit.

Newton Polynomial. Newton formulated a polynomial of least degree that coincides at all points of a finite dataset [26]. Given $n + 1$ data points (x_i, y_i), the Newton polynomial (NEP) is defined as

$$m_{nep}(x) = \sum_{i=0}^{n} \alpha_i h_i(x) \qquad h_i(x) = \prod_{j=0}^{i-1} (x - x_i) \tag{12}$$

where α_i are the coefficients and $h_i(x)$ is the ith Newton basis polynomial. An efficient method for calculating the coefficients is using a Newton divided differences table. Alternatively, LLS regression can be used to estimate the coefficients.

Hermite Polynomial. Hermite introduced a polynomial closely related to the Newton and Lagrange polynomials, but instead of only calculating a polynomial for $n + 1$ points, the derivatives at these points are also considered [22]. The Hermite polynomial (HEP) using the first derivative is defined as

$$m_{hep}(x) = \sum_{i=0}^{n} h_i(x)f(x_i) + \sum_{i=0}^{n} \overline{h}_i(x)f'(x_i) \tag{13}$$

where $h_i(x)$ and $\overline{h}_i(x)$ are the first and second fundamental Hermite polynomials, calculated using

$$h_i(x) = [1 - 2l_i'(x_i)(x - x_i)] [l_i(x)]^2 \tag{14}$$

$$\overline{h}_i(x) = (x - x_i) [l_i(x)]^2 \tag{15}$$

$l_i(x)$ is the ith Lagrange basis polynomial and $l_i'(x_i)$ the derivative of the Lagrange basis polynomial at point x_i. Given the Kronecker delta δ_{ij}, the first fundamental Hermite polynomial adheres to $h_i(x_j) = \delta_{ij}$ and $h_i'(x_j) = 0$. The second fundamental Hermite polynomial has the properties $\overline{h}_i'(x_j) = \delta_{ij}$ and $\overline{h}_i(x_j) = 0$. In the original publication, Hermite used Lagrange fundamental polynomials. However, the concept of osculation can be applied to any polynomial as long as the derivatives are known. Besides the HEP that utilizes osculating Lagrange polynomials, this paper also examines the osculating standard polynomial (OSP) and the osculating Fourier polynomial (OFP).

Splines. Splines are a set of piecewise polynomials where the derivatives at the endpoints of neighbouring polynomials are equal. Given a set of $n + 1$ data points, n number of splines are constructed, one between every neighbouring sample pair. The splines are created as follows:

$$
m_s(x) = \begin{cases} s_1(x) & \text{for } x_0 \leq x < x_1 \\ \vdots & \\ s_{n-1}(x) & \text{for } x_{n-2} \leq x < x_{n-1} \\ s_n(x) & \text{for } x_{n-1} \leq x < x_n \end{cases} \tag{16}
$$

To ensure a smooth connection between neighbouring splines, the first derivatives at the interior data points x_i have to be continuous, that is, $s_i'(x_i) = s_{i+1}'(x_i)$ for $i \in \{1, 2, \ldots, n\}$ [38]. As the order of the individual splines increases, higher order derivatives also have to be continuous. The individual splines can therefore be established using any other kind of polynomial function whose derivatives are known. This paper investigates the standard polynomial splines (SPS) and Fourier polynomial splines (FPS). In practice, cubic splines or lower are mostly used, since higher degree splines tend to overfit the model and reduce the approximation accuracy for intermediate points. Cho provided a theoretical justification for this observation and concluded that cubic splines are sufficient for most practical applications [6].

2.4   Time Series Models

This section provides an overview of some widely used time series models. The autoregressive (AR), moving average (MA), autoregressive moving average (ARMA), autoregressive integrated moving average (ARIMA), autoregressive conditional heteroskedasticity (ARCH) and generalized autoregressive conditional heteroskedasticity (GARCH) models are discussed.

Autoregressive Model. The AR model is an infinite impulse response filter that models a random process where the generated output is linearly depended on the previous values in the process. Since the model retains memory by keeping track of the feedback, it can generate internal dynamics. Given y_i as a sequential series of $n + 1$ data points, the AR model of degree p predicts the value of a point at time delay t with the previous values of the series, defined as

$$
y_t = c + \varepsilon_t + \sum_{i=1}^{p} \alpha_i y_{t-i} \tag{17}
$$

where c is a constant, typically considered to be zero, ε_t a white noise error term, almost always considered to be Gaussian white noise, and α_i the coefficients of the model. A common approach in time series analysis is to subtract the temporal mean from time series y before feeding it into the AR model. It was found that this approach is not advisable with sample windows of short durations, since the temporal mean is often not a true representation of the series' mean and can vary greatly among subsets of the series [12]. The series y is assumed to have a zero mean and to be linear and stationary. A stationary series is stochastic where the joint probability distribution does not change with a progression in time. If the series does not have a zero mean, an additional parameter α_0 is added to the front of the summation in Eq. 17. One of the most widely used methods for estimating the AR model coefficients is solving the Yule-Walker equations with a LLS regression.

Moving Average Model. The MA calculates a series of means from a subset of the input signal. The moving average is a finite impulse response filter which continuously updates the average as the window of interest moves across the dataset. A study on applying the moving average on random events lead to the formulation of what later became known as the MA model where univariate time series are modelled with white noise terms [34]. The MA model predicts the value of a data point at time delay t using

$$y_t = \mu + \varepsilon_t + \sum_{i=1}^{q} \beta_i \varepsilon_{t-i} \tag{18}$$

where μ is the mean of the series, typically assumed to be zero, β_i the model coefficients of order q and $\varepsilon_t, \ldots, \varepsilon_{t-q}$ the white noise error terms. The error terms are assumed to be independent and identically distributed random variables, meaning that all random variables are mutually independent and are subject to the same probability distribution. Since the lagged error terms ε are not observable, the MA model can not be solved using linear regression. Maximum likelihood estimation (MLE) is typically used to solve the MA model, which in turn is maximized through iterative nonlinear optimization methods such as the Broyden-Fletcher-Goldfarb-Shanno (BFGS) [5,16,20,31] or the Berndt-Hall-Hall-Hausman (BHHH) [1] algorithms.

Autoregressive Moving Average Model. The ARMA model is a combination of the AR and MA models. The ARMA model is based on Fourier and Laurent series with statistical interference [39] and was later popularized by a proposal describing a method for determining the model orders and an iterative method for estimating the model coefficients [4]. The ARMA model is given as

$$y_t = c + \varepsilon_t + \sum_{i=1}^{p} \alpha_i y_{t-i} + \sum_{i=1}^{q} \beta_i \varepsilon_{t-i} \tag{19}$$

where p and q are the AR and MA model orders respectively. The ARMA coefficients are typically approximated through MLE using BFGS or BHHH.

Autoregressive Integrated Moving Average Model. The ARIMA model is a generalization of the ARMA model. ARIMA is preferred over the ARMA model if the observed data shows characteristics of non-stationarity, such as seasonality, trends and cycles [4]. A differencing operation is added as an initial step to the ARMA model to remove possible non-stationarity. The ARMA model in Eq. 19 can also be expressed in terms of the lag operator as

$$\alpha(L)y_t = \beta(L)\varepsilon_t \tag{20}$$

where $\alpha(L)$ and $\beta(L)$ are said to be the lag polynomials of the AR and MA models respectively. The ARIMA model is expressed by expanding Eq. 20 and incorporating the difference operator, $y_t - y_{t-1} = (1 - L)y_t$, as follows:

$$\left(1 - \sum_{i=1}^{p} \alpha_i L^i\right)(1 - L)^d y_t = \left(1 + \sum_{i=1}^{q} \beta_i L^i\right)\varepsilon_t \tag{21}$$

where p is the AR order, q the MA order and d the order of integration. The ARMA model assumes a zero mean for the observed data. If the model is applied to a series with a non-zero mean, a summation of AR parametrized means is subtracted from the series' mean and added to the left-hand side of Eq. 21. ARIMA coefficients are approximated with the same method used by the ARMA model.

Autoregressive Conditional Heteroskedasticity Model. ARMA models are the conditional expectation of a process with a conditional variance that stays constant for past observations. Therefore, ARMA models use the same conditional variance, even if the latest observations indicate a change in variation. The ARCH model was developed for financial markets with periods of low volatility followed by periods of high volatility [15]. ARCH achieves nonconstant conditional variance by calculating the variance of the current error term ε_t as a function of the error terms ε_{t-i} in the previous i time periods. Therefore, the forecasting is done on the error variance and not directly on the previously observed values. The ARCH process for a zero mean series is defined as

$$y_t = \sigma_t \varepsilon_t \tag{22}$$

where ε_t is Gaussian white noise and σ_t is the conditional variance, modelled by an AR process as

$$\sigma_t = \sqrt{\alpha_0 + \sum_{i=1}^{q} \alpha_i \varepsilon_{t-i}^2} \tag{23}$$

In order to ensure that the variance is always nonnegative, the coefficients $\alpha_i \geq 0$ must hold true for $i \in \{0, 1, \ldots, q\}$. If $\alpha_i = 0$ for $i \in \{1, 2, \ldots, q\}$, then $\alpha_0 > 0$. If the sum of the coefficients α_i is less than one, the ARCH process is weakly stationary and will have a constant unconditional variance. Since ARCH makes use of an AR process, the coefficients can be estimated through LLS fitting using Yule-Walker equations. Since the distribution of ε_{t-i}^2 is naturally not normal, the Yule-Walker approach does not provide an accurate estimation for the model coefficients, but can be used to set the initial values for the coefficients. An iterative approach, such as MLE, is then used to refine the coefficients in order to find a more accurate approximation.

Generalized Autoregressive Conditional Heteroskedasticity Model.
The GARCH model is a generalization of the ARCH model which also uses the weighted average of past squared residuals without the declining weights ever reaching zero [3]. Unlike the ARCH model which employs an AR process, GARCH uses an ARMA model for the error variance as follows:

$$\sigma_t = \sqrt{\alpha_0 + \sum_{i=1}^{q} \alpha_i \varepsilon_{t-i}^2 + \sum_{i=1}^{p} \beta_i \sigma_{t-i}^2} \tag{24}$$

where α_i and β_i are the model coefficients and p and q the GARCH and ARCH orders respectively. Since GARCH makes use of the ARMA model for the error variance, the model can not be estimated using LLS regression, but has to follow the same estimation approach used by ARMA.

2.5   Artificial Neural Networks

An artificial neural network (ANN) is a model of a biological neural network with a network structure that consists of a number of layered artificial neurons that are connected with artificial synapses and can be used to approximate functions. The input of a feedforward ANN [2] is propagated through the hidden layers to the output layer, where the neurons calculate the net input and pass it through an activation function. The weights of the synapses are updated during training with the aim of improving the approximation of the ANN by reducing the output error [14]. An example of a feedforward ANN is illustrated in Fig. 2, where v and w are the weights, and g, h, and o the neurons in the input, hidden, and output layers respectively.

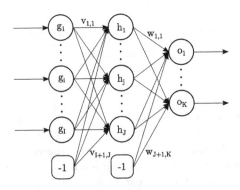

Fig. 2. A feedforward ANN with one input, one hidden, and one output layer.

ANNs are well established in various fields of audio processing, such as speech recognition [11], audio classification [28], and feature extraction [33]. Comparatively little has been published with regards to reconstructing audio signals using ANNs.

Czyzewski proposed a solution for the removal of impulse noise from audio signals that consists of two ANNs, one for impulse disturbance detection and another ANN for the reconstruction of the detected noise [9]. The ANN reconstruction achieved a mean squared error (MSE) of only 0.25. Czyzewski concluded that his approach has limited practical use due to the long training time of the ANNs and even with the extension of his research using self organizing maps (SOM) and rough sets, time complexity still remained the main obstacle [10].

Cocchi and Uncini achieved a better reconstruction with a MSE between 0.002 and 0.04 using a forward and backward predictive subband ANN, without any reference given about the computational time [8].

Seng et al. also utilized forward and backward prediction for the signal reconstruction using a radial basis function ANN [30]. However, the authors neither provide any benchmarking results of the reconstruction performance, nor any indication of the computational time of their proposed solution.

Time delay ANN (TDANN) [25] were investigated in order to determine their ability to approximate an audio signal and interpolate noisy samples. A detailed description for each of the ANN approaches explained below can be found in [37], which includes the network architecture, activation functions, training algorithms, learning rate and momentum. For an audio signal with the longest consecutive noise segment consisting of K samples, the different TDANNs can be applied to any disrupted gap of k samples for $1 \leq k \leq K$ as follows:

Incremental TDANN: The ANN is trained incrementally on historic samples. The ANN has K output neurons with only the first k outputs being utilized. The ANN can be applied in a forward direction (FI-TDANN) or by using bidirectional processing where the results of the forward and backward processes are combined (BI-TDANN).

Incremental Simple Recurrent TDANN: A Jordan recurrency is added to the ANN, where the outputs from the previous iteration are fed in as additional inputs to the input layer [23]. The ANN has only a single output neuron and is trained incrementally. The ANN can be applied in a forward fashion (FI - SRTDANN) or using bidirectional processing (BI-SRTDANN).

Separate Batch TDANN: A set of separate ANNs with between one and K output neurons are batch trained. If a gap of k samples has to be interpolated, the kth ANN is selected from the set, trained, and utilized for the reconstruction. The ANN can be applied in a forward direction (FSB-TDANN) or in both directions (BSB-TDANN).

Complete Batch TDANN: An ANN with K output neurons is batch trained. Only the first k outputs are used for the reconstruction. The ANN has a forward variant (FCB-TDANN) and a bidirectional variant (BCB-TDANN).

Interpolation Batch TDANN: The ANN has two sets of inputs which are delayed by k samples. The first set of inputs consists of the consecutive samples preceding the gap, the second set created from the samples succeeding the gap. A total of K ANNs are batch trained, one for each possible gap duration in $[1, K]$.

3   Empirical Procedure

This section discusses the optimal parameters of the algorithms, the experimental procedures applied during the analysis, the performance measurement used to compare the algorithms and the evaluation of the execution time.

3.1   Parameter Optimization

All algorithm parameters were optimized using fractional factorial design as discussed in [21]. Ten songs in each genre were used to find the optimal parameters. The parameter configurations that on average performed best over all 80 songs were used to calculate the reconstruction accuracy of the entire set of 800 songs. The optimal parameters for the duplication algorithms, polynomials, and time series models are given in Table 1. Table 2 lists the optimal configurations for the ANNs, where the layer structure represents the number of neurons in the

Table 1. The optimal parameter configurations for the duplication algorithms, polynomials, and time series models.

Algorithm	Window size	Order	Derivatives
NNI	2	-	-
SI	284	-	-
STP	2	1	-
OSP	6	2	1
SPS	4	1	-
FOP	250	1	-
OFP	270	10	9
FPS	2	1	-
NEP	2	-	-
HEP	2	-	-
AR	1456	9	-
MA	4	1	-
ARMA	1456	9-2	-
ARIMA	1440	9-1-4	-
ARCH	8	1	-
GARCH	8	1-1	-

Table 2. The optimal parameter configurations for the ANNs.

ANN Type	Layer Structure	Training Algorithm	Learning Rate	Activation Function	Training Epochs
FI-TDANN	832-K	Incr. Backprop	0.1	Sym. Elliot	1
BI-TDANN	832-K	Incr. Backprop	0.1	Sym. Elliot	1
FI-SRTDANN	961-1	Incr. Backprop	0.1	Tanh	1
BI-SRTDANN	961-1	Incr. Backprop	0.1	Tanh	1
FSB-TDANN	224-k	iRprop⁻	-	Sym. Elliot	50
BSB-TDANN	224-k	iRprop⁻	-	Sym. Elliot	50
FCB-TDANN	220-K	iRprop⁻	-	Sym. Elliot	50
BCB-TDANN	220-K	iRprop⁻	-	Sym. Elliot	50
IB-TDANN	256-k	iRprop⁻	-	Sym. Elliot	50

input and output layers. Due to the linear nature of music with a Pearson correlation coefficient of ± 0.6, the ANNs perform better without any hidden layers. A detailed explanation of the linearity of music is given in [37].

3.2 Empirical Dataset

Empirical tests were conducted on a set of 800 songs. The dataset was divided into eight genres, namely classical, country, electronic, jazz, metal, pop, reggae and rock, consisting of 100 tracks each. The songs were encoded in stereo with the Free Lossless Audio Codec (FLAC) at a sample rate of 44.1 kHz and a sample size of 16 bits. The duration of the disruptions in Fig. 1, which will be referred to as *gap sizes*, is typically 30 samples or shorter. To accommodate longer distortions, gap sizes of up to 50 samples were analysed. Although the algorithms are able to reconstruct a gap of any duration, disruptions longer than 50 samples rarely occur and were therefore omitted from the results.

3.3 Reconstruction Performance

Each song was recorded in its original state without any disruptions. The gramophone records were then physically damaged and rerecorded to generate the noisy signals. The noise was flagged with an outlier detection algorithm as discussed in [36]. The reconstructed signal was compared to the original recording to determine the quality of interpolation. The reconstruction performance was measured using the normalized root mean squared error (NRMSE), defined as

$$\text{NRMSE} = \frac{\sqrt{\frac{1}{n}\sum_{i=1}^{n}\left(\tilde{y}_i - y_i\right)^2}}{\hat{y} - \check{y}} \qquad (25)$$

for a set of n samples, where y_i are the samples of the original signal and $\tilde{y}_i$ is the samples of the reconstructed signal. $\hat{y}$ and $\check{y}$ are the maximum and minimum amplitudes of the original signal respectively.

3.4 Execution Time

In addition to the reconstruction accuracy, the algorithms were also compared according to their execution time. The time was measured as the number of seconds it takes to process a second of audio data, denoted as s\s. Hence, a score of 1 s\s or lower indicates that the algorithm can be executed in real time. Based on the concept of the scoring metric in [32], in order to evaluate the tradeoff between the reconstruction accuracy κ and the execution time τ, the speed-accuracy-tradeoff (SAT) is calculated using

$$\text{SAT} = \left(\frac{\kappa}{\hat{\kappa} - \check{\kappa}} + \frac{\tau}{\hat{\tau} - \check{\tau}} \right)^{-1} \tag{26}$$

$\hat{\kappa}$ and $\check{\kappa}$ are the NRMSEs of the best and worst performing algorithms respectively. $\hat{\tau}$ and $\check{\tau}$ are the computational times of the fastest and slowest algorithms respectively. Higher SAT scores indicate a better tradeoff between the accuracy and time. Benchmarking was conducted on a single thread using an Intel Core i7 2600 at 3.4 GHz machine with 16 GB memory.

4 Empirical Results

Figure 3 shows the reconstruction accuracy of the duplication and trigonometric interpolation approaches for an increasing gap size. AWI and MWI achieved a good interpolation for small gap sizes, but quickly declined as the gap increased. LI struggled to reconstruct small gaps, but still outperformed AWI and MWI for gaps of five samples and larger. CI had the best accomplishment for gaps of two samples and greater. The reconstruction performance of the algorithms in Fig. 3 for different genres is given in Fig. 4. CI and AWI achieved the best and worst results respectively for all genres. NNI and SI outperformed LI in all genres, except classical music.

Figure 5 illustrates the interpolation NRMSE for the examined polynomials over an increasing gap size.

The STP, SPS, NEP and HEP achieved almost identical results. Since the best performing spline interpolation utilizes linear piecewise polynomials, the interpolation accuracy of the STP and SPS are equivalent. The STP does not benefit when employed in an osculating fashion. However, the FOP improved with the inclusion of derivatives and clearly benefited when applied as splines. An opposite trend is observed for the FOP and OFP, where smaller gaps were more difficult to interpolate than larger gaps. This trend is caused by a high frequency FOP fitted over smaller gaps. As the gap size increases, the frequency of the sine and cosine waves decreases, providing a smoother interpolation. Figure 6 shows the polynomials' interpolation performance for the different genres. FOP and OFP had a clear inflation compared to the other algorithms. OSP also had a slight surge, with the rest of the algorithms achieving a similar interpolation over all genres.

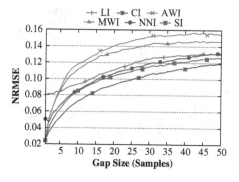

Fig. 3. The reconstruction accuracy of duplication and trigonometric approaches for different durations.

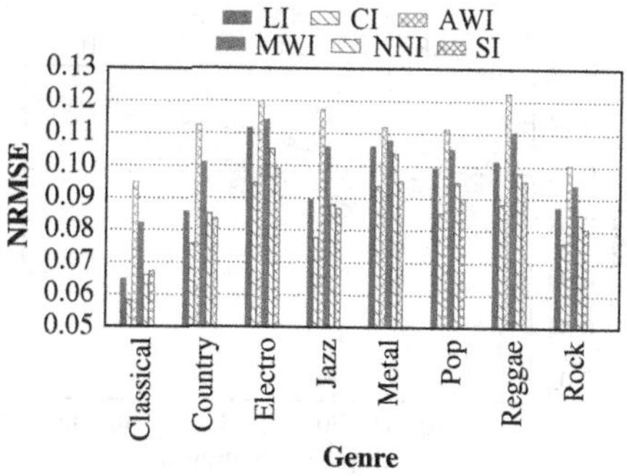

Fig. 4. The reconstruction accuracy of polynomials for different genres.

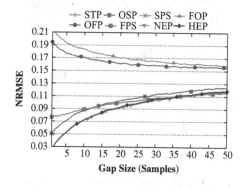

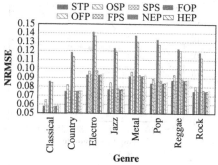

Fig. 5. The reconstruction accuracy of polynomials for different durations.

Fig. 6. The reconstruction accuracy of time series models for different genres.

The time series models' interpolation performance for a growing duration is illustrated in Fig. 7.

The AR and ARMA models had a similar performance, whereas the ARIMA model started deviating from the trend with gaps wider than eight samples. The ARCH and GARCH models had an identical trend, indicating that there is no difference between using and AR or ARMA process to predicting a music signal's variance. On average a music signal's variance is comparatively low compared to high volatile financial markets for which the ARCH and GARCH models were originally intended and therefore do not perform as well as the AR and ARMA models. The corresponding genre comparison for the models in Fig. 7 is given in Fig. 8. The AR and ARMA models performed best for all genres, followed by the ARIMA, MA and then the ARCH and GARCH models.

Figure 9 shows a considerable improvement of the ANNs over all the other models, with all ANNs having a NRMSE below 0.1 for gap durations of up to 50 samples. The IB-TDANN performed best overall, with the BI-SRTDANN

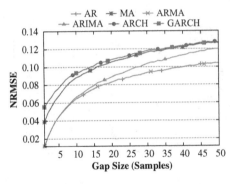

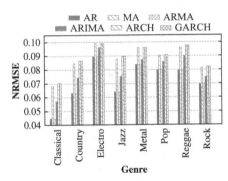

Fig. 7. The reconstruction accuracy of time series models for different durations.

Fig. 8. The reconstruction accuracy of time series models for different genres.

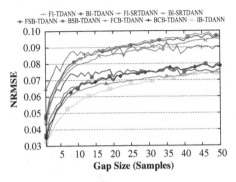

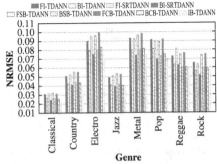

Fig. 9. The reconstruction accuracy of time series models for different durations.

Fig. 10. The reconstruction accuracy of time series models for different genres.

achieving a similar error to theIB-TDANN from 35 samples onwards. The IB-TDANN also performed best for most genres, as indicated in Fig. 10, with the BI-SRTDANN only having a minor decrease in the reconstruction error for metal an rock music. The ANNs also had a notable improvement over the other models for signals showing a strong linear dependency, such as classical, country, and jazz music with a NRMSE between 0.02 and 0.04.

Table 3 lists the overall interpolation accuracy, the NRMSE's standard deviations, the computational speed and tradeoff between the various reconstruction algorithms.

The IB-TDANN performed the best on average, followed by the BI-SRTDANN and the BSB-TDANN. The notable reduction in the interpolation error of the various ANNs shows that more advanced models that adapt over time should be the preferred choice when refurbishing and digitizing music, which is mostly done using AR-based models in existing practical applications. However, the time required to train the ANNs makes them infeasible for most real-time applications, a problem that was also observed by Czyzewski and Krolikowski [9,10]. Due to the

Table 3. The reconstruction accuracy, sample standard deviation, computational time and tradeoff of the restoration algorithms.

Algorithm	NRMSE	NRMSE σ	Speed (s\s)	SAT
AWI	0.111371	0.027830	0.049794	0.593457
MWI	0.104806	0.025612	0.051691	0.628663
NNI	0.090748	0.027156	0.027313	0.735624
SI	0.087269	0.024434	0.054413	0.748390
LI	0.093215	0.026271	0.027908	0.716238
CI	0.081218	0.025435	**0.027128**	0.820088
STP	0.080057	0.024845	0.031490	0.828606
OSP	0.086014	0.025207	0.034523	0.770803
SPS	0.080057	0.024845	0.038588	0.823627
FOP	0.122412	0.031732	0.068523	0.535829
OFP	0.117923	0.029610	5.325502	0.138812
FPS	0.081493	0.023598	0.033035	0.813341
NEP	0.080058	0.024845	0.027329	0.831552
HEP	0.081066	0.025381	0.027557	0.821287
AR	0.071764	**0.023160**	0.092778	**0.870951**
MA	0.087952	0.024475	0.029541	0.757201
ARMA	0.071709	0.023178	2.435243	0.281283
ARIMA	0.080201	0.023740	6.808781	0.122321
ARCH	0.089057	0.024445	0.062245	0.729670
GARCH	0.089057	0.024445	0.062378	0.729598
FI-TDANN	0.068145	0.029736	64.46232	0.014868
BI-TDANN	0.058917	0.025292	129.0510	0.007490
FI-SRTDANN	0.069853	0.033467	2.663952	0.265745
BI-SRTDANN	0.054953	0.025194	5.237380	0.161561
FSB-TDANN	0.071659	0.029915	52.02565	0.018339
BSB-TDANN	0.058147	0.023480	104.2376	0.009259
FCB-TDANN	0.072788	0.032014	89.62463	0.010731
BCB-TDANN	0.058637	0.024168	179.7895	0.005386
IB-TDANN	**0.054247**	0.025009	100.0583	0.009648

single output neuron of the simple recurrent ANNs, the execution speed is up to 67 times faster than that of the other ANNs, which justifies their use in practice even with a slight increase in the output error.

CI was on average the fastest. The tradeoff in the last column shows that the AR model achieved the most effective results for the given execution time. Although not a major improvement over the ARMA model, the AR had a considerable lower computation time, since it was estimated with a LLS fit and not

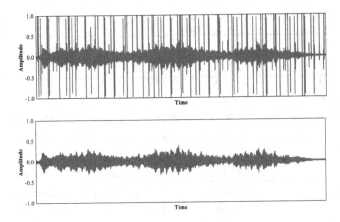

Fig. 11. The sound wave before and after reconstruction.

an iterative gradient-based algorithm. If processing power is of essence, such as in mobile devices, or if real-time restoration is required, the AR model should be utilized. However, most audiophiles and music labels only digitize a record once where higher quality is preferred over a faster execution time and would therefore justify the restoration using an ANN.

The detailed results for the interpolation accuracy is given in the appendix. On average, classical music was the easiest to reconstruct, followed by country, rock and jazz. Electronic, metal, pop and reggae music is in general more volatile, has a wider dynamic range and was therefore more difficult to reconstruct.

5 Reconstruction Example

Figure 11 depicts an example of a sound wave before and after reconstruction using the IB-TDANN. The signal in question is a segment from Mozart's "Eine kleine Nachtmusik". All the impulse disturbances where successfully removed and a reconstruction NRMSE of 0.042 was achieved.

6 Conclusion

Various interpolation algorithms were analysed and benchmarked against each other in order to determine their reconstruction ability on disrupted gramophone recordings. Different approaches to interpolation were considered, including duplication and trigonometric methods, polynomials, time series models, and artificial neural networks. It was found that the IB-TDANN performed the best with an average NRMSE of 0.0542. The CI had the fastest execution speed at 0.0271 s\s. The AR model was the most effective approach by achieving the best interpolation for a given time limit.

Further investigation is needed to determine the capabilities of an ANN when trained in a dynamic environment. A better interpolation accuracy might be achieved if the ANN dynamically adapts to the current volatility of the signal.

One set of parameters may be used when the signal is stable, and another one if the volatility increases. Hence, processing different genres with different models and parameters may produce a more natural reconstruction.

Another problem that needs to be addressed in future research is the long training time of ANNs which can be mitigated by reducing the number of training patterns. Further investigation into recurrent ANNs, which are already considerably faster than other ANN architectures, might prove beneficial. However, a typical consequence of reducing the training time is an increase in the output error which should be taken into account.

Appendix: Detailed Results

Table 4. The interpolation accuracy (NRMSE) for different noise durations.

Algorithm	Noise Duration (Samples)									
	1-5	6-10	11-15	16-20	21-25	26-30	31-35	36-40	41-45	46-50
AWI	0.0610	0.1095	0.1250	0.1369	0.1444	0.1500	0.1531	0.1543	0.1563	0.1553
MWI	0.0600	0.1031	0.1197	0.1302	0.1359	0.1405	0.1438	0.1448	0.1462	0.1460
NNI	0.0566	0.0795	0.0934	0.1039	0.1109	0.1166	0.1210	0.1248	0.1286	0.1313
SI	0.0467	0.0774	0.0918	0.1011	0.1074	0.1129	0.1170	0.1204	0.1235	0.1258
LI	0.0820	0.0902	0.0987	0.1083	0.1157	0.1229	0.1267	0.1287	0.1305	0.1307
CI	0.0401	0.0656	0.0799	0.0900	0.0971	0.1031	0.1078	0.1118	0.1156	0.1184
STP	0.0396	0.0649	0.0790	0.0889	0.0957	0.1017	0.1063	0.1102	0.1139	0.1167
OSP	0.0615	0.0818	0.0924	0.1004	0.1058	0.1108	0.1147	0.1178	0.1214	0.1234
SPS	0.0396	0.0649	0.0790	0.0889	0.0957	0.1017	0.1063	0.1102	0.1139	0.1167
FOP	0.2028	0.1867	0.1782	0.1723	0.1683	0.1658	0.1635	0.1614	0.1605	0.1591
OFP	0.1847	0.1727	0.1666	0.1627	0.1602	0.1590	0.1576	0.1565	0.1565	0.1558
FPS	0.0788	0.0861	0.0925	0.0980	0.1018	0.1054	0.1082	0.1108	0.1135	0.1151
NEP	0.0396	0.0649	0.0790	0.0889	0.0957	0.1017	0.1063	0.1102	0.1139	0.1167
HEP	0.0400	0.0654	0.0797	0.0898	0.0969	0.1029	0.1076	0.1116	0.1154	0.1182
MA	0.0548	0.0815	0.0942	0.1029	0.1088	0.1141	0.1179	0.1211	0.1242	0.1264
AR	0.0300	0.0576	0.0714	0.0806	0.0867	0.0916	0.0954	0.0987	0.1016	0.1036
ARMA	0.0300	0.0575	0.0714	0.0805	0.0866	0.0916	0.0953	0.0986	0.1015	0.1035
ARIMA	**0.0298**	0.0588	0.0743	0.0856	0.0936	0.1008	0.1064	0.1113	0.1157	0.1191
ARCH	0.0666	0.0882	0.0983	0.1060	0.1111	0.1161	0.1195	0.1223	0.1253	0.1273
GARCH	0.0666	0.0882	0.0983	0.1060	0.1111	0.1161	0.1195	0.1223	0.1253	0.1273
FI-TDANN	0.0723	0.0851	0.0868	0.0881	0.0884	0.0891	0.0893	0.0882	0.0900	0.0900
BI-TDANN	0.0587	0.0719	0.0739	0.0747	0.0751	0.0751	0.0756	0.0750	0.0756	0.0756
FI-SRTDANN	0.0593	0.0761	0.0814	0.0853	0.0868	0.0889	0.0911	0.0918	0.0939	0.0949
BI-SRTDANN	0.0441	0.0607	0.0654	0.0680	0.0691	0.0705	0.0718	0.0725	0.0737	0.0742
FSB-TDANN	0.0617	0.0795	0.0850	0.0881	0.0904	0.0919	0.0937	0.0945	0.0961	0.0967
BSB-TDANN	0.0491	0.0644	0.0690	0.0713	0.0734	0.0746	0.0757	0.0766	0.0776	0.0782
FCB-TDANN	0.0587	0.0782	0.0849	0.0885	0.0911	0.0928	0.0947	0.0956	0.0974	0.0978
BCB-TDANN	0.0466	0.0626	0.0682	0.0706	0.0734	0.0745	0.0759	0.0769	0.0780	0.0785
IB-TDANN	0.0405	**0.0537**	**0.0601**	**0.0640**	**0.0666**	**0.0682**	**0.0702**	**0.0719**	**0.0735**	**0.0738**

Table 4 shows the interpolation performance of all reconstruction algorithms for an increasing gap size. The ARIMA model outperformed all TDANNs for durations of five samples or shorter. The IB-TDANN interpolated most accurately for all other gap sizes.

Table 5 provides the detailed reconstruction performance for different genres. The IB-TDANN performed best for all genres, except for metal and rock music, which had a better interpolation using the BI-SRTDANN.

Table 5. The interpolation accuracy (NRMSE) for different genres.

Algorithm	Classical	Country	Electro	Jazz	Metal	Pop	Reggae	Rock
AWI	0.0948	0.1124	0.1199	0.1174	0.1120	0.1115	0.1226	0.1004
MWI	0.0821	0.1010	0.1142	0.1059	0.1079	0.1052	0.1105	0.0943
NNI	0.0659	0.0850	0.1052	0.0879	0.1038	0.0950	0.0981	0.0851
SI	0.0672	0.0835	0.0991	0.0867	0.0955	0.0900	0.0954	0.0807
LI	0.0648	0.0857	0.1116	0.0895	0.1060	0.0994	0.1015	0.0872
CI	0.0582	0.0756	0.0947	0.0777	0.0938	0.0853	0.0881	0.0763
STP	0.0580	0.0748	0.0931	0.0769	0.0917	0.0839	0.0871	0.0750
OSP	0.0650	0.0821	0.0972	0.0846	0.0966	0.0887	0.0934	0.0805
SPS	0.0580	0.0748	0.0931	0.0769	0.0917	0.0839	0.0871	0.0750
FOP	0.0858	0.1182	0.1412	0.1233	0.1373	0.1327	0.1225	0.1184
OFP	0.0845	0.1134	0.1369	0.1185	0.1302	0.1270	0.1204	0.1124
FPS	0.0569	0.0746	0.0978	0.0779	0.0930	0.0870	0.0886	0.0761
NEP	0.0580	0.0748	0.0931	0.0769	0.0917	0.0839	0.0871	0.0750
HEP	0.0582	0.0755	0.0945	0.0776	0.0935	0.0852	0.0880	0.0761
MA	0.0683	0.0846	0.0991	0.0878	0.0959	0.0903	0.0962	0.0814
AR	0.0447	0.0631	0.0895	0.0639	0.0839	0.0798	0.0796	0.0696
ARMA	0.0446	0.0630	0.0895	0.0638	0.0839	0.0798	0.0796	0.0695
ARIMA	0.0573	0.0744	0.0963	0.0753	0.0875	0.0860	0.0900	0.0748
ARCH	0.0704	0.0866	0.0991	0.0898	0.0960	0.0907	0.0976	0.0823
GARCH	0.0704	0.0866	0.0991	0.0898	0.0960	0.0907	0.0976	0.0823
FI-TDANN	0.0311	0.0511	0.0902	0.0492	0.0932	0.0916	0.0731	0.0657
BI-TDANN	0.0267	0.0427	0.0795	0.0411	0.0803	0.0813	0.0633	0.0565
FI-SRTDANN	0.0317	0.0528	0.0959	0.0512	0.0924	0.0895	0.0815	0.0639
BI-SRTDANN	0.0246	0.0413	0.0756	0.0394	**0.0741**	0.0697	0.0630	**0.0519**
FSB-TDANN	0.0324	0.0556	0.0962	0.0536	0.0966	0.0892	0.0753	0.0744
BSB-TDANN	0.0262	0.0441	0.0803	0.0416	0.0806	0.0732	0.0602	0.0591
FCB-TDANN	0.0316	0.0556	0.0997	0.0529	0.0985	0.0921	0.0766	0.0753
BCB-TDANN	0.0256	0.0436	0.0832	0.0403	0.0814	0.0752	0.0606	0.0591
IB-TDANN	**0.0213**	**0.0403**	**0.0748**	**0.0390**	0.0747	**0.0691**	**0.0584**	0.0565

References

1. Berndt, E.K., Hall, B.H., Hall, R.E., Hausman, J.A.: Estimation and inference in nonlinear structural models. Ann. Econ. Soc. Meas. **3**, 653–665 (1974)
2. Blum, E.K., Li, L.K.: Approximation theory and feedforward networks. Neural Netw. **4**(4), 511–515 (1991)
3. Bollerslev, T.: Generalized autoregressive conditional heteroskedasticity. J. Econometrics **31**(3), 307–327 (1986)
4. Box, G.E.P., Jenkins, G.M.: Time Series Analysis: Forecasting and Control. Holden-Day Series in Time Series Analysis, San Francisco, CA (1970)
5. Broyden, C.G.: The convergence of a class of double-rank minimization algorithms. IMA J. Appl. Math. **6**(1), 76–90 (1970)
6. Cho, J.: Optimal Design in Regression and Spline Smoothing. Ph.D. thesis, Queen's University, Canada, July 2007
7. CMU: Complete Music Update - SoundScan may be under reporting US vinyl sales October 2011. http://www.thecmuwebsite.com/article/soundscan-may-be-under-reporting-us-vinyl-sales, 16 April 2014
8. Cocchi, G., Uncini, A.: Subband neural networks prediction for on-line audio signal recovery. IEEE Trans. Neural Netw. **13**(4), 867–876 (2002)
9. Czyzewski, A.: Learning algorithms for audio signal enhancement, part 1: neural network implementation for the removal of impulse distortions. J. Audio Eng. Soc. **45**(10), 815–831 (1997)
10. Czyzewski, A., Krolikowski, R.: Neuro-rough control of masking thresholds for audio signal enhancement. Neurocomputing **36**(4), 5–27 (2001)
11. Dahl, G.E., Yu, D., Deng, L., Acero, A.: Context-dependent pre-trained deep neural networks for large-vocabulary speech recognition. IEEE Trans. Audio Speech Lang. Process. **20**(1), 30–42 (2012)
12. Ding, M., Bressler, S.L., Yang, W., Liang, H.: Short-window spectral analysis of cortical event-related potentials by adaptive multivariate autoregressive modeling: data preprocessing, model validation, and variability assessment. Biol. Cybern. **83**(1), 35–45 (2000)
13. Duchon, C.E.: Lanczos filtering in one and two dimensions. J. Appl. Meteorol. **18**(8), 1016–1022 (1979)
14. Engelbrecht, A.P.: Computational Intelligence: An Introduction, 2nd edn. Wiley Publishing, Chichester (2007)
15. Engle, R.F.: Autoregressive conditional heteroscedasticity with estimates of the variance of united kingdom inflation. Econometrica **50**(4), 987–1007 (1982)
16. Fletcher, R.: A new approach to variable metric algorithms. Comput. J. **13**(3), 317–322 (1970)
17. Fourier, J.J.: Mémoire sur la propagation de la chaleur dans les corps solides. Nouveau Bulletin des sciences par la Société philomatique de Paris. **6**, 112–116 (1807). Paris, France
18. Friedlander, J.P.: News and Notes on 2015 Mid-Year RIAA Shipment and Revenue Statistics (2015). http://riaa.com/media/238E8AC7-3810-A95C-44DC-B6DEB46A3C6E.pdf, 5 December 2015
19. Gearhart, W.B., Shultz, H.S.: The Function sin x/x. Coll. Math. J. **21**(2), 90–99 (1990)
20. Goldfarb, D.: A family of variable-metric methods derived by variational means. Math. Comput. **24**(109), 23–26 (1970)

21. Gunst, R.F., Mason, R.L.: Fractional factorial design. Wiley Interdisc. Rev.: Computat. Stat. 1(2), 234–244 (2009)

22. Hermite, C.: Sur la Formule d'Interpolation de Lagrange. J. für die Reine und Angewandte Mathematik 84(1), 70–79 (1878)

23. Jordan, M.I.: Attractor dynamics and parallelism in a connectionist sequential machine. In: Proceedings of the Cognitive Science Society, pp. 531–546 (1986)

24. Kastner, R., Hosangadi, A., Fallah, F.: Arithmetic Optimization Techniques for Hardware and Software Design. Cambridge University Press, Cambridge (2010)

25. Lang, K.J., Waibel, A.H., Hinton, G.E.: A time-delay neural network architecture for isolated word recognition. Neural Netw. 3(1), 23–43 (1990)

26. Newton, I., Whiteside, D.T.: The Mathematical Papers of Isaac Newton, vol. 1. Cambridge University Press, Cambridge (2008)

27. Niedźwiecki, M., Cisowski, K.: Smart copying - a new approach to reconstruction of audio signals. IEEE Trans. Signal Process. 49(10), 2272–2282 (2001)

28. Ravanelli, M., Elizalde, B., Ni, K., Friedland, G.: Audio concept classification with hierarchical deep neural networks. In: Proceedings of the European Signal Processing Conference, pp. 606–610 (2014)

29. Richter, F.: The LP is Back! January 2014. http://www.statista.com/chart/1465/vinyl-lp-sales-in-the-us 16 April 2014

30. Seng, K.P., Hui, L.E., Ming, T.: Multimedia signal processing using AI. In: Asia-Pacific Conference on Communications, vol. 2, pp. 825–829 (2003)

31. Shanno, D.F.: Conditioning of quasi-newton methods for function minimization. Math. Comput. 24(111), 647–656 (1970)

32. Sidiroglou-Douskos, S., Misailovic, S., Hoffmann, H., Rinard, M.: Managing performance vs accuracy trade-offs with loop perforation. In: Proceedings of the ACM SIGSOFT Symposium and the European Conference on Foundations of Software Engineering, pp. 124–134. ACM (2011)

33. Sigtia, S., Dixon, S.: Improved music feature learning with deep neural networks. In: IEEE International Conference on Acoustics, Speech and Signal Processing, pp. 6959–6963 (2014)

34. Slutzky, E.: The summation of random causes as the source of cyclic processes. Econometrica 5(2), 105–146 (1927)

35. Sprechmann, P., Bronstein, A.M., Morel, J.M., Sapiro, G.: Audio restoration from multiple copies. In: International Conference on Acoustics, Speech and Signal Processing, pp. 878–882. IEEE, Vancouver, Canada May 2013

36. Stallmann, C.F., Engelbrecht, A.P.: Digital noise detection in gramophone recordings. In: International Conference on Signal Processing Systems. Auckland, New Zealand, December 2015

37. Stallmann, C.F., Engelbrecht, A.P.: Gramophone noise detection and reconstruction using time delay artificial neural networks. IEEE Transactions on Systems Man, and Cybernetics, 7th November 2015

38. Wals, J.L., Ahlberg, J., Nilsson, E.N.: Best approximation properties of the spline fit. J. Appl. Math. Mech. 11, 225–234 (1962)

39. Whittle, P.: Hypothesis Testing in Time Series Analysis. Ph.D. thesis, Uppsala University, Uppsala, Sweden (1951)

40. Wile, R.R.: Etching the human voice: the Berliner invention of the gramophone. Assoc. Rec. Sound Collect. J. 21(1), 2–22 (1990)

Beat Analysis of Dimensionality Reduced Perspective Streams from Electrocardiogram Signal Data

Avi Bleiweiss[✉]

Intel Corporation, Platform Engineering Group, Santa Clara, CA, USA
avi.bleiweiss@intel.com

Abstract. Exploration of ECG traces for their spectral characteristics, distinctly discloses a random component that pertains to the triggering of a new cardiac cycle in the inter-beat interval. Yet the stream consistently shows impressive reproducibility of its intrinsic core waveform. Respectively, the presence of close to deterministic structures firmly contends for representing a single cycle ECG wave by a state vector in a low dimensional embedding space. Rather than performing arrhythmia clustering directly on the high dimensional state space, our work first reduces the dimensionality of the extracted raw features. Analysis of heartbeat irregularities becomes then more tractable computationally and thus increasingly relevant to run on emerging wearable and IoT devices that are severely resource and power constraint. In contrast to prior work that constructs a two dimensional embedding manifold, we project feature vectors onto a three coordinate frame of reference. This merits an essential depth perception facet to a specialist that qualifies cluster memberships, and furthermore, by removing stream noise, we managed to retain a high percentile level of source energy. We performed extensive analysis and classification experiments on a large arrhythmia dataset, and report robust results to support the intuition of expert-neutral similarity.

Keywords: Electrocardiogram · Cardiac arrhythmia · Decision trees · Spectral decomposition · Dimensionality reduction · Clustering

1 Introduction

Electrocardiogram (ECG) is a simple and effective tool to assess the electrical and muscular functions of the heart. The shape of the ECG signal [6] is commonly considered a faithful representation of cardiac physiology to assist in diagnosing conditions for the heart to beat in irregular or abnormal rhythm, known as Arrhythmia. The interpretation of ECG tracing requires however a considerable amount of cardiology training. One of the major challenges in automating the analysis of cardiac arrhythmias is the lack of coherency in the captured time series of the heartbeat. Poor repeatability of the recorded ECG signal in a succession of tests administered on the same patient, and variability of patient-to-patient morphologies that lend to extensive waveform shape dissimilarities,

© Springer International Publishing Switzerland 2016
M.S. Obaidat and P. Lorenz (Eds.): ICETE 2015, CCIS 585, pp. 433–453, 2016.
DOI: 10.1007/978-3-319-30222-5_20

make it all but difficult for a clustering algorithm [13] to group complexes consistently, and hence less likely to agree with the more manual process of clinical diagnosis.

In recent years, wearable and Internet-of-Things (IoT) technology for remotely monitoring continuous ECG signals has emerged [2]. These devices use a non-invasive surface recording that employs from three to twelve electrodes, each connected to a different part of the body. Electrodes measure voltage or current change induced by the heart beat over time and conceptually describe heart activity in separable time series streams. Streams represent a high dimensional state space for extracting raw cardiac features, and often follow arrhythmia clustering directly. However, operating on the large state space is compute intensive and conceived practically infeasible to execute on wearable devices that are highly restricted in compute capacity and power envelope.

A number of attempts have been made to analyze cardiac time series in the context of deterministic dynamical systems. Kantz and Schreiber [12] argued that heart dynamics contain a stochastic component in the inter-beat time intervals (RR-interval) [6]. On the other hand, they showed that the single cycle ECG wave, a $PQRST$ complex (Fig. 1), resembles regular structures and can be equally represented by state vectors in a low dimensional embedding space. Inspired by this observation, our work first removes noise from the ECG signal by projecting the original, high dimensional state space onto a lower, three dimensional feature volume, while preserving stream energy to a high percentile. Compared to prior work [14] that resorts to a two dimensional intrinsic space, our 3D projection facilitates a precursory human inspection of arrhythmia formations by means of a vital depth perception. Furthermore, clustering and classification conducted on a dimensionality reduced training set is considerably more computational efficient to better suit portable ECG devices.

As evident from a multitude of research studies that exploit supervised machine learning techniques, an attempt to coerce a cluster to a unique arrhythmia label assessed by a cardiologist, prove unsuccessful and exhibits under par classification rates [22]. Rather, unsupervised learning from presumed unlabeled heartbeat features and clustering a diverse set of ECG morphologies by endorsing neutral similarity in feature space, is better positioned to discover patient groups that span a membership fusion of several arrhythmia types. In our work, we investigate a discovery [18] method that extracts a statistical relation model of arrhythmia bound cases from a large ECG data set, provided by the UCI Machine Learning Repository [21] and constructed of recordings taken from hundreds of patients. The method incorporates both information retrieval [16] and unsupervised machine learning [5] algorithms. Information retrieval (IR) is rapidly becoming the dominant form of data source access, and our work closely leverages IR practices and follows efficient similarity calculations directly from the well known Vector Space Model [20]. Furthermore, we are interested in objectively uncovering the underlying cluster nature of abnormal, cardiac rhythm instances presented in the dataset, without resorting to any prior knowledge of a cardiologist review.

The main contribution of our work is a novel, statistically driven system that combines IR and unsupervised learning techniques to discover instinctive cluster patterns from presumed unsolicited, ECG signal data. We employ Singular Value Decomposition (SVD) [4] for dimensionality reduction of cardiac streams that is equivalent to spectral decomposition of a matrix, known for finding independent linear correlations of feature vectors to yield the best low rank approximation. For arrhythmia clustering, we use the efficient Clustering Using REpresentatives (CURE) [7] method, a hierarchical algorithm that identifies groups of non-spherical shapes with wide variations in size, from perceived inseparable samples. More importantly, CURE is robust to outliers that are prevalent in assembling ECG traces. Owing to a compact cluster representation of a small set of properly scattered points, CURE scales well to large datasets without loss of clustering quality, and the search for cluster similarities is considerably more effective compared to either the all-points or centroid based agglomerative methods. The remainder of this paper is organized as follows. We overview the basics of ECG recording and annotations, and highlight the motivation behind selecting orthogonal features from ECG streams, in Sect. 2. In Sect. 3, we provide preparatory analysis for ranking the importance of cardiac features, by fitting stream data on to a decision tree data structure. Section 4 briefs on the theory of SVD that leads to our compact, 3D embedding space, whereas in Sect. 5, we review algorithm details of the CURE technique. Following in Sect. 6, we present our evaluation methodology of arrhythmia cluster analysis and classification, and report quantitative results of our experiments. We conclude with a discussion and future prospect remarks, in Sect. 7.

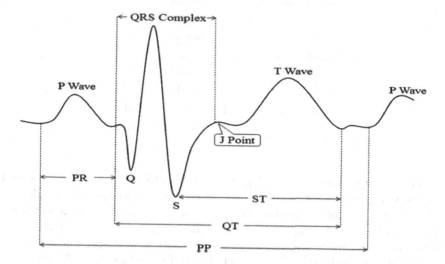

Fig. 1. An end-to-end single cycle of normal ECG characteristics, depicting both waves and basic intervals.

2   ECG Streams

An Electrocardiogram (ECG) provides graphical surface recording of electrical cardiac events. Well established electrode configuration tends to result in a specific tracing pattern, and changes in the ECG signal provides the clinician indispensable data about cardiac physiology. The tracing recorded from the electrical activity of the heart forms a series of prominent waves and complexes that are alphabetically labeled as P, Q, R, S, and T. Each deflection occurs in regular intervals for a healthy heart, and represents depolarization or repolarization of the myocardial tissue. Figure 1 shows an end-to-end single cycle of a normal ECG signal and identifies conventional notations for waves and basic intervals. A standard 12-lead ECG is performed on a patient by attaching to his or her skin a set of electrodes. The leads are grouped into three frontal plane, bipolar limb leads: I, II, and III; three augmented voltage leads: aVR, aVL, and aVF; and six transversal plane, chest or precordial leads: $V1 - V6$ (Table 1). In essence, the 12-lead test supplies spatial information of electrical events in orthogonal directions, hence each separable recorded stream provides a different view of heart activity from a unique angle across the body. The interpretation of the 12-lead ECG is multi-faceted and is based on examining rate, rhythm, the QRS axis, and the various intervals.

Table 1. A 12-lead ECG and their corresponding axes.

Group	Lead	Orientation
Bipolar limb	I	lateral
	II	inferior
	III	inferior
Unipolar limb	aVR	none
	aVL	lateral
	aVF	inferior
Unipolar chest	$V1 - V3$	septal or anterior
	$V4 - V6$	anterior or lateral

The dataset we use in our work [21] is multivariate and coalesces ECG signal features of different categories [8], each described as a vector, possibly combining real, integer, and boolean element types. A patient class leads off with attributes composed of age, sex, height and weight. Eleven global recording parameters succeed next and include the heart rate, measured in beats-per-minute, and a selection of average duration figures, stated in milliseconds, of the QRS complex, the PR and QT intervals, and the P and T waves. Along with frontal plane orientations, calculated in angles, for each of the QRS, P, T, $QRST$, and J axes. To describe the dynamics of the multi-faceted signal shape, a pair of 12-view stream sets follows, one set designated to each of the period and the amplitude cardiac feature groups. Twelve properties form a period view comprised of average width values, expressed in milliseconds, of each of the Q, R, S, R', and S' waves, with R' and S' signifying a small peak right after the R and S waves, respectively. Proceeded by the number of intrinsic deflections and a collection of six categorical flags to indicate the presence or absence of any of a ragged or a biphasic deflection to each of the P, R, and T waves. Similarly, the per-view amplitude class is made up of ten uniform real attributes. Eight elements provide peak voltage measurements of each of the P, Q, R, S, R', S', and T waves, together with the J depression point, all obtained in increments of 0.1 millivolt steps. In addition, an amplitude perspective contains two area-under-curve components, respectively defined as $QRSA = 0.1 \cdot \sum_{i=1}^{k} 0.5 \cdot width_{s^{(i)}} \cdot height_{s^{(i)}}$, where k is the count of segments, $s^{(i)}$, presented in the QRS complex, and $QRSTA = QRSA + 0.5 \cdot width_T \cdot 0.1 \cdot height_T$ that factors in the T wave. For a biphasic T wave, the area derivation only considers the bigger segment.

Table 2. Arrhythmia types and distribution assessed by an expert cardiologist.

Class	Arrhythmia	Dist	Class	Arrhythmia	Dist
1	Normal	245	9	Left bundle branch block	9
2	Coronary artery	44	10	Right undle branch block	50
3	Anterior myocardial infraction	15	11	First-degree atrioventricular block	0
4	Inferior myocardial infraction	15	12	Second-degree atrioventricular block	0
5	Sinus tachycardia	13	13	Third-degree atrioventricular block	0
6	Sinus bradycardia	25	14	Left ventricular hypertrophy	4
7	Ventricular premature contraction	3	15	Atrial fibrillation or flutter	5
8	Supraventricular premature contraction	2	16	Other	22

3   Feature Importance

Our ECG dataset [21] assigns to each patient record one-out-of-sixteen commonly known arrhythmia types (Table 2), previously assessed by a cardiologist. Given this prior classification model, and as a precursory step to our spectral decomposition approach, we sought after fitting each ECG stream data onto a decision tree [3] and rank the importance of the stream-associated cardiac features. A decision tree is a widely used data structure in data mining that is easy to interpret graphically and is highly computationally efficient. A binary classification tree recursively splits the data into two regions by maximizing arrhythmia class homogeneity. Let $X = \{x_1, x_2, ..., x_d\}$ be our input stream vector of d-dimensionality, with x_j in either a numerical or a categorical domain, O_j, and Y a categorical output variable with a domain $O_y = \{1, 2, ..., 16\}$. Then, given n training patient instances, (X_i, Y_i), the task of learning from a decision tree is to predict Y_i based on X_i at a minimal classification error.

Constructing a binary decision tree commences at its root node and repeatedly adding two child nodes, each of either a split or a predictor node type. At each internal node, training patient records are split, not necessarily into equally sized buckets, based on a simple interval checking rule, $x_j < v$, where x_j is an optimally selected attribute and v is a delimiter value. For classification, the cardiac feature and value pair of the highest information gain (IG) [10] determines the split condition of the node. IG is based on the concept of entropy, denoted by H, and strives to maximize the difference between the absolute and the average specific conditional entropy terms of Y, $IG(Y|x_j) = H(Y) - H(Y|x_j)$, where the cardiac feature x_j is iterated over either a numerical or a categorical range of admissible values. Conversely, a split of no information to gain thus constitutes a termination criterion by which a predictor or a leaf node is created. To make a prediction, either a validation or a test perspective stream, X, is traversed down the decision tree until it reaches a leaf node, and its linked arrhythmia class is then fetched and assigned to Y.

In the process of constructing the decision trees for each of the separable perspective streams, cardiac feature selection becomes implicit and has the potential to address non-linear relations between attributes. Comprised of 452 patient instances, the fitting of our ECG training dataset onto an ensemble of disjoint decision trees merits a learning system design that considerably ameliorates a poor relative proportion of feature count to the number of training examples, down from $12 \cdot (12 + 10)/452 = 0.58$ to $12/452 = 0.026$ and $10/452 = 0.022$ for the period and amplitude feature groups, respectively, and hence reduces model overfitting. Still, the cardiologist diagnoses perceived from Table 2 renders a heavily imbalanced class distribution and the prediction of arrhythmia class labels, based on the percentage of training data in each leaf node of the decision tree, is less than optimal. Our goal then mainly revolves around building decision trees that try to minimize the cross-validation error of training as a function of the total number of split nodes in a tree. Figures 2 and 3 provides visualization of a decision tree to each of the separable 12-perspective ECG streams of the period and amplitude feature groups, respectively. Overall, trees bound to the period group express a shallower depth compared to the streams identified with the amplitude collection, and respectively display a maximum of 7 and 10 split nodes. On the other hand, Fig. 4 shows the relative cross-validation error for training our dataset as a function of a non-descending number of tree splits. The error is aggregated for all the ECG stream perspectives that correspond to a feature group. For clarity, the error depicted is absolute and intentionally unscaled by the root node error that stands uniformly at 0.458. As expected, and barring a few exceptions, mean cross-validation error trends a declining curve as the split node count increases.

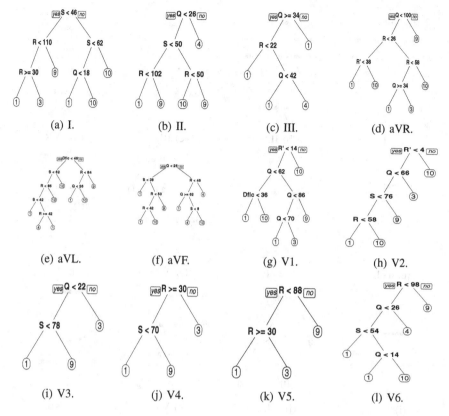

Fig. 2. Cardiac period feature group: graphically illustrated decision trees for each of the separable 12-perspective ECG streams, each learned from a plurality of 452 patient instances.

Lastly, Fig. 5 illustrates the ranking of cardiac feature importance for each stream perspective, respectively for the period and amplitude collections. The higher the intensity displayed for an attribute, the more its weight on impacting an informed arrhythmia class prediction. For the period group, out of twelve features, only four, namely Q, R, S, and the number of deflections, appear dominant as the rest of the elements bear little to no significance. In contrast, a substantially noisier behavior portrays the amplitude group, however, a closer observation singles out T, $QRSA$, and depending on the stream, $QRSTA$ or R, for owning the highest percentile of bias. In all, this orthogonal preparatory analysis that substantiates as prominent less than a handful of cardiac properties in each feature group, endorses favorably our spectral decomposition approach for learning a low dimensional state space. A high level overview of our learning framework that operates on the decomposed ECG streams is illustrated in Fig. 6. Detailed discussion of the pipelined stream transmission from a portable device to the server is outside the scope of this paper.

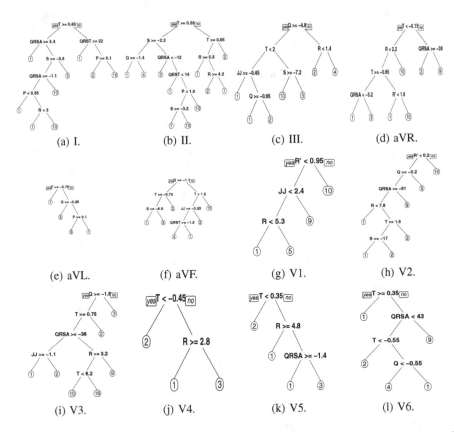

Fig. 3. Cardiac amplitude feature group: graphically illustrated decision trees for each of the separable 12-perspective ECG streams, each learned from a plurality of 452 patient instances.

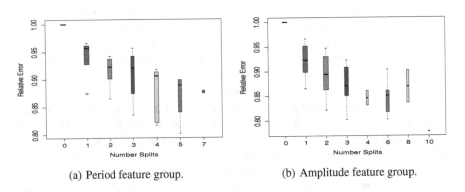

Fig. 4. Cross-validation relative error for training as a function of ascending number of decision tree splits. Visually depicted for aggregate stream perspectives, respectively for each the period and amplitude feature groups.

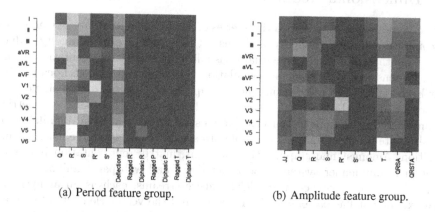

(a) Period feature group.   (b) Amplitude feature group.

Fig. 5. Ranked cardiac feature importance: visually depicted for each stream perspective, respectively for the period and amplitude groups. The higher the intensity displayed for an attribute, the more its weight on impacting arrhythmia class prediction.

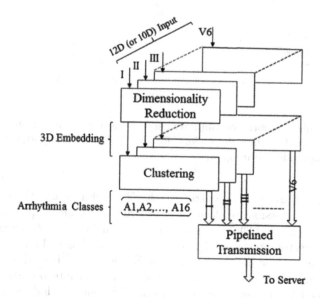

Fig. 6. The input to our learning framework is a set of separable ECG streams in either 12-dimensional or 10-dimensional vectors for the period and amplitude feature groups, respectively. Input streams are each dimensionality reduced to a canonical 3D embedding space, and unlabeled sample points are further clustered into 16 arrhythmia classes. Transmission from any of a wearable or an IoT device to the server is pipelined, one stream at a time.

4 Dimensional Reduction

Directly analyzing an extended time series of the ECG multivariate stream poses a compute efficiency challenge and raises the quest for dimensionality reduction to both explore and perceptually visualize a compact representation of the high dimensional data. In one formulation, Li et al. [14] exploit Locally Linear Embedding (LLE) [19] technique to map the ECG signal onto a single, two dimensional global coordinate system. LLE harnesses neighborhood symmetries of linear reconstructions to learn the global structure of non-linear manifolds. In an alternate prospect, many sources of data are described as a large matrix composition. Amongst many application domains, matrix representation is prominent in recommender systems, social networks, and web page ranking. In our work, we render a collection of ECG feature streams, each as an arrhythmia matrix, A, that has patients as its rows, m, and the vector elements of cardiac features as columns, n. One well established form of matrix analysis is Singular Value Decomposition (SVD) [4] that gracefully leads to data reduction of desired dimensionality at a minimum reconstruction error.

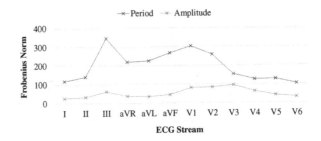

Fig. 7. SVD Frobenius norm for similarity between the original arrhythmia data matrix to its reduced k-rank of three dimensions, for each ECG view and parametrized by the period and amplitude feature groups.

Let our input arrhythmia matrix $A \in \mathbb{R}^{m \times n}$ be of a rank r, then SVD states that it is always possible to decompose a real matrix into a product of three unique matrices $A = U \Sigma V^T$, where $U \in \mathbb{R}^{m \times r}$ and $V \in \mathbb{R}^{n \times r}$ are the left and right singular vectors, respectively, and $\Sigma \in \mathbb{R}^{r \times r}$ is a diagonal matrix comprised of singular values. The diagonal entries of Σ are all positive values and sorted in a descending order ($\sigma_1 \geq \sigma_2 \geq \ldots \geq 0$). For SVD interpretation, columns r of U, Σ, and V are perceived as concepts [18] that are hidden in A, hence U relates patients to concepts, similarly V connects ECG terms to concepts, and Σ attaches a strength or importance to each concept. SVD singles out linear combinations of the data and yields an optimal set of axes to project the data on. Each vector of V constitutes the projection axis of the data, and the corresponding singular value in Σ identifies the variance of data points for the specific dimension. The transformed coordinates in the new projection space are further obtained from the matrix product $U\Sigma$.

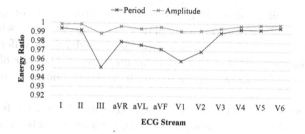

Fig. 8. SVD retained energy ratio for arrhythmia data matrix reduction to a k-rank of three dimensional embedding space, for each ECG view and parametrized by the period and amplitude feature groups.

Reducing the ECG stream data to a k-dimensional space is simplified to zero-ing out the smallest $r - k$ singular values in Σ, and producing the diagonal matrix S. By dropping vectors of small importance, matrix $B = USV$ becomes the best rank-k approximation to A, with maximum similarity quantified by the minimization of the Frobenius norm

$$\|A - B\|_F = \sqrt{\Sigma_{ij}(A_{ij} - B_{ij})^2}. \tag{1}$$

Figure 7 shows similarity between the original arrhythmia data matrix to its reduced k-rank of three dimensions, for each ECG stream and parametrized by the period and amplitude feature groups. For every perspective, matrix columns of importance are markedly reduced from 12 to 3 and from 10 to 3 for the feature groups, respectively. The Frobenius norm distance standard attributes better similarity to the amplitude streams, mostly due to a nonuniform mixture of real and nominal values apparent in a period feature vector. Likewise, Fig. 8 depicts qualitative data reduction measures for each cardiac stream in their respective period and amplitude feature groups. The metrics for selecting the number of matrix dimensions to keep is conventionally governed by the energy ratio term $\sum_{i=1}^{k} \sigma_i^2 / \sum_{i=1}^{r} \sigma_i^2$. A ratio range of 0.8 to 0.9 is commonly deemed acceptable for a reasonable SVD reconstruction error, yet our analysis denotes most energy is retained in the top three matrix columns, with a percentile consistently exceeding 95 %, as amplitude views display no less than a 0.98 proportion.

5 Arrhythmia Clustering

Expert ECG cardiologists largely rely on interpreting visual cues for patient diagnosis, and mainly subscribe to decode recognizable segmentation structures [9]. However, the abundant signal data produced by many small, real-time capture-and-transmit devices necessitate a visual system that is perceptually intuitive and requires effective algorithms to analyze progressively multiple streams of increased dimensionality. In our work, transforming the high dimensional cardiac data to a form both acceptable for human perception and authentic to the original data is facilitated by SVD. Projecting heartbeat data onto a 3D space has the apparent advantage over a 2D planar mapping [14] in allowing arbitrary rotations around the z axis to render the data model from different vantage points. Multiple viewpoints of ECG streams may reveal otherwise obscured patterns that are essential for a domain expert to make an informed analysis about a patient.

Our framework regards the 12-perspective stream data emitted from the ECG Holter as separable, and has each of the cardiac views projected onto a perceptually viable 3D space. Figures 9 and 10 further illustrate stream renditions of the period and amplitude feature groups, respectively. Each frame of reference for a stream, contains 452 patient samples perceived from a prescribed spatial angle, and displayed in a three dimensional space. A closer observation identifies distinct and vital data needed for arrhythmia clustering, but there are also clear indications for instances that overlay each other, although they might belong to a different arrhythmia class, and furthermore, some samples deviate distantly from the formed partitions. Hence, our contention that a clustering method to operate effectively on arrhythmia streams captured from a large number of patients, must grant clusters to form any geometrical shape of variable size, and properly address data point overlaps. In addition, the algorithm is required to be robust in the presence of outliers. We selected the hierarchical Clustering Using REpresentatives (CURE) [7] method, explicitly designed to support our set forth prerequisites.

Cluster analysis of ECG recordings is a powerful tool for discovering patients of similar arrhythmia disorders. In contrast to supervised methods, our evaluation proceeds anonymously on presumed unlabeled cardiac data without resorting to prior knowledge of a cardiologist assessment. Several clustering methods have been devised in the domain of data mining, each of its own strengths and shortcomings. For the sake of keeping the description concise, the reader is kindly referred to an excellent survey of clustering methods, exclusively applied to time series data [15]. CURE stands out as a highly efficient, hierarchical clustering algorithm [11] that has linear storage requirements $\mathcal{O}(n)$ and time complexity of $\mathcal{O}(n^2)$ for low dimensional data of n points, each of d dimensionality, and is no worse than the more constrained, centroid-based hierarchical method. CURE is agglomerative and starts by placing each individual data point in a cluster of its own, and successively merges the closest pair of clusters until the number of clusters reduces to k. Each cluster contains a set of representative points, c, chosen to be well scattered in the cluster extent, who are further shrunk towards the cluster centroid by a fractional factor α. Set apart reference points and the contraction operation that follows, serve the objectives for capturing a cluster of arbitrary geometrical profile and mitigating the effects presented by outliers, respectively. The distance between a cluster pair, u and v, is delineated by the closest pair of representative points, p and q, one from each of the clusters

$$dist(u,v) = \min_{p \in u.rep, q \in v.rep} dist(p,q). \tag{2}$$

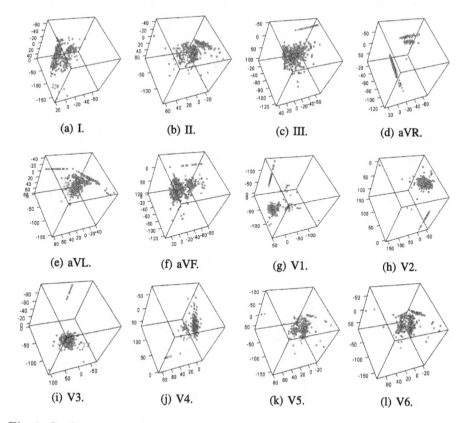

Fig. 9. Cardiac period feature group: visually depicted, separable 12-perspective ECG streams, each contains 452 patient instances viewed from a user set vantage point and displayed in a three dimensional space.

As the distance between two points, p and q, often takes a Euclidean form of L_1-norm or L_2-norm metrics, but also a nonmetric similarity function. Our cardiac feature vectors mix real, integer and boolean components and data points may be rather thought of as directions [1] in the vector space model [20]. Hence, we chose the adjusted cosine similarity for a distance measure that computes a 0 to 180 degrees angle between two zero-mean point vectors and is defined as

$$sim(p, q) = \frac{(p - p_m)(q - q_m)}{\|(p - p_m)\|_2 \|(q - q_m)\|_2}, \tag{3}$$

where p_m and q_m are the mean of p and q, respectively. Adjusted cosine similarity is widely used in the domain of item-based collaborative filtering.

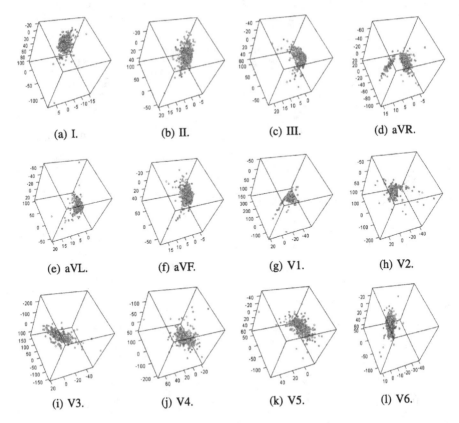

(a) I.   (b) II.   (c) III.   (d) aVR.

(e) aVL.   (f) aVF.   (g) V1.   (h) V2.

(i) V3.   (j) V4.   (k) V5.   (l) V6.

Fig. 10. Cardiac amplitude feature group: visually depicted, separable 12-perspective ECG streams, each contains 452 patient instances viewed from a user set vantage point and displayed in a three dimensional space.

6   Empirical Evaluation

To validate our system in practice, we have implemented a software library that realizes the cluster analysis of ECG streams in several stages. After collecting and cleaning the archived cardiac data, our library commences with extracting patient, global, period and amplitude based feature vectors. Our features are regarded as unlabeled, and follow an explicit clustering process. In addition to detecting the presence or absence of arrhythmia individually, each of the constructed groups represents an objective arrhythmia class and our goal is to further explore and quantify the relations between automatically machine generated clusters to cardiologist diagnoses.

6.1   Experimental Setup

Our work exploits the R programming language [17] to acquire the raw arrhythmia data and fosters cleanup to serve useful in our software environment. We use the extensive and well maintained arrhythmia dataset from the UCI Machine Learning Repository [21], comprised of 452 patient instances with each ECG trace represented as a 279 feature element vector. Occurrences of missing values, primarily manifested in the axis orientation columns, were imputed with the mean of all the feature items present in a data frame column. For our study, we selected the time series attributes held in the 12-perspective streams of each the period and amplitude cardiac groups and total a majority of 264 features, as patient and global properties purposely kept outside the current scope of this work. Measured figures of the dynamic signal were obtained using the ECG system jointly developed by IBM and Mount Sinai University Hospital. As a point of reference, expert cardiologist evaluation is attached to each patient record and lists the 16 types of commonly observed cardiac arrhythmias (Table 2).

Our arrhythmia clustering is entirely autonomous and avoids consulting a specialist diagnosis apriori. Rather than found on a basis of fixed and unique assignment of a single arrhythmia type to a patient [8], our unsupervised methodology clusters objectively by similarity in cardiac feature space, and is therefore impartial to manual process constraints. Hence, our generated arrhythmia groups are each exposed to potentially contain a fusion of a subset of the arrhythmia types specified in Table 2. CURE is handed the input parameter k to follow the generation of 16 logical groups for each of the separable, 12-perspective ECG streams, leading thereof to a 192 multi-class classification paradigm. For our reported experiments, we consistently use in a cluster four representative points, c, that is the minimum set required to ensure concavity of the cluster geometrical shape, and chose a shrinking factor, α, of 0.2 to resonate with the all-points model and distant from a more limiting, single centroid based algorithm.

6.2 Experimental Results

Our clustering process solely relies on automatic feature extraction from natively recorded ECG data and incorporates statistical methods to facilitate the search

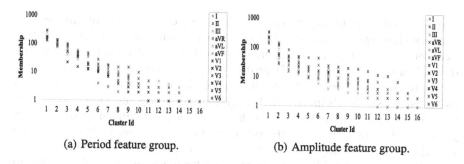

(a) Period feature group.   (b) Amplitude feature group.

Fig. 11. Cluster membership distribution of 452 patient instances for both the cardiac period and amplitude feature groups, each parametrized by an ECG perspective. Patient membership count in each of our unlabeled and statistically learned clusters is shown in a log scale.

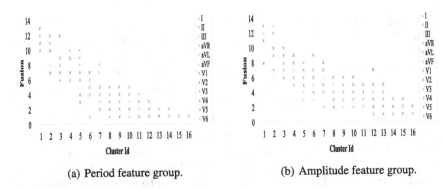

(a) Period feature group.   (b) Amplitude feature group.

Fig. 12. Arrhythmia type fusion in clustering 452 patient instances for both the cardiac period and amplitude feature groups, each parametrized by an ECG perspective. Shown are the number of unique, expertly analyzed arrhythmia classes in each of the unlabeled and statistically learned clusters.

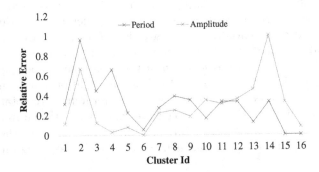

Fig. 13. Comparing membership distribution of machine generated clusters to a manual cardiologist assessment for 452 patient instances. For the former, we take the average across the 12-view ECG streams for each the period and amplitude feature groups. Shown in relative error terms.

of unsolicited arrhythmia patterns, and discover global relations of cardiac irregularities that are not necessarily bound to an individual patient evaluation. Pertinently, our analysis experiments exploit 452 patient records that are SVD dimensionality reduced to a 3D projection space, and are further partitioned across 16 relational arrays. First, we studied the inherent allocation nature of the patient records. Respectively, Fig. 11 shows in a log scale cluster membership distribution of arrhythmia for both the cardiac period and amplitude feature groups, each parametrized by the twelve ECG perspectives. Plotted curves are spread fairly consistently across views, yet the amplitude chart exhibits a higher dynamic range, most likely owing to a uniform vector type of real feature elements.

Next, we examined the relations of our arrhythmia grouping to a human expert analysis, in both the contextual level and proportionality of irregular car-

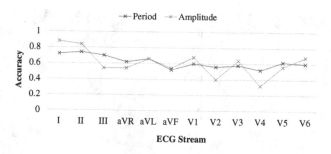

Fig. 14. Classification accuracy in cross validating a combined arrhythmia collection of query and training feature vectors, for each ECG view and parametrized by the period and amplitude feature groups.

diac type assignment. Learning from ECG recordings of a plurality of patients by applying neutral similarity practices is predicted to reveal multiple arrhythmia types attached to a single patient. Hence, grouping cardiac irregularities is equally bound to observe a fusion effect with memberships that span several arrhythmia categories. In our experiments, we inquire the cardiologist evaluation for each person post clustering, and assess the blend of cardiac abnormalities in a cluster. Figure 12 shows arrhythmia type fusion in clustering our dataset for both the cardiac period and amplitude feature groups, each parametrized by the set of ECG perspectives. Some clusters noticeably abide by owning a single and distinct arrhythmia class, however most groups do contain several cardiac anomalies with a count that ranges from two to thirteen. Correspondingly, Fig. 13 shows in relative error terms, membership distribution comparison of machine generated clusters to a manual cardiologist assessment (Table 2). For the former, we take the average across the 12-view ECG streams for each the cardiac period and amplitude feature groups. Evidently, our distributions track well and are for most part inline with the partitions concluded from diagnoses conducted by a professional. Noticeable however are fairly large errors for both the largest arrhythmia classes and for clusters identified by an expert as containing no patients and are therefore statistically unreasoned. For computational stability, we set empty, manually assessed clusters to retain one patient.

We have extended our discovery study to data that is outside the scope of our acquired, ECG training set by artificially generating synthetic cardiac streams. In a sense, this set of query feature vectors is best regarded as means to distort the original ECG signal in a controlled manner. To this extent, a query vector element is randomly selected in the range prescribed by statistically summarizing every feature attribute in the original dataset. For each the period and amplitude feature groups and for each ECG perspective, we produced 50 test vectors to total 600 records per cardiac collection, with an aggregate of 1200 query vectors. In its entirety, query data is fully excluded from any A_{ij}, where $i = \{1, 2\}$ and $j = \{1, 2, ..., 12\}$, our SVD matrix representation of each of the streams in the raw arrhythmia dataset. Each query vector, q, first undergoes transformation

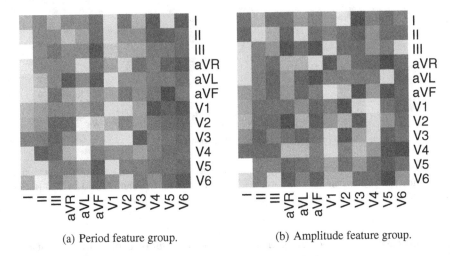

(a) Period feature group.   (b) Amplitude feature group.

Fig. 15. Confusion matrices of query data classification for each the period and amplitude feature groups. Showing predicted against expected behavior of each of the 12-perspective ECG streams.

onto the concept space by utilizing the SVD V matrix and performing qV, and further dimensionality reduced to our working, 3D projection space.

To feature match the query data, we ultimately attempt to correlate a query perspective to a training set cardiac view. We accomplish this by employing a k-nearest neighbor (KNN) [4] baseline classification model that performs a majority voting. Every query vector, q, is sought after the most similar ECG training record by linearly iterating the arrhythmia dataset and computing for each pair the adjusted cosine similarity. The time complexity of this process is $\mathcal{O}(nm)$, with n the number of exclusive training instances and m the number of queries. Throughout, the number of ECG view occurrences for each query perspective collection is accumulated and the highest view score is elected. First, we cross validated each query vector, q, against an inclusive, $m + n$ combined training dataset, using the holdout method with a 90/10 two-way data split. Figure 14 depicts our accuracy rates for each ECG perspective and parametrized by the period and amplitude cardiac group. The period group traces a more smoother curve and tops at a rate of 0.72, in contrast to a 0.88 peak for the amplitude group. Secondly, we provisioned an additional step to evaluate the query test set, m, on the exclusive training set, n. A confusion matrix that enumerates predicted against actual ECG perspectives, for each of the period and amplitude feature groups is further depicted in Fig. 15. Results emerge rather underfitting and strongly imply that the arrhythmia collection we use for training is insufficient to properly represent the highly variant hypothesis space of the query data.

We compared our unsupervised learning results to the ones obtained by the originators of the ECG training dataset [8]. Barring our cross validation methodology that exploits exclusive query data, our overall average accuracy of 0.61 is right on par with their supervised VF15 algorithm that uses however the raw dataset of fully populated attributes and successively processes each into an interval data structure. Unlike our setup that operates on the source cardiac features verbatim, and reduces unassumingly their dimensionality by a factor of 4 and 3.33 for the period and amplitude group, respectively. The work by Li et al. [14] that exploits two-dimensional manifolds uses for evaluation a relatively small and pre-annotated dataset of eight patients, each described by six statistically driven features, and recorded from three perspective ECG streams. A striking disparity from our 452 patient instances, each represented as a pair of 12 cardiac views, to make a fair and sustainable system level comparison on performance. On the other hand, we contend that our 3D visuals of Figs. 9 and 10 reveal authentically both cluster formations and outliers to better assist a specialist in cardiac anomaly analysis, whereas a two dimensional projection is less informative and more limited to exception detection.

7 Conclusions

We have demonstrated the apparent potential in deploying information retrieval and unsupervised machine learning methods to accomplish the discovery of cardiac arrhythmia categories. By disregarding any prior cardiologist knowledge from presumed unlabeled ECG recordings, our proposed system is generic and scalable, and relies entirely on objective closeness metrics in feature space. To accommodate continuous streaming and the immediate response required for detecting abnormal cardiac behavior, our framework separates ECG perspective channels for effective transmission and progressive analysis, and reduces the dimensionality of each to fit the low power and communication constraint, wearables and IoT devices. Furthermore, raw data projection onto a three dimensional embedding space, integrates a vital stage for a specialist to administer preparatory inspection of arrhythmia clusters, and holds a considerable advantage in facilitating spatial data visualization to minimize obstruction, compared to a flat 2D planar mapping.

Utilizing decision trees to rank cardiac feature importance, revealed a small subset of less than a handful attributes to impact the prediction of arrhythmia classes. This markedly benefited our work in providing an alternate interpretation for justifying a learning model that fully operates in a low dimensional reference frame. Our contribution to regard an ECG recording as disjoint and compact perspective entities is substantiated by the efficacy of our cluster analysis, data visualization for human depth perception, and classification. Unlike most systems that tend to aggregate all cardiac view channels into a single discipline. With the intuition of a scheduling scheme that prioritizes the submission of a single ECG perspective at a time, rather than issuing all view channels as a composite, a better overlap of transmission latency, sustained in emitting a decomposed stream from an ECG portable device, with either machine or human expert analysis performed on the receiving end, becomes attainable. Our system classification rate commensurates with a corresponding supervised model that incurs a higher computational cost by employing the unpacked dimensionality of features. However, to ameliorate a fairly impaired performance of cross validating a trained ECG with exclusively generated random test streams, requires an expanded dataset of patient instances.

A direct progression of our work is to extract cardiac features directly from a live ECG signal, and to assess the efficiency of our devised pipelined scheduler for communicating distinct ECG perspectives in a real world, many-devices-to-a-hub network formation. We look forward to advance our study and incorporate an augmented and a more statistically reasoned, ECG training dataset that makes the evaluation of an exclusive test query collection of large variance more robust. Lastly, the flexibility of our software allows us to pursue a higher level correlation of ECG perspective pairs for both clustering and improved recognition of visualization cues, and better understand second order set of arrhythmia relations.

Acknowledgements. We would like to thank the anonymous reviewers for their insightful and helpful feedback on our work.

References

1. Baeza-Yates, R., Ribeiro-Neto, B.: Modern Information Retrieval. ACM Press Series, Addison Wesley, Essex, Boston (1999)
2. Baig, M.M., Gholamhosseini, H., Connolly, M.J.: A comprehensive survey of wearable and wireless ECG monitoring systems for older adults. Med. Biol. Eng. Comput. **51**(5), 485–495 (2013)
3. Breiman, L., Friedman, J.H., Olshen, R.A., Stone, C.J.: Classification and Regression Trees. Wadsworth, Monterey (1984)
4. Cormen, T.H., Leiserson, C.H., Rivest, R.L., Stein, C.: Introduction to Algorithms. MIT Press, McGraw-Hill Book Company, Cambridge, New York (1990)
5. Duda, R.O., Hart, P.E., Stork, D.G.: Unsupervised learning and clustering. Pattern Classification, pp. 517–601. Wiley, New York (2001)
6. Goldberger, A.L., Goldberger, E.: Clinical Electrocardiography: A Simplified Approach. Mosby Year Book, St. Louis (1977)
7. Guha, S., Rastogi, R., Shim, K.: CURE – an efficient clustering algorithm for large databases. In: Management of Data (SIGMOD), pp. 73–84, Seattle (1998)
8. Guvenir, H.A., Acar, B., Demiroz, G., Cekin, A.: A supervised machine learning algorithm for arrhythmia analysis. In: Computers in Cardiology (CIC), pp. 433–436, Lund (1997)
9. Hamameh, G., McIntosh, C., Drew, M.S.: Perception-based visualization of manifold-valued medical images using distance-preserving dimensionality reduction. Trans. Med. Imaging **30**(7), 1314–1327 (2011)
10. Ihara, S.: Information Theory for Continuous Systems. World Scientific, River Edge, Singapore (1993)
11. Johnson, S.C.: Hierarchical clustering schemes. J. Psychometrika **32**(3), 241–254 (1967)
12. Kantz, H., Schreiber, T.: Human ECG: nonlinear deterministic versus stochastic aspects. Sci. Meas. Technol. **145**(6), 279–284 (1998)

13. Kaufman, L., Rousseeuw, P.J.: Finding Groups in Data: An Introduction to Cluster Analysis. Wiley, New York (1990)
14. Li, Z., Xu, W., Huang, A., Sarrafzadeh, M.: Dimensionality reduction for anomaly detection in electrocardiography. In: Wearable and Implantable Body Sensor Networks, pp. 161–165, Aachen (2012)
15. Liao, T.W.: Clustering of time series data - a survey. Pattern Recogn. **38**(11), 1857–1874 (2005)
16. Manning, C.D., Raghavan, P., Schutze, H.: Introduction to Information Retrieval. Cambridge University Press, Cambridge (2008)
17. R Project for Statistical Computing (1997). http://www.r-project.org/
18. Rajaraman, R., Ullman, J.D.: Mining of Massive Datasets. Cambridge University Press, New York (2011)
19. Roweis, S.T., Saul, L.K.: Nonlinear dimensionality reduction by locally linear embedding. Science **290**(5500), 2323–2326 (2000)
20. Salton, G., Wong, A., Yang, C.S.: A vector space model for automatic indexing. Commun. ACM **18**(11), 613–620 (1975)
21. UCI Machine Learning Repository - Arrhythmia Data Set (1987). https://archive.ics.uci.edu/ml/datasets/Arrhythmia
22. Wenyu, Y., Gang, L., Ling, L., Qilian, Y.: ECG analysis based on PCA and SOM. In: Neural Networks and Signal Processing. pp. 37–40, Nanjing (2003)

Traffic Signs Detection Using Tracking with Prediction

Pavel Yakimov[1,2(✉)]

[1] Samara State Aerospace University, 34 Moskovskoye Shosse, Samara, Russia
yakimov@ssau.ru
[2] Image Processing Systems Institute of Russian Academy of Sciences,
151 Molodogvardeyskaya Street, Samara, Russia

Abstract. This paper proposes an efficient algorithm for real-time traffic sign detection. The article considers the practicability of using HSV color space to extract the red color. An algorithm to remove noise to improve the accuracy and speed of detection was developed. A modified Generalized Hough transform is then used to detect traffic signs. The current velocity of a vehicle is used to predict the sign's location in the adjacent frames in a video sequence. Finally, the detected objects are being classified. The detection and classification of road signs algorithms are implemented using CUDA and operate in real time on an Android device. The developed algorithms have been tested using real scene images and the German Traffic Sign Detection Benchmark (GTSDB) dataset and showed efficient results.

Keywords: Traffic signs detection · Advanced driver assistance systems · Computer vision · Graphics processing units · Image processing · Pattern · Recognition

1 Introduction

Traffic Sign Recognition system is designed to provide a driver with relevant information about road conditions. There are several similar systems: 'Opel Eye' of Opel, 'Speed Limit Assist' from the company Mercedes-Benz, 'Traffic Sign Recognition', Ford and others. Most of them are aimed at the detection and recognition of road signs limiting the velocity of movement [1].

Traffic signs recognition is typically executed in two steps: sign detection and subsequent recognition. There are many different methods of detection, and most of them use a single frame from a video sequence to detect an object [2–4]. This means they do not use the additional information about the presence of the sign in the adjacent frames. Such approaches usually have problems of operation in real time and with detection accuracy. On the other hand, several papers describe tracking algorithms, which try to predict the location of signs in a sequence images. In paper [5], the authors show that the integration of the detection and tracking improves the reliability of the whole system due to the decrease of false detections. In [6], it is shown that tracking helps to make the detection faster. However, the described algorithms still have significant computational complexity and cannot be used in real time.

© Springer International Publishing Switzerland 2016
M.S. Obaidat and P. Lorenz (Eds.): ICETE 2015, CCIS 585, pp. 454–467, 2016.
DOI: 10.1007/978-3-319-30222-5_21

Nowadays, vehicles provide a lot of information about its current state, including actual velocity of movement. This paper describes a detection algorithm that uses the velocity obtained from the vehicle in real time. It allows predicting not only the presence of an object but also its scale and location. Thus, the accuracy will be better, while the computational complexity almost will not change.

The performance of existing portable computers is not always enough for the real time detection of traffic signs. Many detection algorithms are based on Hough transform that allows you to effectively detect parameterized curves in an image, but this algorithm is very sensitive to the quality of digital images, especially in the presence of noise. The more noise in the image, the longer it will take to detect objects. Thus, the possibility of detecting traffic signs in real time strongly depends on the quality of the image preparation.

This paper describes the whole technology of traffic sign detection with tracking and recognition. The section with experimental results shows processed real scene images.

2 Traffic Signs Recognition System

Figure 1 shows a road scene model used to design the algorithms of detection and recognition. Here, α is the camera angle in the horizontal projection; W is the width of a road sign image; AC is the distance from the car to the sign. *Image width* is the width of the input image in pixels. In our case, the width of the frame is equal to the width of FullHD, i.e. 1980 pixels.

This paper considers a whole traffic signs recognition technology with three steps: image preparation, detection with prediction and recognition. The detection is based on the color information extracted from images. Therefore, the image preparation starts with color thresholding and denoising. Then, a modification of Generalized Hough Transform (GHT) is used to localize signs in images. A tracking procedure based on the vehicle's velocity is performed to verify a sign presence. Finally, the detected region is being classified.

2.1 Color Analysis and Denoising

Some specific light conditions significantly affect the ability of correct perception of the color in a scene. When taking the actual traffic situation, there are a number of different lighting conditions on the signs.

The signs detection process becomes much more complicated due to such effects as direct sunlight, reflected light, shadows, the light of car headlights at night. Moreover, the various distorting effects may occur on one road sign at the same time (Fig. 2).

Thus, it is not always possible to identify an area of interest in real images by simply applying a color threshold filter directly in the RGB (Red, Green and Blue) color space. Figure 2 shows an example of applying a threshold filter to the red color channel.

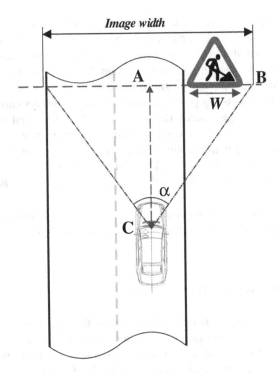

Fig. 1. Road scene model.

Fig. 2. Example of color extraction in RGB (Color figure online).

To extract the red color from the input image it is necessary to use the color information of each pixel, regardless of uncontrolled light conditions. For this purpose, the color space HSV (Hue, Saturation and Value) was selected.

Most digital sensors obtain input images in the format of RGB. Conversion to HSV color space is widely described in [7]. Between the three components of H, S and V there are certain dependencies. H component will not matter if the S or V components are represented by values that are close to zero. The display color will be black if V is equal to 0. Pure white color is obtained when V = 1 and S = 0.

The ideal red (R = 255, G = 0, B = 0) in the HSV color space is defined by the following values $H = 0.0°, S = 1, V = 1$. The experimental method was used to determine the optimal threshold values to extract the red color of traffic signs in the space of HSV:

$$(0.0° \leq H < 23°) \vee (350° < H < 360°) \tag{1}$$

$$0.85 < S \leq 1 \tag{2}$$

$$0.85 < V \leq 1 \tag{3}$$

Figure 3 shows the result of image processing of the road sign from Fig. 2 with threshold values (1)–(3) in HSV.

Fig. 3. Threshold color filtering in HSV.

The binary image obtained using thresholding satisfies the conditions of many algorithms of traffic signs detection. However, one can easily notice the presence of noise in the image. The picture in Fig. 3 is well prepared for further processing, but the situation with the frames captured from a real video sequence is completely different.

The image in Fig. 2 was obtained by a camera with high resolution (8.9 megapixels), and shooting conditions were significantly better than when using a built-in car video sensor. Figure 4 shows a fragment of a frame from the video sequence obtained during the experiments containing a road sign.

Noise in the Fig. 4b appears after thresholding to extract the red color. It not only reduces the performance of the system, but also affects the quality of detection. This can lead to false detection of road signs.

In order to avoid this point-like noise, a modified algorithm based on the results obtained in paper [8] was applied. This article describes the denoising algorithm based on the detection and retouching of point-like glares on the reproductions of works of art. In order to detect these glares the sliding windows algorithm was used. The main advantage of such algorithm is that the parameters can be set in such way that only point-like noise will be removed. At the same time, parts of images of signs stay unfiltered in the processed frames. The result of processing the image from Fig. 4b is shown in Fig. 4c.

Paper [9] shows the effective implementation of the denoising algorithm in the massively multi-threaded environment CUDA. CUDA is a parallel computing platform and programming model provided by NVidia. It enables dramatic increases in computing performance by harnessing the power of the graphics processing unit (GPU). The resulting acceleration on the GPU relative to the CPU reached 60–80 times. Frame

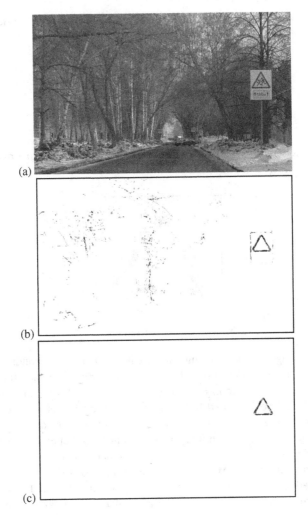

Fig. 4. (a) A frame from video sequence; (b) Binary image with extracted red; (c) Result of image denoising.

size in the video sequence is 1920 × 1080 pixels. Image processing execution time on the CPU is 0.7–1 s. Using CUDA on NVIDIA Tegra K1 has reduced the execution time to 15–20 ms, which helps to process video in real time.

2.2   Detection and Tracking

Modified Hough Transform. Detecting traffic signs is implemented using a modification of Generalized Hough transform (GHT) [10]. Implementing classic GHT in Full HD 1080p images leads to enormous execution time. One of the main objectives of the TSR system is to operate in real time. Therefore, there are maximum 50 ms for processing one frame on the detection step.

Many TSR systems are designed to detect only circular signs. There is no difficulty to detect circles using an implementation of Hough transform, and using CUDA makes it possible to implement it in real time. All processing takes no more than 40 ms including steps of color extraction, denoising, detection and recognition. Other systems use various machine-learning techniques such as Viola-Jones [11] or Support Vector Machine [12], which do not always suit the execution time limitation.

In this paper, we consider detection and recognition of triangular signs in real time. The main difference from the original GHT is in using some other accumulator space (Fig. 5b) and avoiding the R-table construction. After applying a special triangular template to the binary image in Fig. 4c, the point with the maximum value in Fig. 5b is the central point of the sought-for object. The case shown in Fig. 5 is for equal scales of a template object and object in the real scene. The colors in the pictures are inverted in comparison to the images used in the algorithm.

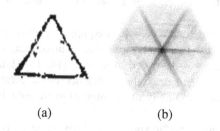

(a)   (b)

Fig. 5. (a) An example of a triangular sign after color extraction; (b) Accumulator space after implementing the developed algorithm.

In case of different scales, we receive some more extremum points in the accumulator, three points when implementing the algorithm using a triangular template (Fig. 6).

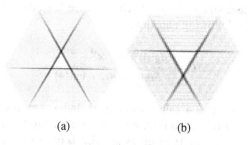

(a)   (b)

Fig. 6. The accumulator space in case of (a) template is smaller than the object in real scene; (b) template is bigger than the object in real scene.

Assuming that the size of a sign is up to 150 pixels, we have found that the distance between two of these points is up to 20 pixels. A sign with 150 pixels of width means that it is located in 6 meters from the camera. There is no opportunity and no need to detect a closer sign, because it moves out from the view of a camera with α equal to 70° (Fig. 1). It allows computing the difference in scales of the template and an object in real scene. Using this value, we can precisely define the area of sign and then pass it to the recognition step. The middle location of these bright points in the accumulator is the coordinates of an object's center.

This paper shows the detection procedure of triangular traffic signs only. However, the described algorithm can also be used to detect rectangular and circular objects in images, thus covering almost all of the traffic sign classes. The main difference is the template images used for detection.

Tracking with Prediction. The above-described traffic sign detection algorithm is designed to localize objects in each two-dimensional frame of a video sequence. However, some researchers propose to use additional information to increase the reliability of traffic sign recognition. For example, in the article [13], the authors propose to combine data obtained with a usual camera and three-dimensional scene obtained with lidar.

In this paper, we assume that a vehicle is equipped with only one FullHD camera. In this case, we can only use two-dimensional consecutive frames of a video sequence. The use of adjacent frames is described in articles [14, 15]. Tracking traffic sign on adjacent frames can not only increase the confidence in the correct detection, but also reduce the computational complexity of the algorithm by reducing the search area in the adjacent frames.

In this article, tracking of traffic signs in a video sequence is performed using the information on the current vehicle speed. Most modern cars are equipped with onboard computers or GPS receivers, which can return the current vehicle speed V. In addition, we know the number of received frames per second FPS. Thus, we can get the exact difference of the distance to the sign in adjacent frames:

$$\Delta AC = \frac{V}{FPS} \tag{4}$$

Consider the case of detecting a triangular traffic sign shown in Fig. 5, using the model of the road scene shown in Fig. 1. The distance from the vehicle to the sign can be obtained using the following equation:

$$AC = \frac{SignWidth_m \times \frac{FrameWidth_p}{2}}{SignWidth_p \times \tan\left(\frac{\alpha}{2}\right)} \tag{5}$$

Here, index $_m$ means that a value is in meters, index $_p$ means a value in pixels.

The actual size of the road signs is known and in our case is 0.7 m. We assume that the sign width in pixels is equal to 31 pixels as this size is quite suitable for the subsequent recognition step. α is equal to 70°. In this case, the distance AC is equal to 30 m.

Using the difference (4) and the distance (5), we can calculate the exact size of the sign on the adjacent frames:

$$SignWidth'_p = \frac{AC \times SignWidth_p}{AC + \Delta AC} \tag{6}$$

A sign image in adjacent frames not only changes its scale but also moves in the frame horizontally. When coming closer to a sign, it will be located further from the center of the image. Finally, it will disappear when reaching the frame bounds. Having the precise sign image's size in the adjacent frames (6), we can also calculate its distance to the center of the next frame:

$$CenterShift'_p = \frac{AC \times CenterShift_p}{AC + \Delta AC} \tag{7}$$

The following code in Matlab shows how to obtain all the above mentioned values:

```
SignWidth_m = 0.7; % Sign width in meters
SignWidth_p = 31; % Sign width in pixels
FrameWidth = 1920; % Frame width in pixels
CenterShift = 200; % Distance to the frame center
angleOfView = 70; % Horizontal angle of view in degrees

% Angle of view in radians
alpha = ( angleOfView / 180) * pi;

V = 30; % Vehicle's velocity in m/s
FPS = 30; % Frames per second

% Distance from camera to a sign in meters
AC = (SignWidth_m * FrameWidth/2) /
     (SignWidth_p * tan(alpha/2));

% Difference of distance to a sign in the previous frame
deltaAC = + V / FPS;
% Distance to a sign on the previous frame
priorAC = AC + deltaAC;
% Resolution of a sign in pixels in the previous frame
priorSignWidth_p = (AC * SignWidth_p) / (AC + deltaAC);

% Difference of distance to a sign in the next frame
deltaAC = - V / FPS;
% Distance to a sign on the next frame
posteriorAC = AC + deltaAC;
% Resolution of a sign in pixels in the next frame
posteriorSignWidth_p = (AC * SignWidth_p) /
                       (AC + deltaAC);

% Sign shift from center of the next frame
posteriorCenterShift = (AC * CenterShift) /
                       (AC + deltaAC);
```

Thus, the detection with tracking uses vehicle speed to predict the sizes of a detected traffic sign in the adjacent frames. This significantly increases the reliability of the correct detection and at the same time reduces the required time for detection.

2.3   Recognition

For the recognition step, the algorithm uses the specially prepared binary template images, which are actually inner areas of traffic signs. Figure 7 shows such etalons.

Fig. 7. Template images for template matching.

After detection, the algorithm obtains images of detected objects, which are quite similar to etalons since they are previously resized to the constant size of etalon images. To determine the type of a found object, we can use any recognition method. However, in case of successful object detection, and due to the execution time limitation, it is expedient to use a simple image subtraction and choose the lowest value, which will point to the most similar etalon. In case of large values, the algorithm gives a false detection message, since no similar etalon images were found.

The execution time of such recognition is 3–4 ms in average with 32 types of image etalons. This performance allows using several etalon images of each type to increase the recognition efficiency and reliability.

3   Experimental Results

In order to evaluate the detection and recognition algorithms accuracy, we used the German Traffic Sign Detection Benchmark (GTSDB) [16] and the German Traffic Sign Recognition Benchmark (GTSRB) [17]. They contain more than 50,000 images with traffic signs registered in various conditions. To assess the quality of the sign detection, we counted number of images with correctly recognized traffic signs. When testing the developed algorithms, we used only 9,987 images containing traffic signs of the required shape and with red contours. The experiments showed 97,3 % of correctly detected and recognized prohibitory and danger traffic signs.

The remaining 2.7 % of traffic signs were rejected on the recognition step with the message "There is no sign in the detected region". When lowing the thresholds of recognition, we can increase the accuracy of the whole procedure. Still, it is much more important to avoid false detection cases in real situation than to miss some traffic signs.

Table 1 shows the resulting accuracy and performance of the detection algorithms from [16] and the method described in this paper.

Table 1. Accuracy and performance of TSR methods.

Method	Accuracy	FPS
Sliding window + SVN	100 %	1
Modified GHT with preprocessing	97,3 %	43
Modified GHT without preprocessing	89,3 %	25
Viola-Jones	90,81 %	15
HOG	70,33 %	20

The accuracy of all methods shown in the table was obtained using the dataset GTSDB. The sliding window method shows the best result with 100 % of accuracy. However, the described in this paper modified GHT reaches the best performance. Testing our method without preprocessing gives worse result in accuracy and almost twice lower performance.

Figure 8 shows some examples of detected traffic signs in the images from the German Traffic Sign Detection Benchmark dataset. The detected objects are marked with green rectangles.

Fig. 8. Traffic signs detection in images from the GTSDB dataset.

In Fig. 9, there are examples of detected and recognized traffic signs from the German Traffic Sign Recognition Benchmark dataset. Despite the bad registration

Fig. 9. Successfully recognized traffic signs from the GTSRB dataset.

quality of some images, most of the detected objects are recognized correctly, because the coordinates of the inner area of a traffic sign are detected quite precisely.

The developed algorithm was also tested on the video frames obtained in the streets of the city of Samara using an Android device Nvidia Shield Tablet built in to a car. Figure 10 shows the fragments of the original images with marked road signs on them.

Fig. 10. Frames from a video sequence with detected and classified traffic signs.

In case of successful classification of the detected sign, localization in the next frame is performed inside an area calculated using (6) and (7). Figure 11a shows the calculated area of interest for the next frame, it is marked with yellow. The vehicle's

Fig. 11. (a) A frame with marked calculated area of interest for the next frame; (b) The next frame with marked area for searching new objects.

velocity is obtained using GPS. Tracking traffic signs in a video sequence reduces the processing time for several subsequent frames. The average time to process one frame is 23 ms. By limiting the search area in the subsequent frames, localization time is reduced to 10–15 ms. An object is being tracked as long as it stays within frame boundaries. The marked yellow area in Fig. 11b is the area of interest for searching new objects.

4   Conclusions

This paper proposes a whole technology for traffic signs recognition, including image preprocessing, detecting with tracking, and recognition of traffic signs. The HSV color model was approved as the most suitable one for the extraction of red color in the images. The modified algorithm for removing noise helped not only to avoid false detection of signs, but also accelerated the processing of images. The developed algorithm can improve the quality and increase the reliability of automotive traffic sign recognition systems, and reduce the time required to process one frame, which brings the possibility to carry out the detection and recognition of signs in Full HD 1920 × 1080 images from the video sequence in real time.

An algorithm for detection of triangular signs is considered in the paper. It is based on the Generalized Hough Transform and is optimized to suit the time limitation. The developed algorithm shows efficient results and works well with the preprocessed images. Tracking using a vehicle's current velocity helps to improve the performance. In addition, the presence of a sign in a sequence of adjacent frames in predicted areas improves the confidence in correct detection. Recognition of detected signs makes sure that the whole procedure of TSR is successful.

In this paper, we consider triangular traffic signs. The developed detection algorithm makes it possible to detect signs of any shape. It is only needed to replace the template image with a sought-for shape.

The use of our TSR algorithms allows processing of video streams in real-time with high resolution, and therefore at greater distances and with better quality than similar TSR systems have. FullHD resolution makes it possible to detect and recognize a traffic sign at a distance up to 50 m.

The developed method was implemented on an Android device with Nvidia Tegra K1 processor. CUDA was used to accelerate the performance of the described methods. In future research, we plan to move all the designed algorithms to the mobile processor Nvidia Tegra X1.

In future research, we plan to create a new traffic sign detection and recognition dataset with annotated videos instead of images, like in GTSDB and GTSRB. Also, we plan to use the convolutional neural networks [18] to improve the efficiency of sign recognition.

Acknowledgements. This work was supported by Project #RFMEFI57514X0083 by the Ministry of Education and Science of the Russian Federation.

References

1. Shneier, M.: Road sign detection and recognition. In: Proceedings of IEEE Computer Society International Conference on Computer Vision and Pattern Recognition, pp. 215–222 (2005)
2. Nikonorov, A., Yakimov, P., Petrov, M.: Traffic sign detection on GPU using color shape regular expressions. In: Proceedings of VISIGRAPP IMTA-4, Paper Nr 8 (2013)
3. Ruta, A., Porikli, F., Li, Y., Watanabe, S., Kage, H., Sumi, K.: A new approach for in-vehicle camera traffic sign detection and recognition. In: Proceedings IAPR Conference on Machine vision Applications (MVA), Session 15: Machine Vision for Transportation (2009)
4. Belaroussi, R., Foucher, P., Tarel, J.P., Soheilian, B., Charbonnier, P., Paparoditis, N.: Road sign detection in images. In: Proceedings 20th International Conference on Pattern Recognition (ICPR), pp. 484–488 (2010)
5. Lafuente-Arroyo, S., Maldonado-Bascon, S., Gil-Jimenez, P., Gomez-Moreno, H., Lopez-Ferreras, F.: Road sign tracking with a predictive filter solution. In: IECON 2006 - 32nd Annual Conference on IEEE Industrial Electronics, pp. 3314–3319 (2006)
6. Lopez, L.D., Fuentes, O.: Color-based road sign detection and tracking. In: Kamel, M.S., Campilho, A. (eds.) ICIAR 2007. LNCS, vol. 4633, pp. 1138–1147. Springer, Heidelberg (2007)

7. Koschan, A., Abidi, M.A.: Digital Color Image Processing, p. 376 (2008). ISBN 978-0-470-14708-5
8. Yakimov, P.: Preprocessing of digital images in systems of location and recognition of road signs. Comput. Opt. **37**(3), 401–405 (2013)
9. Fursov, V.A., Bibikov, S.A., Yakimov, P.Y.: Localization of objects contours with different scales in images using Hough transform. Comput. Opt. **37**(4), 496–502 (2013)
10. Ruta, A., Li, Y., Liu, X.: Detection, tracking and recognition of traffic signs from video input. In: Proceedings of the 11th International IEEE Conference on Intelligent Transportation Systems. Beijing, China (2008)
11. Møgelmose, A., Trivedi, M., Moeslund, M.: Learning to detect traffic signs: comparative evaluation of synthetic and real-world datasets. In: Proceedings of 21st International Conference on Pattern Recognition, pp. 3452–3455. IEEE (2012)
12. Lafuente-Arroyo, S., Salcedo-Sanz, S., Maldonado-Bascón, S., Portilla-Figueras, J.A., Lopez-Sastre, R.J.: A decision support system for the automatic management of keep-clear signs based on support vector machines and geographic information systems. Expert Syst. Appl. **37**, 767–773 (2010)
13. Timofte, R., Zimmermann, K., Van Gool, L.: Multi-view traffic sign detection, recognition, and 3D localisation. Mach. Vis. Appl. **25**, 633–647 (2014). Springer, Berlin, Heidelberg
14. Guo, C., Mita, S., McAllester, D.: Robust road detection and tracking in challenging scenarios based on markov random fields with unsupervised learning. IEEE Trans. Intell. Transp. Syst. **13**(3), 1338–1354 (2012)
15. Mogelmose, A., Trivedi, M.M., Moeslund, T.B.: Vision-based traffic sign detection and analysis for intelligent driver assistance systems: perspectives and survey. IEEE Trans. Intell. Transp. Syst. **13**(4), 1484–1497 (2012)
16. Houben, S., Stallkamp, J., Salmen, J., Schlipsing, M., Igel, C.: Detection of traffic signs in real-world images: the German traffic sign detection benchmark. In: Proceedings of International Joint Conference on Neural Networks (2013)
17. Stallkamp, J., Schlipsing, M., Salmen, J., Igel, C.: Man vs. computer: benchmarking machine learning algorithms for traffic sign recognition. Neural Netw. **32**, 323–332 (2012)
18. Pierre, S., LeCun, Y.: Traffic sign recognition with multi-scale convolutional networks. In: The 2011 International Joint Conference on Neural Networks (IJCNN). IEEE (2011)

A Passive Acoustic Technique to Enhance Lung Diseases Diagnostic

Fatma Ayari[1(✉)], Ali Alouani[2], and Mekki Ksouri[1]

[1] National School of Engineering, University of Tunis El Manar,
B.P.342, Le Belvedere, 1002 Tunis, Tunisia
enit@enit.rnu.tn
[2] Electrical Engineering Department, Tennessee Technological University,
Po Box 5004, Cookeville, TN 38505, USA
equity@tntech.edu

Abstract. Multiple lung obstructive and restrictive lung diseases are considered to experiment a new methodology based on Passive Time Delay Technique (PTDT). Lung sounds were recorded using a multichannel stethoscope on 32 healthy subjects, 20 COPD patients and 20 patients with different lung disorders. The sensors were distributed on the posterior and anterior chest wall. During recordings, all participants were breathing at matching airflow rates. Calculated time delay (TD) was identified for inspiration phase and an average TD value was provided after three repetitive measurements for each inspiration phase. TD computed in COPD patients: 440 ± 87 % ($P < 0.05$) was remarkably greater than time delay computed with normal subjects: 160 ± 10 % ($P < 0.05$) it was also greater than TD recorded with different other lung disorders patients. Results were presented as mean $\pm$ SD, standard deviation of time delay in ms. Significant P values ($P < 0.05$) were indicated using Wilcoxon test. Preliminary results are very encouraging to develop this technique and enhance lung diseases monitoring.

Keywords: Passive time delay · Chronic obstruction · Lung sounds · Lung signal analysis · Multichannel

1 Introduction

Patients with obstructive or restrictive pulmonary disorders are subject to multiple factors that can play a major role in locally changing the airflow behaviour in the lung arteries. Airflow turbulence is revealed by a local transition in the lung sounds. The time delay between lung sounds recorded simultaneously at different lung fields will depend on the obstruction level of the airways. By estimating such time delay, one will determine if airway obstruction exists between two field locations.

This paper presents a new biomedical marker based on the concept of time delay (TD) technique for the detection and localization of obstructive and restrictive pulmonary disorders, using a multichannel stethoscope. In fact, abnormalities in the lung manifested by obstructions or restrictions are causing a local airflow perturbation inside the lung pathways providing an abrupt change in the lung signals recorded over multiple chest sites. To estimate the time delay, the concept of signal correlation is used.

© Springer International Publishing Switzerland 2016
M.S. Obaidat and P. Lorenz (Eds.): ICETE 2015, CCIS 585, pp. 468–489, 2016.
DOI: 10.1007/978-3-319-30222-5_22

In this extended approach to the classical autocorrelation technique, we are using a predictive time delay estimator that allows for the localization of affected lung zones. Results obtained with this new biomedical marker illustrate its performances and show a great consistency with other approaches for detection of lung diseases.

In fact, gas propagation in complex pathways of the respiratory system is accompanied by the spreading of lung sounds that can be collected in various regions of the thorax. Moreover, lung sounds are usually mixed with heart sounds and tissues sounds, caused by any change of the chest movements, during respiratory cycles.

Generally, purely lung signals are highly correlated with mechanical gases vibration along the different pathways as it was mentioned in [1, 2], in their studies. Additional noisy signals must be filtered before dealing with lung signal analysis.

Capturing lung signals using a multichannel stethoscope was a frequent topic in the last decades. Multiple researches were developed using both active acoustic methods (AAM) and passive acoustic methods (PAM).

The AAM consists to transmit a low frequency sound into the chest via a loud speaker placed in the patient's mouth. Then, the delay and frequency response of the lung are used to understand the sound propagation inside the respiratory system [3].

The (PAM) consists on capturing lung sounds from different sites of the chest via digital stethoscope without introducing any external sounds. This dynamic method was used by different authors [4, 5] to analyze the functional properties of different lung diseases. Different authors demonstrated that the PAM provides a better interpretation of the biological signals and adds more precision in the disease diagnose and decision making as mentioned in [6].

In the present study we developed a time delay approach based on the PAM to understand the nature of lung sounds propagation in the case of an obstructive pulmonary disease such as COPD or asthma, but also, to apprehend restrictive defects such as pleural disorders or pulmonary fibrosis. We used the concept of time delay which is motivated by the fact that as the air travels from the mouth to different lung fields, the travel time will depend on the level of obstruction or restriction of the airways in the lung. By comparing the travel time of a healthy lung to that of lung with any obstructive or restrictive disorder, one can detect airways obstruction and the lung area where obstruction or restriction is occurring.

Abnormalities in the lung manifested by obstructions or restrictions are causing a local airflow perturbation inside the lung pathways providing an abrupt change in the lung signals recorded over multiple chest sites.

To estimate the time delay, the concept of signal correlation was used. We developed an extended approach for the time delay estimator that allows for the localization of affected lung zones.

2 Motivation of New Biomedical Markers

2.1 Outline About Biomedical Markers Used in Pulmonary Disorders

Early detection and more precise diagnosis of manifold progressive lung diseases are key features in improving deductions and altering a disease progression. Generally, the presence of visible hallmark symptoms of lung disorders are the first subjective recipes towards a lung disease identification (e.g. breathlessness, crackles, wheeze, fatigue, chronic cough or sputum production, chest tightness, chest infection, swelling, obesity, barrel chest, and rarely cyanosis or hemoptysis so on...). Thus, it is important to get measurable indicators allowing either the detection of a probable lung disorder and also the degree of illness when it is ongoing. The detection of pulmonary disorders using biological markers is widely described over the last decades [7–9]. However, in obstructive, restrictive and mixed pulmonary disorders, airflow and lung volume are varying abruptly. Their measurements are used to characterize biologic markers that describe the lung diseases severities and also measure the lung responses to therapy. Therefore, those markers play important role in monitoring patients with pulmonary diseases. Experimental quantitative measurements of some markers can be ensured with standard tests such as; spirometry instrumentation, gas, body plethysmography and flow-volume loop [11–13]. Spirometry is one of the most recommended tests by Global initiative for Obstructive Lung Disease (GOLD) in multiple lung disorders like COPD, asthma and many others. The pulmonary function tests are performed to evaluate lung function and measure the degree of damage to the lung. According to the history of the patient and its physical conditions, pulmonary tests include CT image scans, Chest X-ray, spirometry, diffusion, plethysmography, bronchoscopy, pulse oximetry, open lung biopsy and blood test that must include (arterial blood gases, hemoglobin with hematocrit levels ...). In fact, doctors can prescribe a pulmonary test according to their experience and also to the patient conditions.

It is well known [14, 15] that in forced spyrometry, inhaled and exhaled air volume in the first second and in the total residual time of breath is used to define the forced vital capacity of the lung (FVC), the forced expiratory volume (FEV1), the pick expiratory flow (PEF), the functional residual capacity (FRC) and the total lung capacity (TLC) Figs. 1 and 2. Till now those markers (designated also by biological markers) are considered as the best indicators used for the detection and the monitoring of the most pulmonary disorders. The problem is that spyrometry requires the patient to inhale or exhale to perform measurements. Based on the health condition of the patient, different measurements may be obtained.

FRC is measured using gas dilution techniques or a plethysmograph (which is more accurate in patients who have airflow restraint). Gas dilution techniques include either Nitrogen scrub down or Helium equilibration which is sharper in some cases. Thus, Body plethysmography uses Boyle's law to measure the compressible gas volume within the thorax and it is more accurate than gas dilution technique. All those indicators are also assumed to be biological pulmonary markers; Tables 1 and 2 illustrate the indexed markers according to pulmonary disorders as defined in references [15–20].

Recently, however, it was suggested that pulmonary embolism severity index (PESI) is used to predict the state of health for patients with pulmonary embolism. The measurements of this biologic marker allow the classification of patient's with risk category based on clinical scores. Table 3 gives the PESI intervals in different stages of the pulmonary embolism according to [21].

In many studies, it was concluded that obstructive defects are caused by increased resistance to flow due to abnormalities within the airway (e.g. tumors, secretions, mucosal thickening). Also, changes in the airway wall (e.g. contraction of smooth

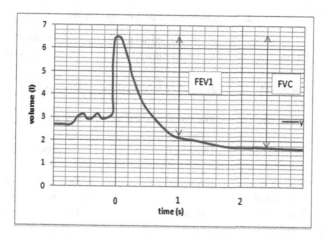

Fig. 1. FEV$_1$ = forced expiratory volume in the first second of forced vital capacity maneuver; FVC = forced vital capacity (the maximum amount of air forcibly expired after maximum inspiration).

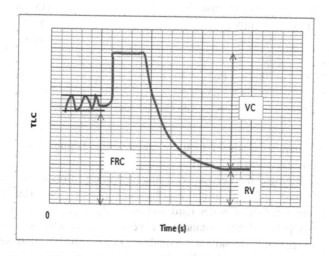

Fig. 2. FRC = functional residual capacity; RV = residual volume; TLC = total lung capacity; VC = vital capacity.

muscles, edema, COPD, emphysema, chronic bronchitis, bronchiectasis and asthma) are induced by obstructive defects. When airflow is decreased, the expiratory phase becomes longer than usual, and air becomes wrapped up in the lungs due to partial drain, in that way lung volume increases [22]. In particular restrictive pulmonary disorders, which include restrictive defects, one can have loss in lung volume (e.g., lobotomy), abnormalities of structures surrounding the lung (e.g. pleural disorder, kyphosis, and obesity), weakness of the inspiratory muscles of respiration (e.g., neuromuscular disorders) and abnormalities of the lung parenchyma (e.g. pulmonary

Table 1. Biomarkers based on spirometry.

Characteristic physiologic changes associated with pulmonary disorders

	Obstructive disorders	Restrictive disorders	Mixed disorders
$FEV_1/$ FVC	Decreased	Normal or increased	Decreased
FEV_1	Decreased	Decreased, normal, or increased	Decreased
FVC	Decreased or normal	Decreased	Decreased or normal
TLC	Normal or increased	Decreased	Decreased, normal, or increased
RV	Normal or increased	Decreased	Decreased, normal, or increased

Table 2. Classification of lung diseases based on FEV1, FVC, TLC.

Severity of obstructive and restrictive lung disorders

		Obstructive	Restrictive
FEV1 /FVC		FEV1	TLC
Normal	≥70	≥80	≥80
Mild	<70	≥80	70–79
Moderate	<70	$50 \leq FEV_1 < 80$	50–69
Severe	<70	$30 \leq FEV_1 < 50$	<50
Very severe	<70	<30 or<50 with chronic respiratory failure	–

fibrosis). The common parameter to these cases is the falling down of the lungs' compliance and/or the chest wall [23].

The overall Biologic markers are carrying important information on the global behavior of the lung under a particular pulmonary disorder. Nevertheless, some of those markers are determined under hard and painfully experiments on the patients. Thus, in particular patients' circumstances, it is very hard to conduct such experimental tests because of patient's weakness. In addition, interpretation of those measured markers depends on patient's effort. Results that do not summon minimum criterions are considered unreliable. It is also notable that most of information carried behind those biologic markers, describe the global functionality response of the lung. They do not inform about location of the problem in the lung. Therefore, in the majority of cases, doctors are recommending complementary tests such as x-ray, CT images scan and so on to trace the infected part of lung when necessary. However, in some few cases (e.g. asthma), parameters deduced from spirometry can be similar to those extracted from normal patients. Also it is noticeable to know that a low PESI (corresponding to risk class I or II as it defined in Table 3 [24, 25]) is sufficient to allow home treatment of low risk patients with pulmonary embolism. Then again, several diagnostic tests are useful for making therapeutic decisions in patients with risk. In view of

Table 3. PESI index.

Points	Risk
≤65	Class I, very low risk
66–85	Class II, low risk
86–105	Class III, intermediate risk
106–125	Class IV, high risk
>125	Class V, very high risk

these considerations, it is important to provide new biologic markers that can provide consistent and reliable estimate of the patient's risk.

In the earliest work of [2], it was demonstrated that there is a relationship between airflow inside the lung and lung sound amplitude. The relationship between lung sound amplitude and airflow is linear and this relationship is very significant for the detection of airflow variation. Nevertheless, it is important to be concerned about the airflow conditions inside the lung because in some lung disorders, airflow limitation is progressive and sometimes worsens overtime irreversibly. In cases when patients are exposed to harmful stimuli like cigarettes, inhalation of coal mine dust, grain dust, silica, or cotton and air pollution, airflow degrade in the lung's airways which take an inflammatory response.

In fact, airflow inside the lung is affected by multiple conditions; pressure inside and outside the lung, volume of lung and alveoli, the state of alveoli and the tubes (by mean of elasticity or plasticity), the wall thickness of tubes and alveoli (they can thin or thick) and obstacles inside the tubes (for example if the tube's mucus secretion is above normal, it congests the tube). However, it is important to understand the most important conditions that are managing airflow change inside the lung are; airway resistance and lung compliance.

2.2 Interest of Lung Sounds Collected Using Multi Sensors

Pulmonary auscultation using a digital stethoscope is being a new efficient tool for objective and noninvasive clinical diagnosis. This technique provides multiple advantages for biological signal analysis, as far as it allows saving, displaying and archiving recorded biological sound signals from any enclosed location in the human body. Thus, it is obvious that this technique provides a better interpretation of the biological signals and adds more precision in the disease diagnose and decision making [26–28].

Assuming that all the sounds recorded over the chest are precious information, reflecting the healthy state of the lung, multiple scientific teams were focalized on the development of new sounds recording tools for the medical diagnosis. Multiple investigations are conducted to explore particularly lung sounds collected from multiple chest sites as it is described in references [29–33]. Authors over the world are completely consent about the fact that in lung diseases diagnosis, it is significantly recommended to collect acoustical information from several auscultation sites in the chest simultaneously. However, this fact surrogate the clinician's daily gesture that is developed nowadays by the multichannel recording sounds.

The usefulness of multi-sensors for pulmonary lung recording is attributed to many advantages. It is possible to cover many important pulmonary sites between apexes to bases. Thus, multichannel records allow for collecting signal information from particular sites simultaneously, as frequently as necessary to follow up the disease development. One of the most recent research dealing with multichannel lung sounds analysis for the classification of lung diseases is due to [34], when author have demonstrated that recorded lung sounds from specific locations in the chest via 16 sensors were used to perform 2D and 3D analysis of lung sounds and he have contributed to classify different lung diseases according to the pathologic markers and lung sound features characteristics. Following the same initiative, we are developing in this study, a new methodology contributing to the detection of pulmonary disorders based on delay produced between lung sounds and lung arteries obstruction that can be associated to various lung diseases. We will explain that abnormal lung sounds due to airway obstruction when the delay between signals is above particular critical value could be an important marker that informs about a specific lung disorder. We will consider multiple time expanded lung waveforms recorded from 8 positions on the chest. For the analysis of those time series, we consider a matrix constituted with vectors corresponding to the different collected time series which is analyzed using a signal processing toolbox implemented in matlab [35, 36]. Furthermore, we are explaining the context and the background towards the development of our methodology to detect particular pulmonary disorders like COPD and cancer lung pathologies using a multichannel stethoscope.

In fact, asthma, bronchitis, and emphysema are all considered as obstructive conditions, but the way each results in an obstructive defect, is quite different. Furthermore, according to GOLD recent definitions (Global Initiative for Obstructive Lung Disease), COPD, is one of the most dangerous and expanded pulmonary disease over the world, and till now it is considered as under-diagnosed and it is very important to distinguish COPD from other pulmonary disorders. In fact, COPD includes the above pulmonary disorders and in the diagnosis of such particular pulmonary diseases, it is worthy to distinguish the degree of damage to the lung clearly and also the severity of the disease. The development of new markers can be very helpful to enhance such lung diagnosis and update rules for early detection and treatment of COPD. Also, it is known that interpretation of doctors to pulmonary function tests is usually arcane. Knowing the value of an objective number that symbolizes the lung state according to a biological marker, in the case of COPD patient is as important as knowing blood pressure or temperature of the body and so on…In fact, either patient and doctors need to have simple indexes that can describe briefly and accurately the healthy state of the patients lungs. That is the reason for which our team as many researches groups are looking for new noninvasive biological markers, providing a measurable index that could be very useful for both patients and doctors.

At least, in some treatable lung pathologies, lung damage has a significant impact on the body and could affect the overall body systems. This fact is thought to contribute to the severity of the lung disease. As soon as we can measure to prevent this lung damage as possible is to minimize the severity diseases progress.

3   Methodology

The methodology adopted in this paper is based on a mathematical model build using experimental data.

3.1   Experiments

The experimental data is given from our own database. This database consists on lung sounds recorded from normal patients and restrictive or obstructive patients. For patients with COPD we collected data from patients with the following symptoms. Chronic bronchitis patients have sputum production such that cough and sputum for at least three months. Prior to recording lung sound phases, we collected information about patients such as name, age, sex, BMI, and thorax size. For other patients with different lung disorders, we have recorded sounds from patients attending hospitals for two years at least and having an updated historical in the hospital department of pulmonary.

Experimental measurements of lung sounds were tabulated in a database that contains smoking subjects and non-smoking subjects. All participants in these clinical experiments were asked to breathe three times and we recorded breath sounds for inspiration phases with time duration of 3 to 6 s. They were also instructed to hold their breath for few seconds and then to breathe easily before each new signal recording.

All participants' lung signals were recorded with an 8-channel stethoscope. This instrument was fully described in the following references [37, 38]. Figure 3 show the multichannel stethoscope used in this study.

Fig. 3. Multichannel lung sound system, capture of the detailed devices used in the multichannel sthetoscope (sensors, I/O box of connexion and DAQ server).

This instrument allowed recording lung sounds during breathing, which are proportional to the gas flow vibrations as postulated by [2].

The monitoring using multichannel stethoscope is insured using a Lab View platform as represented by Fig. 4. Also we can display the 8 signals simultaneously as represented by Fig. 5.

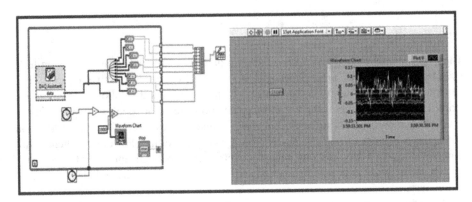

Fig. 4. Capture of the multichannel monitoring using Lab View platform.

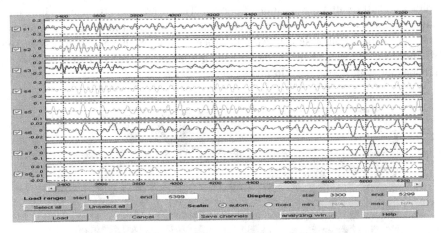

Fig. 5. Capture of the multichannel analysis screen.

The protocol of measurements was executed while subjects were seated. The eight sensors were distributed as follow; four acoustic sensors on the front of the chest and four acoustic sensors on the back. The protocol of recording sounds consists of three breathing cycles to unsure the consistency of the recording sounds. Recorded signals include inspiratory phases and have a time duration ranging between 3 s and 6 s. The goal here was to quantify the health state of patient's lung using a new time delay estimate (TDE) technique based on multichannel lung sounds recording.

3.2   Theoretical Procedure

After collecting data, a preprocessing is used. The captured lung sounds were filtered using a variant of Sgolay filtering algorithm that we developed in references [39, 40]. We built an array of sensors with a distance adjusted according to the body size of the subject. The sounds were acquired via the multichannel stethoscope at a sampling frequency of 11 kHz.

Recorded lung sounds were then sent to computer storage for processing. Collected lung sounds, could then be displayed using appropriate Lab View software. Then, they are converted into a digital wave format and pre-processed so as to reduce noise effect.

The acquisition of captured lung sounds from multiple sites is conducted using a Lab View platform. We developed then a program using Matlab software to extract separate channels and to build the correlation matrix of the eight sensors, after a filtering process based on Sgolay algorithm. Further details about the algorithm that we developed are provided in the next section. A shot screen, of lung signals captured during processing phase.

We developed in this study, a new methodology that aims enhance COPD monitoring, based on time delay produced between captured lung sounds. We considered multiple time expanded lung waveforms recorded from eight positions on the chest. For the analysis and processing of time expanded waveforms, we built a matrix constituted with eight vectors corresponding to the different collected time series of the eight signals.

As we are capturing airflow vibrations which are transformed into electrical signals, digitized further, and displayed on the shot screen as lung signals. Airflow vibrations provoked with abrupt airflow changes, (if any abnormality inside the lung tissues occurred) may amplify the lung signal differently and change its morphology. All depends on the distance traced by the airflow inside the lung pathways; those vibrations reached the sensors at different times. The correlation technique allows measuring this time difference denoted by time delay between captured lung signals.

To compare time delays between sensors, it is important to mention that any time delay estimator is constrained to operate on observations of a finite duration. Also a time delay estimator design is the available amount of a priori knowledge of the captured signals and their noise statistics. Thus, the common method to carry an estimate of the time delay is to compute the cross correlation function first between every couple of signals captured in two different sensors. General cross correlation function is used as a similarity measure function in signal processing, that is described by Eq. (1) in continues signals f (t) and g (t) and Eq. (2) in discrete time series.

$$(f^*g)[n)] = \sum_{m=-\infty}^{\infty} f^*[m]g[n+m] \tag{1}$$

$$(f^*g)[n)] = \sum_{m=-\infty}^{\infty} f^*[m]g[n+m] \tag{2}$$

Where f^* denotes the complex conjugate of the function f.

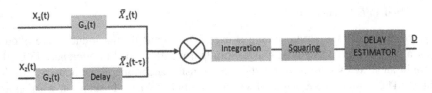

Fig. 6. Received waveforms filtered, delayed, multiplied and integrated for a variety of delays until peak output is obtained.

As described in [41], time delay, estimated in the propagation between two signals across a microphone array is deduced after calculating cross correlation between both signals and pointing in time the point corresponding to maximum of the absolute value of the cross correlation function. This time delay (denoted by D) between both signals is defined as the argument of the maximum of the cross correlation function in Fig. 6.

$$D = \arg\max((f*g)(t)) \tag{3}$$

Signals emanating from a particular lung source mixed with a noise, at two spaced sensors can be modeled as follows:

$$x_1(t) = s_1(t) + n_1(t) \tag{4}$$

$$x_2(t) = \beta s_1(t+D) + n_2(t) \tag{5}$$

Where $s_1(t)$ is the lung signal, $n_1(t)$, and $n_2(t)$ are noise signals associated to both positions and β is a real parameter. It is assumed that the signal s_1 is uncorrelated with noise signals n_1 and n_2.

There are many theoretical approaches which are proposed by researchers to estimate the time delay using different refinement algorithms (Chan 1980), in order to improve the precision in calculating this time delay based on cross correlation function. Some of them are available in the case of stationary signals; the others can be employed in slowly varying environments, where the characteristics of the signals and noise remain mainly stationary only for finite observation time interval T.

For lung signals, we summarized the description of the most important proposed algorithm applied in the case of nearly stationary signals in very small time intervals. Thus, the common method to carry an estimate of the time delay is to compute the general cross correlation function, which is given explicitly between two signals $x_1(t)$ *and* $x_2(t)$ by the following equations as mentioned by (Knapp 1976):

$$R_{x1,x2}(\tau) = E[x_1(t)x_2(t-\tau)dt] \tag{6}$$

In the case of a small sized observation interval T, the cross correlation function takes the following form:

$$\hat{R}_{x1,x2}(\tau) = \frac{1}{T-\tau}\int_{\tau}^{T} x_1(t)x_2(t-\tau)dt \tag{7}$$

As far as it is necessary to carry accurate values of the estimate time delay D, it would be important to undergo a preprocessing of both captured signals $x_1(t)$ and $x_2(t)$. We consider the following filters denoted with G_1 (t) and G_2 (t) as it is illustrated by Fig. 3. The outputs of the two filters G_1 (t) and G_2 (t) are denoted by $\bar{x}_1(t)$, $\bar{x}_2(t)$. The objective of such filters is to smoothen and fine tune the cross correlation signal so that the maximum peak of this function can be sharply defined and therefore the time delay can also be accurately estimated.

The time shift yielding to the peak of the cross-correlation function is an estimate of the time delay D. Thus, to achieve a good and robust resolution of the time delay estimate, the input signals must be weighted.

Those weights are associated to several refinement techniques for example the technique proposed by [42] and the one due to [43]. Most techniques correspond to generalized cross correlation which is conceptually consisting on applying pre-equalization to the signals.

Performance of time delay estimation is strongly affected with noise associated to the captured signal and also to the length of the signal time interval. A low SNR with a relatively extended time interval are both key features for the performance of any refinement TD estimator algorithm. Most of the time delay refinement processors are expressed in the complex domain and their explicit form is done with a Fourier Transform relation. Thus, the cross power spectral density described by the Fourier transform relationship is given by Eq. (8) as mentioned by [44, 45].

$$R_{X_1 X_2}(\tau) = \int_{-\infty}^{\infty} G_{x_1 x_2}(f)e^{j2\pi f\tau}df \tag{8}$$

Generalized correlation between $x_1(t)$ and $x_2(t)$ is given by:

$$R_{\bar{X}_1 \bar{X}_2}^{(ge)}(\tau) = \int_{-\infty}^{\infty} \Psi_{ge}(f)G_{x_1 x_2}(f)e^{j2\pi f\tau}df \tag{9}$$

$$\Psi_{ge}(f) = G_1(f)G_2(f) \tag{10}$$

Among the different existing weight functions [43, 46] we selected the Phase Transform weight algorithm denoted by (PHAT). This algorithm uses a weighting function described with Eq. (11):

$$\Psi_{PHAT}(f) = \frac{1}{|G_{x_1 x_2}(f)|} \tag{11}$$

In the case of non-correlated noise $G_{n_1 n_2}(f) = 0$, the cross correlation will be expressed as:

$$\hat{R}^{(PHAT)}\bar{X}_1\bar{X}_2(\tau) = \delta(t - D) \tag{12}$$

With:

$$\frac{\hat{G}_{x_1x_2}(f)}{|G_{x_1x_2}(f)|} = e^{j\theta(f)} = e^{j2\pi fD(f)} \tag{12a}$$

In fact, the phase transforms denoted with (PHAT) [43], is the most used weighting algorithm and it is very interesting in the case of low noise to signal ratios. The PHAT weighting is the last step before calculating the estimate TD between both signals.

The different steps of our developed algorithm are illustrated by Fig. 7 which indicates the main components of the TDE estimator as it is developed in this study. The weight function applied to two lung signals can be explicitly defined as:

$$\Psi(f) = \frac{1}{|\hat{G}_{x_1x_2}(f)|} \tag{13}$$

And their final form of weighted cross correlation function is defined as:

$$\hat{R}^{new}_{\underset{\bar{X}_1\bar{X}_2}{\equiv\equiv}}(\tau) = \frac{1}{2\pi}\int_{-\pi}^{\pi} \frac{G_{x_1x_2}(f)}{|\hat{G}_{x_1x_2}(f)|}e^{-j2\pi f}df \tag{14}$$

The PHAT weighting processor, used as the last step of TD estimation in our methodology, is justified since it is one of the best weighting functions to be selected in the case of non-stationary and noisy signals as indicated in [44] (Georgiou 1973). To emphasize the importance with applying such a procedure, we computed the time delay

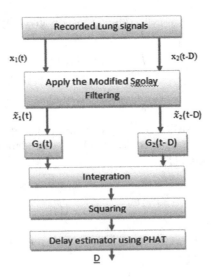

Fig. 7. Diagram of TD using our approach.

using a general cross correlation approach of two captured signals for every patient. Then, we applied the procedure described above to estimate the time delay between those two signals, Fig. 8. We concluded from Fig. 8(a) and (b), that our methodology has effectively strengthened the basic features of the signals. Figure 8(b) shows clearly the difference between general cross correlation technique (a) and the enhanced correlation technique based on PHAT algorithm. From Fig. 8(b), one can distinguish clearly the improved accuracy, and the signals sharpness of the residual peak.

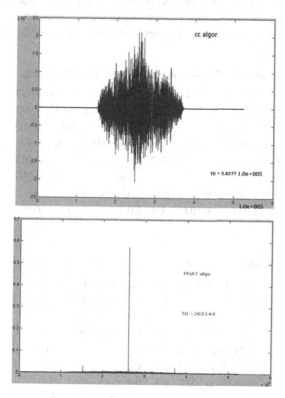

Fig. 8. (a). General cross correlation algorithm of two signals for COPD (the x axis is done in samples), from recorded lung signals of sensor 1 and sensor 8 of patient number 3). (b). Cross correlation of the same two signals using the PHAT algorithm (the x axis is done in samples), from recorded lung signals of sensor 1 and sensor 8 of patient number 3).

4 Results

After calculating the time delay between all couple of sensors, we saved the different time delay values in a matrix denoted by the time delay estimator matrix (TD_{ij}) for every patient. In this matrix, we saved the time delay between two lung signals; among signals captured via the 8 sensors. Columns and rows are corresponding to the reference number of sensors. Each component of the matrix (TD_{ij}) corresponds to a TDE between sensor i and sensor j where $i = [1, 2, \ldots, 8]$ and $j = [1, 2, \ldots, 8]$.

TD values calculated using sampling units are then converted into time delay measured in seconds. The final configuration of the correlation matrix is defined as illustrated by Tables 4 and 5. Differences between recordings at different chest sites for the different patients were highly significant as revealed by statistical tests ($P < 0.001$). To accurately visualize the local TD results distribution, with a statistic interpretation we represented TD using 3D image in Fig. 9, and 2D mapping in Figs. 10 and 11 for different patients. Such graphs can be very useful to localize and highlight the maximum peak of TDE values and also to visualize their distribution on the sensors Map. This representation allowed for localizing the chest zones where the rate flow is the lowest. Those chest zones may represent the most obstructed zones.

Table 4. The TDE matrix in (s) of a COPD patient.

0	0,073	1,374	0	0,967	0,013	1,054	0,938
0,073	0	0,026	0,073	0,751	0,055	0,069	0,071
1,374	0,026	0	1,374	0,723	0,034	0,1	0,103
0	0,073	1,374	0	0,967	0,013	1,054	0,938
0,967	0,751	0,723	0,967	0	1,709	1,016	1,017
0,987	1,055	0,034	0,013	1,709	0	0,006	0,007
1,053	0,1	0,1	1,054	1,016	0,006	0	0
0,071	0,071	0,103	0,938	1,017	0,007	0	0

Table 5. The TDE matrix in (s) of asthmatic patient.

0	0,15	0,03	0,2	0,21	0,12	0,2	0,5
0,2	0	0,01	0,04	0,3	0,1	0,23	0,21
0,3	0,21	0	0,3	0,5	0,2	0,3	0,3
0,35	0,3	0,2	0	0,2	0,04	0,03	0,04
0,23	0,05	0,12	0,04	0	0,12	0,3	0,06
0,02	0,02	0,06	0,02	0,21	0	0,1	0,02
0,01	0,06	0,02	0,3	0,2	0,1	0	0,01
0,02	0,01	0,03	0,1	0,1	0,03	0,2	0

Table 6 is corresponding to experimental measurements of three biomarkers with different patients and lung disorders.

It is observed through Table 6 that values deduced from spirometry of FEV1, TLC and FEV1/FVC are used to describe subjectively the amount of illness in each lung patient. Indexes in Table 6 give an overall idea about the class of each pulmonary disorder (according to comparison with GOLD standards from Table 2). Nevertheless, results provided by TDE of different obstructive and restrictive pulmonary disorders, as classified in Table 2 reveal that the following conclusions can be considered.

The maximum values of TDE extracted from each multichannel analysis of every subject, which are belonging to different classes of pulmonary disorders, are clearly categorized. Thus, the means and standard deviations of all recorded TDE values from

Table 6. Experimental biomarkers for the different patients.

FEV1/FVC	FEV1	TLC	
Subject 1 normal	84	86	90
Subject 2 chronic bronchitis	60	120	72
Subject 3 COPD	Non	Non	Non
Subject 4 asthma	65	80	70
Subject 5 lung tumor	55	50	60
Subject 6 pulmonary fibrosis	Non	Non	Non
Subject 7 pleural effusion	Non	Non	Non

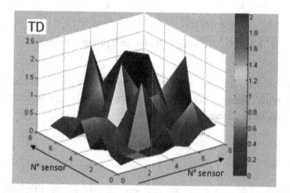

Fig. 9. Example of 3D Map for a COPD patient.

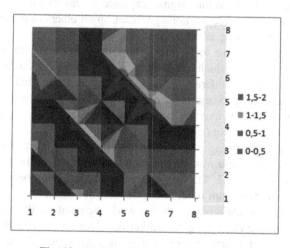

Fig. 10. 2D Map TDE for a COPD patient.

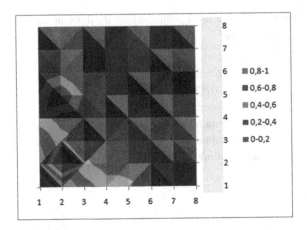

Fig. 11. 2D Map TDE for an asthmatic patient.

each multichannel matrix analysis are well separated. We observe that the max 25 % of TDE are defined with categorized values that are describing efficiently the distinction between considered lung diseases in this study.

5   Discussion

For all the obtained TDE matrices, we observe that in every TDE matrix, among 64 measurements of time delay, few of them were equal to 0. Excluding the diagonal values which are forcibly equal to zero, we observed some symmetric zero delay values i.e. in Table 4 we observed zero TD values between sensors (1–4 and 7–8). This fact means that time delay between lung signals captured at sensors 1 and 4 in one side and sensors 7 and 8 in another side are not significant. In all other combinations we found time delay values are varying asymmetrically.

Two important facts have to be highlighted here; the first one is that we have registered few time delays which are above 1 s; this represents 26.28 % of the total measurements between the different sensors. The second fact is that a delay of 1.709 was found between sensors 5 and 6 for patient ref 3. This value was considered as a relatively high value and it may be used as an index of pulmonary disorder in the airway located between sensors 5 and 6.

TD values were describing respectively the chest zones when the probability of detecting damaged lung zone was important. As an example, in the particular case of the COPD's patient number 3, TD values presented a fluctuation between 0.013 s and 1.709 s which is the maximum delay recorded with this patient.

As illustration to the main finding of this work, we point out that the hypothesis of an objective and measurable biological marker based on Time Delay between multiple nodes distributed on the chest where lung sounds are captured via a multichannel stethoscope. The preliminary results deduced from different patients show a great approbation with this idea. It is shown by the different statistic parameters of Table 7

Table 7. Experimental biomarkers for the different subjects.

TDE	Max	Mean	STD	25 % max TDE	50 % max TDE
COPD	1,709	0,472	0,541	1,202	0,901
Chronic bronchitis	1,054	0,291	0,351	0,836	0,552
Pulmonary fibrosis	0,800	0,223	0,210	0,524	0,392
Asthma	0,500	0,130	0,126	0,303	0,231
Pleural	1,000	0,257	0,226	0,563	0,418
Normal	0,060	0,023	0,018	0,046	0,038

that we have a clear distinction between the different pulmonary disorders. However, to draw definitive conclusions on the statistical TD deducted from a particular lung disease, as a clinical parameter, during a lung diagnose based on those measurable indexes, one can make a comparison with other biological markers to ensure the reliability of TD, as a next step. This step will require more investigations with a larger number of patients and diseases. The results obtained in this work, meet in the particular COPD case the results discussed by Murphy et all in their recent study [34]. In fact, they show according to another methodology used in their work, that a group of COPD patients was identified with a lag time between multiple signals captured via a multichannel stethoscope that is mainly defined with a mean value of 269 ms. This value was estimated as a mean result over couples of signals captured over 14 nodes in the chest. In our methodology we have identified TDE between all couples of lung signals deduced from 8 nodes (8 sensors) and we have highlighted all TDE statistic parameters over the different nodes from the chest in order to target the most damaged areas of the lung based on the TDE calculated using the cross correlation modified technique. The most advantages of this methodology can be illustrated as follows:

- It is very important to deduce via a relatively simple methodology a range of values that characterizes apart each disease objectively.
- Also we need to get a precise idea about the localization of the damaged and soft area of lung via a measurable parameter.
- The implementation of our methodology for TDE definition instantaneously during a diagnosis process is possible via a simple application that can be used on a laptop or any embedded system.
- The measurable parameters deduced via TD estimation can be very practice either for the patient and the doctor to get a preliminary idea about the healthy state of the patient, mostly in critical cases.
- A pulmonary diagnosis based on quantitative and measurable parameters enhances the decision making for the prescription of additional techniques required for a precise description of the pulmonary status.
- Finally, during the monitoring of a pulmonary disease it is very important to quantify the enhancement of the pulmonary sate via simple indexes that can be easily comprehensive by the patient and the doctor.

In this sense, the preliminary results deduced from the little number of studied cases are very encouraging to draw new rules and continue investigations.

6 Conclusions

The development of new markers can be very helpful in enhancing lung diagnosis and update rules for early detection and treatment of multiple lung diseases such as COPD. In fact, both patients and doctors need to have simple indices that can describe briefly and accurately the health state of the patient's lung. That is the reason for which our team as many researchers groups are looking for new noninvasive biological markers, providing instantaneous measurable indexes.

The current study brings significant impact, as we have emphasized a particular attention to the applicability of multiple lung sounds captured via a multichannel stethoscope to enhance lung diagnosis and pulmonary disorders detection, identification and classification.

However, it was necessary to develop a new methodology of lung sounds analysis, based on particular pre-filtering combined to modified cross correlation technique to ensure precise and accurate calculation of TDE and their statistic parameters for every patient. In fact, this development wasn't possible without introducing the fundamental relations between the mechanism of gas transfer inside the lung and also relations with the mechanical characteristics of lung on the example of lung compliance, airway resistance and their relation with biological lung markers.

We reviewed the different biomarkers, before introducing the motivation to our new biomarker based on lung signals processing. This biomarker, which is defined as the time delay between captured lung sounds, can be relevant information to carry out precious diagnosis, and to monitor a lung disorder invasively. In fact, sometimes, it is possible to avoid the use of costly and invasive technologies as well the discomfort of certain patients. Moreover, the use of multiple techniques like x ray or medical imaging can be very critical in many patients cases; i.e. a pregnant woman or an aged person or even a person with high risk to carcinogenic rays. Although we observed acceptable agreement between our results and clinicians symptoms, it would be necessary to include more experiments and measurements to carry general conclusions and standardize rules for this new approach.

We concluded that time delay due to autocorrelation technique has many advantages as it gives more detailed and measurable information on airflow in the pulmonary arteries. Standard clinical auscultation using a classic stethoscope could not detect intensity of this delay, which is related to the degree of illness. Moreover, this technique can be implemented easily on a multichannel stethoscope and could be a helpful tool for clinicians to get precious information on the healthy state of lung before asking for complementary pulmonary tests like spirometry, x-ray and so on.

In summary, computerized analysis of lung sounds using multichannel devices, greatly improve the efficiency of data collection. It can play a very important role in the rapid management of patients with a variety of medical conditions. Results obtained after this experimental investigation are encouraging. At least we can develop different open issues using 2D and 3D maps of TD distribution on the chest. We can exploit easily the contrasts between data for abnormal and healthy subjects which are consistently pronounced.

As a future work, we suggest to enlarge the experimental data and study the effect of other parameters such as (BMI and smoking effect) on the evolution of TD.

References

1. Meirav, Y., Ruben, L., Shaul, L., Yael, G.: Effect of airflow rate on vibration response imaging in normal lungs. Open Respir. Med. J. 3, 116–122 (2009)
2. Kraman, S.: The relationship between airflow and lung sound amplitude in normal subjects. Chest 86(2), 225–229 (1984)
3. Wodicka, G., Aguirre, A., Defrain, P., Shannon, D.: Phase delay of pulmonary acoustic transmission from trachea to chest wall. IEEE Trans. Biomed. Eng. 39, 1053–1059 (1992)
4. Dellinger, R., Parrillo, J., Kushnir, A., Rossi, M., Kushnir, I.: Dynamic visualization of lung sounds with a vibration response device: a case series. Respiration 7, 60–72 (2008)
5. Mor, R., Kushnir, I., Meyer, J., Ekstein, J., Ben-Dov, I.: Breath sound distribution images of patients with pneumonia and pleural effusion. Respir. Care 52, 1753–1760 (2007)
6. Murphy, R.: In defense of the stethoscope. Respir. Care 53, 355–369 (2008)
7. Barnes, P., Chowdhury, B., Kharitonov, S.A., Magnussen, H., Page, C.P., Postma, D., Saetta, M.: Pulmonary biomarkers in chronic obstructive pulmonary disease. Am. J. Respir. Crit. Care Med. 6–14 (2006)
8. Hurst, J.R., Donaldson, G.C., Perera, W.R., Wilkinson, T.M.A., Bilello, J.A., Hagan, G.W., Vessey, R.S., Wedzicha, J.A.: use of plasma biomarkers at exacerbation of chronic obstructive pulmonary disease. Am. J. Respir. Crit. Care Med. 174, 867–874 (2006)
9. Kotyza, J., Havel, D., Vrzalová, J., Kulda, V., Pesek, M.: Diagnostic and prognostic significance of inflammatory markers in lung cancer-associated pleural effusions. Int. J. Bio. Markers 25, 12–20 (2010)
10. Schneider, J.: Tumour markers in detection of lung cancer. Adv. Clin. Chem. 42, 1–41 (2006)
11. Koulouris, N.G., Hardavella, G.: Physiological techniques for detecting expiratory flow limitation during tidal breathing. Eur. Respir. J. 8, 306–313 (1995)
12. DuBois, A.B., Botelho, S.Y., Bedell, G.N., Marshall, R., Comroe Jr., J.H.: A rapid plethysmographic method for measuring thoracic gas volume: a comparison with a nitrogen washout method for measuring functional residual capacity in normal subjects. J Clin Invest. 35, 322–326 (1956)
13. Comroe, J., Botelho, S., DuBois, A.: Design of a body plethysmograph for studying cardiopulmonary physiology. J. Appl. Physiol. 14, 439–444 (1959)
14. Stubbing, D.G., Pengelly, L.D., Morse, J.L.C., Milic-Emili, J.: Pulmonary mechanics during exercise in subjects with chronic airflow obstruction. J. Appl. Physiol. 49, 511–515 (1980)
15. Wanger, J., Clausen, J.L., Coates, A., Pedersen, O.F.: Standardisation of the measurement of lung function testing. Eur. Respir. J. 26, 511–522 (2005)
16. Sud, A., Gupta, D., Wanchu, A., Jindal, S.K., Bambery, P.: Static lung compliance as an index of early pulmonary disease in systemic sclerosis. Clin. Rheumatol. 20(3), 177–180 (2001)
17. Davidson, A.C.: The pulmonary physician in critical care • 11: critical care management of respiratory failure resulting from COPD. Thorax 57, 1079–1084 (2002)
18. Papadakos, P.J., Lachmann, B.: Clinical Applications and Pathophysiology, 688 p. (2008)
19. Goldman, M.D., Smith, H.J., Ulmer, W.T.: Whole body plethismography. Eur. Respir. Mon. 31, 15–43 (2005)

20. Koulouris, N.G., Valta, P., Lavoie, A., Corbeil, C., Chassé, M., Braidy, J., Milic-Emili, J.: A simple method to detect expiratory flow limitation during spontaneous breathing. Eur. Respir. J. **8**(2), 306–313 (1995)

21. Choi, W.-H., Kwon, S.U.: The pulmonary embolism severity index in predicting the prognosis of patients with pulmonary embolism. Arch. Intern. Med. **170**(15), 1383–1389 (2010)

22. Hyges, D.T.D., Empey, D.W.: Flow volume curves. In: Lung Functions for the Clinicians, pp. 82–83. Academic Press, London (1981)

23. Clinical Application Series, Arora V.K., Raghus, S.: Flow volume curves: clinical significance. Lung India **14**(4), 169–171 (1996)

24. Venetz, C., Jiménez, D., Méan, M., Aujesky, D.: A comparison of the original and simplified pulmonary embolism severity index. Schattauer 423–428 (2011)

25. Lankeit, M., Konstantinides, S.: Is it time for home treatment of pulmonary embolism. Eur. Respir. J. **40**, 742–749 (2012)

26. Lichtenstein, D., Goldstein, I., Mourgeon, E., Cluzel, P., Grenier, P., Rouby, J.-J.: Comparative diagnostic performances of auscultation, chest radiography, and lung ultrasonography in acute respiratory distress syndrome. Open Electr. Electron. Eng. J. **4**, 16–20 (2010)

27. Marani, R., Perri, A.G.: An electronic medical device for preventing and improving the assisted ventilation of intensive care unit patients. Respir. Med. **105**(9), 1396–1403 (2011)

28. Gurung, A., Scrafford, C.G., Tielsch, J.M., Levine, O.S., Checkley, W.: Computerized lung sound analysis as diagnostic aid for the detection of abnormal lung sounds: a systematic review and meta-analysis, **105**(9), 1396–1403 (2011)

29. Murphy, R.: Development of acoustic instruments for diagnosis and management of medical conditions. In: Computerized Multichannel Lung Sound Analysis, Respiratory Sound Analysis IEEE Engineering in Medicine and Biology Magazine, January/February 2007

30. Reiser, S.J.: The medical influence of the stethoscope. Sci. Amer. **240**(2), 148–150, 153–156 (1979)

31. Wang, L.Y., Wang, H., Zheng, H., Yin, G.: Multi-sensor lung sound extraction via time-shared channel identification and adaptive noise cancellation. In: 43rd IEEE Conference on Decision and Control, Atlantis, Paradise Island, Bahamas, 14–17 December 2004

32. Jones, A., Jones, D., Kwong, K., Siu, S.C.: Acoustic performance of three stethoscope chest pieces. In: Proceedings of the 20th Annual International Conference of the IEEE Engineering in Medicine and Biology Society, vol. 20, no 6, p 3219–3222 (1998)

33. Maarsingha, E.J.W., van Eykernb, L.A., Sprikkelmana, A.B., van Aalderena, W.M.C.: Histamine induced airway response in pre-school children assessed by a non-invasive EMG technique. Respir. Med. **98**, 363–372 (2004)

34. Vyshedskiy, A., Murphy, R.: Pendelluft in chronic obstructive lung disease measured with lung sounds. Pulm. Med. **2012**, 1–6 (2012)

35. Cardoso, J.F.: Multidimensional independent component analysis. In: Proceedings of the IEEE International Conference on Acoustics, Speech and Signal Processing (ICASSP 1998), Seattle, USA (1998)

36. Hyvarien, A., Oja, E.: A fast fixed point algorithm for independent component analysis. Neural Comput. **9**, 1483–1492 (1997)

37. Alouani, A., ElKeelany, O., Abdallah, M.: Stand-alone portable digital body sound data acquisition device. IJES **4**(3-4), 292–297 (2010)

38. Alouani, A.: A low-cost stand-alone multichannel data acquisition, monitoring, and archival system with on-chip signal preprocessing. IEEE Trans. Instrum. Measur. **60**(8), 2813–2827 (2011)

39. Ayari, F., Ksouri, M., Alouani, A.: Lung sound extraction from mixed lung and heart sounds with FASTICA algorithm. In: Proceeding of the 16th IEEE Electrotechnical Conference (MELECON 2012), Hammamet, Tunisia, pp. 339–342 (2012)
40. Ayari, F., Ksouri, M., Alouani, A.: Computer based analysis for heart and lung signals separation. In: Proceeding of the IEEE International Conference on Computer Medical Applications, (ICCMA 2013) Sousse, Tunisia, pp. 1–6 (2013)
41. Knapp, C., Carter, G.: The generalized correlation method for estimation of time delay. IEEE Trans. Acoust, Speech, Signal Process. **24**, 320–327 (1976)
42. Chen, J., Benesty, J., Huang, Y.: Robust time delay estimation exploiting redundancy among multiple microphones. IEEE Trans. Speech Audio Process. **11**, 549–557 (2011)
43. Kevin, W., Wilson, T.: Learning a precedence effect-like weighting function for the generalized cross-correlation framework. IEEE Trans Audio Speech Lang. Proc. **41**, 2156–2164 (2006)
44. Hyde, D., Nuttall, A.: Linear pre-filtering to enhance correlator performance. Naval Underwater Systems Center, CT, Technical Memo, New London Laboratory, New London (1969)
45. Georgiou, P., Kyriakakis, C., Tsakalides, P.: Robust time delay estimation for sound source localization in noisy environments. In: Proceedings of WASPAA, pp. 1–15 (1973)
46. Li, D., Levinson, S.: Adaptive sound source localization by two microphones. In: Proceedings of International Conference on Robotics and Automation, Washington DC (2002)

Vessel Segmentation for Noisy CT Data with Quality Measure Based on Single-Point Contrast-to-Noise Ratio

A. Nikonorov[1,2(✉)], A. Kolsanov[3], M. Petrov[1,2], Y. Yuzifovich[1], E. Prilepin[4],
S. Chaplygin[3], P. Zelter[3], and K. Bychenkov[4]

[1] Samara State Aerospace University, Moskovskoe shosse 34, Samara, Russia
artniko@gmail.com, yuriyyuzivofich@gmail.com
[2] Image Processing Systems Institute, Russian Academy of Science,
Molodogvardeyskaya St. 151, Samara, Russia
max.vit.petrov@gmail.com
[3] Samara State Medical University, Chapaevskaya St. 89, Samara, Russia
{avkolsanov,chaplyginss,pzelter}@mail.ru
[4] SmedX, LLC, Moskovskoe shosse 34, Samara, Russia
{prilepin,bychenkov}@smedx.com

Abstract. This paper describes a comprehensive multi-step algorithm for vascular structure segmentation in CT scan data, from raw slice images to a 3D object, with an emphasis on improving segmentation quality and assessing computational complexity. To estimate initial image quality and to evaluate denoising in the absence of the noise-free image, we propose a semi-global contrast-to-noise quality metric. We show that total variation-based filtering in the L_1 metric results in the best denoising when compared to widely used non-local means or anisotropic diffusion denoising. To address higher computational complexity of our denoising algorithm, we created two high performance implementations, using Intel MIC and NVIDIA CUDA and compared results. In combination with proposed nearly real-time incremental segmentation technique, it provides fast and framework with controlled quality.

Keywords: Contrast to noise ratio · Total variance de-noising · Liver · Vessels segmentation · CUDA · GPGPU · Xeon Phi · Proximal algorithms · Fast marching · Geodesic Active Contours

1 Introduction

Computer tomography (CT) is one of the most effective and informative methods of abdominal diagnostics. Liver pathology includes numerous focal and diffuse changes, ranging from benign to malignant to metastatic and presents special interest for CT scan image processing and analysis.

Usage of contrast enhancement during CT procedure is mandatory, because different focal lesions are colored in a similar way because they have the same density in Hounsfield units [20].

Minimizing radiation dose has been increasingly important for CT equipment manufacturers [3], which is typically done by reducing amperage and results in higher image

© Springer International Publishing Switzerland 2016
M.S. Obaidat and P. Lorenz (Eds.): ICETE 2015, CCIS 585, pp. 490–507, 2016.
DOI: 10.1007/978-3-319-30222-5_23

noise levels. To maintain acceptable image quality, contrast-to-noise ratio is no longer enough for definitive diagnosis. To address image quality issues, CT scanner manufacturers are working on novel image post-processing techniques that would continue to support reduced radiation levels. Iterative reconstruction protocols in use in CT-coronarography, are not yet widely adopted in liver CT imaging [7].

Liver volumetry is a critical aspect of safe hepatic surgeries. Precise segmentation of the vessel tree topology can be used in an image-guided surgery for liver lobe segmentation, tumor detection, and to reduce incisions and prevent post-operative bleeding, resulting in less blood loss and rapid patient recovery. CT image quality varies widely in different tomograms. Image noise and low contrast between veins and surrounding tissue make automatic and semi-automatic intrahepatic blood vessel segmentation a challenging task.

Image noise is the single most important image quality issue that results from using lower radiation levels. Denoising is thus critical for vascular structure segmentation. Most noise suppression techniques in CT images can be broadly categorized as projection space denoising, image space denoising, and iterative reconstruction [12].

Low contrast problem is caused by non-optimal distribution of the contrast agent during the scan. For example, in venous phase the agent may still be present in liver veins while absent in inferior vena cava. Low contrast in noisy images makes vessel structures indistinguishable from the surrounding tissue.

Differences in CT image quality affect segmentation results, and new segmentation methods have been suggested [23]. Multiple methods exist to perform image restoration both at the scanning and reconstruction stages [24], and at the image processing stage [3].

Quality measure is important for both image and segmentation result evaluation. However, there is no unambiguous solution to measure image quality in practical CT segmentation tasks, because to use a common PSNR metric we would need a noise-free image. Contrast-to-noise measures require a ROI in the image to be selected [24]. This prior knowledge is available only for synthetic tests or when we already have "ground truth" segmentation.

We propose a new contrast-to-noise-based measure with reduced dependency on the prior knowledge, and proceed to using this measure to test different denoising algorithms applied to vessel segmentation. Our incremental vessel segmentation technique is based on fast marching and level-set algorithms.

Total variation denoising using L_1-norm [6] shows the best denoising quality. To make this computational-intensive method practical, we implemented this denoising procedure using two "desktop supercomputing" methods: GPGPU using NVIDIA CUDA and MIC (Many Integrated Core) using Intel Xeon Phi.

Our method not only improves segmentation quality even for noisy images resulting from lower radiation levels present during CT scanning, but can also be implemented in near real-time. In Sect. 3 we discuss how we could speed up segmentation ×8 times.

2   Single-Point Contrast-to-Noise Ratio as an Image Quality Measure

Most of image quality measures developed for signal and image processing, such as PSNR and method noise [4], require prior knowledge about a noise-free image. For example, CT reconstruction quality for different radiation doses is investigated using phantom images [9, 24]. These metrics measure different aspects of image quality: PSNR describes degradation of the best signal, while the method noise measures image edge corruption by denoising procedures. The most important image quality aspect for vessel segmentation is a contrast between vessels and noisy surrounding tissue.

According to [9], contrast-to-noise ratio (CNR) is defined as the ratio of signal difference (contrast) to the noise level in the image:

$$CNR = \frac{M_{object} - M_{background}}{\sigma}, \tag{1}$$

where M_{object} and $M_{background}$ are average object and its background intensities, σ is standard deviation of the image noise.

Details of the CNR estimation vary across different works. Usually, it is necessary to choose one ROI on the object and one – on the background to compute M_{object} and $M_{background}$ [13, 24]. However, it is possible to get incorrect CNR estimation on non-uniform image parts [14].

In [16], Sliver7 [8] training database was used to estimate denoising quality. The training set contains segmented livers that are used to estimate M_{object} in (1) while the surrounding image is used for $M_{background}$ estimation. Unfortunately, this prior knowledge is not available for segmentation tasks found in many preoperative planning situations.

We will use the following image model to estimate CNR on real CT data. We assume that the image consists of only two components: a vessel of an unknown diameter that we need to estimate, and surrounding tissue. This enables us to apply bimodal intensity distribution hypothesis at any local neighborhood.

We used two approaches for CNR-like measure computation. In the simple two-point method we use one point inside and one outside of the vessel object. Similar to ROI selection in [24], a two-point CNR has the following form:

$$q_2(\mathbf{x}^{obj}, \mathbf{x}^{bkg}) = \frac{M(\mathbf{x}^{obj}, R^{obj}) - M(\mathbf{x}^{bkg}, R^{bkg})}{\sigma(\mathbf{x}^{bkg}, R^{bkg})},$$
$$M(\mathbf{x}^{obj}, R^{obj})$$
$$= M\left(\left\{\begin{bmatrix} p(\mathbf{x}), \mathbf{x}: |\mathbf{x}^{obj}, \mathbf{x}| \leq R^{obj}, \\ \|\mathbf{x}^{obj}, \mathbf{x}\|_{\infty} = \max_{i=1,2,3} |x_i^{obj} - x_i| \end{bmatrix}\right\}\right), \tag{2}$$

where $\mathbf{x}^{obj}$ и $\mathbf{x}^{bkg}$ are points at the vessel and surrounding tissue, respectively, x_i, $i = 1, 2, 3$ is i-th component of $\mathbf{x}$, $p(\mathbf{x})$ is an intensity value at the point $\mathbf{x}$, M is an intensity median over a cubic neighborhood, R^{obj} is the size of the cubic neighborhood on the vessel (object), R^{bkg} – on the surrounding tissues (background), $M(\mathbf{x}^{bkg}, R^{bkg})$ is defined the same way as $M(\mathbf{x}^{obj}, R^{obj})$, $\sigma(\mathbf{x}^{bkg}, R^{bkg})$ is standard deviation across the same region as M^{bkg}, $\| \, , \, \|_\infty$ is L_∞ or Chebyshev distance.

The computation of R^{obj} can be done assuming unimodality of the intensity distribution in the cubic image patch centered in $\mathbf{x}^{obj}$. Following [2] if the distribution is unimodal, then

$$\frac{\left| M_{obj} - m_{obj} \right|}{\sigma_{obj}} \leq \sqrt{3/5}, \tag{3}$$

$$\frac{\left| M_{obj} - \mu_{obj} \right|}{\sigma_{obj}} \leq \sqrt{3}, \tag{4}$$

where m_{obj} is mean estimation and μ_{obj} mode estimation over the image cubic neighborhood centered in $\mathbf{x}^{obj}$.

With R^{obj} increasing above a threshold, the distribution loses its unimodality and inequalities (3) and (4) fail.

To separate the object from the background, the value of (2) must be greater than 1, with a value of 2 being a better threshold for a stable separation of the vessel from its surroundings. These values are experimentally obtained, as described in Sect. 6.

Values of (2) vary along with the point on the background selection. A low value for (2) means that the segmentation quality is subpar, however, the opposite is not always true: it does not follow from a high value (2) that the quality is high. It only means that we have not found a bad case, yet. Therefore, the value of metric (2) is a necessary but not sufficient condition for vessel separation from the background.

A typical contrast-to-noise measure is local, because object and background estimation are made in the local neighbourhood. Here we propose a semi-global method for CNR-like measure estimation using only one point inside the object. We use a cubic neighborhood of the point $\mathbf{x}^{obj}$ defined using L_∞ as done in (2):

$$D = \left\{ \mathbf{x} : \left\| \mathbf{x}^{obj}, \mathbf{x} \right\|_\infty \leq R_D \right\}. \tag{5}$$

The distribution inside the cube is unimodal. The tissue surrounding this cube has different intensity distribution and thus the overall distribution becomes bimodal, so inequalities (3) and (4) fail and take the following form:

$$\frac{\left| M_{bkg} - m_{obj} \right|}{\sigma_{obj}} > \sqrt{3/5}, \tag{6}$$

$$\frac{\left| M_{bkg} - \mu_{obj} \right|}{\sigma_{obj}} > \sqrt{3}. \tag{7}$$

At least one of (6) and (7) must be true if the distribution is not unimodal. We can estimate the median over a set of cubic patches centered in $\mathbf{x}^k$ and having the size R^{bkg}, with all patches located in the neighborhood D of the $\mathbf{x}_{obj}$ point:

$$\left\{M_k^{bkg}(\mathbf{x}^{obj})\right\} = \left\{M_k\left(\left\{\begin{array}{c} p(\mathbf{x})\colon \|\mathbf{x}^k,\mathbf{x}\|_{\infty} \leq R^{bkg} \\ \|\mathbf{x}^{obj},\mathbf{x}^k\|_{\infty} \leq D \end{array}\right\}\right)\right\}. \qquad (8)$$

The $\{M_k\}$ set includes only patches with either (6) or (7) to be true, so it is an estimation of the background intensity median. The standard deviation for these patches is estimated as follows:

$$\left\{\sigma_k^{bkg}(\mathbf{x}^{obj})\right\} = \left\{\sigma_k\left(\left\{\begin{array}{c} p(\mathbf{x})\colon \|\mathbf{x}^k,\mathbf{x}\|_{\infty} \leq R^{bkg} \\ \|\mathbf{x}^{obj},\mathbf{x}^k\|_{\infty} \leq D \end{array}\right\}\right)\right\}. \qquad (9)$$

Finally, we estimate median and standard deviation as modes of (8) and (9). So, semi-global CNR-like measure takes the following form:

$$q_1(\mathbf{x}^{obj}) = \frac{M(\mathbf{x}^{obj}) - \mathrm{mode}(M_k^{bkg}(\mathbf{x}^{obj}))}{(\mathrm{mode}(\sigma_k^{bkg}(\mathbf{x}^{obj})) + \sigma^{obj})/2}. \qquad (10)$$

The noise variance often depends on the signal intensity, with the object and the background producing different estimates for the variance. As a result, it is not clear which σ must be used in the denominator of the measure (1). To address this problem, we use a half sum of the object and background noise standard deviations in the denominator of the proposed one-point contrast-to-noise measure (10) as a compromise.

3 Vessel Tree Segmentation

We apply a level set approach to segment vessels. Semi-automatic segmentation is performed in two steps. At the first "interactive initialization" step, Fast Marching Upwind Gradient method is used for a rough segmentation of vascular structure. At the second "precise segmentation" step, Geodesic Active Contours and surface approximation method is used to complete the segmentation. The algorithm is shown in Fig. 1 [1, 5].

At the first step, seed points and optional target points are specified inside the vessel. Seed points indicate the start of the wave front propagation in the Fast Marching algorithm.

The wave propagation is determined by a speed image and stops when one of the specified target points is reached. The original image is used as a speed image after applying a threshold.

At the second step, we use geodesic active contour model to refine segmentation, and surface approximation for final smoothing. This method requires two inputs: The Fast Marching result as the initial level set, and the feature image. We use the gradient magnitude of the original image with the transformation of the nonlinear function (Sigmoid filter) as the edge potential map.

The level-set algorithm produces a real-valued image. The binary image, obtained by applying a threshold, is the final segmentation result.

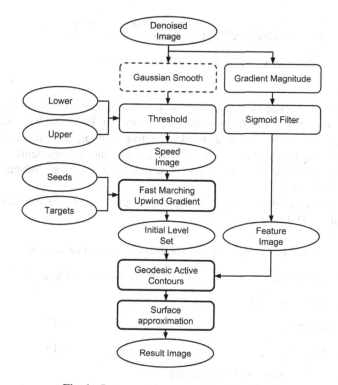

Fig. 1. Incremental segmentation algorithm.

We also use a restricted segmentation region defined by a binary image of an organ or an organ region to improve segmentation speed and increase segmentation precision.

When it is impossible to perform vascular tree segmentation at once, an incremental approach is used. At each iteration, a sub-tree of a vessel tree is processed. The algorithm is shown in Fig. 1 is applied at each iteration. A binary segmentation image obtained at each iteration is then combined with the combined binary image cumulatively achieved at previous iterations.

To improve segmentation quality in low-contrast situations, the original image is smoothed by Gaussian convolution to prevent the leak into the region rich in blood vessels represented as less than one pixel diameter on low-contrast CT data.

The main parameter of the algorithm is a threshold between vessels and surrounding tissues. We automatically estimate its value by using a Mahalanobis-like procedure:

$$T = M_{bkg} + \frac{\left(M_{obj} - M_{bkg}\right)\sigma_{bkg}}{\sigma_{bkg} + \sigma_{obj}}, \tag{11}$$

and using measure (10):

$$T = \text{mode}(M_k^{bkg}(\mathbf{x}^{obj})) + \frac{q_1(\mathbf{x}^{obj})\text{mode}(\sigma_k^{bkg}(\mathbf{x}^{obj}))}{2}, \tag{12}$$

where T is a threshold value, and $q_1\left(x^{obj}\right)$ is defined by (10).

To improve the speed of the segmentation with multiple steps, each step must be optimized. An overview of the segmentation is shown in Fig. 1 diagram and includes preprocessing steps, fast marching, geodesic active contour, and final smoothing by surface approximation. Tests on typical CT data show that each segmentation iteration typically takes more than 12 s (on Intel i7), which is too long for production use and needs to be optimized.

Computation time for each step is shown in the Table 1, averaged over 10 test images taken from IRCAD dataset [10].

Table 1. Computation time for individual segmentation steps.

Segmentation stage	Base scheme	Optimized scheme
Speed image computation	1.52	–
Fast marching	1.06	1.17
Postprocessing	0.31	0.15
Geodesic Active Contour Computation	9.82	–
Surface approximation	0.22	0.22
Total	12.93	1.54

Geodesic active contour step, which is computed after the fast marching, is the most computationally intensive. In the work [1] this step is used to smooth out the final segmentation result. Surface approximation alone provides a similar result, and as our experiments show, excluding geodesic active contour does not significantly affect the final quality of the segmentation. Based on this result, we made a decision to exclude this step as optimization measure.

As described in [22], fast marching is used to propagate the segmentation in the narrow band of the existing front, but we take the whole image during preprocessing and speed image computation. This leads to a significant overhead. We combine preprocessing and speed image computation with the fast marching so that preprocessing computation is applied only to the pixels in the narrow band of the existing front. It allows us to exclude preprocessing at the cost of only a small additional load on the fast marching computation.

After excluding active contour step and replacing global preprocessing with preprocessing in narrow band of current fast marching front only, we reduced segmentation time to just 1.54 s, an 8-fold improvement over the original algorithm, resulting in near real-time segmentation.

4 Denoising Procedures

We compared the performance of four denoising techniques when applied to vessel segmentation: curvature anisotropic diffusion, bilateral filtering, non-local-means filter, and total variance based denoising in L_2 and L_1.

We will briefly describe these methods using the following notation. Let us denote a noisy source image as $\mathbf{p}_0(\mathbf{x})$, while the target filtered image as $\mathbf{p}^*(\mathbf{x})$.

The downside of image denoising/smoothing is that it blurs sharp boundaries that distinguish anatomical structures, such as vessels. Paper [18] introduced anisotropic diffusion as an alternative to linear-filtering. The motivation for anisotropic diffusion (also called nonuniform or variable conductance diffusion) is that a Gaussian smoothed image is a single time slice of the solution to the heat equation that has the original image as its initial conditions. Thus, the solution to

$$\frac{\partial g(\mathbf{x}, t)}{\partial t} = \nabla \cdot \nabla g(\mathbf{x}, t), \tag{13}$$

where $g(\mathbf{x}, 0) = \mathbf{p}(\mathbf{x})$ is $g(\mathbf{x}, t) = G(\sqrt{2t}) \otimes p(\mathbf{x})$, and $G(\sigma)$ is a Gaussian kernel with standard deviation σ. Anisotropic diffusion includes a variable conductance term which in turn depends on the differential structure of the image. Thus, the variable conductance can be formulated to limit edge smoothing in images, as measured by a high gradient magnitude, for example. In our work, we use curvature anisotropic diffusion modification, described in (Shang, 2010) and implemented in ITK [11].

Total variation model was invented by Rudin et al. [21]. This model is based on minimization of the following functional

$$\mathbf{p}^* = \arg\min_{\mathbf{p}} \|\nabla\mathbf{p}\|_1 + \lambda \|\mathbf{p}_0 - \mathbf{p}\|_2, \tag{14}$$

where $\|\ \|_1$ is the robust L_1 norm, $\|\ \|_2$ is the L_2 norm used in the least-squares restoration model, $\mathbf{p}_0$ is the source noisy image, $\mathbf{p}^*$ is the target filtered image and λ is the weighting parameter, which defines the trade-off between regularization and data fitting. The L_1 norm of the image gradient is total variation $\|\nabla\mathbf{p}\|_1$. This filtering is capable of denoising images without blurring edges. We use implementation of total variance filtering based on [6]. We will refer to it as TV-L_1 de-noising.

An alternative denoising technique, based on non-local-mean approach proposed in [4], involves averaging over pixels similar in intensity but distant in spatial domain. It is therefore necessary to scan a vast portion of the image in search of all the pixels that resemble the pixel to denoise because the image can have periodic textured patterns, or the elongated edges. Denoising is then done by computing the average color of these most resembling pixels. The resemblance is evaluated by comparing a whole window around each pixel. This new filter is called non-local means and is computed as follows:

$$p_1(\mathbf{x}) = \frac{1}{C(\mathbf{x})} \sum_{\mathbf{y}} w(\mathbf{x}, \mathbf{y}) p(\mathbf{y}). \tag{15}$$

The family of weights $w(\mathbf{x}, \mathbf{y})$ depends on the similarity between the pixels $\mathbf{x}$ and $\mathbf{y}$, $C(\mathbf{x})$ is a weighting constant:

$$w(\mathbf{x}, \mathbf{y}) = \exp\left(-\frac{\|p(N(\mathbf{x}), p(N(\mathbf{y}))\|_{2,\alpha}^2}{h}\right), \tag{16}$$

where $N(\mathbf{x})$ denotes a square neighborhood of a fixed size and centered around a pixel $\mathbf{x}$.

We also tested a bilateral or Yaroslavsky filter, which we use from ITK package [11].

This approach was previously compared to the anisotropic diffusion and total variation filtering in [4] using method noise measure and comparing visual quality. The main idea of the method noise measure is to estimate how a denoising algorithm alters structures found in the image.

We developed optimization method to de-noise 3D CT data based on the optimal first-order primal-dual framework by Chambolle and Pock (2011). It is a total variation minimization based on L_1 norm, called in this paper TV-L_1 denoising.

Let X and Y be the finite-dimensional real vector spaces for the primal and dual space, respectively. Consider the following operators and functions:

$\mathbf{K}:X \to Y$ is a linear operator from X to Y;
$\mathbf{G}:X \to [0, +\infty)$ is a proper, convex, (l.s.c.) function;
$\mathbf{F}:Y \to [0, +\infty)$ is a proper, convex, (l.s.c.) function;

where l.s.c. stands for lower-semi-continuous.

The optimization framework [6] considers general problems in the following form:

$$\hat{\mathbf{x}} = \arg\min_{\mathbf{x}} \mathbf{F}(\mathbf{K}(\mathbf{x})) + \mathbf{G}(\mathbf{x}). \tag{17}$$

To solve (17), the following algorithm is described in the paper [6]. During initialization, $\tau, \sigma \in R_+$ are set, $\theta \in [0, 1]$, $(\mathbf{x}_0, \mathbf{y}_0) \in X \times Y$ is some initial approximation, $\bar{\mathbf{x}}_0 = \mathbf{x}_0$. For 3D CT data, the final result obtained on the previous slice is used as the initial approximation for the next slice. With $n \geq 0$ as the current step number, values of the $\mathbf{x}_n, \mathbf{y}_n, \bar{\mathbf{x}}_n$ are iteratively updated as follows:

$$\mathbf{y}_{n+1} = prox_{\sigma F*}(\mathbf{y}_n + \sigma \mathbf{K}\bar{\mathbf{x}}_n) \tag{18}$$

$$\mathbf{x}_{n+1} = prox_{\tau G}(\mathbf{x}_n + \tau \mathbf{K}^* \mathbf{y}_{n+1}) \tag{19}$$

$$\bar{\mathbf{x}}_{n+1} = \mathbf{x}_{n+1} + \theta(\mathbf{x}_{n+1} - \mathbf{x}_n) \tag{20}$$

The proximal operator with respect to G in (19), is defined as:

$$prox_{\tau G}(\bar{\mathbf{x}}) = (\mathbf{E} + \tau \partial \mathbf{G})^{-1}(\bar{\mathbf{x}}) = \arg\min_{\mathbf{x}} \frac{1}{2\tau} \|\mathbf{x} - \bar{\mathbf{x}}\|_2^2 + \mathbf{G}(\mathbf{x}), \tag{21}$$

where E is an identity matrix. The proximal operator (18) is defined in a similar way.

The model of denoising is based on the total variance approach [6] and is described by the following functional:

$$\mathbf{p}^* = \min_{\mathbf{p}} \|\nabla\mathbf{p}\|_1 + \lambda \|\mathbf{p}_0 - \mathbf{p}\|_1, \tag{22}$$

where $\|\ \|_1$ is the robust L_1 norm, $\mathbf{p}_0$ is the source noisy image, $\mathbf{p}^*$ is the target filtered image and λ is the weighting parameter, which defines the tradeoff between regularization and data fitting.

In order to apply the described algorithm to (22), we follow the [6]:

$$G(\mathbf{p}) = \|\nabla\mathbf{p}\|_1, \tag{23}$$

$$F^*(\mathbf{p}) = \|\mathbf{p}_0 - \mathbf{p}\|_1. \tag{24}$$

Finally, proximal operators for steps (18) and (19) of the algorithm can be obtained using (23) and (24). Please refer to [6] for further details. The denoising algorithm based on total variance can preserve sharp edges. Also, the use of L_1 makes it possible to efficiently remove strong outliers.

5　High Performance Implementation of Denoising Algorithm

While TV-L_1 denoising algorithm proved to be the best for low-contrast CT data as experimentally shown in the following Sect. 6, it also the most computationally expensive. Not willing to compromise on denoising quality and still obtain real-time performance, we implemented it for two many-core systems, Xeon Phi and CUDA. The work (Pock et al. [19]) mentioned CUDA implementation of TV-L_1 algorithms, but did not provide details.

A general algorithm is shown in Fig. 2. The implementation is based on (11)–(13). Expressions (11) and (12) describe the dual part of the iteration of the proximal algorithm, *UpdateDual()*, and (13) describes the primal part *UpdatePrimal()*.

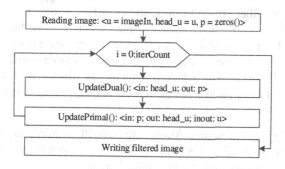

Fig. 2. General algorithm of TV-L_1 filtering.

TV-L_1 is based on proximal algorithms that have a large dimensionality but these algorithms are separable, as shown in (Parikh and Boyd [17]). This property enables efficient parallel implementation.

Each iteration of the computation is divided into two stages: *UpdateDual()* and *UpdatePrimal()*. Inside these stages we have a vector-like processing of the arrays with a size of about 2^{18}. However, these two stages are sequential and require synchronization between them at each iteration.

GPU Implementation. Intensive memory use of TV-L_1 algorithm represents a challenge for GPU implementation. The size of the shared memory is a major constraint of the GPU, which can be expressed as follows:

$$
\begin{aligned}
S_{MP} &= N_{MP} \cdot N_S \le S_{MP}^{\max}, \\
N_{Th\,per\,MP} &= N_{MP} \cdot N_B \le N_{Th\,per\,MP}^{\max}, \\
N_{MP} &\le N_{MP}^{\max}, \\
N_B^{opt} &= N_{Th\,per\,MP}^{\max} / N_{MP}^{\max},
\end{aligned}
\tag{25}
$$

where S_{MP} amount of available shared memory per MP in bytes, N_{MP} - a number of blocks per MP, N_S necessary amount of shared memory per block, $S_{MP}^{\max}$ – maximum amount of shared memory per MP in bytes, $N_{Th\,per\,MP}$ - a number of simultaneous threads per MP, N_B - a number of threads per block, $N_{Th\,per\,MP}^{\max}$ - maximum amount of threads per MP, $N_{MP}^{\max}$ - a number of blocks per MP, N_B^{opt} - an optimal block size in bytes.

In our case, $N_S = (N_B + 1) \cdot S_{type}$, where S_{type} is the size of pixel in bytes. So, the amount of shared memory per multiprocessor is:

$$
S_{MP} = N_{MP} \cdot (N_B + 1) \cdot S_{type} \le S_{MP}^{\max}.
\tag{26}
$$

For both tested GPU platforms we use $N_{MP}^{\max} = 16, N_{Th\,per\,MP}^{\max} = 2048, S_{MP}^{\max} = 49152$, so $N_B^{opt} = 128$ threads per block. Finally, $S_{MP} = 8256$ bytes for single precision and $S_{MP} = 16512$ bytes for double precision, which is lower than $S_{MP}^{\max}$.

An algorithm modified for GPU use is shown in Fig. 3. We use two CUDA kernel calls for each iteration. The first kernel call implements *UpdateDual()*, the second – *UpdatePrimal()*. There is global memory exchange between these two kernel calls, that is why we do not have any overhead caused by shared memory invalidation between the kernel calls. Synchronization is achieved naturally by dividing calculations into two kernels. Each kernel executes in consequent order one after another, because they reside on default CUDA stream.

CPU and Xeon Phi Implementation. Many-core Xeon Phi required an alternative implementation. We use OpenMP for both multicore CPU and Xeon Phi implementation. For Xeon Phi we used a non-shared memory offload model.

We use *omp parallel for private* pragmas for the CPU version. All intermediate variables are made private. Synchronization by *omp barrier* pragmas is made after *UpdateDual()* and *UpdatePrimal()* code sections.

We use *omp parallel for simd private* pragmas for the Xeon Phi version. All intermediate variables are made private. Synchronization by *omp barrier* pragmas is made after *UpdateDual()* and *UpdatePrimal()* code sections, at the same places as in the CPU

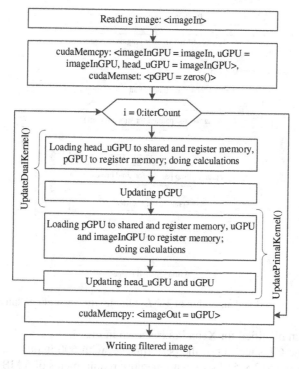

Fig. 3. Modified algorithm of TV-L_1 filtering for CUDA architecture.

version. Private variables are also the same as in the CPU version. Main algorithm iteration loop and all inner loops run on the coprocessor. Parallelization of the for-loops is made by *omp parallel for simd private* pragma. The *simd* modifier allows efficient utilization of the Xeon Phi vector architecture (each core contains a 512-bit wide VPU). We bind OpenMP threads to physical processing units by setting environment variables KMP_AFFINITY to "balanced,granularity = fine" and KMP_PLACE_THREADS to "59C,4T". One core of 60-core coprocessor maintains OS tasks.

Due to difference between CPU and Xeon Phi OpenMP architectures, we had to use platform-specific attributes and pragmas in our Xeon Phi implementation, including pragmas for code sections executed on the coprocessor (*offload target (mic:micID)*) and data copying (*offload_transfer target (mic:micID)*). Data copying occurs only before launching kernel and after its execution. All variables are retained in the coprocessor memory during calculations.

Another convenient feature of Xeon Phi implementation is data initialization for primitive types. Unlike with CUDA implementation, there is no need to explicitly allocate memory on the coprocessor by calling a special. We only need to declare variables with attribute *__declspec(target(mic:micID))*. All the work for copying data into and out of the coprocessor memory is then performed by *offload_transfer* pragma with appropriate parameters.

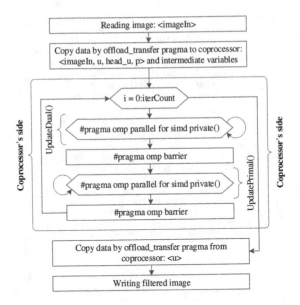

Fig. 4. A modified algorithm of TV-L_1 filtering for Xeon Phi architecture.

An algorithm modified for Xeon Phi is shown in Fig. 4.

We used one CT slice to test the performance, with 600 iterations. The slice is a 16-bit image of the 512×512 size, with memory requirements of 5 MB and 10 MB to process each slice in single and double precision modes, respectively. Testing equipment included Intel Xeon E5-2695 v2, Intel Core i7 4770 K at 4.2 GHz, Intel Xeon Phi 5110P, NVIDIA Tesla K20 m, and NVIDIA GTX770 4096 MB. In the offload model, one Xeon Phi core is reserved for system needs which leaves us with 236 threads out of 240 available at Xeon Phi. Results are shown in Figs. 5 and 6.

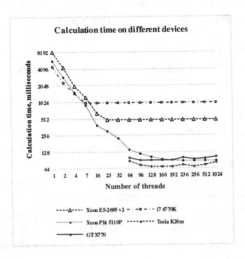

Fig. 5. Computation time for different systems in single precision mode.

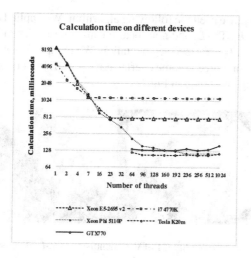

Fig. 6. Computation time for different systems in double precision mode.

As shown in Figs. 5 and 6, NVIDIA Tesla slightly outperforms Intel Xeon Phi, with both systems about 10 times faster than a CPU-based version, and only slightly faster than an implementation based on an inexpensive GTX 770 GPU. A major advantage of Xeon Phi is its capability to run the same OpenMP implementation as a CPU-based version, which makes Xeon Phi a better option for rapid prototyping of computationally-expensive algorithms. GPGPU approach is optimal for production use, when the cost and power consumption considerations become more important. With a typical CT with about 200 slices, the data could be filtered by a GTX 770-based system in about 3.3 s, which is acceptable for production use. Peak memory usage is one gigabyte for single precision and two gigabytes for double precision. Neither GPU nor Xeon Phi architectures limit the memory required for slice-by-slice processing. A similar workflow for large color image filtering was proposed in [15].

6   Results and Discussion

We tested our algorithm on 20 CT images from Sliver7 database and on 8 of our own CT images and used proposed metric and visual quality analysis. We also used 10 CT scans of the abdomen from a publicly available database (IRCAD) in our evaluation of the proposed one-point CNR measure (10).

The implementation of the bilateral filter and the curvature anisotropic diffusion filter can be found in ITK library [11]. The following parameters were used for the bilateral filter: domain sigma of 7, range sigma of 7; and for the curvature anisotropic diffusion [11]: time step of 0.09, 8 iterations and a conductance value of 3.0. The total variance filters have $\lambda \in [0.2, 0.4]$.

We tested different denoising techniques on the CT images from (IRCAD) database. Despite the fact that all images in this database have a good contrast, good quality venous segmentations were only possible after a denoising step.

For our evaluation, we used the following algorithm. We applied different denoising procedures with TV-L_1, TV-L_2 and non-local-means filtering. Then we computed one-point CNR measure and performed segmentation. We compared our segmentation with the ground truth and computed volume overlap error – VOE [8]. Full segmentation result for a sample CT image is shown in Fig. 9.

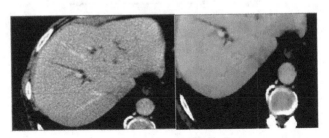

Fig. 7. Low quality CT, TV-L_1 denoising, TV-L_1 denoising.

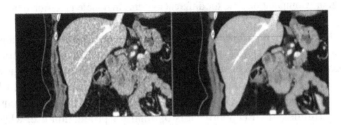

Fig. 8. High quality CT and its TV-L_1 denoising.

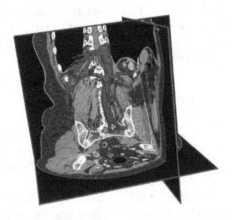

Fig. 9. 3D reconstruction of vessels using proposed segmentation technique.

The value of one-point CNR (10) for different CT images varies, with values typically between 2 and 5, and VOE varies between 5 % and 18 %. To make these values comparable across different images, we apply normalization to CNR and VOE values. Plots of normalized VOE and CNR with its 90 % confidence interval values are shown in Fig. 10.

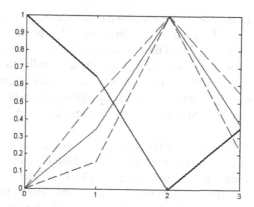

Fig. 10. Normalized VOE (bold), mean normalized value of measure (10) (regular) and its 90 % CI (dashed) for different denoising parameters applied to 10 CT images.

In Fig. 7 a low-contrast CT is shown, the quality measure (10) for this image is 1.45. The result of TV-L_1 denoising has the quality measure of 3.24, for TV-L_2 denoising, 2.83. As shown in Fig. 7, the visual quality for TV-L_1 is also better. This denoised image allowed us to segment a branch portion of the hepatic vein (central-bottom part of the Fig. 7), otherwise not separable. Only TV-L_1 filtering made it possible to perform a complete segmentation of hepatic veins in this CT data using previously described segmentation technique.

A low-contrast example is compared to a high-contrast one shown in Fig. 8. Quality measure for this image is 2.81, the quality increased to 8.62 after denoising.

Table 2. Image quality measure for denoising.

Image type	Image number/quality measure (10)			
	Image #21	Image #3	Image #5	Image #22
Noisy image	1.45	1.86	2.81	2.27
Bilateral filtering	2.11	2.13	5.83	3.12
Curvature diffusion	1.87	2.45	6.17	2.87
Non-local-means	2.30	2.67	8.89	4.13
TV-L_2	2.83	2.44	8.62	3.78
TV-L_1	3.23	2.94	8.17	3.65

Quality measure values for bilateral filtering and curvature diffusion are lower than for the results obtained with non-local-means filter and total variation denoising. Sample results obtained on two low-contrast CT images (with a quality lower than 2) and on two CT images with a normal contrast are shown in Table 2.

These results allow us to make the following conclusions. First, proposed one-point contrast-to-noise based CT image quality measure helps predict the quality of the segmentation and allows detection of the low-contrast CT data. It is also useful in selection of the best denoising procedure and its parameters for individual CT scans.

Second, for CT images with a good contrast and a quality measure exceeding 2.0, results for total variance algorithm using L_1 and L_2 norms and non-local-means are close. Non-local-means produces slightly better denoising results, which is similar to the findings in [4].

Third, TV L1 denoising shows significantly better results for low-contrast images. While these low-quality images represent only 20 % of our data set, only TV-L_1 filtering makes whole venous segmentation technique from Sect. 4 possible.

As shown in Sect. 5, HPC implementation reduces the time of the TV-L_1 denoising procedure while maintains its effectiveness. It makes this denoising method the best practical choice for preprocessing low-contrast CT data with quality measure (10) lower than 2.0.

The results achieved with an HPC-based implementation of TV-L_1 algorithm opens new opportunities in exploring computationally intensive hepatic segmentation algorithms, as well as other aspects of image-guided surgery such as non-rigid registration and real-time tracking. This will be explored in subsequent research.

Improving segmentation for low contrast images is another interesting area to explore. The challenge is that the image requires different threshold values in various areas of the CT. Incorporating threshold prediction in the wave propagation process during the first step of the segmentation could be a promising direction. An HPC implementation of the geodesic active contour segmentation step could further reduce segmentation processing time.

References

1. Antiga, L.: Patient-specific modeling of geometry and blood flow in large arteries. Ph.D. thesis (2002)
2. Basu, S., Das-Gupta A.: The mean, median and mode of unimodal distributions: a characterization. Technical report, 21p (1992)
3. Brenner, D.J., Hall, E.J.: Computed tomography: an increasing source of radiation exposure. N. Engl. J. Med. **357**(22), 2277–2284 (2007)
4. Buades, A., Coll, B., Morel, J.M.: A review of image denoising methods, with a new one. Multiscale Model. Simul. **4**(2), 490–530 (2006)
5. Caselles, V., Kimmel, R., Sapiro, G.: Geodesic active contours. Int. J. Comput. Vis. **22**(1), 61–97 (1997)
6. Chambolle, A., Pock, T.: A first-order primal-dual algorithm for convex problems with applications to imaging. J. Math. Imag. Vis. **40**, 120–145 (2011)
7. Guler, E., Vural, V., Unal, E, Çağatay Köse, I., Akata, D., Karcaaltıncaba, M., Hazırolan, T.: Effect of iterative reconstruction on image quality in evaluating patients with coronary calcifications or stents during coronary computed tomography angiography: a pilot study. Anatol J. Cardiol. (2016)
8. Heimann, T., et al.: Comparison and evaluation of methods for liver segmentation from CT datasets. IEEE Trans. Med. Imag. **28**(8), 1251–1265 (2009)

9. Hendrick, R.E.: Breast MRI. Fundamentals and Technical Aspects. 254p. Springer, New York (2008)
10. IRCAD, 3DIRCADb team, 3D-IRCADb-01 database. http://www.ircad.fr/softwares/3Dircadb/3Dircadb1/index.php?lng=en
11. Johnson, H.J., et al.: The ITK Software Guide, 3rd edn, pp. 1–768. Kitware Inc, New York (2013)
12. Li, Z., et al.: Adaptive nonlocal means filtering based on local noise level for CT denoising. Med. Phys. **41**(1), 011908 (2014)
13. Magnotta, V.A., Friedman, L.: Measurement of signal-to-noise and contrast-to-noise in the fBIRN multicenter imaging study. J. Digit. Imag. **19**(2), 140–147 (2006)
14. Mori, M., et al.: Method of measuring contrast-to-noise ratio (CNR) in nonuniform image area in digital radiography. Electron. Commun. Jpn. **96**(7), 32–41 (2013)
15. Nikonorov, A., Bibikov, S., Fursov, V.: Desktop supercomputing technology for shadow correction of color images. In: Proceedings of the 2010 International Conference on Signal Processing and Multimedia Applications (SIGMAP), pp. 124–140 (2010)
16. Nikonorov, A., et al.: Semi-Automatic liver segmentation using Tv-L1 denoising and region growing with constraints. In: 9th German-Russian Workshop on Image Understanding, pp. 1–4 (2014)
17. Parikh, N., Boyd, S.: Proximal algorithms. Found. Trends Optim. **1**(3), 123–231 (2013)
18. Perona, P., Malik, J.: Scale space and edge detection using anisotropic diffusion. IEEE Trans. Pattern Anal. Mach. Intell. **12**(7), 629–639 (1990)
19. Pock, T., et al.: Fast and exact solution of total variation models on the GPU. In: IEEE Computer Society Conference on Computer Vision and Pattern Recognition Workshops 2008, CVPRW 2008, pp. 1–8 (2008)
20. Prokop, M., Galanski, M., van der Molen, A., Schaefer-Prokop, C.: Spiral and Multislice Computed Tomography of the Body, pp. 1–1104. Thieme, Stuttgart (2002)
21. Rudin, L., Osher, S.J., Fatemi, E.: Nonlinear total variation based noise removal algorithms. Phys. D: Nonlin. Phenomena **60**, 259–268 (1992)
22. Sethian, J.A.: Fast Marching Methods and Level Set Methods for Propagating Interfaces. von Karman Institute Lecture Series, Computational Fluid Mechanics (1998)
23. Shang, Q.: Separation and Segmentation of the Hepatic Vasculature in CT Images, pp. 1–113. Nashville, Tennessee (2010)
24. Shuman, W.P., et al.: Standard and reduced radiation dose liver CT images: adaptive statistical iterative reconstruction versus model-based iterative reconstruction—comparison of findings and image quality. Radiology **273**(3), 793–800 (2014)

Wireless Information Networks and Systems

Scheduling Strategies to Improve Reliability and Fairness for Priority Based Smart Rural Contention Based Applications Over Low-Cost Wireless Mesh Backbone Networks

Sajid M. Sheikh[✉], Riaan Wolhuter, and Herman A. Engelbrecht

Department of Electrical and Electronic Engineering, University of Stellenbosch, Private Bag X1,
Matieland 7602, South Africa
sajid.sheikh@mopipi.ub.bw, {wolhuter,hebrecht}@sun.ac.za

Abstract. Wireless Mesh Networks (WMNs) are viewed as a cheap solution for telemetry networks in rural areas. The main advantages of WMNs are that they allow an easy extension of existing networks to service a wider area by using multi-hop wireless communication and they provide an alternate route when a route becomes faulty. Smart Rural Areas is a new concept for the development of rural areas. It is hypothesized that the Internet of Things (IoT) can help develop rural areas by providing better services resulting in poverty reduction. The widely used carrier sense multiple access with collision avoidance (CSMA/CA) was originally designed for Wireless Local Area Networks (WLANs) consisting of single-hop transmissions. CSMA/CA experiences a rapid decrease in performance when applied to multi-hop distributed networks as an increase in collisions and contention for the medium is experienced. The IEEE 802.11e standard provides data differentiation services for data of different priority levels with enhanced distributed channel access (EDCA) being used in contention based networks. With EDCA, an unfairness problem exists where high priority data can starve lower priority data. To address these problems in low-cost rural smart networks we investigate the performance of six design schemes for wireless backbone networks by assigning different roles to edge and core routers. Simulations were carried out to obtain the results using OMNeT ++ and the INET framework. Simulation results show that hybrid network designs using distributed coordination function (DCF) and EDCA can improve QoS.

1 Introduction

In recent times, wireless mesh networks (WMNs) have gained increasing popularity and usage in rural deployments. WMNs have attracted usage in rural areas mainly due to their self organisation, auto configuration and low cost to extend network coverage compared to other solutions such as fibre optic, cellular networks, Wi-Max or VSATs [1, 2]. With WMNs, many challenges are also experienced such as network capacity, QoS routing, link-layer resource allocation, network security, fairness and seamless roaming [3]. Much research has been done and published in various areas of WMNs which includes routing metrics, optimum routing, security, scheduling, cross layer

© Springer International Publishing Switzerland 2016
M.S. Obaidat and P. Lorenz (Eds.): ICETE 2015, CCIS 585, pp. 511–532, 2016.
DOI: 10.1007/978-3-319-30222-5_24

designs and physical layer techniques. The capacity of WMNs is affected by many factors such as network architecture, network topology, traffic patterns, network node density, number of channels used for each node, transmission power level and node mobility [4].

There are two main categories of MAC scheduling, namely contention based and contention free strategies. The contention free techniques, such as time division multiple access (TDMA), require time synchronization for successful operation which is difficult to achieve in multi-hop networks due to the geographic devices distribution. With TDMA all devices need to be synchronised. The distributed carrier sense multiple access with collision avoidance (CSMA/CA) contention based protocol is therefore, more suitable in WMNs as it does not need time synchronisation. CSMA/CA has been widely deployed in wireless local area networks (WLANs) and ad-hoc networks. CSMA/CA however, has some limitations in multi-hop networks. The original CSMA/CA cannot perform well in wireless multi-hop environments and offers poor throughput performance coupled with unfairness problems [3]. Although CSMA/CA works well in single hop networks, it presents significant challenges when used in ad-hoc networks with collisions, throughput degradation and the collision window increasing significantly, causing an increase in the the end-to-end delay [5].

The distributed coordination function (DCF) in the IEEE 802.11 standard does not provide for data differentiated priority services. The IEEE802.11e standard was developed for data differentiation to provide QoS at the medium access control (MAC) layer. This standard is based both on a centrally-controlled and contention-based channel access strategy [6]. In this work we focus on the contention-based channel mechanism called EDCA, which classifies data into access categories (ACs) depending on the priority level. For the different access categories (AC) or data classes, different values of arbitration interframe spacing (AIFS), different minimum and maximum contention window (CW) sizes are assigned. High priority traffic gets assigned smaller AIFS and CW values compared to lower priority data classes. This gives the higher priority AC a higher chance to access the channel first compared to the lower AC. This results in the fairness problem as higher priority data is given more opportunities to access the medium [7–9]. EDCA can only provide increased statistical chances rather than guaranteed prioritised access to higher priority traffic [3].

The focus of this work is to address the problem of fairness and collision increase in multi-hop networks. Edge nodes or nodes that connect the different network domains are subjected to more traffic load, as they are the gateway to the network domain. We investigate eight design schemes for wireless backbone mesh networks, based on the objective of determining high performance, low cost design implementations. The idea of investigating different roles assigned to edge and core routers has been taken from wired networks that provide differentiated services using Integrated Services (InterServ) and Differentiated Services (DiffServ). The edge routers perform most of the complex operations and the core routers perform simple operations.

These investigations extend our work in [10] by incorporating further investigations. The novel contributions of this work are that we address the fairness and collision increase problems in multi-hop networks by assigning different scheduling strategies to edge and core routers.

The rest of this chapter is organized as follows. In Sect. 2, we present the application domains of the proposed design scheduling strategies for rural low cost networks. Section 3 presents a brief overview of some current priority provisioning techniques and EDCA. Related work is presented in Sect. 4. Section 5 presents an overview of the proposed design schemes. Section 6 presents the simulation experimental setup details. The performance results are presented in Sect. 7 for the proposed design schemes. Section 8 concludes this chapter. Future researches are presented in Sect. 9.

2 Background

In most cases, a rural village in Africa can be characterised as being up to a thousand kilometres away from urban areas and the villages are also normally widely scattered and separated [11]. The cost of covering this distance to reach these scattered rural villages is therefore, very high. As a result, many rural deployments rely on expensive satellite links (usually VSATs) or cellular networks to provide internet access [1, 2].

In rural areas, lower cost and cost effective wireless communication based on WMNs may be more feasible due to cost factors. The settlements in these villages are usually scattered and clustered. The backbone network can be extended and inter-connected in a wireless mesh topology to service these clusters or connect the different network domains for smart rural applications as shown in Fig. 1. Wireless backhaul mesh networks reduce deployment cost and extend network coverage. The existence of multiple routes between source and destination nodes ensures high network availability when node or link failures occur, or when channel conditions are poor [12].

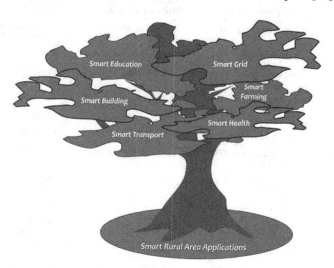

Fig. 1. Some IoT smart rural application domains.

In this chapter, six different IoT smart rural application domain areas are briefly highlighted as possible application areas of the proposed design scheduling strategies as shown in Fig. 1. These application domains are the smart grid which includes energy; smart transport which includes transportation, traffic and parking; smart education which include networks for educational use; smart health; smart farming which include both horticulture and livestock farming; and smart buildings. Smart operations are usually made possible in networks through the use of intelligent sensors and actuators; two-way communications; control and monitoring mechanisms; information and communication technology (ICT); and the internet. Each of these application environments consist of data of different priority levels. We have classified the data into three categories, i.e. high, medium and low priority. The design strategies we investigate in this chapter are therefore, based on these three data priority classes (high, medium and low) to provide improved QoS service in terms of reliability and fairness. Table 1 gives a summarised classification of priority data for these different application domains as above mentioned. Table 2 presents the requirements of a smart grid communication network in more detail. The advanced smart metering infrastructure can tolerate more delay than network data from fault detection networks. Detailed smart grid performance requirements in terms of latency and reliability for different smart grid applications are also stated in [13, 14].

Table 1. Data priority classification for different smart rural application domains.

	High priority data	Medium priority data	Low priority data
Smart grid	Emergency response	Automated demand response (ADR)	Advanced metering infra-structure (AMI)
	Fault detection	Transformer monitoring	Remote connect/disconnect
	Supervisory control and data acquisition (SCADA)	Direct load control	Voltage and current monitoring
Smart education	Online tests	Audio conferencing	Web browsing
	Exams		Emails
	Video conferencing		Online libraries
Smart buildings	Air-conditioning (HVAC) systems	Access control systems	Web browsing
	Video surveillance, safety alarms		Internet access
	Fire protection systems		Smart lighting designs
Smart transport	Ticketing	Digital signage	Sensor object detection for parking
	Payments	Transport logistic	
Smart farming	Renewable energy sources	Tracking of livestock	Sensor readings such as temperature, feed level, soil moisture, Access to stock level for suppliers
Smart health	Tele-monitoring – remote health monitoring of patients	Mobile assistance	Office based applications, medicine use intake by patient, messages to patients

Table 2. Smart grid communication requirements.

Priority category	End-to-end delay	Reliability
HIGH	< 500 ms	99–99.9 %
MEDIUM	500 ms–2 s	99–99.9 %
LOW	2 s–5 s	99–99.9 %

3 Priority Provisioning Techniques

This section presents a brief overview of Integrated Services (InterServ) and Differentiated Services (DiffServ) from where the idea of assigning different roles to nodes in a network for QoS provisioning was taken. This section also presents the EDCA (contention based strategy in IEEE802.11e) and occurrence of the fairness problem.

3.1 Integrated and Differentiated Services

In wired networks, QoS provisioning has been mainly carried out using InterServ and DiffServ. The edge routers have been designed to perform most of the complex operations and the core routers perform the simple operations.

InterServ provides services on a per flow basis. InterServ has three main traffic classes namely, best effort service, controlled load service and guaranteed service. The best effort services are characterized by an absence of a QoS specification and the network delivers the best quality possible. In the guaranteed services classes, users are provided with an assured amount of bandwidth and end-to-end delay. In the controlled load services class, users get serviced as close as possible to that received by a best-effort service in a lightly loaded network [15]. With InterServ, QoS support mechanisms can be provided at the network elements by various packet classifying and scheduling mechanisms such as Class Based Queuing (CBQ) and Weighted Fair Queuing (WFQ). The Reservation Protocol (RSVP) signals the flow requirements. The RSVP protocol carries the QoS parameters from the sender to the receiver to make resource reservations along the path [15].

For DiffServ, flows are differentiated into classes and are treated according to their class, while InterServ provides per-flow guarantees. DiffServ does not need to book resources in advance as compared to InterServ. DiffServ performs mapping multiple flows into a few service levels. The 8-bit TOS (Type of Service) field in the IP header is included to support packet classification. The TOS byte is divided into a 6 bit Differentiated Services Code Point (DSCP) field and a 2-bit unused field [15]. The edge router in a wired system operates using DiffServ included in packet classification, packet marking and traffic conditioning. The core router functions using DiffServ include packet forwarding based on the per-hop behaviour (PHB) that is associated with the packet class. DiffServ provides QoS services by differentiating between service classes. Every class gets a different Behaviour Aggregate (BA). A BA is a collection of packets with the same DSCP crossing a router node in a particular direction. Packets are forwarded according to the Per-Hop-Behaviour (PHB) associated with the DSCP [16]. The edge routers in the network perform the complicated functions such as traffic classification and conditioning, and the core network is kept simple (without per-flow information), which makes DiffServ scalable [3]. DiffServ provide specific treatment known as per-hop treatment depending on the class of the packet.

3.2 Enhanced Distributed Channel Access (EDCA)

The IEEE 802.11 standard for WLANs defines detailed functions of both the Medium Access Control layer (MAC) and the Physical layer (PHY). The MAC layer supports two access mechanisms, i.e. Distributed Coordination Function (DCF) and Point Coordination Function (PCF). Figure 2 presents a summary of the MAC and PHY layers on the most common IEEE802.11 standards.

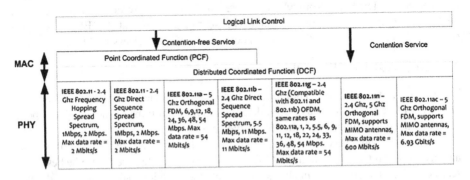

Fig. 2. IEEE 802.11 standards.

DCF is responsible for asynchronous data transmissions to the medium based on the CSMA/CA protocol. It uses the Binary Exponential Backoff (BEB) slotted scheme to try and reduce collisions [17].

DCF includes the carrier sensing mechanisms, inter-frame spacing, and BEB. The DCF technique is a distributed technique where contention to the wireless medium is performed by all the nodes that have data to transmit. The PCF is a centralised technique where access to the wireless medium is given by one node being responsible for controlling access to the medium in an infrastructure based network [18]. The DCF is also referred to as contention-based channel access while the PCF is sometimes referred to as contention-free channel access [19].

CSMA/CA using DCF first senses the medium to determine if any other communication is in process or not. If the medium is sensed to have been idle for a time period greater than the Distributed Interframe Space (DIFS), the station immediately transmits its data. If the medium has not been idle for a time duration greater than DIFS, the station first senses the medium for this DIFS period. If the medium is still idle, the node than performs the BEB procedure where a number is generated randomly in the interval of [0, contention window (CW) -1]. CW is first set to CW_{min} and the backoff time calculated. These time intervals are all integral multiples of slot times. For any unsuccessful transmission, the CW_{min} value is doubled. The value can only be doubled up to the value for CW_{max}. This value of CW_{max} is reset to the minimum value after a successful transmission takes place. The default value for CW_{min} in DCF is 31 and CW_{max} is 1023. After this period, if the medium is found idle, transmission takes place. In the event that during the countdown period, if a transmission is detected, the countdown freezes, and continues only after the channel has again been sensed to be idle for a period of DIFS. After this backoff period, if the medium is found idle, transmission takes place [19].

In CSMA/CA using DCF, the two main Inter-frame Spacing (IFS) timings used are DIFS and Short Inter-frame Spacing (SIFS). The IFS is the time interval in which frames cannot be transmitted. This IFS is a precautionary measure to ensure that frames do not overlap or collide [18]. SIFS is the shortest IFS used. SIFS has the highest priority over IFS frames and is used by urgent messages such as Acknowledgements (ACK), Request to Send (RTS) and Clear to Send (CTS). In CSMA/CA, data frames are transmitted using the DIFS interval while ACK to successful data transmissions are sent back using the SIFS interval. The SIFS interval for the ACK frame takes priority over any other data frames.

Many networking applications require differentiated services. This can be done by giving higher priority data preferential access to the medium. The IEEE 802.11e standard has been developed to provide differentiated services for QoS provisioning. It specifies the use of EDCA and hybrid coordination function (HCF) [18]. EDCA is an extension of DCF and introduces the concept of access category (AC) for data types. Data is mapped at the MAC layer into the corresponding AC. The four access categories are background (BK), best-effort (BE), video (VI) and voice (VO). EDCA introduces a new interframe spacing called Arbitration IFS (AIFS). AIFS is the minimum time period for which the medium must be sensed idle before an Enhanced Distributed Channel Access Function (EDCAF) may start transmission or back off which is a variable value that depends on the AC for which the EDCAF is contending for. The smaller the AIFS number (AIFSN) value for a higher priority AC, the shorter the AIFS duration. AIFS is calculated as given in Eq. 1.

$$AIFS = AIFSN * SlotTime + SIFS \qquad (1)$$

For each of the ACs, the corresponding CW values are shown in Table 3. The Transmission Opportunity (TXOPlimit) is the maximum time interval a node can use the channel to send data without contending for the medium. In other words, a node can

Table 3. Parameters of EDCA assigned to each AC category.

AC	AC type	Traffic type	AIFSN	CW_{min}	CW_{max}	TXOPlimit 802.11a PHY	TXOPlimit 802.11b PHY
AC [3]	AC_BK	Background	7	31	1023	0	0
AC [2]	AC_BE	Best Effort	3	31	1023	0	0
AC [1]	AC_VI	Video	2	15	31	3.008 ms	6.016 ms
AC[0]	AC_VO	Voice	2	7	15	1.504 ms	3.264 ms

send out multiple data packets consecutively until the duration of transmission exceeds the specific TXOP limit [20, 21].

Figure 3 illustrates the different AC's, AIFS and parallel backoff entities in EDCA in a timing diagram. AC[0] has the shortest AIFS period and back off range, compared to the lower priority data. Figure 4 shows the implementation scheduling structure of EDCA. If any queue has data, data is scheduled after sensing the medium to be idle for the AIFS period and CW backoff depending on the priority class. If data from two ACs finish the AIFS period and CW back off period, an internal collision takes place. The internal collision is handled by the virtual collision handler, where the higher priority data is allowed to transmit and the lower priority data has to contend for the medium again behaving as if a collision on the medium as occurred and goes into backoff mode

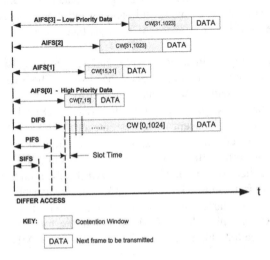

Fig. 3. IEEE 802.11e AIFS and backoff period timing diagram [37].

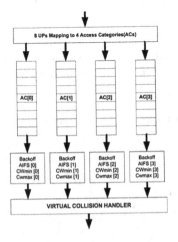

Fig. 4. EDCA implementation model for IEEE802.11e in a node [37]

[22, 23]. This is how the starvation and fairness problem occurs for lower priority data with the higher priority data having higher chances to access the medium [22, 23]. If a node transmits successfully, it sets its CW to the CW_{min}, giving its remaining packets a better chance to be transmitted before packets from other nodes with a larger CW [3] which also results in the unfairness problem. In this study we analyse the performance of EDCA in different design schemes, for suitability in different set of rural applications in backbone WMNs.

4   Related Work

The fairness problem in IEEE 802.11e has been given much attention for Wireless Local Area Networks (WLANs) as in [6, 8, 22, 25–31], while little attention has been given to the fairness problem in multi-hop networks. In multi-hop networks, the fairness problem has been addressed in different ways due to the nature of transmissions.

The fairness problem in multi-hop networks has been addressed by changing the priority of the messages dynamically and not keeping it constant in [20, 32–35]; for intra-class data in [36]; by creating separates queues in [37] or weighted queues in [6, 8, 28, 38]. The fairness problem in multi-hop networks has also been addressed in [20] and [39] by dynamically changing the TXOPlimit value. The fairness problem in multi-hop networks has been addressed in [8, 40] by changing the CW values.

According to the knowledge of the authors, no research has been conducted to address the fairness and collisions problem in multi-hop networks from a design aspect by assigning different roles to edge and core routers except in our work reported in [10]. Not much attention has been given to addressing the fairness and contention increase problems for multi-hop networks such as WMNs with static nodes as well as for low cost networks for rural implementations. Most of the current fairness researches focus mainly on adjusting EDCA parameters such as AIFS, CW values and TXOPlimit, or dynamically changing the priority of the message. This study, therefore, adopts a novel approach by assigning different roles or scheduling strategies to edge and core routers.

5   Proposed Design Schemes

This research is an extension of our research as per [10] where six design concepts were investigated by assigning EDCA and DCF scheduling strategies to edge and core routers in different combinations. The tests were carried out on 4 × 4, 5 × 5 and 6 × 6 square grid topologies. All the schemes were tested on data transmission rates of 100 packets per second for all the data priority classes to expose the fairness problem. In this work we extend our investigations for the design schemes shown in Fig. 5 over a 5 × 5 grid topology and test 8 cases with different data transmission rates (Table 4) for all the different heterogeneous data. In the proposed schemes, we assume a hierarchical backbone mesh network structure consisting of edge and core routers. User clients can connect to the edge routers, while the core routers connect to the backbone routers and carry the data in the backbone. Figure 5 shows the eight design concepts used in our investigation.

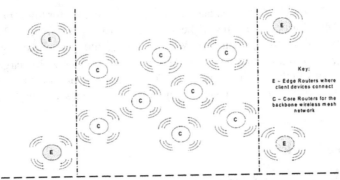

	Scheme	Edge (E) Routers	Core (C) Routers
	SCHEME 1	EDCA	EDCA
Single Radio & Single Channel in the Edge and Core Routers	SCHEME 2	DCF	DCF
	SCHEME 3	DCF	EDCA
	SCHEME 4	EDCA	DCF
	SCHEME 5	EDCA	EDCA
Single Radio & Single Channel in the Core Routers, Two Radios & Two channels in the Core Routers	SCHEME 6	DCF	DCF
	SCHEME 7	DCF	EDCA
	SCHEME 8	EDCA	DCF

Fig. 5. Topology used for the investigation.

Table 4. Simulation data transmission test cases.

	High priority data (Packets/sec)	Medium priority data (Packets/sec)	Low priority data (Packets/sec)
Case 1	50	50	50
Case 2	50	50	100
Case 3	50	100	50
Case 4	50	100	100
Case 5	100	50	50
Case 6	100	50	100
Case 7	100	100	50
Case 8	100	100	100

The schemes are based on the concept of low cost design implementation solutions and hence we investigate designs 1, 2, 3 and 4 for single radio and single channel for both edge and core devices. Schemes 5, 6, 7 and 8 are the same designs as schemes 1, 2, 3 and 4, with the addition of an additional radio in the edge nodes and an additional channel.

The motivation behind adding an extra radio in schemes 5, 6, 7 and 8 is to reduce congestion build-up in the edge routers. It is expected that the multi-radio will help lower congestion build up in the edge routers. In schemes 1, 2, 3 and 4, omni-directional antennas are used. In schemes 5, 6, 7 and 8, omni-directional antennas are used, with 1 radio in the edge devices connecting the user devices and the other antenna connecting the backbone devices. Non-overlapping channels are used. Two radios are only used in a few devices (edge devices) to keep cost of implementation low. Hardware that operates in the unlicensed Industrial, Scientific and Medical (ISM) band can also provide lower cost as compared to the use of licensed spectrum.

In schemes 1 and 5 both the edge and core routers are configured with the default IEEE802.11e EDCA scheduling technique. In schemes 2 and 6, both the edge and core routers are configured with the DCF scheduling strategy. In schemes 3 and 7, the edge routers are configured with DCF and the core routers are configured with EDCA. In schemes 4 and 8, the edge routers are configured with EDCA and the core routers are configured with DCF.

Every node can communicate with their neighbours, provided omni-directional antennas are used and the neighbours being in their coverage range. The tests are carried out on a square grid as square grid topologies provide eight possible neighbours. This provides a high number of alternate mesh routes, as well as creating more contention for the medium between the neighbours which is helpful in accessing the performance of the design schemes under a scenario with high to medium contention. The theme of this work involves mesh networks and the strategies were, therefore, not analyzed in line topologies which do not have mesh links. In random topologies not all nodes have the same coverage, as some neighbours will be able to communicate directly with their 1 hop distant neighbouring nodes depending on the coverage area, while others will be unreachable.

6   Performance Evaluation

This section presents an overview of the simulation setups and performance metric used for the analysis. To investigate the performance of our design schemes, simulations were set up in OMNeT ++ using the INET framework. OMNeT ++ is an open source application. The INET framework offers detailed modelling of radio propagation, interference estimation, implementation of various MAC, network layer, and transport and application layer protocols of wireless network [41]. Table 5 presents the details of the simulation setup implemented in OMNeT ++ using the INET framework. All the nodes were configured with the IEEE802.11 g standard at the MAC and physical layer with nodes to transmit at 54Mbps and operate in the 2.4 GHz band. The standard IEEE802.11e model using AC[0] for high priority data, AC [1] for medium priority data and AC [2] for low priority data was implemented. The traffic type was heterogeneous with different priority levels.

The two ray ground propagation model was applied to represent the physical environment which uses the delay speed to be equal to the delay between the line-of-sight (LOS) ray and the reflected ray. The two ray model was used as in rural areas, these two rays exist predominantly, i.e. direct rays and the reflected rays. UDP packets were sized at 512 bytes as most UDP applications such as Trivial File Transfer Protocol (TFTP) and Domain Name Systems (DNS) use a default packet size of 512bytes. User Data Protocol (UDP) data was utilised in our simulations for the three types of priority data. UDP does not establish connections between the source and destinations (connection-less) and there is no retransmission of lost packets [42]. The use of UDP packets helps determine the unreliability at the lower layers of the network through packet loss meas-ures. On the other hand, Transmission Control Protocol (TCP) is connection oriented and feedback is also received for delivered packets [42]. For each of the eight design schemes, the schemes were each simulated for 100 s and repeated 5 times with different seed numbers generated by the random number generator utility in OMNeT ++. In the next section, depicting the result figures, the top ends of the bars indicate the average from the different seed runs and the error bars represent the 95 % confidence intervals. The simulations were each repeated twice to verify the results. The results from the different seed runs were saved in scalar files (.sca) in OMNeT ++. A python code was written to take the results from all these scalar result files to calculate the averages, error bars, packet loss and fairness. These results were used to draw our result graphs.

Table 5. Simulation environment.

Network setup	
Simulation time	100 s
Topology type	Grid topology
Backbone separation distance	300 m between nodes
Area	2.2 km × 2.2 km = 4.84 km^2
Propagation model	Two ray ground model
Routing protocol	OLSR
Data rate	54Mbits/s
Application data	UDP basic burst packets
Packet size	512bytes

To assess the performance of our proposed design schemes and carry out the compa-rative analysis, end-to-end delay, packet loss (%) and Jain's Fairness Index metrics were used:

1. End-to-end delay: This is the average time taken by a data packet to arrive at the destination from the source. It includes all the delay experienced from the source to the destination which includes route discovery processes, data queuing and packet transmission. Only the data packets successfully delivered to the destinations are included in these calculations [43].

2. Packet Loss: This is the measure of the percentage of packets lost from source to destination. This value was measured at the destination as [44]:

$$\text{Packet Loss } (\%) = \frac{(N_t - N_r) * 100}{N_t} \tag{2}$$

Where N_t is the number of packets is transmitted and N_r is the number of packets received.

3. Jain Fairness Index (JFI): A fairness index is a measure of how fair or unfair the resources are shared among the competing hosts. Equation 2 is used to calculate fairness where x_i is the normalized throughput of station i, and n is the number of flows in the WMN. A JFI of 1 indicates absolute fairness and a JFI of 0 absolute unfair resource distribution [45]. In our case n = 3 as we investigate the fairness for 3 data classes namely for high, medium and low priority classes.

$$f\left(x_0, x_1, x_2, \ldots, x_n\right) = \frac{\left(\sum_{i=0}^{n} x_i\right)^2}{n \sum_{i=0}^{n} x_i^2} \tag{3}$$

$$\text{where } 0 \leq f\left(x_0, x_1, x_2, \ldots, x_n\right) \leq 1$$

7 Simulation Results

The performance of the eight schemes were analysed in terms of packet loss in Figs. 6, 7, 8, 9, 10, and 11. Figure 6 displays the packet loss for high priority data for all the schemes in all the different data transmission rate test cases. Figure 7 displays the consolidated average for packet loss of all the test cases with the different design schemes for high priority data. For high priority data, the schemes which were configured with DCF in all the routers, experienced the lowest packet loss of 34 % average in scheme 2 (1 radio in the edge routers) and 31 % in scheme 6 (2 radios in the edge routers). This was followed by hybrid schemes where EDCA and DCF were configured in either the edge or core routers and vice versa. Scheme 3 had 34 % packet loss, scheme 4 35 %, scheme 7 33 % and scheme 8 35 % for high priority data. The pure EDCA scheme where EDCA was configured in all the routers, experienced the highest packet loss.

Figure 8 displays the packet loss for medium priority data for all the schemes in all the different data rate transmission test cases. Figure 9 displays the consolidated average for packet loss for all the test cases with the different design schemes for medium priority data. A similar trend as for the high priority data was seen for the medium priority data, except that schemes 2, 3 and 4 all experienced 34 % packet loss in the single channel and single radio schemes. Scheme 6 experienced 31 %, followed by scheme 7 experiencing 33 % and scheme 8 with 35 % loss. Again, the pure EDCA schemes experienced the most packet loss for medium priority data.

Figure 10 displays the packet loss for low priority data for all the schemes in all the different data rate transmission test cases. Figure 11 displays the consolidated average for packet loss for all the test cases with the different design schemes for low priority data. Like for medium and high priority data, a similar trend was seen for low priority data as well. Scheme 6 had the lowest packet loss of 31 %, followed by scheme 4 of 33 %. Scheme 7 experienced 34 % packet loss. Schemes 2, 3 and 7 experienced 35 % loss.

DCF in the core routers gives all packets carried in the core network, an equal chance of medium access and packets are transmitted in a first in first out (FIFO) fashion in the core network. DCF also have a larger CW range and contention period compared to the differentiated IEEE802.11e services differentiation scheme. Higher range values of CW with larger back off intervals reduces the collision probability for all the different data priority data classes. In all the schemes, we can see schemes 2 and 6 experienced the least packet loss due to DCF. The performance in terms of packet loss reduction improves with the addition of the additional resource (extra radio and channel) in the edge nodes as can be seen in schemes 5 to 8 for all the data priority data classes compared to schemes 1 to 4 for single radio and single channel schemes. Edge routers in real life networks are usually subjected to more traffic load and congestion. The multi-radio and multi-channel schemes help lower congestion build up in the edge routers.

Packet loss is reduced in the hybrid designs, compared to the pure EDCA schemes as the number of collisions is reduced due to a larger CW range in the core routers. With multi-hop mesh networks, there is more contention for the medium compared to single-hop networks and therefore, EDCA does not perform well in multi-hop networks.

Figures 12, 13, 14, 15 and 17 present the end-to-end delay experienced for the eight design schemes. Figure 12 shows the end-to-end delay for high priority data in all the design schemes for all the different data rate test cases. Figure 13 presents the consolidated average for the end-to-end delay for high priority data for the different design schemes. Schemes 1 and 5 experienced the least end-to-end delay of 6 ms (milliseconds) and 5 ms. Schemes 4 and 8 experienced the next lowest end-to-end delay of 11 ms and 10 ms. Schemes 4 and 8 had DCF configured in the core routers and EDCA in the edge. Schemes 2 and 6 experienced 16 ms end-to-end delay and schemes 3 and 7 experienced the highest with values of 19 ms and 20 ms for high priority data.

Figure 14 shows the end-to-end delay for medium priority data in all the design schemes for all the different data rate test cases. Figure 15 presents the consolidated average for the end-to-end delay for high priority data, for the different design schemes. Again, a similar trend as for the high priority data can be seen for the medium priority, with schemes 1 and 5 experiencing 9 ms and 8 ms delay and schemes 4 and 8 experiencing 13 ms and 12 ms. Schemes 3 and 7 experienced the most delay.

Figure 16 shows the end-to-end delay for low priority data in all the design schemes for all the different data rate test cases. Figure 17 presents the consolidated average for the end-to-end delay for low priority data for the different design schemes. This time, the pure EDCA with low priority experienced the most delay of 77 ms in scheme 1 and 73 ms in scheme 5. The lowest end-to-end delay was experienced with schemes 4 and 8 of 17 ms.

In the hybrid design schemes with DCF, each priority data class is given a fixed DIFS and CW back off interval which results in a decrease in collisions and end-to-end delay.

It can be observed that for the cases of EDCA configured in both edge and core routers, the delay experienced was the lowest for high and medium priority data but the highest for low priority data. For the schemes where DCF was configured in the core routers and EDCA in the edge routers, a higher end-to-end delay was experienced than in the scheme with all EDCA configured routers, but was the lowest compared to all the other schemes.

Figure 18 presents the consolidated average of the Jain's fairness index over all the test cases for all the design schemes. Schemes 2, 4, 6 and 8 provided the highest fairness. These were the schemes where DCF was configured in all the edge and core routers or EDCA in the edge and DCF in the core routers.

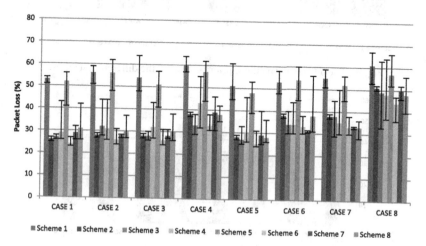

Fig. 6. Packet loss for high priority data for the different test cases.

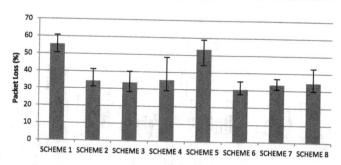

Fig. 7. Average packet loss for high priority data.

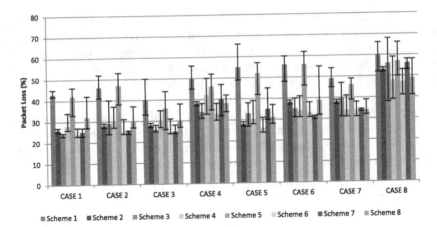

Fig. 8. Packet loss for medium priority data for the different test cases.

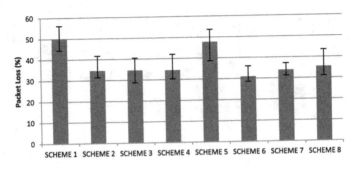

Fig. 9. Average packet loss for medium priority data.

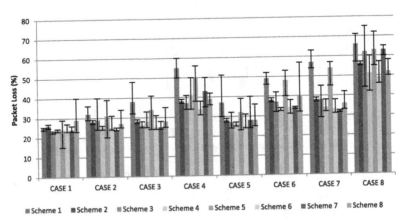

Fig. 10. Packet loss for low priority data for the different test cases.

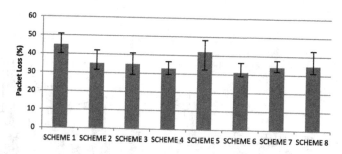

Fig. 11. Average packet loss for low priority data.

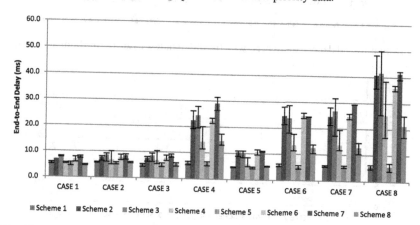

Fig. 12. End-to-end delay experienced with the different test cases for high priority data.

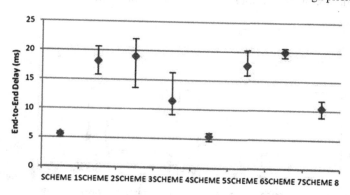

Fig. 13. Average end-to-end delay experienced for high priority data.

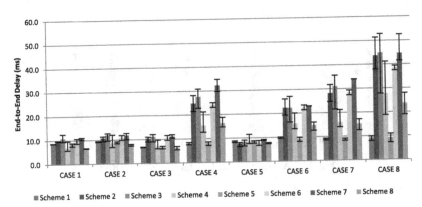

Fig. 14. End-to-end delay experienced with the different test cases for medium priority data.

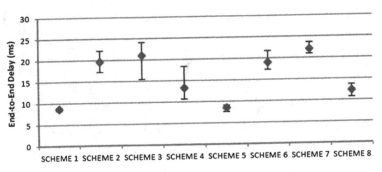

Fig. 15. Average end-to-end delay experienced for medium priority data.

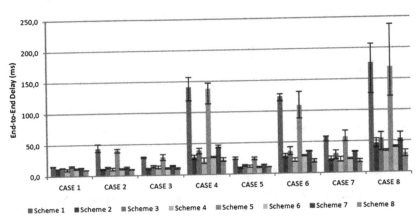

Fig. 16. End-to-end delay experienced with the different test cases for low priority data.

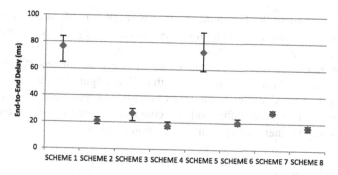

Fig. 17. Average end-to-end delay experienced for low priority data.

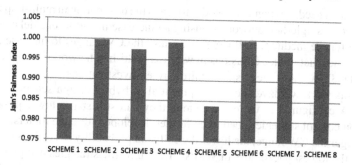

Fig. 18. Jain's Fairness Index for the different design schemes.

8   Conclusion

We have investigated the performance of eight design schemes for wireless backbone mesh networks by assigning different roles to edge and core routers. It was realised that the pure DCF design schemes with all routers configured with DCF experienced the least packet loss, but high end-to-end delay. The pure EDCA design schemes with all devices configured with EDCA, experienced the highest packet loss and the lowest end-to-delay for medium and low priority data, but the highest end to end-to-end delay for low priority data.

The hybrid design scheme where DCF was configured in the core routers and EDCA in the edge routers experienced the lowest end-to-end delay and low packet loss compared with the other hybrid design configured with DCF in the edge routers and EDCA in the core which experienced lower packet loss but higher end-to-end delay. Overall the hybrid design scheme where DCF was configured in the core routers and EDCA in the edge routers gave the best performance, as it had lower packet loss, lower end-to-end delay and provided high fairness. DCF configured in the core routers reduces the number of collisions as DCF have larger CW ranges and contention periods compared to the differentiated IEEE802.11e services differentiation scheme. This results in an improvement in performance. Higher range values of CW with larger back off intervals reduce the collision probability. The different data packets carried in the backbone devices with DCF configured have an equal chance of gaining access to the medium. This scheduling of packets operates as FIFO scheduling in the backbone devices.

From the simulation results obtained, based on design parameters of low-cost rural implementations, a hybrid design scheme, with DCF configured in the core routers and EDCA configured in edge routers improves fairness and reliability. Edge routers are typically subjected to more traffic load and congestion. The multi-radio and channel scheme at the edge routers help prevent congestion build-up.

9   Future Research

In general, data needs to span many nodes to reach the destination in multi-hop networks as compared to single-hop networks causing an increase in end-to-end delay as well as contention for the medium. Collisions also cause the CW ranges to increase for back-off. Techniques that reduce collisions in wireless multi-hop networks using the contention based CSMA/CA strategy still require further investigations.

With this work we have shown the potential of hybrid design schemes. However with EDCA configured in the edge routers, they can still starve lower priority data. Congestion control strategies need to be further developed for edge routers.

The larger the CW range, the lower the collision probability as can be seen for DCF providing the lowest packet loss in WMNs. Deterministic strategies that perhaps make use of large CW values, but ensure corresponding treatment for high priority data, need to be developed and investigated for single channel applications.

References

1. i Direct. Eight Essentials to Implementing Backhaul over Satellite for Mobile Operators, White Paper (2009)
2. Hammond, A., Paul, J.: A New Model for Rural Connectivity, World Resouces Institure, May 2006
3. Jiang, H., Zhuang, W., Shen, X.S., Abdrabou, A., Wang, P.: Differentiated services for wireless mesh backbone. Commun. Mag. IEEE **44**(7), 113–119 (2006)
4. Akyildiz, I.F., Wang, X., Wang, W.: Wireless mesh networks: a survey. Comput. Netw. **47**(4), 445–487 (2005)
5. Yeh, C.-H.: A new scheme for effective MAC-layer diffServ supports in mobile ad hoc networks and multihop wireless LANs. Vehicular Technology Conference, vol. 4, pp. 2149–2155 (2004)
6. Farn, J., Chang, M.: Proportional fairness for QoS enhancement in IEEE 802.11e WLANS. In: International Conference on Local Computer Networks, no. 1, pp. 4–5 (2005)
7. Tseng, K.N., Shih, H.C., Wang, K.: Enhanced fair scheduling for IEEE 802. 11e wireless LANs. J. Inf. Sci. Eng. **1721**, 1707–1721 (2007)
8. Kuppa, S., Prakash, R.: Service differentiation mechanisms for IEEE 802. 11-based wireless networks. Wireless Communications and Networking Conference, vol. 4, pp. 796–801 (2004)
9. Choi, J., Member, S., Yoo, J., Kim, C.: A distributed fair scheduling scheme with a new analysis model in IEEE 802. 11 wireless LANs. IEEE Trans. Veh. Technol. **57**(5), 3083–3093 (2008)

10. Sheikh, S.M., Wolhuter, R., Van Rooyen, G.J.: Performance and comparative analysis of design schemes for prioritised data in multi-hop wireless mesh backbone networks. In: International Conference on Wireless Information Networks and Systems, pp. 13–23 (2015)
11. Johnson, D.L.: Re-architecting internet access and wireless networks for rural developing regions, Ph.D. Dissertation, no. March (2013)
12. Madihian, M.: Multi-hop wireless backhaul networks: a cross-layer design paradigm. IEEE J. Sel. Areas Commun. **25**(4), 738–748 (2007)
13. Gungor, P.V.C.: Smart grid communications: research challenges and oppurtunities, Present. Bahcesehir Univeristy, Turkey (2011)
14. Jeon, Y.-H.: QoS requirements for the smart grid communications systems. Int. J. Comput. Sci. Netw. Secur. **11**(3), 86–94 (2011)
15. Mahadevan, I., Sivalingam, K.M.: Quality of service architectures for wireless networks: IntServ and DiffServ models. In: International Parallel Architectures Algorithms, Networks, pp. 420–425 (1999)
16. Bos, G.: QoS support using DiffServ. In: 6th TSConIT (2007)
17. Elhag, E., Othman, M.: Adaptive contention window scheme for WLANs. Int. Arab J. Inf. Technol. **4**(4), 313–321 (2007)
18. Kaveh Pahlavan, P.K.: Principles of Wireless Networks (2002)
19. Farooq, J., Rauf, B.: An Overview of Wireless LAN Standards IEEE 802.11 and IEEE 802.11e. (2006) B. Chapter
20. Reddy, T.B., John, J.P., Murthy, C.S.R.: Providing MAC QoS for multimedia traffic in 802.11e based multi-hop ad hoc wireless networks. Comput. Netw. **51**, 153–176 (2007)
21. Andreadis, A., Zambon, R.: Improving QoS performance in IEEE 802.11e under heavy traffic loads. Int. J. Wirel. Inf. Netw. **19**, 49–61 (2012)
22. Bourawy, A.A.: Scheduling in IEEE 802.11e Networks with Quality of Service Assurance (2008)
23. Hameed, M.: Performance Evaluation of IEEE802.11e for Industrial Wireless Networks, MSc thesis, University of Applied Sciences (2007)
24. Huiying Liu, J.L., Li, C., Hao, S., Cai, X.: A novel internal collision managing mechanism of IEEE 802.11 e EDCA. In: Asia-Pacific Conference on Communications, pp. 2–7 (2013)
25. Indumathi, G.: Distributed fair scheduling with distributed coordination function in WLAN. In: IEEE International Conference on Networks, pp. 1–6 (2008)
26. Abuzanat, H., Trouillet, B., Toguyeni, A.: Fair queuing model for EDCA to optimize QoS in Ad-Hoc wireless network. In: International Conference on Networks, pp. 306–311 (2009)
27. Somani, A.K. Zhou, J.: Achieving fairness in distributed scheduling in wireless ad-hoc networks. In: Performance, Computing and Communications Conference, vol. 1, pp. 95–102 (2003)
28. Lee, J.F., Liao, W., Chen, M.C.: A MAC-layer differentiated service model in IEEE 802.11e WLANs. Global Telecommunications Conference, vol. 6, pp. 3290–3294 (2005)
29. Ferng, H., Liau, H., Huang, J.: Fair scheduling mechanisms with QoS consideration for the IEEE 802.11e Wireless LAN. In: Vehicular Technology Conference, pp. 840–844 (2007)
30. Hammouri, M.M., Daigle, J.N.: A distributed scheduling mechanism to improve quality of service in IEEE 802.11 Ad Hoc Networks. In: IEEE Symposium Computers and Communications, pp. 1–6 (2011)
31. Keceli, F., Inan, I., Ayanoglu, E.: Weighted fair uplink/downlink access provisioning in IEEE 802.11e WLANs. In: IEEE International Conference, pp. 2473–2479 (2008)
32. Li, J., Li, Z., Mohapatra, P.: Ad Hoc Networks Adaptive per hop differentiation for end-to-end delay assurance in multihop wireless networks. Ad Hoc Netw. **7**(6), 1169–1182 (2009)

33. Wu, Y.-J., Chiu, J.-H., Sheu, T.-L.: A modified EDCA with dynamic contention control for real-time traffic in multi-hop ad hoc networks. J. Inf. Sci. Eng. **1079**, 1065–1079 (2008)

34. Iera, A., Molinaro, A., Ruggeri, G., Tripodi, D., Mediterranea, U.: Improving QoS and throughput in single- and multihop WLANs through dynamic traffic prioritization. IEEE Netw. **19**(4), 35–44 (2005)

35. He, R., Fang, X.: A fair MAC scheme for EDCA based wireless networks. In: International Conference on Testbeds and Research Infrastructures for the Development of Networks and Communities, pp. 1–6 (2009)

36. Zhu, R., Qin, Y., Lai, C.: Adaptive packet scheduling scheme to support real-time traffic in wlan mesh networks. KSII Trans. Internet Inf. Syst. **5**(9), 1492–1512 (2011)

37. Jun, J., Sichitiu, M.L.: Fairness and QoS in multihop wireless networks. In: Vehicular Technology Conference, vol. 1, pp. 2936–2940 (2003)

38. Sheikh, S.M., Wolhuter, R., Van Rooyen, G.J.: A cross-layer adaptive weighted round robin scheduling strategy for wireless mesh networks. In: Southern Africa Telecommunication Networks and Applications Conference (SATNAC), pp. 323–328 (2015)

39. Reddy, T.B., John, J.P., Murthy, C.S.R.: Providing MAC QoS for multimedia traffic in 802. 11e based multi-hop ad hoc wireless networks q. Comput. Networks **51**, 153–176 (2007). Elsevier

40. Zhou, J., Mitchell, K., Hu, R.Q., Qian, Y.: Analysis of express forwarding schemes in wireless mesh networks. In: IEEE International Conference on Communications in China: Communications QoS and Reliability (CQR), pp. 167–172 (2012)

41. Ganlenbein, R.: Virtual mesh: an emulation framework for wireless mesh networks in Omnet ++. University of Bern (2010)

42. Xylomenos, G., Polyzos, G.C.: TCP and UDP Performance over a Wireless LAN, In: IEEE INFOCOM, pp. 439–446 March (1999)

43. Vardakas, J.S., Papapanagiotou, I., Logothetis, M.D., Kotsopoulos, S.A.: On the end-to-end delay analysis of the IEEE 802. 11 distributed coordination function. In: International Conference Internet Monitoring and Protection, pp. 5–9 (2007)

44. Periyasamy, P., Karthikeyan, E.: Comparative performance analysis of AODV and AODV-MIMC routing protocols for mobile Ad hoc networks. Int. J. Comput. Netw. Inf. Secur. (IJCNIS) **6**(6), 54–60 (2014). doi:10.5815/ijcnis

45. Deng, J., Han, Y.S.: Fairness index based on variational distance. In: Global Telecommunications Conference, pp. 1–6 (2009)

Author Index

Printed in the United States
By Bookmasters